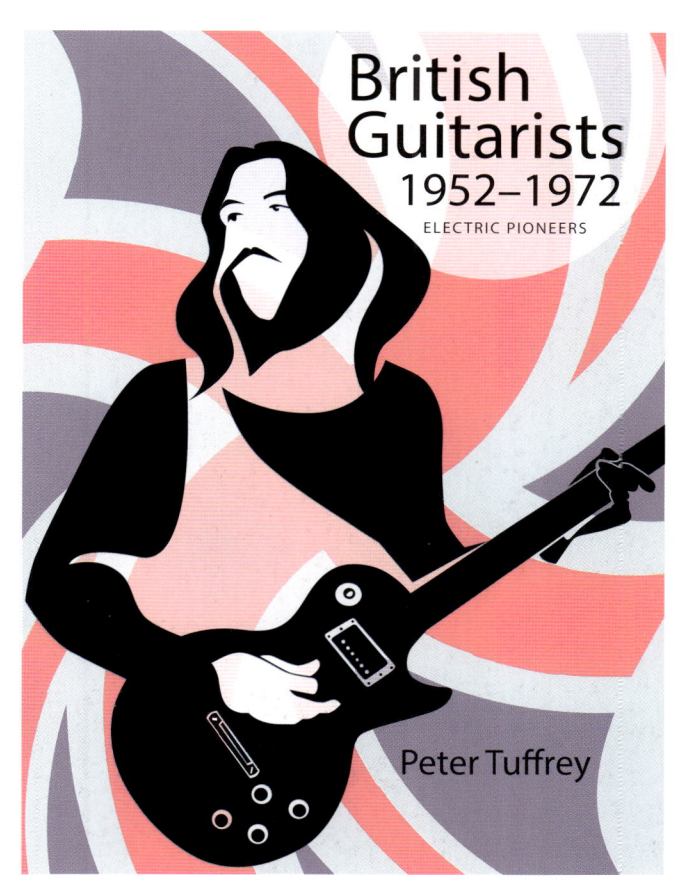

British Guitarists 1952–1972
ELECTRIC PIONEERS

Peter Tuffrey

GREAT NORTHERN

ACKNOWLEDGEMENTS

I would like to thank the following people for their help: Roger Arnold, Roger Askey, Dave Berry, Clive Brown, Joe Brown, David Burrill, Alan Clayson, Clem Clempson, Clement Cachot-Coulom, Peter Crangle, Neil Crossland, Joanna Deacon, Pete Donegan, Vince Eager, Andy Fairweather Low, John Firminger, Barry Gibson, Rob Haywood, Tony Hicks, Peter Jary, Alexander Kretz, Leo Lyons, Tony McPhee, Micky Moody, Richard Henry, Duncan Mangham, David Moffitt, Mike Pender, Graham Platts, Alan Parker, Andy Powell, Alan Rogan, Maggi Ronson, Paul Sandercock, Tony Sherratt, Norman Smart, Jeremy Stewardson, John Taylor, Paul Waller.

Thanks are due to my son Tristram Tuffrey for his help and support throughout the project.

Great Northern Books Limited
PO Box 1380, Bradford, BD5 5FB
www.greatnorthernbooks.co.uk

© Peter Tuffrey 2023

Every effort has been made to acknowledge correctly and contact the copyright holders of material in this book. Great Northern Books Ltd apologises for any unintentional errors or omissions, which should be notified to the publisher.

All rights reserved. No part of this book may be reproduced in any form or by any means without permission in writing from the publisher, except by a reviewer who may quote brief passages in a review.

ISBN: 978-1-912101-27-6

Design and layout: David Burrill

CIP Data
A catalogue for this book is available from the British Library

CONTENTS

INTRODUCTION	4
MARTIN BARRE	7
SYD BARRETT	17
JEFF BECK	22
RITCHIE BLACKMORE	29
MARC BOLAN	37
JOE BROWN	45
ERIC CLAPTON	51
DAVE 'CLEM' CLEMPSON	62
DAVE DAVIES	71
LONNIE DONEGAN	79
ANDY FAIRWEATHER LOW	85
PETER FRAMPTON	91
ROBERT FRIPP	97
DAVID GILMOUR	102
PETER GREEN	111
GEORGE HARRISON	116
TONY HICKS	131
STEVE HOWE	138
TONY IOMMI	145
BRIAN JONES	150
PAUL KOSSOFF	158
ALBERT LEE	162
ALVIN LEE	170
JOHN LENNON	177
PHIL MANZANERA	187
HANK MARVIN	194
JOHN MCLAUGHLIN	202
TONY MCPHEE	209
MICKY MOODY	216
JIMMY PAGE	223
ALAN PARKER	233
MIKE PENDER	238
ANDY POWELL	245
KEITH RICHARDS	253
MICK RONSON	263
MICK TAYLOR	273
PETE TOWNSHEND	278
BERT WEEDON	289
RONNIE WOOD	295

INTRODUCTION

Arguably, from the mid-20th century no other musical instrument developed faster or had a greater impact than the electric guitar. In Britain, many youngsters became enthralled by the look and the sound, leading them to take up the guitar to entertain their peers. Several dozen were able to master the instrument to gain national and international recognition, enjoying careers spanning decades which has resulted in a number being awarded Queen's honours.

Before the Second World War, the technology to amplify the sound of the guitar was not fully developed, though some systems were emerging. Being acoustic, the instrument was limited to accompaniment in either an orchestra setting or to underpin the vocals of a lone singer or group. In the 1930s, some early advancements were made by Rickenbacker and Gibson with 'horseshoe' and 'bar' electronic pick-ups respectively. The latter company produced the P90 pick-up in the early 1940s and this was used in guitars from 1946. A problem experienced from amplifying hollow body guitars was unwanted feedback. The solution to this was the provision of a solid body which allowed much more control over the amplified sound. Leo Fender developed the first mass-produced solid body guitar in the late 1940s with what became the Fender Telecaster series. Gibson followed suit soon after with the Les Paul model, named after the popular jazz guitarist.

In the late 1940s and early 1950s traditional jazz music branched away from big band jazz. The latter focused on performing pieces of music, whereas 'trad' jazz allowed musicians greater freedom for soloing. Ken Colyer's Jazzmen was formed to play 'trad' jazz in the early 1950s and amongst the members was banjo/guitar player Lonnie Donegan. In the break between sets, he performed American folk songs, with two bandmates accompanying on tea chest bass and washboard. This arrangement harkened back to the 'skiffle' style adopted in America during the 1920s where people would use ordinary objects to create music. Many people in post-war Britain recognised this was revelatory as they could now perform with little investment on instruments and time learning musical theory to recreate the songs they enjoyed. For large numbers, one was 'Rock Island Line' released by Lonnie Donegan in the mid-1950s.

This first wave of interest in the guitar was satisfied with cheap acoustic guitars, mainly with high action that left the instrument almost unplayable. Those who could not afford one, or had parents unwilling to indulge their child, resorted to borrowing or making their own guitar. Resources to learn the guitar's basics were hard to come by. Beginners often had to ask friends or relatives to show them a few chords. Bert Weedon's *Play in a Day* was popular for early guitarists, along with *The Complete Guitar Method* by Dick Sadler and Mel Bay's *Modern Guitar Method*, as were books dedicated to chords or general theory. With few sources of distraction at the time, most sat listening to their favourite records learning the music by ear, stopping and starting where necessary, particularly for solos. Tuning the guitar was also a task to be overcome, with a piano, harmonica, or tuning fork amongst several methods employed.

At the same time as the arrival of skiffle, rock 'n' roll music started to gain popularity. This had developed in post-war America with a melding of several different styles: blues; jazz; boogie-woogie; rhythm and blues; country. One of the genre's first hit songs was Bill Haley's 'Rock Around The Clock', whilst a major influence on future guitarists was Chuck Berry, whose playing style was an important starting point. Similarly, Buddy Holly performed prominently with a solid-body Fender Stratocaster, which led several youngsters to dream of acquiring a similar guitar.

Due to import restrictions on American goods, owning a Fender or Gibson model was out of the question for British musicians until the early 1960s. The void was filled by alternatives, such as Hofner, Burns and several other brands, both semi-hollow and solid-body. These were often bought by parents on 'hire/purchase' agreements where the principal sum was paid over weekly instalments. Some musicians experiencing success at the time were able to upgrade to American guitars immediately, such as Joe Brown who bought one of the first ES 335s in Britain, whilst Hank Marvin imported a Fender Stratocaster privately. John Lennon was able to acquire a Rickenbacker through playing in Germany and bandmate George Harrison almost had a Stratocaster if not for a fellow guitarist arriving at the shop before him. Harrison later bought a Gretsch in Liverpool which had been brought home by a merchant seaman.

Amplifiers were also in their infancy. Some guitarists adapted radios or 'radiograms' to hear the instrument's sound electrified. Elpico was a small, dedicated guitar amplifier produced in the mid- to late 1950s. Charlie Watkins started a record shop in the early 1950s and branched into electronics for musicians soon after, initially producing the Westminster amp. Skiffle inspired the company's Dominator and Clubman models in the late 1950s. Similarly, Thomas W. Jennings operated an organ company before a friend, Dick Denney, who played guitar, showed him a prototype amplifier which was developed into the Vox AC15. This became particularly popular for professionals in the late 1950s, early 1960s, especially thanks to the endorsement of Hank Marvin of the Shadows.

As the youngsters assimilated several different styles, their bands began to produce music with a new, distinct sound. At the forefront of this in the early to mid-1960s was the Beatles, with John Lennon's rhythm guitar supporting George Harrison's lead work, and the Rolling Stones where Brian Jones' lead or slide guitar was backed by Keith Richards. Tony Hicks of the Hollies and Mike Pender of the Searchers also provided interesting guitar work to their respective groups.

Some guitarists were particularly dedicated to exploring the roots of rock 'n' roll and found blues music, becoming disciples of people such as Howlin' Wolf, Muddy Waters, Freddie King, Albert King, Robert Johnson, etc. Eric Clapton was one such guitarist and he developed his early reputation on his interpretation of these musicians. He left his first band, the Yardbirds, when the other members followed a more 'commercial' direction and joined John Mayall who shared a passion for the blues. The subsequent album 'Blues Breakers with Eric Clapton' became the foundation for a number of guitarists due to the playing and sound of Eric. Originally wanting a Les Paul Gold Top like Freddie King, Eric could only find a sunburst Les Paul and decided to pair the guitar with a new Marshall 1962 2x12in. combo amp turned up fully to achieve his desired tone. Simple and expressive, his lead was followed by his successors in the group, Peter Green and later Mick Taylor.

As with American instruments, amplifiers were hard to obtain and Jim Marshall, who owned a music shop, was induced by his customers to produce something similar to a Fender amp. The JTM 45 was the first amp of several from Marshall in the mid- to late 1960s built to improve performances for growing audiences. Pete Townshend of the Who was an early customer and was followed by many of his contemporaries. By the end of the decade, several companies had been formed to supply amplification: Orange; Laney; Sound City; Hiwatt.

By the mid-1960s, the arts were enjoying a particular freedom and fertile period of creativity. Musicians were at the forefront. The Beatles started using the studio as a tool for creating interesting sounds for their records. Keith Richards brought the fuzz effect to a large audience with the hit song 'Satisfaction'. Jeff Beck used his guitar to create Indian-influenced sounds for several Yardbirds songs, whilst George Harrison and Brian Jones turned to the sitar for a similar effect. Eric Clapton had a Wah-Wah pedal on a selection of the Cream's songs on the album 'Disraeli Gears'. Whilst some guitarists turned to effects, others sought a new approach to playing the instrument. Syd Barrett drew on his art background to challenge the conventions by changing his playing position and how he sounded notes, using metal objects rather than a pick or his fingers. Pete Townshend similarly used feedback as part of the music, in addition to destroying his instrument as an act of creativity. The art and music world collided several times in the late 1960s as musicians began painting their instruments, with notable examples including Eric Clapton's 'Fool' SG, George Harrison's 'Rocky' Stratocaster and Keith Richards' Les Paul Custom.

The late 1960s and early 1970s were the years of rock, blues rock, heavy rock, jazz fusion, etc. Guitarists mainly favoured Gibson Les Pauls (Jimmy Page, Paul Kossoff, etc), Fender Stratocasters (Ritchie Blackmore, Tony McPhee), or Gibson SGs (Tony Iommi). One of the first custom guitar builders emerged at this time. Tony Zamaitis built both solid-body and acoustic for the guitarists of the day. As the music was popular with the general public and concerts were held at increasingly large venues, amplification was generally multiple 100-watt heads connected to many cabinets, giving rise to the phrase 'wall of Marshalls'. Effects used at the time were generally placed on the stage floor during live performances, though some developments towards a pedalboard occurred in the early 1970s as guitarists such as Robert Fripp and Phil Manzanera acquired units from Pete Cornish.

The author with Mike Pender.

The scope of this book has been limited to this group of around 40 British guitarists that constitutes the pioneers of post-war music in Britain. Several sources have been consulted to develop a history of each and their relationship with the guitars and equipment that created an enduring legacy of music still felt in the 21st century. Interviews have been conducted, whilst historical ones have proved a valuable source of information, particularly *Beat Instrumental* and other magazines. Several books have been published dedicated to guitarists' equipment, such as that by Steve Howe on his own collection, or Andy Babiuk's invaluable resource on both the Beatles' and the Rolling Stones' instruments. In recent years, websites have been founded for fans to contribute to the historical record of their favourite guitarists, such as gilmourish.com or thewho.net. Where there are gaps of information, youtube.com or internet image searches have provided some details, yet the features are not comprehensive or to be considered as such. Rather, they have been compiled to serve as a general source of information and to inform and inspire guitarists of the present.

Martin Barre in performance with Jethro Tull, 1975.
Philip Buonpastore / Alamy Stock Photo.

MARTIN BARRE

Although Ian Anderson is often considered to be the driving force behind Jethro Tull, guitarist Martin Barre has played an equally important role in the band's contribution to classic rock music. Often described as an unsung guitar hero, Martin has also developed a unique solo career. A wealth of information about Jethro Tull's history is provided on www.tullpress.com. The site includes many articles, over the period 1967 to 2001, and whilst these mainly record Ian Anderson's thoughts on music and a whole range of other subjects, information may be gleaned concerning Martin's development as a guitarist and the equipment he used. Other references have also been called upon.

Born on November 17, 1946 in King's Heath, Birmingham, Martin Barre is the son of an engineer. He told *Vintage Guitar* in October 1997 that, to begin with, his father bought him a Dallas Tuxedo guitar on credit.

Recalling his early musical interest and development, he told *Disc & Music Echo* of March 14, 1970: 'I've been playing guitar for eight years … My sister came home from the local community centre talking about this group. I went along to see them and one of them had a red guitar. I just had to have one – it was just the colour really. We used to do music at school but it was all so serious, boring and unexciting … just another subject. It was like doing maths. Music didn't appeal to me, but I suppose if I had taken an interest in it, I would have had the knowledge I yearn for now. I know practically nothing about theory … had guitar lessons at first. When I started, my dad used to play me Barney Kessel records and say, "If only you could play like that…" But at the time, I thought it was a load of crap. I like Barney Kessel now. I don't practice. The only time I ever did was when I was having lessons. I didn't get further than putting your fingers in the right positions. But I've always got a guitar with me. I played in groups at school and then at college but didn't take music seriously. It was while I was at college studying to be a surveyor that I began to care about the music. I started to worry about whether it was good or not. It became more important than college.'

A personal dream was to play a Gibson ES 330 and he eventually bought one on credit. He also played saxophone and flute. During the early 1960s, Martin was a member of a Birmingham band, The Moonrakers, then, in July 1966, he joined The Noblemen, later becoming The Motivation, and they appeared a couple of times at London's Marquee club.

By 1967, he was in The Penny Peeps who were signed to Liberty Records and they released two singles in 1968. Penny Peeps became a blues band called Gethsemane, before disbanding in mid-December 1968. Afterwards, for a brief period Martin was a member of Noel Redding's band, Fat Mattress.

In *Disc & Music Echo* of March 14, 1970, he revealed: 'I developed at first by listening to other guitarists and, now, by not listening to other guitarists. My biggest influence is definitely Clapton. He's the best guitarist in the world, anywhere. And, I listened to Jeff Beck and Jimmy Page. I never really listened to the blues guitarists like B.B. King. I have never listened to the blues riffs. Some people copy phrases but I prefer to half remember phrases and play what I think.'

Amongst the amplifiers he used in pre-Jethro Tull days were: a Watkins Dominator; Vox AC30; and a Laney.

After the release of Jethro Tull's first album, 'This Was', (on October 4, 1968 in the UK), differences of opinion concerning the band's musical direction surfaced, resulting in guitarist, Mick Abrahams leaving. Mick played his final Jethro Tull gig at the London School of Economics on Saturday November 30, 1968. A little later he formed Blodwyn Pig. Auditions were held for a replacement guitarist and amongst those who attended were Tony Iommi (from Birmingham band Earth); Dave O'List formerly of the Nice; and Martin. Whilst playing with Gethsemane at a gig in Plymouth, Martin had met Jethro Tull.

At the audition, Martin played his Gibson ES 330 through an early Laney amplifier but experienced technical problems. In *Melody Maker* 1976, Martin recalled: 'I remember the day I answered Tull's ad in *Melody Maker* for a guitarist – along with about 80 other hopefuls. We all had to audition in front of Ian Anderson while Clive Bunker, the drummer, laid down a 12 Bar beat. When Ian had heard enough, he simply told Clive to stop by tapping him on the shoulder. The sooner he tapped, the worse he thought you were. By the time my turn came around, I was a gibbering idiot. As I walked over to the amp, the room was filled with the sound of coconut shells being knocked together. It was my knees. I can't remember what I played now because my eyes were glued to Clive's shoulder. And when the tap came it was a lot sooner than I had expected. I went home, turned on the budgie, and talked to the telly. I was a total wreck.'

Tony Iommi, (later of Black Sabbath), was successful but his stay was brief. He can be spotted in Jethro Tull's performance on the Rolling Stones' 'Rock and Roll Circus' film of December 1968.

At a second audition, Martin played a Gibson SG Special and was accepted into the band. On www.martinbarre.com, he adds: 'I joined Jethro Tull and had recently bought a very tatty Gibson Les Paul Special, circa late 1950s … I had an early Laney 50-watt head, which I linked to a box 2x12 in. cabinet.'

Martin made his live debut with Jethro Tull on December 30, 1968 at the Winter Gardens, Penzance. In January of the new year, the band embarked on a Swedish tour supporting Jimi Hendrix. Martin recalls the January 1969 gigs were played with his Gibson Les Paul Special through a borrowed 200-watt Hiwatt head and 4x12 in. Hiwatt cab.

Ian Anderson told *Guitar World*, July 1993: 'At that [early] stage Martin was very interested in developing his technique and improving things. He was good for me to work with, I guess, because he was not conditioned to doing things a certain way. He was an open book on which it was possible for me to write – in the sense of coming up with ideas for songs; an important vehicle through which I could develop some ability at writing songs. So, Martin was always a great guy for me to work with.'

At the same time, Martin said, open-minded as he was, he was unprepared for what Anderson had in mind. 'The first week I joined, Ian presented his new songs to Glenn [Cornick, bassist] and Clive [Bunker, drummer] and me,' said Martin. 'And it was quite a shock. They weren't anything like the songs of the Jethro Tull I thought I'd joined.'

On January 18, 1969, Jethro Tull rolled into Manchester University, their final stop in England before they would make their US premiere at New York City's Fillmore East, later in the month.

Martin told *Guitar World* in June 1999: 'Manchester was the gig that finally cracked it for us. The audience went wild for the new songs, and you could hear a huge sigh of relief from the band that the show had gone down so well. It was really the turning point for Jethro Tull – for everything that we were to become and everything we were to inspire in others.'

Jethro Tull went on their first US tour from January 24, 1969 which lasted three months and they recorded the single, 'Living in the Past' there in March 1969.

Jethro Tull's second album 'Stand Up' was recorded between April and May 1969 at Morgan and Olympic Sound Studios in London and released through Island (UK) on July 25, 1969. The album saw Ian Anderson in full control of the music and lyrics and its gatefold cover opened up like a children's pop-up book which allowed a cut out of band members to literally 'stand up'.

Besides contributing guitar and mandolin, Martin played flute on tracks 2 and 9. In *Guitar School*, June 1996, Martin said: 'The guitar solo [on 'We Used To Know'] was all done in one take – I just went for broke. In those days, I never really sat down and worked out the implications of chord changes. I just played by ear; sometimes I'd get lucky and hit a note that worked and on another take it might be a disaster. I suppose all that early emphasis on solos was a hangover from the jazz era where everybody had their solos. In some ways, it reflects on how boring the music was – but we got away with it.'

Martin added that he recorded 'Stand Up' with no effects, only a Dunlop Wah-Wah on the track 'We Used to Know'.

On the BBC World Service in March 1979, 'The Jethro Tull Story', was featured. It was a six-part radio documentary covering ten years in the life of one of the world's leading and most original rock bands, and Ian Anderson recalled Martin's guitar solo on 'We Used To Know': 'That's the definitive Martin Barre track of the era; the first time he had anything other than a Vox AC30. We gave him this big 200-watt deal and said "Play this riff," and it all came out … the engineer actually stood with an 87, a big microphone, on the end of a cord, waving it round in front of the speaker to create a sort of Leslie sound, which is the sound of that particular song. Good old Martin…'

'After we finished Stand Up, we went back to the English blues clubs where Mick [Abrahams] had played,' said Martin. 'There were a few dates where the audience was very quiet. They didn't know what to make of it all. We did some 10 gigs in England, and it wasn't gelling with the crowd. It was a worrying few weeks.'

A second US tour was undertaken in July and a third one in November/December 1969.

Commenting on a Martin Barre's performance during a British tour, Tony Norman for, *Disc & Music Echo*, reported on October 11, 1969: 'Martin Barre is a fine guitarist. He is not on an ego trip. He plays with the group, rather than against it. However, at certain times, noticeably during "We Used To Know", his style really shone through.'

In October 1969, Jethro Tull released their second single 'Sweet Dream' on Chrysalis and written by Ian Anderson. Whilst in Jethro Tull, Martin was happy to remain in the background as confirmed to *New Musical Express* on November 22, 1969: 'I've done just two interviews since I've been in the group. But none of

Martin Barre, with Gibson SG, in performance with Jethro Tull, 1975.
Philip Buonpastore / Alamy Stock Photo.

us mind that. The kind of things Ian has to answer and talk about, all that analysis and comment, I wouldn't care to do that anyway.' In the same interview, he said: 'I was really frightened at first when I joined Jethro Tull. I thought I was an average or maybe slightly above average musician but I soon learned my shortcomings and it was pretty shattering. I discovered that I had been sitting back for the previous two years. At first with Jethro Tull, I really had to force myself to play well. It took me a long time to get any confidence in myself.'

At the end of one gig in the States, it was noted in the *New Musical Express* on December 27, 1969, Martin did not leave with the rest of the band. Instead, he was left, 'trying out Les Paul guitars a friend had brought along for him to buy…'

Talking about touring in America in 1969, Martin said the following to *Beat Instrumental No. 80* of December 1969: 'The trouble with America is that there is so much disorganisation. For example, the sound system is obviously the most important thing, but so often it is handled by a guy who doesn't know anything about it. It's almost as if they are trying to kill off live music in the States. Some of those festivals for instance are terrible. A field filled with 50,000 kids – yet only a couple of thousand can honestly say they can hear or see anything. The distortion is awful…'

Over the next few decades, Jethro Tull would release an album followed by an extensive tour, sometimes across several continents. They experienced various line-up changes and a few disagreements with the music press.

On January 16, 1970, they released another single 'The Witch's Promise'. It opens with Martin Barre playing acoustic guitar. It also marks the use of keyboard; on the B side, 'The Teacher', both Ian Anderson and Martin play guitar.

Martin told *Melody Maker* on February 14, 1970 that the band would be spending around six months of 1970 in America but confessed: 'Everything starts to get on top of you, the way things have happened we've got no time to do anything ourselves and now our personal lives are suffering. I'm going through a stage of depression. We all want to buy houses where you can just sit down with your girlfriend and be on your own. That's very important to me.' He continued: 'Some of the instruments we're playing now are difficult to use on stage especially in the big auditoriums. You can just about get away with a piano but it's difficult to get a good sound. I also play mandolin and flute and Ian plays the piano but generally on stage it's down to the guitars.'

The band received criticism for releasing, what many described as, commercial pop singles, and appearing on 'Top of the Pops'. Martin told *Disc & Music Echo* on February 21, 1970: 'Personally I don't much like "Top Of The Pops" and I can't stand having to mime to our records. It makes me feel completely useless, like a cardboard cut-out, and I can't take it seriously. But on the other hand, I've always been very satisfied with our singles and realise the importance of TV shows like this.'

Between September 1969 and February 1970, Jethro Tull recorded their third album 'Benefit' which was released on April 20, 1970 in the UK and May 1, in the US. The band used piano and organ to add to their sound.

Martin has said he used Hiwatts in 1970. He had a Gibson Les Paul Custom but commented: '[I]t was a fake and didn't stay in the collection very long! But I used it on "Benefit". I started using a Hornby Skewes Treble Booster, which gave the Hiwatts a bit of a kick.' He also began utilising an old Watkins Copycat echo.

Commenting on 'To Cry You a Song' on 'Benefit', Martin said: 'It was more or less live in the studio with a couple of overdubs and a solo, Ian played my Gibson SG and I played a Les Paul on it … It's [Mountain guitarist] Leslie West's favourite Jethro Tull song. I suppose if there is anybody that ever influenced me at all, West was the one. I felt if I could play like he did, I'd be very happy.'

'Sossity, You're A Woman' was on the 'Benefit' album and Martin explained there had been two guitar parts: '[I]t was the first time Ian and I played together. I remember it very well, and I remember which guitar I played – an old Eko acoustic. We played together on that and on "Nothing to Say". We sat in the studio – I played fingerstyle guitar and Ian played with a plectrum.'

Ian Anderson commented about Martin's and his own guitar playing on 'Benefit' to *New Musical Express* April 11, 1970: 'The guitar on "To Cry You A Song" is I think a very good sound, and there are no effects on it. It came out the way Martin wanted it, clean and tight, and it pleases me we got it that way for him. That's important to me … that people are pleased with their own sound … as well as it fitting into the song. I play guitar on all the tracks and initially that was because I was writing songs in terms of guitar, which meant that Martin would have to learn the guitar piece and it became frustrating for him. It was okay when he first started because he wasn't so good then and it gave him the chance to play another person's ideas. On this album, I thought it should be left to him what he wanted to play, just as Glenn and Clive are free to do what they like within the framework of a number written by me.'

Disc & Music Echo, April 18, 1970, stated Martin Barre's lead guitar on 'Benefit' 'features well and more prominently [than previously on 'Stand Up']. A week later, the same newspaper revealed that John Evan who had played on 'Benefit' joined the band as a regular member on organ.

Ian Anderson told *Guitar World* in September 1999: 'I guess you could say that ["Benefit"] was our "guitar riff" album. It was done in a year when a lot of people were working with "the riff", an idea that had obviously come to prominence with bands like Cream, Hendrix and Led Zeppelin. Since that style of guitar playing is very electric, there is very little acoustic guitar on "Benefit".'

Martin remarked on Jethro Tull's stage set-up for an American tour to *Beat Instrumental No. 85* of May 1970: 'We're using smaller amps now, with a monster PA system with echo and everything. John Burns, who is a recording engineer, will be coming with us mixing on the PA. Some things need echo, things come up loud and go right down, so you need someone who's a musician who knows what it's all about to operate it. He's got a more difficult job than we have … We're getting a really tight spread-out sound now. Everything but bass will be going through the PA to get rid of that distortion you get with amps. It needs a lot of thought though, or else it's a dead loss.

PA's a weird thing.'

By the end of 1970 bass player Glenn Cornick had left Jethro Tull and was replaced by Jeffrey Hammond-Hammond a friend of Ian Anderson since schooldays.

The 'Aqualung' album was released in March 1971 and *Sounds* of April 10, 1971 reported: 'There are two qualities in particular that make this album Jethro's finest: taste and variety, neither of which were present in such abundance in their work before. The material ranges from gentle love songs – "Wond'ring Aloud" – to the percussive rock cuts like "Locomotive Breath" with others in between like "Mother Goose", an old English flavoured song, cutely phrased and unusually delivered. Even in "Locomotive Breath" and "Wind Up", the other heavy track, there's light and shade with John Evan's piano introductions providing a contrast to what follows.'

Of Martin's contribution, *Friendz* of May 21, 1971 said: '[The album] includes an exceptional and savoury guitar solo from Martin Barre who also cuts across "Cross-Eyed Mary" and "My God" with a choice sense of drama to complement the commendable lyrics.'

By 1971, Martin said he had met Leslie West of Mountain and as a result bought a Gibson Les Paul Junior which he used on the 'Aqualung' album. This was played through a Fender Super (on 'Cross-Eyed Mary') and 'the rest through Hiwatt plus the Hornby Skewes.' Commenting on the much-revered track 'Locomotive Breath', Martin said: 'That was a Hiwatt amp with a 4x12 in. cabinet, and a Les Paul Junior.'

Jethro Tull enjoyed massive success in front of large crowds and over two successive nights they sold out the Los Angeles Forum (19,000 seats) and Anaheim (9,000). They became one of Britain's hottest rock exports. Towards the end of June 1971, drummer Clive Bunker had been replaced by Barriemore Barlow.

For much of 1971, the music press concentrated on Ian Anderson and his thoughts on music and just about everything else. Martin Barre had his moment when featured as 'Player of the Month' in *Beat Instrumental No. 102* of October 1971. He was pictured with a guitar featuring a Gibson Custom headstock and the top stripped down to the bare wood.

'I like King Crimson, Yes, and the American group Mountain,' he admitted to the magazine. 'At the moment, I find classical music excites me more than anything else. I like Dvorak, Telemann and Vivaldi who, I suppose, were the pop composers of their time but their music endures.'

The magazine added: 'Martin plays mainly guitar although he's just acquired a lute which he's tuned like a guitar. For studio work, he uses a Fender guitar, but on stage uses a Les Paul Standard through Hiwatt amps.'

'I've also got an old Strat but can't handle it on stage,' said Martin. 'I use it just for fiddling about with!'

In March 1972, Jethro Tull embarked on a much-awaited British tour which was sold out; the band's album 'Thick as a Brick' was released in the same month. The original LP cover was designed as a spoof of a 12-page small-town English newspaper, entitled *The St Cleve Chronicle and Linwell Advertiser*, with articles, competitions and advertisements lampooning the typical parochial and amateurish journalism of the local English press.

Martin Barre told *Guitar World* in July 1993: '"Thick As A Brick" was all done in succession – we started off at the beginning and worked our way through the album. And Ian really wrote the material day by day. So, on a Friday we'd finish off with a sort of soft acoustic thing and then Saturday morning, Ian would turn up and say: "Right, we'll go into a guitar solo here, and a riff," or whatever, or, "We'll change key from Bb to Eb," whatever – it was done day by day. And it was good fun because you never really knew where things were gonna go. It was recorded that way as well – in sequence, on the same piece of tape. We'd record an intro, get the tape right and go home. The next day we'd start again right there, either drop in or do an edit, and record the next piece of music.'

Whilst in Australia, as part of a world tour, promoting 'Thick As A Brick', the *Sydney Morning Herald* of July 10, 1972, noted: 'With [Jethro Tull] came 72 pieces of equipment weighing more than 5,000lb and insured for $45,000.'

Jethro Tull's album 'Passion Play' was released in 1973. For the albums, 'Thick As A Brick' and 'Passion Play', Martin states he used Gibson Les Pauls and Hiwatt, though without any effects.

In 1973, Jethro Tull undertook three American tours besides appearing in Europe, the Far East and Australia. But this was the year that Tull fell out with music critics for a time.

A theatrical production of 'Passion Play' at the Empire Pool Wembley in June 1973 was heavily criticised by British music journalists. By contrast, when taken to the US, *Melody Maker* of July 7, 1973 reported: 'The show has sold out three shows at the Los Angeles Forum within one and a half hours of the tickets going on sale, a total of around 53,800 seats.'

Although not a favourite by the music press, 'Passion Play' reached no. 1 in the US – the band's second no. 1 album there, but only no. 17 in the UK. On August 25, 1973 *Melody Maker* ran the headline 'Jethro Retire Hurt', adding: 'Jethro Tull, high in the world's charts with "A Passion Play", amazed the music world this week by announcing their retirement because of "the abuse heaped upon the show by the critics." This extraordinary decision comes after severely critical reviews of both the "Passion Play" album and the band's concert appearances. But Tull are believed to be the first major band to take such criticism to heart.'

Jethro Tull's manager, Terry Ellis commented: 'The abuse heaped upon the [Wembley] show by the critics has been bitterly disappointing to the group and, as illogical as it may be to identify the opinions of the reviewers with those of the public, it has become increasingly difficult for the group to go on stage without worrying whether the audience are enjoying what they are playing.'

Martin Barre told *Record Collector* of October 7, 2013 that he felt that some of the 'Passion Play' music was unnecessarily complex, which made it difficult to play live. 'There was not one gig where I didn't make a mistake – not one, ever! It was impossible, there was so much in it. I mean, not just a slip, but actually making an arrangement mistake, there was so much to remember; it was incredibly complex. Why make it a bar of 7/8 time, did it need to be? And maybe the answer is no, it didn't need to be. I think as a listener, people like to have a rhythm, a groove, to get them involved in the music, and if you're dropping half beats all the way through you can't do it. But as a musician it was a real big lesson, and good to have explored that way of making music complex. But whether you'd ever want to go back and do it again … I don't think so.'

Today, 'Passion Play' is often regarded as a favourite among Jethro Tull fans, and has been listed by contemporary critics as one of the greatest progressive rock albums of all time.

In an interview with *Vintage Guitar* magazine from October 1997, Martin revealed: 'I used a sunburst Les Paul for about four or five years, during the time of "Thick As A Brick" and "Passion Play", but such guitars have become too valuable to take on the road. I met Paul Hamer when he used to deal in vintage guitars. I started playing his guitars because of the value of my old guitars; I hadn't been interested in new guitars for a long time before that. It wasn't a formal endorsement, but maybe they did use me in an ad at one time. It was more of a personal relationship with Paul. I used Hamers for around 10 years.'

Despite the ruck with the press, Jethro Tull were back of the road later in 1974 touring Australia, New Zealand and Japan besides releasing their seventh studio album 'War Child' in October of the same year. In 1975 'Minstrel in the Gallery' appeared. Before Christmas 1975, Jethro Tull parted company with their bass player Jeffrey Hammond-Hammond and he was replaced by John Glascock.

At the end of a long interview with Ian Anderson, by Barbara Charone in *Sounds* January 16, 1976, the equipment used by each Jethro Tull band member was listed. The following is included for Martin: Gibson Les Paul Custom; Fender Broadcaster; Hayman Custom; Martin Acoustic; Yamaha Acoustic; Hiwatt 100-watt amplifier; Hiwatt 4x12 in. cabinets; H/H stereo echo units; Vox amplifier; Marshall tremolo amp; Marshall cabinet; Multi-phase custom-built pedal.

Amongst the albums released during the remainder of the decade was: 'Too Old To Rock 'n' Roll: Too Young To Die!', released in the UK during May 1976. By this time, according to www.jethrotull.com/pastmembers, David Palmer stepped in to fill the void as second keyboard player, concentrating on the provision of the orchestral substitutes then becoming possible with the development of electronic music synthesizers.

In a *New Musical Express* review of 'Too Old To Rock 'n' Roll: Too Young To Die!', it was said on May 8, 1976: 'The songs have simple structures and rely in the main to Anderson's vocal, acoustic guitar and flute, with the band lending unobtrusive musical support – Martin Barre excelling himself on guitar – to what are mainly excellent melodies.'

For 'Too Old To Rock and Roll', Martin admits he 'finally made the transition to Marshall 50-watt heads and, of course 2x12 in. cabs.' He used a Broadcaster on 'Taxi Grab' and also stated 'occasionally a MXR Phase 90 or Flanger crept in.'

In *Rose-Morris International No. 2*, June 1976, headed 'Tull Tour with Marshall', it was announced: 'JETHRO TULL have chosen Marshall amplification to broadcast their music to the world! Now on their first world tour for four years, the band have re-equipped with a complete set of Marshall amplification for the backline sources and a Marshall Equipment Hire P.A. rig … The Marshall amplification was specially selected by the band when they visited Jim Marshall's spacious plant in Britain's newest city, Milton Keynes. It's an indication of the faith that the band has in the products handled by Rose-Morris that the entire backline amps came from Marshall.'

Martin Barre commented: 'When we bought our old one it was the best money could buy. Now this new M.E.H. system is the best – and in a couple of years everyone will be buying one – or hiring one if they can't afford to buy it.'

The Jethro Tull world tour of 1976 was providing Martin with an opportunity to test run the two new Marshall 100-watt stacks he had recently bought from Rose-Morris. He said: 'Actually, I used my old 50-watt amp on "Too Old To Rock 'n' Roll" simply because the 100-watt was too loud. The 50-watt has a good studio sound – really thick – but the 100's will work out good too, once I get used to them. It's really strange because I still feel that tendency to play flat out, to use everything I've got and have it completely wide open – to use all the top, take all the bottom out, put all the middle in, and have the volume flat out. It's psychologically difficult for me to accept that you don't need all that; that you've got some to spare. My main problem is I've never had anything in reserve – I've always had to utilise everything the amp had to offer – and more – because I've had to boost it with pedals. But now I don't have to do this. I've got enough top and good response from all frequencies.'

'Songs From The Wood' appeared in February 1977 and *Melody Maker*, begrudgingly liking the album, commented on January 29, 1977: '"Songs From The Wood" is more durable than its three predecessors, probably because Anderson and his band start fiddling adventurously with the formula, kicking it around and coming up with more experimental arrangements. As well as that, Anderson's vocal blends in much more with the arrangement than it has done. It really sounds as if it is part of the songs.' But the paper stated: 'One of the sadder aspects of this album, in fact, is that Martin Barre is never set loose, which seems to me to be a sad waste of talent, although one of the better aspects of the tracks – and "Pibroch" in particular – is the contribution of the band to the arrangements, especially keyboardists Evans and Palmer.'

Ian Anderson revealed details of Martin's contribution to the album's 'Pibroch (cap in hand)' track on the BBC Radio World Service in March 1979: '…with the guitar piece at the beginning, I said to Martin, "Play me this guitar line" … and he didn't know what for. I said "Go out to the studio and play this little tune," which I played for him on the flute, and then he went out and played it. And he had no idea what was going on inside the control room with all these echo effects … I did everything with that tape to make it sound as if you had about twenty guitars playing, all slightly … different, staggered intervals, playing this thing that was meant to evoke the same emotional thing as a set of bagpipes playing on a windy hill. I mean Martin standing out there thought he was playing a blues riff; had no idea. He then went for a cup of tea and came back, by which time I'd played around with the tapes and done this to it – it absolutely staggered him. He said, "Absolutely fantastic, that! Me…!" You know … "Great!" Which I found was very amusing, and very creative also: it's employing someone's naive involvement in something and then twisting it around and then throwing back something totally different

Martin Barre Band during the Fairport Convention's 40th anniversary at Cropredy Festival in Banbury, 2019.
SOPA Images Limited / Alamy Stock Photo.

as a result.'

An idea of how many records Jethro Tull was selling in the late 1970s is indicated in a statement Ian Anderson made to UK weekly music magazine *National RockStar* on February 5, 1977: 'In a year, worldwide, we will sell 800,000 records. I'll give you my personal guarantee on that, and that's regardless of reviews. But, if we get great reviews, and if we had a hit single from the album in America, obviously where most of our sales are, I'll guarantee you we have two million sales in a year. So things ain't bad.'

'Heavy Horses' was released in April 1978 and Martin commented on the album track 'No Lullaby': 'That was one of those really loud songs played with the amps up full. I played a Hamer guitar in the studio with Marshall amps at 10. I used to use a Gibson Les Paul sunburst, until they got so valuable that I had to buy tickets for it on airplanes. That sunburst went everywhere with me – breakfast lunch, whatever, I couldn't trust it ever going out of my sight. Eventually I thought, "This is wrong," and started playing Hamer guitars.'

On September 16, 1978 *Melody Maker* ran the headline 'Tull to Reach 400 Million by Satellite' and reported: 'Jethro Tull are set to perform in front of the biggest rock audience ever when they play at New York's Madison Square Garden on Monday, October 9. The 20,000 people in the stadium will be joined by an estimated 400 million around the world when the show is televised live by BBC's 'Old Grey Whistle Test' and transmitted in stereo simultaneously on radio. Tull's gig is the first rock concert ever to be televised live from America and, as well as being seen in Britain, it is being broadcast to most of Europe, Australia, Brazil, and America itself … The Madison square Garden concert is part of a six-week American tour by the group which starts on October 1…' In the event, only England took the live pictures.

To coincide with their American tour, the band released their first live album, a double called 'Bursting Out'. All their best-known songs were included as well as two new ones: 'Quatrain', written by guitarist Martin Barre, and 'Conundrum' by Barre and drummer Barriemore Barlow…' Afterwards Tull embarked on a 35-city US tour.

Ian Anderson commenting about Tull's audiences said in *Circus* November 7, 1978, 'Suddenly we've lost the older age group to their domesticity, their mortgages, their family cars, and half-a-swimming-pool average. But it's left a free space for a much younger audience to come in and surprisingly they do. I've queried as to why they come to see Jethro Tull, why they don't want to find their own younger groups to follow. And the only explanation that makes any sense is that, like the Stones or the Who, Jethro Tull has a certain reputation, a mystique that's transcended the generation gap.' Joining Jethro Tull on the tour and playing bass in the band was Tony Williams who replaced John Glascock.

Circus magazine of November 7, 1978 headed a short article, 'Moving Tull', and mentioned: 'Ever wonder, when the lights go up, how all that equipment got there? Behind the seven-week Jethro Tull/Uriah Heep tour, which runs through mid-November, is a logistics effort every bit the equal of the musical performances themselves. The plan calls for trucks (Ryder Rentals) to move from city to city, criss-crossing the country no less than 10 times, for a total mileage of 12,406. Each move is plotted according to a timetable outlined in advance, calculated, for the British group's convenience, in European sequence, where 11 pm is noted as 2300 hours.'

'Stormwatch' appeared in 1979, in the same year the Scottish Ballet Company celebrated its 10th anniversary by including a specially commissioned piece from Anderson and fellow Jethro Tull members Martin Barre and David Palmer. Titled 'The Water's Edge' it dealt with the extraordinary world of Scottish legend and was premiered in Glasgow, at the Theatre Royal, in August 1979. There was another performance at the Sadler's Wells Theatre in London the following November.

Melody Maker July 5, 1980 reported: 'Ian Anderson has re-vamped Jethro Tull with sweeping changes in the line-up. OUT go pianist John Evan, drummer Barriemore Barlow and keyboardist David Palmer. IN comes the highly-rated keyboards player Eddie Jobson from UK plus a 20-year-old Los Angeles drummer, Mark Craney. REMAINING is the exceptional guitarist Martin Barre and top bassist Dave Pegg, the ex-Fairport Convention star who joined Tull a year ago.'

Ian Anderson clarified the situation a week later in *Melody Maker*: 'The changes in personnel and musical direction were ushered in during group discussions over a year ago and involved no ill feeling … I regret any doubts cast over the musical abilities of these three hard-working and talented friends of many years.'

He added that he set about a solo album and because his first thoughts were keyboard-based, he phoned Eddie Jobson, the ex-Roxy Music and Frank Zappa sideman whose outfit UK had supported Tull on the previous year's American tour.

Jobson, it transpired, was on the verge of winding up UK and was delighted to help out on Ian's solo work. Eddie then suggested an American drummer, Mark Craney, whom he had auditioned in the States – and Anderson re-enlisted Martin Barre from Tull, plus Dave Pegg. The scene was set for what Anderson thought would be a period of musical refreshment, with his solo album taking good shape.

When friends and record executives from Chrysalis heard the tapes, they said it was the best Jethro Tull album for some time and, what began as Anderson's private pet, ended up as the 'A' album. It was released at the end of August 1980.

Ray Coleman wrote in *Melody Maker* October 11, 1980: '… dear old Jethro Tull are coming up for air again. A new album, a world tour including concerts at London's Royal Albert Hall next month, and even the traditional single culled from a current LP. Twelve years on the road, 20 million albums sold, but still Ian Anderson is not running out of steam. "Ah, but are they relevant at the dawn of the new decade?" asks a *Melody Maker* reader. It depends entirely on how we measure relevance. To about 13,000 people who will see their two London concerts, and half a million people who will attend their worldwide shows, and enjoy them enough to go and buy Tull's old and new albums, the band is relevant. Judged against, say, the Teardrop Explodes or the Pretenders, Jethro Tull take on a positively paternal, nay grandfatherly, look.'

'Broadsword and the Beast' was released in 1982 and the band used a producer for the first time. Two new band members were included, Gerry Conway (drums) and Peter-John Vettese (keyboards). In 1984, 'Under Wraps' appeared and 'On The Crest Of A Knave' in 1987. Regarding the latter, *Sounds* of September 1987 reported: 'The new LP's opening tracks are stunners: "Steel Monkey" sets a tense keyboard motif against a backdrop of riotous axe-soloing, while "Farm Of The Freeway" [sic] is a contemporary tale of businessmen sweeping away a humble farmer's livelihood. Best of all, "Jump Start" hits the jackpot with an old score being settled between the apparently deranged frontman's flute and the pirouetting guitar of Martin Barre.'

Chris Welch wrote in *Kerrang!*, October 10, 1987: 'There have been many changes in the band's personnel, but Martin Barre remains as Ian's right-hand man, and on ["Crest Of A Wave"] plays some of the most fertile guitar since the invention of the seed drill.' Ian Anderson said in *Billboard* November 21, 1987: 'The songs were constructed to allow the guitar playing to come through and to create the best possible framework to let Martin do his best.'

Martin admits he played a Hamer Chapparal guitar in solid walnut on 'Crest Of A Knave' and 'Rock Island', besides Marshall 15-watt practice amplifiers. Also used on 'Under Wraps', 'Crest Of A Knave' and 'Rock Island' was a Schecter Stratocaster-style guitar.

Following the release of 'Crest Of A Knave', the band launched into yet another world tour. The album turned into one of their most successful for years and won the 1989 Grammy as hard rock/heavy metal album of the year.

Jethro Tull's first album in the following decade was 'Catfish Rising' (1991).

In an interview with both Martin Barre and Ian Anderson in *Guitar World* in July 1993 they both revealed how they have worked together over the long years of Jethro Tull's existence.

Ian Anderson said that Martin was the dominant Jethro Tull personality in the musical sense, explaining: 'Although Jethro Tull has many different facets and characters, according to the finer points of who makes up the band at any point in time, you get the feeling that if you took Martin Barre away, it really wouldn't be Jethro Tull anymore … Very often – especially if it was an improvised section – I would leave him alone for an hour or two and he would do two or three takes. Then I would come and listen to it and say, "Well, the shape of that bit is good," or, "That's a good idea…" We would talk about it and throw it around, and then maybe try and come up with a solo that embraced a few different ideas.'

Explaining how much Ian had influenced the way the guitar came across in Jethro Tull, Martin said: 'Well, he doesn't dictate parts to me, but he's very influential – because I think he's always had a clear idea of how he wants things to sound. And I must say that I've given Ian full control in some areas. I mean, if Ian says, "I think you need this sort of a sound," I'll go with it. As long as I like the sound, I trust his judgment.'

Rolling Stone magazine noted in October 1993, that Jethro Tull were on 'a humongous global tour that would sap the strength of lesser mortals.' In an interview with the magazine Ian Anderson mentioned the following when asked what songs would be played: 'This being notionally a 25th Anniversary Tour, we did try to dig out a few really old ones from the first three albums that we hadn't performed for absolutely ages.'

Around the mid-1990s Martin switched to Soldano Decatone amplifiers coupled with a Marshall 2x12 in. cab and an Ibanez Tube Screamer.

The 'Roots To Branches' album was released in 1995 and 'J-Tull Dot Com' in 1999. Martin played on the latter album (and 'Roots To Branches') Manson guitars and a Matchless Lightning combo.

In 2012, Ian Anderson told Martin Barre and drummer Doane Perry that he had decided to split the band. Martin told www.ultimateclassicrock.com in October 2020: 'Me and Doane were just speechless, really, because Ian has always been a very careful, planned-out person, he knows exactly what he wants and what he's gonna do … It was a very abrupt ending for me and Doane … In a way, it shook me up … I think Tull were getting very lethargic … the sets were becoming very much the same every tour and nobody wanted any change. I always try to get changes within the group and ideas in production and line-up, but there was no interest in doing it. It was a timely occurrence, but it certainly wasn't of my doing or Doane's.'

In *Golamine The Music Collector's Magazine*, Mike Greenblatt wrote on June 20, 2012: 'Jethro Tull has been sliced in half, and it's still bleeding. One half has Ian Anderson resuscitating "Thick As A Brick", and the other half has Martin Barre touring Europe with "The Legends Of Rock" and his own Martin Barre's New Day.'

Since the split with Jethro Tull, Martin has toured and released a number of solo albums.

On his website, Martin admits: 'After a couple of years on Fender Strats I am now a dedicated Paul Reed Smith user. I have two superb 513 guitars and they might just do me for a few years!'

When mentioning his amplifier set-up, he gives these details: '[I use] 2 Soldano Decatone Heads, one feeding one or two 2x12 in. Marshall Vintage Cabs and the other feeding two 1x12 in. Marshall mini-cabs as "front" monitors. From the send of one amp, I route through a simple reverb unit (various makes!) and return to both amps a subtle background hall reverb. An Orchid switching box takes care of the three channels on both amps plus switching in the Ibanez Tube Screamer on the overdrive channel only! I use Samson radio transmitters – they are so simple and so brilliant!'

On www.mansonguitars.co.uk is the following: 'Hugh Manson has been making custom guitars for over 30 years and has earned an enviable reputation within the music industry for innovation and quality. A craftsman and perfectionist Hugh combines technology with inspiring materials to create unique instruments for musicians around the world.'

Matchless Amplifiers was founded in 1989 by Mark Sampson while living in Hollywood, California. He, along with partners Rick Perrotta, Steve Goodale and Chris Perrotta, were the initial force behind the company, often working on Rick's kitchen table.

Sometime in 1965, Syd acquired a Danelectro 3021, a guitar designed by company founder Nathan Daniel and featuring: a semi-hollow body; tempered Masonite top and back; poplar wood neck, core and sides; a rosewood fingerboard, 25 in. scale; and two single-coil pick-ups. Other guitarists such as Jimmy Page and Jimi Hendrix have used the Danelectro during their careers.

Syd Barrett playing the Danelectro guitar with Pink Floyd c.1966.
Pictorial Press Ltd / Alamy Stock Photo.

SYD BARRETT

Whilst Syd Barrett played guitar and wrote songs for a very short period, his influence has been enormous, encouraging many others to move away from accepted practices and boldly create their own individual style.

Born, Roger Keith Barrett on January 6, 1946 in Cambridge, he was the fourth of five children. His father, Dr Arthur Max Barrett was an eminent pathologist and an enthusiastic amateur botanist and ornithologist. A member of the Cambridge Philharmonic Society, he was a skilled classical pianist, watercolour painter and drew plants and fungi. Syd, (adopting this name in his teens) was the only sibling to follow his father's interest in the arts.

Syd's mother, Winifred, was actively involved with the Girl Guides movement throughout her life, as well as running a Wolf Club pack with her husband. Both were practising Quakers.

All Syd's brothers and sisters learned to play the piano. At the tender age of seven, Syd, along with sister Rosemary, won the annual piano prize at the Cambridge Guildhall for their performance of 'The Blue Danube'.

Between 1953 and 1957, Syd attended Morley Memorial Junior School in Cambridge where one of his teachers was Roger Waters' mother Mary. During the latter year, Syd passed his Eleven-Plus and attended Cambridge High School for Boys where he quickly showed an artistic talent.

When Syd was 13, two friends Mick Taylor and Geoff Leyshom, say they showed him how to shape the chords E, A, and D, on a Hofner acoustic guitar. He had played a banjo, picked up in a second-hand shop, for a while and, in his own words, 'pluncked away'. At the age of 14, he acquired his own Hofner acoustic and frequently played in jam sessions with fellow pupils in class at lunch or break times when it was raining and they were unable to go outside.

Syd grew up in the 1950s when social attitudes were changing and arguably this developed further once Conscription ended. In the next decade, the growing popular music scene would flourish and greatly influence everyday life, to create a memorable cultural rebellion that is probably continuing today.

Running concurrent with Syd's growing interest in the guitar was a desire to paint and draw, an ability he had displayed from a very early age. Friends have recollected that he often skipped cross-country running at school and nipped home to paint in his bedroom.

Whilst he was an average student in a number of subjects, he excelled in his early teens with art, and he received much encouragement and advice from his art teacher. He became an avid reader of literature including the works of Hilaire Belloc, Lewis Carroll and Edward Lear, as well as showing an interest in drama. In 1961, he attended a drama summer school in Winchester, involving himself in music-and-movement and improvisation classes and listened intently to a guest lecture from a member of the Royal Shakespeare Company.

During the last month of 1961, Syd's father died. Although deeply upset, his creative urge continued unabated. He was able to shift to a large room in the family home where he could comfortably sleep, draw and paint as well as rehearse. Often, Roger Waters and himself, would strum their acoustic guitars for hours. Amongst Syd's musical influences were Bo Diddley and Joe Brown. He was an admirer of Joe Brown's lead guitar solos and regularly practised playing them.

The final year of Syd's school days saw him being an active member of the school's dramatic society, taking part in several productions. He took an interest in the Theatre of the Absurd movement, and acted in Eugene Ionesco's 'The Bald Prima Donna'.

Syd played in perhaps his first band Geoff Mott & The Mottoes for a brief period during the spring of 1962. He was the band's rhythm guitar player and acquired what has not been convincingly confirmed as being either a Selma Futurama II or Futurama III guitar. They mostly performed renditions of rock 'n' roll numbers and Shadows' instrumentals.

Syd took seven O-Levels in the summer of 1962 and was successful in three of them. His next move was to Cambridge Technical College, enrolling on the Pre-Diploma Art Course. The Pop Art movement's influence had been witnessed in the art world from the mid-1950s and presented a challenge to the traditions of fine art. One exponent of the movement that Syd admired was Jim Dine, known for his contributions to the formation of both Performance Art and Pop Art.

In his Pre-Diploma days, Syd was described as a primitive guitar player and traded Chuck Berry licks with David Gilmour, who was attending the Cambridge Technical College to study for his A-Levels in French and English. Syd occasionally played, from mid-1963 and some months after, with Those Without named after Francoise Sagan's third novel *Those Without Shadows* (1957); the band performed blues and R&B material copying amongst others Jimmy Reed, Bo Diddley and the Rolling Stones.

In Those Without, according to www.groundguitar.com, he sometimes played bass, a 1950s Hofner 500/5, which he bought early in 1964. The website points out he is pictured with the bass in the 2003 BBC Omnibus programme 'Syd Barrett: Crazy Diamond'. Information on the 500/5 is provided on www.guncottonguitars.com: 'Selmer started importing Höfner's 500/5 bass in late 1958 and it instantly became the best bass available in the UK at the time. Many beat combos played one but this beautiful instrument will forever be associated with the Beatles' original bass player, Stuart Sutcliffe.'

Early in 1964, Syd went to the Robert Rauschenberg exhibition at the Whitechapel Gallery where the artist's work led to him producing similar works in mixed media. Syd was also fascinated by the work of abstract expressionist painter, Willem de Kooning, a Dutch-born painter who had settled in America.

When attempting to reach the next stage in his art development, which was the three-year, Diploma in Art &

Design course, Syd applied to both Chelsea and St Martin's schools of art. Although unsuccessful in both these applications, he was delighted to win a place at Camberwell School of Art, starting the course there in September 1964.

The strict figurative disciplines once taught in art schools, especially with the old National Design Diploma course, were soon to be abandoned with the introduction of the Diploma in A&D. Students were allowed to plot their own development attaching themselves to tutors who they considered to be the most useful to their artistic progression. Head of Painting at Camberwell School of Art was Robert Medley, whose work during the early 1960s became increasingly non-figurative.

For his first year at Camberwell, Syd stayed in a large house in Stanhope Gardens, Highgate, owned by Mike Leonard a part-time lecturer at Hornsea College of Art and Regent Street Polytechnic. At the latter place, Roger Waters, Nick Mason and Rick Wright were students who formed a band, known under various names: Sigma 6, the Megadeaths, the Screaming Abdabs, and then the Abdabs.

Syd joined the band in the autumn of 1964 and it also worked as the Tea Set. He was responsible for giving the band a name that has survived decades – Pink Floyd – after two obscure North Carolina blues men Pink Anderson and Floyd Council. Even at this period, Syd was not considered a great guitarist and members continued to perform R&B covers.

Guitars used by Syd over the brief period from late 1964 and into 1965 were a sunburst Hofner Committee with two 'toaster' pick-ups, and a Framus Sorella. A photograph exists of him playing the Framus and it featured a custom-fitted DeArmond Rhythm Chief 1000 pick-up.

Sometime in 1965, Syd acquired a Danelectro 3021, a guitar designed by company founder Nathan Daniel and featuring: a semi-hollow body; tempered Masonite top and back; poplar wood neck, core and sides; a rosewood fingerboard, 25 in. scale; and two single-coil pick-ups. Other guitarists such as Jimmy Page and Jimi Hendrix have used the Danelectro during their careers.

Syd's landlord, Mike Leonard had a great influence on the band, introducing them to light shows and mixed media performances. Light shows were said to have been a significant reason for them to move into a new area. In reality, their live performances became paintings with light and sound.

Syd was encouraged to stop trying to emulate Bo Diddley, and work in a more abstract form. In fact, this may be compared to the way de Kooning approached art, forgetting about past art history and its principles and revel in applying paint to a canvas, and work intuitively from the marks created.

Syd, it has often been conveniently stated, deconstructed his approach to guitar playing. One definition of deconstruct is perhaps applicable here: 'to take apart or examine (something) in order to reveal the basis or composition often with the intention of exposing biases, flaws or inconsistencies.'

In *Beat Instrumental No. 57* of October 1967, Syd stated Steve Cropper and Bo Diddley had a great influence on him and the rest of the group, adding: '[I] don't think they influence me now.' He told the magazine that he had bought a Fender Esquire for £200 and occasionally adjusted the pick-up, 'when I need a different sound.'

Without losing confidence or self-belief, Syd accepted his technical limitations on guitar and pushed himself into other exciting directions. This did not happen straight away as the band continued to play R&B covers during 1965, with Leonard's slides projecting images that washed over them. In the same year, the band submitted their cover version renditions to a few music publishers though without success and entered several competitions with the same outcome. Additionally, they failed an audition for the popular TV programme 'Ready Steady Go!'.

At the beginning of 1966, the band played at private functions and parties, and according to Nick Mason, by this time they had in their repertoire about half a dozen original songs.

When the Notting Hill Free School was established in March 1966, an interesting group of people, with wide-ranging thoughts and ideas, offered help to the ground-breaking institution. Amongst them were John Hopkins, Peter Jenner and Joe Boyd – the latter two would become involved with Pink Floyd.

A great influence on Syd and adding significantly to his move away from straight guitar playing was the work of Keith Rowe, a member of AMM. Rowe did not stand and hold the guitar in the standard way. Instead, he placed it in what has become known as 'a table top position' and created sounds from the guitar by employing different objects such as steel rulers and ball bearings.

In Rob Chapman's *Syd Barrett: A Very Irregular Head* (2010), Keith Rowe explains: 'When the guitar is on the table, the attention's on the table. When people are looking, they're not looking at you any more, they're looking at that. And so, it's this distance thing. I wasn't at the centre of it. It had all those things, which Syd was feeling too.' Interestingly, Rowe says that he could understand why Syd was to withdraw from the music scene a little later. 'In a sense it is already beginning there isn't it [with not wanting to pose with a guitar]. There's a sign of not wanting that gaze.'

In early clips of Pink Floyd playing their classic long improvisational track 'Interstellar Overdrive', Syd may be seen hunched over the guitar on his knee running metal objects up and down the strings. Arguably, he was applying the agenda of Abstract Expressionism to the instrument. Similar to Jackson Pollock, who removed the canvas from the easel and placed it on the floor, so the guitar was removed from a player's body and laid down in a comparable way. Thus, Syd's art school and musical thinking became merged as one.

Syd added silver melinex plastic film and stuck small circular polished metal discs to the white Fender Esquire, with one pick-up, which he bought in 1965, to maybe suggest he wanted to reflect attention further away from himself.

On www.fender.com, an additional detail about the guitar and the part it played in Syd's work is revealed: 'Apart from the visual enhancements, the only other mod to Barrett's Esquire was a raised pick-up, which fattened up the guitar's tone. An early pioneer of creativity over technique, Barrett's guitar work on Pink Floyd's early singles and debut album, "The Piper At The Gates Of Dawn", was fairly basic, something the simplicity of the Esquire lent itself to nicely.'

Peter Jenner, who became Pink Floyd's manager, is quoted as saying that Syd was an inventive musician and inspirational guitar player rather than a technical one.

One effect that Syd made use of successfully was the Binson Echorec, an echo machine produced by the Italian (Milan) company Binson. The company was an early manufacturer of these devices employing an analogue magnetic drum recorder instead of a tape loop.

The latter half of 1966 saw Syd write most of the short compositions that would appear on Pink Floyd's first album, 'Piper At The Gates Of Dawn', though the title was not conceived until a little later. Amongst the records he played at the time was the Beatles' 'Revolver' album.

The band's performances, in the midst of light shows, was described as 'free form pop' and when they appeared at the UFO Club, established in Tottenham Court Road, opening on December 23, 1966, *Melody Maker* described them as the most important band of the year. The *New Musical Express* praised their light shows but were not too impressed with the music.

In 1966 and 1967, AMM played several gigs with Pink Floyd and these were at the Spontaneous Underground events; the Marquee Club; All Saints Hall in Notting Hill; and the *International Times* launch party at the Roundhouse in October. Further, Syd attended the recording session for AMM's debut album in June 1966.

Pink Floyd was filmed in January 1967 playing 'Interstellar Overdrive' and 'Nick's Boogie', for the short documentary 'Tonite Let's All Make Love In London'. Chapman (*op. cit.*) declares Pink Floyd's performance was 'the moment pop liberated itself from blues and its roots.'

Assistant director on the film, Anthony Stern boldly stated: 'It's a magnificent piece of contemporary music. It stands up against [Stravinsky's] "Rite of Spring".' He then gives an observation about Syd's development: 'That sudden switch from Bo Diddley to John Cage – it's a much more abstract style. And that was really the most exciting part about Syd's growth 'cos I think he really was a forerunner of all kinds of stuff. That ability to capture a real rhythmic pulse in "Interstellar Overdrive" which comes from rock music – you can say the one thing he kept from Bo Diddley is that relentless pulse.'

At the end of January 1967, Pink Floyd recorded two of Syd's songs, 'Arnold Layne' and 'Candy and a Current Bun', that were produced by Joe Boyd. A little later Syd took a sabbatical from Camberwell School of Art and a number of his friends there considered this was a wrong move. Pink Floyd turned professional in February 1967 and in the same month they started recording 'Piper At The Gates Of Dawn'. The album features instrumentals and Syd's shorter songs which perhaps drew upon his many literary influences.

The success of the 'Arnold Layne' single, released in March 1967, took the band out of their more familiar London 'underground' club territory and into dance hall venues. Their long improvisations were mostly met with indifference and some hostility and occasionally they were pelted with missiles.

From the mid-1960s, until the end of the decade, popular music fell into basically two categories. One embraced 'underground' bands with the likes of Jimi Hendrix, the Cream, the Nice, and Pink Floyd. In the other category were Soul and Tamla Motown artists, producing music for regular music lovers to dance to in discotheques, Top Rank ballrooms and nightclubs.

Production of 'Piper At The Gates Of Dawn' was placed in the hands of EMI engineer Norman Smith who had worked many times with the Beatles. Besides making pertinent suggestions, contributing some backing vocals, he was intent on making a disciplined commercial record, slimming down a few of the tracks which he considered were burdened by over-long improvisations. Joe Boyd was not involved in 'Piper's' production as EMI wanted one of their own men in control. An argument at the time said Boyd would not have given the album the same commercial focus as Smith. Some of Pink Floyd's ardent London fans decried the finished product as 'commercial pap' though it has since become a 'classic' album.

Amongst the amplifiers that Syd is alleged to have used during the early Pink Floyd days and whilst recording 'Piper' are a Bird Golden Eagle 4/25; a Vox AC30; a 50-watt Selmer Truvoice Treble 'n' Bass; and a Watkins Dominator combo.

Fender Esquire
Officially unveiled in April, 1950, the Fender Esquire was the company's first standard electric solid-body guitar. Although, originally having one pick-up in the bridge position, all bodies were actually routed for two, allowing the option of fitting a neck pick-up.

'See Emily Play' was recorded at Sound Techniques Studio in May 1967, and released in June 1967. It has been hailed as the song that defined the UK music scene's foray into psychedelia as well as epitomising the so-called 'Summer of Love'. Some state that at the time of the recording Syd was changing dramatically. How he changed and for what, if any, reasons has been open to many interpretations and speculations.

Reports state that he was dissatisfied with the final outcome of 'See Emily Play' and even more so with appearing on 'Top of the Pops'. The single spent five weeks in the top ten charts and the band appeared three times on the BBC programme. In one performance Syd appears to mime the song well. On another, he reportedly let his guitar hang low and dropped his head and did not pretend to mime.

Some critics attribute this to the illicit substances he may or may not have been taking at the time. Another argument is perhaps that he was rejecting stardom in a massive way. He still held strong beliefs that were rooted in the work of AMM. Perhaps it is not too dramatic to argue that for him to appear on 'Top of the Pops', amongst all the other chart nonsense, was like de Kooning and Rauschenberg exhibiting alongside parochial artists at a village hall summer show.

In July 1967, he walked out of the BBC 'Saturday Club' session, though this was perhaps not a surprise given the regimented format of the show and the other performers he was expected to line-up alongside. In the following month 'Piper At The Gates Of Dawn' was released and *Melody Maker* reported that Syd was suffering from mental exhaustion.

During late 1967 more of Syd's songs, some of which have been described as having 'dark overtones', were recorded: 'Scream Thy Last Scream'; 'Vegetable Man'; 'Jugband Blues';

Pink Floyd: Their Mortal Remains Exhibition at Victoria & Albert Museum, London May 17, 2017. Courtesy of Alamy.

and 'Apples And Oranges'. Significantly, and perhaps indicating the other members of the band were planning to take their song-writing focus away from Syd, 'Set The Controls For The Heart Of The Sun', by Roger Waters was recorded around the same time.

Guitars and equipment used by Syd through 1967 included a white 1960s Fender Stratocaster, with a rosewood fretboard, which he was seen with at a show at the Queen Elizabeth Hall, London on May 12. Later in 1967, he acquired a c. 1964 white Fender Telecaster with a rosewood neck.

As 1967 progressed, Syd's indifference to the pop world increased. Some have even said he was trying to sabotage the band's success and was incapable of playing any more. In a performance in Copenhagen during September, he was said to have performed well without any problems. During the American tour in early November 1967, at the gig at the old Fillmore West, it was reported he did nothing on stage only blow a referee's whistle. At Venice, Los Angeles, he detuned the guitar on stage and rattled the strings. However, it is worth pointing out that this had occurred during a performance by AMM a year earlier.

When Pink Floyd performed 'Apples And Oranges' on the Pat Boone Show, Syd appeared to be fine. In Rotterdam, the day after the American tour, Syd was said to have played well. During the year, it was noted the band had played nearly 140 gigs.

From November 14 until December 5, 1967, Pink Floyd were included on one of the special 1960s package tours with the Jimi Hendrix Experience, the Nice, the Move, and Amen Corner. On some dates, the Nice guitarist, Dave O'List was asked to be substitute for Syd. This was recalled by him in Dave Ling's article in *Classic Rock* No. 219, February 2016: 'I knew Floyd's music really well – so when they asked me to play with them, it was quite easy.'

A promotional film for Syd's 'Jugband Blues' single shot in October 1967 has him playing a Levin LT 18 guitar. The non-cutaway guitar was Goliath size; featured a spruce top with X-bracing; flame maple back and sides; mahogany bolt-on-neck with adjustable truss rod; single-bound ebony fingerboard with pearloid-block inlays; ebony bridge; nickel-plated strip tuners; and natural finish.

Syd was credited with another good performance on December 20, 1967 when the band appeared on the BBC programme 'Tomorrow's World'. There is enough evidence to suggest Syd was functioning as a creative person though shifting his focus elsewhere. Additionally, it is a legitimate argument that the three other Pink Floyd members took the right decision to continue without Syd, given they had left important university courses to gamble on a career in music.

On January 12, 1968, Pink Floyd appeared at Aston University, Birmingham as a five piece with David Gilmour joining them. They played four gigs as a quintet. On April 6, 1968, there was an official announcement that Syd had left Pink Floyd.

When studying Syd's immediate post-Pink Floyd years, I read about his early return to the studio to record several tracks with Peter Jenner in May 1968. I looked with compassion and sometimes detachment at stories of his excesses in a number of London flats.

Wading through accounts of the recordings of 'Madcap Laughs', released January 3, 1970 and 'Barrett' appearing on November 14, 1970, and the forensic examination of the lyrics of both albums, I found everything fascinating. His use and manipulation of words in most cases was exciting and I suspect they have been influential to a number of song-writers over subsequent years.

I noted with sadness the reviews of his last performances, particularly the final one at Cambridge. Syd, allegedly, was devastated by one review and never performed in public again. However, to detail all this is far beyond the remit of this book.

One author whose judgement and opinions I have trusted to form a basis for writing this Syd Barrett piece has been Chapman *(op. cit.)*. A comment he made about Syd's guitar playing after he left Pink Floyd is most relevant: 'Without the drive and cohesion formerly supplied by his old bandmates, Syd falls back on uninspired blues runs, which merely emphasise his lack of conventional virtuosity. Within months of leaving [the band] he permanently abandoned the sonic voyaging he had once so eagerly pursued…'

A final comment about Syd might be left to his sister, Rosemary Breen. In an interview, at an exhibition of Syd's work in London, 2011, she said: 'If ever he was asked what he did, the reaction would always be "I'm an artist", never "I'm a musician".' She argues that music had side-tracked him away from art but after he left Pink Floyd and took up painting once more, he was a more contented person. She underlines that Syd never understood about being a 'celebrity', and never wanted it in any way.

> **Levin Guitars**
> *Herman Carlson Levin founded the Swedish company which used his surname and was active producing guitars, banjos and lutes from 1900 to 1978. For many years, Levin was the largest instrument manufacturer in Scandinavia.*

JEFF BECK

In a career spanning 60 years, Jeff Beck developed a reputation, with the public and professional musicians alike, as an innovative guitarist always ready to surprise with a moment of brilliance. Often with a Fender Stratocaster and Marshall amplifier, over the years he embraced several musical styles – blues, rock, 'fusion' – and collaborated with a number of top artists. This was in addition to releasing many of his own well-regarded albums, such as 'Truth', 'Blow By Blow' and 'Jeff Beck's Guitar Shop'.

Jeff grew up in a musical environment. His uncle could play the violin, whilst his mother and older sister were also competent on the piano. Yet, he did not find an affinity with either instrument, or the cello, despite attempting to do so. An early inspiration for Jeff to turn to the guitar was Les Paul, who was often heard on the family's radio, and a makeshift instrument was created by Jeff using a box and an elastic band. A school friend with an acoustic gifted the guitar to Jeff, though the instrument had just two strings and he had to improvise to replace the missing ones. His mother and father tried to interest him in Segovia and Django Reinhardt but he was particularly inspired by Gene Vincent and his guitarist Cliff Gallup. This led to another homemade guitar, which he had help in creating into a Fender Stratocaster shape from a neighbour. He then stole a pick-up from a local music shop and built an amplifier in school.

At 14, Jeff attended a Buddy Holly concert and doubled his efforts in learning the guitar, briefly attending lessons before teaching himself and studying the country fingerstyle playing of Chet Atkins. In local bands for a time, Jeff moved into the professional world at 16 with the Bandits which was a backing band. His homemade guitar was deemed unsuitable and Jeff persuaded his father to help buy a Guyatone LG 50. His position in the band was just a short-term arrangement and Jeff enrolled at art college. An opportunity soon arose to join local group the Deltones and Jeff took the role as lead guitarist with a recently acquired Burns Vibra Artist. He later swapped this for a Futurama and upgraded completely to a Fender Stratocaster a little later.

The Deltones eventually disbanded and Jeff worked several jobs throughout 1962. In the following year, he joined another local band – the Nightshift – which he remained with for a couple of years though not finding any success. Jeff joined the Tridents in 1964 and the band was playing blues orientated music as part of the 'British Blues Boom', in addition to his own experiments with sound in between. He had again changed guitars and was playing a Fender Telecaster with a Vox AC30.

Formed in 1963, the Yardbirds also adopted American blues music and after original lead guitarist 'Top' Topham left, he was replaced by Eric Clapton. When the band veered slightly towards a 'pop' sound with the 1965 single 'For Your Love', Eric decided to leave. Session musician Jimmy Page was initially approached, yet he recommended Jeff, a friend of several years' standing. Jeff joined the group around April 1965 which was just in time to experience the band's first success with the aforementioned single. A contemporary performance of the song on American TV show 'Shindig!' sees Jeff playing a Guild 12-string acoustic with added pick-up. On the same programme, the Yardbirds played the follow-up single 'Heart Full Of Soul' and Jeff changed to a blonde Fender Esquire with maple neck. He mainly used the guitar during this early period – firstly with white pick-guard then black – though he was also seen with a rosewood neck Telecaster; Jeff told *Beat Instrumental No. 29* of September 1965 that he had bought one for £125 and 'I like it the best … I don't think I'd play anything else now.' Amplification was from a Vox model.

A feature of 'Heart Full Of Soul' was the 'Indian-style' riff which Jeff devised in the studio using Jimmy Page's fuzz pedal, built by Roger Mayer, though Jeff later obtained a Tone Bender to achieve a similar sound.

With the success of the singles, the Yardbirds travelled to America and performed in several cities, also recording a version of Bo Diddley's 'I'm A Man'. Returning to England later in the year, the next single was the brooding 'Evil Hearted You', which was again written for the group. The following release was 'Shapes Of Things' and this was the first single written by band members. Jeff contributed a particularly interesting guitar solo incorporating an Indian sound with his Tone Bender and feedback. He would achieve a similar sound on the next single 'Over Under Sideways Down'. The Yardbirds quickly recorded their first album 'Yardbirds', also referred to as 'Roger The Engineer', in spring 1966 and featured several moments of note from Jeff, including 'Jeff's Boogie'.

During early 1966, a sunburst Gibson Les Paul was purchased by Jeff and this had a black pick-guard in place of the standard cream one; the pick-up covers were later removed to reveal 'double white' PAF humbuckers. Soon after, he moved on from Vox amps to Marshall and favoured a JTM 45. In mid-1966 the Yardbirds' bassist, Paul Samwell-Smith decided to leave the group and Jeff was quick to enlist friend Jimmy Page on the instrument. This was to be a short-term arrangement as second guitarist Chris Dreja learned the bass over an American tour in the summer. Jeff and Jimmy were able to develop a dual guitar sound when the switch occurred and – though short lived – the pair performing together was captured in the film 'Blow Up' directed by Michelangelo Antonioni. The Yardbirds played 'Stroll On' which was a renamed version of 'Train Kept A Rollin' and Jeff was seen using a sunburst Hofner Senator with a Vox amplifier. Originally, the director wanted Jeff to smash his Les Paul though was soon advised, in no uncertain terms, this was unacceptable and a number of Hofners were purchased for the destruction scene. On working with Jimmy, Jeff commented to *Beat Instrumental No. 45* of January 1967: 'I found that my technique was improving and that Jimmy and I were getting a much closer sound. We'd play separate solos and then, when we played together, we'd find that our ideas were running into each other. Each of us would play separate solos but, when one of us started a phrase the other would slide into it, so that in the end we got sort of a stereo-sound effect between the two guitars.' In the June issue of the same magazine, Jeff was asked why he did not use a semi-hollow body guitar: 'I don't use one because, if I ever started to play one I know I'd never play anything else. I'd rather chop and change. The only time I have used a semi was on the Beatles tour with the Yardbirds. I busted two strings at once on the Telecaster, and Mal Evans fetched George's Gretsch for me, within seconds of us going on. It was in a different pitch from the group's guitars. I had to play "Smokestack Lightning" in Eb!'

The year ended with a package tour across America which pushed Jeff to exhaustion and he decided to leave the group. After a break over the festive period, Jeff recorded his first single 'Hi Ho Silver Lining' b/w 'Bolero' (also known as 'Beck's Bolero'), with the latter dating from a previous session that occurred in summer 1966. The record was a hit for Jeff and spent a number of weeks in the chart. Just before the single was in the shops, Jeff recruited singer Rod Stewart and Ronnie Wood on bass, then permanently hired Mickey Waller on drums after several musicians had been trialled.

The Jeff Beck Group slowly built up a following playing blues around the country. Yet, the band's manager, Peter Grant – who had also worked with the Yardbirds – decided that the American market should be their focus and in mid-1968 the quartet left Britain. Their first gig was at the Fillmore East, playing before the Grateful Dead, and this was particularly successful in announcing the band to American audiences. Jeff travelled with his Les Paul, though the top finish was now stripped to natural, and pushed through a Marshall stack.

Before leaving England, the Jeff Beck Group hastily recorded the album 'Truth'. This mainly featured covers, with three of the ten tracks composed by Jeff and Rod Stewart. Jeff was mostly working with his Les Paul, though used a lap steel on a cover of the Yardbirds' 'Shapes Of Things', and a Marshall, probably using his JTM 45 or a 200-watt head acquired for work in America. A Tone Bender pedal also sounds present, as well as a Wah-Wah, being used in 'I Ain't Superstitious'. Thanks to the popularity gained by the band in America over the summer, the record was quickly released in July 1968 and broke into the US top twenty.

Two further tours of America were carried out in late 1968 and early 1969. The band then returned to the studio to record 'Beck-Ola', which saw drummer Tony Newman recruited and Nicky Hopkins added to the line-up. Jeff had a new Les Paul for the sessions as his other was broken during one of the preceding US tours and later repaired with a new neck that Jeff did not like. The second sunburst Les Paul had been purchased from Rick Nielsen, later of Cheap Trick, and featured a distinctly striped maple top. A new guitar used was a Fender Stratocaster, whilst amplification continued to be Marshall heads and cabs.

The Jeff Beck Group imploded following more dates in America in the summer of 1969. In the winter, Jeff was involved in a serious car accident and suffered multiple injuries, requiring months of convalescence. During mid-1970 he had recovered enough to recruit Cozy Powell on drums and record at Motown's studios in the US, though these proved fruitless and remain unreleased. Retaining Cozy's services, Jeff went on to secure the assistance of new musicians in 1971 for the 'Rough And Ready' album, including Clive Chaman on bass, Max Middleton on keyboard and Bobby Tench singing and playing rhythm guitar. Jeff chose to move his sound away from the heavy blues rock of 'Truth' and 'Beck-Ola' to Soul. For this he mainly concentrated on using his Stratocaster, which had been stripped of the finish and had a maple neck with a three-ply pick-guard broken at the lower horn. A Wah-Wah pedal was also used on some tracks, such as 'Got The Feeling', and on 'Short Business' Jeff played slide, which was a technique he had been nurturing for several years.

Jeff turned to Steve Cropper to produce the next album, 'Jeff Beck Group', in an attempt to find the sound he still thought eluded him. Whilst recording in Memphis, Jeff went to a local music store and purchased a Gibson Les Paul. This was a 1954 model that had been recently refinished in a dark brown or 'oxblood' colour and fitted with humbuckers in place of the original P90s, though the wrap tailpiece was retained.

Before his car accident in 1969, Jeff was set to join forces with former Vanilla Fudge members, Tim Bogert and Carmine Appice. His long recovery forced the idea to be dropped until mid-1972 when the Jeff Beck Group came to an end. Though initially billed under the latter title, also featuring Max Middleton and Bobby Tench, a trio was formed soon after a number of pre-booked gigs were completed and named Beck, Bogert, Appice. The band took a heavy rock direction and Jeff used both his new Les Paul and a contemporary Fender Stratocaster in white with rosewood fingerboard. *Beat Instrumental No. 155* of April 1976, looking back at Jeff's career, noted him using a Gibson SG at this time and pictures exist of him with a late 1960s model. He also used Sunn Coliseum amp heads with Univox 6x12 in. cabinets. The Sunn heads were solid state and remained clean to high volume without the classic breakup associated with tube amps, leading Jeff to play with a Fender Champ as a preamp to distort the signal from his guitar. He continued to use Wah-Wah and slide, whilst a talk box was utilised at certain points. Beck, Bogert, Appice recorded a self-titled album in late 1972/early 1973 and a 'Live In Japan' record in mid-1973. By early 1974, the band had disintegrated despite work progressing on a second album.

Jeff collaborated with the 'jazz-rock' band Upp for the BBC special 'Five Faces of Guitar' during 1974, performing the Beatles' 'She's A Woman' and 'Get Down In The Dirt'. For both songs Jeff used his Les Paul and the Fender Champ amp, as well as the talk box for 'She's A Woman'. Footage of the performance is available on YouTube and is worth seeking to view Jeff's command of the effect, in addition to his dynamic use of the guitar's controls.

Whilst on tour with Beck, Bogert, Appice, the band had supported the Mahavishnu Orchestra, led by John McLaughlin on guitar. Jeff was particularly impressed with the latter's mastery of the instrument and the music the group was playing – a mixture of jazz, rock, eastern music, etc. This found success with audiences and critics alike and Jeff decided to take elements to make his own music. Jeff again joined forces with

Jeff Beck playing with the Yardbirds on 'Ready Steady Go!' 1966.
Pictorial Press Ltd / Alamy Stock Photo.

Jeff Beck performs at Rock 'n' Horsepower, 2014.
Russell Kirby / Alamy Stock Photo.

Max Middleton and added Richard Bailey on drums with Phil Chen on bass for the 'Blow By Blow' sessions produced by George Martin. Jeff played both Les Paul and Stratocaster on the album through Marshall amps, with aforementioned effects as well as newly acquired octave and custom volume pedals. A new guitar provided by future pick-up manufacturer Seymour Duncan – then working for Fender – was a 1959 Telecaster which was heavily modified by a previous owner and further altered by Seymour through the addition of two re-wound PAF humbuckers. This is known to have been used on two or three tracks. The record, which was completely instrumental, sold particularly well in America and a joint tour with the Mahavishnu Orchestra was also successful.

'Wired', released in 1976, followed a similar musical path, with George Martin again producing, and helped along by Max Middleton, though was joined by Mahavishnu Orchestra members Jan Hammer and Narada Michael Walden, in addition to bassist Wilbur Basscomb. Jeff again began to favour a Stratocaster and used a similar pedal arrangement to 'Blow By Blow', whilst a contemporary interview (*Guitar Player* November 1975) has Jeff noting the amplification was Marshall heads with Fender speaker cabinets. Touring across America for the album, Jeff was using his old Stratocaster, a sunburst model with maple neck, as well as a contemporary white guitar with rosewood neck; the latter was later paired with the stripped Stratocaster. Amplification was from Marshall and Univox 6x12 in. cabinets.

At the end of the 1970s, Jeff teamed up with American bassist Stanley Clarke, drummer Simon Phillips and keyboardist Tony Hymas for a tour in the Far East. Jeff was using a white Stratocaster with rosewood neck and black pick-guard, though the pick-ups were also black, with two control knobs and three small switches. This instrument was issued soon after by Greco as model SE-600J and the controls for this were master tone, master volume, switch for all pick-ups either on/off or phase reverse. On the tour, Jeff was also pictured using a Roland synthesizer guitar. The band decided to continue in early 1979 and played a number of dates in Europe during which Jeff had a 1954 sunburst Stratocaster with later 1950s maple neck and changed pick-ups, in addition to his Seymour Duncan Telecaster.

Stanley Clarke departed to work with the New Barbarians before Jeff entered the studio to record 'There And Back' with the other band members, and Mo Foster came in to add bass; Jan Hammer also added keyboards to some songs. Released in 1980, the album continued the precedent set by 'Blow By Blow' and 'Wired' in both sound and success, with the equipment being similar to the latter. An American tour occurred in late 1980, followed by Japan and two nights at the Hammersmith Odeon in 1981, which was Jeff's first show in Britain for several years – a naked bagpiper announced the event on the 'Old Grey Whistle Test'.

In the early 1980s, Jeff took a step away from playing his own music, though still made guest appearances at events and on record. In 1981, he was on stage with Eric Clapton for Amnesty International's 'The Secret Policeman's Other Ball' fundraising event. The pair played three songs: 'Cause We've Ended as Lovers'; 'Further On Up The Road'; 'Crossroads'. Jeff used his Telecaster throughout. Later in the year, Jeff played on Cozy Powell's 'Tilt' record, in addition to performing on a track of Simon Phillips and Tony Hymas's band Ph.D., 'Is It Safe?'. For American TV show 'Rock'n'Roll Tonight', Jeff took the opportunity to play with Les Paul and had an early 1950s sunburst Stratocaster. Jeff also made a small contribution to a Yardbirds reunion album – rechristened 'Box Of Frogs' for legal reasons. In support of Ronnie Lane (of Small Faces and Faces), Jeff was also involved with all the concerts for Action into Research for Multiple Sclerosis (ARMS), with which the former was suffering. Jeff performed a set of material amongst those from Eric Clapton, Steve Winwood and Jimmy Page. The first show was in London, though later travelled to America. Jeff used a Stratocaster for some shows and also played a newly acquired Jackson Soloist in pink (with Kahler locking tremolo), as well as another in orange (utilising a Floyd Rose unit), along with a Telecaster. The first half of the decade was topped with Jeff playing lead guitar on several tracks for Mick Jagger's first solo album 'She's The Boss'.

In the mid-1980s, he returned to working on his own material and enlisted record producer Nile Rogers to work with him on 'Flash'. The latter, after much persuasion, had Jeff record vocals on two tracks – 'Get Workin'' and 'Night After Night' – for the first time in many years, whilst the others had Jimmy Hall take over singing duties; Rod Stewart was a guest on 'People Get Ready'. In *Hot Wired Guitar: The Life of Jeff Beck* (2014) by Martin Power, the author notes that the interesting solo in 'Get Workin'' was created by Jeff 'popping the strings of his '53 Tele against the pick-ups, the treble rolled right back so as to enhance the overall percussive effect.' Power also notes that a Seymour Duncan 100-watt Convertible amp was employed for the sessions – Jeff later promoted the product in advertisements – in addition to a Rat overdrive pedal.

Though experiencing a successful tour of Japan in support of 'Flash', the album was a disappointment commercially and Jeff was subsequently dismissive of the project – and the 1980s in general – as being too rooted in the period. In the latter part of the 1980s, Jeff again worked with Mick Jagger on his second solo album, 'Primitive Cool' and was due to be part of a tour in support of the record, though 'creative differences' led Jeff to leave the band.

Now with some free time, Jeff headed into the studio with drummer Terry Bozzio and Tony Hymas to record, with the results released as 'Jeff Beck's Guitar Shop' in late 1989; the trio won 'Best Rock Instrumental Performance' at the 1990 Grammy awards for their efforts. Jeff continued to favour his Stratocasters, though the Les Paul made an appearance, as did a Gretsch Duo Jet, whilst amplification was from Marshall and Fender models; the Rat continued to provide overdrive. There were several high points on the album, including 'Where Were You', which is a beautifully haunting piece thanks to Jeff's mastery of the instrument, seamlessly controlling the tremolo bar and creating volume swells at the same time.

In 1991, Jeff's association with the Fender Stratocaster was recognised by the company as he received a signature model. This had some modern appointments, such as roller nut, rosewood fretboard with 9.5 in. radius, 1950s neck shape, polyurethane finish, Sperzel locking tuners, Fender lace sensor pick-ups in neck and middle positions with lace sensor humbucker in the bridge, five-position switch, push-pull pot and two-point tremolo. Production of this continued through to 2001 when upgraded.

In the early 1990s, Jeff again turned to session work, including film scores for 'Young Guns II' and 'Days Of Thunder', and guest appearances with other artists, such as Buddy Guy and Roger Waters. A career-spanning retrospective of outtakes and rarities was also assembled – 'Beckology'. In 1992, Jeff worked with Jed Leiber on the soundtrack to the Australian TV series on the Vietnam war, 'Frankie's House'. Power (*op. cit.*) notes Jeff using a Digitech GSP 21 Legend guitar signal processor during the recording of this project, with the unit used between the Stratocaster and recording console. Jeff and Jed went on to win a BAFTA TV award for 'Best Original Television Music'.

Jeff returned to his roots for 1993's 'Crazy Legs', with the Big Town Playboys, which honoured Gene Vincent and his guitarist Cliff Gallup. For the record Jeff decided to source the same Gretsch Duo Jet as used by the latter, but had a false start with a 1963 model when Cliff used a 1954 guitar with fixed-arm Bigsby tremolo. Jeff had to settle with a 1956 Duo Jet with swivel-arm Bigsby, though later had a fixed-arm Bigsby-equipped Duo Jet. Several Fender amps from the period were also used to recreate a similar sound to what Cliff achieved on the original records. Jeff also had to change his picking technique as Cliff used two fingerpicks and a plectrum between thumb and index finger. Of the project, Jeff is quoted on www.gretcsch.com: 'The guitar parts were difficult to get right … I put myself in Cliff's shoes for a month and I've got to take my hat off to him – if he came out with those solos off the top of his head then the guy was more of a monster than I ever believed.'

At the end of the 1990s, Jeff started working on his next studio album, 'Who Else!', with Steve Lukather producing and Jennifer Batten recruited for second guitar duties. Randy Hope-Taylor was on bass, Steve Alexander on drums and Tony Hymas on keyboards, though the latter also produced when Steve and Jeff parted ways amicably due to 'creative differences'. The record saw Jeff experimenting with electronic dance music backing overlaid with his guitar, such as 'What Mama Said', 'THX 138' and 'Psycho Sam', whilst also providing a more familiar sound for long-term fans in 'Brush With The Blues', 'Blast From The East' and 'Angel (Footsteps)'. The album inspired Jeff to continue with this mixture of musical styles and these were present on 'You Had It Coming', which was released in early 2001. On tour in support of the latter record, Jeff was using a Stratocaster with two Marshall JCM 2000 DSL50 heads and two Marshall 4x12 in. cabinets, though – according to an article on www.guitarworld.com – these had been heavily modified from the stock configuration.

In the midst of several guest appearances with other artists, Jeff made his ninth album, 'Jeff' and this was released in 2003. Then he went on tour with B.B. King and played dates in Britain during 2004. He favoured a white Stratocaster with rosewood neck from the Fender Custom Shop at this time, still with the Marshall amplification. Jeff had upgraded his signature guitar in 2001 with softer 'C' shape neck, dual coil ceramic noiseless pick-ups, contour heel and five-way selector. In 2004, the Custom Shop also began producing his Stratocaster guitars, and later a recreation of the Esquire from the Yardbirds was released as a limited edition. During 2006, Jeff performed at the company's 60th anniversary show.

Jeff played a series of intimate gigs at Ronnie Scott's club in London towards the end of 2007 and these were recorded for a special DVD release. He performed with a cream-coloured Stratocaster and had his two Marshall JCM 2000 heads along with two reissue Marshall JTM 45 heads. Jeff had a similar arrangement when he was inducted into the Rock & Roll Hall of Fame in 2009, performing with Jimmy Page on the latter's 'Immigrant Song' during an interlude to 'Beck's Bolero'. Jeff had assembled a pedal board and favoured a Klon Centaur for distortion, whilst having a ring modulator, flange pedal, Wah-Wah, octave pedal and delay.

'Emotion & Commotion' was released in 2010 and was particularly successful for Jeff in both the US and UK, as well as Japan. The record mainly featured classic and popular songs interpreted by him, with guest vocals provided by Imelda May, Joss Stone and Olivia Safe. 'Hammerhead', which was written by Jeff and keyboardist Jason Rebello, went on to win a Grammy award in 2011 for 'Best Rock Instrumental Performance', providing Jeff with his sixth win in the category; this was the last year the award was offered.

During June 2010, Jeff paid tribute to Les Paul, who had died a year earlier, in New York at the Iridium Club, playing a number of rock 'n' roll standards. Whilst using the Stratocaster, he also had several other guitars, including a Gibson ES 175, Fender Telecaster and sunburst Gibson Les Paul 1958 reissue, with amplification from several Fender Pro Juniors.

Jeff continued to play consistently throughout the 2010s, with a recording made of a night in Tokyo during 2014 and at the Hollywood Bowl in 2017. For much of this period Jeff used a signature Stratocaster with rosewood neck possessing a reversed headstock. In 2016, Jeff released 'Loud Hailer' which was a collaboration with Rosie Bones (vocals) and Carmen Vandenberg (guitar) of Bones UK.

Jeff worked with actor/musician Johnny Depp in the early 2020s. The duo created new material and covered a number of songs, which saw release on the album '18' in mid-2022. Following a short illness, Jeff died in January 2023 and many tributes were paid to him by friends/musicians, such as Jimmy Page, Ronnie Wood and Mick Jagger, as well as millions of fans across the world.

Ritchie Blackmore with Deep Purple, 1974.
MARKA / Alamy Stock Photo.

RITCHIE BLACKMORE

Known as an eccentric personality, Ritchie Blackmore's career in music has been equally unconventional. Starting out working with Joe Meek playing mainstream pop music, Ritchie subsequently moved to the forefront of the heavy rock genre with Deep Purple and Rainbow. More recently, Ritchie has concentrated his efforts on performing medieval/renaissance pieces with his wife Candice Night under the name Blackmore's Night.

Music began to interest Ritchie early in life, particularly that of Elvis Presley, Duane Eddy, Buddy Holly and Tommy Steele. At age 11, Ritchie was given a Framus acoustic guitar by his father, with the stipulation that he had to take lessons. Finding a classical tutor, Ritchie was taught for around a year. He later received advice on playing contemporary songs from noted musician Big Jim Sullivan, who was a friend of Ritchie's older brother.

The Framus was later modified through the addition of three pick-ups and Ritchie used a portable radio for amplification. His first 'real' amplifier was a Watkins Dominator, though he experienced problems with several examples and changed to a different model.

Ritchie's second guitar was a blonde Hofner Club 50 which he acquired from Jim Marshall's shop in the early 1960s. In Gordon Giltrap and Neville Marten's *The Hofner Guitar – A History* (1993), Ritchie comments: 'The Hofner Club line were wonderful guitars, although I wouldn't play them much on stage because they didn't cut through that well. But, like everyone else, I remember looking through the magazines at fourteen and thinking how wonderful they all were.' Ritchie possessed the instrument for around two years and in this time, he fitted a Bigsby tremolo unit to the guitar.

During the skiffle boom of the mid-1950s, Ritchie was involved with a group, though not playing guitar. After acquiring the Club 50, he joined the Vampires – later the Dominators – which also embraced this new style. Ritchie performed with the group for a time before deciding to become a professional guitarist. He auditioned for Screaming Lord Sutch & the Savages, narrowly missing out to his fellow guitarist in the Dominators. Soon after, Ritchie was asked to join Mike Dee & the Jaywalkers and began playing at venues outside his local area.

Thanks to the continued support of his father, Ritchie was able to upgrade all his equipment for this new endeavour. He bought a cherry Gibson ES 335 with 'dot' neck and Vox AC30, as well as a Vox echo unit. Again, the guitar was fitted with a Bigsby B5 or 'horseshoe' tremolo. The band pushed for success, recording a demo for Decca and briefly featured on a Billy Fury tour, yet this proved elusive. When Ritchie was approached by Screaming Lord Sutch to join the band in early 1962, there was no hesitation from the 17-year-old guitarist.

Ritchie was only with the group for six months, though the time was formative as the naturally shy young man was required to join in with the stage antics of Screaming Lord Sutch. The large number of gigs also promoted Ritchie's talent with the guitar, particularly the speed of his playing at this time. Following his departure from the Savages, Ritchie was approached by Joe Meek to join the Outlaws which the latter produced.

Whilst Lord Sutch provided stage experience, the time spent with the Outlaws educated Ritchie in the studio. The group recorded as backing musicians for many of Joe Meek's performers, such as Glenda Collins, Freddie Starr and Heinz, in addition to releasing singles under their own name. The band's first record saw a release in early 1963 – 'The Return Of The Outlaws'. Extensive touring was also undertaken and the Outlaws backed Jerry Lee Lewis on one package event, in addition to Gene Vincent. An appearance in the film 'Live It Up!' was arranged and the band performed the instrumental 'Law And Order'; Ritchie energetically plays his Gibson ES 335.

The Outlaws reached the end of their time together in 1964. For a final single, the group recorded 'Keep A Knockin', backed with 'Shake With Me', which featured a particularly impressive solo from Ritchie. He continued his association with Joe Meek and was given the role of leading the latter's protégé Heinz's band the Wild Ones (later changed to the Wild Boys).

Though Heinz was moderately successful, Ritchie was soon ready to move on and in early 1965 he joined Neil Christian & the Crusaders. Finding few gigging opportunities, the band took an offer from Screaming Lord Sutch to back him for some dates.

In the midst of sessions for other performers, Ritchie was able to record two tracks for release under his own name – 'Getaway' with 'Little Brown Jug'. On both tracks, Ritchie achieves an unusual guitar tone. Mick Underwood, who was drummer on the session (also playing with Ritchie in the Outlaws), explains in *Black Knight: Ritchie Blackmore* (2008) that this was achieved by using his amp with 'cheap little speakers … [that] … didn't last very long but they fuzzed and he could get the sustain.' The single was released in March 1965 but received little attention.

At the end of the year, Ritchie was in Germany to back Jerry Lee Lewis in Hamburg. Following the conclusion of this spell, he decided to remain in the city with two other musicians forming the Three Musketeers. The band played a number of gigs in clubs, mainly fast instrumental songs, with Ritchie being particularly inspired by Les Paul over this period. In early 1966, this group dissolved and Ritchie rejoined Neil Christian & the Crusaders, then Screaming Lord Sutch, before forming the Trip for a tour in Italy.

Following the hustle and bustle of the previous years, Ritchie had a quiet year in 1967, having relocated to Hamburg following the breakdown of his first marriage. He attempted to form a band whilst there, though this came to naught. At the end of the year, Ritchie was contacted by Chris Curtis (formerly of the Searchers) with a view to founding a new group. The latter quickly lost interest, yet Ritchie persisted with others contacted by Curtis – organist Jon Lord and bassist

Nick Simper – whilst suggesting drummer Ian Paice and Rod Evans on vocals. Originally known as Roundabout, the band changed names to Deep Purple in early 1968.

During the first few months of 1968, Deeves House, near South Mimms (just north of London), served as the group's base for rehearsals of new material and covers. With backing from a management group, the band was able to buy new equipment and Ritchie acquired a Marshall stack, as well as a Wah-Wah pedal. He chose to continue with his Gibson ES 335 and this was present for the group's first recorded performance – of the Beatles' 'Help!' – in Denmark at the end of April 1968.

Before leaving England for the Danish tour, Deep Purple had recorded demos with a view to being signed by the American label Tetragrammaton. With these accepted, the band booked recording sessions for May. The result was several tracks forming the 'Shades Of Deep Purple' album released in America during July 1968. The record was preceded by the single 'Hush' which was a cover of a Billy Joe Royal song written by Joe South. This was a big hit for the group in North America, reaching no. 4 on the Billboard chart, also helping the album into the top thirty. With this success, Deep Purple was soon on tour in the States and appeared on the 'Playboy After Dark' TV programme performing 'Hush'. Ritchie again has his ES 335 and briefly demonstrates a few chords to the programme's host (and magazine founder) Hugh Hefner in a segment before the performance.

Little attention was paid to Deep Purple in Britain at the time and both the single and album did nothing to broaden the group's fan base. A promotional video was made for 'Hush', with the band miming to the song in an outdoor setting. Ritchie is seen with a new guitar which is a Fender Telecaster in black with Bigsby tremolo.

For the American tour in late 1968, Deep Purple was obliged to quickly produce a second album. 'The Book of Taliesyn' was similar to the first record in that original compositions were mixed with covers. Neil Diamond's 'Kentucky Woman' was the first single, followed by Ike and Tina Turner's 'River Deep, Mountain High'. Both failed to capture the success of 'Hush', as well as the album falling short of the top fifty.

Ritchie had been particularly influenced by Jimi Hendrix following his emergence in 1967 and around 1968/1969 he decided to obtain a Fender Stratocaster. His first came from Eric Clapton, though Ritchie found this difficult to play, despite liking the sound. During an interview with *Guitar Player* magazine in 1978, he commented: 'The transition [from Gibson to Fender] was really hard. I found great difficulty in using it [the Stratocaster] the first two years. With a Gibson you just race up and down [the neck], but with a Fender you have to make every note count; you have to make the note sing or otherwise it won't work.'

Following the American tour, Deep Purple returned to the studio and recorded tracks for their third album 'Deep Purple'. This proved to be the last for Tetragrammaton, as the company ran into financial difficulties, and for singer Rod Evans and bassist Nick Simper. The pair left in mid-1969 and replaced by Ian Gillan and Roger Glover, who were known to be song-writers.

The 'Deep Purple' album again failed to interest the British public and did not see strong sales in America. Similarly, the band's next single 'Hallelujah' failed to make an impression despite being chosen for perceived commercial potential. During a performance of the song on the German TV programme 'Beat-Club' in 1969, Ritchie makes an early appearance with a 1968 Fender Stratocaster which is black and has a maple neck with large headstock.

In September, the band played a concert with the Royal Philharmonic Orchestra. Jon Lord had written 'Concerto for Group and Orchestra' specifically for the project. Broadcast by the BBC, the event served to promote Deep Purple and was successful, as was the subsequent album recoding of the performance. Ritchie returned to his ES 335 and Vox AC30.

Whilst Deep Purple had produced material that reflected music popular at the time, from mid-1969 a focus was placed on hard rock music and this was spearheaded by Ritchie. The band honed this change through a series of gigs in Britain and Europe through the end of 1969 and into 1970.

Ritchie continued to play his ES 335, though his Fender Stratocaster was often in evidence and both were sent through a pair of Marshall 200-watt 'Major' stacks, which became his favoured set-up going forward. Ritchie's sound from these was mainly achieved by modification of the head's preamp circuit and the use of a Hornby Skewes Treble Boost pedal. Ritchie had both the germanium and silicon transistor versions and later had a unit custom-made. The AC30, which was used for 'Wring That Neck' on stage during this period, perhaps also remained in service in the studio for a time. Ritchie particularly liked the sound of the Vox and modification of the Marshall 'Major' heads was an attempt to recreate this for the large concert halls the band played in. Ritchie has commented in several interviews over the years that he would go to the Marshall factory and ask the technicians to change components to suit his preferences.

Between concerts, the group spent time in the studio recording material for the next album, 'Deep Purple In Rock'. The record was released in June 1970 and was particularly successful in the UK, peaking at no. 4 in the charts. Following the lead of the album was the specially-written single 'Black Night', which reached no. 2. Both records similarly brought the band to the attention of the public worldwide and a tour was undertaken in Europe, America and Australia to the end of 1970, as well as most of 1971.

Early in this period, Deep Purple appeared on the Granada TV show 'Doing Their Thing', performing 'Speed King', 'Child In Time', 'Wring That Neck', and 'Mandrake Root'. Ritchie starts off with his black Fender Stratocaster, before taking up his Gibson ES 335 for two songs, then ending with the Fender. His Marshall stacks and the AC30 are used. Also of note is Ritchie's theatricality with the guitar, particularly the Stratocaster on 'Mandrake Root', where he swings the instrument several times and ends by playing the guitar with his foot on the floor, to mention just two instances.

Whilst touring took up most of the band's time, sessions were booked in various studios between dates. Though struggling to be inspired, 'Fireball' was released in June 1971. This was preceded in February by the single 'Strange Kind Of Woman' which entered the top ten of the UK chart. In a performance of the song on Italian TV in May 1971, Ritchie

Ritchie Blackmore with Deep Purple.
Pictorial Press Ltd / Alamy Stock Photo.

Ritchie Blackmore with Deep Purple at the California Jam, April 6, 1974 at the Ontario Motor Speedway in Ontario, California.
Pictorial Press Ltd / Alamy Stock Photo.

has a white Fender Stratocaster with maple Telecaster neck. In Jerry Bloom's *Black Night: Ritchie Blackmore* (2008), Deep Purple roadie, Ian Hansford, comments that Ritchie's first Strat, which was bought from Eric Clapton, was one fitted with a Telecaster neck.

At the end of 1971, Deep Purple travelled to Switzerland to record their new album. Following the problems experienced producing 'Fireball', the group decided to concentrate on capturing their live sound, using the Rolling Stones Mobile Studio. A handful of new songs had been developed during the preceding tours, though a new song was penned after the original venue for the sessions, the Montreux Casino, caught fire in the midst of a Frank Zappa concert. 'Smoke On The Water', with the distinctive riff developed by Ritchie, was not particularly popular with the band when recorded, yet the song later gave Deep Purple a resurgence of interest in America thanks to heavy airplay on the radio.

Around this time, Ritchie acquired a new Fender Stratocaster, which had a sunburst finish, maple neck and scalloped fretboard. This latter feature – where the wood between the frets is removed – was done by Ritchie himself and he tailored the modification to suit his own playing style. The main benefit of this is to allow faster playing as friction is reduced between fingers and the fretboard. Ritchie would favour a scalloped fretboard going forward.

The resulting 'Machine Head' album was an immediate

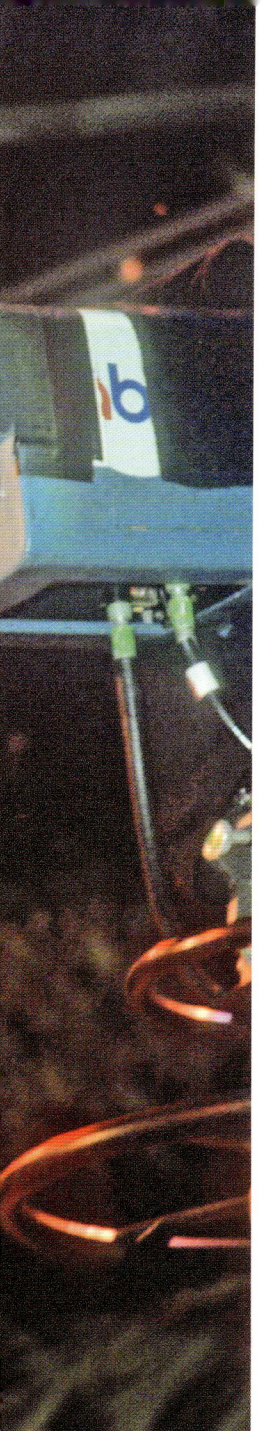

success in Britain when released in March 1972 and did break into the top forty in America, though in 1973, the album climbed to no. 7 on the back of the success of 'Smoke On The Water'. Much of 1972 was spent on tour, with Ritchie using both the black and sunburst Stratocasters through two Marshall 200-watt heads and cabinets. Footage exists of the March concert in Copenhagen, where Ritchie uses the black Stratocaster exclusively until the encore when a switch is made to the sunburst. The latter is used on a 'Beat Club' performance in June, with the camera often closely following Ritchie's finger movements and also providing a glimpse of the scalloped fretboard.

When the band was in Japan during August 1972, the opportunity was taken to capture several dates on tape and tracks from these were assembled for release in that country only. Yet, the album was ultimately available worldwide and provided the group with another hit record. Though Deep Purple was very popular around the world at this point, internal tensions were surfacing, partly due to the heavy workload. At the end of 1972, lead singer Ian Gillan announced he was to leave the band after booked concerts had been completed; bassist Roger Glover also subsequently departed from the group.

'Who Do We Think We Are' was the last album to feature the second line-up of Deep Purple and was recorded towards the end of 1972 at several venues; release occurred in early 1973. The year did not start well for the band as a riot occurred at a concert in Holland in late January and much of the equipment was destroyed. Marshall had to send replacement amplifiers with just three days' notice before the next date.

By the end of 1973, David Coverdale had become the band's vocalist, whilst Glenn Hughes filled the bassist position. Ritchie had spent much of the downtime developing ideas for the band's next album, 'Burn'. This was recorded when Deep Purple returned to Switzerland in November 1973 and appeared four months later. Soon after the release, the band performed at the 'California Jam' festival. Ritchie used a new Stratocaster with natural finish, later turning to a mid-1970s white model. At the end of the set, he discarded the instrument at the front of the stage and picked up another white Stratocaster, which he completely destroyed (damaging a film camera in the process). For a finale, the central amplifier stack of a trio exploded and was again dumped in front of the stage. At the end of this carnage, a new and integral piece of Ritchie's sound is glimpsed – an Aiwa TP-1011 reel-to-reel tape recorder. He used this as an echo unit, though further changes to his Marshall Major amps were necessary for the pair to work to his liking. Also, around this time, the preamp modification was superseded by the addition of an extra output stage.

Following 'California Jam', Deep Purple returned to Britain and began a UK tour in Scotland during late April, moving through England in May. Ritchie continued his Stratocaster use and added a 1970s left-handed sunburst model with maple neck in an apparent homage to Jimi Hendrix. With a break scheduled for June, the band reunited in July for writing sessions for the next album, 'Stormbringer'. At this time, Ritchie's tastes were seriously diverging from those of David Coverdale and Glenn Hughes, with the pair favouring a move away from the hard rock of earlier albums to funk. Ritchie meanwhile was increasingly immersing himself in the music of several centuries earlier, particularly medieval and baroque pieces.

An American tour was completed at the end of 1974, featuring American band Elf as support. Ritchie became friendly with the band, especially the singer Ronnie James Dio, and decided he wanted to use them – minus the guitarist – for a solo project during time off from Deep Purple in early 1975. The tracks subsequently recorded formed the album 'Ritchie Blackmore's Rainbow' released in August 1975. Ritchie retained his foundation of a distinctive riff with flamboyant solos and fills whilst incorporating classical elements. On a radio interview at the time – partially reproduced in Bloom (*op. cit.*) – he comments: '…a lot of the progressions we used were classical progressions. That's not as drastic as it sounds, they're still rock progressions because I believe that Bach even in the 16th century [sic] was still playing in a way that was very relative to the way that people are playing today which is very rhythmical … We used a lot of modes instead of scales. And modes meant we used weird chords. But we found out it worked with a rock backing.'

Before the album went on sale, Ritchie agreed to fulfil his obligation to Deep Purple's Eastern European tour in the spring of 1975. Whilst initially remaining silent on his future with the band, by the middle of the tour continued tensions resulted in Ritchie's decision to quit at the end of the dates.

'Ritchie Blackmore's Rainbow' was relatively successful and reached no. 11 in the UK charts and no. 30 in America. Ritchie was determined to improve on this and attain the level of success of Deep Purple with his own band, as well as drastically reducing the pressure that had been placed on the old group. Although there were no complaints with the musicians used on the album, Ritchie decided to retain just Ronnie James Dio and went on to recruit Cozy Powell on drums, bassist Jimmy Bain, who was an old friend from Hamburg and American keyboard player Tony Carey. The new band – renamed just Rainbow – briefly rehearsed before going on a short tour of North America at the end of 1975. Ritchie continued to play through his two Marshall stacks, using a natural Stratocaster.

In early 1976, Rainbow reunited to record the next album – 'Rising'. This had a similar sound to the preceding record, though a new element was Ritchie's use of a slide, which he had used sparingly in the past. Two tracks featured the slide, 'Run With The Wolf' and 'Starstruck'. Later footage of Ritchie using the slide shows his preference for grasping the slide rather than on the finger, as in the bottleneck style.

Speaking to Paul Guy of Guy Guitars in 1998 (with the interview reproduced on www.guyguitars.com), Ritchie comments: 'I find you can get a better vibrato by grasping [the slide], because you can move the whole wrist and hand, as opposed to just a finger, which is a little bit more jerky.' In another interview (recorded while with Blackmore's Night and available on youtube.com), Ritchie revealed he liked to slacken and move the low E and A strings off the fretboard to just sound the top four strings when playing slide.

The 'Rising' album appeared in mid-May and the band was soon on the road in support. For the previous tour, Ritchie had pressed for a giant illuminated rainbow crossing the stage, yet this proved problematic, not least with the guitar pick-ups receiving interference from the lights (commonly known as 60 cycle hum). This lighting feature was retained for the second tour, with the problems worked out to an extent. Ritchie modified his guitar to use the middle pick-up as a second coil that cancelled any hum received and switched to low impedance pick-ups as a further deterrent. These had reduced windings and the signal was boosted to be like a normal single coil. Ritchie's preference was to use the neck and bridge pick-ups exclusively, so the loss of the middle position was not a problem. Also of note is the frequency with which Ritchie would change pick-up positions during songs, particularly solos.

On the tour, Ritchie was seen with several Stratocasters, including a sunburst guitar with maple neck, a white Strat with rosewood neck and white pick-guard and another white model with black pick-guard and pick-up covers. The latter, which later received a white pick-guard, became a main guitar for Ritchie and utilised Red Rhodes' 'Velvet Hammer' pick-ups.

Rainbow's schedule during 1976 and 1977 was particularly intense, with touring undertaken through the end of 1976 in Britain, Europe, Australia, Japan and America. In 1977, the band began by recording material for the next album, 'Long Live Rock 'n' Roll'. These sessions were broken by a European tour and the recruitment of bassist Bob Daisley and keyboardist David Stone. Ritchie used several Stratocasters over the aforementioned period, including those mentioned above, not least because a number were destroyed during his on-stage antics, such as Munich in 1976 and the Empire Theatre, Liverpool, 1977, when he went in a box at the end of the set and smashed his guitar – as well as some decor.

Released in April 1978, 'Long Live Rock 'n' Roll' breached the top ten in the UK, but was perhaps disappointing elsewhere, particularly America. Ritchie's use of the slide was pronounced and featured on several tracks, including 'Lady Of The Lake', 'LA Connection', 'The Shed' and 'Sensitive To Light'.

A standout song from the record was 'Gates Of Babylon', which featured an unusual chord sequence, providing Ritchie with a chance to deliver an impressive solo. He later cited this amongst his favourites, commenting to *Guitar Player* magazine in 1978: 'It is the best because it's the most intricate solo, yet at the same time it's not clinical … There are so many weird chords involved that I could go back to my old way of playing, which is just to have the chords in front of me and play the solo … Because I love musical theory I was well into that … I love playing a few augmented and diminished runs and not just the usual blues licks.'

Before the album appeared, Rainbow toured Japan extensively and then later in the year supported REO Speedwagon across America. Over this period, Ritchie's relationship with Ronnie James Dio deteriorated and at the end of the year he was ready to reform Rainbow with new musicians. Ex-Deep Purple bassist Roger Glover was recruited, along with Don Airey on keyboards and Graham Bonnet for vocals.

Ritchie decided he wanted to appeal to a broader audience with the new record – 'Down To Earth' – and the lead single was a cover of Russ Ballard's 'Since You Been Gone'. This was particularly successful in Britain and a promotional video was filmed. Ritchie has a white Stratocaster with rosewood neck and black pick-ups, which were Schecter F400 models and wired in the manner previously stated. The guitar was a favourite for Ritchie and found use on the second American tour in late 1979, the Japanese and European tours of early 1980 and for the inaugural 'Monsters of Rock' festival at Donnington in August.

The gig marked the end of this line-up of Rainbow, as drummer Cozy Powell decided to leave and Graham Bonnet soon after felt at odds with Ritchie's new direction. This was a move towards high-tempo rock. Drummer Bob Rondinelli was brought in, along with singer Joe Lynn Turner for the sessions that yielded the next album, 'Difficult To Cure'. The lead single was 'I Surrender' (another track by Russ Ballard) which turned into the band's biggest single, climbing to no. 3 in the British Charts; the album reached a similar position.

Rainbow quickly followed up the album with their sixth record 'Straight Between The Eyes', which was released in mid-1982. A tour of the US was undertaken at the time and at the end of the year, Rainbow was in Japan and Europe. Ritchie continued to use his white Stratocasters with Marshall amplifiers.

In the early 1980s, plans were formulated to reunite the second line-up of Deep Purple. Ritchie eventually agreed after they completed on the seventh Rainbow album, 'Bent Out Of Shape', and a tour of Japan in early 1984. This culminated with a performance of Beethoven's 'Ode To Joy', with orchestra. Ritchie used his white Stratocaster with Schecter pick-ups through Marshall cabinets covered in white tolex, which look to be from the period.

Deep Purple came together in mid-1984 to record a new album – 'Perfect Strangers' – and tour. This latter began in Australia before going across to America, then Japan and Europe, concluding with a small number of US shows in August. The reunion was a huge success with the record selling very well and the tour was amongst the top grossing of the year.

Whilst the band initially found enthusiasm for the reunion, the tensions that originally caused the split soon surfaced. A second album, 'The House Of Blue Light', was released in 1987 to a lukewarm response and a live album – 'Nobody's Perfect' – fared similarly. During this time, Ritchie broke a finger in the midst of performing stunts with his guitar and an American tour had to be cancelled. In 1989, Ian Gillan left Deep Purple and was subsequently replaced by ex-Rainbow singer Joe Lynn Turner for Deep Purple's thirteenth album 'Slaves And Masters'.

At the end of a worldwide tour supporting the record, Deep Purple began writing a follow-up, yet conflict developed between Turner and the rest of the group with the direction of the music, as the former wanted to create songs in line with contemporary bands. This resulted in Turner's dismissal and after several months looking for a new vocalist, Ritchie was pressured into accepting Gillan back into Deep Purple.

Aptly named, 'The Battle Rages On…' album was released to celebrate the band's 25th anniversary in July 1993. Faring well in Europe and Japan, the record performed poorly in the UK and America and the supporting tour reflected this, with no US dates scheduled. Ritchie continued to play his favoured Stratocasters, though changes to the pick-ups had been made, with lace sensor types being installed, along with a Roland GK-1 synthesizer unit (mounted below the bridge and the pick-up mounted between the bridge and bridge pick-up). Contemporary white Marshall cabinets were used, though the heads were no longer visible.

Ritchie only managed to perform on the European leg of the tour as his dissatisfaction with the group reached such a level that he forfeited his lucrative salary for appearing in Japan. He was ultimately replaced by Joe Satriani on those dates and Deep Purple decided to continue subsequently with Steve Morse.

In 1994, Ritchie brought a new band together, though he was obliged to return to the Rainbow name by his record deal. Released as 'Ritchie Blackmore's Rainbow', the group's album 'Stranger In Us All' appeared in late summer 1995. Whilst the record was only moderately successful, the subsequent tour of Europe and Japan attracted many of Rainbow's fans. Ritchie continued to use the above-mentioned Stratocaster, although a change had been made to his amplifiers. After many years of service, the Marshall Majors had been replaced by Engl 'Savage' 120-watt heads and 4x12 in. cabinets.

Rainbow played more dates in Europe during 1996 and crossed America for a series of gigs in 1997. Yet, Ritchie was ready to explore a new musical venture with his girlfriend, Candice Night, who was classically trained on the piano. The couple shared a love of medieval/renaissance music and worked on tracks from the mid-1990s, eventually accumulating enough for an album – 'Shadow Of The Moon' – under 'Blackmore's Night' in mid-1997. An early appearance of the pair on Japanese TV has Ritchie playing a Taylor acoustic and at this time he also had an Alvarez-Yairi acoustic. For subsequent live shows he played a Fender Telecaster acoustic (of which there were two, a black one and a natural) fitted with a Roland GK-1 unit. Both Telecasters had rosewood necks, though these were not scalloped as with Ritchie's electric guitars; he also occasionally used his Stratocaster for Deep Purple and Rainbow songs which were usually played during the encore. A Crate amplifier was used during this period, along with the Engl 'Savage' and 'Sovereign' (50-watt 2x12 in.).

'Shadow Of The Moon' was particularly successful in Japan and Germany and this stimulated Ritchie to prolong the project, rather than reform Rainbow, which he regularly mentioned doing in contemporary interviews. The public's interest in Blackmore's Night was reflected by his own enthusiasm of the music and a follow-up record – 'Under A Violet Moon' – was completed in 1999. Whilst Ritchie continued to play guitar, he also learned to play instruments contemporary to the music, such as a mandolin, mandola, mandocello and hurdy gurdy,

which he found rewarding. Talking to Dr Matt Warnock for guitarinternational.com in 2011, Ritchie commented on the challenge of switching between the instruments: 'I have to readjust whenever I pick up the mandola or mandolin as they are tuned in 5ths, and I have to feel my way around the instrument. When I'm playing a mandolin or mandola, I don't know sometimes what chord I'm playing or what key I'm in, but I find it refreshing because it's a sense of adventure not knowing exactly what I'm playing. I tend to go to different places that are not familiar.'

During the late 1990s, Ritchie was honoured by Fender as the company produced a Stratocaster with the specifications of his favourite guitar. This was white with Seymour Duncan pick-ups in bridge and neck positions, with dummy middle coil, and scalloped fretboard. Initially made in Japan, his signature model has also been manufactured in Mexico and the Custom Shop made a tribute Stratocaster in 2013, taking inspiration from the black guitar used during the early Deep Purple years. Ritchie endorsed Engl amps around this time and had a signature 100-watt amp head built. This was similar to the 'Savage' model, though slightly simplified.

Blackmore's Night continued to be active throughout the early 2000s, with several more albums produced: 'Fires At Midnight' (2001); 'Ghost Of A Rose' (2003); 'The Village Lanterne' (2006); 'Winter Carols' (2006); 'Secret Voyage' (2008); 'Autumn Sky' (2010); 'Dancer And The Moon' (2013); 'All Our Yesterdays' (2015). Two live concerts were filmed of the band in Burg Veldenstein and Paris in 2004 and 2006. In these, Ritchie primarily used custom-made Kawakami guitars, of which there were two, one with a classical headstock and another with a contemporary style, though both had sitka spruce tops and maple back and sides with mahogany neck and scalloped fretboards. Ritchie was also known to use custom-made Lakewood guitars for the Blackmore's Night project, such as the 'moon' model, 'A32', and a 12-string lute. Amplification was provided by an Engl combo, as well as a Fender Acoustasonic. Of particular interest in the Burg Veldenstein concert is Ritchie playing a hurdy gurdy, likely made by Helmut Gotschy.

Ritchie used a similar set-up in the 'A Knight in York' live show recorded in England during 2011, though a Flyde mandola was more prominent than previously. This make was favoured by Ritchie for both mandola and mandolin, whilst the Kawakami guitars continued to feature, along with the white Stratocaster; a different Fender Acoustasonic was now in evidence.

In 2015, Ritchie decided to reform Rainbow for a small group of three gigs in 2016, recruiting vocalist Ronnie Romero, Jens Johansson on keyboards, David Keith on drums and Bob Nouveau on bass. Ritchie used his white Stratocaster, which was now fitted with black lace sensor pick-ups and the synthesizer unit painted white. The Aiwa reel-to-reel had a prominent position behind Ritchie and amplification was provided by a pair of Engl combo amplifiers. A brief tour of England was arranged in 2017 and the band played several dates in Europe during 2018. In the main, Ritchie continued to use the aforementioned set-up, though for acoustic tracks he turned to his Kawakami guitars.

Marc Bolan early 1970s.
Pictorial Press Ltd / Alamy Stock Photo.

MARC BOLAN

Marc Bolan had a steady rise to fame developing several styles before finally achieving the recognition he had craved from an early age. His music divided critics, but today his influence is still heard. Many known guitarists readily acknowledge the part he has played in their development.

Born Marc Feld on September 30, 1947, he was the second son of Simeon and Phyllis Feld. Harry was Marc's elder brother. For a time after Marc was born, they all lived at Stoke Newington Common, Hackney. According to www.marc-bolan.net: 'The Felds were a working-class Jewish family. Simeon, known as Sid, was a van driver and sometime cosmetics salesman; who also ran a stall in Petticoat Lane at weekends, selling jewellery. Phyllis ran a fruit stall in Berwick Street Market, in the Soho district of London…'

The above website mentions that at the age of nine, Marc had a Suzuki acoustic guitar. This was acquired on hire purchase by his mother. However, brother Harry says on a documentary that Marc had his first guitar at 11. Also, a photograph with scant details on the internet shows Marc at an early age playing what appears to be a Gallotone guitar.

Marc attended Northwold Road Primary School, Stoke Newington until he was 11, and then moved to William Wordsworth Secondary Modern School. His early musical influences included Gene Vincent and Chuck Berry. He liked the way Eddie Cochran held his guitar, Little Richard placed a foot on the piano while playing, and Elvis Presley's outrageous stage movements. Marc is quoted as saying: 'I've always been a fan of early rock and roll – it's really good music. The first Elvis records were incredible … My first experience of rock came after I heard 'Ballad of Davy Crockett' by Bill Hayes. My Dad went out to buy that record but instead bought one by Bill Haley. I was so disappointed – until I heard the record. Then I threw Bill Hayes out of the window and rocked.'

Commenting on Marc's early years, elder brother Harry has said that Marc was a very different character than himself. Also, that Marc was lively, had no professional tuition on the guitar and just strummed away until he taught himself.

Whilst in his early teens, Marc joined his first band, Suzie and the Hula-Hoops, featuring vocalist Helen Shapiro. Mark became absorbed by the 'Mod' culture taking particular interest in clothes. He regularly missed school to visit the fashion shop Sportique in Old Compton Street, London. He appeared in the men's magazine *Town* in September 1962. Around the same time, the family moved to Summerstown near Wimbledon. He was registered with a model agency and featured in a Littlewood's autumn/winter mail-order catalogue. Additionally, he modelled for John Temple's 'Styles to Suit You, Suits to Style You' brochure.

Marc was dyslexic and left school without any qualifications. His parents knew he had no interest in school and let him go his own way. He took odd jobs, like working in a Wimpy bar and a clothes shop. He showed an interest in poetry and by 1964 he became impressed with Bob Dylan's music. He befriended Allan Warren, a child presenter of the 'The Five O'Clock Club'. Warren became Marc's manager and arranged for him to record a version of Dylan's 'Blowin' in the Wind'. The first session was at Regent Sound Studios and then at Maximum Sound Studios. A photograph exists from this period of Marc looking like a Dylan acolyte, holding an acoustic guitar with a pick-up fixed to the sound hole. Warren recalls that Marc would sit cross-legged on the floor of his flat playing acoustic guitar and singing to himself.

Around the summer of 1965, Marc performed at the Pontiac Club, Putney, under the name of Toby Tyler. On August 9, 1965, Marc, becoming Marc Bolan, signed to Decca Records. He appeared on 'Ready Steady Go!' on Friday November 12 performing 'The Wizard', and on 'Five O'Clock Fun Fair' on November 18. The single was officially released a day later and flopped. He performed at the 'Glad Rag Ball' at Wembley on November 19, 1965 and on 'Thank Your Lucky Stars', on December 18, 1965.

A second single titled 'The Third Degree' was released by Decca on June 3, 1966 without any success and the company lost interest in him. Undaunted, Marc contacted record producer Simon Napier-Bell who is quoted on www.marc-bolan.net: 'His guitar playing was appalling … he was absolutely unaware of his shortcomings.' Under Napier-Bell's guidance, Marc was able to record the single 'Hippy Gumbo' which came out on EMI's subsidiary Parlophone. This too, was a flop. One reviewer said the single sounded like a crazy mixture of an incredibly bad blues singer and Larry the Lamb.' Marc performed the song on 'Ready Steady Go!' on December 16, 1966. On the same bill was the Jimi Hendrix Experience.

Napier-Bell was the manager of John's Children, and in early 1967 suggested that Marc joined them. Marc was expected to write for the band, play guitar and perform backing vocals. He played a Gibson SG with P90s and his first performance with them was during March 1967. Chris Townson of John's Children has made the following comments about Marc's electric guitar playing: 'His first rehearsal with us was deafening, even by our standards! I think the band got worse when Marc first joined, because all he did was stand there and make this messy blurge. It was so bad, that I used to sneak round before a gig and retune his guitar … He seemed to think it didn't matter.' Another member Andy Ellison gathered Marc had never played an electric guitar before.

Cliff McLenehan in *Marc Bolan 1947–1977 A Chronology* (2002), under the heading German Tour, mentions: 'Stories regarding John's Children's tour of Germany supporting the Who have now passed into rock legend.' The tour began on April 8, 1967 and only lasted for five dates before they were asked to leave. The band's performances were quite theatrical. Uwe Witsch wrote a review in the *Rheinische Post* after their appearance supporting the Who in Dusseldorf on April 11, 1967: 'The climax of the spectacle came with John's Children … they wildly stamped around the stage, jumped into the audience, lashed out with metal chains and guitars, kicked around the amps, slit open a pillow and finally rolled among the feathers.'

On the way back home, the band stopped off in Luxembourg to watch a performance by Ravi Shankar and a tabla player. Marc, it was reported was fascinated by the performance and several John's Children members suggest this may have sparked him a little later to establish the slimmed down Tyrannosaurus Rex.

John's Children played at the much celebrated '14 Hour Technicolour Dream', held at Alexandra Palace, London on April 29, 1967. Marc wrote the single 'Desdemona' for the band and this was released on May 5. Peter Jones writing a review in *Record Mirror* said: 'Strong guitar in parts and the beat is just right.'

Marc left John's Children in early July 1967. A short time afterwards, Tyrannosaurus Rex was formed. The first incarnation may have been a five-piece electric band proffers McLenehan (*op. cit.*) but this was short-lived. He adds: '[Signed to Track Records] the record label repossessed the electric equipment that Bolan had been using, which could explain why right from the very outset all the early Tyrannosaurus Rex material was basically acoustic.' Tyrannosaurus Rex featuring Marc, guitars, and Steve Peregrin Took, percussion, probably made their first appearance as a duo in late July 1967.

Over the next few weeks, they undertook recordings and appeared regularly around London, particularly at Middle Earth, Covent Garden. On November 5, 1967 they were heard on John Peel's 'Top Gear'. This began a long association with the DJ. Their performance received mixed reactions and this was to continue throughout their existence. A setback at the end of 1967 was that Track Records ended their interest in the duo.

On Friday, 19 April, 1968, they released first single 'Debora' on Regal Zonophone. It peaked at no. 34 in the singles charts. One critic said: 'A versatile and very underrated group…' Another commented: 'This is ever so clever, ever so different…'

In *Beat Instrumental No. 62* of June 1967, Rick Sanders reported: 'Marc plays a £14 Suzuki guitar, and insists he knows nothing about music – "we're interested in vocal and percussion effects" – although he did tell me of a special Moroccan tuning he sometimes uses. "You take the top E to G and the bottom E to 7th, and you get some really weird sounds." The rest of the time he uses normal tuning, but "not knowing the chords too well," just plays what he feels.'

On July 5, 1968, Tyrannosaurus Rex released their first album 'My People Were Fair And Had Sky In Their Hair … But Now They're Content To Wear Stars On Their Brows.' The album appeared on Regal Zonophone, was produced by Tony Visconti and peaked at no. 15 in the album charts. Part of a *Disc & Music Echo* review of the album said: 'Marc is one of the most prolific composers we know and the strength of the album lies in his excellent, totally individual songs…' *Record Mirror* added: 'The duo's sound is the brainchild of Marc Bolan whose career has spawned many phases … Most of the tracks are a kind of jugband psychedelia…'

On Friday August 23, 1968, Tyrannosaurus Rex released their second single 'One Inch Rock'. This peaked at no. 28. *Beat Instrumental No. 67* of November 1968 offered a glimpse into how Marc wrote his songs: 'If I get a particular feeling then it just has to come out. I can just sit down and get a song written down straight away; it takes me as long to do it as it takes to physically write it down. As soon as I start to think about it, then I might as well forget it. It has to come out unconsciously. Once I've got it down, I usually play it to myself about 20 times on the trot, getting the music worked out, and then tape it on my little recorder. Maybe we use it – maybe not…'

The duo played the first Isle of Wight Festival on Saturday August 31, 1968. They toured for much of September and part of October as well as recording a radio session for John Peel's 'Top Gear'.

The second album 'Prophets, Seers And Sages, The Angels Of The Ages' was released on Friday November 1, 1968. *Melody Maker* commented: 'A mere acoustic guitar jumbles merrily, while bongos plink and plonk like gnomes tap dancing on flower pots … Marc's guitar seems to be improving…' The album failed to dent the charts.

A third single 'Pewter Suitor' appeared on Friday, January 17, 1969, but was less successful than the previous two. A YouTube video shows Marc with capoed acoustic guitar performing the song in Paris during March 1969. Derek Johnson from *New Musical Express* said: 'Set to an urgent driving beat which intensifies throughout, it also spotlights some really exciting guitar playing.'

At the beginning of March, Marc's book of poems *Warlock of Love* (1969) was published. In the same month, according to McLenehan (*op. cit.*): 'Bolan bought a Fender Stratocaster (the famous guitar with the teardrop symbol), and slowly began to introduce the electric guitar into the live set.' The author adds that the first 'electric gig' was at London's Lyceum in April.

When Tyrannosaurus Rex's third Album 'Unicorn' appeared on Friday May 16, 1969, Marc was credited with playing guitars and harmonium. Nick Logan in *New Musical Express* wrote: '"Unicorn" marks the start of the duo's excursion into electronic backing. Half is traditional Rex. The rest, recorded after a six-month break, is new Rex plus electricity … the [songs] I liked best were those with the fascinating electric backing…'

The 'King Of The Rumbling Spires' single was in the record shops from Friday July 25, 1969. It only reached no. 44. The duo undertook their first and only American tour during August and September 1969. They played support to Country Joe and the Fish as well as the Turtles, MC5 and It's a Beautiful Day.

By October 1969, Steve Peregrin Took had been replaced by Micky Finn and a British tour started on Friday, November 21, 1969. The last single to be released under the Tyrannosaurus Rex name was 'By The Light Of The Magical Moon', released on January 16, 1970. It failed to chart.

On the 'Beard Of Stars' album, which appeared on Friday, March 13, 1970, Marc is credited with playing acoustic guitar, electric guitar, bass guitar, percussion and chord organ. Nick Logan wrote in *New Musical Express*: '[The album] marks young Mr Bolan's emergence as guitar star extraordinaire. In fact, it's Marc's string bashing that makes this their most distinctive and perhaps most successful album so far.'

Marc mentioned about 'Beard Of Stars': 'I suppose there is more electric guitar … I've been staying down at Eric Clapton's home quite a bit recently and you can't be around Eric and not be influenced.' A *Melody Maker* article headed 'Bolan Goes Electric,' stated: 'Never before has T. Rex sounded so heavy or exciting … "Elemental Child" will come as a considerable surprise. It features Marc's untutored but energetic and groovy heavy rock guitar work.'

Tony Visconti told www.guitarworld.com on July 21, 2021: 'Eric Clapton was another player Marc loved. June [Bolan's wife] was Eric's girlfriend before she met Marc. She took him to Clapton's house for a weekend and Marc told me that he sat on the floor and watched Clapton play for the whole weekend. He said to me: "I sat at the feet of the master." He copped a lot of blues techniques from watching Clapton. He was a very quick learner.' Photographs exist on the internet of Marc at Clapton's house and these are dated 'circa late 1969 or early 1970.'

Tyrannosaurus Rex appeared as the headline act at the first Glastonbury Festival on Saturday, September 19, 1970. A photograph exists of Marc sitting cross-legged playing an Epiphone acoustic guitar.

McLenehan (*op. cit.*) states the name Tyrannosaurus Rex was officially shortened to T. Rex in October 1970 adding: '…though many concert promoters continued to bill them as Tyrannosaurus Rex.'

Marc Bolan's most commercial single to date, 'Ride A White Swan', was available from October 9, 1970. Looking back, in November 1971, Bolan told Michael Wale about the crisis of 1970 and his musical change. The following is quoted from www.tilldawn.net: 'It came because I'd done four albums and we were boogie-ing along … things looked really nice, but they were comfortable, you know? I was very unhappy with the way that we were really being ignored by the media of all sorts, the papers and the radio and that. So, what I did really was a gamble; either we've got to get a hit record, or I'm going to be a writer. End of story. Like I was just going to back off, because I was beginning to be bored with what I was doing, the way I was doing it. That was, I suppose, just before 1970. Just before White Swan. We cut it and it sounded like a hit … so I thought, Well, **** it, I'm going to put it out and if it's not a hit there ain't no way I'm ever going to get a hit record.'

T. Rex's final broadcast for 'Top Gear' was November 7, 1970. The band appeared on 'Top of the Pops' for the first time, performing 'Ride A White Swan' on Thursday, November 12, 1970. The single eventually reached no. 2 in the charts.

Marc commented to *Beat Instrumental No. 94* of February 1971 after the success of 'Ride A White Swan': 'Reaching a wider public is what we want. If "underground" means being on a show screened at midnight watched by 15 people – then we're out of it. If we're asked to do 'Top of the Pops', we do it and if we're asked to do John Peel, we do it.'

The album simply titled 'T. Rex' was released on Friday, December 18, 1970. Marc was featured on vocals, acoustic guitar, electric guitar, bass guitar and chord organ. Howard Kaylan and Mark Volman (former Turtles and Frank Zappa band members) were on backing vocals. Tony Visconti provided string arrangements. The album cover shows Marc holding a Gibson Les Paul.

Reviewing a T. Rex concert at The Lyceum, London, on January 25, 1971, Chris Welch of *Melody Maker* wrote: 'The best moments were during Marc's electric guitar freak-out on "Elemental Child", where his fantasies of being a heavy rock star were fully played out.'

Further success with singles in 1971 was encountered with 'Hot Love', released February 19. It climbed to no. 1 and stayed there for six weeks. A performance on 'Top of the Pops', on Thursday, February 25, 1971, reveals Marc with a sunburst Fender Telecaster. According to Steve Turner in *Beat Instrumental No. 109* of June 1972: '[Marc] has a Fender Custom Telecaster which he's fitted with a Gibson pick-up. This model was bought the year it came out – 1968.'

In a subsequent performance of 'Hot Love' on the same show, Marc has a Gibson Les Paul. This guitar was thought be from the late 1950s and acquired by Marc around 1970. In *Beat Instrumental No. 109* of June 1972, Steve Turner wrote: 'This guitar was soon to be having a new neck fitted as the original neck had been broken by a fall. As a result, Marc took it to be refitted but unfortunately neglected to take it back to its makers – Gibson. Because of this, the new neck which was put in by a small firm began twisting and he's now been forced to take it back to Gibson to have it refitted in the correct manner.' This information has been updated on www.mistymist.wordpress.com, where it is said: 'During the time Marc owned the [Les Paul] it went through a few modifications – including being refinished in a translucent orange colour dubbed "Bolan Chablis", similar to his hero Eddie Cochran's Gretsch guitar, and having three neck replacements/repairs when the original neck was broken in 1971.' The guitar was later seen with a Gibson Custom neck and headstock.

T. Rex embarked on a US tour from April 6, 1971 to May 3, 1971 where on several gigs they supported Humble Pie, Emerson Lake and Palmer and Procol Harum. The band returned to begin a British tour starting on May 9.

The band's second no. 1, 'Get It On', was released on Friday, July 2, 1971. It remained at the top of the charts for seven weeks. Nick Logan of *New Musical Express* observed: 'I'm sure a lot of Rex aficionados have found themselves wavering recently in the face of all the anti-Rex sniping. But there is a simple cure … listen to the music. Of course, T. Rex is now commercial, but they … are playing today in a different context as well as they have ever done.'

During a 'Top of the Pops' performance of 'Get It On' in July 1971, Marc is seen with a black Gibson Flying V.

According to *New Musical Express*'s Tony McNally reporting on T. Rex live in Birmingham on July 2, 1971, the band's performance featured 'a nice balance … Marc Bolan opens things with his screeching guitar effects, the rest of the band join in for some solid rock, and then we have the acoustic set, followed by the T. Rex hit parade.'

Between July 1971 and the end of the year, Marc was busy playing at festivals, recording, appearing on TV and touring. He released the 'Electric Warrior' album which was a great success and topped the LP charts. It reached no. 32 in America. The final single before the end of the year was 'Jeepster' which was released on Friday, November 5.

An informative double-page article written by Steve Turner appeared in *Beat Instrumental and International Recording Studio No. 103* of November 1971. It was revealed that in his new Maida Vale home, 'Marc has a music room where he puts down ideas on tape. The room itself has posters of Jimi Hendrix hanging on the walls while guitars lay around on the

Marc Bolan early 1970s.
Tom Hanley / Alamy Stock Photo.

floor.' Steve Turner gives guitar details: 'Marc has a total of nine guitars laying around in his room. He has two Fender Stratocasters, one Fender Telecaster with a Gibson pick-up, one 1952 Les Paul, one SG Special (Les Paul), one Gibson Flying Arrow, one Gibson acoustic and one Epiphone acoustic.'

During 1972, Marc and T. Rex released the following singles: 'Telegram Sam' (January 21); 'Metal Guru' (May 5); 'Children Of The Revolution' (September 8); 'Solid Gold Easy Action'. On a 'Top of the Pops' performance of 'Telegram Sam' Marc has the Gibson Les Paul Standard, not yet fitted with the Custom headstock.

Performing 'Metal Guru' for 'Top the Pops', he has a guitar made by Tony Zemaitis. On a Christmas version of the programme, he performs the song with the Gibson Les Paul that now has a Custom headstock. He is seen with a Veleno guitar when playing 'Children Of The Revolution' on 'Top of the Pops'. The Gibson Les Paul with Custom headstock is seen when he promotes the 'Solid Gold Easy Action' single on the BBC.

The Veleno guitar is discussed by Jeff Nolan on The Hard Rock Vault on YouTube. Jeff says John Veleno, a former machinist, made the guitar for Marc Bolan in 1970 and it was one of the first that he built. Jeff adds that he believes it was one of the first guitars John sold. It was bought by Marc at a gig. In total, John produced about 200 guitars and many are owned by noted players. Jeff explains that the Veleno guitars are made entirely out of aluminium. The pick-ups on Marc's guitar are DeArmond single coil. Marc's name is engraved on the front of the guitar.

The only 1972 T. Rex album was 'The Slider' (released July 21) whilst tours were undertaken in Europe, North America (twice), and the Far East. The film 'Born to Boogie' was premiered in December.

Further information about Marc's guitars and amplifiers may be gleaned from Steve Turner's June 1972 *Beat Instrumental* article. The details were provided by Mike O'Halloran, Marc's roadie of the previous two-and-a-half years. Specific information is given about the guitar which was especially made for Marc to his own specifications by A.C. Zemaitis: 'The front is silver plated and has the maker's name engraved on it with the year 1972.' Also mentioned is a Les Paul Special 1961 and a 1958 Fender Stratocaster. Amongst the acoustics: an Aria, Astoria, a Gibson Special and a 1969 Epiphone. According to Mike O'Halloran, Marc took a number of guitars to all of his gigs. During a performance, he had them standing along the side of the stage and often swapped guitars after a number. With regard to amplification O'Halloran explained: 'We use custom-built Vampower amps for the bass with 16 12-inch speakers. Marc has custom-built cabinet[s] as well as two H & H amps. He has two spare Vamps and a Vox Supreme … For practice amps we use Vamp or we've also got two Fender Champ amps and a Vox AC30 tune-up amp.'

Additional comments about Marc's Vampower and H & H amps in conjunction with his use of a Dallas Rangemaster may be found on www.analogman.com. Research has been put on the site by a Paul of Doncaster. Under several headings he offers erudite comments. Here is one example. '"Electric Warrior" – By the sounds of it and the few photos in existence … this appears to have been mainly Fender Strat into Vampower and Vox amps. His Rangemaster was probably used all the time, but can be clearly heard in particular on the rhythm tracks on "Motivator", "Lean Love" and "Rip-Off" (this latter track has some great overdriven "separation" in the chord work), and the solos on "Lean Love", "Get it On" (short solo at the end when it hits the "G").'

Only one album, 'Tanx' would be released in 1973. The singles were: '20th Century Boy' (March 2); 'The Groover' (June 1); 'Truck On Tyke' (November 16).

An appearance on the 'Cilla Black Show' on Saturday, January 27, 1973 saw Marc playing a 1950s Gibson CF-100E single cutaway acoustic with a pick-up.

T. Rex toured North America, West Germany, Europe and the Far East, but they did not perform in the UK. In performances of '20th Century Boy', Marc has the Gibson Les Paul with the Custom headstock. Around the time of 'The Groover', Marc is sporting an Ovation Breadwinner guitar produced by the Ovation Guitar Company around 1973.

In September/October, Marc split with his wife June and moved into a new flat with Gloria Jones. He kicked off 1974 with the 'Truck Off' British tour which included two sax players. Backing vocals were provided by Gloria Jones and Sister Pat Hall.

'Teenage Dream' was in the record shops from January 25, 1974. In a video from February 7, 1974, Marc performs the song solo with a Non-Reverse Gibson Firebird that has a customised top. Existing on the internet is a picture of Marc with a collection of guitars hung on a wall behind him. Clearly visible is the aforementioned Firebird. In the same picture another Non-Reverse Firebird can be spotted. Marc has been photographed with a white Gibson three pick-up SG Custom; a black Gibson 1954–1956 Les Paul Custom; and a 1964 Sea Foam Green Fender Jaguar.

On www.frettedamericana.com are the comments: 'Only four Foam (or Sea Foam) Green Jaguars from this year are known, and this is the only one known with gold hardware.

> On www.vampoweramp.com is the following information: 'Vampower was originally manufactured by Triumph Electronics along with VOX® AC50, AC100, and 7-series amplifiers used by the Beatles. Despite having only been produced in very limited numbers from 1968 to 1973, Vampower quickly earned a legendary reputation due to its distinct sound and design. In early 2015 Vampower was reestablished…'

> The CF-100 was produced by Gibson from 1951 until 1959. It was the only 1950s Gibson flat top acoustic with a cutaway and produced with and without the option of a pick-up.

> There were several types of Ovation guitar introduced including the Breadwinner, the Deacon and Breadwinner Limited. Photographs exist of Marc playing a black Breadwinner.

Marc Bolan with Burns Flyte guitar.
Trinity Mirror / Mirrorpix / Alamy Stock Photo.

Jim Burns designed the Flyte guitar and it appeared under the name Burns UK Ltd in 1974. At the time the body and headstock shape were quite exciting. The body was mahogany and there was a bolt-on maple neck. Two Mach One Humbuster humbuckers were fitted with novel five-sided metal covers.

It was owned by Marc Bolan of T. Rex and later by Henri Padovani of The Police.'

The long-titled album 'A Creamed Cage In August/Zinc Alloy And The Hidden Riders Of Tomorrow' was released on March 1, 1974. It received mixed reviews with its funk and R&B influences and was not released in the USA. Chris Welch of *Melody Maker* said: '…with the help of Tony Visconti, the Bolan sound has become even more vibrant, slightly dotty and sharply professional … It's a futile exercise to probe too deeply into T. Rex music.'

The album saw B.J. Cole on steel guitar and Jack Green as a second guitarist. This album was to be Marc's last association with Tony Visconti.

In a piece on www.thequietus.com from March 3, 2014, Neil Kulkarni commented about 'Zinc Alloy' under the heading Pop, Fragility & Dissolution: A Marc Bolan Reappraisal: '"Zinc Alloy" can be heard now as a glorious document of a man at his mental breaking point, a man heroically still trying to find new ways to sing his songs, and crucially a man really now engaged in the full-on engagement with black music (through his long obsession with US black radio) that his rivals (Bowie, Ferry) STILL didn't have the smarts or inclination to try yet.'

A single 'Light Of Love' was released on July 5, 1974, and then at the end of September, Marc embarked on what was to be T. Rex's final tour of America. After the performance at the Tower Theatre, Pennsylvania on September 26, 1974, Steve Weitzman wrote in *Zoo World*: '[Marc] switched from his Les Paul to a Fender Stratocaster … tambourined its fretboard to death, laid his instrument down, whipped it repeatedly, picked it up and hurled it [at] an amp which had been electronically rigged to explode upon impact amidst a cloud of smoke. The kids were wide-eyed.'

On some of the US gigs T. Rex played support to Blue Oyster Cult and ZZ Top.

Another single 'Zip Gun Boogie' was in the record shops from November 1, 1974. A live filmed and elongated version of the song has Marc soloing on the Les Paul with Custom headstock.

Singles released in 1975 were 'New York City' (June 20, 1975) and 'Dreamy Lady' (September 26, 1975). 'New York City' received poor reviews including one from John Peel. Marc performed the song on 'Top of the Pops' on July 3, 1975, with a Fender Stratocaster. Albums which appeared in the same year was the solitary 'Bolan's Zip Gun'. The album did not dent the charts. In 1975 a few gigs were performed by T. Rex during July.

The album 'Futuristic Dragon', released on January 30, 1976, received poor reviews and did not sell well, only reaching no. 50. Nonetheless, a tour to promote the album was undertaken, starting from February 5 to March 6.

In a break from the tour on February 17, 1976 Marc filmed an appearance on 'Supersonic'. He performed 'London Boys' with a Burns Flyte guitar. Towards the end of the song, he flung the guitar from a raised platform.

'London Boys' was available from February 20, received some scathing reviews and stalled at no. 40 in the charts. Another single 'I Love To Boogie' appeared on June 14 and pushed Marc back into the top twenty peaking at no 13. But it failed to garner any critical acclaim. On 'Top of the Pops' June 17, Marc appears after losing weight, hair shorn and playing the Gibson Les Paul. The 'Laser Love' single appeared on September 17. On 'Top of the Pops' October 7, 1976, Marc still sports the Les Paul, but Miller Anderson (formerly Keef Hartley Band) has joined on second guitar. Marc performs solo with the Les Paul on 'Supersonic' October 16, 1976. Reports state the Les Paul was eventually stolen in late 1976 or early 1977 from outside a rehearsal studio.

Marc revived his fortunes for a time in 1977. He embarked on a British tour with the Damned, on March 10, 1977. He embraced the new wave of music about to sweep the country. In turn, those involved embraced him with affection, many having grown up listening to his music. On March 11, the album 'Dandy In The Underworld' was released. The British tour of the same name received some favourable reviews and the album eventually peaked at no 26. A single 'Soul Of My Suit' was taken from the album though stalled at no 42. An official video of Marc performing the single has him with a sunburst Fender Stratocaster, that has a rosewood board and a large headstock. The single 'Dandy In The Underworld' released on June 3, 1977, failed to chart. An appearance on Granada Television's 'Get It Together' on June 29, 1977, has Marc performing with a black Gibson Les Paul Standard. Miller Anderson is on second guitar. Another single 'Celebrate Summer' from August 5, 1977, failed to dent the charts. Marc plays the black Les Paul again when promoting the single.

On August 24, 1977, the first of five shows titled 'Marc' was transmitted. Amongst those appearing on the shows with him were the Jam, Generation X and David Bowie.

Marc's world ended in the early hours of September 16, 1977, when he was killed in a car crash at Barnes, London. Gloria Jones was the driver and she survived. They were only a mile away from their home.

In 2007, Marc's Gibson Flying V from 1968, serial no. 907116 was sold at Christie's for £36,000. In 2012, Gibson produced the Custom Marc Bolan Les Paul in a run of 100. It included the replacement Custom model neck and headstock, uncovered humbucking pick-ups, the zebra coil neck unit and the orange 'Bolan Chablis' body finish.

Summing up Marc's guitar playing, his long-time friend and producer, Tony Visconti, commented on www.guitarworld.com: 'He was more of a blues guy than me. He listened to the early blues players a lot … His technical knowledge guitar-wise was not great at all. He knew a handful of chords, the right ones, of course, for rock 'n' roll … One thing that he did that was really weird was that he might be soloing in the key of E, but then he'd slide up three frets and be playing solos out of the G blues box. Some of those notes are modally not the correct notes but he just played with abandon. I think that explains some of his unusual note choices.'

Visconti is also quoted on www.rockcellarmagazine.com: 'The positive thing I'd like to say is that what [Marc] did leave behind is basically the germ, the seed, that he planted that gave rise to 150 rock and roll bands, from U2 to the Cars, to you name it. There's a T. Rex lick in there in so many bands, and that feel. The things that he took from the 50s and turned into new things in the 70s spawned a whole new genre after Marc died.'

Joe Brown with Grimshaw guitar.
John Taylor Management.

JOE BROWN

In the late 1950s/early 1960s, Joe Brown was a session man playing with Gene Vincent, Johnny Cash, Eddie Cochran and Billy Fury. He was also a successful solo artist and his clever guitar breaks were heard on unique hit records.

Although speaking with an unmistakeable cockney accent, Joe was born in Lincolnshire on May 13, 1941. Later, he moved with his mother, father and brother Pete, to his paternal uncle Joe's pub, the Sultan, in Grange Road, Plaistow, London. Joe's father was not a well man and spent time in and out of hospital, dying when Joe was only 12.

As a young lad, Joe was involved in several small lucrative ventures: selling shellfish, jellied eels and scrap metal as well as running for a local bookie. Sometimes in school holidays he travelled up to uncle Ern's farm at Melton Mowbray and worked there. He hated school but managed to pass his Eleven-Plus, attending Plaistow Grammar School only to leave shortly afterwards for another school, Pretoria Road Secondary Modern.

Georgie Dance, a member of a musical family was often seen playing a guitar with a matchstick for a plectrum, in and around the Sultan pub. When Joe first heard guitar, he fell in love with the sound. He bought his first guitar from Georgie for £1. This was 1953, the year Frankie Lane's 'I Believe' was the biggest selling single of the year, staying top of the chart for 18 non-consecutive weeks. Lane also had the most top 12 entries in that year, with eight in total.

'I knew nothing about music so Georgie tuned the guitar for me and I marked all the notes on it in chalk,' recalled Joe, adding: 'He always tuned the guitar to an open chord, and of course I thought that was the way to tune it, so if ever I broke a string, I'd put another on and tune it the same. I think I played the bloody thing like this for five years until I suddenly realised that I'd better do something about it and start again.'

While still at school Joe began playing in a skiffle band, the Ace of Clubs Rhythm Group, and made appearances at a local youth club. On escaping school, Joe worked as an electrician's apprentice in a packing department, then on the railway, during steam days, as a cleaner and later a fireman. Whilst in the latter job he played in another skiffle group, the Spacemen. Joe later recalled in a newspaper interview: 'It was a wonderful time because it was the first time the youth of England had their own music. Before that it was all geezers in white suits singing with megaphones. Kids had no fashion of their own either, it was all demob suits.'

The Spacemen skiffle group played around the local pubs and clubs and gradually Joe moved from skiffle to rock 'n' roll, and left his job as a locomotive fireman. Said Joe: 'Everyone loved skiffle but then rock 'n' roll came along and when we heard Little Richard for the first time it all changed. Luckily, the transition was easy for me because I was one of the few skifflers who played an electric guitar – and not only that, because I'd been playing for so many years, I actually knew four chords, so I was the king!' With the Spacemen, Joe played through a Selmer amplifier and occasionally used a Watkins Dominator.

Joe's reputation as a guitarist grew and he was in demand. He played a summer season at Filey, East Yorkshire, 1959/1960 with Clay Nichols and the Blue Flames, which he hated.

A guitar he was using around this time was a Hofner Club 50 played through a Selmer Truvoice amp. Joe states in Giltrap and Marten (*op. cit.*) that Hofners were the only real, decent guitars available in the UK around the late 1950s. He bought his Hofner from Selmer's in Charing Cross Road. For him they were good guitars, having their own sound. He argues that in the old days there was no British rock sound but the Hofners gave character to British rock 'n' roll. He also quips that Bert Weedon played Hofners all the time and was later described as 'the only man who made a fortune out of a yard of German plywood.'

The Hofner Clubs were sold in the UK by Selmer from 1956 and their distinctive shape was clearly inspired by Gibson's Les Paul. They were popular with young skiffle combos, the short scale and compact size made them easy to play. They featured two Hofner 'Bar' pick-ups and the control panel provided an interesting range of sounds.

On www.vintagehofner.co.uk it is stated: 'Photographs abound of John Lennon, Paul McCartney, Dave Gilmour, Justin Haywood, etc, clutching a Hofner in their youth until they were weaned away by such modern developments as the Futurama III or, if really lucky, an American guitar.'

Skiffle music first appeared in the United States during the 1920s. Played on simple instruments, it was revived in Britain during the austere and impoverished post-World War Two years by young musicians. They were delighted to discover that skiffle music could be played on makeshift instruments: a cheap guitar, a washboard scraped with thimbles, and a tea-chest (a broom handle and string fixed to a wooden case used for exporting tea). The music had one foot in the blues and the other in folk music. The main British Skiffle exponent was Lonnie Donegan who had a massive hit with 'Rock Island Line' in 1954.

Rock 'n' roll originated and evolved in the United States during the late 1940s and early 1950s via a number of musical styles: jump blues, jazz, boogie-woogie, rhythm and blues, and country music. A piano or saxophone was often the lead instrument being subsequently replaced or joined by guitar which became a symbol of modernity, tapping into a cultural fascination with technology in the decade. Not acquiring its name until 1954, rock 'n' roll is really a blues rhythm with an emphasised backbeat, mostly provided by a snare drum.

Looking for something better to play than Hofners, Joe went along to the Grimshaw Guitar Company in south London to choose a guitar. He is pictured on the Grimshaw website with a number of the company's models including an SS Deluxe and a TA63 Troubadour with a cutaway body. The website also has a picture of Pete Townshend with a Grimshaw SS Deluxe having purchased it from Ivor Mairants 'because Joe Brown had one.'

Joe Brown's Grimshaw guitar was once borrowed and played by Johnny Cash whilst they were doing a live TV show. Joe said the guitar 'looked comical being so small on Johnny who was huge.'

After being involved with a number of Butlin's holiday jobs, Joe came into contact with impresario Larry Parnes who had a stable of rock 'n' roll singers with distinctive names such as Vince Eager, Johnny Gentle, Dickie Pride, Duffy Power and Marty Wilde. Parnes was always looking for new talent and regularly held auditions. Joe came into contact with him when asked to play guitar in one of these auditions held in Southend. Parnes was aiming to provide singers for Jack Good's new TV show 'Boy Meets Girls'. Joe was paid ten shillings for playing in the auditions but was also expected to play two shows with Parnes' band, the Beat Boys.

Jack Good told Parnes he was not impressed by any of the singers but would like to have Joe playing lead guitar in the orchestra for the 'Boy Meets Girls' shows. Parnes suddenly announced he was Joe's manager. A little later, Joe signed a contract with Parnes but rejected having his name changed to Elmer Twitch.

The 'Boy Meets Girls' show started on September 12, 1959, and lasted until February 1960. Good had been responsible for earlier popular music shows such as 'Six-Five Special' (February 16, 1957 to December 27, 1958) and 'Oh Boy!' (September 13, 1958 to May 30, 1959), the first UK teenage music programmes. Joe Brown made regular appearances on 'Boy Meets Girls' which featured Marti Wilde as presenter and performer.

The programme introduced American rockers Eddie Cochran and Gene Vincent to British teenagers. Joe Brown is pictured on the show with Gene Vincent playing a Grimshaw SS Deluxe guitar in December 1959. A little later he's also pictured with Eddie Cochran on the show.

When Selmer's became Gibson agents in the UK, Joe Brown says that he and many of his contemporaries switched over to Gibson guitars. From Selmer's, Joe chose a Gibson ES 335 sunburst around 1959/1960. He had taken the opportunity of asking Larry Parnes to buy it as part of signing a management agreement with him.

Banjo player, Emile Grimshaw (b. 1880) established a company with Emile Jr in 1930 to produce banjos and guitars. On www.grimshawguitars.co.uk mention is made that the early guitars were constructed in a similar fashion to the banjo – the guitar had a separate detachable back. After Emile Snr's death in 1943, his son increased guitar production and in the following decade the company manufactured both acoustic and electric models: G3, G5, and G6. The website claims the most popular model of the 1950s was the SS (short scale) Deluxe, the style a cross between a Gibson ES 335 and a Gretsch White Falcon. The model featured an individual style of unequal cutaways and could be bought in a variety of colours at a time when many guitars were dark sunburst. The website concedes Grimshaw guitars were good substitutes for the American guitars which were not imported into the UK (due to austerity measures post-war). The SS models found popularity with early rock 'n' rollers.

Kevin Swift in *Beat Instrumental No. 37* of May 1966 said that anybody who is around their twenties and plays guitar, looks back to Joe Brown's early days with a certain respect for the shock-haired guitarist and singer. 'Remember the publicity angle that was used to promote him? The-loveable-cockney-with-the-guitar-which-knocked-him-back-well-over-the-100-quid-mark. That Sunburst Gibson ES 335 TD aroused a lot of interest. Must have been one of the first to come into the country.'

Joe said: 'When I first got [the guitar] I filed all the frets down to make the action even lower. It's a real pleasure to play. I had the "twang" sound before most people even thought about it. You know that guitar must be really solid because it's been under a train when it fell off a platform, it's been dropped on stone floors, and it's even been in two bad car crashes.'

In the same *Beat Instrumental* article, Joe talked proudly of a rare Maccaferri guitar which he had picked up in Glasgow. After giving a demonstration, he said: 'Just listen to it. Django Reinhardt had one of these; it's got a very individual sound, sharp, punchy, ideal for a rhythm section in a band, it cuts through so well. Mind you, it's got a pretty hard action. I practice on it so that when I play any of my other guitars it's ridiculously easy.'

In *Beat Monthly No. 8* December 1963, Pete Goodman said: 'On stage Joe purveys the big beat but also includes acoustic – unamplified – guitar. And the fans lap it up, quiet though it is. He's one of the few beat specialists who can cope with this intricate type of music. He studied "finger-style" in his quieter moments during the summer.'

Mick Farren's *Gene Vincent: There's One in Every Town* (2004) recalls Gene Vincent arriving in England on December 5, 1959, and amidst a furore of press, fans and bike-riding rockers there was Joe Brown and the Bruvvers playing 'Be-Bop-A-Lula'. Then, 'with Joe Brown flanking him as his first UK guitar player, he headed on to Manchester where he taped eleven songs with the house rhythm section, and the Vernons Girls singing back up.' During January 1960, Gene headlined a twelve-date tour of the UK. Joe Brown and the Rockets made up his backing band. On the short tour Joe played lead on the Gibson ES 335 through a Vox AC30.

Spencer Leigh in *Things Do Go Wrong: Eddie, Gene And The UK Tour* (2008) says surviving recordings from the Gene Vincent's first visit to the UK (audio only and inferior sound quality) are very competent. Leigh added: 'In interviews, Gene said that he had been apprehensive about the quality of British musicians, but he could see that Joe Brown and Red Price were world class. The ferocity of Joe Brown's playing in "Rocky Road Blues" rivals the Americans and nobody hearing the session

Joe Brown with Gibson Dot ES 335.
John Taylor Management.

The American Gibson Guitar Corporation introduced its ES (Electric Spanish) guitar series in 1958. A 1958 catalogue reveals the price of a natural finish ES 335 retailed for $282.50; sunburst finish $267.50; and the case $46. Shipping totals for the sunburst guitar were as follows: 1958 (267); 1959 (521); 1960 (405).

Joe Brown with Gibson ES 345.
John Taylor Management.

would think the Brits couldn't play rock 'n' roll; they had risen to the challenge.'

Between January 24 and April 16, 1960, Larry Parnes organised a tour featuring Gene Vincent and Eddie Cochran. It was a combination of complete weeks in large cities and one-night stands elsewhere. Also on the bill were Parnes' own artists including Joe Brown. Joe says he was paid 'something like sixteen quid a week in those days, regardless of whether we were on a TV show, a tour, or topping the bill in Grimsby.'

In his book *Brown Sauce: The Life and Times of Joe Brown* (1986), Joe states he learned a lot from Eddie Cochran: 'Eddie had a great trick. He put a second string instead of a third string on his guitar, so that he could bend it and get those bluesy sounds that you never heard in England. I nicked the idea and got lots of session work as a result.' Joe added: 'We'd sit up most nights, picking and strumming and if anyone taught me to play the guitar, it was Eddie Cochran.'

Joe Brown was part of the backing band for the whole show but also had a solo spot where he used the Vox AC30 and the Gibson ES 335. Joe said: 'I rate Eddie Cochran very highly as a rock 'n' roll guitarist. He was great. He could play a good lead guitar but he said: "Oh, you can play the lead. I'll play rhythm". Eddie used to play rhythm on stage and he hardly took any solos. He was brilliant. He had an old Selmer amp which we wouldn't use because we didn't think they were any good. We had Vox AC30s 'cause no-one could get hold of Fenders in those days. He used this old amp and got a great sound from it, a sound nobody else could get, perhaps because he used a Gretsch guitar and we didn't have them over here.'

When opening with 'Be-Bop-A-Lula', Gene Vincent, in part of his act, swung his leg in a circle over the microphone stand. But, on one occasion cracked Joe at the side of the head.

A photograph showing an impressive line-up on stage of some of the star musicians on the tour reveals Joe's Gibson ES 335 plugged into a small Gibson GA series amplifier. Gibson's first amplifier was introduced in 1935; the company developing an electric guitar shortly before this time. Joe recalls that the picture was taken at a TV show and the amp was supplied rather than brought in by himself. Later, a line-up of Joe and the Bruvvers illustrates several Vox AC30 amplifiers.

On March 23, 1960, Joe charted with 'The Darktown Strutters Ball' on Decca, its peak position was no. 34.

Whilst working as a session guitarist for Jack Good, Joe played guitar for Johnny Cash. But Joe's snap decision to include a fill in a song being recorded live brought him the sack. Signals were being sent down telephone lines from Manchester into an Ampex recording machine in London and it was far from economical to make more than one take.

'Joe,' Cash drawled. 'Thar'll be no pickin' thar.'

After the second recording, Joe was sacked but eventually reinstated and, in time, Cash sent him a pair of cowboy boots.

Joe Brown played guitar on Billy Fury's 'Sound Of Fury', recorded at Decca, West Hampstead, London on April 14, 1960. Joe seems to recall that the Vox AC30 and Gibson ES 335 were used once again. Radio, television presenter and author, Paul Gambaccini has said it is the best British rock 'n' roll album and one of the best ever.

After the last American Rock 'n' Roll show at the Bristol Hippodrome, on Saturday, April 16, 1960, Eddie Cochran was killed in a car accident whilst travelling to London in an unlicensed cab.

Other Joe Brown hits during the early 1960s were: 'Shine' (February 1961, peak position no. 33) with quite an adventurous guitar break; 'Crazy Mixed-Up Kid' (April 1961); 'What A Crazy World We're Living In' (January 1962, peak position 37); 'A Picture Of You' (May 1962, peak position no. 2); 'Your Tender Look' (September 1962, peak position no. 31); 'It Only Took A Minute' (November 1962, peak position no. 6). Joe is seen playing 'It Only Took A Minute' on 'The Lenny the Lion Show' and his Gibson ES 335 has acquired a Bigsby.

To promote his hits, Joe toured with his band the Bruvvers, which contained two members of the former Spacemen band, brothers Tony and Pete Oakman. When he appeared at the Cambridge Hall, Southport and Tower Ballroom, New Brighton on July 26 and 27, 1962, the Beatles played as support on the bill with Pete Best on drums. Whilst at one of the venues, George Harrison had his photograph taken with Joe's Gibson ES 335.

It was during the early 1960s that Joe showed Hank Marvin an early Italian-made Meazzi Echomatic and the latter made good use of the effect in his playing. Joe has not always performed with electric guitars. On a television performance of 'Joe The Carter Lad' he is playing a Gibson 12-string.

In the 1962 *New Musical Express* newspaper poll, Joe was voted Top UK Vocal Personality and presented with the award by Roy Orbison. Further hits continued in the following year: 'That's What Love Will Do', released in February 1963, peaked at no. 3; 'Nature's Time For Love', July 1963, reached no. 26; 'Sally Ann', October 1963, peaked at no. 28.

Whenever showcasing his hits on TV, Joe put in an energetic performance, playing fills and fluent lead parts. The Gibson ES 335 was purchased without a Bigsby, but Joe fitted one for a period, then it was removed.

In his autobiography, Joe states that when the Beatles and other beat groups took centre stage in the early 1960s, it was time for him to start looking in different directions for work.

Over the Christmas period 1962/1963, he had played Wishee Washee in 'Aladdin' at the Globe theatre in Stockton-on-Tees and it was to acting he turned. He appeared in a number of films, pantomimes and stage musicals. Amongst these were: the film 'What a Crazy World' (1963) including Marti Wilde and others; and musicals 'Charlie Girl' and 'Three Hats for Lisa'. He presented the children's television series, 'Joe & Co.', and three series of the 'Joe Brown Show' for ITV.

During the 1970s, he formed, Brown's Home Brew, playing rock 'n' roll, country and gospel. The band featured his wife, Vicki Brown, a former member of the Vernons Girls. A photograph in his autobiography shows the band with Hiwatt amplifiers.

After becoming tired of the Gibson ES 335 in the 1970s, he part-exchanged it for a Les Paul, though he now regrets the transaction. Roy Wood of the Move, ELO, and Wizzard now owns the ES 335.

Since the 1970s, other television appearances and accolades have followed. Joe still performs to sell-out audiences. In 2008, his 50th anniversary celebrations included UK gold album sales for over 100,000 copies of 'Joe Brown – The Very Best Of'; a 37-date spring tour; an all-star concert at the Royal Albert Hall; and a 36-date autumn/winter tour. In recent years he has been seen playing a Gibson ES 345 as well as numerous ukuleles.

Joe Brown was appointed MBE in the 2009 Birthday Honours for services to music and in the same year he was presented with a *Mojo* lifetime award for outstanding contribution to music.

Eric Clapton with ES 335 c. 1969.
UMA Press, Inc. / Alamy Stock Photo.

ERIC CLAPTON

For much of his life, Eric Clapton has been the electric guitar's greatest ambassador. His guitar playing earned him the plaudit, 'Clapton is God' in the 1960s while using a Gibson Les Paul. In the same decade, he employed a Gibson SG which was painted in psychedelic designs by Marijke Koger and Simon Posthuma (later forming the Fool collective) perhaps introducing the first art guitar. Other guitars such as the Gibson ES 335 have taken on lives of their own. When sold in 2004, to raise funds for his Crossroads treatment centre, it raised nearly £1m.

Being a celebrated guitarist has also brought its troubles for Eric, having to cope with several addictions, but it has also brought salvation. Whenever he wanted a road out of a predicament, he turned to making music, with his guitar ultimately leading the way forward.

A number of guitars Eric has used during his career have been launched as signature models by various manufacturers and this must be one of the best accolades for a guitarist. Besides writing songs, Eric has created music for film scores such as 'Edge of Darkness'.

His *Eric Clapton: The Autobiography*, published in 2008, covers in great detail the ups and downs of his life. A film, 'Life in 12 Bars' (2018) gives a further insight into the high and low points of his career.

Eric was born on March 30, 1945 and, in his early years, was raised by his grandparents Rose and Jack Clapp (her second husband). Eric takes his name from Rose's first husband, whose surname was Clapton. Rose played piano as well as harmonium. His maternal great-grandfather could play accordion and violin. Eric's first musical efforts saw him winning an award for playing 'Greensleeves' on a recorder.

Attending Ripley Church of England Primary School, Eric showed an early aptitude for art. When he was around ten years old, he attempted to play violin though this did not last very long. His uncle Adrian introduced him to jazz records and he was an avid listener to the BBC radio programme 'Children's Favourites', on Saturday mornings. When he heard Sonny and Brownie's 'Whooping And Hollering', he was greatly impressed.

In 1956, Eric failed the Eleven-Plus and attended St Bede's Secondary Modern School. This was the time Elvis Presley and rock 'n' roll rose to prominence and one of Eric's friends had a copy of 'Hound Dog' which was released in July 1956. A year later, Eric received his first record player, a Dansette. The first single he bought was 'When' by the Kalin Twins; the first album was 'Chirping Crickets' by Buddy Holly. In March 1958, when he saw Buddy Holly, on television's 'Sunday Night at the London Palladium', playing a Fender Stratocaster guitar, he was most impressed.

Whilst in his early teens, Eric's artistic talents were recognised by an art teacher, Mr Swan, though on his 13th birthday he received his first guitar. This was purchased by his grandparents from Bell Musical Instruments store and was a Hoyer acoustic made in Germany.

Eric recalls the guitar had steel strings and was difficult to play and tune. The first song he chose to learn was 'Scarlet Ribbons' and he recorded his efforts on a Grundig tape machine.

Passing the 13-Plus examination, Eric moved to Hollyfield School, Surbiton, becoming increasingly aware of folk music, New Orleans jazz and rock 'n' roll. The Hollyfield School contained a junior art department of Kingston School of Art and for a couple of days a week, Eric attended art classes. The art department was close to Bell's music store and he would admire guitars displayed in the windows.

In 1960, Eric persuaded Rose and Jack to buy another guitar, a Washburn parlour acoustic, which had a painting of a naked lady on the reverse. He found the guitar comfortable to play and he began to learn the styles of a number of blues men, steadily becoming a proficient player.

At 16, he attended Kingston School of Art and was placed in the graphics department. In the evenings, he went to the L'Auberge club near Eel Pie Island where performers such as Ken Colyer appeared. Eric seriously explored the blues, feeling the music was soothing. Meticulously trying to adopt various finger techniques, as well as play like his heroes such as Jimmy Reed, he listened to his efforts after recording them on the Grundig. His stint at art college did not last, realising the career of a graphics designer was not for him. Afterwards, he worked for his grandfather, who was a skilled builder, adept at turning his hand to plastering, brick-laying and carpentry.

In the early 1960s, Eric's record collection grew and he became captivated by the electric blues performed by B.B. King and Muddy Waters. When his Washburn guitar was damaged beyond repair, he turned to a guitar he had watched Alexis Corner playing, a Kay Jazz II. Bought around 1962, Eric has admitted that this was a poor man's version of a Gibson ES 335. Acquired from Bell's shop, it cost £10 whereas an ES 335 at that time would have been £100.

Eric's Kay guitar reveals several differences to the standard model: instead of uniquely shaped inlays, it has simple block inlays; a black round pick-guard, contrasting with other Kay Jazz II guitars which have a distinctively shaped pick-guard in white. Quickly finding the Kay difficult to play – the strings were too high off the fretboard and the neck began to bow – he was disappointed but pressed on regardless, picking up

> *The Hoyer website, www.hoyerguitars.com informs that the Hoyer guitar brand started in 1874 when Franz Hoyer opened a workshop in Schonback (today Czech Republic). Initially, lutes and zithers were made until classic and folk guitars were built. The company passed down several family members before the Hoyer name was established in Germany becoming known for producing good quality instruments.*

influences and interpreting them. One major inspiration, acquired during the early 1960s, and which was to stay with him for the rest of his life, was the music of bluesman Robert Johnson. However, when he tried to copy Johnson's technique, he found it challenging.

In January 1963, Eric joined Tom McGuiness (later of Manfred Mann) in a band, the Roosters, where each member played through one amplifier. They turned out some R&B and blues cover numbers. It was during this period that Eric was first introduced to Freddie King's playing, where the guitar was being employed as a lead instrument and not as part of an accompaniment. Discovering how King 'bent' the guitar strings particularly impressed Eric, encouraging him to develop his own guitar solos on the Kay guitar, played through a Selmer Futurama III amplifier. The Roosters supported Manfred Mann at London's Marquee Club though blues music was not popular at the time as most young people were turning to the Beatles and the Mersey Sound. Eric lasted with the Roosters until the final gig at the Marquee on July 25, 1963.

His next band was Casey Jones and the Engineers, though this group only performed seven gigs and he played through small Vox or Gibson amplifiers, with a repertoire of mainly top ten covers. During the time with the Roosters and Casey Jones, he was still working regularly on building sites with his grandfather.

In October 1963, Eric joined the Yardbirds. His main recording and gigging guitar, from the outset, was a Fender Telecaster which belonged to the Yardbirds' management. He pushed this through a Vox AC30 and used light gauge strings on the guitar with a very thin top E to bend notes more easily. Playing with the band provided Eric with a weekly wage and he moved into London and appeared regularly within the capital as well as other areas of the country. During 1964, he picked up the nickname 'Slowhand'; played over 200 gigs; toured with Jerry Lee Lewis and the Ronettes; and performed at the Richmond Jazz and Blues Festival.

The Yardbirds became known for stretching out numbers to five or six minutes in length as could be heard when the 'Five Live Yardbirds' album was released in December 1964. In the same month, the Yardbirds played at the Hammersmith Odeon with the Beatles and other 1960s bands. Eric became friends with George Harrison. Eric explained how he used light gauge strings, bought from Clifford Essex's store in Earlham Street, while George showed Eric his Gretsch guitars.

The guitars used by Eric in the Yardbirds, apart from the Telecaster, included a Gibson ES 335 with block markers and a black Fender Jazzmaster. There are pictures of Eric with the ES 335 during his Yardbirds days and it was also played by the band's rhythm guitarist Chris Dreja. Around August 1964, the guitar was smashed in an accident on stage and replaced by a dot marker ES 335 which Eric also played.

Fed up with the direction in which the Yardbirds were heading, following the release of the single 'For Your Love' in March 1965, he left the band and moved back to live with his grandparents. His next action was joining John Mayall's Bluesbreakers in April 1965 where he felt much more comfortable with the music being created. He lived in a small room in John's house in Lee Green, earned £35 a week, and was on the road constantly, appearing at a variety of venues including the Twisted Wheel, Manchester; Club A'Gogo, Newcastle; Boathouse, Nottingham; Starlight, Redcar; and Mojo, Sheffield.

There were a number of highlights whilst a Bluesbreakers member: he worked with Mayall and Bob Dylan in the studio, though nothing was finished; Mike Vernon asked him to play some studio sessions with Muddy Waters and Otis Spann; and the slogan 'Clapton is God' appeared on London street walls.

During his first performances with John Mayall, Eric can be seen with a Fender Telecaster with a rosewood neck and the body stripped down to the wood. But for most of his time with the Bluesbreakers, he played a 1960 Gibson Les Paul Standard.

In 'The Guitar Show' on YouTube, a short story may be heard about how Eric acquired the guitar. Jimmy Nolan, an employee at Selmer's Charing Cross Road store, bought a Gibson Les Paul from his workplace and played it in his jazz band around London. Quickly finding the guitar was not suited to this type of music, he is quoted as saying that he sold the guitar to Eric Clapton for around £200–£250 and the price included the case.

Eric's original intention was to have the same Les Paul guitar that he had seen Freddie King pictured with on an album cover. But, this was a Gold Top and he decided on the sunburst Les Paul Standard instead. Eric amplified the Les Paul through a stock 45-watt Marshall 2x12 in. combo with the original tubes replaced by KT66s. He was noted for playing the amp with the volume turned up full, even in the studio.

During the summer of 1965, Eric had a brief interlude away from the Bluesbreakers forming a band, the Glands, residing for a period in Greece. On his return to England, he found Jack Bruce had joined the Bluesbreakers and Eric was impressed with the bass player. Jack's stint with the band was short lived. Eric first recorded with John Mayall in mid-August 1965 on the single 'I'm Your Witchdoctor' with 'Telephone Blues' on the B-side. Produced by Jimmy Page, the record was issued on the Immediate label. The recordings are often considered to represent the birth of the modern rock guitar. Jimmy Page commented on Eric's guitar playing in the American *Trouser Press* magazine (which existed from March 1974 to April 1984): 'Eric was the first to evolve the sound with the Gibson and the Marshall amps; he should have full credit for that.'

For the legendary, John Mayall/Eric Clapton Bluesbreakers album, recording took place at Decca's studios at West Hampstead at the beginning of May 1966. Eric's Les Paul, pictured during recordings, has both pick-up covers removed and this was played through the Marshall 45-watt combo amplifier. The album was produced by Mike Vernon and engineered by Gus Dudgeon. The aim of the album was to capture the exciting stage performance and basic set on vinyl. Initially, there were problems over the high volume at which Eric wanted to play, though he would not compromise. Eric envisaged a sound similar to Freddie King's, though this was transcended when a much fatter result was achieved. All the bass was turned up on the bridge pick-up and both the guitar and amplifier volumes were on maximum settings. The guitar was then on the edge of distortion and a unique sustain was achieved. Eric sang on the side two track, 'Ramblin' On My Mind', marking his vocal debut and his first cover of a Robert

The Cream on 'Ready Steady Go!'.
Pictcrial Press Ltd / Alamy Stock Photo.

Johnson composition.

On May 13, 1966, Ginger Baker approached Eric with the suggestion of forming a band. When Jack Bruce agreed to join them, the trio had a work-out at Ginger's house in Neasden north-west London during late May 1966, where they just improvised. Afterwards, all three instantly agreed they had a certain magic together.

Around May 11, *Melody Maker* announced that Eric, Jack and Ginger were forming a band. A little later, publicity stated that the three musicians would call themselves Cream, with Robert Stigwood as manager.

Eric's last gig with the Bluesbreakers was in mid-July; the Bluesbreakers' album was officially released on Friday, July 22, 1966. Over a period, from Friday July 22 to Friday July 29, Cream rehearsed at a church hall in Kensal Rise, working out a basic repertoire. During this time, Eric had his Gibson Les Paul stolen from the church hall.

Cream's first gig was at the Twisted Wheel Club in

Manchester on Friday, July 29, 1966. At the same time, Elektra Records released an album 'What's Shakin' with Eric and the Powerhouse playing on three tracks: 'I Want To Know', 'Crossroads', and 'Steppin' Out'.

Cream appeared at the Windsor 6th National Jazz & Blues Festival, Royal Windsor Racecourse on Sunday, July 31, 1966 and Eric 'borrowed', as some people have argued, a Gibson Les Paul with a Bigsby. He played this on several occasions during the early Cream days. Before the Cream show at the Klooks Kleek Club on August 2, someone cheekily stole the guitar case of Eric's first Gibson Les Paul. On August 16, 1966, the band performed at the Marquee Club with Eric playing a Gibson Les Paul Special double cutaway guitar with a Bigsby and single coil pick-ups.

Andy Summers (later of the Police) had acquired a 1960 Gibson Les Paul just before Eric had bought the one that was stolen. In *One Train Later: A Memoir* (2007), Andy Summers recalls that Eric made contact in September 1966, offering to buy his guitar and a deal was completed. Andy delivered the guitar to Advision studios where Cream was recording 'Fresh Cream'. Tony Bacon in *Million Dollar Les Paul: In Search of the Most Valuable Guitar in the World* (2008) writes that it was used 'to record most of the group's first album Fresh Cream…' He adds that it was also heard on the single 'I Feel Free'.

Eric removed the pick-up covers to show double black bobbins on the Summers' burst. Several other items were removed, including the plastic truss-road cover, pick-guard and pick-up selector surround. Noticeable on the Summers' burst were reflector knobs, exclusive to the 1960s Les Paul models, instead of the bonnet knobs.

In *Beat Instrumental No. 40* of August 1966, Eric was asked to define his style of playing: 'Modern Chicago Blues style – that's what it is although I wouldn't pretend for one moment that it is the complete statement of the scene in Chicago, because, I must, naturally, be exposed to the outside influence of English guitarists.'

Commenting on the Gibson Les Paul, he stated: 'I thought the Telecaster had great tone, but being solid it didn't feedback very well, so I couldn't get that sustained effect. The semi-acoustic is great for this. I hate a thin treble sound. I always give myself plenty of bass and treble so there is some bite to my sound.' When asked about the army of people who followed him from gig to gig, shouting 'Clapton is God', he answered: 'It's all very encouraging but I'm not sure that people are interpreting the whole thing properly. I am not a great guitarist, it's just that they enjoy the style of guitar I play. It's rare if not unique in Britain. The acclaim puts a great weight on my shoulders and I feel a great deal of responsibility to the audience because I am supposed to be the greatest. I am expected to play better all the time, and this is hard.' He mentioned two British guitarists he admired were Jeff Beck and George Harrison.

After only being in Britain a week, Jimi Hendrix played 'Killing Floor' with Cream at the Regent Street Polytechnic, central London on Saturday October 1, 1966. Eric in his autobiography states: 'I remember thinking that here was a force to be reckoned with, because he was clearly going to be a huge star, and just as we were finding our own speed, here was the real thing.'

Whilst many people felt that Cream's first single 'Wrapping Paper' was a disappointment when released on October 7, 1966, they were rewarded after hearing the instrumental B-side 'Cat's Squirrel' where Eric's guitar playing is strongly in evidence. The band's second single 'I Feel Free' was released on December 9, 1966, and their first album 'Fresh Cream' on the same date.

For the first few months of 1967, Cream played a number of colleges, clubs and small theatre gigs as well as short trips to West Germany, Ireland and Scandinavia, performing much of the 'Fresh Cream' album. During a gig at the Marquee Club on Tuesday, March 21, 1967, Christopher Hjort notes in *Strange Brew: Eric Clapton and the British Blues Boom* (2007), Eric played 'his newly acquired black three pick-up Gibson Les Paul Custom model.' For the second set of the evening, he borrowed the 1964 Gibson EDS 1275 Doubleneck guitar belonging to John Whitney of support band Family.

Cream embarked on their first American visit from March 25 to April 6, 1967. Appearing in Murray the K's Music in the Fifth Dimension in Brooklyn, New York, Eric showcased his 1964 Gibson SG, having been painted by Dutch artists Simon Posthuma and Marijke Koger. The guitar included a Maestro tremolo and the pick-guard was fastened to the body with six screws, a detail which appeared from the beginning of 1964.

In time, Eric would remove the vibrato arm from the SG. Initially, during the Murray K shows, Cream used the amplifiers belonging to The Lovin' Spoonful but later played through those belonging to the Who. Whilst in the US, Cream undertook recordings at the Atlantic Records studio in New York. There is a picture on the www.angelfire.com website, from this period, showing Eric playing a 1954 black Les Paul Custom.

In *Beat Instrumental No. 48* of April 1967, under the heading 'The Sounds I Like by Britain's Top Guitarists', Eric mentions: 'As I can't stand a thin, weak sound, I use a lot of bass when I'm playing. Both on the stage and in the studio … My stage set up consists of a Marshall 100-watt amplifier with two sets of 4x12 in. speakers … Can't say I like to use a fuzz-box. I prefer to rely on the quality of my pick-ups. You don't need fuzz unless your pick-ups are bad, or if you're using a treble sound. Then it needs filling-out…'

On May 7, 1967, at the Swan, Yardley, Birmingham, Eric is identified with a Danelectro guitar. Cream flew out to Atlantic Studios on May 12 until May 15, 1967, and took with them their guitars and Marshall amplifiers. For the recording of

---

The Gibson Firebird was designed for the company by car designer Ray Dietrich and was their first solid-body guitar to use neck-through construction – the neck extended to the tail end of the mahogany body. The neck is made up of five plies of mahogany interspersed with four narrow strips of walnut to provide added strength. Amongst the other features were: 24.75 scale; rosewood or ebony fretboard with trapezoid, block, or dot inlays; reverse headstock; and banjo-style planetary geared tuning keys.

'Disraeli Gears', it is submitted that Eric used the SG and a Gibson Black Les Paul Custom. Speculation exists around how he created the jangling guitar sound on 'Dance The Night Away'. It was most likely a Fender XII. The 'Classic Album' DVD series featured 'Disraeli Gears' and when discussing the song, Eric plays a Fender XII with 'hockey stick' headstock.

Eric, along with 'Disraeli Gears' producer Felix Pappalardi, visited Manny's Music on West 48th Street, New York to buy a Wah-Wah pedal for use on 'Tales Of Brave Ulysses'. 'Strange Brew', the single, was released on May 26, 1967, with 'Tales Of Brave Ulysses' on the reverse.

Eric explained in *Beat Instrumental No. 52* of August 1967 some details about his guitar sound: '…I'm playing more smoothly now. I'm developing what I call my "Woman Tone". It's a sweet sound, something like the solo on "I Feel Free" … You wouldn't think that it was a guitar for the first few passages. It calls for the correct use of distortion.'

At McGoos, Edinburgh, August 6, 1967, Eric was spotted playing a Fender Stratocaster. From August 20 to October 1967, Cream embarked on their first US tour and carried out more recording at Atlantic Studios. In September 1967, Eric played for the first time with B.B. King.

Cream's tour opened on August 22, at Bill Graham's Fillmore Auditorium. The www.angelfire.com website shows Eric playing a sunburst Fender Stratocaster. Beginning on Tuesday, September 26, Cream played three nights at the Whisky a Go Go in Los Angeles and Eric was seen with the Gibson SG with Marshall stacks to the rear. In one picture, there is a sunburst Fender Strat in the background. 'Disraeli Gears' was released on November 10, 1967. In *Beat Instrumental No. 57* of January 1968, Eric talks about the new direction Cream are taking: 'The emphasis is more and more on playing. Our music is much more free, and improvised, than it was.'

Eric is seen on a flat-bed lorry with a 1962 Custom Telecaster in the Danish film 'It Was a Saturday Evening', shot on February 5 and 6, 1968, in Copenhagen. The guitar was fitted with a late 1960s Fender Stratocaster neck with a large headstock and rosewood fretboard.

On February 12, 1968, Cream departed for a second extensive tour of the US. This was besides spending more time recording their third Album, 'Wheels Of Fire'. Whilst in the Atlantic Studios, Eric employed a Leslie rotating speaker and found time to jam with B.B. King at the Au Go Go in New York.

On the American tour, Bruce McCaskill from Liverpool was in charge of guitars. Noted amongst Eric's guitars were the painted Gibson SG and the Gibson Les Paul Custom in black with three pick-ups. For amplification, Eric used Marshall stacks besides Fender Dual Showman amps with a split lead. McCaskill told *Melody Maker* as recalled in Hjort (*op. cit.*): 'It was done so that the musicians could adjust one amp to treble and the other to bass. They have tried it with three amps, but it is normally used only with two.'

During Cream's US tour and appearance over three nights March 8–March 10, 1968, at Winterland, San Francisco, live recordings were made. Amongst the tracks is 'Crossroads', which many people will claim is not only Cream's, but Eric's finest moment. Jack, Ginger and Eric were interviewed during the Winterland appearances by film-maker, Tony Palmer. Eric demonstrated how his guitar runs were put together as well as revealing details of the 'woman tone' and use of the Wah-Wah pedal.

On March 29, 1968, Eric was spotted playing a 1953 Les Paul Gold Top at Hunter College Auditorium New York. In the same year he appeared in a Guild guitar catalogue with a Guild F-50 acoustic.

A 1964 Gibson Firebird I was probably acquired, according to a Cream concert tour expense ledger (quoted on www.groundguitar.com), on April 13, 1968. It was bought from either 8th Street Music or Music City Store both based in Philadelphia. The guitar was first played by Eric at Philadelphia's Electric Factory around the same date.

Eric's Vintage Sunburst Firebird I featured a single mini-humbucker in the bridge position, two knobs (volume and tone) and a wraparound tailpiece. He used it on a number of live dates in the USA as well as during the band's final show at the Royal Albert Hall in November 1968.

A Cream performance was taped for the 'Smothers Brothers Show' in May 1968 and Eric played an acoustic when performing 'Anyone For Tennis', which was released as a single in the same month. After Cream's American tour ended in mid-June 1968, Hjort (*op. cit.*), states that Eric gave the psychedelic SG to George Harrison.

Melody Maker's front-page headline in July 1968, read: 'Cream to Spilt Up'; and this was to happen before the end of the year. In an interview, Eric explained: 'With Cream, solos were the big thing, but I'm really off that virtuoso kick. It was all over-exposed.' He states being impressed by the Band's music and Bob Dylan's 'Basement Tapes', adding: 'I want to be in a group where I can control the music but be at the back.' On August 9, 1968, Cream's 'Wheels Of Fire' was released in the UK.

Early in September, George Harrison invited Eric to a Beatles recording session at Abbey Road. Several weeks earlier, Eric had given George a red Gibson Les Paul guitar and he played that, double-tracked, on 'While My Guitar Gently Weeps'.

Cream began their US farewell tour at Oaklands-Almeda County Coliseum, CA, on Friday, October 4, 1968. Amongst the guitars that Eric used, were: a 1958 Gibson Les Paul dark burst; the one pick-up Firebird; and at the LA Forum in October 1968, he has a Gibson ES 355.

A Gibson ES 335, according to Gerry Donohue, working at Selmer's store in Charing Cross Road, was bought by Eric two weeks prior to Cream's shows at the Albert Hall on November 26, 1968. There were two concerts: one at 5.45 pm, and the other at 9.00 pm with Eric playing a Gibson ES 335 and the Firebird I. The shows were filmed by Tony Palmer and became a BBC programme and a full-length movie. Eric appears in the Rolling Stones' 'Rock and Roll Circus' film during December 1968 performing with the Dirty Mac band where he uses a Gibson ES 335.

A guitar luthier attracting Eric's attention by the late 1960s was Anthony Zemaitis. The pair collaborated to co-design a 12-string guitar in 1969, nicknamed 'Ivan the Terrible'. It featured a mahogany top, decorated with wood inlay in a heart

Eric Clapton's Gibson SG Electric Guitar. Artwork by Marijke Koger and Simon Posthuma. ZUMA Press, Inc. / Alamy Stock Photo.

motif. The back and sides were rosewood, the fingerboard bound and inlaid with silver.

In mid-February 1969, Eric, Ginger and Steve Winwood got together and recorded several versions of Buddy Holly's 'Well Alright', where it is noted that Eric plays a Fender guitar through a Leslie speaker. In late February, Cream's 'Goodbye' album was released and in mid-March, Eric played his Gibson Firebird I in 'Supershow' (with a subtitle 'The Last Great Jam of the 1960s'), a music documentary film that included a cross section of jazz and blues musicians. Eric plays 'Slate 27' with Roland Kirk, joined by Jack Bruce, Jon Hiseman, and Dick Heckstall Smith. In 'End Jam' Eric's seen alongside Buddy Guy.

Early in April 1969, Eric, Ginger and Steve Winwood announced they would play a free concert in Hyde Park on June 7, though they had not found a bass player. A little later, Rich Grech of Family joined the trio, named Blind Faith by early May 1969. In photographs of the band in Eric's Hurtwood home, he is seen holding a painted double-cut Danelectro guitar. Blind Faith performed in Hyde Park in front of approximately 120,000 people who mostly found the band's performance disappointing. Many fans thought they would be witnessing how Cream ought to have developed, with Steve Winwood added to the line-up. For Eric, there are no Gibson guitars in sight, playing instead, the Custom Telecaster, seen previously in Sweden, though this time with a maple neck. Film of the event was not seen until 2006.

Blind Faith started on a week-long Nordic tour on June 12 with Eric initially using the Custom Telecaster/Stratocaster neck guitar, though he switched to a Gibson Les Paul.

On July 12, Blind Faith began their American tour at Madison Square Garden. During this period, the band is supported on some gigs by Free, and at one point Eric talked to Paul Kossoff about his finger vibrato technique. Eric swapped a Gibson Les Paul sunburst for a black Gibson Les Paul Custom belonging to Kossoff.

Eric played his cherry ES 335 during the Blind Faith tour and Steve Winwood may be seen with the Telecaster/Strat necked guitar. The band's album was released in the UK on August 22, 1969. In an American review of the record, one critic said of Eric's guitar playing on the track 'In The Presence Of The Lord': 'Never has a guitarist said so much so beautifully in such a short space of time.' Blind Faith completed their US tour on August 24 and never played together again.

Eric performed with his black Les Paul Custom (not the one obtained from Paul Kossoff) in the Plastic Ono Band at the Toronto Rock 'n' Roll Revival Show on September 13. At the end of the month, he played on John Lennon's Plastic Ono Band single, 'Cold Turkey'. By the middle of October 1969, he was recording with: Delaney & Bonnie; on a Ric Grech session; tracks for Doris Troy; and Leon Russell.

Near the end of October, Eric became a sideman with the Delaney & Bonnie entourage as they began a European tour. On the 'Beat Club' performances, Eric plays a black Gibson Les Paul Custom with three pick-ups through Fender amplifiers. The band then toured Britain where, on some dates, Eric played alongside George Harrison. Later in Copenhagen, Delaney was using Eric's Firebird while he stuck with his Gibson Les Paul Custom. Delaney & Bonnie's single 'Comin' Home' was released as a single December 5, 1969, the same month as their European tour ended.

During January 1970, Eric completed his first solo album, apart from a number of finishing touches made later in California. Much of the album was recorded with the Delaney & Bonnie band, augmented with a few others. The new decade would see Eric switch, for much of the ensuing years, to Fender guitars. His solo album was recorded employing a 1956 sunburst Fender Stratocaster with a maple neck and which became known as 'Brownie'. In the early months of 1970, Eric found time to play on a King Curtis record and lead guitar on several tracks by the Crickets.

In February 1970, Eric was back on the road with Delaney & Bonnie for a US tour. Speaking to *Guitar Player* June 1970, Eric mentions the following about his Stratocaster: 'It's just right for the kind of bag I was playing with [Delaney & Bonnie] … [With the guitar] I just set the switch between the first and middle pick-ups. There is a little place where you can catch it so that you get a special sound somehow.'

On www.fendercustomshop.com, information about the Stratocaster is given: 'Eric Clapton bought the Stratocaster he affectionately nicknamed "Brownie" second hand at Sound City in London May 7, 1967…' The guitar was illustrated on the front of Eric's first solo album; the neck had been seen at Hyde Park, fixed to the Fender Custom Telecaster body. By the beginning of March 1970, Eric had performed for the last time with Delaney & Bonnie, but was involved in various sessions as a guest guitarist with: Stephen Stills; Taj Mahal; and Howlin' Wolf (playing some slide guitar).

Eric's first solo album was finally mixed by Tom Down in May 1970 and around the same time 'Delaney & Bonnie & Friends On Tour With Eric Clapton' was released. In June 1970, 'Live Cream' appeared.

In the middle of June, Eric played with a number of mostly former Delaney & Bonnie musicians at a concert for Dr Spock's Civil Liberties Fund and they adopted the title of Derek and the Dominos. In a session with Dr John, Eric is mentioned in *Melody Maker* of July 18, 1970: 'The new, more withdrawn Clapton was also in evidence, quietly sitting down to play his Telecaster with a steel bottle neck.' Richard Williams, author of the article added: 'What came out was the most satisfying Clapton I've ever heard, very reticent but adding a whole lot to the ensemble sound with sweet sliding fills and brief glistening solos.'

At the same time, a three-leg tour was announced for Derek and the Dominos. Eric gave details on his equipment set-up in *Melody Maker*, August 8, 1970: 'At present I play a [1956] Fender Stratocaster with a Fender Dual Showman amplifier and speakers, a Fuzz-Face fuzz box and a Wah-Face Wah-Wah pedal…' Derek and the Dominos began live performances on August 1, 1970. Songs included those from Eric's solo album (released on August 7, 1970) and others that were to be featured on their projected album with recording starting towards the end of August 1970.

After the Allman Brothers played at the Miami Civic Centre, they jammed with Eric and his band at the Criteria studios. Afterwards, Duane Allman played on most of the tracks that made up the album 'Layla And Assorted Love Songs', released November 1970. On the album, Eric plays his Fender Stratocaster 'Brownie', though on the second leg of the band's British tour he was seen playing the three-pick-up Gibson 'Black Beauty' Custom. For recording the album, a Fender Champ was the main studio amp, whereas on stage Fender Dual Showmans and Marshalls were employed with Fender cabinets.

From mid-October, the band began its first and last US tour. About this time, Eric's laid-back guitar playing received much praise. Some critics preferred that style to the long breath-taking guitar solos witnessed in Cream's US tours, though, for some, opinion was still divided.

Whilst in Nashville to record for the 'Johnny Cash Show', Eric saw a batch of Fender Stratocaster guitars in the city's Sho-Bud shop selling for around $100 each. Later, Eric stated he bought a handful of them: 'I gave one to George Harrison, one to Stevie Winwood and one to Pete Townshend. I kept three, and out of them I made one, which is 'Blackie'. I just took the body from one, the neck from another, and so on.'

During the Derek and the Dominos tours, Eric squeezed in time to record with John Mayall for his album 'Back To The Roots'. Derek and the Dominos played their last gig together in New York on December 6, 1970, and during the following week the album was released.

Over the ensuing three years, Eric was absent from the spotlight for a while. However, he did emerge to play at the 'Concert for Bangladesh' in August 1971 where, amongst the guitars he used, was a 1950s Gibson Byrdland and the 'Brownie' Fender Stratocaster. However, it has been an old debate on guitar forums about whether the first guitar was a Byrdland or a 350T.

Arguments for it being a Byrdland are: the headstock inlay; fingerboard is pointed at the end; the top seems to be spruce; tuners have gold-plated metal buttons. Alternatively, the 350T submissions are: double parallelogram fretboard inlays; pick-guard appears to be black. Summing up, one forum contributor argues that maybe the fingerboard was modified or perhaps it was custom guitar, ordered that way, but the evidence gathered and considered 'points more to Byrdland than 350T.'

Eric was persuaded to take to the stage once again by friend, Pete Townshend and Lord Harlech (whose daughter Alice was living with Eric) on January 13, 1973. A concert was performed at the Rainbow Theatre in London with a band that included, Pete Townshend, Ronnie Wood, Steve Winwood, Ric Grech, and Jim Capaldi. There were two shows and Eric used the 'Blackie' guitar with tremolo still attached and a Gibson Les Paul.

Between April and May 1974, Eric had recovered sufficiently to team up once more with Carl Radle and start recording again. The result was '461 Ocean Boulevard', released in July of the same year. The album was recorded in Miami with contributions made by Yvonne Elliman and guitarist George Terry; Tom Dowd was producer. Several tracks were adaptions of songs by Blind Willie Johnson, Elmore James, and Robert Johnson. Eric used 'Blackie', his cherry ES 335, a Dobro, and Martin acoustic guitars on the album. Quite surprisingly, the Bob Marley covered track, 'I Shot The Sheriff' reached no. 1 on the Billboard Hot 100. Noticeable on this album was that Eric's vocals had matured from previous attempts in the past. '461 Ocean Boulevard' topped the charts in the USA and Canada and broke into the top ten in several other countries. Looking back at the album in *Uncut* December 1, 2004, Nigel Williamson stated: '[with "461 Ocean Boulevard" Eric] rediscovered the primacy of music in his life.'

For the remainder of 1974, Eric toured extensively in Europe, the US, Canada, Japan and fitted in two shows at the Hammersmith Odeon. Eric was noted around 1974 to acquire a Gibson Explorer, which was modified by having the long protruding horn chopped down. By 1977, it had been sold to Junior Marvin. In 1975, Eric built on the success of the previous year and recorded 'There's One In Every Crowd' in Miami and Jamaica. Amongst the tracks were four originals by Eric as well as a collaboration with George Terry. There were adaptions of others, most notably a track by Willie Johnson, along with 'Swing Low, Sweet Chariot'. Although similar in style to his 1974 album, the 1975 release did not enjoy the same critical acclaim. Throughout 1975, Eric was mostly touring in Hawaii, Australia, the US, and Japan. In the same year 'E.C. Was Here', a live album, appeared and on some of the tracks Eric played the Gibson Explorer.

'No Reason To Cry', Eric's fourth studio album was recorded at the Band's Shangri-La studios between December 1975 and May 1976. Bob Dylan contributed a song 'Sign Language', and there were other compositions from Rick Danko, Richard Manuel and Marcy Levy. Critics picked out Otis Rush's 'Double Trouble' as the standout track, one saying it 'features some exceptional playing by Clapton.' The album peaked at no. 10 in the UK. Eric toured in the UK and US during the remainder of 1976. In November 1976, he appeared as one of the guests at the farewell performance of the Band in 'The Last Waltz'. He performed 'Further On Up The Road', in spite of having trouble with his guitar strap at the beginning of a solo.

Before the end of the decade, Eric would release two more albums: 'Slowhand' (1977) and 'Backless' (1978). By this time, Eric had married Pattie Boyd though was struggling to cope with alcoholism. Nonetheless, 'Slowhand' featured the two singles 'Lay Down Sally' and a song for Pattie Boyd 'Wonderful Tonight'.

Albert Lee joined Eric's band around 1978 and was given a Gibson Les Paul Custom guitar. Said Albert: 'That's the one [Eric] used with Delaney & Bonnie and Cream … It's one of my treasures.' In 1979, developments in Eric's life included rekindling his relationship with his mother.

The following decade began badly for Eric. His good friend, bassist Carl Radle, died in 1980, and in March 1981, he collapsed through complications with ulcers. At the end of that year, Eric admitted he was an alcoholic. During early 1982, he booked into Hazelden Minneapolis alcohol treatment centre. Despite setbacks with his health, there were interesting developments with his work and the guitars used. In the 1980s, Eric offered the following albums: 'Money And Cigarettes'; 'Behind The Sun'; and 'Journeyman' with notable assistance from Phil Collins.

In 1983, he was presented with the Silver Clef Award from Princess Michael of Kent for outstanding contribution to British music. According to Tom Wheeler in *The Stratocaster*

Chronicles: Celebrating 50 Years of the Fender Strat (2004), Eric was presented with one of the first 1982, '57 reissue Fender Stratocasters, by John Page and Freddie Tavares. This was during the time of the 1983 ARMS concert tour, in which Eric was involved.

Roger Waters asked Eric for assistance in the studio and to join his touring band for his 'Pros and Cons of Hitchhiking' project between August 1983 and May–July 1984. Eric ventured into film music, joining forces with Michael Kamen to write the score for 'Edge of Darkness', originally screened by BBC2 in 1985. The score won a BAFTA award for Best Original Television Music.

On www.giffinguitars.com, the company announces it built two Custom 'Strat' guitars 'for Eric Clapton's 1985 World Tour. Both were exact copies of "Blackie" except for the colour, (one was blue, the other green).'

In 1987, Eric retired his 'Blackie' and started to play his new signature model developed by Fender. In fact, this was the first signature model produced by Fender. Eric was involved in designing the guitar after an approach was made to him in 1985. He told Fender he wanted an exact copy of 'Blackie'. He required a soft V-shape neck comparable to the Martins he played: a 1939 000-42 and a 1966 000-28. Additionally, he asked for a 'compressed' pick-up sound and this was achieved with gold lace sensor pick-ups and adding mid-boost circuitry and a bypass mini-switch. George Blanda in the Fender Custom Shop was responsible for building a number of prototypes for Eric's signature model. One was in Torino Red and the two others in Pewter Grey Metallic.

During the late 1980s, Eric began his annual stints at the Royal Albert Hall. In 1991, a record 24 nights, between February 5 and March 9, 1991, were performed at the venue by him. The shows were divided into four different configurations: Four Piece; Nine Piece; Blues Band; and a Full Orchestra. The shows were filmed and recorded.

Eric suffered a parent's worst nightmare on March 20, 1991, when his four-and-a-half-year-old son, Connor, was killed. However, in the immediate aftermath of the event he somehow coped with the tragedy by immersing himself in work. He composed music for the film 'Rush' which included a song 'Tears In Heaven' written by Eric and Will Jennings about Connor's death.

In December 1991, Eric and his band, including Andy Fairweather Low, toured with George Harrison in Japan for 'The Rock Legends Tour'. The following year saw an important development in Eric's career. On January 16, he filmed an episode of the MTV Show, 'Unplugged', at London's Bray Studios. The TV show, and subsequent DVD and CD releases, proved to be a great success bringing three Grammy Awards for Eric at ceremonies in Los Angeles in 1993. At the same ceremony, 'Tears In Heaven' from the 'Rush' soundtrack received three Grammy Awards. Walter Carter in *The Martin Book: A Complete History of Martin Guitars* (2006) states that Eric used a Martin 000-42 on 'Unplugged'. Afterwards, the Martin company was prompted to issue the signature 000-42 EC model in 1996 'that ten years later had passed the 4,000 mark in sales.' The success continued with two limited-run Clapton signature models: the 000-42EC in 2000 and the 000-28 two years later (both also came in ECB versions with Brazilian rosewood back and sides).

A musical shift for Eric occurred in 1997 when he teamed up with Simon Climie to release 'Retail Therapy', featuring jungle, techno, R&B and ambient music. The album was issued under the band name of TDF. Amongst Eric's other album releases in the 1990s were 'From The Cradle'; 'Pilgrim'; and 'Blues'. Of course, many concerts were undertaken at home and abroad to promote these albums.

In 1997, Eric founded the Crossroads Centre at Antigua, a drug and alcohol rehabilitation treatment clinic. To raise funds for this project, he auctioned 100 of his guitars in June 1999 along with several amplifiers and Versace guitar straps. The sale was held at Christie's auction House in New York City. Amongst the items sold were: a 1956 Fender Stratocaster (sunburst), known as 'Brownie'; a 1958 Gibson Explorer (natural) used during the 1983 ARMS Tour; a 1974 Martin 000-28 (natural); and a 1986 Pewter Fender Stratocaster Eric Clapton signature model.

Eric recorded an album with blues legend B.B. King titled 'Riding With The King', released in June 2000 and it was a major success earning a gold disc in a short space of time. He re-introduced art onto his guitars in 2001 after a collaboration with the well-known American graffiti artist, John 'Crash' Matos. At a Royal Albert Hall performance in March 2001, he appeared with a vividly painted Eric Clapton Signature Stratocaster, that became known as the Crashocaster or Crash 1. Several more graffiti guitars were commissioned from 'Crash' as well as other artists: Stas, She One, Kaws, Next Sky, D'Zine, Daze, and Futura.

On June 24, 2004, Christie's New York sold 88 lots that included some of Eric's guitar collection along with instruments donated by friends. The proceeds, (approximately $6.4 million) benefited the Crossroads Centre in Antigua. Amongst the top three prices paid for Eric's guitars were his legendary Fender Stratocaster 'Blackie'; the Gibson cherry red Gibson ES 335; and the 1939 Martin 000-42 used on MTV's 'Unplugged'.

At the long-awaited Cream re-union concerts in 2005, the following were amongst Eric's equipment: four Fender black Stratocasters; 1957 Fender Custom Shop reissue Tweed Twin amplifier; a Leslie speaker; Samson wireless pack; and a Wah-Wah pedal.

In the same year, Digitech launched the Crossroads Artist Series Pedal which was endorsed by Eric. Seven selectable 'sounds' generated by the pedal were named 'Sunshine Of Your Love'; 'Crossroads'; 'Badge; 'Layla (Acoustic)'; 'Layla (Electric)'; 'Lay Down Sally'; 'Reptile'.

After years of admiring the work of J.J. Cale, Eric collaborated on an album with him. Released in November 2007, it was titled 'Road To Escondido' and won the Grammy Award for Best Contemporary Blues Album at the 50th Annual Awards Ceremony in Los Angeles 2008.

Eric was reunited with his friend Stevie Winwood for a tour in 2009 and his equipment included: Eric Clapton Signature model Fender Stratocasters in black; Martin signature model 000-28EC; Fender Custom Shop 1957 Tweed Reissue amplifier; Leslie speaker; Samson Wireless pack; and Vox Wah-Wah pedal.

The Eric Clapton 'BLACKIE' Fender Stratocaster guitar. One of 275 reproductions made by the Fender Custom Shop in 2006.
ZUMA Press, Inc. / Alamy Stock Photo.

A third auction of Eric's guitars was staged by Bonhams in New York on March 9, 2011, and the catalogue conveniently illustrated Eric with some of the items. Lot 2 shows him playing through c. 1974 Pignose amplifier; Lot 26, with Jim Marshall and a 2003 Marshall 1962 Jag Limited Edition model amplifier; Lot 51 with a 2001 Gibson ES 335, serial no. EC001; Lot 55 pictured playing a 1982 Strings & Things in Memphis Custom 'St Blues/Bluesmaster'; Lot 74, seated playing a 1948 Gibson L-5P; Lot 77 standing in front of a 1970s Music Man HD-130 Reverb Stack; Lot 92 seen in front of a 1957 Fender Twin Amp – Model 5E8A; Lot 98 sitting behind a 1998 Fender Woody Jr; Lot 121 seated holding a circa 1970 Gibson LP-2; Lot 138 with a 2008 Fender Stratocaster Eric Clapton signature model.

The early years of the 21st century had seen Eric using amps built by Dennis Cornell. On www.bonhams.com, there is the following information about a 2002 Cornell Custom 80 that was sold at the March 2011 sale: 'After working on Clapton's Vibro King amps, Lots 95 and 96 [in the sale], an English amplifier technician Dennis Cornell was asked to build a custom amp for him using the shape of the Tweed Twin cabinet but adding his own circuitry incorporating Clapton's tonal requirements … The Cornell Custom 80 serial number DC-2 and it[s] companion DC-1 served as Clapton's main stage amplifiers over the period 2002 until approximately 2004, which encompassed several world tours as well as the Concert for George and John Mayall 70th Birthday concert at Liverpool docks on July 19, 2003 and the first Crossroads Guitar Festival in Dallas, 4–6 June 2004.'

In the years leading up to the 2020 Covid-19 Lockdown, Eric continued to tour and release albums. For the 2014 Japan/Mid East Tour, Eric's fan website www.whereseric.com, mentions he used the following equipment: 'Eric Clapton signature model Fender Stratocasters in Pewter; 6-string Martin acoustics – OM-ECHF Navy Blues; Fender 57 Bandmaster; Leslie speaker; BAE 1073 DMP DI-Box (for his acoustics); Dunlop Cry Baby Classic GCB895 F; Box to switch from the amp to the Leslie or to select both.'

Eric Clapton on stage at the Brighton Centre, Brighton, February 1, 1992.
Trinity Mirror / Mirrorpix / Alamy Stock Photo.

DAVE 'CLEM' CLEMPSON

For much of Clem Clempson's early life he was a dedicated pianist but all that was to change when an aunt took him to see 'Rock Around The Clock' in the late 1950s. He was mesmerised and is sure that sparked his ambition to become a professional guitarist. 'The solo in the title track still blows me away,' said Clem.

Clem was born in Tamworth, Staffordshire on September 5, 1949, and is the eldest of three brothers. His father, Dennis, worked at Royal Doulton, the ceramic manufacturing company producing tableware and collectables. His mother, Betty was a housewife. Whilst his parents had no formal musical training, they were both keen members of a local Methodist church choir. His maternal grandfather was a violinist with his own semi-pro band, the Elite Dance Band, and played at events around the Tamworth area. He died when Clem was only an infant.

Aged four, Clem was given a toy piano and his family was astonished when he immediately picked out tunes heard on the radio. His parents arranged piano lessons with a local teacher, Kitty King, paying her 2/6 (12½p) for each session.

'We had a piano at home and I was required to practice for a minimum of 30 minutes each day. Apart from the tasks Kitty gave me each week, I enjoyed tinkling around on the piano and improvising.'

Kitty King was a piano teacher for the Royal College of Music and this meant Clem had to sit examinations once a year at the Royal School in Birmingham. Having his performances judged was a terrifying ordeal but he always attained high marks and still has, somewhere, all the certificates up to grade 7.

Clem was also obliged to enter piano competitions, usually at Tamworth Assembly Rooms. 'It was horrible really. After we'd performed our pieces, someone would stand up on stage and tell us what we were doing wrong. Whilst the criticism could be quite brutal, I always managed to bring home some silverware which made my mum, dad and grandma very happy.' Kitty King taught Clem to read and write music which was a bonus for his future career and made things easy when teaching himself to play guitar.

Clem's first school was Wilnecote Infants, then Wilnecote Junior. He liked school and did well, passing the Eleven-Plus exam before moving to Atherstone Grammar School where his best subjects were English language, English literature, French and Latin. 'I think my parents hoped I would become a teacher, possibly a music teacher, but in my early teens I had no firm idea of what I wanted to be.'

As well as having a keen interest in music, Clem was fanatical about football and played at every opportunity, mostly in the street or on some patch of public land, with the obligatory jumpers for goal posts. Supporting West Bromwich Albion, he saw his first home match against Manchester City in 1953. Clem's hero was Davy Burnside, West Brom's number 8, or inside right as it was once called. Clem played for his school, Atherstone Grammar School until he was banned for refusing to wear the school cap on Saturday match days.

On seeing her star pupil becoming disenchanted with classical piano lessons, Kitty King told Clem's parents that it would be best if he was not allowed to have a guitar. Initially, Clem 'made' a guitar from a piece of cardboard for a body, an old stick for a neck and a few elastic bands for strings. In 1963, he sold an electric train set for five pounds, went to a music shop, passed many times on the way to West Brom's ground, and bought his first guitar – a six-string acoustic. The piano lessons would eventually cease.

Donato Joseph 'Danny' Cedrone (1920–1954) played a key role in Bill Haley and the Comets' first recording session for Decca Records on April 12, 1954 when they recorded 'Rock Around The Clock' in New York City. The song's guitar break is widely considered to be one of the greatest rock 'n' roll guitar solos of all time. On June 17, 1954, Cedrone died after falling down a staircase and breaking his neck. His place as guitarist in the Comets was taken by Franny Beecher.

'I only knew one lad in the neighbourhood who had a guitar. This was a six-string Hawaiian guitar which had an instructional manual which I borrowed. I didn't realise that a Hawaiian guitar is tuned differently to a regular instrument and so I first played a guitar in an open G tuning.'

Clem acquired Bert Weedon's *Play in a Day* (1957) and quickly retuned his guitar. After finding his way round the instrument, he now needed a band. He persuaded his two oldest and best friends to buy instruments and join his new outfit. They included Kevin Day on bass, and Karl Robinson on rhythm guitar. Billy Sanders was recruited to play drums and David Cotton to handle vocals. 'We were nicknamed "Adders" though it was suggested "The Vipers", being another name for the adder, was cooler.'

After teaching themselves to play a bunch of Shadows instrumentals and around 20 chart hits, they were ready to start gigging. But amplification was needed. Karl Robinson's dad said that if pick-ups were fitted to their acoustic guitars, the sound could be amplified by plugging into the back of a couple of old radios.

Clem decided that an electric guitar shouldn't have a sound-hole so covered up the one on his instrument with a piece of black Formica, cut roughly into the shape of a Fender Stratocaster scratch-plate. The band's first public appearance was at Wilnecote Methodist church and very soon they were entering talent competitions, frequently held in the many working men's clubs in villages around Tamworth. Being regular winners enabled Billy Sanders' dad to get them proper bookings, charging a fee of around £5 or £6. After expenses, they were each earning around ten shillings, which was big money when a lad's normal weekly pocket money was about two shillings.

Steve Marriott and Clem Clempson of Humble Pie perform on stage in Bilzen, Belgium, August 17, 1974.
Gijsbert Hanekroot / Alamy Stock Photo.

The top band in the Tamworth area was called the Wanderers, playing mostly Shadows tunes with the lead guitarist using a white Fender Stratocaster. Clem dreamed of owning a proper electric guitar similar to that as the action on his makeshift electro/acoustic was too high to play comfortably beyond the 5th fret. Saving up his cash from gigs provided enough funds to buy a red Hofner Galaxie solid-body guitar.

'Made to give all the effects and variety of tone colour that today's music demands', read the blurb for Hofner's top-of-the-range solid, the Galaxie.

Clem's bandmate, Karl Robinson bought a very exotic-looking instrument and Kevin Day purchased a Hofner Violin bass. Then, it was time for Clem to acquire some proper amplification and he chose a Selmer Treble and Bass 50 mark II.

The band was content to be gigging and rehearsing regularly and entertaining working men's club audiences with chart hits until they heard blues music. Clem had purchased a cut-price Chess sampler album including tracks by Muddy Waters, Little Walter and Howlin' Wolf. To him, the sounds were raw and exciting. Soon afterwards Clem's first girlfriend bought him 'Five Live Yardbirds', released in December 1964.

Guitar playing was certainly becoming very interesting for Clem and he definitely needed a new instrument.

Produced in Germany, the Hofner Galaxie, was one of the company's most popular guitars in the 1960s and cost around £60 in the UK. It featured a one-piece maple neck with a 22-fret rosewood fingerboard which had full-width fret markers of double mother-of-pearl alternated with black. There were three Nova sonic humbucking pick-ups activated by simple single sliding switches, three tone controls and one master volume control. There was a tremolo, moveable bridge and a flick-down damper for playing staccato. The Galaxie was a striking guitar finished in bright red but ultimately could not compete with American rivals.

Clem Clempson.
MARKA / Alamy Stock Photo.

'I found my first serious instrument in the strangest of circumstances. The school swimming pool was undergoing refurbishment and somehow, I found myself chatting to one of the workers about guitars. He said he owned a Gibson SG Junior which he planned to sell for £40 and suggested bringing it into school the next day for me to look at. Once I'd bought the guitar, it was such a joy to play especially after the cheap ones I was used to. I was also getting closer to the sound I wanted to create.'

Clem left school in 1966 and in the same year he heard the most extraordinary guitar sound he'd ever experienced, following the release of 'John Mayall's Bluesbreakers With Eric Clapton' in July of that year. Living in a small town like Tamworth, guitar information was not so easily found, and Clem was totally at a loss to understand how Eric Clapton was producing such an incredible guitar sound on the record.

'The sustain was immense and I initially thought this might be obtained through playing at high volume. But, on the working men's club circuit we had to adhere to strict orders regarding our volume so I couldn't experiment fully. Also, I recalled that Bert Weedon had said the way to obtain the best tone from a guitar was to have the guitar's volume high, while having the volume setting of the amp only as high as necessary.' Clem speculated Eric must be using a fuzz box, so he bought the best one he could afford and whilst that had given more sustain, the overall sound was not right.

By the mid-1960s, Clem's band, the Vipers, were introducing some blues into their set and decided on a name change to reflect a more progressive approach to their music, becoming 'Harwell Reaction'. Frustrated playing the local circuit, coupled with the other band members not having the same drive and ambitions as himself, Clem joined the Pinch, based in Lichfield. John Hinch played drums and Dave Mason guitar, but was willing to switch to bass once Clem joined them. John and Dave had similar aspirations to Clem and in the past had played at colleges. Another advantage was that they had their own van so Clem couldn't resist the opportunity of joining them.

During one of the Pinch's early dates – a college dance in a large hall in Lichfield – Clem finally solved the mystery of the Clapton sustain. They were due to play quite late and by the time they appeared on stage, Clem was emboldened by the drinks downed at a nearby pub. He had recently acquired a Vox 'Beatle Master' and feeling a little reckless, turned the amp up to 10, played some lead lines and quickly discovered the sound he had been searching for. For Clem, it was a wonderful magical moment.

Clem traded the Gibson SG Junior for a Stratocaster at Ringway Music, Birmingham. It was the morning after watching Jimi Hendrix playing 'Hey Joe' on television. He was disappointed when the guitar didn't replicate the sounds Jimi made. Shortly after, Dave Mason was replaced on bass by Terry Foole, and the Pinch entered a talent contest at Birmingham's Locarno Ballroom. In the audience's opinion, the Pinch were no match to the Geno Washington-type bands they were competing against. Nonetheless, the judges were impressed and awarded the band second place. One of the judges was a local entrepreneur and jazz trumpeter, Jim Simpson who, over the band's first Indian meal, offered to manage them. This was to be the beginning of Clem's professional music career.

The SG-type Les Paul Junior was in production by December 1961. It was available in cherry with nickel-plated hardware. On the headstock 'Les Paul' appeared in gold script with 'Junior' in gold print below. The fingerboard was rosewood, unbound and with dot inlays. There were white side dots from the third fret. A single-coil pick-up, designed by Walter Fuller, and known as the P-90, was used. Other features were a height adjustable wraparound tailpiece; two knobs for tone and volume; and Kluson three-on-a-strip tuners with small white plastic keys.

After leaving school in 1966, Clem had taken a job at the Reliant Motor Company as a technical author and illustrator, producing driver's handbooks and advertisements. To Clem, it was boring work but at least he learned a little about photography and kept his old acoustic guitar hidden on the top of a cupboard in the darkroom and practised playing whenever time allowed.

Jim Simpson harboured ambitious plans for the Pinch and soon the band was signed to the Harold Davidson Agency. 'At Jim's suggestion, we changed our name to Bakerloo Blues Line (BBL). We opened our own blues club, Henry's Blueshouse, above the Crown public house, near Birmingham's New Street Station, where we played most Tuesday evenings. Local musicians, including Robert Plant and John Bonham, would often sit in with us.'

Realising that the output of Vox AC30 was perhaps no match for the deafening screams of beat group fans of the early 1960s, Jennings Musical Industries' (JMI) response was to develop 50- and 100-watt tube amplifier circuits. The first 50- and 100-watt amps, without effects or other options, just simple and loud, were produced in late 1963. The Beatles first used versions of the 50- and 100-watt heads in Paris and the USA in early 1964.

A major break for the band came when Jim persuaded John Peel to watch them play and were subsequently invited to perform a live set on the DJ's BBC 'Top Gear' radio show. After that, BBL were booked into top blues clubs around the country, including the Marquee Club in London's Wardour Street. Their first gigs were supporting bands such as Jethro Tull and, quite memorably, Led Zeppelin on their first ever UK date.

As Clem's band was travelling further afield for gigs, his time with the Reliant Motor Co. came to an end. He left by mutual agreement with the managing director who had caught him up to no good in the darkroom with a girl from the typing pool.

Bakerloo Blues Line had great fun on a tour Jim Simpson organised, featuring all the acts he was managing: Tea and Symphony, Locomotive and Earth, who would, a little later, become Black Sabbath.

Up to 1969, Clem had tried out a number of guitars and

settled for a period with a Gibson ES 335, though dreamed of one day acquiring a Gibson Les Paul. Apart from holding Peter Green's Les Paul, while he opened a case to put it away after a gig with John Mayall at Birmingham's Metro Club, Clem had never got close to one. His dream would soon be realised.

'A friend of Terry Poole's called Tony Crosby was visiting us for a few days. He played guitar and was a student at Nottingham College of Art. When Terry and I had to drive into Birmingham for a meeting with Jim Simpson, Tony asked us to drop him off at Ringway Music, Birmingham. Returning a couple of hours later, we found Tony holding a 1958 Gibson Les Paul Gold Top which had arrived at the shop that morning. I was devastated. I was a regular customer at the store but had missed the opportunity to purchase the guitar of my dreams!'

Tony Crosby had spent his entire student grant on the Gold Top and a few weeks later offered it to Clem, provided an exchange could be made with a Gibson SG and some cash. Hurriedly, Clem hitch-hiked to London, swapped his ES 335 for an SG Special, then hurtled directly up to Terry in Nottingham where he finally got hold of the guitar that he has been playing ever since.

Jim Simpson took impresario and publisher, Tony Hall to see Bakerloo Blues Line play at Henry's and soon afterwards an offer came from the newly-formed EMI label, Harvest. The band was booked into Trident Studios, just off Wardour Street, where the 'Bakerloo' album (Blues Line was dropped by this time) was the label's first production by Gus Dudgeon. He had produced the John Mayall-Eric Clapton album.

'We knew nothing of recording techniques and simply set up our gear to play as if we were performing at a gig. On the playback, when Gus had completed the mix, I was a little startled to hear my guitar solos seemingly flying round the room.'

During the recording session Clem played his Gold Top through a Laney 100-watt amp. He also played harmonica and keyboards. With the exception of one track, all were written by Clem and Terry Poole. Bakerloo split up around May/June 1969, a number of months before their first album was released in December 1969. During the summer of 1969, Clem formed a band with Dave Pegg and Cozy Powell and they performed a gig at Nottingham University.

Clem received an offer from Jon Hiseman to join Colosseum, as James Litherland, singer and guitarist with the band, was leaving. Although Clem was sad to accept, the band he'd been planning with Cozy and Peggy might not happen, he couldn't resist Jon's offer. Colosseum had 'blown him away' when on seeing them play at the much-celebrated Mothers Club in Erdington, Birmingham.

Clem borrowed a copy of the first Colosseum album 'Those Who Are About To Die Salute You', and learned every track. A few days later, he met up with the band in a church hall at Elephant and Castle, London. They played the title track from the album and Jon told Clem straight away he'd got the job. Clem performed his first Colosseum gig a few days later. He stayed with Jon and his wife, Barbara in their house in Shepperton until Dave Greenslade, Tony Reeves and himself found a flat together, at 8 Aylestone Avenue, Queens Park. It became their 'Big Pink'. Clem was still using Laney amplification and subsequently got an endorsement deal with them.

'Jon was always driving the other members to be creative, not only in our compositions but also with the instrumentation, and I enjoyed doubling on keyboards on occasion – notably on an instrumental Dave and I had written called "Bring Out Your Dead", which onstage featured the two of us switching between Hammond organ, electric piano, vibraphone and mellotron.'

Colosseum's third album 'Grass Is Greener' was released, only in the United States and Canada, in January 1970. It features four tracks recorded with Clem in the winter of 1969 and three tracks from the 1969 Vertigo LP 'Valentyne Suite' but with vocal and guitar parts provided by Clem instead of James Litherland.

The 1970 Bath Festival of Blues and Progressive Music was a highlight of Clem's time with Colosseum; it was one of the legendary UK festivals of the period. He was always reluctant about being the vocalist, and before the band recorded the 'Daughter Of Time' album, through the summer of 1970, he convinced Jon Hiseman a singer was needed with the power to match the band's formidable instrumentation. Juicy Lucy's Paul Williams was a candidate, but Chris Farlowe joined instead. He was certainly able to provide the technique as well as the sheer vocal power that was required.

'I celebrated my 21st birthday at the Fehmarn festival of September 1970 which is now legendary because it was Jimi Hendrix's last performance. Also appearing were Canned Heat, Sly and the Family Stone and Alexis Korner. We all travelled together by train from Hamburg to the island of Fehmarn, and I remember Jimi was very quiet and soberly dressed in a pale blue suit. A few days later he was dead.'

In December 1970, Colosseum's 'Daughter Of Time' album was released. It was recorded at Lansdowne Studios London with the exception of 'Time Machine' taken from a Royal Albert Hall live performance of July 2, 1970. Out of eight tracks, Clem co-wrote four. He was trying out different guitars regularly, including Fenders, a Gibson ES 335, and an Ampeg Dan Armstrong Lucite, but always returned to the Gold Top.

'The high point for me in Colosseum was around the release of the live album in September 1971 (recorded at Manchester University March 18, 1971, and the Big Apple, Brighton March 27, 1971). Our performances made us one of the biggest acts in Europe, especially at festivals, where Rory Gallagher was the only act that could live with us. He was dynamite onstage! We had a great tour of Germany as joint-headliners with Free, who were enjoying the success of "All Right Now". The low point was the period before we split in October 1971, when the creative juices just seemed to have run out. We were getting tired of some of the old material in our show but couldn't seem to come up with anything new.'

Later in 1971, Clem accepted Steve Marriott's invitation to replace Peter Frampton in Humble Pie. Generally, Clem was the lead guitarist and Steve rhythm, but occasionally Steve would play a little lead, and sometimes they would play harmony parts together. Humble Pie recorded 'Smokin'' at Olympic Studios in February 1972 and it was released a month later. The album includes guest appearances by Stephen Stills, Madeline Bell and Alexis Korner. Clem played guitar, keyboards, and was heard on backing vocals. He was co-writer on 'Hot 'n' Nasty', 'The Fixer', 'Sweet Peace And Time', and 'Roadrunner'. Although mainly using his Gold Top, he bought, during the recording sessions, a Gibson Flying V and a white Gibson SG Custom, which he played on the hit single 'Hot 'n' Nasty'.

Humble Pie toured extensively in the 1970s, across the USA, Europe and Japan. In the USA they played some of the largest venues including Philadelphia Spectrum, Detroit Cobo Hall and Madison Square Garden.

'I went through masses of gear during my time with Humble Pie. On trips to the USA, Steve and I would visit the pawn shops at every opportunity. In those days, you would always find a selection of Fenders, Gibsons, Epiphones and usually some of the more unusual models. That's how Steve came to use a Dwight guitar. And the prices were so cheap. We would give some of the guitars away to the crew at the end of a tour. My most memorable find was a 1953 honey Telecaster, exactly like the one used by one of my heroes, Roy Buchanan. I picked it up in a San Francisco pawn shop for $200. We bought loads of late 1950s and early 1960s Strats, Les Pauls and Martin acoustics for next to nothing.'

Most of the time, Steve and Clem both used Marshall 100-watt amps. Bass player Greg Ridley always favoured Acoustic bass amps. When the company introduced guitar amps, Clem used one for a while, then went back to the trusty Marshalls.

In April 1973, Humble Pie released 'Eat It' – a double album with the fourth side recorded live. Clem played guitar and added backing vocals. He had a writer's credit for 'Up Our Sleeve' and played a variety of guitars, amongst them being a Gibson ES 5 Switchmaster, the 1953 honey-coloured Telecaster, the Gold Top and a cherry Les Paul, which Steve had given to him. Later, Clem discovered it belonged to Keith Richards.

During February 1974, the 'Thunderbox' album appeared with Clem having three song-writing credits. 'I played the same guitars I used on "Eat It". I'm not sure which I used for the slide part on "Black Coffee". Most likely it was the Les Paul I'd acquired just prior to the tour of Japan. A 1960 model, it was the prettiest Les Paul I'd ever seen, with a very faded sunburst body and two cream humbuckers – very rare.'

The mixing of 'Street Rats', released in February 1975, was done by someone outside the band and on hearing it they were horrified. 'It was a very depressing and frustrating time. But, there's one interesting little anecdote; the title track, which as Steve has said, was recorded in his own studio with Ian Wallace and Tim Hinckley. It was originally the backing track for a version of "Paperback Writer". Steve thought the track was great and decided to write new lyrics. The opening guitar riff is a total giveaway.'

In the same year, Clem left Humble Pie to form Strange Brew with Cozy Powell. Rehearsals took place in Clem's studio at his home in Essex but an accident curtailed the band's plans. During a five-a-side football match on a concrete indoor pitch, Clem fell and damaged his left hand.

'An X-ray showed I'd broken a bone just below my left thumb. While putting my forearm in plaster, a nurse informed me that there was a possibility that the bone wouldn't heal, being so fine. I was dumbstruck. She asked me which hand I wrote with, and when I answered, my right hand, she beamed and said, "Oh, that's lucky, isn't it?".'

Clem recovered fully from the injury, though in the meantime, Ritchie Blackmore had persuaded Cozy to join Rainbow. Damon Butcher and Clem accompanied Steve Marriott on a solo tour in 1976.

'I decided to play my 1953 Telecaster on the tour. I took a 1954 Les Paul Black Beauty as a spare, but swapped it for a lovely 1963 red Stratocaster whilst in San Francisco.'

After the tour, Clem and Damon Butcher formed Rough Diamond releasing an album in February 1977 and then another band, Champion, but the latter soon folded. 'This all happened as the Punk movement seemingly took control and I felt it was all over for my generation in terms of making a living in the music industry.' However, Clem's assumption was to prove wrong.

Champion's lead singer, Gary Bell was a talented writer and became involved producing advertising jingles for Jeff Wayne, noted for his musical adaption of H.G. Wells's science fiction novel *The War of the Worlds*.

'Gary and I were great friends, and I was very happy to play guitar on his sessions. This quickly led to my being hired by other producers and writers, and before long I was one of the busiest guitar players on the London session scene. Often, I was racing between as many as four different studios in a day to play on film scores, TV jingles and album tracks. I very much enjoyed this work after spending so much time on the road and usually being ripped off and ending up with nothing to show for it. Even in Humble Pie, after many US tours headlining huge arenas, we ended up struggling to pay our bills in the last year or so of the band's existence. That was probably the biggest factor in our demise.'

Over the next few years, Clem found time to tour with ex-Family front man, Roger Chapman's Shortlist. 'I used a cherry ES 335 which I'd just acquired by swapping a '57 sunburst Strat with Bernie Marsden, and a fantastic Mesa Boogie amp. It was one of the first to be built and belonged to Bobby Tench but had originally been with George Harrison.'

During 1979, Clem played guitar on two tracks of Cozy Powell's album 'Over The Top' and appeared with the drummer's band on the 'Old Grey Whistle Test' on January 8, 1980. 'I played my Gold Top on album tracks, "The Loner" and a cherry Gibson ES 335 on "Killer".' Later in the year, Jon Anderson called on Clem to play on two tracks of his album 'Song Of Seven'. Before the year was out, Clem was recording with Jack Bruce on the album 'I've Always Wanted To Do This'.

'Recording and touring with Jack's band of breathtakingly-talented people was one of the proudest moments of my career, and the beginning of a long and precious friendship with Jack.'

Jon Anderson called on Clem once more in 1982 to play guitars on his album 'Animation'. 'I needed an acoustic with a pick-up, which I didn't have. So, Jon dispatched his assistant to London's West End and he came back with two Adamas acoustics, a six-string and a twelve, which I subsequently used on countless sessions and still have them. They were great for

Clem Clempson, left, with Colosseum.
Philippe Gras / Alamy Stock Photo.

recording, except when the batteries suddenly died during a session. Replacing them was a nightmare and keeping an 80-piece orchestra waiting while I fumbled around inside the body was not good.'

Throughout the 1980s, Clem worked as a session guitarist with Roger Daltrey, Paul McCartney and Roger Waters. He was also involved in the film soundtrack 'Hearts Of Fire' in 1987 with Bob Dylan, Ronnie Wood, Ian Dury and Reg Presley.

Although Clem's career has many magical moments, a new pinnacle was reached in 1993 when he joined Jack Bruce for two concerts held in Cologne to celebrate the bass player's 50th birthday.

'We spent a very happy few days in Cologne rehearsing. Jack had brought together a great line-up of musicians including Simon Philips, Garry Husband and Ginger Baker on drums; Dick Heckstall-Smith, Henry Lowther, were among the brass section; Bernie Worrell on Hammond organ, and Gary Moore and myself on guitars. Gary was only there for the second night, so on the first night I had to play the whole show, including a "Cream" spot with Jack and Ginger – one of my teenage dreams came true that evening.'

On June 24, 1994, Colosseum reunited at the Freiburg Zelt Musik Festival with exactly the same line-up as when they split in 1971. On October 28, 1994, they played a concert in Cologne at E-Werk which was recorded for a TV special and later released in 1995 as a CD and video (and a DVD in 2004). A second tour followed in 1997 to promote their new studio album 'Bread And Circuses'. In 1999, he was featured in the film soundtrack for 'Notting Hill'.

'My main guitar continued to be the '58 Gold Top, which I'm playing on the video of the E-Werk concert. For amplification, I was using a Groove Tubes set-up – a Trio preamp through a Dual 75 stereo power amp into a stereo 4x12 in. speaker cab. Colosseum continued recording and touring until 2015, when sadly Barbara Thompson was forced to retire due to Parkinson's disease.'

Clem was thrilled in 2005 to be guitarist and musical director for B.B. King's 80th birthday album 'B.B. King and Friends 80' recorded at London's Olympic Studios.

'We spent the first day rehearsing the band, just talking through the songs B.B. wanted to do. It was obvious that he needed some help with the arrangements, so as I'd had quite a bit of experience in that by this time, I ended up in that role. When, first Roger Daltrey, then Van Morrison came in to do their respective tracks, I took them through the arrangements we'd decided on – the tempos, who would sing which verses, when the solos would happen etc. No big deal really, but those things needed to be decided otherwise there's inevitably a lot of hesitation during the sessions. Anyway, it all went very well,

The Gibson Les Paul Gold Top was launched in 1952 and cost $210. Les Paul claimed the gold colour of the original Les Paul was his idea. 'Gold means rich', he said, 'expensive, the best, superb.' Tony Bacon and Paul Day in The Gibson Les Paul Book: A Complete History of Les Paul Guitars *(1993) mention Gibson had made a one-off all-gold hollow-body guitar in 1951 for Paul to present to a terminally-ill hospital patient. 'The presentation guitar may have prompted the all-gold archtop electric ES 295 model of 1952, and it could also have been the inspiration for the colour of the first Les Paul model.' Before the end of the decade the Gold Top would undergo several changes: the original 'trapeze' bridge/tailpiece was replaced by a one-piece, bar-shaped combined bridge/tailpiece in 1953; a Tune-o-matic bridge was fitted in 1955; humbucking pick-ups replaced P90s in 1957.*

I particularly enjoyed seeing Roger again, and Van was very amicable and easy to work with. At the end of the sessions, BB signed my copy of 'Live At The Regal' – one of my all-time favourite albums – with a very nice message.'

From 2003, Clem had played a few gigs as a guest with the Hamburg Blues Band and subsequently became a permanent member until around 2012. One of the highlights was returning to the Fehmarn festival which Colosseum had played on his 21st birthday. This time it was his 60th birthday. On the HBB album 'Mad Dog Blues' released in 2008, Clem played Les Paul guitars and Marshall amplifiers.

Having formed his own band by 2013, Clem played Les Pauls and an Orville 335 on his solo album 'In The Public Interest'. His amps included a 1970s Fender Bandmaster, customised by Brinsley Schwarz and a wonderful Gomez 'El Sonido'. For the Colosseum album 'Time On Our Side' (2014), and tour, Clem employed a Marshall JCM 100 for lead and a Groove Tubes Trio/Dual 75 for rhythm. The same amplification was used for the Colosseum farewell concert held at Shepherd's Bush Empire on February 28, 2015.

During 2017, Jon Hiseman decided to make an album featuring the songs and instrumentals associated with people who he had played with but were no longer alive. Clem and Mark Clarke became involved and the band became known simply as JCM. An album, 'Heroes' was released and a tour organised.

'I used my Gold Top for almost every guitar part on the album, a couple of things on the Orville 335, which is a fantastic and inexpensive guitar, and a couple of rhythm parts on a Stratocaster. For the lead sounds, I used one of my Marshall JCM 100 heads and a 70s Park 50-watt head that I'd bought a few years back, though hardly ever used. I used a Dude overdrive pedal most of the time, and of course the same Cry Baby Wah-Wah I've been using since the 60s. For rhythm sounds, I had a couple of combos that I picked up during my session musician days – a Mohave Coyote, a Top Hat and a 60s Fender Vibrolux. On the tour, which began in April 2018, my set-up was the El Sonido and a Fender DeVille ML in stereo, with the Bandmaster in between, going through the Groove Tubes 4x12 in. speaker cab.'

Clem Clempson with Gibson Gold Top and Gretsch guitars. Peter Tuffrey photographs.

Dave Davies on stage with Guild Guitar.
Photo 12 / Alamy Stock Photo.

DAVE DAVIES

Dave Davies tasted massive success at an early age, gathered many admirers through the ground-breaking 'You Really Got Me' riff, squabbled with his brother Ray, went painfully through the rock 'n' roll lifestyle, played lead guitar all over world, and suffered a massive stroke in 2006. Yet, he is still performing.

Dave was born on February 3, 1947, the last of eight children and one of two boys (Ray Davies was the seventh) of Annie Florence and Frederick George Davies. During the Second World War, George had worked as a slaughterman. He also played banjo at family gatherings.

Dave was exposed to music at an early age, admitting that the most important piece of furniture in the family's front room was a piano, which all six of his sisters could play. Dave's sisters also boasted a wind-up gramophone though he states the greatest form of family entertainment occurred on Saturday nights when family members gathered together and partied. Continuing until the early hours of the morning, the songs performed included old musical hall favourites: 'Bye, Bye Blackbird', 'If You Were The Only Girl In The World', 'My Old Man Said Follow The Van'.

Dave failed his Eleven-Plus and attended the William Grimshaw Secondary Modern School in Muswell School, initially excelling at French, English and boxing. He won a silver medallion after representing his school in the Middlesex School Boxing Championships. In his own words, he gave up the sport in favour of music, football and girls.

Dave received his first guitar in 1959. Full details of the hire purchase agreement, taken out by his father, from Selmer's store on Charing Cross Road, London, are reproduced in Dave's *Kink: An Autobiography* (1996). The guitar was a Harmony Meteor and the total amount of HP was £29 14s 6d. The Monthly Hire of £1. 9s 5d was due on 23rd of each month commencing 23rd December 1959.

In his early career, Dave admits that music was a great awakening for him and he would listen intently to records, enjoying picking out riffs. He would skip school and spend hours playing blues records as well as the music of Django Reinhardt, Buddy Holly, Eddie Cochran, Little Richard and Lonnie Donegan.

During late 1960, Dave began performing instrumental duets with brother Ray – who took the lead parts and Dave rhythm – for family and friends, and at their dad's local pub the Clissold Arms. They were billed as the Kelly Brothers and amongst their influences were Chet Atkins and the Ventures.

By Autumn 1961, Peter Quaife had teamed up with the two Davies brothers and the line-up, becoming the Ray Davies Quartet, was augmented with drummer John Start possessing, as Dave describes, 'a "whole" drum kit.' The first gig was perhaps at a William Grimshaw School autumn dance, playing a mixture of instrumentals and rock 'n' roll numbers.

Before the end of 1961, the band, with Pete Quaife switching to bass, would play a number of dances at the Athenaeum ballroom Muswell Hill, with all three guitarists playing through Ray's little Watkins Dominator amp. Into 1962, the Ray Davies Quartet was playing in and around the Muswell Hill area at pubs, social clubs and youth clubs. On one occasion the band played with Rod Stewart on vocals. At this period, Dave possessed a small 10-watt Elpico combination amp, bought from a local radio shop, and an old 60-watt linear amp acquired through *Exchange & Mart*.

Dave was disillusioned with school, his only interest being art lessons until being expelled at 15 years old in June 1962. A little later, Dave found employment at Selmer's music shop but, disappointing for him, it was not in the guitar department, but in a warehouse repairing brass and woodwind instruments. During spring 1963, he was sacked for falling asleep after gigging late the previous night.

Early in 1963, Dave saw Duane Eddy at the Finsbury Park Empire in North London. '[Duane] eventually appeared on stage and it was one of the most thrilling experiences of my life … The sound was amazing: he used a very small Gibson Amp. He

---

Founded in the USA during 1892 by Wilhelm Schultz, a German immigrant from Hamburg, the Harmony company made many types of string instruments including, ukuleles, acoustic and electric guitars and violins. An estimated ten million guitars were produced between 1945 and 1975. The company ceased trading in the latter year. On www.chasingguitars.com it is mentioned that Harmony was capable of turning out guitars with good workmanship though they were never positioned to compete with D'Angelico, Gibson, Gretsch or Fender. The site adds: 'Harmony-built guitars were many times a player's first instrument … Harmony peaked in 1964-1965 selling 350,000 instruments.'

An early picture of Dave performing shows him with an Eko 400 by the Italian manufacturer Eko. This was the company's first electric guitar and was often called the 'Ekomaster' produced in a number of variations from 1960 to 1962. The guitar had four pick-ups, tone-changing push buttons, and two palm rollers, altering volume and tone. The Eko played by Dave had the 3+3 headstock configuration with block inlays, details that were subsequently changed.

Elpico amplifiers were available between the early 1950s and c.1970. They were initially built by Lee Products (International) Ltd, the company changing its name several times: Lee Products, Lee Products (GB) Ltd, and Elizabethan Electronics.

looked so cool, so nonchalant,' recalled Dave.

Ray and Dave's four-piece played local halls and school dances. They appeared under a number of names during the early 1960s including the Ramrods, the Ravens, and the Bo Weevils. Once signed by an agent, Danny Haggerty, they were found work on US air bases in England and at private events. Parting company with Danny Haggerty, they joined a management team of Robert Wace and Grenville Collins. For a time, Robert Wace fronted the band which appeared as Robert Wace and the Bo Weevils (from September 1963) and they played according to Dave 'at society dos, parties thrown by wealthy aristocrats and posh friends of Robert's.'

Ray Davies eventually took over the lead vocals, and in late 1963, Robert and Grenville invited Brian Epstein to one of the band's rehearsals but it came to nothing. In spite of this, the band made demos at Regent Sound Studios in Denmark Street and by the start of 1964, there was a change of name to the Kinks. Producer Shel Talmy persuaded Pye to sign them. Drummer John Start had left the band in the Summer of 1963 and the trio used fill-in drummers for a time. When the band auditioned for a new drummer, Viv Prince was in contention, but did not turn up and later became a Pretty Things member. Mick Avory who had played with Mick Jagger and Keith Richards in a developing line-up of the Rolling Stones was given the job on January 27, 1964. However, Bobby Graham played drums on recording sessions for a period.

The Kinks first recorded at Pye's studios in ATV House near Marble Arch, London, on January 20, 1964, with Dave playing lead on his Harmony Meteor guitar and adding backing vocals. 'Long Tall Sally' from the session, produced by Shel Talmy, would be released as a single on February 7, 1964. The first gig with the band listed as the Kinks was at the Town Hall Oxford on Saturday, February 1, 1964. Six days later the band made their first appearance on 'Ready Steady Go!'. Dave is seen with the Harmony guitar.

There is footage on YouTube of an early performance of 'Long Tall Sally' and although Dave almost has his back to the camera, he is clearly playing the Harmony Meteor. *Beat Monthly No. 12* April 1964 has the following to say about the band: 'The Kinks, art-students now on the Pye label, surely wear the most way-out gear of any group – short of Lord Sutch and the Savages. And they design it themselves, even those thigh-length leather boots. They're co managed, by the way, by Larry Page … Kinks debut disc, "Long Tall Sally", still selling well.' 'Long Tall Sally' peaked in the UK charts at no. 42.

The Kinks first played the Cavern Club, Liverpool on Friday, February 21, 1964, and during the following month they would appear alongside Gene Vincent; they began the Dave Clark Five show on March 29, receiving a number of indifferent reviews. The tour lasted until May 14. Songs performed included 'Bo Diddley', 'You Really Got Me' (in an embryonic form), 'Long Tall Sally', 'Smokestack Lightning' and 'Too Much Monkey Business'. The Kinks reputedly donned the 'famous' red riding jackets during the tour – at Bournemouth Winter Gardens on April 25, 1964.

The Kinks' second single 'You Still Want Me', recorded around January 20 at the Pye Studios session, was produced by Shel Talmy and released on April 17, 1964. Dave played lead guitar and contributed vocals on the track, but it did not reach the UK charts. From May 15, 1964, the Kinks embarked on a busy tour schedule taking them to Lancashire and Yorkshire. Advertising for the performance at the Public Hall Wallington, Surrey, states: 'If you like the Rolling Stones, you will love the Kinks.' At Bath Forum Cinema on Sunday, June 7, 1964, the Kinks opened for Gene Vincent.

According to Dave, the unmistakeable 'You Really Got Me' riff was initially worked out one afternoon, on piano by Ray Davies as F G G F G in the brothers' parents' front room in Muswell Hill, during early March 1964. Recalled Dave: 'I wondered what it would sound like as bar chords on my guitar with my new amp sound. So, I tried it. It was as if something magical had descended upon us … Ray shifted the riff a tone. G A A G A. Then, he repeated the same riff in D. I blared out the chords on my Harmony guitar. It was wonderful, instinctual. Ray went away and a day or so later came back with some lyrics [for "You Really Got Me"].' Reflecting on his and brother Ray's guitar styles, Dave said: 'My style of playing was rough and ready, self-taught, more natural, Ray had a better hook on remembering notation and reading music.'

Recording of 'You Really Got Me' started on June 14, 1964, at Pye Studios with Shel Talmy as producer and went through some development before actually reaching the version recorded. Ray was dissatisfied with the first attempts. A final recording of the song at the Independent Broadcasting Company's Studios was financed by the Kinks themselves on July 12, 1964. The UK charts at this time reflected an R&B boom with the Animals at the top with 'House Of The Rising Sun' and the Rolling Stones at no. 2 with 'All Over Now'.

In *The Kinks: All Day and All of the Night: Day-by-Day Concerts, Recordings and Broadcasts, 1961–1996*, (2004), Doug Hinman gives information about the 'You Really Got Me' riff: 'Dave plays his Harmony Meteor through his Elpico amp with a punctured speaker to get the distinct guitar sound, which is in turn fed through a Vox AC30 amplifier.' In a December 1965 copy of *Melody Maker*, Ray Davies said: 'To clear up anything that's ever been said … Dave Davies plays every solo on every record we've ever made and does it better than anyone else.'

By slashing the Elpico speaker cone with a razor blade, Dave says in *Kink* he discovered a 'new' sound.

'You Really Got Me' was released in the UK on August 4, 1964, and subsequently reached no. 1 in the UK. When released in the USA a little later it peaked at no. 7. A review by David Gell in *Beat Monthly No. 17* September 1964 mentions the following: 'The one to give the group a major breakthrough. All that staccato beat-purveying, with wildie, way-out vocal work. Number is slap in the modern idiom and could fair zip through, given enough plays by deejays. It's one of those numbers that builds and builds, with a fine guitar lead in the middle. Very clever … but atmospheric, too.'

Beat Instrumental Monthly No. 18 of October 1964 has the Kinks as 'Group of the Month'. A full-page picture shows the band with the following included in the caption: '… Dave is leaning on Pete's Fender bass, whilst his own Epiphone looks as if it's going to slip from Pete's grasp at any moment.' The editorial notes: 'DAVE DAVIES plays Epiphone lead guitar and sings.' In footage of the band playing 'You Really Got Me',

Dave is playing an Epiphone Casino which he recalls was his 'second ever guitar used on early package tours with the Hollies and the Dave Clark Five and on the "Kinda Kinks" [album].'

In an interview with Jonathan Clarke on New York's classic rock station Q104.3, during 2014, Dave said this about the 'You Really Got Me' sound and riff: 'When talking to Jimi Hendrix [in the late 1960s] he did mention the sound [on the record] was a landmark. That was a real compliment.'

After the outstanding success of 'You Really Got Me', the remainder of 1964 saw a further single released 'All Day And All Of The Night', an EP and an LP. Guitars used by Dave on film performances during 1964/1965 include a sunburst Epiphone Casino, a Vox Phantom, and a 'Special' Guild DE-500. An Epiphone Casino in 1965 was priced at £170 2s 0d, with Bigsby £182 14s 0d, and with Tremetone £192 3s 0d.

'Arguably,' states Hinman (*op. cit.*), '1965 was the defining year for the Kinks' with a number of hit singles released, TV appearances, tours in the UK and the rest of the world.'

Dave was 'Player of the Month' in *Beat Instrumental Monthly* No. 23 of March 1965 and he admits the following: 'I reckon I've got pretty wide tastes in music. For instance, I'll spend hours listening to Big Bill Broonzy – his voice is fantastic and he's also one of my favourite instrumentalists … I used to practice like mad. I'd listen to any type of guitarist back in those early days.' The article argues Dave's guitar style is a most important part of the Kink sound adding: 'Technically, it's fluent and punchy.'

Dave comments: 'But I've not tried to copy anybody else. I don't like to think too closely about it – it's much better to just let it sort of happen. I believe more in "feeling" a number than getting something that is too precise, too exact.'

In *Beat Instrumental Monthly No. 26* of June 1965, Dave describes once again how he obtained the 'You Really Got Me' distorted amplifier sound in the studio but that it turned out to be impractical to use on stage: 'So I decided to simplify matters a bit, and disconnect one of the speakers on my usual amp. It buzzes a bit on normal volume, but when it's turned up to meet my requirement, it gives out a fabulous "Fuzz" sound. Pete's bass does the same. When we play together at full volume, the noise is unbelievable.'

According to Dave, in *Kink*, before the American tour, which began June 18, 1965, someone had loaned him a Guild guitar – the DE-500. Dave then relates how the guitar was nowhere to be seen when the Kinks arrived in LA. He did not have another to play, on a scheduled performance on the TV show 'Shindig', but a hurried trip to a guitar store unearthed a Gibson Flying V which he liked and bought for two hundred dollars. 'I used the Flying V for the first time on "Shindig",' said Dave who would often be seen playing the V between its 'wings'.

Dave owned the 1958 Korina solid-body Flying V guitar serial No. 8-4643 until 1992 when it was sold. Accompanying the sale was a letter of authenticity from Dave confirming the 'Shindig' appearance and detailing the guitar was used on 'Till The End Of The Day', recorded in November, 1965. For a period, it was part of the Dr George Borst Electric Guitar collection and put up again for sale at Heritage Auctions, 2019 in Dallas, Texas. Sales details about the V mention it had been refinished, with a heel crack and a broken Gibson logo having also been repaired.

For the 'Shindig' appearance, backing tracks were pre-recorded for 'All Day' and 'Long Tall Shorty' and these were performed by the house band, the Shindogs, with Dave the only Kink present, playing rhythm guitar. The Shindogs included, on lead guitar, James Burton, one of Dave's all-time heroes and who he said later inspired his solo on 'Till The End Of The Day'. On the pre-recording backing track, Burton had borrowed Ray's Fender Telecaster.

Of the many Kinks hit singles, Dave states one of his favourites is 'See My Friends' released at the end of July 1965. It has a unique guitar hook almost sounding like a sitar. Dave explains in *Kink* there was experimentation with different tunings to get the right kind of droning noises, an influence of Davey Graham's album 'Folk, Blues And Beyond'. Dave adds they were initially disappointed with the sound until 'the engineer came up with the idea of pushing the output of the multi-track (4-track) into the input of their two main compressors. He pushed the volume as high as it would go before audible distortion. We went back into the studio and tried it again. It was amazing.'

In performances of the song, Dave is seen with several guitars: an Epiphone Casino; a double-cut Gretsch (on a pilot episode of 'Discothec' introduced by Simon Dee, 1965); and a Guild Starfire III.

Beat Instrumental No. 31 of November 1965 mentions Dave was looking for a brand of strings that he bought while the group were on the last USA trip. 'They're called Ernie Ball

---

Introduced in late 1965, the Fender Electric XII featured a body style similar to a Fender Jaguar/Jazzmaster; a maple neck; a long, curved headstock, earning it the nickname the 'hockey-stick' headstock; it was purpose-built to attract a part of the folk-rock market. The 12-saddle bridge allowed precise adjustments of individual string heights and intonation. Colours available included Sunburst (standard), Candy Apple Red, Olympic White, Lake Placid Blue and Firemist Gold. Not particularly popular, the Electric XII was dropped from the Fender line in 1969 though reintroduced during 2019.

In Dave Hunter's Acoustic Guitars The Illustrated Encyclopedia *(2003) a background to the Malibu's development is given: 'As Fender's success grew [in the 1950s and early 1960s], its sales team was drooling for a bite at the acoustic guitar sector … In the early 1960s, Leo [Fender] hired former Gibson and Rickenbacker designer Roger Rossmeisl to oversee design and manufacture of flat top [acoustics].' The result was a range that included the Malibu; a distinctive feature was the inclusion of a Stratocaster-shaped headstock. However, as pointed out by Dave Hunter, 'by the end of 1971 each of these models had been discontinued.'*

Dave Davies with Flying V guitar.
Tracksimages.com / Alamy Stock Photo.

The Gibson Korina Flying V and the companion Gibson Korina Explorer were released in 1958 with *Gibson Gazette* announcing: 'Gibson looks to the future and finds truly inspirational ideas.' Gibson president Ted McCarty wanted a guitar to compete against Leo Fender's popular solid-body Stratocaster. Shipments to dealers began in April 1958 and Larry Meiners in *Flying "V": The Illustrated History of This Modernistic Guitar (2001)* writes: 'The total number of Flying V guitars shipped in 1958 is estimated at 81, with another 17 in 1959. The modernistic pair was a failure. By 1960, these guitars were eliminated from the Gibson catalogue.'

Rock 'n' Roll Strings,' said Dave. 'I bought quite a stock while I was there but I haven't got many left ...' The magazine added: 'Dave is now playing a Gibson Flying Arrow guitar – after having two models stolen. He mislaid an Epiphone, then bought a Guild and lost that.'

In *Beat Instrumental*'s 1965 'Gold Star Awards', the results published in the magazine's No. 36 issue January 1966, Dave came 7th in the Lead guitar section; Hank Marvin was first. The new year, 1966, saw an increase in pressure on Ray Davies, eventually causing him to have a physical and nervous breakdown. Pete Quaife was involved in a car accident and would later leave the band, being replaced by John Dalton. Dave was also ill for a period with nervous exhaustion. In addition, there were management, record company and publishing disputes. However, the chaotic touring at home and abroad continued even though quite a number of performances were cancelled. In March/April Ray was absent forcing Dave to take over lead vocals for some concerts with a stand-in guitarist, Mick Grace of the Cockneys, added to the Kinks' line-up.

The first hit single of 1966 'Dedicated Follower Of Fashion' released in February with Dave contributing to writing the B side 'Sitting On My Sofa'. The record peaked at no. 2 in the UK and 36 in the US.

Beat Instrumental No. 35 March of 1966 ran a feature 'On Stage with The Kinks' and commented on Dave's playing: 'Dave Davies is officially the lead guitarist, but uses a very bassy tone on his Guild thus reversing the accepted practice of lead being trebly and the rhythm being invariably bassy. He squeezes a lot of life out of his guitar and moves it about a great deal, now and then giving the impression that he is fighting to keep it within his grasp.'

The 'Sunny Afternoon' single appeared in June and reached no. 1 in some UK charts. A music video, showcasing the song, has Dave with the Gibson Korina Flying V while on a 'Top of the Pops' performance he's with a Fender Electric XII. Dave recalls the Fender Electric XII was used on 'I'm Not Like Everybody Else' – the B side of 'Sunny Afternoon'.

An appearance on 'A Whole Scene Going', on June 8, reveals Dave has the Guild Starfire III. He gave some details about his guitar playing on this single to *Beat Instrumental No. 39* of July 1966 under the heading 'A Vibrant Kink': 'On Sunny Afternoon I used the Guild and the Vox AC30, about the only thing I did, which meant a change for me, was to alter the stringing on my guitar. As a rule, I have it understrung, starting at the 6th with an A and working up. I found that I couldn't get a full enough sound so I swapped over to normal stringing.' In the same article Dave elaborated on his stage set-up which included two Vox AC30s: 'I've got a lead which splits up into four jacks, two go into two inputs on one, and two go into inputs on the other. I stick one amp on full treble the other on full bass – it gives a good thick sound.' When asked why he chose to put two jacks in each amp he said: 'Well I figure that if I stick everything I can into everything I see, I just can't go wrong.'

Towards the end of June 1966, the Kinks were refused visas for working in the US. The band released their 'Face To Face' album at the end of October with Dave taking lead vocals on several tracks. Their final single of the year 'Dead End Street'/'Big Black Smoke' appeared from November 18. An early example of a music video was created for the single's B side. The 'Face To Face' album released at the end of October witnessed the Kinks step away from the hard-driving style of early rock music that had brought them international acclaim from the early 1960s.

During 1967, a number of events occurred: Dave emerged as a successful solo artist; the band strived for a better balance between touring and time spent in the studio; Ray took over from Shel Talmy as producer; some of their business commitments were resolved. Ray and Dave also found time to play football in the *Melody Maker* Ravers Sunday football matches and in a Showbiz XI football team. The band was still refused visas for the USA in 1967 and this thwarted an approach to appear at the now world-renowned Monterey International Pop Festival, Monterey, CA.

A still from 'The Daily Express Record Star Show' on April 16, 1967, shows Dave on stage playing the Flying V. Just under three months later, his first single 'Death Of A Clown' (written with Ray), was released. It reached no. 3 in the UK and was a success in Europe. The B side 'Love Me Till The Sun Shines' was written by Dave. Promoting the single, he made a number of solo performances dressed in outlandish hired costumes. One guitar he was seen with was a Fender Malibu natural acoustic.

The success of 'Death Of A Clown' brought the obvious questions: was Dave leaving the Kinks to pursue a solo career? Did he intend to release any more singles or even an LP? Whilst there was no question of him leaving the band, another single 'Susannah's Still Alive' with 'Funny Face' on the B side appeared towards the end of November 1967. One promotional performance shows him playing the Fender Sunburst Electric XII which he had been seen with before. On the Kinks' final single of 1967, 'Autumn Almanac', released on October 13, Dave performs on 'Top of the Pops' with a Vox XII string acoustic – a V240 Folk Twelve Electro.

Two Kinks singles were released in 1968 – 'Wonderboy' and 'Days', before Dave's third single 'Lincoln County' in

www.voxshowroom.com states the Vox V239 Folk Twelve Acoustic was built by the Italian manufacturer, Eko; it was really a 'rebadged Eko 12 guitar.' The website adds: 'Both Eko and Vox offered a version of this guitar with a pick-up. The Eko version was named the "Ranger 12 Electra", the Vox version was the V240 "Folk Twelve Electro".'

Fender Telecasters with rosewood fingerboards were introduced by the company in 1958/1959 along with custom-coloured paints and a shift from five to eight screws on the pick-guard.

The Les Paul Gold Top with combined bridge/tailpiece, often known as the 'wrap around' tailpiece, was introduced by Gibson in 1954 and followed on from Les Paul Gold Top with the 'trapeze' tailpiece of 1952.

Dave Davies on stage with Fender Malibu acoustic.
Photo 12 / Alamy Stock Photo.

August. In a clip of 'Wonderboy' on a German television show, Dave has a sunburst Fender Telecaster with a rosewood fingerboard; a performance of 'Days' sees Dave return to the Flying V. Unfortunately, for Dave 'Lincoln County', which was written by him, failed to chart even though it received favourable reviews and good advertising.

The year 1968 saw the band still banned from playing in America, but their album 'The Kinks Are The Village Green Preservation Society' was adventurous for the time, embracing the gentler aspects of traditional English life with some great Ray Davies' songs. A fourth single by Dave 'Hold My Hand', written by him and produced by brother Ray, was released in January 1969.

Footage of the Kinks playing on 'Once More With Felix' – performing 'Last Of The Steam Powered Trains' on January 7, 1969 – illustrates Dave playing a sunburst Fender Telecaster with rosewood fingerboard. He also plays a Fender Telecaster on a music video of 'Plastic Man', released in March 1969.

The good news for the band in 1969 was that they were allowed back into the US. This was following the lifting of the American musicians' union ban and they embarked on a tour in October.

The Kinks' poor showing in the singles charts towards the end of the 1960s was halted at the start of the following decade with the release of 'Lola' in June 1970. The single revelled in success all around the world. Enlarged now to a five-piece, with John Gosling on keyboards, the Kinks appeared on 'Top of the Pops' to promote 'Lola' and Dave is present with a black Gibson Les Paul Custom. 'Lola' catapulted the band back to prominence in the public eye, particularly in the USA for much of the 1970s and they concentrated on promoting Ray's ambitious theatrical productions of albums such as 'Arthur'; 'Lola Versus Powerman And The Moneygoround: Part One'; 'Everybody's In Show-Biz-Everybody's A Star'; 'Preservation Act 1' and 'Preservation Act 2'; along with the 'Percy' soundtrack album; 'Muswell Hillbillies' and 'The Kinks Present Schoolboys In Disgrace'.

Later in the decade, the band would expand in personnel to include a brass section and, on occasions, female backing singers. They would take charge of their own destiny, controlling their business interests and eventually establishing their own Konk Studios. A live appearance on Germany's 'Beat Club' recorded in April 1972, reveals Dave playing a sunburst Fender Stratocaster with a maple neck. Dave relates that he used a 1954 Fender Stratocaster 'a lot during the "Everybody's In Showbiz" and "Preservation" live shows period around 1972–74.'

He informs a 1952 Fender Telecaster was played on 'some of the 'Preservation' recordings and on 'Hard Way' from 'Schoolboys In Disgrace' and on 'Stormy Sky' from the 'Sleepwalker' album. For 'Sleepwalker', and tours around that time – in the late 1970s – Dave played a Gibson Les Paul Gold Top which he said was 'a favourite of mine I bought in the States for about $400.' He adds the guitar was used on 'Father Christmas' and the 'Misfits' album (on 'A Rock'n'Roll Fantasy').

'The Kinks In Concert' at the BBC on March 28, 1977, shows Dave with a Gibson Les Paul Gold Top with P90s and a 'wrap around' tail piece.

A backline featuring Marshall and Hiwatt heads and Hiwatt 4x12 in. cabinets were amongst the amplifiers seen and used by the Kinks during the decade.

Towards the end of the 1970s, the Kinks had slimmed down to mainly a five-piece band. At the same time, they found credibility with the Punk/New Wave movement which had rejected a number of the Kinks' 1960s contemporaries.

During an appearance in the USA on 'The Mike Douglas Show', broadcast March

Introduced in 1977 the Gibson Les Paul Artisan was an ornate Les Paul Custom model with a hearts and flowers inlay pattern on the neck, and a pre-war style 'Gibson' script logo. Amongst the other features were: a stopbar tailpiece (later models had a TP-6 fine tuning tailpiece); three pick-ups (two Gibson Series VI humbucking pick-ups, and a middle position Gibson Super Humbucking pick-up); a pick-up selector switch wired to three settings; ebony fingerboard; and gold hardware. The finish colours included mainly Ebony, Walnut and Tobacco Sunburst. In 1978, the Artisan sold for $1,039; a case was supplied for an extra $99.50.

8, 1977, Dave is with a Gibson L5S in cherry sunburst. In an interview with Arlene R. Weiss for *Guitar International Magazine* in May 2002 Dave said: 'I wish I had kept the L5[S]. It was a custom-built [one] that I had. It was nice, it had more of a jazzy kind of feel to it and a contour body.'

In the 1980s, Dave and Ray Davies pursued solo projects whilst, at the same time, the Kinks continued to tour at home and around the world with gigs in Japan and Australia. In the US, they broke into the arena-sized venues circuit and played at the vast Madison Square Garden. Success was achieved with the single 'Come Dancing' which reached no. 12 in the UK and no. 6 in the USA. Several albums reached the top twenty in the USA including: 'One For The Road'; 'Give The People What They Want'; 'State Of Confusion'. Dave released several solo albums and singles during the decade.

A Gibson Artisan was used by Dave for a concert on April 3rd/4th, 1982, at the Grugahalle, Essen, Germany. The concert was broadcast on German, Swedish, Danish and French television. Dave says the Artisan was used on 'Low Budget' (1979), 'Give The People What They Want' (1981) and 'Chosen People'(1983) as well as on the major stadium tours of the USA during the 1980s. He admits using a 1983 Fender Elite Telecaster on the 'UK Jive' (1989) and 'Phobia' (1993) albums.

On www.equipboard.com it is stated: '[Dave's Gibson Les Paul Artisan] is now on display in the British Invasion exhibit at the Rock 'n' Roll Hall of Fame in Cleveland.'

The 1990s started well for the Kinks as they were inducted into the Rock and Roll Hall of Fame in January 1990. In April of the same year, the band won an Ivor Novello Award for Outstanding Service to British Music. Doug Hinman (*op. cit.*) notes only two singles were released in 1990 and appearances were minimal. In the following year, there were no single or album releases but 1993 was quite different. Two singles and an album were released and touring was extensive with appearances in the UK, Europe, the USA and Japan.

In an appearance on 'The Tonight Show With Jay Leno', on May 26, 1993, Ray and Dave are backed by members of the Branford Marsalis Band when performing songs 'Hatred' and 'Celluloid Heroes'. Dave is filmed playing a sunburst Fender Elite Telecaster – manufactured 1983–1984. The guitar has a maple neck, four controls, two white plain top humbucker pick-ups and a white pick-guard. For the video promoting the single 'Scattered', Dave has a natural Ovation single-cut guitar.

After 30 years in the business in 1994, the Kinks were sadly not far away from winding down as a successful recording and performing outfit. Tours were undertaken in the UK and Scandinavia in 1994 and the year after in Japan, the USA and Australia. Dave Davies released his autobiography in February 1996 and after his 50th birthday celebrations, organised by Ray at the Clissold Arms pub in North London, the band came to a halt.

In the years afterwards, Dave pursued a solo career, gathering a group of musicians around him to tour. Several live and studio albums followed and he also collaborated with son Russ Davies.

In the Arlene R. Weiss *Guitar International Magazine* interview from May 2002, Dave gave an insight into the

Dave Davies performs at Islington Assembly Hall, December 18, 2015.
WENN Rights Ltd / Alamy Stock Photo.

equipment used on the 'Bug' album, released in May 2002 and a few other details of what he had employed in preceding years: a Fender Telecaster with lace sensor pick-ups; a Dobro; a six-string Guild; and a Gibson Les Paul Recording guitar. For amps, he used a Mark Two Mesa Boogie head pushed through a 4x12 in. Marshall cabinet with Celestion speakers. The pedals plugged into were mainly Boss, that he'd possessed for a while.

Whilst leaving an interview on June 30, 2004, Dave suffered a debilitating stroke spending several months in hospital. A little later, whilst recuperating in a village near Dartmoor, Devon, Dave was the subject of a film by Julien Temple, 'Dave Davies: Kinkdome Come', released in 2011.

On picking up the guitar again, he told the *New York Post*, on January 16, 2017, the first chord he played was E, adding: 'E will always have a special place in my heart because of when I picked up a guitar in the first place, and then when I was in rehab.'

Lonnie Donegan c. 1962.
ZUMA Press, Inc. / Alamy Stock Photo.

LONNIE DONEGAN

Few guitarists – even great ones – are privileged to have their own signature guitar built by a celebrated guitar manufacturer. The most important player in the development of British popular music, Lonnie Donegan, was honoured with such an instrument – a 000-28LD – by C.F. Martin in 2002.

'He was more impressed with that fantastic accolade than receiving an MBE in the same year,' revealed Pete Donegan, Lonnie's son, who is still performing Dad's popular songs as well his own unique compositions. Pete explains the Martin Company first contacted Lonnie by appearing at a show and announcing they wanted to build a commemorative guitar for him.

Of course, he was highly delighted, and the Martin Company used the 1967 000-28 as a starting point. 'I had quite an input into the design,' announced Pete. 'Dad wanted a sunburst guitar and I suggested that people sometimes favoured fancy inlays up and down the neck. He said he didn't want all that garishness. Instead, first and foremost, he wanted a nice, playable guitar. I said, if I can come up with something that you'll like will you consider it? He agreed. I was 18 at the time and devised a design that included a crown, at the top of the fretboard, the word SKIFFLE was spelled out in pearl at the 5th, 7th, 9th, 12th, 15th, and 17th frets, and Lonnie Donegan was placed in stylized letters between the 18th and 20th frets. Thus, the neck symbol and letters were intended to read King, SKIFFLE, Lonnie Donegan. The headstock is fitted with gold Grover enclosed tuners. Also included on the headstock is the C.F. Martin gold foil logo with a Water Rat symbol and G.O.W.R. pearl inlays. When Martin build signature models, they ensure that a portion of the proceeds from the guitar sales go to a charity of a guitarist's choosing. In Dad's case it was the Grand Order of Water Rats.'

The Lonnie Donegan signature guitar was featured at the 2002 California NAMM Show. There are two prototype models but they have different woods: one has Indian rosewood, the other Brazilian rosewood. The East Indian rosewood model was presented to Lonnie in a ceremony at Hank's Guitars, Denmark Street, London in 2002. Van Morrison, a great friend of Lonnie, has the other prototype. The tops on both models combine Sitka spruce and hand-scalloped $5/16$" X-bracing for rich balanced tone. The low-profile neck with diamond volute is carved from mahogany. Both the fingerboard and belly bridge are black African ebony. For optimum tone, genuine bone is utilised for both the nut and compensated saddle.

When travelling with his dad's signature guitar, Pete Donegan says he has a certificate of authenticity with him at all times due to rosewood being protected worldwide.

Explaining some of Lonnie's prototype guitar features, Pete says: 'The guitar is finished entirely in polished gloss lacquer with a dark 1935 sunburst top, has a custom case, a special socket for a stereo jack, a bridge pick-up, and a small condenser microphone which sits behind the strings. This only activates when using the stereo jack. A stereo jack is also fitted to Van Morrison's prototype model.'

A limited number of the signature models have been produced by Martin but do not include the stereo jack. Pete is known to play a signature 000-28LD model on stage and, if a string breaks, reaches for the prototype.

Sadly, a few months after being presented with the signature guitar in 2002, Lonnie Donegan died.

Lonnie Donegan was born Anthony James Donegan on April 29, 1933 in Glasgow's Strathclyde district. His mother, Mary Josephine, was Irish, and his father, Peter, Scottish. For a period, Peter Donegan was a violinist with the Royal National Scottish Orchestra and then he moved his family to London when Lonnie was three.

'My dad was born with a faulty aortic valve in his heart,' began Pete Donegan, 'and he was told he would never play football or any other sports and the best thing he could do was stay at home and do nothing. Dad was not that kind of person. What young boy is? So he said, "Sod it. If I'm going to go out before my time, I'll do what I want to do." He played football, ran down the left wing and received sports awards.'

Lonnie's father said to him, 'Whatever you do don't become a musician. There's no money in it.' That advice went unheeded too. Spencer Leigh in *Puttin' On the Style: The Lonnie Donegan Story* (2003) mentions that when Lonnie was four, he was fascinated when he saw an uncle's guitar. He liked the shape of a guitar, but his parents initially had not encouraged him to have one.

Interviewed by Mo Foster, for *British Rock Guitar* (2011), Lonnie said he got his first guitar at the age of 14. After leaving school in 1946, he worked as a stockbroker's runner, and met a lad three years older than himself who played guitar in a dance band. Lonnie learned some basic instruction on that guitar and then bought it when the friend moved on to another instrument. Lonnie's mother bought the guitar for him as a Christmas present and paid 25/- (£1.25). Lonnie said it 'was really a Spanish guitar and would not tune up – I broke the machine heads trying to get it in tune.'

After that, Lonnie's father bought him a £12 cello-top instrument from a store in East Ham High Street.

'Dad had some guitar lessons but got kicked out of them,' began Pete Donegan. 'The teacher was suspicious that he wasn't actually reading music, he was playing by ear. Dad was asked to play a particular song with something written in it which wasn't a regular sequence. He went away, came back, and played the song. The tutor said "you've played the song beautifully but it's not what is written here, you're playing it by ear. Get out." That was the end of lessons but Dad kept learning bits and pieces.'

Spencer Leigh (*op. cit.*) states one of Lonnie's first guitar heroes, following an early interest in jazz, was Neville Scrimshaw adding: [Lonnie] rehearsed with an amateur band in Ilford and his first stage appearance was playing "Muskrat

Ramble" at a school dance.'

After being sacked from his position as a stockbroker's runner, Lonnie found employment in a storeroom at a laboratory for King's College. Later, Lonnie worked at Meaker's men's clothing store and then as a builder's labourer. He was conscripted in 1949 though shortly before this he had bought a Gibson Kalamazoo. It cost about £20, from Selmer's in Charing Cross Road and he took it away with him. Posted to the Royal Army Medical Corps, at Woolwich, it was during this period that he befriended trombonist, Chris Barber, who ran an amateur band.

Chris asked Lonnie if he could play banjo and the reply was 'yes'. This was untrue, though Lonnie quickly purchased one and not knowing the banjo tunings, tuned the first four strings like a guitar and dispensed with the fifth. During Lonnie's first performance, Chris quickly realised Lonnie's lack of knowledge with the banjo but didn't dismiss him.

After being demobbed in 1951, Lonnie worked at an electrical store, then at Ryman the stationers, and Millets Army Surplus Store in Oxford Street. At night, he performed solo spots with his guitar during the intervals at jazz nights held at the Fishmonger's Arms in Wood Green. He sang Lead Belly and American folk songs and began introducing himself as Lonnie Donegan.

Lonnie joined trumpeter Bill Brunskill's band, a New Orleans-style outfit, though the name was soon changed to the Tony Donegan Jazz Band. Again, during intervals, Lonnie appeared singing American roots music with a guitar and his reputation began to grow. He was to say later: 'at Wood Green, I would sing the songs with a mixture of ineptitude and amateurism.'

Lonnie told Mo Foster (*op. cit.*) he acquired a mahogany Martin guitar for £6 from a Walthamstow market stall. This was a nod to hero Lonnie Johnson who played a similar instrument. Lonnie Donegan admitted that he used this model for a long time. Amongst the strings he used were Black Diamond and Cathedral. He also mentioned that it was a great struggle to buy anything related to the guitar during the 1950s. The only guitars available were the imported German cello-type guitars, like the Hofners, or some second-hand Gibsons and Epiphones. Pete Donegan mentions that his father initially tuned a guitar using tuning forks.

Lonnie's reputation for playing American roots music as a soloist landed him an appearance – his first as Lonnie Donegan – at the Royal Albert Hall on June 2, 1952. It was proclaimed to be the greatest jazz event to be staged in Britain. Lonnie was not liked by reviewers but loved by the audience. A little later he appeared as a solo artist at the Royal Festival Hall where his hero Lonnie Johnson was also on the bill.

Shortly afterwards, Lonnie left his band and met up once more with Chris Barber. Forming a new band, they made a debut at the Club Creole, in Soho on Christmas Eve 1952. The band recruited 'high priest' of the New Orleans sound Ken Colyer for a tour in Denmark, and they appeared as Ken Colyer's Jazzmen – a six-piece outfit – with Ken's brother Bill as manager.

According to a *Record Mirror* reviewer the music played was 'the nearest thing we have heard to genuine New Orleans music.' A breakdown group also featured during the tour. A photograph reproduced in Billy Bragg's *Roots, Radicals and Rockers* (2017) illustrates the breakdown group performing in Denmark with Lonnie Donegan taking centre stage, singing and playing guitar. The importance of the moment is not lost on Bragg who eruditely points out: 'The picture embodies a revolutionary moment in British popular music, when the guitar, for so long at the back of the bandstand, an often inaudible part of the rhythm section, comes to the front and takes control.'

On returning to Britain and playing a gig at Acton Town Hall, the band was seen by Pete Townshend, then a mere youth, and later the Who's inimitable guitarist. In a radio interview with Billy Bragg, Townshend underlined Bragg's above statement, by saying the sight of the guitarist taking centre stage made him grasp the enormity of what was happening: 'The [guitar] was going to change the world. For me this was absolutely massive because my father was a saxophone player. I could see the end of my father's world – I was going to get this guitar and it was going to be bye-bye, old timer, and that's exactly what happened.'

During a review of Ken Colyer Jazzmen's performances, Brian Nicholls, in the *Jazz Journal* of June 1953, paid particular attention to the breakdown group, calling it a 'skiffle group'. Bragg (*op. cit.*) astutely mentions Nicholls was the first journalist 'to use the word "skiffle" in reference to music played by British musicians.' He adds: 'In memoirs and interviews over the years, those who were there at the time [early 1950s] tend to credit Bill Colyer [Ken's brother] as the man who introduced the term "skiffle".'

Whilst in New Orleans, during early 1953, Ken Colyer had used 'skiffle' to describe music improvised on homemade instruments but, Bragg informs, 'it was Bill who first applied it to the guitar-led music that the [Ken Colyer Jazzmen] breakdown band were playing in the UK.'

Pete Donegan adds a little more information about the word 'skiffle': 'It first appeared in the States in the 1920s and 1930s as a term to describe a musical or social event at a rent-house party. If someone was short of rent money, they would hold a party and their mates would come round with guitars, make-shift instruments, spoons or whatever they could find to make a noise. The music was very improvised, a bit folky and a little jazzy. Sometimes a small admission fee was charged or a collection organised to try and raise much needed cash for rent. In short, "skiffle" originally was not always used to describe the type of music, perhaps more the event itself. Later, of course, in my dad's time, in the 1950s, it was a term for a hybrid music that embraced blues, country, folk and other genres.'

Pete explains that his father rather stumbled on some of the American roots music that he admired and performed: 'He found a small section of the field recordings made by John Lomax and son Alan for the Library of Congress could be

Kenneth Colyer (1928–1988) played trumpet, cornet and guitar. Devoted to New Orleans jazz, he joined the Crane River Jazz band in 1949; where members were noted for including breakdown sets during their show intervals.

Lonnie's son, Pete Donegan playing his father's signature model Martin 000-28LD.
Peter Tuffrey.

Christian Frederick Martin was born on January 31, 1796, in Markneukirchen, Germany, a small town noted for constructing musical instruments. His ancestors were cabinet makers and woodworkers. According to Johnston, Boak and Longworth in Martin Guitars: A History *(2008), C.F. Martin by the age of 15 was apprenticed to well-known Vienna guitar maker George Stauffer. Once his apprenticeship was completed, he returned to Markneukirchen to open his own guitar shop only to become embroiled in a controversy concerning the guild system. Believing that was too inhibiting he moved to New York in 1833 and Nazareth, Pennsylvania six years later, the company remaining there ever since.*

listened to or borrowed on vinyl from the American Embassy. That's where he discovered Woody Guthrie doing "Gypsy Davy".'

Following an internal argument everyone, except Ken Colyer, left the band during May 1954. The rest, including Chris Barber and Lonnie Donegan, assumed the name once again of the Chris Barber Jazz Band. In July of the same year, the band recorded an album, for Decca, titled 'New Orleans Joys'. At the same time during a break in the sessions, Lonnie recorded for the album several songs with a breakdown or skiffle group which included: Lonnie, guitar; Chris Barber, double bass; and Beryl Bryden on washboard. Of the five songs recorded only 'Rock Island Line' and 'John Henry' appeared on the album.

'Rock Island Line', the third single from the 'New Orleans Joy' album, was not released by Decca until November 1955. It was attributed not to the Chris Barber Band but the Lonnie Donegan Skiffle Group.

For the recording, which he did not think was very good, Lonnie had only been paid £3 10s (£3.50p) as a session fee with no royalty payment. But he once said: 'It did give me a career.' Neither Lonnie nor Decca could have predicted the massive impact the single would have on the music scene.

In 1956, 'Rock Island Line' peaked at no. 8 and almost immediately encouraged working-class teenagers with little or no musical knowledge to interpret skiffle in their own way on simple instruments. John Lennon is known to have played 'Rock Island Line' over and over again.

When Lonnie bumped into Bert Weedon whilst playing 'Rock Island Line' accompanied by the Cyril Stapleton Orchestra, the *Play in a Day* guitarist, congratulated him and said: 'You're the first man to have made any money out of the guitar. Bloody well done.'

'Rock Island Line' was successful in the USA, reaching no. 8, the same position as in the UK and Lonnie followed this up with a tour over there. He was only allowed to sing, not play, with the exception of a rock 'n' roll show in Detroit where Spencer Leigh (*op. cit.*) notes he 'was alone with a little Martin.'

Decca released 'Diggin' My Potatoes'/'Bury My Body' in 1956 and the Lonnie Donegan Skiffle Group EP in the same year. Before the year was out, several more releases were made, Lonnie having transferred to the Pye Nixa label.

During 1957, Britain was awash with skiffle bands. *Record Collector* of April 1982 noted: 'Unlike rock 'n' roll, skiffle didn't need expensive electric guitars, amplifiers and drums. Anyone could play it (or thought they could) on cheap Spanish guitars, with washboard and 'tea chest' bass accompaniment.' The magazine goes on to say by the end of 1957, Britain resounded to an army of amateur groups pounding out mainly American folk songs and the guitar – previously an unusual instrument in Britain – suddenly started selling in vast quantities, setting the stage for the British Beat explosion which followed in the early sixties.

An example of how once traditional music shops switched to selling guitars following the success of 'Rock Island Line'

Clarence Wilson, a member of the Rock Island Colored Quartet, a 'booster' singing group, comprising employees of the Chicago, Rock Island and Pacific Railroad, is credited with writing the earliest-known version of 'Rock Island Line' in 1929. The lyrics to this version differ to the one that later evolved and became well-known. John Lomax and his son Alan researched African American work songs for the Archives of Folk Music at the Library of Congress, from the early 1930s. In September and October 1934 John Lomax, accompanied by Huddie Ledbetter, known as Lead Belly, made recordings of versions of 'Rock Island Line' at Tucker Arkansas prison and Cummins State Farm prison. Lead Belly subsequently recorded adaptations of the song first in 1937 and several more times before he died in 1949.

is given in *Eric Clapton: The Autobiography* (2007). The author mentions that Bell's music store, which he would walk past regularly, had made its name selling piano accordions when they were all the rage. 'Then, when the skiffle boom took off … Bell's changed tack and became a guitar store …'

Whilst the skiffle musical movement had a limited lifespan, it did much to push popular music down a number of avenues and ultimately gave way to rock 'n' roll and in time the Beat Boom.

Between 1957 and 1966, Lonnie had a number of outstanding hits in varying styles, two examples being the novelty numbers 'My Old Man's A Dustman' and 'Does Your Chewing Gum

Lonnie Donegan with band.
Pictorial Press Ltd / Alamy Stock Photo.

Lose Its Flavour'.

'Dad had a deep love of making people happy and laugh so he wanted to do one or two novelty songs,' said Pete Donegan. 'Everyone's got a fun number somewhere in their repertoire, Chuck Berry has "My Ding-a-Ling" and the Beatles, "Yellow Submarine". When asked much, much later to be in soaps and dramas, he said he didn't want to be serious, didn't want to make people sad or cry. He wanted people to be happy. He was a massive all-rounder, and game for anything.'

Lonnie hosted his own television show and was busy with a publishing company, Tyler, established in the late 1950s. One guitarist he signed was Justin Hayward and he also co-wrote and published Tom Jones's hit 'I'll Never Fall In Love Again'.

During 1978, Adam Faith produced an album for him, 'Puttin' On The Style', with top stars flocking to be part of the backing band. Amongst these were Elton John, Ringo Starr, Rory Gallagher and Brian May.

'Many people in the music industry recognise the influence of Lonnie Donegan,' said son Pete, 'but outside he is extremely under-appreciated for what he did. Many remember him mainly for "My Old Man's A Dustman". But, his influence is really underrated. Without him, people don't realise there would have been no Beatles, no Rolling Stones, and the list really goes on and on.'

Andy Fairweather Low with Custom Telecaster.
John Taylor Management.

ANDY FAIRWEATHER LOW

Andy Fairweather Low is still a busy, working musician, his long career stretching back over many decades. Nearly always seen with a warm smile on his face, Andy admits determination and self-belief have always kept him going.

He was born August 2, 1948, in the town of Ystrad Mynach, Wales, near the Penallta colliery which in 1935 held the European record for coal wound in a 24-hour period. Andy's dad was a dustman. Not all Lonnie Donegan fans liked the single 'My Old Man's A Dustman', regarding it as a flimsy novelty song, while Andy readily admits: 'It was a big favourite in our household. We proudly sang along when it came on the radio.' He admired Lonnie's other songs from the 1950s, especially the gospel and Woody Guthrie songs. Whilst on holiday in Great Yarmouth, Andy's parents took him to see Lonnie perform.

Andy's mother had a number of jobs but he remembers one in particular: 'She worked in a cake shop, and regularly brought home lots of goodies.' He is the middle brother of three and, initially, his elder brother started playing accordion though did not make any significant progress. Andy was not interested in music at school though does recall a music teacher, Mr Silman, allowing pupils to bring into class and play a Beatles album.

'There were no other family connections with music, except my dad surprised me, much later, when he was in his 70s, at a New Year's Eve party. He suddenly pulled out a harmonica and played it very well.'

Andy had a flirtation with classical music at school when playing Papageno in Mozart's 'The Magic Flute'. In his teens, he attended a Saturday club at the Capital Theatre where records of the day were played. Then, on one occasion, Dave Edmunds' band, a rockabilly trio, the Raiders performed. Dave was playing a Burns guitar and sang 'I'm Henry The VIII', and Andy was impressed.

Whilst still at school and working part-time on Saturdays – along with Dave Edmunds – at Barratts' Music Store, he bought his first guitar. 'It was a Hofner Verithin on HP and my dad had to sign for it. I wanted a Futurama but didn't get one.'

Until buying the Verithin, Andy played football and wanted to be a goalkeeper yet accepted his small stature would be a problem. Whilst there were no guitar lessons at school, his parents did pay for a solitary session with a private tutor. 'I played on a Spanish guitar, trying to learn "Oh, Little Town Of Bethlehem", and have to admit, I struggled.'

Andy wasn't encouraged by his parents to play guitar but it didn't matter, he practised constantly. 'When I went to bed, I'd take the guitar with me and tried to play it quietly. My dad, who was already in bed because he had to get up early for work, would constantly tell me to stop making a racket and put the guitar down.'

Andy learned to play guitar through sheer perseverance, often on a guitar that had an incredibly high action. 'I wanted to play "Diamonds" by Jet Harris and Tony Meehan and made a reasonable attempt. I found it was all about being obsessed with the instrument and about practising.'

During the last year at school, he would skip classes and listen to records. 'My mother would see us out in a morning. Then, I'd wait round the corner, until she'd left for work and sneak back into the house. I listened all day to the early Rolling Stones albums, paying particular attention to "Route 66" and "I'm A King Bee".'

On leaving school nobody thought Andy would achieve much. 'I wasn't very good at things. One brother took an apprenticeship in a steel works, the other as a mechanic.'

The part-time job at Barratts' became a full-time occupation and Andy recalls selling Fenders, Gibsons, Rickenbackers, along with Barratt, Selmer, Marshall and Vox amps. His favourite guitars in the store included a Gretsch White Falcon and a Gretsch Country Gentleman.

During the first half of the 1960s, Cardiff – a few miles from Andy's home – boasted an exciting music scene where bands could be seen at a number of venues including the Astorian, Top Rank, Capitol Theatre, and Gaumont.

Peter Finch in *The Roots of Rock: From Cardiff to Mississippi and Back* (2016) gives the following details: 'Cardiff is not the centre of the music universe by any means but it has had its moments. Bill Haley came here in 1957 and played the Cardiff Capitol. Lynyrd Skynyrd did the same thing in 1975. John Lee Hooker was here in 1964 at a surf club on the Wentloog flatlands. Jerry Lee played Sophia Gardens in 1962. Dion wandered to the Capitol in 1964. Chuck Berry duck walked there a year later. Johnny Cash visited in 1966. Elvis never …'

The Rolling Stones played two shows at Sophia Gardens on February 28, 1964. 'They were all leather waistcoats and long hair,' recalled Andy. 'I loved them and the concert left a lasting impression on me. The Beatles played Vox amps at the Capitol Theatre in November 1964. The Kinks were at the same venue during May 1965 where Mick Avory and Dave Davies had a fight on stage.'

Andy saw a Soul package tour at Cardiff Top Rank on

> On www.vintageguitarandbass.com it is recorded: 'The Verithin, like so many other Hofner models was clearly inspired by the guitars of American manufacturer Gibson, who's 'thinline' range, launched in 1958, had been a massive success. Guitars like the ES 330TD and ES 335TD (generally known as the ES 330 and ES 335) were very expensive in Europe, typically out of reach of the majority of musicians, and no British manufacturer was capable of making anything even vaguely similar. So it is no surprise that the Hofner Verithin, debuting in 1960 was an instant success. It was built in Germany, but distributed by Selmer in the UK and Commonwealth, and was first included in Selmer's 1960 catalogue with a price tag of 52 gns.

Monday April 3, 1965, featuring Otis Redding, Arthur Conley, Sam and Dave, and Booker T and the MGs featuring Steve Cropper. 'Each band played an extended set. Steve Cropper was amazing, his simplified riffs flawless. Whenever working on a song now I'm thinking about Booker T and the MGs.'

Booker T and the MGs were the Stax Records house band, which backed artists such as Otis Redding, Sam and Dave, Carla Thomas, and Rufus Thomas. He also acted as the producer of many of these records. On the early Stax recordings, Cropper is known to have played a 1956 Fender Esquire, and later used a blonde Fender Telecaster.

Andy listened to music on Radio Luxembourg and at Spillers Records, a record store in Cardiff which presently boasts on its website to be the 'Oldest Record Store in the World.' The first band he joined was the Taff Beats – they all lived in the Taff valley. Andy had a Gibson ES 330 by this time and each member of the band plugged into a Bird amplifier. Andy was the lead guitarist because he could competently play 'Johnny B. Goode'. The band also performed numbers by Lazy Lester, Chuck Berry and Jimmy Reed. 'To tune the guitar, we just got an A off a piano and only changed a string when one broke.'

By 1965, Andy was in another band, Sect Maniacs, which included Charlotte Church's granddad on sax. Andy played a white Stratocaster through a Vox AC30 with a treble boost. The music played was Soul, including Rufus Thomas's 'All Night Worker' and 'Walking The Dog'. During the following year, Amen Corner came together through Andy pulling musicians from other bands. The name was derived from The Amen Corner, a weekly disc spin at the Victoria Ballroom in Cardiff, where every Sunday night a Dr Rock would play the best Soul music from the USA.

'Together, I thought we would all make a great band playing Soul. As I'd formed the band, I decided there was nothing else for me to do but sing. Every song was either on Stax or Atlantic. Whilst I didn't read music, I worked out all the song arrangements. On hearing an original song, I said this is how we're going to do it. We set a rough track down then I worked with other band members to create their parts. We were happy just to do covers. I'd only sang a little before because I wanted to be Eric Clapton. But, if Soul music is performed, you don't need an Eric Clapton-type guitar player. I wrote Amen Corner's B sides on guitar and mainly started with an E chord.'

Andy vividly remembers being very impressed witnessing Eric Clapton performing with John Mayall's Bluesbreakers at the Flamingo Club during early 1966. Little did he know at the time, both he and Eric would have a close working partnership in later years.

Whilst Amen Corner played on the same bill as Jethro Tull and the Only Ones, the band was recommended to Ron King, who signed them to his company Galaxy Entertainments. King boldly decided 'they were going to be successful' and their first single 'Gin House Blues' reached no. 12 in 1967. This was followed by 'The World Of Broken Hearts', a UK no. 24.

Beat Instrumental No. 53 of September 1967 gives the following information: 'The Amen Corner line-up consists of a baritone sax, tenor sax, guitar, bass, drums, organ and vocals which is pushed through Triumph amplifiers and a Selmer 100-watt PA, with a set of Marshall 4x12 in. columns.'

'All seven of us were living at the Madison Hotel, Sussex Gardens, in one room where you start hating the colour of people's socks. If you didn't go down for breakfast, you didn't eat. Ten Years After were also there. Ron King got us the deal with Triumph amps but they were not very good. We had to have two of everything as they kept breaking down. Whether the amps were on or off, we couldn't hear anything. A good or a bad gig would be judged on how many people in the audience fainted. It was frustrating driving all over the country just to play 20 or 30 minutes.'

Towards the end of 1967, Amen Corner joined a package tour organised by impresario Tito Burns that included the Jimi Hendrix Experience, the Move, Pink Floyd, and the Nice.

'We played a straight 15 minutes set twice nightly without stopping each time. Jimi Hendrix was very friendly and quiet. The only topic of conversation was the weather. He was so far ahead in a different world.'

Amen Corner's third hit, 'Bend Me, Shape Me' was suggested in 1968 by Ron King and went to no. 3. 'The song had been covered in the USA by the Models, the Outsiders and the American Breed. We took the main riff from Smokey Robinson's "Going To A Go Go".'

By the time 'High In The Sky' was released in 1968, the band had been sold by Ron King to Don Arden. Two more singles were

---

According to the Rock and Roll Hall of Fame, Soul is 'music that arose out of the black experience in America through the transmutation of gospel and rhythm & blues into a form of funky, secular testifying. Catchy rhythms, stressed by handclaps and extemporaneous body moves, are an important feature of Soul music …'

Bird amplifiers: On www.vintagehofner.co.uk it is mentioned Bird Amplifiers have all-but been forgotten for forty years. 'They seem to have only been produced for about five years or so in the early to mid-sixties, and not that many were sold compared to Selmer, Watkins, and Fenton-Weill. That is a pity, because they are well-built amps with features that were in the forefront of UK amplifier design in the early 1960's. They were produced from about 1960 onwards by Sydney S. Bird & Sons of Poole, Dorset who, amongst many other things, were into the manufacture of electronic organs.'

The Flamingo Club was a nightclub in Soho, London, between 1952 and 1967. It was located at 33–37 Wardour Street from 1957 onwards and played an important role in the development of British rhythm and blues and jazz. The club had a wide social appeal and was a favourite haunt for musicians, including the Beatles.

hits in 1969, 'If Paradise Was Half As Nice' and 'Hello Susie' (written by Roy Wood). 'Get Back' in the same year failed to chart. Andrew Oldham had become manager by the end of the decade and just as the band were about to be sold once more to EMI, Amen Corner disbanded.

'Events were moving apace in the music industry and I desperately wanted to play guitar again. I bought a second-hand Gibson Les Paul and played it through a Vox AC30. I formed, Fair Weather, which was Amen Corner without the brass section. RCA gave us some finance to pay off some bills and we started again. I also had a white Strat which used to belong to Steve Marriott. Later when touring we used a Hiwatt backline.'

Fair Weather released four singles and two albums between 1970 and 1972 with little success and afterwards disbanded.

'After finishing a gig, I told them to drop me at Paddington. I'm going home. It's all over.'

Despite a downturn of fortunes, the remaining years of the decade were eventful. Andy worked as a backing vocalist for Richard and Linda Thompson and played guitar with Leo Sayer and Gerry Rafferty. 'I played on Baker Street, though not credited.'

Prior to the early 1970s, Andy had always used a plectrum when playing, but began to take an interest in other techniques – picking and playing with his fingers. 'Whilst back home, I listened to cassettes and studied instructional books by Stefan Grossman. He opened up a completely new door for me. I wanted to play with my fingers and learned the tunings and guitar tricks used by Lightnin' Hopkins, Mississippi John Hurt and Robert Johnson. I always found these players used tricks and it was great discovering what they were.'

Andy got married in 1973, and the couple are still together today. 'She's put up with a lot but has always been very supportive,' declares Andy.

During 1974, Andy won a deal with A&M for three albums and he mainly wrote all the songs himself. For the first album, 'Spider Jiving', he went to San Francisco for three happy months, though it only took 12 days to record from beginning to end. He spent nine days recording the backing tracks in San Francisco and then three days in Nashville with some fabulous musicians, including the Memphis Horns, who had played with Otis Redding. The producer was Elliott Mazer. At this point, Andy played a white Strat through a Fender Twin.

The solo career brought some chart success especially with the single 'Wide Eyed And Legless'. Produced by Glyn Johns, the track featured ex-Eagle Bernie Leadon on acoustic guitar while Andy used a 12-string with a Nashville or high-strung tuning.

'I wrote "Wide Eyed And Legless" on an old, late 1940s parlour guitar. A friend, Micky, found it down the Bay in a skip. Although it had been in a fire, Micky had it renovated and I bought it off him for £47. Glyn wasn't convinced about the song and, initially, it had a third verse but was dropped. I toured some of the time as a soloist using a Gibson 12-string but I kept breaking strings. Of course, there were no guitar techs in those days to run to your assistance.'

Leaving A&M, Andy signed a seven-album deal with Warner Brothers and was dropped after the first year, only producing one album. His languid laid-back music had been kicked into touch by the savage onslaught of Punk.

Struggling to pay bills, he sold his Les Paul and white Strat, went home, borrowed money from his mother, who also let him use her car. Fortunately, Andy had a good working relationship with Glyn Johns and opportunities were sent his way. 'I realised I couldn't play lead guitar as good as I wanted to though I was competent playing rhythm. I spotted some of the "Premiership" guitarists sometimes needed a rhythm guitar and there was a niche for me in that area.'

Andy was with Glyn Johns when Faces' Ronnie Lane called seeking volunteers for a benefit concert for ARMS (Action into Research for Multiple Sclerosis), a disease that Lane was suffering from. The first (and initially planned to be the only) event took place at the Royal Albert Hall on September 20, 1983. Andy appeared alongside Eric Clapton, Jimmy Page, Bill Wyman and Jeff Beck.

Much work followed for Andy after the event and the ARMS American tour. This included a long working relationship with Bill Wyman's Rhythm Kings and Roger Waters – in the studio and on tour. Andy featured in Waters' tours of 'The Pros And Cons Of Hitchhiking' and 'The Wall' as well as contributing to 'Radio Kaos'. Throughout this period, Andy played both bass and guitar using Waters' noted black Strat and Precision bass. He also used his own Fender Vibro-King amps.

Flying home from a USA tour, Roger Waters announced to Andy he was going to take a break for a while. Luckily, around the same time, Andy received a phone call from Roger Forrester, Eric Clapton's manager. He was invited to join Eric's band, backing George Harrison on a tour of Japan. That was 1991, and it was to be the first time a Beatle had returned to perform in Japan since 1966.

'George wanted me to play slide guitar. I said I'm not a slide player but will play slide if you want me to. He said, "I've never heard you play but everybody seems to like you." Later, during a band meal, he told me I wasn't the first choice. I was actually the seventh, the others included Alvin Lee and Gary Moore. But he assured me I was the right choice.'

On the Japanese tour, Andy played the well-known lead riffs from George's fabulous songs. Naturally, he felt nervous having to play them in exactly the same way they had been heard millions of times before around the world. 'I'd listened to all the bits and was quite conversant with how to play them. Whilst I experienced a lot of pressure and didn't sleep very well

> *During the 1970s and later, Grossman saw a niche in the market for solo acoustic guitar records which were accompanied by a tablature book to allow the buyer to try playing the arrangements and, with his friend Ed Denson taking care of the US side of business, founded Kicking Mule Records. Grossman also released his own original and instructional albums on KM, the latter including seminal works such as* Fingerpicking Guitar Techniques, How to Play Ragtime Guitar *and* Famous Ragtime Guitar Solos *which had a major influence on acoustic guitarists in Europe, the UK and the US.*

Andy Fairweather Low with Gibson L5.
John Taylor Management.

on some nights, thankfully everything went OK, particularly when I played lead on "Give Me Love". On George's tour, I had one guitar and had to borrow everything else. Afterwards, as a way of saying thanks, George gave me an Eric Clapton signature Strat to keep.'

Being involved with George was a life-changing moment for Andy as he began a long working relationship with Eric Clapton. He became involved with Eric's Royal Albert Hall concerts and the now celebrated 'Unplugged' recording for MTV besides a number of other albums.

'The best time of my life was with Eric. He liked to laugh and provided everything I wanted regarding guitars. Prior to "Unplugged", I spent a week at his house going through songs. There were only two guitars there – one for me and the other for him. I played a 000-28 that his tech, Alan Rogan, had sourced from Gruhn's Guitars in Nashville. It was slightly altered and became known as Andy's guitar. Later it was sold at Eric's guitar auction in Dallas. We had three weeks rehearsing in Bray and during the MTV performance the songs took care of themselves. The parts were already written. They were Eric's ideas and I played along. The only real work I did was on "Malted Milk". During the concert, I played several guitars, amongst them was a Gibson Super 300.'

In the 1990s, Andy undertook session work with other artists, including Joe Satriani and Stevie Nicks. 'On the Satriani sessions I had a Supro with a lap-steel pick-up and a Bajo-Sexto guitar, that Fender made for me. I'd seen Ry Cooder playing one during a Hammersmith Odeon concert. I played a mandolin and put a diagram on the floor to help me along because there was a complicated arrangement of chords.'

Through Glyn Johns, Andy worked with Stevie Nicks on 'Street Angel' and used a baritone guitar and a number of Fenders. 'When

Andy Fairweather Low with Vox guitar.
John Taylor Management.

playing through a vintage Fender Twin, I blew a speaker and have never been forgiven for it.'

Performing with Eric Clapton allowed Andy to request guitars from manufacturers including Gibson. 'I fancied a Black L5 and Gibson sent me one. To stop it feeding back, I had to resort to drastic measures, including filling the body with foam. When I asked if they wanted it back, they said no, you can keep it.'

Other highlights of his time with Eric Clapton were performing with B.B. King, Billy Preston and Jimmy Vaughan. Andy played on 'From The Cradle', 'Riding With The King' and 'Me And Mr Johnson'.

Roger Waters called on his services once again in 1999 and 2007 respectively to be part of the 'In The Flesh' and 'Dark Side Of The Moon' tours. 'Roger used to say get out there and make a statement only don't play too much. That's what I did when playing an energetic version of "Money". I started on a B chord, making a big statement. It's something I learned from Pete Townshend.'

In 2011, Kate Bush invited Andy to perform on her track, 'Wild Man', saying he had the perfect voice for the song. Later, when released as a single, it appeared as Kate Bush and Andy Fairweather Low.

Over the last few years, Andy has moved away from being an integral part of other bands to establish his own outfit, Andy Fairweather Low and the Low Riders. He released his first solo album in 26 years, 'Sweet Soulful Music', in 2006.

The guitars in his arsenal at the moment include a light blue Airline; a Teisco; Supro; and a Knight guitar made by Gordon and Robert Wells. Many of them are fitted with Gibson Burstbucker pick-ups. An amplifier currently in use is a Cornell Duke 3 Custom. 'I wanted Dennis to build me an inefficient amp which slightly confused him. I just wanted treble and bass without any gimmicks, simple but effective. I like to drive the amp hard so the output has three wattage settings.'

Guitar brands featured here amongst Andy's collection include: Gibson, Airline, Eko and Martin.
Peter Tuffrey.

Peter Frampton with Humble Pie.
Trinity Mirror / Mirrorpix / Alamy Stock Photo.

PETER FRAMPTON

A child prodigy on guitar, Peter Frampton first found success at an early age as part of the Herd and Humble Pie. Embarking on a solo career, he built a strong catalogue of material which was recorded on the multi-million selling album 'Frampton Comes Alive!'. This cemented his status as an exciting and innovative guitarist, particularly through employing the relatively obscure 'talk box' effect on the tracks 'Do You Feel Like We Do?' and 'Show Me The Way'.

Peter grew up in the 1950s, the son of an art teacher in a South London school. Peter briefly lived with his grandparents when young. There, he had an early introduction to music as an upright piano was played regularly for family entertainment. Later, Peter became interested in rock 'n' roll, as well as the Shadows and, like many others, was struck by the playing of Hank Marvin. Around age seven, Peter was gifted a banjolele from his grandmother and quickly picked up several simple English music hall songs which his father taught him. Soon after, Peter acquired an acoustic for Christmas. He had a natural affinity with music and was soon inseparable from his guitar which he took to school to play for both classmates and teachers. This led to his first public performance at an end-of-term show.

In secondary school, Peter studied music during his final year. He formed his first group with fellow students on piano and bass. Still armed with the acoustic guitar, he fitted a pick-up during this period. Peter's father encouraged his son's interest and paid for guitar lessons which broadened Peter's knowledge of musical principles. Around age 12, Peter was able to write instrumentals which he performed with another group he founded, the Trubeats. The band performed at venues across South London. By this time, Peter had acquired a Hofner Club 60 electric guitar. In his teenage years, Peter worked in local music stores which acquainted him with the area's musicians. Drummer Tony Chapman invited Peter to join his new group, the Preachers. Tony knew Bill Wyman of the Rolling Stones and this led to a recording session for the Preachers that yielded the single 'Hole In My Soul'. This was besides a TV appearance when the Stones took over 'Ready Steady Go!'. Whilst with the Preachers, Peter was pictured using a Guild Starfire III with a Vox amp.

At a Preachers gig, Peter was approached by members of the Herd to join them for the summer of 1966 and afterwards this turned into a permanent position. Peter began as the rhythm player, but with band rearrangements he became the lead guitarist. In early 1967, the Herd went into the studio and recorded 'I Can Fly', an upbeat pop song. Although ultimately not troubling the charts, a promotional video was made for the track and Peter was seen using a Gibson Melody Maker. The next single, 'From The Underworld', proved much more successful and peaked at no. 6 in the UK, in addition to Europe and elsewhere. For TV appearances promoting the track, Peter was using the Melody Maker, as well as a Fender Stratocaster in sunburst. The success of the single helped the Herd gain a

Peter Frampton c. 1967 with Epiphone acoustic during his time with The Herd.
Pictorial Press Ltd / Alamy Stock Photo.

position on a package tour of England with the Who.

The Herd followed 'From The Underworld' with 'Paradise Lost' which peaked at 15 in the charts, whilst 'I Don't Want Our Loving To Die' came out in early 1968 and reached no. 6. Later in the year, the Herd made an appearance on the German TV music programme 'Beat Club' to perform the two previously mentioned tracks. Peter played his Stratocaster and a 1954–1956 specification Gibson Les Paul Custom.

Disagreement and subsequent separation with the band's management affected the next release 'Sunshine Cottage'. This was written by Peter with bandmate Andy Bown and produced with the help of Small Faces' Ronnie Lane and Steve Marriott. The lack of success of the single, which had a 'rockier sound' than the previous pop-styled hits, coupled with growing disillusionment in the Herd and his position of singer/guitarist/teen idol, led Peter to leave during late 1968. He had immediately bonded with Steve Marriott, who initially helped Peter look for musicians to start a new band before the pair decided to team up and form Humble Pie.

In mid-1969, the band released the album 'As Safe As Yesterday Is' and single 'Natural Born Bugie'. A performance of the latter took place on 'Beat Club' and Peter was filmed using a c. 1960 Gretsch Duo Jet with Elgen amp head and Orange speaker cabinets. The single was in the blues rock genre and fared well as the band's initial offering, peaking at no. 4 in the UK. The album saw two writing credits for Peter – 'Stick Shift' and 'I'll Go Alone' – as well as a co-written track with Steve, 'As Safe As Yesterday Is'. Humble Pie quickly followed up with 'Town And Country', which was a departure from the first album, adopting a mellower acoustic sound, though still with some electric guitar. Peter was pictured during his Herd tenure using an Epiphone acoustic and he continued with the brand by purchasing a Texan model around the time of Humble Pie's formation. Again, two tracks had his sole credit: the lead track 'Take Me Back' and 'Only You Can See'. He shared recognition with Steve and bassist Greg Ridley on 'Home And Away'.

Peter Frampton performs at the 2016 We're All for the Hall benefit concert supporting the Country Music Hall of Fame.
The Photo Access / Alamy Stock Photo.

Humble Pie went to America in 1969 and toured for six weeks. Upon the group's return to England, Immediate Records, which had released the first two albums, folded and A&M Records subsequently won the band's signature. 'Humble Pie' was produced for the label and appeared in mid-1970. Only one credit for Peter was on the record, 'Earth And Water Song', which was primarily acoustic guitar. Peter was pictured with two SGs in 1969/1970. One was a Custom with sideways Vibrola and the second was a Standard with short pick-guard and stopbar tailpiece. In *Do You Feel Like I Do?: A Memoir* (2021), Peter relates that he swapped an SG for a Gibson ES 335 around 1970. When in America during the year, another change occurred after a fan, Marc Mariana, gifted Peter a 1954/1955 Gibson Les Paul Custom that had been reworked to include three humbucker pick-ups and a thin neck shape.

Early in 1971, Humble Pie recorded 'Rock On' at Olympic Studios in London. As with 'Town And Country', a track from

Peter opened the album. This was 'Shine On' and followed by the co-written 'Sour Grain'. Peter's other sole credit was 'The Light'.

At the end of May, the band was in America touring and a night at the Fillmore East was recorded for the live LP 'Performance: Rockin' the Fillmore' which appeared at the end of the year. On the 'Discover Music' channel on youtube.com, Peter informed that on the night he was using a late 1960s Marshall 100-watt Super Lead and Marshall 50-watt with 4x12 in. cabinets. The 50-watt head was used as a monitor for Steve Marriott on his side of the stage.

Peter's involvement with Humble Pie came to an end in late 1971 as he felt the time was right to become a solo artist. He assembled several friends to complete 'Wind Of Change' for release in mid-1972. The songs were mainly acoustic-led with electric guitar sections. Peter toured the material in 1972/1973 under the name 'Frampton's Camel' and supported several acts, including Humble Pie and ZZ Top. The band's name served as the title for Peter's next album which was recorded in New York at Electric Lady Studios with Eddie Kramer in early 1973. Peter informs in *Do You Feel Like I Do?: A Memoir* that the solo for 'Lines On My Face' was recorded using his Les Paul Custom and an Ampeg ET-1 combo amp with 2x12 in. speakers.

'Somethin's Happening' was recorded in early 1974 and continued the direction established with the previous solo albums. Cryptically, on the rear cover of the record, Peter is credited as using a 'guitar synthesizer', though details of what this is has proved elusive. In addition to electric and acoustic guitars, Peter also played piano and organ on the record. 'Somethin's Happening' was poorly received, yet Peter was honing a reputation for his live performances and supported the album through 1974. Around the end of the year, Peter wrote material for his fourth solo album, 'Frampton', in the Bahamas. He mainly used his acoustic to write songs, which were recorded on a Sony 550A tape player. Peter had his electric on hand and states in his autobiography that he tuned the instrument to open A when he wrote 'Nowhere's Too Far For My Baby'.

In March 1975, 'Frampton' was well-received by both critics and the public, selling around 300,000 copies. Following the pattern set by Humble Pie, a live album of the ensuing tour was planned. Dates were recorded at Winterland, San Francisco, using 24-track tape machines. Though originally to be a single album, the material warranted a double record and two shows in New York state were later captured using 16-track tapes. 'Frampton Comes Alive!' appeared at the start of 1976 and reached no. 1 in America during April. The record went on to be the biggest-selling of the year. On the tour, Peter was mainly using his Les Paul Custom into two 100-watt Marshall heads and cabinets. In conversation with record producer Rick Beato on youtube.com, Peter revealed he plugged into the second channel and 'jumpered' to the first channel. He used two Leslie speaker cabinets, with one on stage and another off to the side, whilst a Binson Echorec was also present. A particularly distinct piece of equipment acquired by Peter for the 'Frampton' album was the 'talk box'. This diverted the output from a speaker cabinet to another speaker connected to a plastic tube which the musician put in their mouth. The sound was manipulated by the shape of the mouth cavity and the ensuing distortions were picked by the microphone. Peter had first become aware of the effect in 1970 when working with George Harrison on the 'All Things Must Pass' album as Pete Drake, the Nashville-based pedal steel player, was present and showed him a device he made along similar lines. Audio engineer Bob Heil developed a talk box in the mid-1970s and an early user was Joe Walsh who utilised the effect on the Barnstorm track 'Rocky Mountain Way'. Peter was gifted one just before 'Frampton' by Bob Heil and featured the talk box as part of 'Do You Feel Like We Do?' and 'Show Me The Way'. In his autobiography, Peter said of the effect: '… I love it. I love its humour; it's very funny … there's nothing like when the guitar starts talking to you.'

Footage of Peter from the period was captured on the 'Midnight Special' TV programme, and he was using the previously mentioned equipment, in addition to a 1955 Fender Stratocaster in red with tortoiseshell pick-guard on 'Show Me The Way'. His Les Paul had also acquired the distinctive white pick-up surrounds, whilst a second Les Paul Custom in white performed 'Nowhere's Too Far For My Baby'.

With the success of 'Frampton Comes Alive!', Peter was under pressure to reproduce this with his next studio album. 'I'm In You' was recorded over six months at the end of 1976, into 1977 and had guest appearances from Mick Jagger and Stevie Wonder. Debuting at no. 1 in America, 'I'm In You' subsequently reached 'platinum' status and spawned Peter's first number-one single with the title track. In addition to playing electric and acoustic guitar on the album, Peter was credited with using several keyboard synthesizers, including Moog and ARP models. On stage in 1977, Peter was seen performing with an Ovation six-string acoustic for his opening mini-set of songs using that instrument, followed by previously mentioned guitars and equipment.

Peter was involved in a serious car accident in 1978 which curtailed his activities for several months. He returned to touring with dates across Asia later in the year and in the winter returned to the studio for 'Where I Should Be'. The lead track was also the single, 'I Can't Stand It No More', which broke into the top twenty, whilst guitarist Steve Cropper and bassist Donald 'Duck' Dunn made guest appearances on a couple of the album tracks. For the follow-up, 'Breaking All The Rules' (May 1981), Peter obtained the services of Steve Lukather on guitar and Jeff Porcaro on drums, both from the band Toto. Whilst on tour in South America during 1980, the cargo plane carrying Peter and the band's equipment crashed on take-off, destroying all items.

In 1982, Peter completed his eighth solo album, 'The Art Of Control'. In promotional videos for the record, he was seen with a Telecaster with neck humbucker for the track 'Sleepwalk', and 'Back To Eden' had a Les Paul Custom in black with two pick-ups (with cream surrounds) in use through a Marshall head and one 4x12 in. cabinet. Following the release of the album, Peter left his record company and took an extended break to spend time with his family.

'Premonition' marked Peter's return in 1986 and he supported Stevie Nicks on tour following the album's release. Afterwards, he was contacted by childhood friend David Bowie to play guitar on the latter's 'Never Let Me Down' record, in addition to being credited with providing sitar on one track. Peter was on the subsequent 'Glass Spider' tour. He played a Suhr 'Super Strat'-type guitar with two humbuckers (bridge and neck positions), single coil in the middle and Floyd Rose tremolo, with a wireless system used to allow movement during the energetic stage show. Peter was obliged to play several guitar parts devised by other guitarists on songs as part of the set, such as Robert Fripp on 'Heroes' and Stevie Ray Vaughan for 'Let's Dance'. On taking the challenge of sounding like the original recording for the fans, Peter commented in *Do You Feel Like I Do?*: '… I played my version of their parts. It's pretty much written as to what you play, so it was a challenge …' In the book, he reveals some of his home studio equipment of the period: '… 3M M79 24-track analogue machine, Studer 2-track Amek Angela console … Mac SE and performer MIDI software …' This set-up was used to gather the material for Peter's next album, 'When All The Pieces Fit' which appeared early in 1989.

In the early 1990s, Peter attempted a reunion with Steve Marriott and the pair wrote together for a time before going their separate ways. Sadly, soon after his arrival back in Britain, Steve perished in a house fire. One of the tracks from the collaboration, 'Out Of The Blue', appeared on 1994's 'Peter Frampton' record. In 1992, Peter embarked on a small tour of America – his first in several years – and he continued to use his Suhr, with this going through a vintage Marshall head and one 4x12 in. cab as well as a modern Marshall head paired with another cabinet. He had acquired a Gibson Les Paul Custom with three pick-ups and acoustic tracks saw a Taylor in use.

The 20th anniversary of 'Frampton Comes Alive!' was celebrated in 1995 and for this Peter recorded two dates at the Fillmore which were later released as 'Frampton Comes Alive! II', in addition to a film of the performances being made. Peter started the set with a Gibson Les Paul Junior, later moving on to the Suhr, Les Paul Custom, natural Gibson Nighthawk with two pick-ups, Telecaster-type guitar, Taylor acoustic, Guild acoustic and sunburst Gibson Nighthawk. Marshall amplifiers stood behind Peter and he had a custom pedalboard, apparently for rack-mounted effects.

In 1997/1998, Peter was part of Ringo Starr's All Starr Band, along with Jack Bruce, Gary Brooker, Simon Kirke and Mark Rivera. The band played a medley of the constituents' songs and Peter was required to tailor his gear as a result. A video made of a concert in New Jersey has him using a Gibson Les Paul Custom Florentine, Fender Telecaster, Les Paul Standard (for a time in the 1980s/1990s Peter had an original 1960 Les Paul which he subsequently sold), black electro-acoustic guitar and Taylor 12-string acoustic. Amplification and effects appeared to be as mentioned earlier.

In the early 2000s, Peter teamed up with song-writer and musician Gordon Kennedy to work on 'Now', Peter's twelfth solo album. The pair collaborated on 'Fingerprints' from 2006, which featured several other well-known musicians. The record went on to win a Grammy award as Best Pop Instrumental Album. Around this time, Peter was honoured by Gibson guitars with a signature Les Paul Custom, as well as a Les Paul Junior with three P90 pick-ups.

Peter had recorded mostly in his home studio from the early 2000s and around 2010 he moved to Nashville and was able to buy a studio, later named 'Phenix'. This came with much of the equipment installed, whilst also allowing Peter to house equipment he had accumulated from the 1970s. He talked to *Guitar World* magazine about his live rig on YouTube, revealing a custom set-up made by Mark Snyder. Effects were rack-mounted and set to be easily removed if required. A Fender Bassman head was used for clean tones, whilst a 1970s Marshall head with master volume modification was selected for overdrive. The signal was then taken into several other effects processors before delivered to the Marshall 4x12 in. cabinets. Another Marshall head was used for the talk box. An Axess Electronics programmable pedalboard controlled the amps and effects. Peter states in his autobiography that he was still using guitar cables at this time as he did not care for the sound the wireless system produced.

In 2012, Peter's original Les Paul Custom was returned to him, having survived the plane crash in 1980 and used by a local musician for a time. The instrument was partially restored by Gibson but remained the same cosmetically with charred headstock and partially missing custom inlay. Gibson later offered a very limited number of replica 'Phenix' Les Paul Custom guitars. Peter's first public performance with the guitar was appropriately at the 35th anniversary show for 'Frampton Comes Alive!'.

Severe flooding struck Nashville in 2010 and affected some musicians, particularly equipment in storage. Peter lost over 40 guitars, though was insured and able to replace them. One survivor was his Epiphone acoustic which he had owned from his days with Humble Pie. His new guitars included a 1959 ES 335 – in an extremely rare cherry finish – a 1960 Gibson Les Paul Standard (previously owned by J.J. Cale), vintage Fender Jaguar and Jazzmasters, and a 1959 Fender Telecaster. On his new acquisitions, Peter told the reverb.com channel on youtube.com that he wanted a variety of guitars that inspired him. This also stretched to his choice of amplifier and in his studio during the interview he had a few Fender tweed combo amps, as well as Ampeg and others.

Several albums were recorded by Peter in the 2010s: 'Thank You Mr Churchill'; 'Acoustic Classics'; 'All Blues'; 'Frampton Forgets The Words'. He continued touring, being seen with a collection of previously mentioned instruments, including his original Les Paul Custom. Whilst touring in the mid-2010s, Peter noticed a loss of muscle strength and was later diagnosed with Inclusion Body Myositis. Initially keeping the affliction at bay, by the end of the decade this had progressed to the point he noticed an effect on his playing. During 2019, Peter embarked on a 'Farewell' tour of the USA. Peter mainly used his Les Paul Custom, but also had his ES 335, a sunburst ES 335, 1962 SG Standard, cutaway six-string acoustic, and 1960 Les Paul Standard. He continued to use Marshall and had his own-brand talk box, the Framptone, which was made by Keeley Electronics.

Robert Fripp, with Roland synthesizer guitar.
dpa picture alliance / Alamy Stock Photo.

ROBERT FRIPP

As the constant member of King Crimson, Robert Fripp has steered the band through several line-up changes whilst managing to keep the integrity of the music. Highly regarded for his technique, Robert has also been innovative, creating 'Frippertronics' in his work with Brian Eno and pioneering 'New Standard Tuning' as part of his Guitar Craft teaching courses.

Robert was interested in music from an early age, first liking traditional jazz, then rock 'n' roll. His mother supported this curiosity, buying Robert a Manguin Frere acoustic guitar when aged 11. Robert immediately took to the instrument, though being naturally left-handed, he found the guitar initially hard to play right-handed. He progressed from playing rock 'n' roll to jazz in just a few years. This was thanks to guitar lessons taken from local teacher Don Strike, who introduced Robert to several jazz guitarists, including Django Reinhardt. By age 15 (in 1961), Robert was at an advanced stage in terms of theoretical musical knowledge and decided to take the next step of joining a band and putting this to practical use.

By this time, Robert had also graduated from his acoustic to a Hofner President with Watkins amplifier. He eventually formed a group with school friends and local boys. First was the Ravens, which was active for approximately a year before Robert left to pursue his O-Levels. In the summer, Robert took a job with his father and subsequently decided he wanted to become a professional musician. For a period, Robert worked as a guitar teacher in Boscombe, though his parents thought he should consider another career path and he returned to school for his A-Levels. He did form another group, the League of Gentlemen, and was in the house band for the Majestic Hotel, Bournemouth. During this time, he had a sunburst Gibson ES 345, bought new in 1963.

Set to attend university, Robert decided instead to forge a career as a musician. During late summer 1967, he answered an advert for a singing organist which had been placed by the Giles brothers, Michael and Peter. Both had been in a group called the Trendsetters which failed to find a sustainable following. After a month's rehearsal, and a booking as support for the Flowerpot Men, the band moved to London. This gig fell through, and the trio was left to develop their own act. They created a sound, which was a fusion of various styles, through 1968. With little money to enter a studio, they improvised by turning the living room of their rented house into a space to record demos. One of these was sent to Decca Records, which offered Giles, Giles and Fripp a record deal and they recorded an album 'The Cheerful Insanity Of Giles, Giles And Fripp' which was released in September 1968. Most of the tracks were written by the Giles brothers, but Robert contributed 'Little Children', 'Suite No. 1' and 'Erudite Eyes'. 'Suite No. 1' was in the jazz style and found Robert playing with a clean tone, whilst 'Erudite Eyes' has an experimental or 'psychedelic' sound.

Despite their best efforts, Giles, Giles and Fripp failed to achieve any success and Peter Giles left the band towards the end of 1968. Robert and Michael recruited multi-instrumentalist Ian McDonald, Greg Lake on bass and vocals, as well as lyricist Peter Sinfield, who also worked on the stage presentation. The new group was christened King Crimson.

Ian McDonald had a wealthy relative willing to invest in the band and this allowed Robert to upgrade from his ES 345 to a 1959 Gibson Les Paul Custom. The pick-up covers were removed exposing double black PAFs in bridge and middle positions and a 'zebra' in the neck. Talking to Tony Bacon in 1991 (and reproduced on www.reverb.com), Robert commented that he purchased two Marshall bass stacks for the band, and used one himself. The group's first booking was a week's residency at Newcastle's 'Change Is' club. Discussing the presentation of King Crimson soon after, the band members concluded that all should feel comfortable and reflect their personalities. Robert decided that he was most at ease sitting down when playing guitar, as his technique was geared towards this position. Additionally, he was a naturally shy/reserved person who did not gravitate towards the traditional 'guitar hero' theatrics – he preferred to let the music represent him.

King Crimson soon developed a reputation on the London club scene. This was part of the reason the band was able to support the Rolling Stones at their free concert (with an estimated attendance of 500,000) in July 1969. Robert was using his Les Paul Custom with Marshall stack. At this time, the band recorded their first album 'In The Court Of The Crimson King' which was released in October 1969. Initially signed to Decca, the group became frustrated with the first recordings and left, later joining Island Records. Robert was possibly using Marshall amps on the album, though at some time during the second half of 1969 switched to a Hiwatt 100-watt head and favoured this for several years. He had a volume pedal, fuzz and Wah-Wah, whilst the acoustic guitar present on some tracks could have been a borrowed Guild according to information on frippgear.wordpress.com. The buzz around the album, which peaked at no. 5 in the UK, resulted in Atlantic Records signing the band for American distribution. This also saw a tour mounted in late 1969, yet the quick success of the group proved too much for Ian McDonald and Michael Giles. Both decided to leave upon their return to England.

Greg Lake felt that the loss of Ian and Michael fundamentally changed the dynamic of King Crimson and he left to pursue other musical projects, forming Emerson, Lake and Palmer. However, Greg was persuaded to provide vocals for the follow-up King Crimson album 'In The Wake Of Poseidon'. Robert eventually recruited old friend Gordon Haskell (vocals/bass) and Greg recommended drummer Andy McCulloch. Robert contributed Mellotron parts, as well as keyboards using a Hohner pianet and celesta on the record. Photographs from the studio show Robert with his Gibson ES 345 and a Hiwatt head with 4x12 in. cabinet. Despite the upheaval, 'In The Wake Of Poseidon' was met with many positive reviews and very

Robert Fripp (far right) with King Crimson.
MARKA / Alamy Stock Photo.

good placings in the UK and US charts – no. 4 and no. 31 respectively.

In 1970, King Crimson stayed off the road, with a lone appearance on 'Top of the Pops' being recorded for the single 'Cat Food' (Robert had his Les Paul Custom). At the end of the year, the band returned to the studio and recorded 'Lizard', with the addition of Mel Collins to the line-up on saxophone/flute. Robert bought a Martin acoustic to play on the album, whilst Peter Sinfield acquired a VCS3 synthesizer which was used by the band. A feature of 'Prince Rupert Awakes', which was part of the 'Lizard' suite, was Robert's backwards guitar part.

King Crimson returned to touring in 1971 (Mel Collins, Boz Burrell and Ian Wallace formed the band), and started with a residency at the Zoom Club, Frankfurt, before embarking on a UK-wide series of appearances. Robert seems to have mainly used his Gibson Les Paul Custom with Hiwatt and effects, though around this time he purchased a spare guitar, which was a contemporary Les Paul Custom with two pick-ups.

Buoyed by the success of the tour, Robert was ready to record 'Islands' in late 1971 before King Crimson travelled to the US for a tour at the end of the year. On the track 'Sailor's Tale', Robert used the VCS3 for a delay effect and consequently a very unique guitar sound was achieved. 'Ladies Of The Road' also featured backwards guitar parts and an interesting solo.

Tension between Robert and Peter built for some time before the latter was asked to leave at the end of 1971. The remaining members were back in America early in 1972 and some dates were recorded for the 'Earthbound' live album which appeared in mid-1972. At the end of this period, Robert decided to reform King Crimson with ex-Yes drummer Bill Bruford, John Wetton on bass/vocals, Jamie Muir playing percussion and David Cross on violin/keyboards. The new band toured to the end of 1972 developing a rapport which was displayed to full effect on 1973's 'Larks' Tongues In Aspic'. The title track, part one, has Robert developing a fuzz guitar sound and playing a Mellotron M400, whilst 'Book Of Saturday' has another backwards part and 'Talking Drum' has Robert manipulating his fuzz and Wah-Wah.

Jamie Muir left for personal reasons before a tour through Britain, Europe and America occurred between March and July 1973. With further dates scheduled in America and Europe later in the year, the band took the opportunity to make live recordings of the on-stage improvisations. The results were mixed with two studio recordings and released as 'Starless and Bible Black' in March 1974. The pace did not slacken for King Crimson in early 1974 as further concerts were held in America during the spring, then immediately after 'Red' was recorded. 'Fallen Angel' had Robert playing an acoustic guitar, yet this would prove to be one of the last times he played such an instrument on a King Crimson track. For 'Providence' he produced a flute part using the Mellotron, while on 'Starless' Robert devised a single note theme and used just two strings.

A short time before 'Red' went on sale in late summer 1974, Robert decided to split the group as he had recently experienced a spiritual awakening and needed to explore the matter further. A second live King Crimson album was released in 1975, featuring recordings from the US in 1974 and Robert also

assembled a retrospective album in 1976 – 'A Young Person's Guide To King Crimson' – featuring several highlights.

Robert had been active with other interests outside King Crimson. In 1972 he recorded 'The Heavenly Music Corporation' with Brian Eno of Roxy Music. The track was made using two Revox reel-to-reel tape recorders connected. Brian made 'loops' using a VCS3 for Robert to play over; then recorded certain passages which also looped creating a new part on top of those already recorded – a process that was later christened 'Frippertronics'. 'Swastika Girls' was created in a similar manner in the following year and the two tracks were released as an album, '(No Pussyfooting)'. Robert and Brian continued to collaborate and produced 'Evening Star' in 1975 using similar techniques. Robert contributed to Brian's solo albums, playing guitar for some tracks on 'Here Come The Warm Jets', 'Another Green World' and 'Before And After Science'. The pair played a series of live dates in 1975.

During late 1976, Robert worked with former Genesis member Peter Gabriel, providing guitar parts, and banjo, to the latter's eponymous debut solo record. Robert later joined Peter for a tour, but wanted to remain anonymous and played guitar off stage, also using a pseudonym to hide his identity.

Shortly after moving to New York in 1977, Robert was contacted by Brian Eno, who was working with David Bowie on the 'Heroes' album in Berlin. Robert was invited to provide lead guitar to several tracks. He was pictured in the studio with his Les Paul Custom and was possibly using a Marshall head and one 4x12 in. cabinet. The title track features a particularly well-known guitar part from Robert. Brian Eno initially played two synthesizer parts then Robert emulated them, playing while moving back and forth between the speakers to create controlled feedback from the guitar, whilst Brian was also manipulating the notes through the VCS3. Robert produced two more guitar parts which producer Tony Visconti then used together to create the overall sound.

After the David Bowie sessions, Robert produced Daryl Hall's album 'Sacred Songs' and featured on a group of tracks. He made a sole appearance on 'Urban Landscape' which was included on the record despite being in the vein of a Fripp/Eno collaboration. Daryl's record company deemed the whole album as too polarising to existing fans and shelved 'Sacred Songs' until 1980.

At the end of the 1970s, Robert worked with several 'new wave' artists, such as Blondie – 'Fade Away And Radiate' on the album 'Parallel Lines' – and Talking Heads ('I Zimra'), whilst also producing the Roches, a vocal trio consisting of sisters from New Jersey. Robert provided 'fripperies' to the group's 'Hammond Song'. He found time to work on two more Peter Gabriel albums, producing the second, known as 'Scratch'.

Hiwatt was started by Dave Reeves in the mid-1960s and in time became a significant competitor to Marshall in the UK. Reeves contracted wiring expert Harry Joyce to help cope with the demand for Hiwatt amps which came to be used by major acts such as Jethro Tull, the Moody Blues and the Who. Hiwatt amps, featuring high-quality Partridge transformers, and master volume controls, were available in 50-, 100-, 200- and 400-watt versions. Following Reeves' untimely death in 1981, Hiwatt has undergone a number of ownership tussles, but the amps are still available and as popular today.

In 1979, Robert's first solo album – 'Exposure' – was released and featured several collaborations with artists from recent years: Brian Eno, Daryl Hall, Terre Roche and Peter Gabriel. Appearances were made at record stores to promote the record, at which Robert played songs from the album, as well as demonstrations of 'Frippertronics'. A follow-up was quickly made – 'God Save The Queen'/'Under Heavy Manners' – mainly consisting of 'Frippertronics'. Under the title 'The League Of Gentlemen', Robert toured in 1980 with Barry Andrews (organ), Sara Lee (bass), Johnny Toobad (drums), though the latter was later replaced by Kevin Wilkinson. A live album was captured during the run of dates and appeared in 1981. Robert was using a Roland Jazz Chorus amp.

King Crimson was reformed in 1981, with Bill Bruford returning, whilst Adrian Belew was recruited as a second guitarist and Tony Levin came in on bass and Chapman 'Stick'. Initially performing as 'Discipline', the group toured in England and Europe, with Robert using a Roland GR-300 synthesizer guitar with the Jazz Chorus and a Roland SA09 'Saturn' keyboard, as well as aforementioned effects. Of the GR-300, Robert later commented in an interview for *Sound on Sound* magazine (December 1993): 'The GR300 is the only practical guitar synthesizer that I've ever used – it's exceptionally limited, but if you work within those limitations

Robert Fripp in performance.
John Atashian / Alamy Stock Photo.

there's nothing else to replace it. It does things nothing else will do.' Following the success of these initial gigs, the quartet decided to resurrect the King Crimson name as the music was fitting to what had been created previously, in addition to being an easier way of connecting to the existing fanbase. In the summer of 1981, the album 'Discipline' was recorded. The track 'Frame By Frame' is an example of Robert and Adrian's guitars working together, with the latter playing the main riff while Robert performs the same passage with accents in different places, in addition to double-time parts in the background. 'Thela Hun Ginjeet' also saw experiments with different time signatures as the band used 4/4 and Robert 7/8; 'Discipline' also employed a similar technique.

Touring Europe, the UK and US in late 1981 and 1982, 'Beat' was recorded soon after, with Robert providing keyboard parts on 'Sartori in Tangiers' and 'The Howler' in addition to guitar on all tracks. During a break in the band's commitments, Robert recorded with Andy Summers, who he had known from the 1960s. 'I Advance Masked' was the debut of the duo in late 1982, whilst a second collection of songs was produced as 'Bewitched' in 1984. In that year, the newest line-up of King Crimson released their final album, 'Three Of A Perfect Pair' before a tour of Japan and America.

In late 1983, Robert developed 'New Standard Tuning' for the guitar. This saw the low 'E' (sixth) string tuned to 'C', then descending to 'G', 'D', 'A', 'E' and 'G'. This made each open string 'perfect fifth' intervals, though a minor third had to be settled for between the 'E' and 'G' as the tension was too great to tune up to 'B', and expanded the range of ideas available on the guitar.

With the second demise of King Crimson, Robert was able to fully explore and promote the New Standard Tuning, founding Guitar Craft in 1985 to teach students this, in addition to technique, such as picking exercises. For the course, an Ovation 1867 electro-acoustic guitar was recommended by Robert. Talking to Tony Bacon in 1991 (and reproduced on www.reverb.com) Robert said he had become acutely aware of the limitations of standard tuning and was looking at alternatives when 'New Standard Tuning' presented itself out of the blue one day. He decided to fully embrace a new system at the end of King Crimson, as well as with the chance to teach arising. The tuning was seen as an opportunity to create new music as standard tuning had become associated too much with various styles. Whilst some musicians taking the course went on to use both standard and New Standard Tuning, Robert chose to concentrate solely on the latter.

At the end of the 1980s, Robert worked on Guitar Craft and performed live with the band formed from students of the course, the League of Crafty Guitarists. He made a record with his wife Toyah Willcox – 'The Lady Or The Tiger' – and began an association with David Sylvian (of the band Japan), playing on the latter's track 'Steel Cathedrals'. The pair later created an album together, 'The First Day', in 1993 and subsequently toured with a live album taken from the dates, 'Damage: Live'.

A change of guitars was made over this period as Robert wanted the option of whammy bar effects. Initially willing to modify a vintage Les Paul, he was dissuaded by a conscientious luthier and chose a Tokai Les Paul-style guitar, which was at the time building a reputation as a cheaper and quality alternative to the Gibson model.

Robert's Tokai was in black with Kahler tremolo, humbucker pick-ups with coil split and phase switch, whilst a hexaphonic midi pick-up was later added. Around the early 1990s, Robert also acquired Fernandes Les Paul-style guitars in gold and red sparkle finishes with a similar specification to the Tokai, whilst he had a custom sunburst Les Paul-style instrument built by 48th Street Guitars. After working with David Sylvian on 'The First Day' in 1993, Robert told *Sound on Sound* magazine (December 1993) about his set-up at the time. He used the Roland GR-300 and a fuzz pedal as a basic sound before combining other effects, such as from a Korg A2 multi-effect processor (also the A1 model) or the Zoom 9030. Robert had a Roland GP16 unit and Eventide 3000SE for octave pitching.

The Revox recorders had been retired and two TC Electronics TC2290 dynamic digital delay units were employed in their place, in addition to an Electro Harmonix 16-second delay. There was a Yamaha echo/harmonizer in use and a TC Electronic parametric EQ. A Carver Professional amplifier was directing sound to Tannoy speakers housed in Lockwood cabinets; a Sansamp simulator could also be called upon.

In the early 1990s, Robert left his management company after 20 years and formed his own record company Discipline Global Mobile. At this time, he decided to reform King Crimson. Initially, he wanted David Sylvian to join, though the latter did not feel comfortable working for such an established act. The members of the last incarnation agreed to play together again, along with Trey Gunn on Chapman Stick and Pat Mastelotto as a second drummer. Initially, an EP for Japan was recorded – 'Vroom' – before 'Thrak' was released in April 1995. An extensive tour of Europe, America and Japan was mounted in support, with a visual recording made of the

Robert Fripp at Fairport's Cropredy Convention. Banbury, UK. August 11, 2022.
MusicLive / Alamy Stock Photo.

gig at the Nakano Sun Plaza, Tokyo, later released.

King Crimson found themselves creatively drained by the mid-1990s. An opportunity for live improvisational shows arose which prompted Robert to come up with the idea of 'FraKtals' where members of the band joined together, though not all, in order to devise new music and develop the ideas before presenting to the complete King Crimson line-up. The smaller bands were known as 'ProjeKcts' and several variations were formed through to the new millennium, all of which featured Robert. Live recordings mainly resulted, though 'ProjeKct 2' (Robert, Adrian and Trey) did make a studio album.

When King Crimson next assembled for recording, Bill Bruford had left to pursue other musical interests and Tony Levin was busy with other projects. The remaining members created 'The ConstruKction Of Light' which was completed in May 2000. The title track features Robert and Adrian playing the melody line individually in alternate notes, whilst on 'The World's My Oyster Soup Kitchen Floor Wax Museum' Robert plays an interesting solo using a synthesized piano sound.

Around this time, an improvisational album was released under the 'ProjeKct X' title, despite featuring King Crimson members, called 'Heaven And Earth'.

After touring and releasing two EPs in the early 2000s, King Crimson's final studio album to date was produced in 2002 and released in March 2003 – 'The Power To Believe'. In 2004, Robert and Brian Eno completed a new album of music, 'The Equatorial Stars' and followed this in 2006 with another record of collaborations spanning the period 1992–2006. For King Crimson's 40th anniversary in 2008, Tony Levin rejoined and drummer Gavin Harrison became a member of the group.

Robert collaborated with Jakko Jakszyk and Mel Collins for 2011's 'A Scarcity Of Miracles'. Though an announcement of retirement was made by Robert in 2012, he recanted the following year and King Crimson began touring in 2014, with Jakko and Mel added to the existing line-up. The band continues to be active up to the present. In 2019, Robert was featured on *Premier Guitar*'s 'Rig Rundown' series and his guitar tech Biff Blumfumgagnge went through the equipment. Robert mainly used his Fernandes Les Paul-style guitar, of which he had several and at the time using a gold top, with sustainer neck pick-up, Seymour Duncan bridge pick-up, midi pick-up in front of the bridge, on/off switch, synthesizer switch, sustainer, Kahler tremolo and Sperzel locking tuners. A Roland GR1 guitar synthesizer unit was employed, along with two Eventide H8000 effects processors and two Eventide H3500 Ultra Harmonizers for delay. Robert had several volume controls and a Digitech Whammy II, whilst an Axe-FX II XL preamp and effects processor was employed. The Omenie Mellotronics M3000 app for iPad was used to provide Mellotron effects. To aid grip on the pick Robert used Mr Zog's Sex Wax, which was originally created as a substance for coating surfboards.

DAVID GILMOUR

Widely regarded, David Gilmour has achieved his reputation thanks to thoughtful and melodic guitar playing with Pink Floyd. This is demonstrated on the incredibly popular albums 'Dark Side Of The Moon', 'Wish You Were Here', etc.

David's interest in music began in the mid-1950s with the rock 'n' roll boom. He initially liked Elvis and Bill Haley before favouring the Everly Brothers. At 13, David borrowed a guitar from a friend and soon discovered an affinity for the instrument. He was encouraged by his parents and they presented him with *The Folksinger's Guitar Guide* by Pete Seeger which helped David to master the basics.

Around 1962, David was playing in a local band, the Ramblers, using a Burns Trisonic. Yet, he did not like the instrument and by 1963 had changed to a Hofner Club 60 which was favoured for several years. David is pictured playing the guitar with another group, Jokers Wild, and appears to be using a blonde Vox amplifier. While studying for his A-Levels, David decided that he wanted to seriously pursue a career in music and left his studies to perform with Jokers Wild in and around Cambridge. The band developed a reputation locally and was even scouted by a representative for Brian Epstein, though the interest went no further.

Despite this setback, David continued to push forward with Jokers Wild and a residency at a hotel in Marbella was arranged for the summer of 1966. With this a relative success, the band was able to book similar gigs on the continent in Belgium and Paris towards the end of the year. Early in March 1967, David celebrated his 21st birthday and to mark the occasion his parents bought him a Fender Telecaster, which was white with a rosewood neck. He had little opportunity to show off his present to a paying audience as the group found work difficult to obtain in Paris.

Jokers Wild, then known as Flowers, returned to London later in 1967 and David got temporary work to make ends meet. His appearance on the London music scene coincided with the growing problems with the band Pink Floyd, started by close friend Syd Barrett, who was withdrawing from the pressure experienced by their success. At the end of the year, David was approached by the members of Pink Floyd to act as a second guitarist, though soon became the main guitarist when Syd left in early 1968. David was thrust into his new role, performing in the UK at several gigs. An early recorded appearance of the band was made on the French TV show 'Bouton Rouge' and David used his Telecaster to perform 'Astronomy Dominie', 'Flaming', 'Set The Controls For The Heart Of The Sun' and 'Let There Be More Light'. He had a similar Telecaster as backup, which was Syd's guitar, and is using a Selmer Stereomaster amp with 2x12 in. cabinet. This was 100 watts when used with one cabinet, or two channels at 50 watts to achieve a stereo sound. The amp was likely used for much of David's work through to mid-1969 and he also utilised a Binson Echorec, a fuzz and Wah-Wah pedal.

Late in 1967, Pink Floyd had begun recording the second album 'A Saucerful Of Secrets' as a follow-up to the impressive 'Piper At The Gates Of Dawn'. Sessions continued in early 1968 and David was involved in the process, playing electric guitar on all but two tracks ('Remember A Day' and 'Jugband Blues'). David mainly contributed to the group's textured compositions – in the main spearheaded by bassist Roger Waters – rather than bringing his own tracks to Pink Floyd. Released in late June 1968, 'A Saucerful Of Secrets' reached the top ten in the UK, though did not quite receive the acclaim of the debut record, despite some strong moments.

When not in the studio, Pink Floyd had heavy touring commitments during 1968, appearing in Europe and England up to the summer when a series of gigs were arranged for America. Whilst travelling in the country, David's Telecaster was lost by an airline. He had to switch to a white Fender Stratocaster with rosewood fretboard (mid-1960s model with large headstock and Fender logo), which had been obtained shortly before the tour, and soon after purchased a new Fender Telecaster in natural with a maple neck. American musician, Frank Zappa used this guitar during a guest appearance with the band in France during October 1969 and the neck pick-up had the cover removed. During the American tour in 1968, Pink Floyd did not transport amps from Britain and used those provided at venues or loaned from local stores, being a mixture of several brands.

The band continued to promote the new album in Europe to the end of the year. One filmed performance for the French show 'Samedi et Compagnie' in September 1968 has David with an unusual and unidentified guitar. This was a thinline Gibson ES-style guitar in white with neck featuring Gretsch-type 'thumbnail' markers. Another French TV appearance, on 'Forum Musiques' in January 1969 sees David with a Gibson ES 345 guitar with stopbar tailpiece.

The band's first project of 1969 was the soundtrack for the Barbet Schroeder feature 'More'. This was a mixture of instrumental music and songs, which featured David on lead vocals. Of particular interest for his guitar playing are the tracks 'Nile Song', 'Up The Khyber', 'More Blues', 'A Spanish Piece' (his first solo writing credit within the band) and 'Dramatic Theme'. The film was unfavourably reviewed at the time, mostly because of sex and drug themes, which also led to poor distribution. Nevertheless, the soundtrack album was unhindered and reached the top ten in the UK during mid-1969.

In the spring, Pink Floyd developed an idea for performing music with scenes acted on stage. Called 'The Man and the Journey', this was toured in England from April to September. On some dates, the band performed songs from the two albums and early in the tour two nights in Birmingham and Manchester were recorded for inclusion on a live album. This project later evolved into the band's third studio album, 'Ummagumma', which featured one disc of live tracks and a second of pieces written by the four band members. David's

David Gilmour with Pink Floyd performing live on stage at Ahoy in Rotterdam, Holland in February 1977 during the Animals tour.
Gijsbert Hanekroot / Alamy Stock Photo.

contribution was 'The Narrow Way', on which he played all the instruments and wrote his first lyrics. The song starts with an acoustic section, which was likely played using David's Levin acoustic, then being joined by a slide part on electric guitar. A second section begins with an electric guitar using fuzz before descending into 'experimental' sounds. For the final part, David uses a Leslie speaker, as well as echo for a slide part.

David made a change to his amplifiers in the summer of 1969, adopting the newly formed Hiwatt's 100-watt DR-103 head. Initially, he used two which powered four WEM 4x12 in. cabinets equipped with Fane Crescendo speakers. Around a year later, a third head was acquired and often appeared with the other two on stage in a custom-made housing, though one was only a spare.

The end of the 1960s saw Pink Floyd in Rome working on tracks for acclaimed director Michelangelo Antonioni's film 'Zabriskie Point'. Despite completing several tracks, only three were included on the soundtrack: 'Heart Beat, Pig Meat'; 'Crumbling Land'; 'Come In Number 51, Your Time Is Up'. The second mentioned is interesting for the acoustic guitar part David played, whilst the other two songs continue the experimental/soundscape theme of other compositions from this period.

A start was made on the next album – 'Atom Heart Mother' – in early 1970, while the band played some dates in Britain. A US tour was organised for the early summer and soon after arriving, David acquired a second Fender Stratocaster – a late 1960s model in black with a rosewood neck. He is seen playing the guitar in footage of a performance made for a local TV station in San Francisco. In mid-May, when in New Orleans for a gig, the band's equipment was stolen. Most of the items were later recovered, apart from David's white and black Stratocasters. Before returning to England at the end of the tour, David visited Manny's Music in New York and bought another black Stratocaster (again a late 1960s model) though with a maple neck.

Work continued on the album in early June and the main 'Atom Heart Mother' suite was completed. Running nearly 25 minutes in length, David weaved a variety of guitar textures into the track, including slide, blues-style soloing and multiple guitar parts. The second side of the album also featured solo compositions from the four band members and David contributed 'Fat Old Sun' which was mainly acoustic (possibly a Gibson J45), though featured a rock guitar solo. The 'Atom Heart Mother' suite was performed at the Bath Festival in late June 1970, with a choir and brass section joining the group on stage in the early morning. David first used his new Stratocaster publicly during this appearance.

Another new Stratocaster was seen with David a little later. This was gifted to him and had a 1959 sunburst body paired to a 1963 neck with rosewood fingerboard. David played the guitar during the Hyde Park Free Concert in July 1970.

Pink Floyd continued to perform 'Atom Heart Mother' through to the end of the year at both home and abroad in Europe and America for a second time. The promotion helped the album to reach no. 1 in the UK and no. 55 in America. Whilst David was in the US, he purchased a Gibson Les Paul Special (double cutaway) and a Bill Lewis custom-built guitar. This was made from mahogany and had an ebony fingerboard with 24 frets. Two Lewis humbuckers were provided and these had the ability for coil-split.

Over the period, January to August 1971, Pink Floyd developed material for their sixth studio album, 'Meddle'. Notable features of David's guitar playing over the tracks were the use of slide and open or alternate tunings, with open Em used on 'One Of These Days', open G on 'Fearless', and for 'Seamus' the guitar was tuned down one whole step. David mainly used a Stratocaster, though an acoustic also featured, along with a Fender twin-neck lap steel guitar. A Dallas Arbiter fuzz continued to be used, along with the Binson Echorec and Vox Wah-Wah. The latter provided the interesting 'seagull-like' effect around halfway through the epic 'Echoes', as David plugged the leads into the pedal the opposite way. David's Bill Lewis guitar was used for one of the early solos in the track.

David Gilmour at Merriweather Post Pavilion, Columbia, Maryland in June 1973.
Gado Images / Alamy Stock Photo.

Whilst a proportion of 1971 was spent in the studio, the band was also on the road, starting off in England before travelling to the Continent. A maiden excursion to Australia and Japan followed in August before a tour of America at the end of the year to promote the release of 'Meddle'. This did not perform well there in comparison to 'Atom Heart Mother' owing to poor publicity. In contrast, the album continued Pink Floyd's success in England, reaching no. 3 in the album charts.

Several pieces of footage from this period exist, most notably the 'Live in Pompeii' film made in October and later released in September 1972. The band were seen in the empty Roman amphitheatre playing live two tracks from 'Meddle' – 'Echoes' and 'One Of These Days' – as well as others from the back catalogue still in the touring repertoire – 'Careful With That Axe Eugene', 'A Saucerful Of Secrets' and 'Set The Controls For The Heart Of The Sun'. David uses his touring equipment in the film and this included the trio of Hiwatt heads and WEM cabinets, with Binson Echorec, as well as fuzz and Wah-Wah pedals. New additions to his rig were a volume pedal and a Leslie speaker cabinet. David primarily used his black Fender Stratocaster throughout the year.

Pink Floyd soon moved on to new ideas for their next project. Initially titled 'Eclipse', the suite of music developed from early 1972 was subsequently released on the album 'The Dark Side Of The Moon' in March 1973. The band began playing some of the songs during a tour of England which took place between January 17 and February 20. Shortly after this concluded, Pink Floyd was again approached by director Barbet Schroeder to complete a soundtrack for his film 'La Vallée'. The band had just two weeks to complete this task and produced a concise group of songs to fit various points in the film. The soundtrack was released in June 1972 as 'Obscured By Clouds' and again performed well in the UK charts.

In March 1972, Pink Floyd returned to Japan for a small number of gigs, then in mid-April began the first of two American tours during the year, with this concentrating on the East Coast, whilst the second in September took in the south, West Coast and Canada. The year ended with a number of dates in Europe. There were several changes in David's equipment. A Colorsound Power Boost was added to his pedals, along with a Univox Uni-Vibe. Around mid-1972, David decided to switch the necks between his two Stratocasters. The black model had the 1963 rosewood neck, whilst the 1959 sunburst model the late 1960s neck with maple fretboard. A third Stratocaster in black was seen for a time in the year and this was a contemporary model with 'bullet' truss rod and three-bolt neck.

Between dates in the busy touring schedule during 1972, Pink Floyd began recording 'The Dark Side Of The Moon' in June and completed the record by January 1973. David mainly used his black Stratocaster, with certain parts played on the Bill Lewis Custom – 'Money' (last solo), 'Brain Damage' and 'Eclipse' – and the Fender pedal steel for 'Breathe' and 'The Great Gig In The Sky'. For both the latter tracks, David tuned the pedal steel to an open G6 chord, which was like open G with low to high strings (6–2) D, G, D, G, B, though the high E remained that note instead of being tuned down to D. The Binson Echorec was used for most of the tracks and either the Uni-Vibe or Fuzz had a role on most, sometimes both. David also utilised a Leslie speaker on 'Brain Damage' and 'Eclipse'. Highlights of David's guitar playing on the album were 'Time' (both fills and solo), 'Money', which had a double-tracked solo and an automatic double-tracked solo on the Bill Lewis guitar, and 'Any Colour You Like' for the double Uni-Vibe guitar part and solo.

In conjunction with the album release in March, Pink Floyd embarked on another US tour across much of the East Coast. One noticeable change was made to David's black Stratocaster early in 1973, and lasting to the middle of the year, was the addition of a Gibson humbucker between the middle and bridge pick-ups. Evidently, this change was not successful, as David swapped the pick-guard and pick-ups from the black Stratocaster with bullet truss rod for the second tour of the US which ran from June 17 to 29.

Despite 'The Dark Side Of The Moon' being highly successful in the UK and America (for the first time in the latter country), Pink Floyd had become weary following years of hard work. To the end of 1973, the band only played a benefit concert for Robert Wyatt, formerly drummer in Soft Machine, who had become disabled after a fall from a window. Though the band returned to the studio in early 1974, the sessions were not particularly productive. Some new songs were again worked into the live set when Pink Floyd toured France in June 1974, then later in the year when a number of gigs took place in Britain. For both tours, David acquired two new pedal steels by Jedson in blonde and red, and tuned to open G6. Also, during 1973, David had started to use a pedal board occupied by earlier-mentioned models, with the addition of an MXR Phase 90 in 1974. Further changes included the purchase of new Hiwatt amp heads and WEM cabinets and David's black Stratocaster was transformed again through the fitting of a black pick-guard, yet the pick-ups and knobs remained white. A new guitar on the tour was a 1959 Custom Telecaster with humbucker in the neck position.

Between January and July 1975, Pink Floyd recorded the tracks they had been working on and these were assembled for the 'Wish You Were Here' album released in September. The first track on the record was 'Shine On You Crazy Diamond' which was a five-part suite of music of varying textures. David is pictured in Abbey Road studio one recording the track with his Binson Echorec through a Fender Showman 100-watt head and 2x15 cabinet, as well as his usual Hiwatt and WEM cabinet; the Phase 90 and Colorsound boost also appeared on the song. 'Welcome To The Machine' followed and this had an acoustic part David played, using his 1969 Martin D-35.

According to the catalogue for the sale of his guitar collection in 2019, he had purchased the Martin in 1971 and first committed the guitar to tape during the 'Obscured By Clouds' sessions. 'The Dark Side Of The Moon' did not feature acoustic guitar and he returned to the Martin for the 'Wish You Were Here' sessions. David also added 12-string acoustic to 'Welcome To The Machine' and again used a recently-acquired Martin. Starting side two of the original album, 'Have A Cigar' has David playing a rock guitar part and noteworthy solo at the end, which interestingly segues through an imagined switch via a radio dial into title track 'Wish You Were Here'. This has a Martin 12-string intro riff, then followed by the Martin D-35 and a Fender pedal steel solo slightly lower in the mix. The pedal steel makes a follow-up appearance on the conclusion to the 'Shine On You Crazy Diamond' suite and David's tone is coloured by several of his effect pedals. Whilst perhaps overshadowed by 'The Dark Side Of The Moon' in terms of sales and critical acclaim, 'Wish You Were Here' has been cited by both David and Rick Wright to be their favourite Pink Floyd album.

The release of 'Wish You Were Here' in September 1975 was preceded by a tour of America over tour legs (April 8–27, June 7–28) and an appearance headlining the Knebworth Festival on July 5. The band decided not to promote the new record and scheduled no concerts for 1976. Pink Floyd used this time to rest, build a recording studio and work on new material. Though existing from the 'Wish You Were Here' sessions, the tracks 'Sheep' and 'Dogs' were revisited for the 'Animals' project and added to the new compositions, 'Pigs (Three Different Ones)' and 'Pigs On The Wing', which was split into two parts bookending the record. 'Dogs' saw the acoustic rhythm guitar part played by Roger Waters on an Ovation Custom Legend six-string, which was one of a pair (the other a 12-string) ordered by the band, though these later became part of David's collection. The electric guitar parts and solos were played by David on his Custom Telecaster tuned down one whole step, mainly using a Yamaha rotating speaker as well as a fuzz pedal. The last-mentioned was custom-built by Pete Cornish, being similar to an Electro Harmonix 'Big Muff' pedal, which David ultimately preferred and returned to later. During the sessions David had completely upgraded his pedal board with a bespoke unit assembled by Pete Cornish. 'Pigs (Three Different Ones)' saw David play a fretless bass as Roger Waters had a rhythm part he wanted to play, though the other guitar parts were David's. He used several effects including, boost, fuzz and delay, in addition to new effects – an Electro Harmonix 'Electric Mistress' flanger and a talk box.

'Animals' was completed at the end of 1976 and released in early 1977. The band toured Europe in the first three months of the year, then played concerts in America, again over two legs (April/May, June/July). David mainly used his Stratocaster and Custom Telecaster, which was tuned down and now fitted with an exposed Stratocaster pick-up, through the Hiwatt and WEM amps and cabs. The Leslie speaker was replaced by the Yamaha model used in the studio and the pedals were assembled on the new Pete Cornish board. Many of the previously mentioned units were incorporated into this, alongside master tone and volume pedals. 'Snowy' White joined the band as second guitarist for the tour.

After a busy 1977, the band broke for a time to pursue their own interests. David reunited with former Jokers Wild bandmates Rick Wills on bass and Willie Wilson on drums to record his first solo album – 'David Gilmour'. He used his Stratocaster mainly, though added a 1954 model in white and anodised gold pick-guard with serial number 0001 to his collection just before the sessions, as well as a Gretsch Duo Jet in silver sparkle finish. This likely found use, in addition to the Custom Telecaster and lap steel on 'No Way'. Amps continued to be as mentioned for 'Animals'. The Pete Cornish pedal board was slightly modified by changes in pedals, with the Electro Harmonix 'Big Muff' taking a permanent position in place of the custom-built unit, whilst the Uni-Vibe was taken off and used in isolation on 'Cry From The Street'. A promotional film was recorded and released to promote the record in place of a tour. David played five songs – 'There's No Way Out Of Here', 'So Far Away', 'No Way', 'I Can't Breathe Anymore' and 'Mihalis'. David employed his black Stratocaster for three of the tracks, though changed to a well-worn mid-1950s sunburst

Fender Esquire (with neck pick-up fitted) for 'No Way' and a black Gretsch Duo Jet on 'I Can't Breathe Anymore'. As well as the Hiwatt, David had a Fender Dual Showman 100-watt head.

Whilst David had been recording his solo album, Roger Waters began formulating plans for Pink Floyd's next project. Semi-autobiographical, 'The Wall' told the story of 'Pink', from his childhood to rise as a 'rock star', his disillusionment with life as a famous musician, then redemption through enlightenment. David's amp and pedal use continued mostly unchanged from his solo album through 'The Wall' sessions, yet Pete Cornish provided a more compact pedal board for studio use. The black Stratocaster continued to be David's main guitar which was modified to have a DiMarzio single coil pick-up in the bridge position and a Charvel maple neck was installed. A new guitar used by David on the track 'Another Brick In The Wall (Part Two)' was a 1955 Gibson Les Paul in all-gold finish with two P-90 pick-ups and a wrap tailpiece. The instrument was used for the solo and plugged directly into the mixing desk and recorded before being fed out through a Mesa Boogie amp to be captured again. David also used a variation on 'Nashville tuning' for the song 'Hey You'. This involved taking the E, A, D and G strings off his Ovation acoustic and replacing them with octave strings from a 12-string set, though in this instance David used a high E for the low E string which achieved a two-octave increase in the note rather than one for the others. Released in late 1979, 'The Wall' was supported with a series of shows in 1980 and 1981. Owing to the staging of the concept and songs, the concerts were limited to Los Angeles, Uniondale (Long Island) and London in 1980 and Dortmund and London in 1981. David used the same rig as on the 'Animals' tour, though added his Gibson Les Paul to the guitar line-up. This was in addition to the Fender Esquire used on his solo film and two Ovation acoustics – one with steel strings, the other with nylon.

A follow-up release to 'The Wall' was planned using some of the out-takes from the sessions, yet in 1982 Roger Waters was concerned with the British government's handling of the Falklands conflict. He was moved to repurpose some of the recordings for a new project criticising war in general. David held a similar view, though did not like the musical direction of the project and tempers between the pair became strained. David contributed to many of the tracks on 'The Final Cut' album, however, using much of the same equipment as 'The Wall' sessions. The black Stratocaster saw further changes as a Seymour Duncan single coil was fitted in the bridge position and another Charvel maple neck was used, though this had 22 frets, rather than 21 as previously.

Following the animosity generated during 'The Final Cut' sessions, Pink Floyd entered an uncertain period during the mid-1980s. David recorded his second solo album in 1983, 'About Face'. Released in 1984, featuring a more 'commercial' contemporary rock sound than much of Pink Floyd's material, the record matched the modest success of his debut. At this time, David made several changes to his equipment. He started to limit the use of his black Stratocaster, which had been fitted with a Kahler locking tremolo, and received several contemporary Fender Stratocaster 1957 reissues directly from the company. David favoured these on the ensuing tour in support of 'About Face', particularly a white model then later a red guitar. The Pete Cornish pedal board was also afforded a break from the road and a Boss SCC-700 controller was used with a number of the company's pedals; overdrive, distortion, equaliser, delay and chorus. David also used a Mesa Boogie head as a drive for two Fender Twin Reverb heads into the WEM cabinets.

After working on his own project, David was keen to return to Pink Floyd, though Roger Waters was reluctant and an agreement was reached for him to leave. Pink Floyd began recording new material in late 1986 with producer Bob Ezrin, who had previously worked on 'The Wall'. The sessions took place on David's recently acquired houseboat that was converted into a studio – Astoria. This influenced David's sound as his usual amps were too powerful for the confined conditions and he adopted a Fender Super Champ amplifier, as well as a Gallien-Krueger 250ML 100-watt lunch-box size combo. The use of Boss pedals continued though others were mixed in. David used his red Stratocaster, which – along with the other Stratocasters – had been fitted with EMG SA pick-ups to reduce noise interference, and a recently arrived Steinberger GL 3T.

'A Momentary Lapse of Reason' appeared towards the end of 1987 and an extensive tour followed, beginning in September in Canada, taking in much of North America to the end of the year. Early in 1988, Pink Floyd played Australia, New Zealand and Japan, then returned to America before a stint in Europe over the summer, with a climax in the USA during August. In 1989, the band had more dates which focussed on Europe and in 1990 a one-off gig was held at Knebworth. The red and white Stratocasters were David's main guitars and he also used a reissue Fender Telecaster in blonde. For acoustic songs, David adopted a Takamine guitar and the Jedson lap steels again found use. Pedals continued to be a mixture of Boss and other brands, whilst rack-mounted effects were also present. David started with the Fender Twin Reverb heads, though later reverted back to Hiwatt.

In 1994 'The Division Bell' was the product of fruitful sessions conducted at several London studios (including David's Astoria) throughout 1993. David was pictured recording with a Gretsch 6121 Chet Atkins model, in addition to his Telecaster 1952 reissue. A Gibson J200 'Celebrity' (limited to 90 guitars) acoustic was used for several tracks, most notably 'Take It Back' and 'Keep Talking' where David played with an Ebow into a Zoom effects unit plugged into the recording console. On 'Poles Apart' David tuned his acoustic guitar to 'DADGAD', whilst 'Keep Talking' sees a return to the talk box effect and a Digitech Whammy was present on a small number of tracks. In the studio, David appears to have used Fender Bassman amps in partnership with Hiwatt 2x12 in. combos and a Maestro Rover rotary speaker.

In contrast to 'A Momentary Lapse Of Reason', 'The Division Bell' tour schedule was modest, though still travelled throughout North America and Europe in 1994. David travelled with an extensive rig, with instruments comprising three Stratocasters (two red and one white), two Telecasters (both 1952 reissues), two Gibson J200 'Celebrity' acoustics

David Gilmour with Custom Telecaster.
Pictorial Press Ltd / Alamy Stock Photo.

David Gilmour performing on stage, Live 8 Concert, Hyde Park, 2005.
PA Images / Alamy Stock Photo.

and the Jedson lap steels. A large number of effect pedals were carried to achieve various sounds in the set which spanned Pink Floyd's career, with several rack-mounted units also employed. Hiwatt 100-watt heads continued to be David's main amplifiers, though these now fed two Marshall cabinets in addition to a pair of WEM cabinets. A duo of custom-built rotating speakers was also employed.

David took a step back from music in the last half of the 1990s, though returned to the stage early in the new millennium with a small number of acoustic shows in London and Paris. David's main guitars were a Martin D-28 and a Taylor 712-CE. Whilst continuing to work on solo material into the mid-2000s, a benefit concert to end world poverty was organised for July 2005. The 'Live 8' event was held in five countries, with the four members of Pink Floyd reunited for the first time in two decades as part of the London show. The band played four songs, 'Breathe', 'Money', 'Wish You Were Here' and 'Comfortably Numb'. David returned to his black Stratocaster and also played his Gibson J200 'Celebrity'. Amplification and effects were similar to the previous Pink Floyd tour.

Soon after the 'Live 8' performance, David released his third solo album 'On An Island' and this was a worldwide success. A European and American tour followed in support of the record and this saw David continue the use of the black Stratocaster, along with several other old favourites, in addition to new guitars – a 1956 Gibson Les Paul with Bigsby tremolo and a 1958 Gibson 'Country and Western' acoustic. David commissioned a new pedal board from Pete Cornish, who also worked on many of the pedals to reduce signal losses and preserve the integrity of the tone. The final show from the tour was recorded and filmed for release later as 'Live in Gdansk' during 2008.

In the years following 'On An Island', David worked with a number of other artists, both guest appearances and a collaboration with electronic group the Orb on the album 'Metallic Spheres'. He continued to develop new material for his own album and released 'Rattle That Lock' in 2015. David continued to use the black Stratocaster on the ensuing tour along with the 1956 Gibson Les Paul with Bigsby, while also bringing the sunburst Fender Esquire back on stage. A new pedal board was assembled to control the various effects and David used just one 50-watt Hiwatt head with an Alessandro head into WEM cabinets.

David has been a patron of several charities over the years and in June 2019 he auctioned well over 100 guitars from his collection to raise money to help reduce climate change. Included was his black Stratocaster, which sold for over £3,000,000 and was for a time the most expensive guitar ever auctioned. In total the sale amounted to nearly £17,000,000.

Peter Green playing at the Rhodes Centre, Bishops Stortford, Hertfordshire, England in 1968.
CJM Photography / Alamy Stock Photo.

PETER GREEN

At the forefront of the British 'Blues Boom' of the mid-1960s, Peter Green influenced a generation of guitarists with his melodic phrasing and restrained approach. First playing with John Mayall, he went on to found Fleetwood Mac. With the band, he expanded his reputation by becoming a distinctive song-writer, achieving success with 'Albatross', 'Black Magic Woman', 'Man Of The World', 'Oh Well' and 'The Green Manalishi (With The Two Prong Crown)'. Many of Peter's songs were created with his 1959 Gibson Les Paul Standard, featuring a reversed pick-up that provided a unique voice for an inimitable guitarist.

Peter came of age in the skiffle and rock 'n' roll boom of the mid- to late 1950s and his first record purchase was 'Whole Lotta Shakin' Goin' On' by Jerry Lee Lewis. Around this time, Peter's older brother Len returned home with a guitar and demonstrated some chords for the enthralled youngster. Along with his other brother Michael, Peter soon had a Spanish-style guitar and the pair would play together. Peter was more adept at performing lead and would solo as his brother played chords. Both soon had several self-penned songs at their disposal.

Despite his ability with the guitar, Peter decided to take up the bass when joining his first group, the Ken Cats, later Bobby Dennis and the Dominoes. He bought a Star bass and a Fenton Weill 15-watt amp. The group did not stay together very long and he moved on to another local band, the Muskrats. Whilst playing mainly pop songs of the day, Peter developed an interest in the growing British blues movement and would attend Yardbirds gigs to study the work of Eric Clapton.

In early 1966, Peter decided he wanted to be a professional musician, returning to the guitar. He found work with Peter B's Looners, which was busy on the London club circuit (also featuring Mick Fleetwood on drums), and played a Harmony Meteor acquired from a fellow bandmate in an earlier group. One single was recorded (as The Peter B's) – 'If You Wanna Be Happy', with 'Jodrell Blues' as the B-side. The lead track was organ-led, yet the B-side allowed Peter to display his soloing skills with the blues-based song. By this time, he had likely acquired a Gibson Les Paul Standard. Perhaps influenced by Eric Clapton's effective use of the model, Peter bought the guitar second-hand from a central London music shop.

Peter B's Looners soon metamorphosed into Shotgun Express with Rod Stewart and Beryl Marsden on vocals. Peter was only involved with this line-up for a couple of months, as the opportunity to join John Mayall's group presented itself following Eric Clapton's departure.

John Mayall commented to *Beat Instrumental No. 42* of October 1966: '… in Peter Green we have a replacement who is a young genius. He's better known than Eric was when he joined, and for my money he'll be better than Eric … Peter is more interested in playing blues than being a star. Eric's gone all "show biz".'

Audiences declined for a short period whilst Peter grappled with performing much of the recently released 'Blues Breakers With Eric Clapton' album in a way that pleased both fans and himself. Peter used his Gibson Les Paul and an early Marshall JTM 45 50-watt head and 4x12 in. cabinet.

Initially, Peter had the neck pick-up in the standard orientation (with the pole pieces close to the fingerboard), then around 1967 this changed 180 degrees. This was due to an issue with the pick-up which required repair at the point of purchase; Peter apparently continued to play the Les Paul with just the bridge pick-up for a time. When reinstalled, the pick-up was the 'wrong' way round and had been repaired, yet a further mistake had occurred as the magnet had been removed and reinserted the wrong way, reversing the polarity. Evidently, Peter thought the repair was good enough and made no further changes. The modification resulted in the bridge and neck pick-ups being 'out of phase' when both selected, producing a 'thinner' sound than usual.

Shortly after Peter joined John Mayall, the group recorded two tracks, 'Looking Back' and 'So Many Roads'. Further sessions undertaken to the end of the year saw songs completed for the album 'A Hard Road', released in February 1967. Peter provided vocals for 'You Don't Love Me' (a cover of the Willie Cobbs song), whilst also writing 'The Same Way', which he sang, and 'The Supernatural'. The latter is a standout track, with Peter using the sustain of his guitar and reverb to good effect.

After completing these sessions, the band backed American harmonica player and singer Paul Butterfield on several songs, with an EP released – 'John Mayall's Bluesbreakers With Paul Butterfield'. The group kept a busy schedule of gigs through to the end of 1966 and into 1967. The latter year started well with 'A Hard Road' peaking at no. 8 in the UK charts. Yet, changes were soon made to the line-up, with drummer Aynsley Dunbar replaced by Mick Fleetwood on Peter's suggestion. This new roster was short-lived and in June 1967 Peter decided to leave the band.

Originally unsure of the direction to take, with a stint playing the blues in Chicago considered, Peter decided to form his own band. His first recruit was Mick Fleetwood, followed by slide guitarist Jeremy Spencer, who had been recommended to Peter by producer Mike Vernon, then bassist Bob Brunning. John Mayall's bassist John McVie was undecided over an offer to join, though ultimately accepted and replaced Brunning. The group was named Fleetwood Mac after an instrumental track recorded by Peter and the rhythm section of John Mayall's band at a session earlier in the year; Peter had considered forming a 'power trio' like Cream or the Jimi Hendrix Experience.

Fleetwood Mac rehearsed for around a month before the first gig at the Windsor Jazz and Blues Festival in mid-August. Peter was dedicated to making a success of the venture and spent much of his free time obtaining gear for the band, microphones, etc. Yet, for the festival Fleetwood Mac used equipment provided by the organisers as Peter's Les Paul was plugged in to a WEM PA system. This was inadequately powered and contemporary reports detail technical problems

Peter Green's Gibson Les Paul.
Richard Henry.

marring performances. Nevertheless, *Melody Maker* gave a favourable notice for Fleetwood Mac.

Up to the end of 1967, the band played gigs across the country, whilst recording tracks for a debut album – 'Fleetwood Mac' – released in February 1968, reaching no. 4 in the UK charts. The songs were a mixture of covers and originals, with Jeremy Spencer sharing the credits with Peter. The album was faithful to the blues and allowed Peter to display his mastery of the style. He shows his skill with the harmonica on 'Looking For Somebody' and resonator for 'The World Keep On Turning'. Peter almost certainly used his Les Paul for much of the album, though his amp choice is unclear. He might have continued with the Marshall, though he was also pictured, around the period, with a Vox AC100 head and a Vox bass cabinet with 1x12 in. and 1x18 in. speakers.

Fleetwood Mac's first single of 1968 was released at the end of March. 'Black Magic Woman' was written by Peter after he found inspiration from the Otis Rush song 'All Your Love'. The song peaked at no. 38 in the UK charts, though this was considered a disappointment. Later, the track was popularised by Mexican-American guitarist Carlos Santana, although some changes were made to the song. In April, Fleetwood Mac was busy with a Scandinavian tour and attending recording sessions for the second Album 'Mr Wonderful', which appeared in late August. Half of the 12 tracks were written by Peter. Yet, the band chose to incorporate a horn section to the recordings, as well as enlisting Christine Perfect on piano and keyboards.

Soon after the album had been recorded, Fleetwood Mac travelled to America for their debut tour. This proved to be quite unsuccessful, as poor PR and a lack of chart success failed to attract audiences. Peter did have the chance to meet many of the original blues artists, such as Freddie King and Howlin' Wolf, as well as some of the contemporary American musicians. Another opportunity for Peter was the acquisition of new guitars. While in America he bought a sunburst Stratocaster with maple neck. He commented in his column for *Beat Instrumental No. 66* of October 1968: 'I'm using that Stratocaster I picked up in the States all the time on stage now, and my Les Paul has gone to rest. I'll probably get it polished and hang it on the wall.' Peter was later seen performing the song 'Need Your Love So Bad' with the Stratocaster on a Dutch TV show.

When Fleetwood Mac returned to Britain in late summer 1968, guitarist Danny Kirwan was invited to join the band. He had been a fan of Peter for some time and was guitarist for Boilerhouse beforehand. Peter initially wanted to support Danny through the formation of a new band but was impressed enough with his playing to add a third guitarist to Fleetwood Mac. Danny's style was quite different from Jeremy Spencer's and allowed greater interplay within songs. This aspect was soon implemented on Peter's track 'Albatross', which he had been working on for some time. Peter was particularly keen to record the track to his satisfaction and spent two days in the studio. He was ultimately pleased with the result and commented in *Beat Instrumental No. 67* of November 1968: 'I've recently realised that I have been neglecting my own guitar playing while I've worried more about good lyrics … I intend to sort this out. I've written an instrumental … titled "The Albatross" I think it's going to be a real classic in the

Peter Green.
Pictorial Press Ltd / Alamy Stock Photo.

instrumental field, along with "Apache" and "FBI"…' Peter was accurate in his prediction as the song was the band's first UK number one single and widely well-regarded. Danny was the featured guitarist on the B-side 'Jigsaw Puzzle Blues'.

Just before the success of 'Albatross', the band received a set of amplifiers from the recently founded Orange company. Peter used a 100-watt GT120 head with a pair of 2x12 in. cabinets and also had a reverb unit, which was often prominent atop the amp. In *Beat Instrumental No. 68* of December 1968, Peter was enthusiastic about his new equipment: 'Anyone looking for a quality amp and one that can give out any sound you want is well advised to try one. They do a great reverb as well, which has become my pride and joy.'

In late November 1968, the band was in Paris to record 'Surprise Partie' for French TV and later broadcast on New Year's Eve. Performing at least two songs, 'Homework' and 'My Baby's Gone', Peter used his Les Paul through an early 1960s (blonde) Fender Bandmaster head and 2x12 in. cabinet.

Despite the poor reception received in America earlier in the year, Fleetwood Mac returned for a tour in late 1968. Early in 1969, the band followed in the footsteps of the Rolling Stones by making the pilgrimage to Chicago and Chess Records. A day was spent there recording a number of tracks with Otis Spann, Willie Dixon, Buddy Guy, David 'Honeyboy' Edwards, Walter 'Shakey' Horton, J.T. Brown, and S.P. Leary. Peter used his Les Paul through the studio's Fender combo amps. Otis Spann was impressed enough with Fleetwood Mac to have them (minus Mick Fleetwood, who was replaced by Spann's drummer S.P. Leary) back him for an album recorded in New York a week later – 'The Biggest Thing Since Colossus'.

Whilst in America, Fleetwood Mac recorded a new single to follow up the successful 'Albatross'. This was the haunting 'Man Of The World' written by Peter. The track was released in April and managed to reach no. 2 in the UK chart. Around the time of reaching this position, the band appeared on the German TV programme 'Beat Club' and Peter performed the song using a Dallas Tuxedo guitar.

In early 1969, Fleetwood Mac's contract with Blue Horizon

records lapsed. The band's manager negotiated a lucrative deal with Immediate, though this proved short-lived as the company folded later in the year and Warner Bros signed them to the Reprise label. Despite the lure of more money from a different label, there was a major downside to the change, mainly the loss of producer Mike Vernon, who had worked successfully with the group and Peter from the beginning.

Peter decided to take the lead when sessions began for the next album. These were much different to the relatively simple methods previously used, as live play gave way to jamming, editing and overdubs. Danny Kirwan was given encouragement to write material and seven of the 14 tracks were credited to him. Even though Jeremy Spencer continued to play live with the band, he did not perform on any of the new songs; later the band backed him for his solo album released in 1970. Peter's new songs were a mixture of the blues – 'Rattlesnake Shake' – country blues with slide – 'Showbiz Blues' – slow instrumental – 'Underway' – and contemporary blues rock – 'Fighting For Madge' and 'Looking For Madge'.

Peter undoubtedly used his Les Paul, along with a resonator for 'Showbiz Blues' and a Spanish-style acoustic for 'Closing My Eyes' (likely his Ramirez). He had acquired a Fender six-string bass and perhaps used the instrument during the sessions. The songs were later released on the record 'Then Play On', which broke into the UK top ten albums at the end of 1969.

Further evidence of the evolving musical interests of Peter was the 'Oh Well' (Part One and Two) non-album single release in September 1969. Whilst 'Oh Well Part One' was a relatively straightforward blues rock song, 'Oh Well Part Two' saw Peter playing classical guitar to a melancholy, yet ominous background. He performed all the other instruments, apart from the piano which was by Jeremy Spencer and the recorder, as Peter enlisted his girlfriend, Sandra Elsdon. 'Oh Well Part One' continued Fleetwood Mac's chart success, attaining the no. 2 position in the UK, and was the group's first inroad into the American Chart, almost breaching the top fifty.

Footage of the band performing 'Oh Well Part One' on 'Monster Music Mash' – a BBC TV programme – has Peter with his Les Paul and behind the group is a line-up of Fender amps. The Orange equipment had lasted for much of the first half of the year as the group toured with B.B. King in April and appeared at the Bath Festival in June, amongst other gigs. By the end of the summer, the group chose to incorporate Fender equipment, with Peter picking a Fender Bandmaster Reverb model and 2x12 in. cabinet.

At the end of 1969, Fleetwood Mac toured in Europe and footage was recorded of the concert in Oslo, Norway, during November. 'I'm Worried' was followed by 'Like It This Way' where Danny breaks a guitar string. This prompted Peter into a solo version of 'The World Keep On Turning' before the film ends with 'Rattlesnake Shake'. Throughout, Peter uses his Les Paul with the Fender Bandmaster head with matching cabinet, as well as a Tremolux 2x10 cabinet (blonde tolex with oxblood grill cloth, indicating very early 1960s model) and another unidentified Fender cabinet, possibly with 2x12in speakers.

A three-month tour of America was undertaken at the start of 1970. Three nights in Boston were recorded for an official release at the time, but this project ultimately did not come to fruition until the mid-1980s when an album was made available; later a three-volume set was offered for fans. Whilst in the US, the band appeared on the 'Playboy After Dark' TV programme, performing (perhaps appropriately) 'Rattlesnake Shake' and 'Coming Your Way'. Peter had his Les Paul and a Fender amp was provided. Another task undertaken was recording Fleetwood Mac's next single, Peter's 'The Green Manalishi (With The Two Prong Crown)'. Contrasting to this extended heavy rock track was the B-side, 'World In Harmony', which was co-written by Peter and Danny, featuring both guitars with a clean and 'shimmering' sound. The single reached the UK top ten in mid-1970.

Fleetwood Mac performed in Europe soon after returning from the US. Stress caused by the band's recent success and leading the group musically, coupled with drug abuse, induced Peter's decision to quit after the tour. Yet, instead of taking time off to recover, he threw himself into new projects, such as playing with the band Gass on two tracks for their 'Juju' album – 'Juju' and 'Black Velvet' – attending sessions for Memphis Slims' album 'Blue Memphis', providing guitar parts for Peter Bardens' first solo album 'The Answer' and appearing with John Mayall at the Bath Festival.

Peter's decision to leave Fleetwood Mac had been germinating for some time before. In *Beat Instrumental No. 86* of June 1970, were the following comments: 'The one thing that emerges most strongly from talking with him is that, despite the suggestions of some people that he's lost it, he has kept his head far more than most who have become successful in such a short time.' Peter also elaborated on his reasons for quitting: 'I want to play a lot … jam a lot with people whether in public or at home. I used to be a respected musician and I want to pick up some of that again. I just want to carry on entertaining the good people and anyone else who wants to listen. I want to be free of the pressures that make you feel "Got to be good tonight because we are Fleetwood Mac and people have paid to come hear us".' He went on: 'We [Fleetwood Mac] were successful both as a blues group and a singles group, but that isn't enough if you're not happy with it. I was feeling very frustrated and fed up with being successful. I felt I was doing nothing with my life, because there was no challenge.' Peter added: 'Five years ago I was just getting along in life, and like most people I just wanted a bit of fun … Because of work, I didn't have time to think of anything else … Now I have time to think, I feel a strong communion with some force controlling my life. No one person can control my life.'

Peter recorded his own solo album quite soon after leaving Fleetwood Mac. 'The End Of The Game' was assembled from a long jam with Zoot Money on piano, Nick Buck on keyboards, bassist Alex Dmochowski and Godfrey McLean (of Gass) provided drums and percussion. Whilst the album was much different from the Fleetwood Mac output, Peter's playing remained distinctive and evidently inspired by the progressive rock of the period, also having jazz elements, such as free-form expression. Another standout feature of the album is Peter's use of the Wah-Wah pedal, which he had not previously incorporated into his music.

Later in 1970, Peter travelled to America for a break, returning to England energised to form a new band. Yet, this task was

Peter Green with Fleetwood Mac's Danny Kirwan, left, and John McVie in recording studio.
Pictorial Press Ltd / Alamy Stock Photo.

interrupted early in 1971 when Fleetwood Mac requested that he return to help fulfil dates in America following the departure of Jeremy Spencer. A daunting stipulation for the band was that Peter was allowed to jam with them rather than play any of the old songs, which was accepted and happened for many of the remaining shows. Upon his return to England, Peter recorded his first solo single 'Heavy Heart' and 'No Way Out' as the B-side. Both featured distinct percussion sections with his guitar filling in certain parts and continued in the style of tracks on 'The End Of The Game'. Performing the single on BBC TV in 1971, Peter used a sunburst Fender Stratocaster with rosewood neck.

The single was not looked on favourably by the press and added to Peter's already well-founded disillusionment with the music industry. He decided to spend time away from the business and worked for much of the second half of 1971 in Mortlake cemetery. Peter's musical output in 1972 was limited to the single 'Beasts Of Burden' b/w 'Uganda Woman', which had been recorded in 1971, and in 1973 he appeared on 'Night Watch' by Fleetwood Mac. In the early 1970s, Peter sold his Les Paul to Skid Row/Thin Lizzy guitarist Gary Moore, who owned the instrument for over 30 years.

Further deterioration of Peter's mental health during the mid-1970s saw him hospitalised for a time and an incident with an unlicensed firearm resulted in a brief stint in prison, followed by a return to hospital. At the end of the decade, Peter became involved with music again thanks to his brother Michael, who had taken a job at PVK Records, run by Peter Vernon-Kell. Gradually, Peter was inspired to play the guitar again and used a Fender Jaguar owned by the studio. He had lost confidence with the instrument due to the extended layoff and was assisted in much of the sessions by 'Snowy' White. The resulting songs were collected and released as the 'In The Skies' album in mid-1979.

Reaching the top thirty of the UK charts and selling particularly well in Germany, Peter recorded a follow-up album, 'Little Dreamer' in 1980. This was largely written by his brother Michael, though the title track was a co-effort and harks back to 'Albatross'. Peter continued to be active in the early 1980s, with further releases 'Whatcha Gonna Do?', 'White Sky' and 'Kolors'. He had several guitars during this period including a Gibson Les Paul 'Firebrand', Aria Les Paul copy, Fender Stratocaster and an Ibanez, using a Marshall amplifier. Peter played the Aria Les Paul for touring in the early 1980s with Afro-Caribbean-inspired band Kolors. He has the guitar in a recorded performance for the German festival 'Rockpalast' in 1982.

Again, the money-driven side of the music industry disillusioned Peter by the mid-1980s and he retired from the limelight. Ten years elapsed before Peter felt able to return, forming a band, the Splinter Group, with friend and guitarist Nigel Watson which played in Europe during 1996 and 1997. Peter decided to use a black Gibson Howard Roberts Fusion semi-hollow guitar, as well as a Fender Stratocaster, through a Fender Blues DeVille 4x10 in. amp. Much of the material was covers of blues standards and these were assembled for an album ('Peter Green Splinter Group') in 1997. This was followed in 1998 by 'The Robert Johnson Songbook' and 'Soho Session', which was a recording of a gig at Ronnie Scott's Jazz Club. The Splinter Group recorded several other albums featuring mainly covers until disbanding in 2004. Peter briefly returned to the stage in 2009 and 2010 before retiring. He died in July 2020.

GEORGE HARRISON

Although initially overshadowed in the Beatles by the songwriting partnership of John Lennon and Paul McCartney, George Harrison arguably became more than an equal to his contemporaries. In the early days, he was a driving force with the guitar before spearheading an interest in new instruments, particularly the sitar, in the mid-1960s. George later returned to the guitar with a highly individual and melodic style of slide playing.

By the summer of 1957, John Lennon had joined the skiffle craze and formed a band called the Quarry Men. Paul McCartney was invited to one of their gigs by a mutual friend and later played guitar for John, who was quite impressed. Paul was eventually asked to join the group. The Quarry Men performed a few gigs to the end of the year, then in early 1958 the band evolved to play more country and rock songs with a different line-up. John and Paul were still present and there was a drummer and pianist.

George knew Paul after meeting him on a bus, with the pair living quite close to each other, and both soon found they shared an interest in guitars. Paul later introduced George to John – coincidentally also on a bus – and George auditioned for the band. He was admitted after playing the song 'Raunchy' which John thought required suitable skill to master. George learned the guitar in his early teens and his first instrument was a cheap Egmond acoustic he purchased from a school chum. It cost £3/10s and fascinated him, so much so that he wanted to see how it went together and removed the bolt-on neck but could not get it back on. His older brother came to the rescue and George was able to continue. He was inspired by Lonnie Donegan and initially learned skiffle songs.

Before joining the Quarry Men, George had upgraded from his acoustic to a Hofner President. He soon fitted a pick-up to the guitar as the band moved away from playing acoustically and took steps towards amplification. Paul had the first documented amp for the band, which was an Elpico model.

In mid-1958, the Quarry Men made their first recording, which was a primitive affair conducted in a makeshift Liverpool studio. They recorded Buddy Holly's 'That'll Be The Day' and a track written by George and Paul, 'In Spite of all the Danger'.

The band continued as a hobby through the end of 1958 and into 1959. A disagreement with the drummer early in that year led the Quarry Men to become a three-piece with just guitars. Yet, this was often met with derision at clubs and eventually caused the band to disperse. For a time, George played with the Les Stewart Quartet.

This group was booked to play on several occasions at the Casbah Coffee Club, yet before they began, all but George and another guitarist – Ken Brown – left the band. Still wanting to perform, George contacted John and Paul to make up the numbers. With the prospect of playing a number of appearances, George decided he needed a new guitar. This was a Hofner Club 40 which he swapped with Ray Ennis of the Swinging Blue Jeans. At the Casbah, all the guitarists apparently used Ken Brown's Watkins Westminster Amp.

After the run of gigs at the club finished, George, John and Paul banded together to form Johnny & the Moondogs and auditioned for a contest known as Mr Star Maker. They had applied as the Quarry Men but had been rejected. This time they made the finals in Manchester, but failed to win with a performance of 'Rave On'.

George was not disheartened and just five days later went to Hessy's Music and bought a Futurama on hire-purchase. This was a Czechoslovakian-made copy of the Fender Stratocaster and was the closest George could get to the latter at the time due to import restrictions.

In early 1960, John Lennon's friend, Stuart Sutcliffe joined the band on bass and soon the band became known as the 'Beatals', but shortly after switched to 'The Silver Beetles'. Under this moniker, the band, along with a quickly recruited drummer, auditioned for Larry Parnes. This was to be a backing band for a singer under his management. The group did not get the job but were instead rewarded with a spot supporting Johnny Gentle on a Scottish tour. At both the audition and on tour, George was playing his Futurama. He perhaps first came into contact with a Selmer Truvoice amplifier at the audition, as this was provided for use by all the bands, and could have influenced a decision to purchase his own from Hessy's following the conclusion of the tour.

This new amp would be useful for the band's new venture. A friend had recommended them to a German promoter with clubs in Hamburg. They jumped at the chance of playing there and, after recruiting Pete Best on drums, travelled in late summer 1960. George took his Futurama and Truvoice, which was shared with John Lennon. George was forced to return to England shortly before the end of the band's run due to an issue over his age. He was soon joined by his bandmates after they had encountered further troubles with the promoter.

A tentative deal to appear in Hamburg, but at a different club, had been made before the problems had occurred. As 1961 progressed, the Beatles found that the agreement would be honoured and travelled to Germany for appearances to begin in April. George was still playing his Futurama through the Selmer Truvoice. With Stuart Sutcliffe leaving the band to concentrate on his Art studies, George inherited his Gibson 16-watt amp with a 12-inch speaker. The Selmer was transferred to Paul and used with his new Hofner 500/1 'violin' bass. In the midst of the club dates, the band was approached to do a recording session, along with Tony Sheridan, who was appearing at the same venue. The Beatles were able to record two tracks on their own: 'Ain't She Sweet' and 'Cry For A Shadow', the latter being an instrumental written by George and John.

George was on the lookout for a new guitar as he was not satisfied with the Futurama. One night, he received information that his dream guitar – a Fender Stratocaster – was for sale and went to buy it. Yet, a rival had also heard the news and

George Harrison with Gretsch guitar and Vox amplifier.
PA Images / Alamy Stock Photo.

acquired the guitar before George. The Futurama remained with George as the band returned to England in early summer 1961 and for subsequent gigs in Liverpool at the Cavern Club, which had welcomed the group for the first time earlier in the year. The Futurama's days were numbered though and George soon spotted an ad in a Liverpool paper offering a Gretsch Duo Jet for sale. The owner, a merchant seaman, had purchased the guitar in America during a trip and had added a Bigsby tremolo.

The Beatles continued to perform in and around Liverpool during the remainder of the year, increasing their exposure and popularity. This brought them to the attention of music store owner Brian Epstein, who eventually persuaded the group to let him manage them. As part of the deal, Epstein prioritised finding the Beatles a record deal. He was able to secure session with Decca on January 1, 1962.

The band did not have a good start as a label representative was adamant that their equipment was not good enough and made them use the studio amplifiers. The Beatles recorded over a dozen songs, with a small number being originals. The Beatles' first single was released early in the year through the Polydor label and the track was culled from the German session that took place the previous year. The track – 'My Bonnie' was recorded with Tony Sheridan and credited to both.

Decca declined to sign the group. Not deterred, Epstein and the Beatles began looking elsewhere and eventually contacted George Martin at Parlophone who was tentatively interested.

In the meantime, the Beatles were booked to return to Hamburg for another three-month stay. The band only took their instruments and left the amplifiers at home. The venue provided Fender Bandmaster heads and cabinets for George and John to use during their residency.

Whilst in Germany, the band received news from Brian Epstein that George Martin had been in contact to formally arrange a test session. This took place on June 6, and the group took their equipment to Abbey Road. Again, the amps were met with some derision by the engineers and repairs had to be made to get them up to a standard suitable for recording. George took along his Gretsch and Gibson GA-40 amp and these were used on the four tracks recorded: 'Ask Me Why', 'Besame Mucho', 'Love Me Do' and 'PS I Love You'.

Epstein soon solved the problem with the amplifiers by entering into an endorsement deal with Jennings Musical Industries, which produced Vox amplifiers. These were the most popular in Britain at the time and Epstein managed to source them even though the band had not yet had a hit record. As part of the deal, George and John's Gibson and Fender amps were taken in part exchange. The two guitarists then received AC30 models with tan covers and were in use by the end of July 1962.

The Beatles were obliged to return to Abbey Road for further recording sessions. This time the group had new amplifiers and a new drummer as Ringo Starr replaced Pete Best. 'Love Me Do' was rerecorded and George Martin asked them to perform 'How Do You Do It?' by Mitch Murray. George was using his Gretsch through the Vox for the session.

George Martin was still unhappy with the recordings and the group had to return the following week to try again. In the meantime, both George and John had acquired two new guitars. These were a pair of Gibson J-160E acoustic guitars, which had a pick-up mounted on the top. Ordered from Rushworth's in Liverpool, the guitars had taken around two months to travel from the USA and cost around £160 each. George and John later mixed up the guitars and John had his (originally George's) stolen. The remaining guitar was subsequently used by both George and John on a large number of recordings.

The third session at Abbey Road yielded the group's first single: 'Love Me Do' with 'PS I Love You'. Released in early October 1962, the record reached no. 17 in the charts. George played acoustic guitar, likely his new Gibson, on both tracks. With a single in the charts, the Beatles were busy promoting the release in Liverpool, around the country and on radio and TV throughout the remainder of 1962. The band spent a short period in residence at the Star Club in Hamburg, both during November and December.

Following the relative success of 'Love Me Do', George Martin arranged a session to record a follow-up single in late November 1962. The band pushed for another original composition and 'Please Please Me' was chosen. George played his new Gibson J-160E on the track, providing melodic parts mirroring John's harmonica and the vocal. A similar theme was at work on the B-side 'Ask Me Why' which also saw George playing the acoustic. The single was released early in 1963 and proved to be the band's first hit.

With the release of a new single on the horizon, Epstein arranged for the Beatles to embark on a British tour with star of the day Helen Shapiro. In preparation for this, both George and John's Vox AC30 amplifiers were sent away for overhaul. This included recovering the amps and this was done with black tolex. George took his Gretsch on the tour, in addition to his Gibson acoustic.

In the midst of the tour, George Martin called the group into the studio to record their first album. They did not have enough originals, so had to add some covers. The album, 'Please Please Me', drew on the increasing popularity of the single. George took his current pair of guitars into the studio, along with his amp. Whilst he had provided backing vocals for the previous recordings, George sang lead vocals on two of the album's tracks: a cover of the Cookies' 'Chains'; and the Lennon–McCartney 'Do You Want To Know A Secret?' The latter was later released as a single in America and reached no. 2 in the Billboard Chart.

The Beatles made their first appearance on 'Thank Your Lucky Stars' on February 17, 1963, performing the single 'Please Please Me' which was about to reach the top of the charts. George was featured playing his Gibson J-160E.

Following the conclusion of the British tour, the Beatles returned to Abbey Road to record their third single. This was the recently penned 'From Me To You'. George used his Gibson acoustic through his Vox amplifier. The Beatles were very busy during the summer of 1963 as their popularity increased and two further tours of Britain were undertaken. George was able to indulge in his passion for guitars and purchased from Sound City in London, a Gretsch Chet Atkins 'Country Gentleman'.

The guitar was used during the Roy Orbison/Beatles tour,

taking place from mid-May to early June 1963. George favoured the guitar for recording the band's fourth single, 'She Loves You' with 'I'll Get You' as the B-side. For the former track, George played rhythm guitar and some lead lines between verses using the 'Country Gentleman' through his Vox AC30. During the summer, George's amp was replaced by a new AC30, which was basically the same apart from small detail differences.

Not too long after buying the Gretsch 'Country Gentleman', the guitar required repair work and George took up a Maton MS-500, which was an Australian-made solid body, rather than revert to his old Duo Jet. George bought a new guitar in the autumn during a visit to his sister, who lived in America. This was a single pick-up Rickenbacker 425, which he had refinished black at the store. George did not use the guitar for very long, but was pictured with the Rickenbacker on 'Ready Steady Go!' shortly after his return from the USA.

By November, George's 'Country Gentleman' was still not playable and he had a new guitar sent to him from Sound City. This was almost the same as the original, but had switches that operated the string mutes, rather than knobs. For the upcoming British tour, George decided to take this guitar and continued to play through a Vox AC30. Before the end of the year, Vox delivered a new AC50 model as the band increasingly became overpowered by the sound of the screaming audience. The new amp consisted of a separate 'head' connected to the speaker cabinet containing two 12-inch speakers.

George continued with Gretsch guitars as in early 1964 he was first seen playing a Chet Atkins 'Tennessean' model. This was similar to the 'Country Gentleman' but was intended to be a budget version and was therefore plainer. The British Christmas tour finished in mid-January and only a few days later the band travelled to Paris for a residency at the Olympia Theatre. George's new guitar was present, along with his 'Country Gentleman' and both were used with the new Vox AC50 amplifiers.

Early in 1964, 'I Want To Hold Your Hand' reached the top of the American charts and this prompted the band to fly over for an appearance on the prestigious 'Ed Sullivan Show'. Their Vox amplifiers were shipped out and George also took his 'Country Gentleman', which featured on the recorded performance.

George and John both playing Rickenbacker guitars during 1963 was not lost on the company. Thus, Rickenbacker attempted to obtain an endorsement deal with the Beatles using the company's amps. This was not to be, but a selection of guitars was brought along to a meeting in New York, including the new Rickenbacker 12-string. This was given to George and he would use the guitar extensively on future recordings.

Following their appearance on the 'Ed Sullivan Show', the Beatles performed gigs in Washington and New York to sell-out audiences. The band then had some time off in Miami before recording another appearance on the 'Ed Sullivan Show'. Throughout this period George was playing his Gretsch 'Country Gentleman' with the Vox AC50.

Upon returning to England, the Beatles went to Abbey Road to record more songs, and specifically a B-side to the new single 'Can't Buy Me Love', which had been recorded in France the previous year. George used his Rickenbacker 360-12 for the first time in the studio, playing rhythm on 'You Can't Do That' and the introductory guitar part, which appears several times throughout the song. The 12-string was also used for 'I Should Have Known Better', specifically the solo. For another track completed during the session, 'And I Love Her', George brought his new Ramirez Spanish acoustic guitar and produced several distinct passages of playing throughout the song, in addition to the solo. The AC50 was used for the previously mentioned two tracks. These recordings would form the basis of the group's next album 'A Hard Day's Night', which was also the soundtrack to the feature-length film of the same name. Both were released in July 1964. George continued to use his current line-up of guitars, with particular emphasis on the 12-string Rickenbacker.

In light of the group's experience playing gigs over the last six months or so – where screaming girls drowned out the band playing – the Vox AC50s were decidedly underpowered. The Beatles turned again to Vox to come up with more power. The result was the 100-watt AC100 amp head connected with a 4x12 in. cabinet. Three prototypes were delivered in late summer just before the band embarked on a USA tour. For the 23 dates, along with three in Canada, George used his Gretsch 'Country Gentleman' and Rickenbacker 360-12. Along with the Gretsch 'Tennessean', these instruments (and Vox AC100) continued to be used when George returned to England, both in the studio as the group recorded songs for the upcoming 'Beatles For Sale' album and the autumn British tour.

Over the festive period of 1964/1965, the Beatles performed a number of shows in London. They then began sessions for their new album – 'Help!' – which would also form the soundtrack for their second film, sharing the title of the record. The first track recorded was 'Ticket To Ride'. The introduction was played by George on his Rickenbacker 12-string, whilst some of the lead fills were provided by Paul on his Epiphone Casino.

The Gretsch Guitar Co. introduced the Duo Jet in 1953 and was the company's first solid-body model – although the instruments featured chambering under a solid top – launched in response to the success of the Fender Telecaster and Gibson Les Paul. The Duo Jet was fitted with two DynaSonic pick-ups and had a volume control for each pick-up, as well as a master volume, and a master tone.

The 'Country Gentleman' was developed from an existing hollow body guitar by rising country star Chet Atkins and originally featured a Bigsby tremolo, melita bridge and DeArmond pick-ups. The guitar was adorned with images with a connection to the 'old west' but these were later phased out. By the early 1960s, it featured double cutaways, 'Filter'Tron' pick-ups, screw-operated mutes and false 'f' holes (the mutes subsequently being switch-operated).

George Harrison performs 'I Need You' on the movie set of 'HELP!'. Filmed on Salisbury Plain, Wiltshire. May 4, 1964.
From Original Negative / Alamy Stock Photo.

The sessions saw George experiment with his guitar sound through the use of a Vox volume pedal, which allowed the volume to be raised or lowered whilst playing, not manipulating the controls on the guitar. A primitive version of this had been attempted by George and John previously, where the latter sat in front of George and manually turned the volume control on the guitar at the required moment. The volume pedal was first used on George's composition 'I Need You' in partnership with the Rickenbacker 360-12. George played rhythm guitar on his Ramirez acoustic. 'Yes It Is', which was the B-side to 'Ticket To Ride', saw George use the volume pedal with the 12-string.

The Beatles recorded scenes for the film, as well as tracks for the album when the schedule permitted. George's guitars remained unchanged and both the records and film feature his instruments: Gretsch 'Tennessean', Gretsch 'Country Gentleman', Rickenbacker 360-12 and Gibson J160-E.

When finished with the film and album, the Beatles were back on the road in Europe, then Britain. George had his two Gretsch guitars and Rickenbacker to play through his Vox AC100. These also made their way to America for a summer tour. Another appearance on the 'Ed Sullivan Show' kicked off the visit, with George playing his Gretsch 'Tennessean' on a selection of the group's recent recordings.

Apart from older covers and hits of their own, the Beatles performed songs from 'Help' at Shea Stadium. This would be the group's largest concert, with over 55,000 people attending. George played his Gretsch 'Tennessean' and Rickenbacker 360-12, also leading the Carl Perkins song 'Everybody's Trying To Be My Baby'. A further nine shows were staged in America, as well as one in Toronto before the group returned to England.

George did not land empty-handed as he had been presented with a new Rickenbacker 12-string whilst in the USA. During a stop in one of the cities, a local guitar store gave him a 360-12 in the new shape. This was a lot more rounded than his other guitar and there were other small detail changes.

Following an extended break, the Beatles were in Abbey Road Studio, preparing a new single and album. The first session yielded two tracks: 'Run For Your Life' and 'Norwegian Wood (This Bird Has Flown)'. The latter song saw George turn to the sitar. George had first come across one during the filming of 'Help!' and the name of a famous player, Ravi Shankar. George found a sitar in London and familiarised himself with it. Taking the sitar along to the recording sessions, he felt that the sound would suit 'Norwegian Wood (This Bird Has Flown)', breaking new ground in the process through the cross-pollination of musical styles.

The Beatles moved on to record the next single, promoted with both tracks as the A-side, 'Day Tripper' and 'We Can Work It Out'. The first track saw George use his Fender Stratocaster to play the signature riff, which John had devised. The guitar had been purchased earlier in the year by road manager Mal Evans along with another for John. Both were in Sonic Blue – a rare custom colour.

The new singles saw the Beatles develop a far-reaching innovation. As requests for performances and appearances were arriving all the time, the decision was taken to record the band performing the tracks and this would then be sent out for TV programmes to play on air. In effect, this was the birth of the music video. For 'Day Tripper', George played his Gretsch 'Tennessean' and 'We Can Work It Out' sees him with a new guitar, a Gibson ES 345 in sunburst finish. The instrument was only with George briefly, though he did take it on the short British tour in late 1965.

George had two tracks featured on the new album – 'Rubber Soul' – released in early December 1965. 'Think For Yourself', which featured Paul playing a distinctive bass line utilising a Vox Tone Bender fuzz pedal, and 'If I Needed Someone'. This saw George playing a memorable opening, using his Rickenbacker 12-string.

'Rubber Soul' achieved worldwide success and marked a new direction for the group. Growing increasingly dissatisfied with life on the road and constant engagements, the band decided to concentrate on recording and create interesting songs and sounds in the studio. They had plenty of time to make plans for their seventh album as the first three months of 1966 were devoted to relaxation following at least five years of near constant work.

George used some of his free time to shop for new guitars. He acquired a Gibson

SG Standard (1964 model, with nickel hardware) and an Epiphone Casino in sunburst with a Bigsby vibrato. For the start of recording sessions in early April, the band acquired some new Fender amps. These were the Showman models, with an 85-watt head connected to a 1x15 cabinet. Vox sent over their latest offering – a 120-watt solid state amplifier with a 4x12 in. cabinet.

Between April and June 1966, the Beatles spent time recording tracks for 'Revolver', released in August. On the album, George was featured with three tracks, including the opener 'Taxman'. He used his Fender Stratocaster on this to provide the rhythm track, whilst Paul performed the solo. George followed John's lead by moving his song-writing away from traditional themes of love and relationships and wrote 'Taxman' in protest at the amount of money lost in taxes.

The fourth 'Revolver' track, 'Love You To' was written by George and he returned to the sitar and employed other Indian instruments. During the previous three months, George had studied Indian music and the sitar in London, growing increasingly fascinated and influenced. In mid-1966, he began lessons with world-renowned sitar player Ravi Shankar. George's final composition on the album was 'I Want To Tell You', featuring a distinctive riff played on his Fender Stratocaster.

The same guitar was used on 'I'm Only Sleeping', particularly the backwards guitar solo, both the clean and fuzz versions. George took his time over the solo and worked one out that sounded good when played backwards.

George used his Epiphone Casino effectively on 'And Your Bird Can Sing', playing the lead parts in partnership with Paul. The guitar is likely used on 'She Said She Said'. The Gibson SG made an appearance on 'Doctor Robert' and was prominent on the promotional videos filmed for singles, 'Paperback Writer' and 'Rain'. Yet, pictures from the studio during the recording of the two songs show George with a Burns Nu-Sonic bass.

At the end of the sessions, the Beatles began a world tour which would prove to be the last time they went on the road. The first dates were in Germany before travelling to Tokyo for three days at the Budokan arena, then they made their way to Manila. Whilst there, a misunderstanding with the local dignitaries caused the group to flee fearing for their safety. This incident would cement the group's – and particularly George's – increasing dislike of touring. After a month back in England, the Beatles were in the USA for a string of dates which concluded in San Francisco.

Throughout this period, George favoured his Epiphone Casino and used his Gibson SG as a backup instrument. He had his second Rickenbacker 360-12 for use on appropriate songs. George shipped his new Vox 7120 amp for the gigs in Europe and the Far East. In America, the US Vox distributors provided their own version of the 7120, named the 'Super Beatle'.

Several factors contributed to making the 1966 world tour less than rewarding for the Beatles and they collectively decided to concentrate on recording new material in the studio. Following three months on holiday, everyone returned to Abbey Road in late November 1966 to begin work on a new album for 1967. George had spent a considerable period of his free time in India, studying the sitar with Ravi Shankar.

George continued to use his Epiphone Casino, Gibson SG Standard, Fender Stratocaster and Gibson J160-E for the recordings, whilst various combinations of amplifiers were used. The band had AC30s in the studios and Vox sent over their new range of solid-state amplifiers, which comprised heads with cabinets.

Surprisingly, given his contributions to 'Revolver', only one track of George's appeared on the new album 'Sgt Pepper's Lonely Hearts Club Band'. This was the Indian-influenced 'Within You Without You' on which George played sitar. This was amongst other instruments of that country, accompanied by musicians from the Asian Music Circle. The use of the Indian Tambura, which was present on the track, would seep into other songs on the album, such as 'Lucy In The Sky With Diamonds' and 'Getting Better'. For the single 'Strawberry Fields Forever', George played the swarmandal (an Indian type of zither) to bridge the short gaps between the chorus and verses.

Perhaps George's standout guitar performances for the album are on the songs 'Fixing A Hole' and 'Sgt Pepper's Lonely Hearts Club Band (Reprise)'. He uses his Stratocaster to create a distinct rhythm pattern and then with a distorted tone delivers a memorable guitar break on 'Fixing A Hole'. He also uses a similar sound to create interesting fills between gaps in the lyrics.

At the end of recording tracks for 'Sgt Pepper's Lonely Hearts Club Band', the Beatles continued to work in the studio. They had committed themselves to creating songs for a soundtrack to an animated film based on 'Yellow Submarine'. Paul conceived an idea for a film featuring the group where they embark on a trip and get into interesting scenarios. These would be interspersed with songs, and work was soon underway on the title track – 'Magical Mystery Tour'.

Of the six songs the band produced for the 'Yellow Submarine' album, two were from George. The first was 'Only A Northern Song', written earlier in the year for 'Sgt Pepper'. It did not feature a guitar part, but George played a Hammond organ. This also featured on the other song, 'It's All Too Much' and George employed a distorted guitar tone for the part, also using 'feedback' for the intro and some backing sections. The guitar played was likely the Fender Stratocaster, given the use of the tremolo arm to raise and lower the pitch of the feedback.

George's Fender Stratocaster was about to undergo a makeover at this time. In the USA and Britain, there was a growing trend to move away from the staid and restrictive culture of the period and people wanted to be more individual and forthright. One area where this was displayed was fashion and during 1966 and 1967 there was a distinct move towards bright, colourful and unique clothing. The Beatles adopted this mindset and it soon affected their instruments. George chose his Stratocaster to receive a new multi-coloured finish which he hand-painted; the guitar was rechristened 'Rocky'. The Stratocaster would be visible on the 'Our World' TV special, which saw the band perform the song 'All You Need Is Love', and more prominently in the 'Magical Mystery Tour' film shown at Christmas on the BBC.

After the 'Our World' broadcast, the group took some time

off before continuing with the 'Magical Mystery Tour' project. George contributed one song to the soundtrack, 'Blue Jay Way'. Again, he preferred to omit the guitar on the song and instead plays a Hammond organ throughout, whilst a cello plays melody lines. In general, the songs on 'Magical Mystery Tour' lack distinct guitar parts and either orchestral accompaniment or that of the Hammond organ is favoured by the Beatles.

The group rounded off 1967 by recording a video for the new single for the Christmas market, 'Hello Goodbye'. Band members were filmed miming to the song on stage at the Saville Theatre dressed in their Sgt Pepper costumes. George chose to play his Epiphone Casino with a Vox Defiant amplifier.

Although the Beatles had ended their commitments for the year, George had signed up to produce the soundtrack for Joe Massot's film 'Wonderwall'. From late November until early 1968, he recorded a number of instrumental tracks to suit film scenes. George was particularly pleased to have landed this task and even flew to India at his own expense to record. The songs relied heavily on Indian instrumentation and technique, particularly the use of drone.

Few tracks featured the guitar and those that did mainly used guest performers. On 'Ski-ing' Eric Clapton plays a riff with a fuzz effect, although George added a backwards guitar solo, and 'Party Seacombe' saw Remo Four guitarist Colin Manley using a Wah-Wah pedal, whilst he also played steel guitar to 'Cowboy Music'. George continued with the idea of 'the studio as instrument' by employing various effects and using tape loops, particularly on the track 'Dream Scene'.

'Wonderwall' saw only limited release in 1968 due to its low budget which also precluded the release of the soundtrack album. Later, the record was released as part of Apple Records, the Beatles' own label created in 1968, and became the first solo record from one of the bandmembers. Receiving mixed reviews at the time, the album has gained more favour in recent years.

'The Inner Light' was recorded during the sessions and did not make the album, yet became George's first song to appear as part of a Beatles' single when paired with 'Lady Madonna'. This was another of George's tracks to be heavily influenced by Indian music and he only provided the vocal.

George returned to the guitar in sessions arranged just before the group left for India to spend time studying the Transcendental Meditation technique with Maharishi Mahesh Yogi. The Gibson SG Standard was used on 'Lady Madonna' and 'Hey Bulldog', with the former serving as a single for release during the group's time away. The latter appeared on the 'Yellow Submarine' soundtrack. The process of recording 'Hey Bulldog' was filmed for use as the video for 'Lady Madonna' and George is featured regularly with his Gibson, which was likely played through a Fender Showman amp, performing the lead guitar part and the solo.

The Beatles spent differing amounts of time in India, with Ringo and Paul leaving earlier than George and John who remained with the Maharishi for nearly two months. Nevertheless, the time spent there was fruitful for the group as a large number of songs were amassed for when they returned to England.

Starting in mid-May, sessions for the new album, which turned into the two-disc 'The Beatles' or the 'White Album', were spread over the following four and a half months. Generally, the group toned down the use of orchestral arrangements for the new songs and the guitar was featured prominently.

Several of George's songs were recorded and four were used. The Indian influence was more restrained and he returned his focus to the guitar. This is demonstrated in his first song on the album, 'While My Guitar Gently Weeps'. Yet, Eric Clapton was the soloist, George just played the rhythm part on his recently acquired Gibson J200 acoustic. Eric played a 1957 Gibson Les Paul Standard which he had bought in America and gifted to George earlier in the summer. The instrument, subsequently nicknamed 'Lucy', had been owned by American guitarist Rick Derringer who had it refinished by Gibson from the original gold to a translucent cherry a short time earlier. The guitar would be heavily used by George, in addition to his Stratocaster and to a lesser extent the SG.

The Gibson J200 was used for the backing to the next track, 'Piggies', but the song's prominent feature was a harpsichord. The acoustic was heard more distinctly on 'Long, Long, Long'. George turned to the Gibson Les Paul Standard for both the lead and rhythm guitar parts on his final track on the album 'Savoy Truffle'.

During the recording of the album, the Beatles' long-standing agreement with Vox to use their amplifiers was broken. This led Fender to approach the group with an endorsement deal. Whilst no official agreement was reached, Fender sent equipment to the band and a number of amps arrived, along with a Bass VI. The latter was used by George on the album ('Birthday' and 'Honey Pie') and also in the video for the single 'Hey Jude' where he is connected to a Fender Showman amp. The B-side to the single was 'Revolution', which was slightly different from the album version, and also had a video recorded. On this, George is seen with his Gibson Les Paul Standard plugged into a Fender Deluxe Reverb.

When released in November 1968, 'The Beatles', or 'White Album', was an immediate success. Yet, the content polarised some fans and critics following the accolades for 'Sgt Pepper' the previous year. The album is certainly a progression from the latter as the group mixes the experimentation of the previous two years with a return to the pop/rock sound of their earlier years. This was particularly the case with George as his devotion to Indian music tempered slightly, allowing a return to the guitar.

Early in 1969, the Beatles began a new project. This saw the band gather at Twickenham Studios to film the creation of a new album. The songs from this were to be performed at a special concert. George took his Gibson Les Paul Standard to the sessions and used a 1968 Fender Twin Reverb amplifier, also moving to the Fender Bass VI from the 'White Album' sessions on occasion and playing through a Fender Bassman. Unfortunately, tensions had been building within the band from the end of the 'Sgt Pepper' sessions and these came to a head in early 1969 when George walked out on the group.

After concessions were made, George returned to the recording sessions which were moved to the Apple offices on Savile Row where a studio had been built. During recording,

George received a new guitar from Fender which was specially built for him. This was a Telecaster model made with a rosewood body and neck and he would use it for a short time. The guitar was featured on tracks such as 'Two Of Us', 'Dig A Pony', 'I've Got A Feeling', 'One After 909', 'Get Back' and 'Don't Let Me Down'. The sessions culminated with a performance on the roof of the Apple offices. George used the Telecaster through a Fender Twin Reverb amp.

Two of George's songs were recorded during the project. 'I Me Mine' was inspired by the problems the group were having and saw George playing rhythm on his Gibson J200 with lead sections on the Gibson Les Paul Standard. The other track was 'For You Blue' which again had the Gibson J200 on the rhythm part, whilst John played a lap steel guitar. The animosity created during the sessions led the group to shelve the project and the album, which was initially titled 'Get Back', did not appear until mid-1970 as 'Let It Be'.

In the downtime following the end of the sessions, George turned to an experimental project begun in late 1968 using a Moog synthesizer. The record, 'Electronic Sound', consisted of two sides, with one – 'Under The Mersey Wall' – solely created by George using various sounds at his disposal. The Moog would find its way onto the Beatles' album 'Abbey Road'.

The new album was begun quite early in 1969, but stalled as the band took an extended break through to the spring. Resuming in April, the band worked on George's 'Old Brown Shoe' which was to be the B-side to the next single, John's 'The Ballad Of John And Yoko' recorded by just him and Paul. 'Old Brown Shoe' had been gestating from the 'Get Back' sessions and the final song saw George use his Telecaster, as well as playing a rhythm part on a Hammond organ. An impressive guitar solo was recorded by George and he made the tone distinct by using a Leslie speaker as well as automatic double-tracking.

Over the ensuing months a number of songs were captured for 'Abbey Road', including two of George's – 'Something' and 'Here Comes The Sun'. On 'Something' George played his Gibson Les Paul through a Leslie speaker whilst the Gibson J200 was featured on 'Here Comes The Sun' in addition to the earlier-mentioned set-up. For the latter, a capo was used on the seventh fret of the guitars. George employed the Gibson Les Paul for much of the album but also turned, on occasion, to the Telecaster, in particular for the solos on the final track 'The End'. Paul, George and John (in that order) took turns soloing for two bars, three times each.

In late September, shortly before the release of 'Abbey Road', John announced to the group that he would no longer be involved with the Beatles. Yet, there was no public announcement as the band wanted to protect their business interests.

George was free to pursue the production of his own songs, which had been stifled under John and Paul, at the end of 1969. He even went on a brief tour of Europe in December with American group Delaney & Bonnie and Friends, who he had been introduced to by Eric Clapton. The latter was also on the tour and would swap guitars with George and Delaney. George could be seen playing either his Fender Telecaster, which he later gifted to Delaney, the Stratocaster (still painted), his Gibson Les Paul Standard or Eric's Gibson Les Paul Custom with three pick-ups. Amplification was provided by Fender heads and cabinets. The group appeared at a concert for UNICEF, which featured John and his Plastic Ono Band, and on this occasion, George had Eric's Gibson Les Paul Custom.

George began 1970 by finishing some tracks for the 'Let It Be' album before moving on to record traditional songs by the Radha Krishna Temple. He had worked with the group the previous year on the 'Hare Krishna Mantra' and in February they recorded 'Govinda'. During 1971, an album was released on Apple. In March, George moved into a new home, Friar Park, a Victorian Neo-Gothic mansion. He would spend several years renovating the house and gardens and in 1972 he installed a recording studio. This was used for nearly all his subsequent albums.

By mid-1970, George was ready to produce a solo record as he had a large stockpile of material waiting to be released. He had grown friendly with producer Phil Spector, who was working on the 'Let It Be' project, and George asked him to listen to a number of demos with a view to working together. Spector was impressed and agreed to get involved on the album, beginning in late May 1970.

George worked on the demos with a large number of musicians – with some debate as to who actually made the finished recording. Along with George, Eric Clapton provided guitar parts, as well as Dave Mason from Traffic, Peter Drake played pedal steel guitar and Peter Frampton contributed acoustic to some songs. Apple-signed band, Badfinger appeared with their three guitarists, whilst members of the Delaney & Bonnie band played on some tracks. Ringo was asked to play, along with recent Beatles collaborator Billy Preston, who was signed to Apple, as well as Klaus Voormann.

With a number of guitarists involved with the album, many of the songs naturally have prominent guitar parts. Several, such as 'I'd Have You Anytime', 'Wah-Wah', 'Let It Down', 'Plug Me In' and 'Art Of Dying', feature the lead work of Eric Clapton, whilst pedal steel guitar player Peter Drake contributed to 'Behind That Locked Door', 'Ballad Of Sir Frankie Crisp (Let It Roll)' and 'All Things Must Pass'. The acoustic guitar underpins many of the tracks and, as mentioned, was provided by several guitarists.

As various guitar breaks were left to Eric, George chose to contribute his lead parts using a slide. He had taken up this aspect of playing, thanks to Delaney Bramlett. A song in the group's set called for a slide part and George was asked to perform using a bottleneck. Evidently, he became quite interested in adding this new sound as seven of the songs on the album – 'All Things Must Pass' – contain a slide part: 'My Sweet Lord', 'Isn't It A Pity', 'What Is Life', 'Beware Of Darkness', 'Awaiting On You All', 'I Dig Love' and 'Hear Me Lord'. Whilst slide guitar appears to have been George's focus during this time, he played the main riff on 'Wah-Wah' and 'What Is Life' and he also turned his hand to the blues-rock style on the 'jam' third disc of songs.

Just as the personnel of the album is not particularly clear, the guitars George used for specific tracks is similarly open to debate. He likely continued to use his Gibson Les Paul and Fender Stratocaster, which might have been for the slide parts, but some were recorded using a newly acquired resonator guitar; this was the first of several George would own. The acoustic George used is unidentified. A number of sources point to the Gibson J200 and, whilst this might have been present on some of the demos, George is said to have given it to Bob Dylan for his performance at the 1969 Isle of Wight Festival. George does not appear to have been seen with the instrument subsequently. The J200 is rumoured to be pictured with Bob Dylan for the cover of his 1969 album 'Nashville Skyline', with George spending time at Dylan's home during late 1968. George could have used a Harptone L-6 which appeared around the time of the album along with a 12-string model. The amps used were likely to be the Fenders left over from the Beatles. George used a fuzz tone effect on 'What Is Life', whilst Eric played through a Wah-Wah pedal, appropriately, on 'Wah-Wah'.

'All Things Must Pass' was released in late November 1970 as an unprecedented three-record set. The album was an immediate success, both critically and commercially, as was the lead single 'My Sweet Lord'.

In early 1971, George worked with John Lennon on the 'Imagine' album. George contributed both slide guitar parts and rhythm and lead. The process was filmed and later released allowing an intimate glimpse at the sessions, many sections featuring George. On 'Crippled Inside', George used one of several resonator guitars John had in his home studio, adding a slide part. On his Gibson Les Paul, he played a delicate rhythm piece on the track 'Oh My Love'. For 'How Do You Sleep?' George used a Fender Stratocaster in light blue (reminiscent of the original colour of his own Stratocaster 'Rocky') and with a maple neck. The lead fills and solo are played with a metal slide. For the fills, George used his fingers, then for the solo turned to a pick.

The Stratocaster is of an unknown origin and appears to be a body from the early 1960s, as it possesses an 11-screw pickguard, mated to a neck pre-1959 when a change was made to rosewood for the fingerboard. There is a very slight possibility this is a rare custom-ordered guitar, but more likely the two pieces were joined latterly.

In the early summer of 1971, George was in the studio producing a new Badfinger record 'Straight Up', even contributing slide guitar to 'Day After Day'. He then went to America to continue production on the soundtrack to the documentary film of Ravi Shankar, *Raga*. During these sessions, Ravi talked with George about the continuing humanitarian crisis in Bangladesh and George was compelled to respond. He built on an idea by Ravi to hold a fundraising concert by making it a rock show to help draw in the crowds. There was the further idea of recording proceedings both in sound and on film in order to maximise the earning potential of the event.

The concert was organised for August 1, 1971, at Madison Square Garden, New York. Ravi was scheduled to perform a set of his music first and then be followed by George. The latter assembled a band from the members of Badfinger, Klaus Voormann, the Hollywood Horns, Ringo, Leon Russell and Billy Preston. Eric Clapton agreed to play, whilst George managed to persuade Bob Dylan, who had been on an extended break from live performances, to play a short set at the end of the show.

George recorded a single – 'Bangla Desh' – to promote the cause and the concert and this was released just before the event. The track was piano-led, but George contributed a slide solo, likely on his Stratocaster.

George's set list comprised songs from 'All Things Must Pass', as well as some of his popular Beatles songs: 'Something', 'While My Guitar Gently Weeps' and 'Here Comes The Sun'. He primarily used a Fender Stratocaster with maple neck. This does not appear to have a factory finish and could be the same guitar from the 'Imagine' sessions, but from after being stripped of the paint. George had done this before with his Epiphone Casino and has been noted as saying this improves the guitar's tone. For the acoustic tracks he switched to a Harptone 6-string acoustic guitar. Amplification was provided by a Fender combo and George had his Gibson Les Paul on hand as a standby.

The Concert for Bangladesh was a success and helped raise funds for the relief efforts there. The event even spawned follow-up shows, which did not feature the participation of George, in England and Australia.

George would concentrate on working with other artists over the next year or so, as well as having some time off. He ended his time in America after the Bangladesh concert by helping Billy Preston complete his album 'I Wrote A Simple Song' and played slide on a resonator guitar for the title track. Ringo also received assistance from George in the creation of the single 'Back Off Boogaloo'. George recorded a succession of particularly forceful slide guitar parts. The number of George's production credits also increased as he worked with Cilla Black and Apple artists Lon and Derrek Van Eaton, as well as overseeing another Ravi Shankar album 'In Concert 1972'. George played with Harry Nilsson on the latter's track 'You're Breaking My Heart' and made a thinly disguised guest appearance – being credited as George O'Hara – on Nicky Hopkins' solo album 'The Tin Man Was A Dreamer'. Slide guitar continued to be George's preferred method of playing and he provided parts for the tracks 'Speed On', 'Edward' and 'Waiting For The Band'.

At the time of George's work with Nicky Hopkins, the pair were also involved in George's next release. This was 'Living In The Material World' produced over the winter of 1972/1973 at Apple and Abbey Road studios, as well as his new state-of-the-art recording facility installed at Friar Park.

In comparison to 'All Things Must Pass', George worked with a small core of musicians and kept the songs relatively simple. He provided all the guitar parts, with the possible exception of 'Try Some, Buy Some', which had a backing track dating from 1971 likely featuring members of Badfinger. The guitar sounds on 'Living In The Material World' were quite straightforward and generally clean, with the use of a Leslie speaker adding a change of tone at certain points, such as on 'Who Can See It' and 'That Is All'. The title track provided an example of the use of the Leslie, in addition to a rare instance of an overdriven guitar on the album. This song is also interesting for the 'duelling' guitar and saxophone parts during the solo. George continued to use a slide for the solo in this song and the others on the record, such as 'The Light That Has Lighted

George Harrison performs with Fender Stratocaster during the Concert for Bangladesh, 1971.
Keystone Press / Alamy Stock Photo.

The World' and 'Don't Let Me Wait Too Long'.

In similarity with the previous album, 'Living In The Material World' does not appear to have been well documented with regards the instruments or amps George used. We can surmise from listening to the record and the guitars in his possession at the time that he almost certainly used a Fender Stratocaster, either one of at least three he had, and could have played the Gibson Les Paul on the title track. George's acoustic was probably the Harptone 6-string, as well as the 12-string, and a resonator was used on 'Sue Me, Sue You Blues'. Amplification likely continued to be one of several Fender models George owned.

Whilst the album received mixed reviews from critics, success was found with the public and the record went to the top of charts around the world. The lead single from the album was 'Give Me Love (Give Me Peace On Earth)', which was a hit. This featured George on acoustic guitar for the rhythm part and several lead sections on slide guitar provided melody.

Early in 1974, George took a break and visited India. With his friend Ravi Shankar he toured several sites of religious significance and this inspired George to write new material. Upon his return to England, George set about launching his own record label – Dark Horse – as Apple Records was no longer concentrating on new artists. George brought Ravi over to the new label for the release of the latter's latest record 'Shankar Family And Friends' which was produced by George and he played acoustic guitar on the western-styled single 'I Am Missing You'. Joining Dark Horse at this time was the vocal duo Splinter, and George produced and played on their first album 'The Place I Love', released in September 1974. George is prominent on the tracks 'Drink All Day', 'The Place I Love', 'Situation Vacant', 'Elly May' and 'Somebody's City'; the latter showcases George's lead-playing in the blues-style. The guitar parts were mainly acoustic and electric slide, with the addition of a resonator.

George gave Bobby Purvis from Splinter his Harptone 12-string guitar at some point during the sessions and the instrument can be seen during the group's performance on the 'Old Grey Whistle Test'. This gift was likely influenced by George's acquisition of a new 12-string guitar in late 1973/ early 1974 from guitar builder Tony Zemaitis. This instrument was accompanied by a 6-string counterpart and a small version for George to use when travelling. The guitars were made with a spruce top, mahogany back, sides and neck, an ebony fingerboard with mother-of-pearl 'Om' spiritual symbol, and a wooden flower petal design around the soundhole; engraved metal plates, which were distinguishing features of Zemaitis guitars, adorned the headstock.

Despite being heavily involved with production on Splinter's album, working with Ravi on the 'Music Festival From India' album and subsequent tour, setting up the record label and producing the film 'Little Malcolm', George worked on new songs for his own album, 'Dark Horse'. This was released at the end of 1974. Spread over several months, the sessions featured a variety of musicians, including guitarists Alvin Lee and Ronnie Wood on the song 'Ding Dong Ding Dong' and Robben Ford on three tracks, 'Hari's On Tour (Express)', 'Simply Shady' and 'Dark Horse'.

George continued to favour either acoustic rhythm or slide lead on the album. The latter is highlighted on the opening track 'Hari's On Tour (Express)' and 'Māya Love', which has a funk-influenced rhythm with a blues-style slide lead part. 'So Sad' showcases George's acoustic playing and the 12-string part harks back to 'Here Comes The Sun', whilst 'Dark Horse' has a memorable acoustic rhythm figure.

The end of 1974 saw George tour the United States and Canada with Ravi Shankar, who opened the show. A relatively large band accompanied George, including Robben Ford on guitar. The set list for the concerts comprised new and old material and as a result George took several guitars to provide the sounds he needed. He had three Fender Stratocasters, including 'Rocky', a sunburst mid-1950s model (gifted from Eric Clapton), which featured two prominent stickers – one of the Dark Horse Records logo and the other depicts a man playing a saxophone – and another in a light brown finish. Interestingly, this has the same Dark Horse Records sticker as the other. The Gibson Les Paul was present, as was the Zemaitis six-string acoustic. For amplification, George appears to be using a Mesa Boogie Mark I.

The song 'Dark Horse' was released as a single in mid-November 1974, followed around three weeks later by 'Ding Dong Ding Dong'. For the latter, George filmed his first post-Beatles promotional video and he features a number of his guitars that intend to mimic different periods of his career. He starts off with a Gibson ES 5 'Switchmaster', which he was first seen with in 1968 during sessions for a Jackie Lomax recording, and a Fender tweed amp is in the background. George then appears with his Rickenbacker 12-string and a Fender Solid State amplifier (either a Deluxe or Twin Reverb model) before being filmed with the small Zemaitis acoustic. The Epiphone Casino from the mid-1960s is visible while George plays his Gibson Les Paul. These two guitars are joined by 'Rocky', as all three are propped up against the Fender Solid State, and a new addition to George's collection is seen for the first time. This is a custom-made Greven resonator with bespoke inlay work. Finally, George uses his Zemaitis 12-string guitar.

George suffered from laryngitis during the end of 1974, so in early 1975 he spent time pursuing other interests. He was in LA during the spring to record Splinter's second album, but the band were unable to use the studio time so George decided to take it himself and came up with some new songs in addition to developing older ideas. The result was the album 'Extra Texture (Read All About It)' which was a departure from the sound of 'Dark Horse' as George relied more on pianos, keyboards and horns rather than his guitar. However, there are some standout performances with the guitar on the album, such as 'This Guitar (Can't Keep From Crying)' which showcases George with the slide over his acoustic rhythm part. Also, 'Tired Of Midnight Blue' features melodic slide fills.

George followed up 'Extra Texture (Read All About It)' with 'Thirty Three & $\frac{1}{3}$' which was recorded over the summer of 1976. It was the first of his solo records to appear on his Dark Horse label. The album saw an increase in guitar-based compositions, although George played synthesizer on a number of tracks and piano and horns continued to be prominent.

'Woman Don't You Cry For Me' was a song George made

early in his study of the slide technique which was resurrected for the album. 'Beautiful Girl' offers an example of how George had developed with the method as he used two slide parts to create a layered solo. 'Crackerbox Palace' demonstrates how effectively he could employ the sound to a simple riff, creating a distinct part in the song. 'Thirty Three & ⅓' sees George dispensing with the slide for guitar parts, such as the arpeggio-laden electric guitar backing of 'Beautiful Girl' reminiscent of his early Beatles work. Three tracks have a solo played conventionally: 'This Song', 'Pure Smokey' and 'Learning How To Love You'. The latter is interesting for being a solo on the acoustic.

The album was released in November 1976 and George promoted it (and the lead single 'This Song') in America and Europe at this time. He appeared on the American TV programme 'Saturday Night Live' and performed with Paul Simon on several tracks, including 'Here Comes The Sun' and the latter's 'Homeward Bound'. For this George used a Martin D-35S and he also played a guitar built by the company briefly in the promotional video for 'This Song'. On the German TV programme 'Disco', George performs to the track with the 1950s sunburst Stratocaster heavily used during the 'Dark Horse' tour.

'Thirty Three & ⅓' was a success for George both critically and commercially and on the back of this he decided to take a year off from music to concentrate on travelling. Although continuing to write songs during the interval, George did not return to the studio until early 1978 when sessions began for the self-titled album 'George Harrison'. The year proved particularly eventful for George, as his son Dhani was born, he married for the second time and he formed a film company – HandMade Films – to release Monty Python's 'Life of Brian'.

Recording proceeded through to the end of 1978 and 'George Harrison' was released in mid-February 1979. The style of songs throughout was consistent with recent releases in that tracks featured acoustic or electric rhythm guitar by George with mainly slide solos or lead parts. These attributes are highlighted in the songs released as singles from the album: 'Blow Away', 'Love Comes To Everyone', 'Faster'. The first and last-mentioned songs were also accompanied by videos featuring George playing the guitar. For 'Blow Away' and 'Faster' he is seen with the Zemaitis six-string acoustic whilst the Gibson Les Paul also appears in the former.

George's next album, 'Somewhere In England', was completed during 1980. Yet, his record company did not feel that the songs were commercial enough and forced George to record four new songs. One was 'All Those Years Ago', which had initially been written for Ringo, but was repurposed following the murder of John Lennon on December 8, 1980, to reflect on this tragic event.

The interference from the record company and the death of John contributed to George's disillusion with the recording industry and he quickly produced 1982's 'Gone Troppo' to fulfil his contract with Warner Brothers. Afterwards, he produced several movies for HandMade Films and even made cameo appearances in 'Shanghai Surprise', which also saw George arrange music for the soundtrack, and 'Water'. The latter sees George performing in a band with Ringo, Eric Clapton and Billy Connolly; he uses an unidentified guitar.

In 1985, George made his first appearance on stage since 1974 as he participated in 'Blue Suede Shoes: A Rockabilly Session' which was a tribute to Carl Perkins. George was joined by Eric and Ringo, as well as several other musicians, to play with Carl Perkins. He used a Gretsch 'Chet Atkins Nashville', possibly with a Mesa Boogie amp, although Fender and Vox amps are also present on stage. In 1986, George made a guest appearance at the 'Heart Beat 86' event to raise money for Birmingham Children's Hospital and played a Fender Telecaster during a performance of Chuck Berry's 'Johnny B. Goode'.

George's interest in making music again had evidently been revived and in early 1987 he began recording songs for a new album, 'Cloud Nine', which was released at the end of the year. Co-produced with Jeff Lynne (previously of the Electric Light Orchestra), the album was a worldwide success with fans and critics alike. This was spurred on by the singles 'Got My Mind Set On You' (a cover of a James Ray song from 1962), 'When We Was Fab' and 'This Is Love'.

The use of slide continued to be favoured by George and appeared on all tracks on the album. A particular highlight was the complementing guitar parts on the opening track 'Cloud 9' with Eric Clapton playing lead together with George on slide. 'Someplace Else', 'That's What It Takes', 'Just For Today' are also noteworthy for the use of slide.

George promoted 'Cloud Nine' through videos for the singles, particularly 'Got My Mind Set On You' which received substantial airplay on the MTV channel. Two versions were produced and both saw George appearing with guitars. In the first – where he is seen as part of a 'nickelodeon' film – he plays a black Fender Stratocaster and in the second – with just George appearing in a room full of objects moving to the song – he has a cream-coloured Fender Telecaster with maple neck. The Fender Stratocaster was also prominent in the video for 'When We Was Fab', which featured appearances from Ringo and Elton John, whilst 'This Is Love' sees George with a sunburst Fender Stratocaster (possibly vintage), a Rickenbacker 450 from the 1960s and, briefly, his Zemaitis six-string acoustic. The cover of the 'Cloud Nine' album also saw George posing with his Gretsch Duo Jet which had returned recently to his possession.

During the recording of the 'Cloud Nine' album, George and Jeff Lynne discussed forming a band. In early 1988, George was asked to provide a song for the B-side of 'This Is Love'. He was in America at the time with Jeff and asked Bob Dylan if they could use his home studio as no others were available. This was arranged and Roy Orbison was invited to attend, along with Tom Petty. George decided that with all these great musicians in the same place it would be foolhardy not to have them contribute the track, which was 'Handle With Care'. The record company was taken aback by the song and its line-up and decided that the track deserved a release of its own.

All the musicians were amiable about continuing with the project for an album and the Traveling Wilburys was formed. Over a short period in May 1988, the group completed basic acoustic backing tracks and vocals for several songs which were then embellished by George and Jeff in England. The album

'Traveling Wilburys Volume 1' was released in late 1988 and was a major success.

'Handle With Care' was the lead track from the album and was released as the group's first single in October 1988. A music video was recorded and featured George playing his rhythm parts and slide solos (with metal slide) on a Gretsch Traveling Wilburys TW-300 guitar. This was one of several models created by Gretsch as a promotional tool following the re-launch of the company in the late 1980s. They were cheaply produced solid-body instruments made in Asia and featured themed graphics on the tops with white paint covering the rest of the guitar.

'End of the Line' was the follow-up single, released in early 1989, and for the song's performance George played a Gretsch 'Electromatic' with a metal slide. An early 1950s guitar, this was the precursor to the 'Country Club' model. George had been pictured with the instrument in mid-1988 when the group assembled for the recording sessions in LA and posed with a number of vintage Gretsch guitars.

Although both singles were credited to all the Traveling Wilbury members, they were basically composed by George and featured his trademark slide solos. Yet, the rest of the album is relatively free of them and only two other tracks have slide parts, 'Congratulations' and 'Tweeter And The Monkey Man'; the latter sees George play slide on a resonator.

The positive reaction to 'Traveling Wilburys Volume 1' led the group to record a follow-up, which was mischievously titled 'Traveling Wilburys Volume 3' by George, in mid-1990. However, the group no longer featured Roy Orbison as he passed away at the end of 1988. Sessions for the album took place in April and May 1990 and during rehearsals George was pictured with a Silvertone 1448 electric guitar.

Two singles were released in late 1990 and one in 1991; 'She's My Baby', 'Inside Out' and 'Wilbury Twist' respectively. In the video for the first-mentioned, George plays a Gibson ES 150-style guitar which does not have a pick-up, whilst in the second he has a Gibson ES 175. For the final one, he has two unidentified acoustics, a six-string and a 12-string (with slotted headstock) and in the last scene appears to have a Gibson Les Paul Junior double cutaway.

Despite discussions about mounting a Traveling Wilburys tour, the group disbanded. Yet, at the end of 1991, George enlisted Eric Clapton for a tour of Japan. Over 12 dates, the band performed a set spanning George's career, in addition to a small group of Eric's songs in the middle. An album of the performances was released the following year as 'Live In Japan'. George took several guitars on the tour including: a Fritz Brothers Roy Buchanan Bluesmaster, which was a Telecaster-style guitar; a red Fender Stratocaster; a Fender 12-string from the late 1960s; a Gibson J200 cutaway acoustic. George appears to have played through a Fender tweed amp, which looks to be a Bassman, and used a glass slide for at least one song ('Cheer Down').

Early in 1992 George performed his first and only solo show in London at the Royal Albert Hall. This comprised a similar set list to those songs performed in Japan and George used a similar set of instruments, but mainly played the Roy Buchanan Bluesmaster and Gibson J200 cutaway acoustic with a Fender tweed amp. He did take the Gibson Les Paul on stage for 'While My Guitar Gently Weeps' which saw Gary Moore playing the lead parts.

In October 1992, Bob Dylan staged a concert to celebrate his 30 years in music. George performed 'Absolutely Sweet Marie' and was part of an ensemble rendition of 'My Back Pages'. For both songs George used a Martin D-28 acoustic.

During the mid-1990s, George took part in 'The Beatles Anthology' project which saw a documentary series produced along with three albums of rare and unreleased songs. He then collaborated with Ravi Shankar on the 'Chants Of India' album. George was diagnosed with cancer in the late 1990s and fought the disease into the early 2000s. Yet, he succumbed on November 29, 2001, at age 58.

In the midst of his illness, George worked on his final album, 'Brainwashed', and he was nearing completion when he died. Jeff Lynne and George's son Dhani later finished the work according to instructions left by George.

A rendition of the standard 'Between The Devil And The Deep Blue Sea', which appears on the album, was filmed – featuring Joe Brown and Jools Holland – and sees George playing a Kamaka six-string tenor ukulele. He was particularly fond of ukuleles and would often gift them to friends.

A standout track for George's slide playing is 'Marwa Blues', which later won the 2004 Grammy Award for Best Pop Instrumental Performance. Similarly, 'Any Road', which was paired with the aforementioned as George's last single.

Tony Hicks with Gibson ES 345.
Hollies Management.

Gibson's ES 345 was first produced in 1958 and differed from the ES 335 with the inclusion of a multi-position 'Varitone' switch situated above the lead tone and volume controls. This added various combinations of inductors and capacitors to the guitar's electronic pick-up circuit, altering its resonant frequency and giving an unmistakeable character to the sound. The position markers on the ES 345 are 'double parallelogram' rather than block inlays and the vibrato (Vibrola or Bigsby) was an option for the guitar. Other features included an optional stereophonic output jack, gold-plated hardware and a thicker three-ply edge binding than that of the ES 335.

TONY HICKS

During the mid-1950s Tony Hicks was fortunate that an aunt was ready to launch him into a guitar-playing career. She bought him not one but two guitars sparking an interest, or perhaps an obsession, with guitar playing that has enabled Tony to have a long, distinguished career. He is currently amongst a small, yet revered group of British guitar players, who are still performing to appreciative audiences today.

Tony was born on December 16, 1945, and by his own admission was not from a musical family. His dad possessed an accordion but he never saw it being played.

'The first guitar,' began Tony, 'was an acoustic made by a neighbour. It was absolutely massive – no exaggeration. It was deep-bodied and looked like something a player from one of those Mexican Marimba bands might use. The second one – an acoustic Spanish guitar – was purchased from a shop in Nelson, Lancashire. I don't think we could afford a case so it was wrapped in brown paper and tied up in such a way that when I was walking home people could see it was a guitar.

'I had lessons with a guitar teacher and it involved learning to read music and playing classical pieces. But, no way did I become a classical guitarist. I can read music but have never used it.'

Tony first performed in a seven-piece outfit called Les Skifflelets comprising several guitarists, all playing rhythm, one washboard and a tea chest bass.

'I can't remember what kind of guitar I had with Les Skifflelets though we all played acoustically. The first guitar I actually amplified was through my dad's radiogram. In the early stages of my career, the one thing that moved me and gave me the shivers and got me interested in music was not the guitar but the trumpet. The trumpet solo in Glen Miller's "A String of Pearls", with a brass section thumping out chords behind it, I still find fantastic to this day. But thank God I didn't take up the trumpet.'

Working semi-pro, Les Skifflelets passed an audition for 'The Carroll Levis Discovery Show' in London. First playing a radio version of the programme at the playhouse on the Embankment, they returned for a TV presentation at the Hackney Empire, which was then the home of the 'Oh Boy!' pop show.

Tony often trekked from his home in Nelson to Barratt's Manchester music store where, on a regular monthly basis, an American guitar would appear in a window display. After admiring Buddy Holly and the Crickets on ITV's 'Sunday Night at the London Palladium', Tony convinced himself that there was a chance, with a bit of luck, for a working-class Lancashire guitarist to be a success. His favourite record at the time was Buddy Holly's 'Peggy Sue', recorded and released as a single by Holly in 1957. In the late 1950s, guitarist Scotty Moore's work on early Elvis Presley recordings left a deep impression on Tony.

'Scottie Moore played remarkably considering the guitar and amp he used with no studio effects.'

On a trip to London, Tony saw Tommy Steele perform, and grew up loving Johnny Kidd and the Pirates, as well as Cliff Richard and the Shadows. He was also impressed with Ricky Nelson's lead guitarist James Burton whose playing on 'Hello May Lou' (released 1961) he thought was 'wonderful'.

'I always wanted to be a lead player and used to watch the Shadows on the television. I must confess I observed Hank play more than Bruce. Much later on I actually sold Hank a mint condition mid-1950s Stratocaster.'

On leaving school, Tony became an apprentice electrician, playing guitar at weekends in a band, Ricky Shaw and the Dolphins.

'Like most people, I had a Hofner Club 60 which was very good, a Futurama, the nearest thing in those days to a Strat. The first decent guitar I had was a Gibson cherry red ES 335. Originally it belonged to the Dolphins' rhythm player and I always liked the look of it. When he couldn't afford the payments on it, I took it over. I had an Australian Maton MS-500 guitar that eventually ended up in Barratt's Manchester store. George Harrison played it for a time while his Gretsch Country Gentleman was being repaired at the store. It was then bought by Dave Berry's guitarist and much later sold for an enormous amount. I played the Maton and the ES 335 through a Vox but also recall using a Selmer Truvoice amp.'

Ricky Shaw and the Dolphins played gigs around Manchester for £15 a night. For Tony, this lasted until 1963 when guitarist Vic Farrell left the Hollies – the band only holding the Hollies name from December 1962 – and he was asked to join them. Initially, Tony was invited to listen to the group at the Manchester club, the Twisted Wheel and agreed to join them as a full-time professional, provided he was paid £18 a week.

'Soon after joining the Hollies, I swapped my ES 335 for a Fender Jazzmaster which was owned by the band's manager.'

Tony first recorded with the Hollies when they auditioned on April 4, 1963, at EMI's Abbey Road Studio No. 2. The songs he played on included a cover of the Coaster's 'Ain't That Just Like Me' and two Allan Clarke, Graham Nash originals, 'Hey What's Wrong With Me' and 'Whole World Over'. 'Ain't That Just Like Me' was the band's debut single, released in May 1963 with 'Hey What's Wrong With Me' on the flip side.

'I used the Jazzmaster on the early Hollies' recordings pushed through a battered beige-coloured Vox AC30 that they owned. One of the speakers was virtually kicked in but it sounded great. Then, when I'd earned a few quid with the Hollies I bought myself a Vox AC30 with a treble boost. This

Bill May founded Maton Guitars in Australia during 1944, turning out a fine array of archtop guitars. Later, the company started producing electric guitars, with the MS-500 appearing around 1958. Only a very small number of Maton guitars were shipped to the UK during the early 1960s.

was before Vox started giving us equipment.'

Hollies lead singer Allan Clarke said Tony was a perfect match for the music they were playing. His guitar style was personal. Graham Nash adds that quite by accident they discovered Tony could sing as well as play lead guitar. This allowed them to work on three-part harmonies which became very much a part of the Hollies' sound and 'happened quite naturally.'

Tony states that EMI producer Ron Richards – an assistant to George Martin – was instrumental in helping him play guitar in a 'simpler' way.

'The one thing he always professed was that the important notes in a solo were just as much the ones you don't play as well as the ones you do play. In my solo lead parts for the Hollies, I was always aware they had to fit comfortably between the vocals and to have unique melody and inspiration.'

In a rare 1963, but good quality, promotional film, Tony is playing some neat lead licks on the track 'Little Lover' using the sunburst Fender Jazzmaster. On the promotional film and on the back cover of *Beat Instrumental No. 7* of November 1964, Tony is pictured with the Jazzmaster.

The Hollies' second single was 'Searchin' followed by 'Stay', written by Maurice Williams and released in November 1963. 'I picked up a version of "Stay" in a junk shop and worked out how we would record it with Bobby Elliott. Ian Paice of Deep Purple, once said he was greatly influenced by Bobby Elliott's drumming on "Stay".'

By the end of 1963 Tony, like several other Hollies members, was living in London and for a time he became their man for finding songs. He often trawled the Denmark Street (England's Tin Pan Alley) publishing houses collecting acetates of songs the Hollies might consider recording.

'Just One Look' appeared in February 1964. 'I first heard a version of that record at a party in Manchester and I knew we could do something with it. Obviously, the songs that we adapted or heard as demos did not have any lead guitar introductions or breaks and I used to sit down and create them.'

Initially, the Hollies recorded on a two-track machine, eventually progressing to four-track. They invariably recorded in Abbey Road's Studio 2 and sometimes Studio 3.

'Just One Look' peaked at no. 2 for the Hollies in the British charts and when promoting the single on the New Musical Express Poll Winners Show 1964, Tony is playing a cherry Gibson ES 345 Stereo with a Bigsby (though he is also known to have used the guitar without the Bigsby) and the pick-up covers removed. Tony played the Gibson through a backline of Vox amps.

The Fender Jazzmaster was first introduced at the 1958 NAMM Show and Tony Bacon and Paul Day in 50 Years of Fender: Half a Century of the Greatest Electric Guitars (2000) provide a few details: 'The sound of the Jazzmaster was richer and warmer than players were used to from Fender. The name had not been chosen at random, for Fender was aiming this different tone at jazz players who at the time largely preferred hollow body electrics and principally those by Gibson.'

London's Denmark Street, a short thoroughfare, stretches from the east side of Charing Cross Road to St Giles High Street. A 1960 trade directory includes quite a number of music publishers. The street also boasted a number of recording studios, including Regent Sound where the Rolling Stones recorded early singles and LPs.

'I'd always been a fan of Big Jim Sullivan and when I saw him backing artists of the day with a Gibson ES 345, I liked it and ordered one from Selmer's on Charing Cross Road. I picked it up one day whilst we were all in the van ready to drive to a gig in Gravesend. I took it straight out of the case – a Selmer one not a Gibson case – and played it on stage the same night. I always loved it. In those days when places were filled to the rafters, I'd have the Vox AC30 turned full on and make good use of the ES 345's filter switch to produce great rhythm and lead overdriven sounds – over the top of the crowd. This was of course in the days before channel switching. Much later, the guitar was sprayed black. I haven't got it now and believe it's somewhere in Germany. I should have kept it.'

In *Beat Instrumental No. 19* of November 1964, under the heading 'Price Is No Object', there was an article discussing the merits of guitars over 200gns. Tony had this to say about his 205gns, Gibson ES 345. 'The Gibson is "me" if you get what I mean. It's the sound I like. I think it's become a part of The Hollies as well. Of course, you can't just take a sound or a tone setting and build a group around it, but I know that a lot of people would be surprised if they suddenly heard a Fender sound on one of our records. The Gibson fits beautifully – that's why I consider it well worth the money.'

The first single to be written by Clarke, Nash and Hicks was 'We're Through', released in September 1964 and it reached no. 7. The song was credited to a pseudonym L. Ransford, the name of Graham Nash's grandfather. Commenting in *Melody Maker* about the song, Brian Jones of the Rolling Stones said: 'Liked that guitar run. I don't know who it is, but I'm pretty sure it's British. Great guitar solo, very tight and pleasant.'

Tony added a Gibson Les Paul Standard to his arsenal during an American tour in April 1965. The instrument, priced at $80, was bought for him from a pawn shop by CBS who were filming the tour. 'The guitar had a Bakelite switch installed and when I got it back home, I had Barratt's take it out and repair the hole. I never felt the Les Paul guitar sound suited the Hollies and the guitar itself eventually ended up with Spencer Davis.'

For a TV show in Scotland in the mid-1960s, Tony had to borrow a Fender Stratocaster but Stratocasters did not appeal to him.

The Hollies released 'I'm Alive', written by Clint Ballard, in May 1965 and it became their first no. 1 UK hit. In a promotional film for the single, Tony plays the Gibson ES 345. On the Hollies DVD 'Look Through Any Window 1963–1975' (2015), he explains that he picked a melody out of a chord for the solo 'which seemed to work for what we were doing at the time.'

Tony Hicks second from left with The Dolphins.
Hollies Management.

Recording of 'Look Through Any Window', written by Graham Gouldman and Charles Silverman, took place at Abbey Road at the end of June 1965 and was released in August 1965. When appearing on German TV's 'Beat Club' in 1966 the Hollies performed several hits live. On playing 'Look Through Any Window', Tony used a 12-string Framus acoustic 'Texan' (with a pick-up).

The Hollies' spot on 'Sunday Night at the London Palladium' on October 3, 1965, featured 'Look Through Any Window' and Tony is playing a Vox 12-string. Graham Nash admits that at the time they had heard the Byrds' version of Bob Dylan's 'Mr Tambourine Man' and wanted to get a 12-string 'jangly' sound.

'Amazingly, I did live shows like that one with only one guitar – no spare one in case I broke a string – and only one amp. I never thought about calamities like that.'

During the summer of 1965, Clarke, Hicks and Nash formed their own publishing company (under an imprint of Dick James Music) Gralto Music (recognising part of their Christian names GRaham, ALlan, and TOny).

In *Beat Instrumental No. 31* of November 1965, Tony features in a large full-page advertisement headed 'ALL-VOX Man ... that's TONY HICKS'. The advertisement includes the following text: 'It's no secret! The Hollies feature VOX, the Sound Equipment that gives the most, sounds best! Tony Hicks features the VOX Phantom 12-string, partnered by the superb VOX AC50 Super Twin Amplifier. If you dig the Hollies' sound ... you dig VOX'.

Both guitar and amplifier were made by Jennings Musical Industries Limited in Dartford,

During the early 1960s, Vox were determined to design guitars that would be instantly recognisable as being produced by the company. Thus, Vox sought the help in 1962 from the London Design Centre, to conceive appropriate body shapes for a new range of guitars. The first to appear was the 'coffin'-shaped V209 Phantom VI guitar followed by the V210 Vox Phantom Bass and V221 Vox Phantom 12-string. Other than Tony Hicks, members of the Dave Clark Five and Peter Jay and the Jaywalkers used Vox Phantom guitars.

Kent.

In *The Vox Story* (1993), David Petersen and Dick Denney comment: 'For a British-made instrument, the Phantom represented a great improvement in build quality, typified by its heavier body and an advanced neck-building technique including the use of laminated sections as well as the usual tensioning rod.'

Beat Instrumental No. 31 of November 1965 gave the following offered Tony's comments about the Phantom 12-string and the AC50 Super Twin:

'I must admit that I found it difficult to play 12 strings and didn't like the thicker string above the thinner one. In fact, I mostly used them as six strings and never toured with a 12-string. It was marvellous being associated with Vox. We were supplied with their amps in America. They had a place in New York and we could go there and choose what we wanted. Often, I would nip down to the Dartford factory and discuss with the technicians, certain amp tweaks I would like. For instance, I was a bit of a treble maniac and they would make adjustments to an amp straight away. On one occasion I got them to install a tweeter into a T60. I never really got involved with their effects pedals.'

Beat Instrumental's 1965 'Gold Star Awards' published in the magazine's No. 33 January 1966 edition, revealed readers had voted Tony at no. 5 in a top ten of lead guitarists. The list was topped by Hank Marvin with Eric Clapton at no. 6. The Hollies were voted 'Best Group on Stage' and Bobby Elliott won the 'Best Drummer' award.

On one of Tony's many hunting trips to publishing houses he found 'I Can't Let Go' by Al Gorgoni and Chip Taylor at Dick James Music. Recorded at Abbey Road Studios, it was released in February 1966. 'With this single I played the lead parts with the Rickenbacker mapleglo and the ES 345 is chugging along behind.'

Around this time, it was stated by Pete MacLaine, a Manchester musician and close friend of the band: 'Tony Hicks was probably the musical leader of the group.' Abbey Road sound engineer, Ken Townsend also commented favourably: 'Tony Hicks was musically the strongest Hollie and, without doubt, he led the band in the studio.'

In June/July 1966, Eric Haydock, a founder member of the Hollies, left the band. The 'Bus Stop' single, released in the same year, was the first recording with Bernie Calvert – a member of the Dolphins – playing bass.

The Phantom 12-string
Fitted with six-pole maximum frequency, adjustable pick-ups, separate tone and volume controls, adjustable bridge. Reinforced slim-line neck with adjustable truss-rod, fast action fingerboard. Tuned with E and B in unison – other strings in octave separation. Available in white, black, light blue, dark blue or green polyester finish.

AC50 Super Twin
A 50-watt model with built-in glass-shattering treble, and full, deep tone bass boost. Two channels (bass and treble) each with two inputs. Two 12" loudspeakers and a high frequency pressure horn with cross-over network in separate case. Combination, swivel and rigid stands available.

Supreme
Dick Denney and David Peterson (op. cit.) state the following about the amplifier: 'Perhaps the handsomest amplifier ever made, the Supreme. It began life as the "British Beatle", heavily influenced by the Thomas Organ Company design [Vox USA], and sharing most of its features.' But, they say, by the time the amplifier was introduced, the third channel and the tuning tone had vanished and the distortion feature made variable by a panel control.

The itinerary for the Hollies in 1966 embraced trips to Holland, Sweden, Iceland, America and Poland. The band also waxed an EP in French with the main tracks 'Look Through Any Window' and 'We're Through'.

In *Beat instrumental No. 39* of July 1966 Tony is featured in an article titled 'Tony Hicks … Zealous Hollie' by Mike Crofts. The article revolves around Tony being an Everly Brothers fan, meeting Don and Phil and writing some songs for them. Tony, Allan and Graham Nash took some songs they had written to Decca's West Hampstead studios to catch the Everlys in session. While Tony demonstrated the basic song idea on his guitar, occasionally adding little phrases, Graham and Allan went through the words with Don and Phil. Tony said: 'They were all new songs, and the fact that the Everlys chose several, gave us a lot more confidence as far as writing was concerned. It was interesting to hear how different their versions sounded …'

Eight of the Clarke, Hicks and Nash compositions appeared under the pseudonym, L. Ransford, on the Everly Brothers album 'Two Yanks In England' released in 1966. Tony commented: 'I ended up playing guitar with them on [the] album which they recorded in just a week. Jimmy Page was working as a session guitarist then and he joined us along with John Paul Jones on bass – so, basically, it was the Everly Brothers with Led Zeppelin and myself.'

In the same article, Tony gave details of the Hollies' recent tour of America and he mentioned the band went to see Simon and Garfunkel recording 'I Am A Rock' in New York and then the Mamas and the Papas in California recording an LP 'Stop Stop Stop' appeared in October 1966 and saw Tony Hicks playing a banjo acquired from Barratt's. The instrument, according to Tony, was quite a primitive one, tuned like a guitar and recorded in a way that made it sound like a balalaika. The overall feel of the song suggests the influence of Middle Eastern and Greek music. Graham Nash relates the song was inspired by seeing a belly dancer in a New York nightclub. It was the first big hit which Nash, Clarke and Hicks had written themselves, reaching no. 2 in the UK and no. 1 in Canada and New Zealand.

During an American tour in late 1966, the band ran into union trouble with their PA, as Graham Nash explains: 'We [carried] our own PA equipment … cost about £1,000 and came from Sweden … Anyway, it costs a fortune in excess baggage to cart it off to America.

So what happens? At one date, the unions move in and say our bloke can't work it. The unions apparently own the hall. There's all the threatening and ruddy stupid talk. We weren't working without it; they said we couldn't work with it, unless their man operated it. Eventually we reached a deal … our man set it correctly, then their fellow sat by it for the show.'

Tony added: 'The PA was revolutionary at the time and Benny England was the maker. The system had loads of 8-inch speakers and we took it wherever we went. We shipped the speaker cabinets to Australia without flight cases just with pieces of plywood nailed to the fronts to protect the speakers.'

Beat Instrumental No. 45 of January 1967 includes Tony in a feature titled 'Vox Hall of Fame: No.2' and mentions: 'Tony plays a Phantom 12-string guitar through a 120-watt Solid State amplifier.' The article illustrates a 12-string Vox guitar leaning against a Vox Supreme amplifier – one of three lead guitar Solid State models introduced mid-1966; the other two were the Conqueror and Defiant.

The Hollies' 'On A Carousel', penned by Allan, Graham and Tony was released in February 1967. In a performance of the track in Abbey Road Studios 1967 from the 'Reelin' in the Years Archive', Tony is using a black Gibson Les Paul Custom with a P90 and an alnico pick-up. 'On that single I played the guitar through the Solid State amp with the mid-range boost pushed up.'

By February 1967, it was revealed that the Hollies had a new contract with EMI. This enabled them to record independently and also to record other artists.

According to Graham Nash, the Hollies' 'Carrie Anne' song was written about Marianne Faithfull but confesses they were too shy to use her real name. The single released in May 1967, featured a solo using steel drums.

In an article titled 'The Sounds I Like by Britain's Top Guitarists' in *Beat Instrumental No. 48* of April 1967, Tony said: 'I don't believe in padding-out all my lead passages with wild string-slurring, but try to play as many notes as possible in the most exciting way. I love a good, thick, chunky sound. I've never really gone for all this whining guitar stuff. Mustn't be too bassy either. Somewhere just in the middle. That's one of the reasons why we like the new Vox Solid State amps.'

A performance of 'Carrie Anne' on 'The Smothers Brothers Show' reveals Tony with a mapleglo (natural) Rickenbacker. *Teen Beat* magazine, first published in August 1967, features a picture of him holding the mapleglo guitar with six strings.

In 1967, with the 'Evolution' (June 1967) and 'Butterfly' (November 1967) albums, Graham Nash admits he was trying to push the band into being more experimental than in previous years. On 'Butterfly', Tony plays a Danelectro sitar.

Allan Clarke admits this was the period where the band started moving away from an instantly recognisable Hollies sound to one featuring Graham Nash. In a promotional video for 'Dear Eloise', taken from the 'Butterfly' album, Tony strums the Rickenbacker mapleglo guitar.

Written by Graham Nash, 'King Midas in Reverse' was released in September 1967 and though a critical success it did not reach the same dizzy heights in the charts as had become a regular occurrence previously for the band. In an effort to bring the Hollies back to more customary chart success, they released 'Jennifer Eccles'.

Tony mentions in *Beat Instrumental No. 55* of November 1967 that he had hoped to be the first to use the Vox Wah-Wah pedal on discs. 'It's on our soon out LP. But Hendrix beat me to it – so I'm not the first. But I think it's great. But it's true that electronic devices are coming in, on all instruments, and I suppose you can see a time when the musician will be more or less a push button star …'

Graham's desire to change his life, experiment more and develop his song-writing skills were amongst the reasons for him leaving the band on December 8, 1968, to be replaced by Terry Sylvester formerly of the Escorts and the Swinging Blue Jeans. He played guitar, sang and made contributions to the established song-writing team of Clarke and Hicks.

At the end of the 1960s and into the 1970s, the band moved into another successful phase and continued to make single and LP hits. 'Sorry Suzanne' reached no. 3 in the UK singles chart and no. 1 in South Africa and Switzerland. In a video of the band performing the song, Tony plays some neat lead licks on a black Gibson Les Paul Custom with three pick-ups (without a Bigsby).

'We were doing a show in Germany and a guy in the orchestra there was playing a black three pick-up Les Paul Custom. He was desperate to offload it and buy a Gretsch so I bought the Les Paul off him. It looked great, it didn't have a Bigsby, or gold Grover heads just plastic ones.'

The 'Hollies Sing Dylan' album was released in May 1969 and the band's last single of the 1960s was 'He Ain't Heavy, He's My Brother'. It was another song 'discovered' by Tony: 'I found it at Cyril Shane Music Ltd and thought it would make a good change of pace for us.' The single was no. 1 in the UK and South Africa with further respectable positions around the world.

Gibson's first version of the Les Paul Custom was produced between 1954 and 1957. At that time it was priced at $325 which was $100 more than the Gold Top. Introduced in the same year as the Junior, the black Custom featured an all-mahogany body, black finish, multiple binding, block-shaped position markers in an ebony fingerboard and gold-plated hardware. Les Paul is quoted saying in Tony Bacon's 50 Years of the Les Paul: A Half-Century of a Guitar Icon *(2002) that he chose the black colour for the Custom guitar: 'When you're on stage with a black tuxedo and a black guitar, the people can see your hands move with a spotlight on them. They'll see your hands flying.' The Custom was advertised in Gibson guitar catalogues as 'the fretless wonder' because the low fret wire employed enabled some guitarists to play faster.*

Between 1957 and 1961 Gibson produced the 'second version' of their Les Paul Custom. It was similar to the first, except three metal-covered humbucker pick-ups were provided. A Bigsby vibrato unit was optional.

Tony Hicks with a selection from his guitar collection.
Hollies Management.

'Hollies Sing Hollies' – their ninth studio album – featured all the songs written by the band and was released in November 1969. Failing to chart in the UK, it did well in the USA, reaching no. 32.

Several singles, including 'I Can't Tell The Bottom From The Top' and 'Gasoline Alley Bred', appeared in 1970. After the release of the 'Distant Light' album in October 1971, Allan Clarke departed to pursue a solo career, with Swedish singer Mikael Rickfors joining the band.

'Long Cool Woman In A Black Dress', was released in April 1972 and reached no. 2 in the USA, but was only a moderate success in the UK. One video showing the band performing the song reveals Tony had switched to a Gibson Les Paul Special double-cut in TV yellow with P90 pick-ups.

'Over the years I've had loads of Gibson Les Paul Specials, single and double-cuts. Some of them were bought from Gruhn's Guitars in Nashville. I've also had a Gibson Korina Explorer and a single pick-up Firebird, bought from noted guitar tech, Alan Rogan. Now, I only have a cherry Les Paul Junior but I reckon if I'd kept some of my guitars, I'd be at least a million pounds better off.'

Allan Clarke rejoined the Hollies in 1973 and the band went on to achieve a UK no. 2 (or no. 1 depending on which chart is referenced) with 'The Air that I Breathe' when released in January 1974. The Hollies' version of the song achieved worldwide top ten positions. During a performance of the single Tony is seen playing the lead parts on a Rickenbacker mapleglo 450/12.

'It took some time devising the unmistakeable lead guitar intro to that song. Someone once told me that they'd heard Eric Clapton say he would have liked to have written it. Maybe that's true, I don't know.'

The band enjoyed singles chart hits during the remainder of the 1970s, only these were mainly in Europe and New Zealand. The early 1980s saw Calvert and Sylvester leave the Hollies. In 1981, Tony Hicks edited a medley of Hollies' hits and it was released as 'Holliedaze' which returned them to the top thirty. For a 'Top of the Pops' promotion, the BBC insisted that the original members of the band performed on the show. Thus, Graham Nash and Eric Haydock briefly rejoined in September 1981. For the performance, Tony has a sunburst Gibson Les Paul.

Graham Nash made some recordings and appearances with the band until around 1984. Afterwards, there was no let-up for the Hollies continuing to record and tour round the world. Ray Stiles, formerly of the band Mud, joined the band on bass from 1986. 'He Ain't Heavy' was re-released in 1988 and reached no. 1. The 1990s were marked with Graham Nash once again reunited with the band to record a new version of 'Peggy Sue Got Married' that featured pre-recorded lead vocals by Buddy Holly. This was taken from an 'alternate' version of the song given to Graham Nash by Holly's widow, Maria Elena Holly. In the middle of the decade, the Hollies were awarded an Ivor Novello Award for Outstanding Contribution to British Music.

Allan Clarke's last Hollies show was on November 27, 1999, and he was replaced by former Move front man, Carl Wayne. Between 2000 and 2004, the band toured extensively and a New Zealand 'Hollies Greatest Hits' collection made it to no. 1 in that country. Wayne only recorded one song with the Hollies, 'How Do I Survive' which charted at no. 21 in the UK.

Following Carl's death in 2004, Peter Howarth replaced him and the band was introduced into the 'Vocal Group Hall of Fame' in the US in 2006. In the same year the Hollies released

> *Paul Reed Smith, born in 1956, began building guitars in the mid-1970s and launched his company in 1985, quickly finding a niche in the upscale guitar market. His first factory was in Annapolis, Maryland, followed by a move to Stevensville on Kent Island. By the end of the 20th century, PRS was producing 700 guitars a month with a staff of 110.*

Tony Hicks playing a Paul Reed Smith. Hollies Management.

their first studio album since 1983, 'Staying Power'. Three years later another one appeared, 'Then, Now, Always'.

Hollies members, Allan Clarke, Graham Nash, Tony Hicks, Bobby Elliott, Eric Haydock, Bernie Calvert and Terry Sylvester were inducted into the Rock and Roll Hall of Fame in 2010 in recognition of their achievements. Three years later, the Hollies' 50th year of existence, was marked with a worldwide tour, with over 60 concert performances.

Tony had some guitars made for him by Roger Giffin who established the Giffin Guitar workshop and developed the Steinberger 'M' guitar before being offered a job running Gibson's West Coast Custom Shop.

Over the last few years, Tony has become accustomed to using PRS guitars. 'Doug Chandler, who along with his wife, established Chandler Guitars in Kew during 1979, said I ought to try the PRS range. When I did, I was sold straight away. I've got a PRS Metal guitar. When I first saw it, I thought, no, that's not for me, it's too fancy. It must have been in the store three or four weeks before I tried it. Quickly, liking the sound, I bought it. I'm glad I did as it's been a hell of an investment. When I told Paul Read Smith, I'd got a Metal guitar he congratulated me. He said he'd only ever made a few and wanted them to appeal to heavy metal people but disappointingly struggled to sell them. I've got about 15 PRS guitars and a number are from the early production years featuring the T & B pick-ups. I must admit that at first, I was suspicious of the Sweet switch but have found it very useful.'

With regard to his use of amplification, Tony said: 'I actually got someone at Vox to convert an amp to switch channels and give an overdrive. But, after that I turned to Mesa Boogie. One of our road crew went to the Mesa Boogie factory and asked if I could use one. After a while, I got an amp with a graphic equalizer which I used for a period. But now, I go straight into the board.'

STEVE HOWE

As part of the progressive rock band Yes, Steve Howe has created a legacy of music, particularly his guitar work on such records as 'The Yes Album', 'Fragile', 'Close To The Edge' and 'Going For The One'. He has also released solo albums showcasing his diverse musical interests. Mainly known for using a Gibson ES 175, Steve has built around this guitar an assorted collection of instruments. He adds these – such as a lap steel or classic acoustic – to his songs to create interesting tonalities.

Steve was one of four children. There was no musical ability in his family and he became interested around age ten when he would listen to his parents' records. Later, he took notice of the rise of rock 'n' roll in Britain. This likely inspired a desire for a guitar and at Christmas in the late 1950s he received a German-made acoustic archtop. Steve learned from records, including those by Chet Atkins, the Shadows and Duane Eddy. He obtained Eric Kershaw's *Dance Band Chords for the Guitar* (1946) which assisted him further. He continued to investigate guitarists in his early teens – Django Reinhardt, Wes Montgomery, Tal Farlow.

Leaving school at 15, Steve developed an interest in woodwork by taking a job as an apprentice piano maker. Yet, he discovered the noise of the factory was potentially detrimental to his hearing and found employment elsewhere. Steve was still honing his guitar playing at this time and eventually decided he was ready to join a group. At age 17, he formed the Syndicats with other local musicians. To allow him to play gigs, a Guyatone LG50 and matching amp, later upgraded to a Watkins Dominator, were purchased from a friend.

Around early 1964, Steve and the Syndicats entered Joe Meek's studio to record a cover of Chuck Berry's 'Maybellene'. He used equipment mentioned previously, yet soon made a dramatic upgrade. With the financial help of his father, Steve ordered a Gibson ES 175 and partnered this with a Fender Tremolux head and cabinet. The pair were first heard on the group's next session with Meek which yielded 'Howling For My Baby' – a cover of Howlin' Wolf's 'Howlin' For My Darling'. A more interesting effort is the group-penned B-side 'What To Do'. Steve's new guitar and amp can be seen on an appearance for the TV programme 'Beat Room' available on youtube.com where the band plays a medley of Bo Diddley songs.

'On The Horizon' was the group's last single and this saw Steve using a DeArmond volume pedal. Around the end of 1965, Steve left the Syndicats and joined The In Crowd. He first appeared on the band's next single 'Stop, Wait A Minute' and the B-side 'You're On Your Own'. The latter saw the DeArmond pedal in use and Steve had a particularly driven lead tone thanks to an unidentified 'fuzz box'. The In Crowd recorded another single and continued to play gigs around Europe. The group evolved to embrace the 'psychedelic' music of the period, with long jams taking favour over standard songs and covers of before. This led to a change of name to Tomorrow. The band recorded an album in mid-1967, with a single, 'My White Bicycle', released at the time, though the LP did not appear until early 1968. The single featured Steve's backwards guitar and recording effects applied to some of his contributions. 'Now Your Time Has Come' on the album allowed Steve a chance to demonstrate his guitar capabilities.

Keith West, Tomorrow's singer and song-writer, experienced some success out of the band and, in addition to diverging musical interests, the group folded during 1968. Steve did contribute guitar and bass to some of Keith's tracks, whilst also performing session work for others. A new band, Bodast, with Steve on guitar was formed in mid-1968. An album of material was recorded for Tetragrammaton in the late 1960s, though the company folded before the release. The sessions were later released as 'The Bodast Tapes' in the 1980s. In late 1969, Steve was asked to back P.P. Arnold in a band that toured in support of Delaney & Bonnie and Friends.

The new decade provided Steve promising opportunities. The band Yes had been formed in 1968 and recorded two albums. The second one brought conflict within the group and resulted in guitarist Peter Banks departing. Steve auditioned for the band in early 1970 and was accepted into the line-up by the middle of the year. Soon after, Yes rented a cottage in Devon to work on the next record – 'The Yes Album'. The first track 'Yours Is No Disgrace' demonstrates Steve's ability to create several textures amidst the group's sound. He achieves this using his Gibson ES 175 which moves from clean to distorted sounds, sometimes with echo and others with Wah-Wah. A volume pedal is employed, as is a studio stereo-panning effect. Steve played a Martin 00-18 acoustic on the song, in addition to the following track 'Clap'. He had acquired the guitar several years earlier. Similarly, a Portuguese 12-string instrument was gifted to Steve by his sister in the early 1960s and this found use on 'I've Seen All Good People'. In *The Steve Howe Guitar Collection* (1999), he mentions the guitar has an unusual tuning – Ab, E, B, E, B, E – which he developed, though whether this was the case at the time of recording the previously mentioned or later songs is unclear. The same publication notes Steve was using a Solid State Vox 100-watt head in the late 1960s and went on to buy a Fender Dual Showman before the next album was recorded in early 1971, leaving a speculative gap for 'The Yes Album'. An image of the band rehearsing in Devon is reproduced in Steve's book *All My Yesterdays* and the amp he is using appears to be a Vox head with cabinet. When released in early 1971, the record achieved no. 4 in the UK and peaked at no. 40 in America. It also received critical acclaim.

Yes toured for much of late 1970 and the first half of 1971. For the European dates in early 1971, the band was supported by Iron Butterfly. The American group later sold their PA system to Yes and it consisted of Ampex equipment. An early visual appearance of the Fender Dual Showman amp used by Steve, with an extension cabinet, was on the German TV series 'Beat Club' in April 1971 when the band performed 'Yours Is

No Disgrace'. Steve continued to play his ES 175 and had his Martin and Portuguese 12-string acoustics on hand. Whilst on tour, the seeds were being sown for songs that would appear on the next album 'Fragile'. Sessions for this began at the end of the American leg of the tour, starting August 1971. These saw the departure of Tony Kaye on keyboards and Rick Wakeman join. A mixed approach was made to song-writing, with individuals contributing their own compositions and the group coming together for longer tracks. One of the first songs, 'Roundabout', which subsequently appeared first on 'Fragile', saw the collaboration between Steve and singer Jon Anderson. Steve uses his Martin initially on the track before switching to a new guitar – a 1959 Gibson ES 5 'Switchmaster' in blonde finish. He employed the guitar on the remainder of the album, apart from final track 'Heart Of The Sunrise', as well as his solo contribution 'Mood For A Day', recorded on a classical guitar.

Sessions for 'Fragile' concluded in early September and by the end of the month Yes were on the road in support – the album was available from November. 'Fragile' built on the success of 'The Yes Album' and breached the UK top ten and went to no. 4 in the US. The tour began in the UK and ran through to late October before going to the States until the end of the year. A round of British and European dates occurred in January 1972 and again followed by two months in America.

Whilst in the latter country, Steve was approached by Gibson to promote the company's strings. As a result, he was able to acquire a Gibson ES 345 Stereo guitar, which had an ES 5-style tailpiece – a custom request from Steve. He went on to use this for some of the electric guitar parts on the title track for the next album, 'Close To The Edge', recorded throughout the first half of 1972. He also played a Coral Sitar guitar and a Gibson BR9 lap steel. The latter was featured on the second-side tracks, 'And You And I', and 'Siberian Khatru'. For the featured guitar solo on the last-mentioned song, Steve divulges in *All My Yesterdays* that he did not listen to his guitar at that point and just allowed the music to flow. Happily, the part fit and has been recognised as a highlight of 'Siberian Khatru'. 'Close To The Edge' was a top-five album following release in September 1972 in the UK and US, also receiving much critical acclaim.

Despite the band working on the new album, time was found for continued touring in summer 1972 (USA), as well as later in the year (both Europe and America again). As the gap was bridged between 'Fragile' and 'Close To The Edge', the material played changed and Steve added to his guitars. With 'Close To The Edge', as well as 'And You And I', featuring both 6-string and 12-string guitar parts, he purchased a white Gibson EDS 1275 Doubleneck guitar (with distinctive upper pick-guard) in order to play both parts seamlessly. The lap guitar also made appearances as 'Siberian Khatru' joined the set list. Recordings were made from live shows during 1972 and some of the best performances of the main songs were compiled for the band's first live album, 'Yessongs', appearing in mid-1973.

Towards the end of 1972, a concert at the Rainbow Theatre, London, was filmed and later released in 1975. Steve started with the Portuguese 12-string, then moved on to use the Gibson ES 5 'Switchmaster' for 'I've Seen All Good People'. For Steve's spotlight showcase on 'Clap' he turned to the Martin 00-18. This was followed by 'And You And I' which called for the lap steel and Gibson EDS 1275. 'Close To The Edge' had the Gibson ES 345 and Choral Sitar, which was fitted to a stand in playing position for Steve to perform without switching instruments. After Rick Wakeman's solo spot – featuring a medley of his own 'Six Wives Of Henry VIII', which Steve contributed guitar for on 'Catherine Of Aragon' – the band played 'Roundabout' and Steve returned to the ES 5. For the encore, 'Yours Is No Disgrace', Steve's Gibson ES 175 made an appearance. Amplification appears to have continued to be the Fender Dual Showman rig mentioned previously, with at least Wah-Wah/volume pedal and reverb effects applied at various points – a pedalboard is visible though not featured enough to note individual items.

With a break taken over the Christmas and New Year period of 1972–1973, Yes returned to the road in March 1973 for their first tour of Japan and Australia. Amidst these dates, Jon Anderson had an idea for the next album when reading *Autobiography of a Yogi*. He thought of modelling four songs on the author's description of four aspects of how to look at different subjects. With Steve, Jon developed ideas for this subsequently and into the following American tour in April. After this ended, Yes recorded 'Tales From Topographic Oceans' over the summer. Stretching over a double album, four lengthy songs took up each side. Steve varied his guitars in order to achieve the right tonality to fit each track. 'The Revealing Science Of God' started the record and he used the Gibson ES 345, followed by a recently-acquired Danelectro 12-string on 'The Remembering' covering side two. 'The Ancient' featured Steve on a lap steel on several sections, a classical acoustic and a Gibson Les Paul Junior. The latter also provided guitar parts on 'Ritual' which closed the album. Yes toured 'Tales From Topographic Oceans' in Britain during late 1973 and America and Europe during early 1974. His equipment over these dates appears to have been similar to the above, with the addition of the Les Paul Junior.

Another round of summer recording sessions took place in 1974 as Yes assembled 'Relayer'. The band returned to the single-album format, though again favoured longer songs in which several musical themes were developed. Steve made a break with Gibson guitars for the record and primarily played a 1955 Fender Telecaster, though this was tempered by the fitting of a humbucker in the neck position. He changed his lap steel to a Fender Dual 6 Professional pedal steel which had two necks. In *The Steve Howe Guitar Collection*, Steve records that one neck was tuned to E major, whilst the other varies according to his requirements, but could be standard tuning or E minor. The steel guitar was featured on the lead track 'Gates of Delirium'. A visual record was made of the band performing at Queens Park Rangers football ground in the middle of promotion for the album in mid-1975. The two earlier instruments were used on stage by Steve, along with the ES 345, Martin 00-18, a lute, classic acoustic, EDS 1275, Les Paul Junior and ES 175.

Steve recorded a solo album in 1975 as Yes took a break from their collective commitments. 'Beginnings' was an eclectic mix of material and featured several friends backing Steve. He publicised the record with a short film of three tracks,

Steve Howe with a collection of his string instruments.
Victor Watts / Alamy Stock Photo

Steve Howe with Gibson ES 175 guitar.
Pictorial Press Ltd / Alamy Stock Photo.

Steve Howe at Saratoga, California, USA, July 7, 2013.
ZUMA Press, Inc. / Alamy Stock Photo.

two of which were performed. The first was 'Ram' and had Steve playing all the instruments using an editing technique and these consisted of: Martin 00-18; unidentified lap steel, possibly a Fender model; Bacon and Day 'Blue Bell' banjo; Gibson EMS 1235 Doubleneck mandolin; washboard. The title track was featured and saw Steve with a Kohno No. 10 classical acoustic.

Yes returned to the stage in mid-1976 with an American tour, then at the end of the year entered the studio to record new material. The band decided to relocate to Switzerland to do this and 'Going For The One' was the product. This took a different format from previous efforts and songs were shorter than previously, though the final track 'Awaken' stretched to 15 minutes. A few new instruments appeared on the record, including a mid-1960s Fender Stratocaster, a Rickenbacker mapleglo 12-string, Gibson L5, 'Sho-Bud' pedal steel, Gibson Les Paul, Gibson Les Paul Junior double cutaway with Bigsby Palm Pedal, whilst aforementioned Martin 00-18, Kohno No. 10 classical acoustic, 1955 Fender Telecaster and Fender Dual 6 were also used. From footage taken of the recording process, Steve appears to be using a Fender amp.

'Going For The One' was the band's second UK no. 1 album and found similar success in America, breaking into the top ten during summer 1977. Yes filmed their first music video for the single 'Wonderous Stories' and this saw Steve with the Portuguese 12-string before playing a Gibson ES 225 thinline with two P90 pick-ups. The track was popular and peaked at no. 7 in the singles charts. Touring was undertaken during the second half of 1977, with the band visiting the US, Britain and Europe. Several shows were organised for the Empire Pool, Wembley, and these were particularly successful for the group. Footage of the appearance at Glasgow's Apollo Theatre shows Steve with a mid-1960s Fender Stratocaster, Rickenbacker mapleglo 12-string, Portuguese 12-string, pedal steel and Gibson ES 175. Steve's amps were hidden as part of the stage design.

The band continued in 1978 with the recording of 'Tormarto' [sic] taking place in London over several months early in the year followed by a tour in support in the second half, as well as 1979. In the latter year, another concert film was made of the group performing in Philadelphia. Over this period, Yes played on a revolving stage which was stylised. This appears to have resulted in Steve switching to a pair of Fender Twin amps covered in a matching material to the white colour scheme of the stage. His instruments remained relatively static. The Gibson Les Paul featured as part of the video for the album's single release 'Don't Kill The Whale'. Similarly, when Steve completed his second solo record in 1979, 'The Steve Howe Album', many previously mentioned guitars were used – Steve helpfully indicated for those interested which were used on the ten tracks in the inner of the original gatefold vinyl sleeve. Those perhaps new to sessions were Gibson and Martin mandolins, a Gibson EB-6 bass and a Gibson Les Paul Recording, though the latter was with Steve for the 'Going For The One' sessions but not filmed in use and seen on a stand in the background.

Jon Anderson and Rick Wakeman became the driving forces behind the proposed direction for the tenth Yes album in late 1979. Yet, this diverged from the other three members and, after fruitless sessions in Paris and London, a break occurred between the two factions. Steve, Chris Squire and Alan White decided to continue as Yes and joined forces with the Buggles' Trevor Horn and Geoff Downes. The duo was recently lauded for the single 'Video Killed The Radio Star' and brought fresh impetus to the group. The new Yes completed one album – 'Drama'– and embarked on a worldwide tour before disbanding in 1981. Two promotional films of the line-up were recorded for the songs 'Into The Lens' and 'Tempus Fugit'. Steve has his Fender Stratocaster in the latter, whilst the former has the Telecaster, Fender Dual 6 and Choral Sitar through a Fender Twin combo amp.

Steve soon turned to establishing a new group. He was referred to John Wetton, the former bassist of King Crimson who was also looking for a new project. The pair went on to join with Geoff Downes and drummer Carl Palmer to form Asia in 1981. A self-titled album was recorded over the summer and appeared in March 1982. A more 'commercial' rock sound was employed quite successfully as the record spent over two months at the top of the US chart and several months in the UK charts. The three singles – 'Heat Of The Moment', 'Only Time Will Tell' and 'Sole Survivor' – fared similarly well, particularly in America. Steve notes several facts about 'Heat Of The Moment' in *All My Yesterdays*, including that a number of the guitar parts were performed on his Gibson Les Paul Junior through multiple amps to gain particular sounds for each and he used a Koto for the 'middle eight' section. At the time of release, the band performed in America and later in the year was live across Europe. On the video for the single, Steve is filmed using his Gibson Les Paul exclusively. For the tour, Steve played four Gibson ES Artist guitars, which were based on the ES 335 though with different controls, built-in effects – limiter, 'expander' and treble boost – and no f-holes. They were custom modified to feature an extra pick-guard above the pick-ups. He played the ES Artists through a Fender Twin amp with 15-inch speakers.

Asia recorded a second album, 'Alpha', in 1983 and again performed in America. Yet, this was cut short and John Wetton left the group. A commitment in Japan ('Asia in Asia') had to be fulfilled, resulting in the recruitment of Carl Palmer's bandmate Greg Lake for the dates. One concert at Tokyo's Budokan was broadcast live by MTV and Steve is seen playing his Gibson ES Artists. Again, in *All My Yesterdays*, Steve notes he was obliged to alter the tuning of each guitar in order to suit Greg Lake's vocal range on certain songs.

Despite Wetton returning to Asia, conflicts remained and Steve left the band. He soon teamed up with former Genesis guitarist Steve Hackett to form GTR. A successful single, 'When The Heart Rules The Mind', and album, 'GTR', appeared in 1986, being generally similar to the music Asia had produced. Over this period, Steve favoured the use of synthesizer guitars, though not exclusively. He had a Roland G505 Stratocaster-type guitar with effects unit, as well as a Gibson Les Paul Studio Custom fitted with a Roland LPK-1 pick-up and electronics which could connect to either GR-300 or GR-700 synthesizer systems. Although Steve, in *The Steve Howe Guitar Collection*, informs that he also used an Ibanez emulator unit with the guitar.

The GTR project ultimately went no further, despite Steve attempting to move forward with other musicians. In the late 1980s, he performed on sessions and worked on a third solo album – 'Turbulence' – which ultimately appeared in 1991. A short time after the dissolution of GTR, Steve was contacted by Jon Anderson with a view to working together again outside of Yes, which was continuing separately under Chris Square and Steve's replacement on guitar, Trevor Rabin. Jon and Steve later recruited Rick Wakeman and original Yes drummer Bill Bruford, as well as noted bassist Tony Levin, becoming Anderson Bruford Wakeman Howe. A self-titled album was recorded between 1988 and 1989, with Steve adding guitar to tracks in a London studio. In *All My Yesterdays*, Steve writes that he had 40 guitars stored there for use when required, likely being many instruments mentioned earlier. Similarly, several favourites went on tour in 1989 and 1990, with both the new and Yes material played. A concert film – 'An Evening Of Yes Music Plus' – and album was recorded amidst these dates.

Work began on a follow-up album before the decision was taken to merge Anderson Bruford Wakeman Howe with Yes for the album 'Union'. This was not universally accepted and subsequently conflicts arose as to the direction of the record. Anderson and the producer, along with the record company, wanted to retain the commercial aspect of Yes of the 1980s and some of Steve's and Rick's parts were replaced by those of session musicians. Nevertheless, Steve's solo piece 'Masquerade' was left free from tampering and was later nominated for a Grammy award.

In the early 1990s, Steve concentrated on his solo material. As noted, 'Turbulence' appeared in 1991 followed two years later by 'The Grand Scheme Of Things', featuring appearances by Steve's sons Virgil and Dylan on keyboards and drums respectively. Steve was active touring his new material and old Yes songs, with a focus on playing acoustic guitars. His first live album was a recording of this set list and appeared as 'Not Necessarily Acoustic' in 1994. Steve used the Kohno No. 10, a Martin 6-string and a Steinberger headless electric guitar.

Yes underwent further personnel changes in the mid-1990s and resulted in Steve and Rick reuniting with the band to recreate the main 1970s line-up. The first project was a mixture of live and studio recordings which appeared as 'Keys To Ascension' and 'Keys To Ascension 2' in 1996 and 1997. In the latter year the studio album 'Open Your Eyes' was completed and before the end of the decade the band recorded 'The Ladder'. Steve continued with his solo material and released the first of his 'Homebrew' series which comprised of new and old material presented in a 'demo' format. 'Quantum Guitar' featured several instruments from Steve's collection and was completed in 1998 and 'Pulling Strings' was created from live recordings of performances earlier in the 1990s. Steve collaborated with Martin Taylor on 'Masterpiece Guitars' which utilised over 50 instruments from the Scott Chinery collection. He teamed up with several musicians to record a tribute album to Bob Dylan in 1999.

At the start of the 2000s, Yes toured with an orchestra which played new material from the 'Magnification' record and songs from the past. Steve produced a solo album, 'Natural Timbres' using only acoustic guitars from his collection and followed this with several instrumental albums to the mid-2000s – 'Skyline', 'Elements', 'Spectrum'. In the early 2000s, Gibson guitars honoured Steve and recognised his use of the ES 175 with a signature model which was in production for several years. 2004 saw Steve record a live album and film, 'Remedy Live', and for the set he used many previously listed instruments – Fender Telecaster, Fender Dual 6 Professional, Kohno No. 10, Gibson Les Paul Studio Custom, Gibson ES 175 – and two new guitars. This included a red Fender Stratocaster and Martin MC-28 acoustic. Amplification was from a pair of Fender Twin Reverb amps and Steve had a pedalboard, though it is unclear what was in use specifically here. Steve recalls in *All My Yesterdays* that at this time he had three volume pedals for use when working in stereo, a 'Big Muff' fuzz, a distortion, and a delay unit.

Asia reunited in 2006/2007 for a tour and this saw Steve adopt Line 6 amplification, initially a Vetta II combo amp. On the film captured from the tour Steve was mainly using his sunburst ES Artist guitar. Yes planned a tour but this was delayed owing to the ill health of Jon Anderson, then Chris Squire. Steve decided to recruit Oliver Wakeman and Benoît David and tour when Squire had recovered. This took place from mid-2009 to late 2010, with a number of these dates featuring Asia as support, with Steve playing in both sets.

In the early 2010s, Steve recorded albums with both Asia and Yes – 'Omega' and 'Fly From Here' respectively – and toured with the two groups, as well as the Steve Howe Trio which was jazz-orientated. For Yes and Asia, Steve mixed his classic guitars with new technology in the form of a Pod HD500 digital modelling unit and a Line 6 Bogner DT50 combo amp with 1x12 in. speaker. During spring 2013, Steve was interviewed by *Premier Guitar* magazine as part of the 'Rig Rundown' series and made available on youtube.com. Several abovementioned guitars were in use for the Yes tour being undertaken at the time (where the group started performing complete albums), in addition to a 1956 Gibson Les Paul Custom and Line 6 Variax guitar. The latter utilised digital modelling to present the sounds of several well-known guitar makes. In this instance, Steve was employing the instrument to achieve a sitar tone in place of the Coral Sitar. The Pod HD500 had each track in the set list stored in the memory with relevant effects selected to achieve the required tonality of the original recording.

Steve left Asia in 2013 and has concentrated subsequently on Yes and his solo material, continuing to be particularly active touring for both projects. 'Love Is', Steve's most recent solo album, was released in 2020.

Tony Iommi in Milan, Italy, September 18, 1995.
Fabio Diena / Alamy Stock Photo.

TONY IOMMI

The loss of two finger ends when a teenager might have thwarted the aspirations of many young guitarists. Not Tony Iommi. With great courage and determination, he overcame the problem by devising his own unique method of playing. In doing so, he created some of the most memorable riffs that rock has ever heard and unwittingly laid the foundations for what became known as Heavy Metal.

Tony was born in Birmingham on February 19, 1948. His parents were Italian and he was an only child. Initially, he played the accordion but soon lost interest. Whilst attending Birchfield Secondary Modern, Tony became involved with judo, karate and boxing. He found the only instrument he could learn to play at school was the recorder. This did not interest him. Instead, he wanted to play the guitar after hearing Hank Marvin of the Shadows. From a catalogue, his mother paid about twenty pounds for his first guitar and amplifier – a left-handed 'Watkins Rapier' and a Watkins Westminster amplifier. This was paid off in instalments. One of the first songs he learned to play, together with a friend, was Frankie Laine's 'Jezebel'. Collaborations with other friends were also made and this led to him playing his first pub gigs.

Recalling the early 1960s, Tony said: 'I'd listen to the Top 20 and wait for The Shadows to come on. Later, I got one of their albums and learned the songs from playing it over and over again. I've always tried to make my guitar playing melodic. That stayed with me and it has always been a part of my song-writing.'

Tony left school at 15 and was employed in a number of jobs. He played with the Rockin' Chevrolets who were noted as a good live band and they enjoyed regular work around Birmingham. The band played Shadows songs plus rock 'n' roll numbers. On www.brumbeat.net the band's vocalist Neil Cassin recalled: 'Tony was a very versatile guitarist. He was playing blistering rock 'n' roll with us plus Shadows' stuff. He also loved jazz, in particular, Joe Pass. We started getting bookings very quickly, including several resident nights.'

As the Rockin' Chevrolet's workload increased, Tony decided to splash out on another guitar, a left-handed Burns Trisonic. He also acquired a Selmer amp with an echo unit. After internal disagreements, Tony left the Rockin' Chevrolets in 1965 and soon joined the Birds and the Bees who were about to play a number of gigs in Germany. At this point, Tony was working as a welder. Just after lunch on the day he was due to quit the job, and go to Germany as a full-time musician, he was injured in a terrible accident. For a time, this threatened to ruin his career as a guitarist. The ends of two fingers on his right hand were sliced off by a machine he was operating. Whilst recuperating he was grateful for a manager at the factory giving him a Django Reinhardt EP. Reinhardt had lost the use of two fingers in a gypsy caravan fire accident some years earlier, yet played skilfully. Tony considered switching to playing guitar right-handed though soon dismissed the idea. He made a few crucial adjustments to a Fender Stratocaster he was playing and experimented with banjo strings (as the B and high E) and soft plastic tips or thimbles attached to the ends of his fingers. He was determined to continue as a left-handed guitarist. His signature sound then eventually developed by tuning down three semitones.

He said: 'Before the accident I could play in the normal way, using full chords and everything, but after[wards] I had to play differently. I came up with fatter chords that I could play with less fingers.'

Prior to Black Sabbath being formed in the late 1960s, Tony played in several bands including the Rest, Mythology, Polka Tulk and Earth. When lead guitarist, Mick Abrahams left Jethro Tull, Tony went to an audition that was held to find a replacement. To his surprise, he got the job and in late 1968 attended rehearsals for the band's second album, 'Stand Up'. He performed with his white Fender Stratocaster when Jethro Tull were featured in the Rolling Stones' film 'Rock and Roll Circus'. Originally, the Stratocaster had a sunburst finish but was subsequently painted white. Not long after appearing in 'Rock and Roll Circus', Tony left Jethro Tull and rejoined Earth.

Deciding to change their name, Earth took Black Sabbath from the American title of the classic Italian horror movie 'I Tre Volti Della Paura'. Their first appearance as Black Sabbath was on August 30, 1969.

Tony was using Laney LA100BL amplifiers built by Lyndon Laney. On October 16, 1969, Black Sabbath began recording their first album at Regent Sound Studios, Denmark Street, London. During the session, one of Tony's Stratocaster pick-ups faltered. He then switched to using a Gibson SG for the remainder of the session. Tony told *Hit Parader* magazine of July 1993: 'Back then, fixing a guitar pick-up wasn't as easy as it is today and it was real work to change them. We only had two days in the studio to finish the entire record, so there was no time to waste. It was at that moment that I switched over to [a Gibson SG], and I never played the Stratocaster again.' Whether this guitar was a right-handed SG guitar turned upside down or a 1965 left-handed SG is unclear from various published reports.

The 1965 SG Special in a red finish became Tony's main guitar for a number of years. Black Sabbath's first album was released on Friday February 13, 1970.

On Gibson TV March 26, 2020, Tony described his many attempts to acquire really light gauge strings so that he could play, bend strings and use vibrato without causing damage to his prosthetic fingertips. On www.stringsdirect.co.uk it is stated that many string manufacturers appeared to be unwilling to help him. It adds: '[B]ut eventually Tony found a UK company, a heritage brand here with Strings Direct, Picato. They managed to meet his requirements and help him towards his ideal solution. From there, Tony progressed to GHS Strings and now resides with the prestigious La Bella [from 1990] to fulfil his specific requirements.'

In *Iron Man: My Journey Through Heaven and Hell with Black Sabbath* (2012), Tony states: '[In comparison to Led Zeppelin, Black Sabbath's direction] … was the riff, the heavier sound of the guitar. Where Zeppelin relied on thundering drums, we had our massive guitar and bass wall of sound.' On www.allmusic.com the band's first album was reviewed by Steve Huey who said: 'Black Sabbath's debut album is the birth of heavy metal as we know it,' adding 'guitarist Tony Iommi's loss of two finger tips, which required him to play slower and to slacken the strings by tuning his guitar down [created] Sabbath's signature style.'

For their first American tour, the band took a Laney PA which was damaged in transit. They used monitors for the first time at the Fillmore East. The second album 'Paranoid', recorded between June 16 and 21, 1970, was released on September 18 of the same year. It appeared on Vertigo Records in England and Warner Bros Records in the US. The album contains several of the band's familiar songs, including 'Iron Man', 'War Pigs'. The title track, 'Paranoid' was their only top twenty hit. It reached no. 4 in the UK charts. Around 1970, Tony befriended guitar luthier John Birch who undertook modifications to the left-handed SG Special.

On www.groundguitar.com further information is provided: 'His left-handed SG received a brand new Simplux pick-up in the neck, which was John Birch's take on the P90. The bridge pick-up was taken out and re-wound, and then re-covered in metal casing. The neck was refinished with a coat of polyurethane lacquer to improve playability, and a zero-fret was installed next to the nut. He decorated the guitar with a sticker of a monkey playing a fiddle. Tony used the "Monkey" guitar on "Paranoid" (1970), "Master of Reality" (1971), and "Vol. 4" (1972).' During the 'Paranoid' period, Tony was also seen playing a 1962/1963 Gibson Les Paul/SG Custom with three humbucker pick-ups and a Maestro Vibrola. It was a white, left-handed guitar.

In a documentary about the 'Paranoid' album, Tony mentions the following about the guitar solo in the track 'Warning', 'I always tried to keep the bottom string ringing so it fills out nicely.'

Ozzy Osbourne has commented '… Tony Iommi turned out to be one of the greatest heavy rock riff-makers of all time. Whenever we went into the studio, we'd challenge him to beat his last riff – and he'd come up with something like "Iron Man" and blow everyone away.' Commenting on Paranoid in *Rolling Stone's 500 Greatest Albums of All Time*, Joe Levy (ed.) said: 'Sabbath ruled for bummed-out kids in the Seventies and nearly every heavy-metal and extreme rock band of the last three decades owes a debt of worship to Iommi's "crushing" guitar riffs …'

The 1970s would see Black Sabbath release a number of albums with the classic line-up of Iommi, Butler, Osbourne and Ward. Each album would be followed up with a number of tours in Europe, the US and in other parts of the globe.

For the band's album, 'Masters Of Reality' recorded in February and March 1971, Tony mentions that on certain tracks 'we tuned down three semitones. It was part of an experiment: tuning down together for a bigger heavier sound … Tuning down just seemed to give more depth [to the sound]. I think I was the first one to do that.' Besides electric guitar, on the album Tony played, on certain tracks, synthesizer, flute, piano and acoustic.

On www.sputnickmusic.com, these comments are made about 'Masters Of Reality': 'The down tuning of the guitars and bass brought about an even heavier sound than what was heard in earlier records. The heavy, down-tuned sound also helped take Sabbath's slow, sludgy sound a step further. [The opener] "Sweet Leaf", showcases the updated element in the band's arsenal exceedingly well, and has been very influential in the likes of Stoner metal … The most enjoyable song spawned by this riffy variation of Black Sabbath is easily "Children of the Grave". Driven constantly by a mid-paced (yet pretty fast for Sabbath's standards) rhythm, it employs every trick that the British metallers had learned within the last year.'

By the end of the band's third tour of America, Tony was suffering from exhaustion and on the verge of a nervous breakdown. He was forced to take a rest along with the others who were also not in good health.

In Tony Bacon's *The SG Guitar Book: 50 Years of Gibson's Stylish Solid Guitar* (2015) John Birch employee, John Diggins, mentions it was around 1972 that 'they made Iommi that first twenty-four-fret SG-style guitar, an all-maple creation.'

By 1973, Tony was describing himself as the driving force in the band. He argued that this determination arose from his parents telling him he wasn't going to do anything constructive with his life. It was coupled with comments made by several people after his accident who said he would never play guitar again. He frequently made the band rehearse and tried to give them a focus. He felt the pressure of devising the music and riffs, because if he didn't, he thought nothing would happen.

'Sabbath Bloody Sabbath' was recorded at Morgan Studios, London and according to Tony the band produced the album themselves. Rick Wakeman played on 'Sabbra Cadabra'. Tony experimented with bagpipes and a sitar for the album but to no avail. He is credited with playing on certain tracks: piano, synthesizer, harpsichord, organ and flute. BBC DJ Alan Freeman used 'Laguna Sunrise' as a theme tune for his radio show. Talking about 'Sabbath Bloody Sabbath' to Jeff Kitts in *Guitar World* in February 19, 2021, Tony said the album was a real turning point for the band. They began recording it in LA but switched to renting Clearwell Castle in the Forest of Dean, Gloucestershire. '[We] rehearsed in its spooky old dungeon. After we wrote [the title] track things just started coming fast and furious.'

On www.kerrang.com the following is noted: 'By the time Sabbath were recording ["Sabbath Bloody Sabbath"], excess was beginning to take its toll and creative doubt was beginning to creep in. By Geezer Butler's own admission, the members felt their time was up – until Tony came out with the initial riff for "Sabbath Bloody Sabbath" [and] we went "We're baaaack!"' The album was released on December 1, 1973. A departure from the norm for Tony on the album was an acoustic instrumental titled 'Fluff'. It also incorporated piano and strings.

Around 1975, John Diggins built Tony another SG-style guitar which became known as the Old Boy. Diggins in Bacon (*op. cit.*) says he made the Old Boy from mahogany, adding: 'But I overlapped the heel with the body so they were glued together, as opposed to just the neck joining to the body. That made it stronger.' The Old Boy featured 24 frets, cross inlays, as well as one Birch and one Diggins pick-up. However, the guitar was not used until later in the decade when Tony retired the earlier John Birch guitar. Later, John Diggins progressed to establish Jaydee Custom Guitars and he states on the company's website: 'I couldn't make [Tony's] guitar in John Birch's time so I made it at home. It was made on the kitchen table and was completed in about 2 weeks … the guitar was not given a proper unveiling until I had produced the pick-ups that could deliver the sound that Tony was happy with.' The Diggins' Old Boy was retired in 2013.

Albums that followed from 1975 to 1979 were 'Sabotage', 'Technical Ecstasy', 'Never Say Die'. 'Sabotage' was produced by Tony and Mike Butcher. Tony is also credited with playing on the album: piano, synthesizer, organ and harp. Billy Altman in *Rolling Stone* September 25, 1975, wrote: '"Sabotage" is not only Black Sabbath's best record since "Paranoid", it might be their best ever. Even with the usual themes of death, destruction and mental illness running throughout this album, the unleashed frenzy and raw energy they've returned to here comes like a breath of fresh air.'

'Technical Ecstasy' was produced by Tony and he made these comments to *Guitar World* in 1992: 'We recorded the album in Miami, and nobody would take responsibility for the production. No one wanted to bring in an outside person for help, and no one wanted the whole band to produce it. So they left it all to me!' He commented: 'Black Sabbath fans generally don't like much of "Technical Ecstasy". It was really a no-win situation for us. If we had stayed the same, people would have said we were still doing the same old stuff. So we tried to get a little more technical, and it just didn't work out very well.'

'Never Say Die' was the last album recorded by the original Black Sabbath line-up until the 2013 album '13'. It was recorded at Sound Interchange in Toronto and released in September 1978. Tony for the first time sang backing vocal on 'A Hard Road'. The title track was released as a single and it was performed on 'Top of the Pops'. Tony appeared on the show with a left-handed Gibson Les Paul.

By 1979, it was decided that the band's output needed revitalising as their slow riffs were seen, by some, as out of sync against several bands – Judas Priest and Motörhead – leading the charge of the New Wave of British Heavy Metal. In the summer of 1979, Ozzy Osbourne was replaced with Ronnie James Dio, the former vocalist for Rainbow. Dio said in an interview with Tommy Vance for BBC Radio 1's Friday Rock Show, broadcast 21 August 1987, transcribed by editor Peter Scott for Sabbath fanzine *Southern Cross* No. 11, October 1996: 'Sabbath was a band that was floundering. And, with my inclusion in it, we pulled ourselves up by our bootstraps, cared a lot about each other, and knew that we could do it again – especially under the banner of a band that had been so successful.'

With Dio, Black Sabbath produced the 'Heaven And Hell' album which appeared in April 1980 and was very successful. Further line-up changes occurred within the band as Bill Ward was replaced for a period by Vinny Appice. In his autobiography Tony wrote: 'Ronnie liked singing across the riff instead of with it, [and to] come up with a melody that was different from that of the music, which musically opens a lot more doors … Ronnie's approach opened up a new way for me to think.'

Mick Wall in *Black Sabbath: Symptom of the Universe* (2014) wrote: 'The reborn Black Sabbath, with their glistening new sound, incomparable new singer and top-drawer new album, were seen as part of a widespread revival in rock fandom.'

Commenting on the album, www.allmusic.com said: 'Upon its release, "Heaven and Hell" was one of Black Sabbath's more commercially successful albums, bringing the group into the '80s with a renewed spirit and a coat of production polish that saved them from the brink of demise they'd been teetering on.' To promote 'Heaven And Hell' Black Sabbath toured Europe, the US and Japan.

In 1981, Tony asked John Diggins to build him another guitar which became known as his Jaydee SG Custom. It served as a backup for the Old Boy. Although the body was shaped in the SG design, the headstock was different. There were two double-rail humbucker pick-ups, and the body finish was maroon with light and dark brown stripes extending down the middle. A similar guitar built for Tony had a black finish and a stainless-steel pick-guard. It is thought that Tony used the Jaydee SG Custom between 1981 and 2012.

'Mob Rules' was Black Sabbath's tenth album and featured Ronnie James Dio and drummer Vinny Appice. It appeared in November 1981. According to Tony in his autobiography, the band wanted to record in their own studio and bought a sound desk. But this didn't work out. 'We just couldn't get a guitar sound. We tried it in the studio. We tried it in the hallway. We tried it everywhere but it just wasn't working. We'd bought a studio and it wasn't working.'

Fred Thomas in his review of 'Mob Rules' on www.allmusic.com commented about Tony's playing: 'Tony Iommi's signature guitar playing takes on new forms throughout the album, with Zeppelin-esque riff-ing on "Slipping Away", slithering bluesy rock playing on "Voodoo", and a strikingly different approach to soloing, shifting from the laser-focused slow burn of early Sabbath albums to a more frenetic, technically showing style on some tracks.' Commenting about the fast song 'Turn Up The Night', Tony said: 'Working with Ronnie, somehow the faster ones came easier than before.'

From 1982, it is claimed on www.guitarlobby.com that Tony used a black B.C. Rich Mockingbird. Also, probably dating from 1983, a B.C. Rich Ironbird Pro was played. As well as the cross inlays, the guitar had a Kahler bridge, two DiMarzio pick-ups, two built-in preamps, and a scalloped fretboard. The latter was undertaken by B.C. Rich's master builder Neal Moser. The guitar featured in Tony's 'Star Licks Series' video lesson from the early 1980s.

By November 1982, Dio and Appice had left Black Sabbath. In the following year, Ian Gillan took over vocal duties for the band. The line-up on the 'Born Again' album, recorded in May 1983, was Tony Iommi, Ian Gillan, Bill Ward and Geezer Butler. Additional musicians included Geoff Nicholls on keyboards. Released in August 1983, the album was promoted with Bev Bevan occupying the drum stool during the remainder of the year and into 1984 when Gillan left.

A lesser-known guitar that Tony used from around 1983 was a Steinberger GM4T. The guitar was 'headless' with tuning machines integrated into the bridge. By the end of 1984, Black Sabbath only consisted of Tony Iommi. Ward and Butler had left and there was no vocalist.

The original Black Sabbath reformed for a performance at Bob Geldof's Live Aid. They appeared at the Philadelphia show on July 13, 1985. 'Seventh Star' was recorded in the same year and released in January 1986. It was originally intended to be Tony's first solo album but due to pressure from Warner Bros Records appeared under the title of 'Black Sabbath featuring Tony Iommi'. None of the original Black Sabbath members were present and Glenn Hughes was the vocalist. Dave Spitz was on bass guitar, Eric Singer drums and Geoff Nicholls keyboards. For a tour promoting the album the band brought in Ray Gillen after a few shows to replace Glenn Hughes.

Other Black Sabbath albums released during this decade were 'The Eternal Idol' (1987), and 'Headless Cross' (1989). Tony used the Steinberger GM4T guitar when performing a cover of the song 'Apache' by the Shadows in Russia during 1989.

The 1990s were marked with the following Black Sabbath releases 'Tyr' (1990), 'Dehumanizer' (1992), 'Cross Purposes' (1994), and 'Forbidden' (1995). In the early 1990s, Tony met Gibson luthier J.T. Riboloff who built him a black SG with a Floyd Rose vibrato. This impressed Tony and he met Riboloff and several other Gibson staff at the 1996 Frankfurt Music Fair. This resulted in Gibson producing the Tony Iommi Signature pick-up. It was a first for the company. Information of Tony's website states: 'It was decided that the pick-up would be a standard humbucker size to allow retro-fitting and the sound would be based on the bridge pick-up in the Jay Dee SG. This pick-up is not only quite different in size, but it is sealed in epoxy resin as an anti-feedback measure, which also renders it impossible to disassemble without destroying it …'

In late 1997, the Gibson Custom Shop in Nashville built as prototypes two SGs for Tony – one black and one red. They were intended for the Limited Edition Tony Iommi Special Custom Shop model. The features included 24 frets, cross inlays, four controls (bridge pick-up tone disconnected), Sperzel machine heads and Tony Iommi Signature Pick-ups as made by Gibson.

The early 1990s saw Tony forge links with Patrick Eggle Guitars. According to www.groundguitar.com the company produced for him the Patrick Eggle Artist Model Prototype and the Patrick Eggle Tony Iommi Artist Model. One Artist Model Prototype guitar was in a natural finish and two others in black. The Tony Iommi Artist Model featured a Brazilian mahogany body and neck, 24 frets (w/zero fret), cross inlays, Sperzel locking tuners, Schaller fine-tuning bridge, and two special designed Seymour Duncan pick-ups. Tony received four of these guitars. They were all finished in black.

In December 1997, the original Black Sabbath line-up reunited to record two shows at the Birmingham NEC. This was released as a double album 'Reunion' on October 20, 1998.

Between 2000 and 2005 Tony released three solo albums, 'Iommi' (2000), 'The 1996 DEP Sessions' (2004), and 'Fused' (2005). Under the heading 'Equipment' on Tony's website the following is mentioned about the guitars used on the DEP Sessions Album: 'Gibson SG and Les Paul guitars, the Jaydee Custom SG, a Fender Telecaster in the 'overstrung' or 'Nashville tuning' mode, a Steinberger TransTrem guitar, a Gibson J50 acoustic and a Fender nylon strung classical guitar.'

For amplification, Tony employed Laney GH100TI amplifiers, a Laney VC30 amplifier, a Marshall 2554 amplifier and Laney speakers. The guitar effects included a Peavey TubeFex unit. All the guitar strings used were by La Bella.

Epiphone introduced the Tony Iommi Signature G-400 guitar in 2005. In a review, *Total Guitar* magazine of March 2005 said that it was: 'Probably the best Epiphone electric we've ever seen.' The guitar included a mahogany body and neck, rosewood fingerboard, crucifix inlays and 24 frets. This was besides a Tune-o-matic bridge, fixed tailpiece and Grover machine heads. Production models came with a plain black scratch plate.

In the 2005, *Metal Hammer* magazine ranked Tony number 1 on the poll of the 'Riff Lords', praising his 'highly distinctive style of fretsmanship that's economical yet crushingly effective.'

Tony joined forces again with Dio, Geezer Butler and Vinny Appice but under a new name Heaven and Hell. The band released a studio album 'The Devil You Know' in April 2009. Following Dio's death in May 2010, 'Neon Nights: 30 Years Of Heaven And Hell' appeared. On www.guitarplayer.com, Jesse Gress in an article dated January 29, 2014, said: 'In 2009 with Heaven and Hell, Iommi used an Engl Powerball head in addition to his GH 100 TI Laney Tony Iommi Signature amp along with both amps' respective 4x12 in. cabinets (loaded with Celestion Vintage 30 speakers), replaced his Tycobrahe Parapedal with a Chicago Iron Parachute wah, and experimented with several additional effects, including an Ibanez Tube Screamer and a Boss OC-3 Super Octave.'

During November 2011, Black Sabbath announced that the original line-up would reform in the following year to tour and cut a new album. This was delayed due to Tony being diagnosed with the 'early stages of lymphoma'. After initially being part of the reunion, drummer Bill Ward left the band. A warm-up show was performed in Birmingham on May 19, 2012, then the Download Festival on June 10, 2012, and the Lollapalooza Festival in Chicago on August 3, 2012. Black Sabbath returned to the road in 2013–2014. They performed in New Zealand, Australia, Japan, North America, South America and Europe. Meanwhile Tony underwent successful treatment for his illness. He wrote a song 'Lonely Planet' which was performed by Dorians for Armenia in the 2013 Eurovision Song Contest. The song finished 18th in the final scoring 41 points. In November of the same year Tony received an Honorary Doctorate of Arts Degree from Coventry University. The university said the degree came 'in recognition of his contribution to the world of popular music,' and recognised 'his role as one of the founding fathers of heavy metal music and his status as one of the industry's most influential figures.' Tony also became Visiting Professor of Music at Coventry University.

The Black Sabbath album '13' was released on June 13, 2013. Featuring Tony Iommi, Ozzy Osbourne and Geezer Butler, it was the 19th and final studio album made by the band. Brad

Tony Iommi at Tinley Park, Illinois, USA, September 4, 2016.
ZUMA Press, Inc. / Alamy Stock Photo.

Wilk played drums. The album '13' received positive reviews and was a no. 1 album in several countries, including the UK and USA. According to Tony's website, amongst his guitars used on the '13' album, 'were custom built "New Boys" (replicas of Tony's stalwart "Old Boy") made by the original luthier John Diggins (Jaydee) along with a couple of his signature Gibson SG models. There were also some lovely Taylor acoustics which sound brilliant. The ever-present Steinberger GM4T was used for clean parts.' Amplifiers used included his signature Laney TI100, and old Laney Klipp and a Laney Supergroup.

On www.reverb.com 'Master of Reality: Sound like Black Sabbath's Tony Iommi', Jamie Wolfert wrote: 'The essential elements of Tony Iommi's playing style, which were considered quite unusual in the early 1970s, have become the standard way to make heavy guitar sounds today. Two-note, root-plus-fifth power chords on the low strings is a definitive Iommi manoeuvre, which, though brilliantly innovative, probably seemed overly rudimentary and caveman-like to other guitarists at the time. Playing in unison with the bass is another trick that many of Iommi's contemporaries would have eschewed as being too simplistic, but which Iommi and his equally innovative cohort Geezer Butler embraced fully for the monolithic quality it gave to their beastly riffing.'

Black Sabbath embarked on their final tour, appropriately titled 'The End Tour', on January 20, 2016. They performed 81 shows across North America, Europe, Oceania and South America. The final concert took place on February 4, 2017. Founding members Ozzy Osbourne, Tony Iommi and Geezer Butler were present along with session drummer Tommy Clufetos filling in for original drummer Bill Ward. Also included was keyboardist and guitarist Adam Wakeman. The final concert took place in the band's home city of Birmingham.

Around the time of the End Tour, Laney issued in their 'Black Country Customs' the TI Boost. The Laney website states the pedal was designed in conjunction with Tony Iommi 'to be a significant part of his tour rig for the final ever Black Sabbath tour. The TI-BOOST replicates the significant bass cut and mid boost of Tony's original "modified" Dallas Arbiter Range Master pedal, but we have included a little more gain and some enhanced EQ options to make it more appealing to every player looking to find their own sounds.'

BRIAN JONES

'Brian Jones, of the Rolling Stones, is one of the most exciting guitarists in the business' was the first sentence of a feature produced on Brian in *Beat Monthly No. 12* April 1964. As we approach (at the time of writing) the 54th anniversary of his death this statement is perhaps lost on a whole generation of the group's fans. In the ensuing years much has been made of Brian's drug use and alienation from the band near the end and has served as a detriment to the fact that Brian was a vital force in the Stones' formation and early recordings.

At a young age, Brian was encouraged by his parents to take an interest in music. His mother played piano and she initially taught Brian before sending him for lessons. From the piano, Brian moved to the clarinet and he was first chair in Cheltenham Grammar School's orchestra, also singing in the school's choir, and later took up the saxophone. Brian comments in *Beat Monthly*, referenced above, that these early experiences served as a 'good grounding' for his future musical endeavours.

During his teens, Brian became interested in jazz music and this led him to the guitar when he was about 17. He bought a Spanish-style acoustic for his birthday to learn and, with his musical background and the aid of a teaching book, quickly picked up the instrument. He moved on to purchase a Cromwell archtop guitar, which he later regretted selling.

Brian came from a quite conservative background and was expected to take a career when he left school. Yet, during his middle teens, Brian became increasingly rebellious and this culminated in his leaving home at 17 with ambitions to become a professional musician. He lived locally for a time before travelling around Scandinavia.

From the early 1960s, Brian featured in a succession of jazz bands in Cheltenham, mostly playing alto saxophone. He persevered with his acoustic guitar before trading the Cromwell for a Hofner Committee in late 1961.

With no fixed abode, Brian moved between several houses, eventually teaming up with Richard Hattrell. A blues devotee, he helped kindle Brian's early interest in the music by unearthing recordings by Bo Diddley, Muddy Waters and Chuck Berry.

Alexis Korner appeared in Cheltenham at this juncture and became a guiding light for Brian. Korner played a set of blues music as part of a Chris Barber jazz band concert which Brian witnessed. The two talked after the show and Korner advised Brian to leave Cheltenham behind and enjoy the growing London blues scene.

Over the winter of 1961/1962, Brian made many pilgrimages to London. On one occasion, Alexis Korner played Brian an Elmore James album and he became an important early influence on Brian. He was encouraged to take up slide guitar, which was virtually unknown in Britain at the time, and used a piece of pipe in substitute for the traditional bottleneck. Brian would listen to James's albums constantly, trying to decipher his favourite phrases and was not satisfied until he had memorised them correctly. He would later say: 'I discovered Elmore James and the earth seemed to shudder on its axis.'

Brian decided to move to London around March 1962. Soon afterwards he appeared with Alexis Korner's Blues Incorporated band and played Elmore James's 'Dust My Broom'. In attendance were future bandmates Mick Jagger and Keith Richards. Both were very impressed by his rendition of the classic song, which he played on his Hofner Committee through an Elpico AC55 amplifier, and were eager to make his acquaintance.

Invigorated by his success, Brian placed an advert in *Jazz News* looking for prospective members of a rhythm and blues band. One of the first responses was from Ian Stewart, who played piano, and others soon followed. The new band, which did not receive a name, only rehearsed and was never booked for a gig.

At a rehearsal, Mick, Keith and Dick Taylor turned up and Brian quickly decided that a new group with these three and Ian Stewart would be a better proposition and immediately joined forces with them. Brian became the leader as he possessed experience of being in a band and had the most musical knowledge.

Following several practice sessions, the as-yet unnamed group received their first booking at the Marquee Club. Whilst Brian was on the phone with the manager of the establishment, the band had to hastily come up with a name. Someone suggested 'the Rolling Stones' after a line in a Muddy Waters song and this eventually stuck.

The gig occurred on July 12, 1962, and consisted of several blues numbers. Brian played his Hofner Committee through the Elpico AC55. The night was relatively successful and led to further engagements for the band at the Marquee and also

---

Cromwell was amongst a series of budget guitars built at Gibson's Kalamazoo factory during the 1930s (other brands included Fascinator, Recording King and Kalamazoo). The ranges mimicked the low-end models from Gibson's catalogue, but were built without truss rods and archtop models had pressed tops, rather than carved tops which were more expensive and time-consuming to produce.

The Hofner Committee was a top-of-the-range archtop model available from 1954 through to the late 1960s. Available in both acoustic and electric versions (Brian had an acoustic which had been modified to carry a pick-up), the guitar had a carved spruce top with 17.5 in. diameter lower bout, maple back and sides and laminated maple/mahogany neck, initially with no truss rod, but this was later provided.

the Ealing Jazz Club.

This increasing exposure led Brian to decide to quit his job and concentrate on the Rolling Stones full time. Keith Richards was also unemployed and along with Mick Jagger, who was studying at the London School of Economics, the trio obtained accommodation in Edith Grove, Chelsea.

Brian and Keith spent most of their days listening to music, learning guitar parts and developing a way of pairing their two guitars within a song. Brian worked on his slide guitar technique and experimented with new tunings.

In an interview given in early 1965, Brian would say of the early Stones guitar sound: 'I play a lot of lead guitar and I am not really interested in rhythm guitars … In the Stones we have two lead guitar patterns going and we never use straight rhythm guitar as in the old Shadows days. We also use a heavy bass riff pattern … a Chuck Berry thing.'

Towards the end of 1962, Brian's old friend from Cheltenham, Richard Hattrell, visited Edith Grove. Brian managed to obtain some money from Hattrell to buy a new guitar, which was a Harmony Stratotone Mars H46 model. This was a semi-hollow body guitar with bolt-on maple neck and two pick-ups. He paired the guitar with a recently acquired Harmony H306 amplifier with a 12 in. speaker.

Late in 1962, Bill Wyman was taken into the group to replace Dick Taylor on bass and brought along a spare Vox AC30, which was out of both Brian and Keith's means at the time. Charlie Watts was persuaded to play drums for the band early in the following year.

At the start of 1963, the Rolling Stones were offered a slot at the Crawdaddy Club, located within the Station Hotel, Richmond, after another band failed to materialise. The manager, Giorgio Gomelsky, was impressed by the band, in spite of an initially low turnout, and, sensing a change in musical tastes, decided to book them for a residency, also taking over managerial duties from Brian at the same time. After just a few weeks, the venue was packed and people travelled from miles around to see the band.

The Stones obtained another residency at Studio 51 in early 1963 and made their first studio recordings. Five songs were demoed from their repertoire using their current equipment (Brian's Harmony Stratotone with either a Harmony or Vox AC30 amp). Yet, the record companies were not interested in this new sound and the Stones returned to gigging, not disheartened.

Gomelsky was replaced as manager by Andrew Loog Oldham, who was in partnership with the more experienced Eric Easton. The pair set about pushing the Stones back towards the record companies as the buzz around them continued to grow. Two immediate additions were made to the group's gear in the form of Vox AC30 amplifiers in black.

In mid-1963, the Stones were finally signed by Decca, which took the group in the hope that they would become as popular as the Beatles, who had been turned down by the executives over a year earlier. Oldham took the Stones to Olympic Studios to record their first single which was a cover of Chuck Berry's 'Come On' with Muddy Waters' (although written by Willie Dixon) 'I Want To Be Loved' on the B-side. For both numbers Brian played a Hohner Echo Super Vamper harmonica (also referred to as a 'blues harp'). Even though the group did not like the end product, believing the song unrepresentative of their overall sound, the single was released by Decca in early June 1963 and ultimately fell just one place short of the top twenty.

Shortly afterwards, Brian went to Sound City in Central London and bought a Gretsch G6118 Anniversary in smoke green. It had a hollow maple body and a maple neck with ebony fingerboard, as well as two 'Hilo'Tron' pick-ups. Brian dispensed with the Harmony and the Gretsch became his guitar of choice for the time being. Brian received a new Vox AC30 to go with his new guitar. A Vox promotional campaign featuring the Stones resulted in a set of amps given to the group.

The Stones were in the studio several times during the summer of 1963 attempting to craft a follow-up to 'Come On', yet the band found a suitable number elusive. Brian played his Gretsch through a Vox, in addition to providing harmonica and some acoustic guitar. He continued with this set-up through several gigs and television appearances, then on a 36-date tour of Britain as the band supported Bo Diddley and the Everly Brothers.

During the tour, the band broke away for a day to record their next single, the Lennon–McCartney penned 'I Wanna Be Your Man'. Brian gave the record a touch of distinction through a slide solo using his Gretsch and AC30. The single improved on the previous offering by reaching no. 12 in the charts. 'I Wanna Be Your Man' was also the first song the group performed on 'Top of the Pops' at the start of 1964 and Brian could be seen playing his Gretsch with a slide. Throughout the first half of the year, on tour and on sessions for the upcoming first album, the guitar was consistently used, along with an acoustic and his Echo Super Vamper 'blues harp'.

The hectic first few months of 1964 culminated with the release of the first album – *The Rolling Stones* – which reached

The Vox Mark VI followed on from the Vox Phantom guitar released in 1962. The styling was similar, but the new model was much more rounded, and the specifications also matched closely. The body was solid maple or ash, with a maple neck topped by a rosewood fretboard and a 25.5 in. scale length. Two or three pick-up versions were offered with a vibrato unit and Tune-o-matic bridge.

Following the failure of the 'modern' series of guitars and increasing competition from Fender, Gibson approached retired car designer Ray Dietrich in 1962 to design a stylish new guitar. The result was the Firebird model which appeared during the following year. The guitar featured a neck-through body made from laminated mahogany and walnut, with mahogany wings attached at either side. As with other models in the Gibson ranges, the Firebird had varying appointments to meet certain price brackets. At the top of the range was the Firebird VII, with ebony fingerboard, block inlays, three pick-ups and maestro Vibrola; all hardware was gold-plated.

Brian Jones with Gibson Firebird VII.
Pictorial Press Ltd / Alamy Stock Photo.

no. 1 in the charts after just a handful of days on the shelves. Brian commented: 'I'm knocked out by the album. A lot of experimenting went into it … I think it is a lot better than we originally expected.'

Off the success of the album, the Rolling Stones were booked on a tour of America during June 1964. Brian only took his Gretsch and Hohner harmonicas, relying on rented amplifiers for gigs and TV appearances; he used Gibson and Fender amps during the tours.

Attendances on the tour were disappointing for the band, yet a highlight was stopping off in Chicago to record for two days at Chess Records. Many of the group's favourite tracks had been made there and the Stones were given unprecedented access, as the facilities were only available to the company's artists. The Stones were inspired to record several tracks, including the Valentinos' 'It's All Over Now'. Brian played the rhythm part with his Gretsch through one of the studio's Fender amps. When released during July, the track reached no. 1 in the English charts and performed well in America. A version of Muddy Waters' 'I Can't Be Satisfied' was also captured and Brian's efforts on slide particularly pleased him as commented to the *New Musical Express* during the following year: 'It has one of the best guitar solos I've ever managed.'

Brian received a new guitar in late summer 1964. Already having a good relationship with Jennings Musical Industries, which produced Vox amplifiers, the company presented Brian with the new Vox Mark VI or 'Teardrop' guitar, which was in fact the prototype. Brian's differed from future production guitars by having an ebony fingerboard, a Fender bridge unit, which could not be used for vibrato, and colour-matched headstock.

Brian immediately liked the guitar and the Gretsch was

Brian Jones with Gretsch G6118 Anniversary Model in smoke green.
Pictorial Press Ltd / Alamy Stock Photo.

relegated to a backup position, with Keith also playing the latter instrument on occasion. The same was true of a Vox Mark XII 12-string guitar also presented to Brian around this time, although this would be mostly used in the studio and rarely taken out for gigs or TV appearances.

Keith made additions to his own arsenal around this time, with a Gibson Les Paul Standard and Fender Telecaster. The last-mentioned was mainly kept in reserve and Brian was known to play the guitar, especially on the British tour in late summer of 1964. The two guitars were also taken to the US in October for another tour and Brian used the Vox as his main instrument. This guitar was prominent for the group's first appearance on the 'Ed Sullivan Show', which was broadcast on October 26. For the tour, Brian and Keith again used rented Fender amps.

Once more, the group recorded while in the US, spending time at RCA in Los Angeles and returning to Chess in Chicago. Unfortunately, Brian became ill whilst in the latter city and was hospitalised for the remainder of the dates.

The Stones returned to Britain in mid-November to find their rendition of Howlin' Wolf's 'Little Red Rooster' had reached no. 1 in the charts. The song showcased Brian's mastery of slide guitar and the end of the track featured him on his 'blues harp'. For the rest of the year, the band was promoting the song on TV shows and Brian continued to use the Vox guitar.

In the new year, the Stones took to the road and were in the States to record in mid-January. At RCA they cut 'The Last Time', with Brian playing the distinctive riff on his Vox, through a Fender Showman belonging to the studio. The single became the band's third successive no. 1 in Britain and the first for the song-writing duo of Jagger/Richards. The record fared well in America, breaking into the top ten.

Exposure to Fender amps in America led the two Stones guitarists to buy a pair of Showman heads and 2x15 cabinets. At 85 watts the Showman was much more powerful than the AC30s used thus far and was perhaps part of the reason for the switch, given the increasing size of venues being played. The amps went straight into service during February 1965. The band began another tour of Britain, with 'The Last Time' and 'The Rolling Stones No. 2' album in the charts, and on to Europe during March and April, then a third tour of America.

The Stones' popularity in America led the Gibson guitar company to enter into an endorsement deal with the band. Both Brian and Keith received Firebird VII guitars and Heritage acoustic guitars, along with a Titan V amp with matching 2x12 in. cabinet, a Maestro Fuzz-Tone effect unit.

The guitars went into use at recording sessions that took place at RCA during mid-May 1965. Brian used his Vox and Keith's Telecaster during the recording of several new tracks, including '(I Can't Get No) Satisfaction', released soon after and became the group's first American no. 1. Directly following the sessions, a number of TV appearances were scheduled and on the 'Hollywood A Go-Go' show both Brian and Keith are seen playing their new Firebird VIIs.

The Stones returned to London in early June and were soon off on a tour of Britain and Europe, which lasted through to late August. Brian continued to bond with his Firebird VII, but struggled to let go of his Vox and both featured heavily on the tour.

In September, the band was scheduled for more recording sessions in LA at RCA, which had become their favoured studio. Before travelling, Brian bought a 12-string Rickenbacker 1993 electric guitar. This was almost identical to the 330 model, but Rose-Morris (distributor of the company's instruments) received versions with an f-hole rather than a curved hole on instruments sold in the USA and were reclassified as a result. The guitar was used on the sessions, particularly 'The Singer Not The Song' and 'Blue Turns To Grey' and also the Stones' next no. 1, 'Get Off Of My Cloud', although the sound of the 12-string is not as distinct, sitting lower in the mix.

Just as Brian strayed from the guitar earlier in the Stones' career and played harmonica on a number of songs, during this period he began using an organ for certain tracks. Initially, this was provided by the venue when on the road, but Brian received a Vox Continental model towards the end of 1965 and the organ was used on the subsequent British tour. On this, Brian was mainly playing his Firebird VII and the Rickenbacker through the Fender Showman amp. The set-up continued on the North American tour which began in late October and finished in early December.

No visit to America at this time would have been complete without a visit to the RCA studio. A number of tracks were recorded and several would later appear on the group's next album, 'Aftermath'. Brian took the above-mentioned instruments into the studio, minus his Rickenbacker, which had been stolen towards the end of the tour. He was quick to replace the guitar, however, with the similar 360/12. This was the slightly upgraded model from the 1993 or 330/12, with contoured body, 'shark-tooth' inlays and traditionally shaped sound hole.

The sessions were the start of Brian's move away from the guitar. Keith explained to *Trouser Press* magazine in 1979: '[Brian] lost interest in guitar and wanted to play anything – harmonica, tambourine, organ … On "Aftermath", I think he was only playing guitar on two or three tracks.' One example from the session was 'Doncha Bother Me' which sees Brian adding a slide riff to the blues number.

Whilst Brian's instrument choice for the studio became more eclectic, on the road he was still playing the guitar. In early 1966, the Stones went to Australia for a tour and, just before, both he and Keith received Gibson 'Non-Reverse' Firebird VIIs. Brian would go on to use his throughout 1966, with the 'Reverse' VII favoured as a backup.

After two years of production, sales of Gibson's Firebird guitars were relatively disappointing. In an effort to boost popularity, the company modified the design and 'flipped' the shape, also dispensing with the neck-through construction, which made the guitars very expensive to manufacture, and reverted to a set neck. The Non-Reverse Firebirds were offered with similar variations to the 'Reverse' models and the VII featured three mini-humbucking pick-ups and maestro Vibrola (all gold-plated), but with a rosewood fretboard and dot inlays.

From Australia the group returned to RCA and recorded more tracks for the 'Aftermath' album, released in Britain during April 1966. The sessions were very productive and cemented the Jagger/Richards song-writing partnership. Brian's early role as leader of the group was now at an end, yet the album reinforced his importance within the Stones as a multi-instrumentalist who could contribute defining sounds to the group's output. 'Lady Jane' sees Brian playing an Appalachian Dulcimer (an electric version would be created for him by Vox – the 'Bijou' model – which he can be seen playing during a performance of the song on the 'Ed Sullivan Show'), marimba on 'Under My Thumb', and sitar on 'Paint It Black'.

Brian had become interested in the sitar late in 1965. This was around the time 'Rubber Soul' was released by the Beatles and featured George Harrison playing a sitar on the track 'Norwegian Wood'. Brian told *Beat Instrumental No. 38* of June 1966: 'Atmospherically, it's my favourite track by the Beatles. George [Harrison] made simple use of the sitar and it was very effective.'

Brian took sitar lessons from a friend – Hari-Hari – and was able to work out a method of playing it to suit the Stones' music. The result was a distinct sound to one of the group's most enduring and recognisable songs. Again, in *Beat Instrumental No. 38* of June 1966, Brian explains his sitar contribution on 'Paint It Black': '… I used a flattened 3rd in fret position [to achieve a Western diatonic scale]. The sound you get from a sitar is a basic blues pattern, which resulted in the flattening of the 3rd and 7th as a result of the super-imposition of primitive Eastern pentatonic (5 notes) system on the well-known Western diatonic scale.'

Bill Wyman in *Rolling with the Stones* (2002) comments on the sessions: 'Brian was at his creative peak with the band around this time. While the songs were all written by Mick and Keith, it was Brian's musical abilities that made those recordings sound so much better than they might otherwise have done.'

In the summer of 1966, the Stones promoted 'Aftermath' and several singles at both home and abroad, particularly America, where the band reached new heights. For the US tour, Brian took his Reverse and Non-Reverse Firebird VIIs, the Rickenbacker 12-stirng, his dulcimer, the Vox Continental and a variety of 'blues harps', using his Fender Showman for amplification.

Touring Britain during the autumn of 1966, Brian finished the year creating the soundtrack for Volker Schlöndorff's film 'Mord und Totschlag' ('A Degree of Murder'), which starred his girlfriend, Anita Pallenberg. The music – composed in partnership with Mike Leander – saw Brian continue to use different instruments from the guitar. He chose to add parts featuring harmonica, dulcimer, organ, sitar and recorder, which he would use on the Stones' 'Between the Buttons' sessions (particularly 'Ruby Tuesday'). Guitar parts were provided by future Led Zeppelin guitarist Jimmy Page, then working as a session player, and Nicky Hopkins and Kenney Jones provided piano and drum parts respectively.

A particularly difficult year awaited the Stones in 1967, with Brian, Mick and Keith all arrested for drugs offences. This caused the band to lose their focus in the studio and the rigorous touring schedule adopted hitherto was abandoned after the European tour ended in mid-April.

The year began with the Stones promoting the single 'Let's Spend The Night Together'/'Ruby Tuesday', along with the 'Between The Buttons' album, in both Britain and America. From mid-March the group was on the road and Brian was using Keith's newly acquired Gibson ES 330 guitar through a Vox Supreme head and cabinet. The amp was a new 100-watt model which replaced the Fender Showmans of both Brian and Keith for a time during the year.

Just before and after the tour, the Stones were continually in the studio working on tracks for the next album – 'Their Satanic Majesties Request'– which would be released before the end of the year. Brian had virtually abandoned the guitar at this point, only playing an acoustic on a couple of tracks. His new interest was the Mellotron. Two had been bought by both Mick and Keith and the latter's was mainly used during the sessions.

The Mellotron was introduced in 1963 and was subsequently adopted by bands such as the Moody Blues and the Beatles. It featured a large number of audio tapes with different sounds that played when a key on the keyboard was de-pressed. The keys were very touch sensitive and this caused fluctuations in the sounds, giving the Mellotron an interesting voice.

As with other instruments, Brian mastered the Mellotron quickly despite the intricacies of operation and provided sounds for several tracks that would appear on 'Their Satanic Majesties Request', including '2000 Light Years From Home', and the single 'We Love You' which was recorded at the time.

Brian also played the recorder, dulcimer and harmonica on the sessions, along with a recently acquired soprano saxophone. During the year, he was present at a recording session held by the Beatles and played the instrument on the track 'You Know My Name (Look Up The Number)', which was released as the B-side to 'Let It Be' in 1970.

The stress of the court case against Brian for drug possession had a lasting effect on his mental health. During 1968, he appeared at few of the Stones' recording dates, but he did provide a sitar part on 'Street Fighting Man' and slide guitar on 'No Expectations'.

Brian was arrested for drug possession in mid-1968 and when the case was resolved later in the year, he was lucky to receive only a fine. Yet, his criminal record, which barred him from entering America – the prime destination for the Stones' tours – and deteriorating health and mental state, signalled the end of his time with the group.

Although appearing with the Stones at their 'Rock and Roll Circus' performance, playing a Gibson Les Paul Gold Top, Brian's contribution was minimal and this was the last time he shared the stage with the band. He formally left the group six months later and tragically died on July 3, 1969.

Brian Jones with Vox Mark VI or 'Teardrop' guitar.
Pictorial Press Ltd / Alamy Stock Photo.

PAUL KOSSOFF

The combination of a Gibson Les Paul guitar and Marshall amplifier is synonymous with music in the late 1960s and early 1970s, just as drug use is by musicians of that period. Sadly for Paul Kossoff, his addiction to illicit substances ultimately took precedence over creating music with his Les Paul and Marshall. Yet, Paul's guitar playing was always tasteful, dynamic and packed full of emotion, with his vibrato technique particularly unique, and his style often admired by fellow musicians and fans alike.

Born on September 14, 1950, Paul Kossoff was the youngest son of actor David Kossoff. Paul developed an early interest in music after listening to Hank Marvin of the Shadows and his father encouraged his son by arranging lessons with a local guitar teacher. A Spanish-style acoustic was Paul's first guitar and he used this into his teens.

Paul was later adamant that the lessons only helped him with his finger dexterity, rather than theoretical knowledge. He was taught for several years before ending his tuition, frustrated that he was limited to the classical style. At this juncture he had already obtained his first electric guitar – an Italian-made Eko, which was in the style of a Fender Jaguar – and went on to receive a Gibson Les Paul Junior (SG style) from his father in the early 1960s.

If his interest in the guitar had been waning, Paul found renewed enthusiasm after witnessing Eric Clapton play with John Mayall and the Bluesbreakers at Golders Green just before Christmas, 1965. Clapton had developed a reputation as one of the best young guitarists around, playing blues influenced by B.B. King and Freddie King. He was also at the forefront of a new sound, created by using a Gibson Les Paul guitar through a Marshall amplifier set at a high volume.

During an interview with *Melody Maker* in early 1975, Paul commented: 'I can still remember … hearing Clapton in Mayall's Bluesbreakers. That feeling – it was an amazing sound … I'd never heard that on guitar before.'

In the new year, Paul formed a band and was armed with a newly acquired 1955 Gibson Les Paul Custom, which his father had obtained for him while in America. Paul does not appear to have bonded with this instrument and sometime around late summer he moved on to a later model Les Paul Custom (1957–1960) with three pick-ups.

The latter guitar was purchased from Selmer's music shop and around this time Paul became employed there, selling many guitars to the famous players of the day. He likely bought his first Marshall amplifier at Selmer – a JTM 45 – and this was used with a homemade 4x12 in. cabinet.

During 1966, Paul explored the music of various blues artists, becoming increasingly adept and was acknowledged as being an up-and-coming guitarist. His ability piqued the interest of the members of Black Cat Bones, a local blues band, and he was admitted also partially because of his possession of a real Gibson Les Paul guitar.

Black Cat Bones was a five-member group, the line-up of which changed several times throughout 1967. Paul was a constant on lead guitar and the band quickly gained a reputation around London. They supported artists such as Ten Years After, John Mayall and Fleetwood Mac; the latter band's lead guitarist Peter Green was also an inspiration to Paul. This period culminated with Black Cat Bones supporting Champion Jack Dupree and Paul, along with drummer Simon Kirke and bassist Stuart Brooks was featured on the 'When You Feel The Feeling You Was Feeling' album released in 1968.

Paul was unimpressed with his Les Paul Custom, and, during late 1966 or early 1967, he found a guitarist that was willing to swap a Les Paul Standard with him. This was a late model from 1960 and had a cherry sunburst finish with prominent 'tiger stripe' figuring in the maple top. This guitar was used throughout 1967 and into early 1968, likely being present at the Champion Jack Dupree sessions, before being traded back for the Les Paul Custom as the new owner decided he did not like the guitar.

During early 1968, Paul became frustrated with Black Cat Bones and left, joining forces with drummer Simon Kirke to found a new group. One night, he came across Paul Rodgers performing with a blues group in a North London pub and soon recruited him, with bassist Andy Fraser arriving later via a recommendation.

The first rehearsal occurred in mid-April 1968 and was quite successful, lasting for several hours, and resulting in the composition of 'I'm A Mover' and 'Walk In My Shadow'. Alexis Korner attended the session and suggested that the band should adopt the name Free and also offered them a slot opening for him on a forthcoming tour.

Paul was back using his black Les Paul Custom and soon after the band's formation had a 50-watt Marshall head with two 4x12 in. cabinets. This set-up continued through the early days as Free played opening slots for other bands and became the prime attraction in smaller venues. As their reputation grew, the group was given a residency at the Marquee Club on Wardour Street.

This spot, which took place on a Monday night, brought Free to the attention of Island Records, which quickly signed up the band despite misgivings about the name of the group. The label

Introduced in 1954, the Gibson Les Paul Custom differed in several ways from the Standard. The body was of all mahogany construction (no maple top), the fingerboard was ebony (in place of rosewood), low frets were provided (in deference to Les Paul's preference, earning the sobriquet 'Fretless Wonder' for the Les Paul Custom guitars), a stopbar tailpiece and ABR-1 Tune-o-matic bridge were installed and a P90 pick-up was paired with the Alnico Five or 'Staple' pick-up. From 1957, the Custom featured three of Gibson's new humbucking pick-ups.

Paul Kossoff playing at the Isle of Wight Festival August 30, 1970.
Philippe Gras / Alamy Stock Photo.

pushed Free to gigs around the country and began making plans for the band to record their first album. Paul Rodgers and Andy Fraser took up responsibility for song-writing, with suggestions provided by Paul and Simon Kirke. Rodgers and Fraser developed Free's sound using the traditional blues as a basis.

To ease Free into recording their album, producer Guy Stevens decided to have them play most of their live set in the studio, capturing their distinct energy in the process. Eight of the ten tracks were original compositions, with the two covers being 'Goin' Down Slow' and 'The Hunter'. Highlights of Paul's playing (incredibly, he had just turned 18) are heard on 'Walk In My Shadow', 'Goin' Down Slow', 'I'm A Mover', 'The Hunter' and 'Moonshine'.

Paul gets a number of distinct sounds out of his Les Paul Custom which showcase his mastery of not only the blues but the guitar. His meaningful lead lines compliment the singing of Paul Rodgers effectively on tracks such as 'Walk In My Shadow' and 'Goin' Down Slow'. Of particular note is Paul's vibrato technique which is expressive and instantly recognisable. Paul's idol, Eric Clapton, later asked him to demonstrate his vibrato technique after a gig in mid-1969.

At the time of release (early 1969), the album – 'Tons of Sobs' – did not fare well in the British charts, and neither did the singles, yet the band's reputation as a dynamic force in the burgeoning blues rock scene was cemented.

Despite the debut album's commercial failure, Island Records continued to support the band. The label quickly had the group back in the studio to record a follow-up to 'Tons Of Sobs'.

Paul diversified his guitars and amps for the sessions, using a Gibson ES 355 and a Fender Stratocaster through a Fender Super Reverb in addition to his Les Paul and Marshall. Early in 1969, for live dates, Paul had acquired a Marshall Super Lead 100-watt head and used a pair of Marshall 4x12 in. cabinets. These were fitted with bass speakers and changed the tone more to Paul's liking.

Free's second album, simply titled 'Free', was a departure from the sound of 'Tons Of Sobs' as the guitar-driven blues sound of the latter was replaced by several 'gentler' songs. Paul toned down his energetic and forceful guitar playing and provided a calmer rhythm accompaniment. Yet, there was still room for tracks that recalled the band's early sound, such as 'I'll Be Creepin', 'Trouble On Double Time' (the only track on the record that was credited to the whole group, not just Fraser/Rodgers), 'Woman' and 'Broad Daylight'. 'Free' was released in late 1969 and performed better in the British charts, almost breaking into the top twenty.

Following the 'Free' recording sessions, the band was booked to support Blind Faith on their upcoming American tour. This started on a sour note for Free at Madison Square Garden, New

York, as numerous technical difficulties frustrated the group. Paul was still playing his Les Paul Custom at this time, but during the tour he swapped the guitar with Eric Clapton for a 1958 Les Paul Standard. The instrument had a dark sunburst finish and would become one of Paul's favoured guitars, along with another Les Paul Standard he acquired during mid-1969. This had a distinct natural finish, created by a previous owner stripping the paint from the guitar's top.

The sunburst Les Paul was used when Free appeared at the 1969 Isle of Wight Festival, just before the Who. The slot was just 15 minutes long, but the band managed to stay on stage for 25 minutes, delivering an impressive performance. Paul used Who guitarist Pete Townshend's Hiwatt amplifiers.

Free continued to play gigs through to the end of 1969 and into the early 1970s, when the concert at the Sunderland Locarno was recorded. Some of the set was used on the 'Free Live', which was not released until late 1971; the other tracks were culled from a 1970 gig at the Fairfield Halls, Croydon. During this period (and for the recordings), Paul played either of his two Les Paul Standards through a Marshall Super Bass and two Marshall Super PA heads (all 100 watts) in partnership with three 4x12 in. Marshall cabinets fitted with bass speakers.

At the same time, Andy Fraser and Paul Rodgers prepared new material for the band's next album. This was recorded on several occasions during the first half of 1970 and ultimately consisted of seven tracks released as 'Fire And Water' in late June 1970. The disc turned out to be the group's most successful to date, reaching no. 2 in the British charts and no. 17 in America, and this was partially the result of the incredible success experienced by the first single.

'All Right Now' was chosen without any inclination from the band or management that the song would prove to be so popular after release in May 1970. It climbed to no. 2 in Britain and no. 4 in the US. Whilst devised by Andy Fraser, the riff is brought to life by Paul through his Les Paul and Marshall, and he then goes on to deliver a typically tasteful solo, which was unfortunately cut down for the single.

Speaking to Steven Rosen in 1976 (and reproduced in his book *Free at Last: The Story of Free and Bad Company* (2001), Paul commented: 'My playing is very primitive and was on ["All Right Now"]. I work from a few chord shapes, but it's really pretty basic … I use a lot of open strings and the chords are neither major or minor. I don't like to play a major chord unless it's necessary … [the solo] wasn't exactly worked out but at the time we were thinking more of effect than virtuosity.'

'All Right Now' was the standout track for the public in the summer of 1970, but several others on 'Fire And Water' are worthy of mention. The title song 'Fire And Water' is similar to 'All Right Now', featuring a distinctive rhythm pattern played by Paul and a melodic, yet biting solo. 'Oh I Wept' was Paul's sole song-writing credit on the album (apart from the group compositions) and he provided an interesting chord progression that underpins Paul Rodgers' lyrics and vocals. 'Mr Big' is a reminder of Free's earlier music, being a slow, riff-based blues number that allows Paul to shine through a lengthy guitar solo.

The success of 'All Right Now' and 'Fire And Water' made sure that Free were the in-demand band during the summer of 1970. The culmination of this period was the group's appearance at the Isle of Wight Festival. Staged on the island for the two previous years, the event had quickly grown in scope, attracting more people and bands. In 1970, the attendance reached over 500,000 and dozens of acts appeared over several days. Free's appearance was initially scheduled for Saturday, but delays forced the band to wait until Sunday. Unlike the previous year, Free played a long set featuring songs from all three albums, culminating with an encore of 'All Right Now' and 'Crossroads', which had been a firm favourite of the band at gigs. For the performance, Paul used his natural finish Les Paul Standard through three 100-watt Marshall heads and cabinets (with the earlier-mentioned specifications).

Free continued to tour through to the end of the year, but were obliged to find time to record a quick follow-up album to 'Fire And Water'. The band modified their sound, using less of Paul's guitar and more of Andy Fraser's piano, yet Paul still shines on tracks such as 'The Highway Song' and 'Be My Friend'. Continuing to use his Les Paul and Marshall amps, Paul added a new sunburst Les Paul (with highly figured top) to his collection and also employed a Fender Stratocaster.

'Highway' was released just before the end of 1970 and struggled to break into the top forty album chart. The single 'The Stealer' also failed to generate any interest, leaving Free disheartened. Early in 1971, differences between the group members, which were exacerbated by the highs and lows of the previous year, caused Free to disband. Paul was disillusioned with the band's move away from their roots and this contributed to his growing addiction to drugs.

During the summer of 1971, Paul founded, with Simon Kirke, a new group – Kossoff Kirke Tetsu Rabbit – with bassist Tetsu Yamauchi and keyboardist John 'Rabbit' Bundrick, which tried to recapture Free's earlier sound, and did for the most part on the band's self-titled album released in 1972. 'Blue Grass' and 'Just For The Box' are two tracks of the set that showcases Paul's playing. For the sessions, he continued to use his Les Pauls, along with a white Fender Stratocaster (acquired around mid-1971) and played through Marshall amplifiers. Paul experimented at this time with a Leslie rotary speaker, such as on the track 'Colours'.

Kossoff Kirke Tetsu Rabbit did not remain together for long as Paul's personal problems increased during the sessions and he was unable to continue. In an attempt to help him, the other members of Free decided to reform in early 1972. A tour took place soon after, but Paul often struggled. Remarkably though, recording sessions that took place at the same time saw Paul well enough to make meaningful contributions. His presence is felt on several tracks on 'Free At Last', released during mid-1972, entering the British charts' top ten, but performing poorly in America. In the studio, Paul carried through his set-up from the 'Kossoff Kirke Tetsu Rabbit' sessions, including the Leslie speakers. Speaking to Steven Rosen in 1976, Paul commented: 'To me, I think it was Free's most complete album. I liked my playing on that album.'

Although the sessions for 'Free At Last' went relatively well, on tour in America during the summer matters deteriorated and Andy Fraser decided he was ready to move on. Tetsu Yamauchi and John 'Rabbit' Bundrick were drafted in, with the latter hired to help underpin the sound when Paul was unable to play to his usual standards; Paul Rodgers also filled in on guitar on several occasions. The last Free tour of Britain occurred at the end of 1972 and the final album – 'Heartbreaker' – was recorded concurrently and released in early 1973, with William 'Snuffy' Walden and Paul Rodgers providing all of the rhythm guitar and Paul some solos.

Paul officially left Free at the end of 1972 and during the following year recorded a solo album, 'Back Street Crawler', featuring a number of musicians, including his ex-Free bandmates. Paul demonstrates that when in the right frame of mind, he was still able to deliver forceful and emotional lead guitar work. Highlights are 'Tuesday Morning', an extended jam that ebbs and flows over the first side, 'Time Away' where Paul solos over an atmospheric backing and 'Back Street Crawler (Don't Need You No More)'. Paul used his Gibson Les Pauls and white Fender Stratocaster (which he is pictured with on the album cover) on the record, going through Marshall heads and cabs, with a Leslie speaker again employed. 'Time Away' (in fact part of a larger jam with guitarist John Martyn which was edited down) was played using the Stratocaster, Marshall and Leslie combination and Paul commented about the track in *Sounds* magazine: 'The way I was playing on that track is the way I like to express myself. I think it's a good example, it's a very bluesy track and just drifts.'

'Back Street Crawler' did not make any waves at the time and Paul fell back into drug addiction, even selling many of his guitars during 1974 to fund his habit. In 1975, Paul talked in several interviews to the music press about this period: 'I found myself sitting in my flat doing fuck-all and I met up with … you know, characters who wanted to be associated with Paul Kossoff … I went through a period of thinking there's other people playing, not so much better than me, but they don't need me … It [drugs] was an escape from playing as well, 'cause that's a big responsibility in itself; you have to prove yourself. I didn't want to pick up a guitar.'

Paul managed to revive himself enough later in the year to attempt to retrieve some of his guitars. He was reunited with his figured sunburst Les Paul (acquired in late 1970) and continued to use this for the remainder of his life.

Despite several proposals, Paul was unable to solidify a position in a new band until early 1975 when he teamed up with vocalist Terry Wilson-Slesser (previously of Beckett), bassist Terry Wilson, drummer Tony Braunagel and keyboardist Mike Montgomery (all American session musicians). The band took the name of Paul's solo album 'Back Street Crawler' and began recording early in 1975 with a record deal from Atlantic Records. The result of the sessions was 'The Band Plays On', released in October 1975. Several tracks see Paul on good form: 'Hoo Doo Woman', 'Survivor', 'It's A Long Way Down To The Top', 'Train Song'. 'The Band Plays On'.

The year did not end well for Paul as he was hospitalised twice through his drug use, then in early 1976 he broke fingers on his left hand, which severely limited his guitar playing. Yet, he was in America to record Back Street Crawler's second album, '2nd Street', which saw Mike Montgomery replaced by John 'Rabbit' Bundrick and William 'Snuffy' Walden was drafted in to provide rhythm guitar parts; Paul added solos and fills later.

Shortly after the completion of the record, Paul was travelling from Los Angeles to New York when he sadly died during the flight: he was just 25 years old.

Paul Kossoff's 1959 Gibson Les Paul Standard offered for sale at Bonham's Entertainment Memorabilia Sale 2015.
PA Images / Alamy Stock Photo.

ALBERT LEE

Without any fuss and always with a beaming smile on his face, guitarist Albert Lee has made an exceptional contribution to the music of many performers. Amongst them are: Chris Farlowe, Eric Clapton, Emmylou Harris, the Everly Brothers, and Bill Wyman's Rhythm Kings. This is besides developing a successful solo career, which has run alongside a heavy workload as a session player.

He hails from a Romany family and was born in Lingen, Herefordshire, on December 21, 1943, though not long after, his family moved to Blackheath, London. His father was a builder and could turn his hand to playing music: Hawaiian-style guitar, fiddle, piano and accordion. Aged around seven or eight, Albert studied piano for a couple of years until losing interest, though an appreciation of music was born. Passing his Eleven-Plus, in 1955, he attended Roan School for Boys, Maze Hill, London, and developed an appetite for rock 'n' roll, particularly the music of Jerry Lee Lewis, as well as skiffle music, and Lonnie Donegan.

By 1957, Albert was teaching himself guitar – initially on borrowed instruments – eventually absorbing Bert Weedon's *Play in a Day* (1957) and Eric Kershaw's *Dance Band Chords of the Guitar* (1946).

Between 1956 and 1958, the skiffle craze led to the formation of numerous makeshift bands across the UK and Albert played in one titled the Dewdrops, performing mostly in pubs and youth clubs. Albert practised continually, working out guitar solos, being influenced by Scotty Moore and, in particular, Cliff Gallup (of Gene Vincent and the Blue Caps) as well as Buddy Holly.

Although enjoying sport, Albert did not excel academically at school and days before his 15th birthday, his headmaster suggested that he ought to leave. His interest in music was encouraged by his parents and at Christmas 1958, they bought for him a second-hand Hofner President archtop acoustic for about £20.

Early in 1959, Albert started work at the Plan Reproduction company in Brockley while still continually practising and soaking up influences. He was especially interested in the way Cliff Gallup played with a wound third string and James Burton with an unwound G.

Forming his first rock 'n' roll band, Albert and his pals played at the Rivoli in Crofton Park every Sunday night for a while and for little money. His Hofner was traded in, part exchange, for a Grazioso guitar. He received £20 for the Hofner and his dad signed HP papers for the other instrument which cost £85. Albert and bandmate 'Bugs' bought a Selmer Truvoice 19T, though three members of the group plugged in for amplification. They largely played Buddy Holly and Gene Vincent material and appeared during Saturday morning cinema intervals as well as at the same venues on Sunday nights. Calling themselves, for a very brief period, Johnny Vincent and the Delroys, the band recorded four tracks in a church hall in Kidbrooke Park Road around August 1959. Later, the band became known as Johnny Lane and the Cruisers.

Early in 1960, Albert and two of his band members were booked on a short tour of Scotland providing backing for Dickie Pride, from Larry Parnes' stable of pop stars. Returning from Scotland, Albert and the two others met up briefly with Eddie Cochran discussing a variety of musical subjects. Following another Scottish tour, Albert returned to London and bought a Supro amp with a 15-inch Jensen speaker. A German Klemt Echolette was also acquired.

Albert undertook various menial jobs as well as becoming impressed with the country music of Chet Atkins, Don Gibson and Hank Snow. In the summer of 1960, Albert was known to have been playing a borrowed Stratocaster at gigs in a small basement club in Lee Green. In March of the following year, Albert met Bob Xavier, a saxophone player, who wanted him to join his band, the Jury. To Albert's surprise, Xavier provided him with a new 1960 Gibson Les Paul Custom complete with three gold pick-ups and a Bigsby. The band played London clubs and American airbases while Albert undertook some session work. Xavier had acquired the Gibson on hire purchase and, after a while, Albert took over the payments.

Playing with the Jury in the well-known 2i's coffee bar, backing Jackie Lynton and others, and working as a session guitarist, Albert met other musicians including Big Jim Sullivan and Jimmy Page. He also adopted a style of playing with a flat pick and fingers together.

Around early October 1962, Albert met Everly Brothers' guitarist Don Peak and they discussed the playing of B.B. King and Howard Roberts. He was introduced to Phil Everly who was on tour in the UK during that month. After the Jury folded, Albert joined together with other musicians to form Nightsounds and in late October 1962, performed in Hamburg, Germany, for about three weeks. Although the band played long hours for little money it gave them much experience and they exchanged ideas and musical tips with other performing band members.

After Christmas 1962, Albert was back in Hamburg playing in Don Adams and the Original Rock 'n' Roll Trio. A photograph exists from this period showing Albert with the band and playing the Gibson Les Paul Custom. On returning to Britain after about six weeks away in Germany, Albert quickly joined a German band, Mike Warner and the Echolettes – and flew back to the country. For performances, over a three-month period, he continued with the Gibson Les Paul Custom and his Supro amp before someone spilt beer over the latter.

Back in Britain in May 1963, Albert was happy to listen to Hank Garland's 'Jazz Winds From a New Direction'. He also bought his first Fender Telecaster – one from 1959 with a rosewood fingerboard – for £53 from Selmer's and largely used it as his main guitar.

When Gene Vincent toured the UK in May 1963, Albert substituted for the rocker's guitarist who was down with flu.

Albert Lee, with Gibson Everly Brothers' guitar.
Glasshouse Images / Alamy Stock Photo.

He then played with XL5, an R&B band, for a few months appearing at military bases in the UK amongst other venues. From XL5, he joined the Crusaders fronted by Neil Christian and earned £15 a week. Then it was back with Mike Warner, who provided Albert with a new red 1962 Fender Stratocaster as well as a Fender Bassman head with 2x12 in. speaker cabinet. But, about a year later, Albert swapped the amp for a Fender Bassman 4x10 in. combo acquiring another one a little later.

During February 1964, Albert joined the Method, for a Gene Pitney and Billy J. Kramer 20-date tour. A picture exists of the band showing Albert holding his Gibson Les Paul Custom. In June 1964, Albert won an audition to replace the guitarist in Chris Farlowe's band the Thunderbirds; the outfit enjoying a good following on the club circuit.

Early in 1965, Albert traded his Gibson Les Paul Custom for a Gibson Super 400, a guitar used by his hero Scotty Moore. Unimpressed with the instrument, Albert sold it and acquired a white Gibson SG Custom. In June 1965, Albert recorded 'Stormy Monday Blues, Part 1 and 2' with Chris Farlowe who, for contractual reasons, changed his name to Little Joe Cook. With Albert's remarkable guitar playing, the track, over the ensuing years, has been cited as 'the greatest British blues record ever made.'

Information about an adaption to a Fender Telecaster used by Albert was outlined in *Beat Instrument No. 32* December 1965: 'He has taken a pick-up from an old Gibson Les Paul and fitted it in the bass position of the Telecaster. He has also fixed the toggle switch so that it will give either pick-up or a combination of the two.'

Chris Farlowe's major commercial success came with the Jagger/Richards composition 'Out Of Time' recorded in May 1966 and released in June of the same year and reaching no. 1 in the charts. Although Albert did not play on the single, he helped Farlowe create some of his own compositions by adding chords and arrangements.

Albert was praised by Chris Farlowe in *Beat Instrumental No. 40* of August 1966: 'We get about half-a-dozen groups at every booking. They all come to watch Al. He's respected by so many people you know. The other day I was talking to Big Jim Sullivan and he said to me, "It's about time Al got the recognition he deserves". "You're bloody well right," I said. To me Al is the number one guitarist in the country … Al is versatile. He can change his mood so often in one night. He'll do one solo and it'll be out-and-out rock, then he'll do

Albert Lee playing guitar at the Buddy Holly Hall of Performing Arts, Lubbock, Texas.
Tim Board / Stockimo / Alamy Stock Photo.

another and it'll be pure Chet Atkins. Another solo might be jazzy. He's a progressive guitarist. He usually steers clear of the B.B. King stuff … He's quiet, cool, and he likes to stay in the background – out of the limelight.'

Beat Instrumental No. 41 of September 1966, featured Albert as 'Player of the Month' and this mentions that since his first pro gamble he has hardly been out of work and is respected by many of the contemporary music scene as one of the top boys. His secret was dedication to his instrument. 'When I was at school, I used to come home every night and practise. Didn't go out much, just stayed home every night and practised.' He then added: 'I've never gone too much on blues guitar, but rock and country and western music are still my favourite styles. I first started the picking style, which I use now after seeing a bloke called Mickey King play. He used to be with the Rebel Rousers. I always wanted to get Scotty Moore's sound but I didn't realise that he used his fingers as well as plectrum. This bloke opened my eyes, and I've played this way ever since. There was another player as well, his name was Harvey, played with the Cresters and at one time with Mike Berry.' Of his role with Chris Farlowe's Thunderbirds, Albert said: 'I try to fill the sound out, use good full chords. This is one advantage of my picking method …'

Throughout 1967, Albert remained a member of Chris Farlowe's Thunderbirds and toured extensively, though found time to appear on Gerry Temple's album with Jimmy Page, Big Jim Sullivan and Clem Cattini.

By May 1968, Albert had quit the Thunderbirds, unhappy with the direction the band was heading as well as the rock scene generally. He drifted towards a more country style of playing – reflecting that of Buck Owens – something he had wanted to embrace for several years. This interest led him, along with other like-minded individuals, to form Country Fever with Jon Derek. The new band backed country performers and appeared at American bases, and on the Fuller's pub circuit. Often the band toured with the Tumbleweeds and sometimes Albert would appear with them, though was earning little money, country music not being popular in the UK at this time.

To supplement his income, Albert turned to more session work and teamed up with producer Derek Lawrence being part of a studio band that included Ritchie Blackmore, Ian Paice, Big Jim Sullivan, and Nicky Hopkins. Songs were recorded under the names of Country Fever (not connected with the band Albert formed with Jon Derek) and Black Claw. Lawrence recorded 12 tracks which featured Albert on a solo album titled 'The Bell', during late 1968 and May 1969, though this was not released until 1991.

During 1969, Albert gigged with Jon Derek's Country Fever appearing at country venues such as the Nashville Room,

Albert Lee with Lonnie Donegan.
Pete Donegan collection.

London. This band recorded for Decca though the two tracks produced were never released. In May 1969, the band toured extensively and backed many visiting country singers. On signing with Lucky Records, Albert sang on their single 'Did She Mention My Name'. Near the end of the year, the band recorded an album for Lucky, 'Listen To The Country Fever', as well as one for Rediffusion titled 'Mountain Music Jamboree'. Both albums demonstrated Albert's proficiency, as a guitarist, fusing both rock and country picking, as well as revealing his competence as a vocalist.

Albert featured on the two albums recorded under the name of Poet and the One Man Band with a group of session musicians intended to feature the songs of Tony Colton and Ray Smith. These were released early in 1969 and Albert played several gigs with the band as well as with Country Fever. In a feature on Poet and the One Man Band in *Beat Instrumental No. 74* of June 1969, it is mentioned: 'One interesting feature of the band is the three-guitar line-up in addition to bass, drums and keyboards. As well as Ray smith on guitar, there is Jerry Donahue, who does backing-vocals behind Tony Colton's lead singing, and Albert Lee who has had various enthusiastic tags stuck on him such as the "guitarist's guitarist", and "the fastest guitarist alive". Albert is very unwilling to push himself forward, but it is said that a few years back certain budding British guitarists were to be seen listening to Albert, taping his phrases on portable recorders and learning them off. Albert is highly rated by Chet Atkins …'

At the end of 1969, Albert left Jon Derek's Country Fever and during the beginning of the following year was working with Steve Gibbons besides Derek Lawrence on the 'Green Bullfrog' album that included Ritchie Blackmore, Chas Hodges, Big Jim Sullivan, Ian Paice, Rod Alexandra, and Tony Ashton. His versatility was shown when playing guitar on the Mike D'Abo album released in July 1970 and recording with Shirley Bassey.

Albert's next major involvement, from around July 1970, was with Heads, Hands and Feet, that included: Chas Hodges on bass, fiddle and keyboards; Tony Colton; and Ray Smith. Albert contributed to the song 'Country Boy' for the album 'Heads Hands And Feet' and this has since become his trademark piece. The recording of the song featured Albert playing a Baldwin Electric Classic.

In the summer of 1971, Heads, Hands and Feet embarked on an American tour and were well received. Albert met a number of people that were to become important in his continuing development as a guitar player, in particular Sterling and Ernie Ball. The band visited the Ernie Ball factory in Newport Beach.

In several interviews with the music press in the latter half of 1971, Albert mentions a few snippets of information about the equipment he was using. Whilst in America he bought a maple neck '53 Fender Telecaster, a B-Bender mechanism, an amp, pedals, and an Echoplex. Mention is made that he sold a 1959 Telecaster, bought in 1963 with the neck inlaid with mother of pearl, to bandmate Ray Smith. He added that he possessed a Martin 000-28 which he'd acquired for £130 some two years earlier.

Heads, Hands and Feet appeared in Hyde Park London 1971 with Grand Funk Railroad and Humble Pie as well as appearing at several other festivals. They released two more albums. A review of the band in *Melody Maker* included the following about Albert: 'It is easy to comprehend the reasons for the aura of superlativeness that surrounds Albert Lee. Simply, he is a natural, uncluttered and attractive guitarist who has obviously never heard of the word "cliché" in relation to the versatility of his instrument …' But the review pointed out: 'Unfortunately, it seems that his full talents are left rather unexploited on a good deal of Heads, Hands and Feet material …'

The band was the first to appear on the 'Old Grey Whistle Test' in September 1971 where Albert is seen playing slide on a 12-string guitar. Before the end of 1971, Albert was involved in John Lord's rock symphony 'Gemini Suite' besides touring with Heads, Hands and Feet. The latter band never achieved its full potential for a variety of diverse reasons though toured in America again and released two more albums: 'Tracks' and 'Old Soldiers Never Die'. Albert contributed songs, sang and played piano as well as guitar. Heads, Hands and Feet split at the end of 1972.

Early in 1973, members of Heads, Hands and Feet, along with a host of other musicians attended four days of recording sessions backing Jerry Lee Lewis. Afterwards, Albert continued with session work, contributing to the music of artists such as folk singer Carolanne Pegg, Jaki Whitren, and tenor sax player Eddie Harris.

Through Ric Grech, Albert met and played with the Crickets on a British tour in 1973. Albert's connection with the Crickets' Jerry Allison, led him to strike up a friendship with Don Everly. He had a brief meeting with Gram Parsons shortly before the latter's death in September 1973. Whilst the pair had agreed to play together, that did not happen. Albert played on the Crickets' 'Remnants' album (released in 1973) and, eventually 'A Long Way From Lubbock' (appearing during 1975).

In 1974, Albert contributed to Don Everly's 'Sunset Towers' and moved to the US. He played Telecaster on a Crickets album produced by Duane Eddy and in the summer of 1974, he toured with the Crickets in the UK. He is noted as playing some impressive guitar solos 'though were largely unappreciated.'

Settling in the US, Albert tried to carve out a career for himself on the session music scene and he regularly played at impromptu music gatherings in local LA clubs, including the Sundance Saloon. At these appearances, Albert is known to have sometimes played his B-Bender Telecaster. There is also a quote mentioning Albert Lee had 'recently acquired his Evans Pull-String Tele.'

He played on sessions, with Glen Campbell producing, and then teamed up with fellow Englishman Joe Cocker for a tour – Joe Cocker and the Cock 'n' Bull Band – in the Autumn of 1974 and into 1975. Albert contributed to the Cocker album 'Stingray' and started on his first solo album organised by Jerry Moss, the co-founder of A&M records.

In 1975, Albert was in demand playing with Marvin Rainwater, at the Country Music Festival at Wembley, flautist Herbie Mann, Chris Farlowe once more, and Jackson Browne. He also found time to work, in stages, on his solo album.

The early part of 1976 saw Albert take over from James Burton in Emmylou Harris's Hot Band and it was mentioned that he fitted in very well from the outset to form a great country rock band. Besides touring with Emmylou, during 1976, Albert played on her 'Luxury Liner' album, contributing acoustic guitar, electric guitar, mandolin as well as backing vocals. A little later in the year, he played on Lonnie Donegan's 'Puttin' On The Style' album as well as with Joan Armatrading.

Albert appeared in Emmylou's Hot Band on the 'Old Grey Whistle Test' in April 1977 where he is seen with a maple neck Telecaster. He had a treat at Easter 1977 when Don Everly invited him to become an 'Everly Brother' and sing 'Bye Bye Love' with him at the three-day International Festival of Country Music, staged at Wembley, London. Albert then toured with Emmylou and appeared on her album 'Quarter Moon In A Ten-Cent Town', contributing piano, acoustic and electric guitar, and mandolin.

By the spring of 1978, Albert had left the Hot Band to concentrate on his first solo album, begun three years earlier. Members of the Hot Band appeared at the sessions along with Emmylou, Don Everly, Chas Hodges and Dave Peacock. For the remainder of 1978, Albert contributed to many sessions by other performers, including Marcia Ball.

Albert appeared on Emmylou's album 'Blue Kentucky Girl', released in 1979, where he played electric guitar, acoustic guitar and mandolin. Early in 1979, Albert was invited by Eric Clapton to join his band as a 'second guitarist' for a 40-date world tour. In February 1979, Albert's solo album 'Hiding' was released.

During early rehearsals for the world tour, Eric gave Albert his black Les Paul Custom guitar with three pick-ups. Albert has mentioned that in a moment of craziness he had sold his own Les Paul Custom that he had played from the early 1960s. He adds that he considers the three pick-up Les Paul Custom to be one of the best guitars ever made.

At Eric Clapton's warm-up gigs in Ireland, Albert is noted playing a cream-coloured Telecaster with black binding. This was a Telecaster copy built by renowned guitar designer and builder, Phil Kubicki. Albert has talked about one of his Kubicki Telecaster guitars which has Seymour Duncan pick-ups and a B-Bender. He mentions the mechanism, built into the back of the guitar, is 'a lot of fun' and is operated by pulling on the strap button which raises the second string a whole tone, producing steel guitar sounds.

During a break in the Clapton world tour, Albert played his Fender B-Bender on Dave Edmunds' 'Sweet Little Lisa', and mostly mandolin on sessions for Emmylou's 'Roses In The Snow' album. Back on the Eric Clapton tour, in late 1979, Albert played in two concerts in Tokyo, December 3 and 4, that appeared as a double live album, 'Just One Night', in 1980.

He was pleased to play the lead solo on 'Cocaine' which was used on the live album. In the early 1980s Albert appeared at Wembley with Don Everly, Emmylou and Ricky Skaggs, as well as undertaking a 13-date UK tour with Eric Clapton. The tour nights were opened by Chas and Dave and Albert often played with them.

In August 1980, Albert married for the second time and at an all-day jam session a number of players turned up including Lonnie Donegan (playing Albert's 1958 Telecaster), Rodney Crowell, Rosanne Cash, and Emmylou. Albert was amongst a number of musicians involved in Paul Kennerley's 'The Legend Of Jesse James', contributing vocals, guitars, and mandolin; the same year saw him contributing to Eric Clapton's 'Another Ticket'. The latter album was intended to be promoted during 1981 over 60 nights, though was postponed after seven, due to Eric Clapton being hospitalised.

For a period, Albert turned increasingly to session work, helping Emmylou, Bobby Bare, and Bert Jansch on 'Heartbreak' as well as appearing on a Rodney Crowell album. During the autumn of 1981, Albert was back on tour with Eric Clapton. Then, in the spring of 1982, he worked on a second solo album which had a more rock 'n' roll feel than his first one and included Rodney Crowell, Larrie Londin, Emory Gordy, and Vince Gill. Sessions were undertaken for Gail Davies before touring once more with Eric Clapton where on some dates Muddy Waters joined them.

Amongst the players on Eric's next album 'Money And Cigarettes', recorded in late 1982 at a studio in the Bahamas, was Ry Cooder. A tour promoting the album began in 1983 and spots were given to Albert to showcase tracks from his second solo album. Later in the year, he parted company with Eric. Not downhearted about this set back, he was able to play a role in the reunion of Don and Phil Everly who had not played together after a fall-out since 1973. Their comeback was staged at the Royal Albert Hall, London on September 22 and 23, 1983, and Albert had the honour of being chosen to be in the backing band. After rehearsals one night, Albert had an amplifier stolen, though it was retrieved a little later. The concerts were performed without any warm-up gigs and Albert employed one of his Telecasters at the Albert Hall concerts.

Albert is noted as acquiring one of the new Ernie Ball Music Man amplifiers in 1984 as well as giving his opinion on a range of guitars including the Silhouette, Axis and eventually the Albert Lee signature model.

When the Everly Brothers were awarded a recording contract in early 1984, Albert was recruited by producer Dave Edmunds for the sessions which took place in April 1984. Afterwards, Albert joined the brothers for a ten-week tour of the USA and Canada, making a huge contribution with his guitar playing which was often highlighted in concert reviews. After the US tour, the brothers and Albert played 15 dates in the UK.

It was in the 1980s that Don Everly and his wife Karen gave Albert a 1958 black Gibson J200 with two white pick-guards. Albert had played and admired the guitar for a number of years. In a YouTube video, Albert states that it is a guitar with a lot of character and he has used it whenever he could but does not like to drag it around the world too much. He adds that it is a prototype for the Everly Brothers Signature guitar introduced by Gibson in 1962.

In January 1985, Albert played a Telecaster with John Fogerty in a gig for an invited audience before the former Creedence Clearwater ex-member began recording and performing again. Albert toured and recorded once again with the Everly Brothers and whilst involved in more session work during 1985 he recorded his first solo instrumental album, 'Speechless'. On this, he played mandolin and piano as well as writing five of the eight tracks.

At the beginning of 1986, Albert was present for the recording of 'Trio', harnessing the talents of Dolly Parton, Emmylou, and Linda Ronstadt. On two of the tracks, Albert played a high-strung guitar as well as featuring heavily on acoustic guitar. Besides touring with the Everlys in 1986, Albert played for a short period with Duane and the Rebels on a tour with Huey Lewis and the News.

Albert's 'Speechless' album enjoyed success and he produced another instrumental album, 'Gagged But Not Bound', released in 1987 and featuring a wide variety of styles: country, blues, jazz and bluegrass.

Albert fronted a band at a steel guitar festival at Newbury, Berkshire in 1987. This led to him loosely forming Albert Lee and Hogan's Heroes and the band toured intermittently later in the year. In the following year, Albert was involved with the Everly Brothers as well as Hogan's Heroes. In pictures of the latter band playing at the New Pegasus in April 1988 Albert has a Music Man guitar. In the same year, he was in the USA playing lead guitar and mandolin on Pattie Loveless's, 'Honky Tonk Angel'. He also worked with Dolly Parton, Ricky Skaggs and many more in sessions.

Albert appeared with the Everlys on a two-week tour of Australia on the 'Legends of Rock' package tour. Shortly afterwards, when the brothers played Las Vegas, Albert is noted as using his 1953 Telecaster and a 1913 Gibson F4 mandolin. In a YouTube video, Albert says he has a few Gibson and Fender mandolins, some four strings and some with eight. Talking about a solid-body Gibson from the 1950s, one of the few 'solids' they made, he states that although not playing this kind of instrument a lot or practising with them, he does enjoy their sound. He recalls he used mandolins quite often with Emmylou who liked to hear them.

In the same YouTube video, Albert talks about this 1953 Telecaster, mentioning it's one of four or five Fenders he owned. He had about half a dozen in total, including some copies and tended to choose those which were light in weight. He found them more comfortable to play and the sound was not so hard as it could be with an instrument that was much heavier. A feature of his 1953 Telecaster body is a collection of autographs of people he has played with over his long career, making the guitar a real collector's item.

The 1953 Fender was not his oldest, as he possessed one from 1952, but he confesses the 1953 guitar was his favourite. Instantly noticeable is that the guitar has no finish. Albert points out it has a phase reversal switch, reversing the polarity on one of the pick-ups for an out of phase sound. The guitar is strung with Ernie Ball extra slinky strings and he uses a 24 instead of a 22 in the set-up, finding the former a little too light.

Albert Lee on stage at National Folk Festival in Salisbury, Maryland, USA.
Edwin Remsberg / Alamy Stock Photo.

Albert admits to having what he describes as a 'nut fetish' – often filing the nut down too much – but adjusts by putting paper beneath the strings to raise them and avoid 'buzzing'. He adds that he uses a Boss Chromatic Tuner throughout a set, admitting that previously he had always considered himself to be always in tune whilst on stage. However, he found that his guitar would drift about a quarter tone down and the tuner had been invaluable as a reference point for him. He demonstrates using a flat pick and several fingers to play, dismissing the theory that most people had of him using a thumb pick.

Albert was in Australia in January 1990 appearing with Tommy Emmanuel, and whilst there, Maton produced a prototype guitar for him. Then, he was back on tour with the Everlys, Linda Ronstadt, as well as Tal Farlow and Jerry Douglas. Session work was with Carlene Carter, and in the same year he toured with Hogan's Heroes, appearing on Jools Holland's 'The Happening'. By this time, he was often seen using his Ernie Ball/Music Man Prototype guitar.

In 1991, Albert told *Musician* magazine that although he had not made a lot of money from music, he had enjoyed his time playing. This was the year he stopped appearing for a while with the Everlys and involved himself with more work on the road and in the studio.

He began a 53-date tour with Hogan's Heroes in 1991 and is noted as playing a red and white Music Man guitar. In 1992, he appeared at the Royal Albert Hall in the 'Return of Spinal Tap' followed by a 30-date tour with the Everlys. At the end of the year Albert was at Wembley in a rock 'n' roll package that included Duane Eddy, Jerry Lee, Little Richard and Chris Montez. Albert played on both the Duane Eddy and Jerry Lee sets and in the show's encore with Little Richard.

A press release on August 17, 1993, announced that Ernie Ball Music Man was to unveil the Albert Lee Model guitar. It featured an angular Axis prototype, body style; three Seymour Duncan single-coil pick-ups; five-way switch; figured maple neck and matching fingerboard; and Schaller tuners. Albert played a part in promoting the guitar by undertaking clinics and workshops in the US and Europe. At the same time, he was involved in a short tour in Australia with Biff Baby's All-stars that included Steve Morse. More session work and a 34-date European tour with the Everlys followed. On an autumn tour with Hogan's Heroes, Albert is mentioned as using one of his Ernie Ball signature guitars. In the following year, he carried out sessions with Randy and Rachel Parton as well as playing once more with the Everlys and Hogan's Heroes.

Albert recorded some sessions with Bill Wyman's Rhythm Kings during 1996. Around this time, he was persuaded, after using a Music Man amp for quite some time, to try a

Albert Lee playing guitar with Vince Eager and James Burton.
Vince Eager collection.

Fender Tonemaster amplifier, which he liked. In 1997, Albert played some gigs with Bill Wyman and he received a 'Lifetime Achievement Award' at the British Country Music Awards in April of that year.

During 1998, Albert toured with Hogan's Heroes, the Everlys and Bill Wyman. In New Mexico, Albert's 1913 Gibson mandolin, and a Music Man HD130 head were stolen. A year later, he toured with Hogan's Heroes, the Everlys and played at the 'Eddie Cochran Rock 'n' Roll Weekend' in Chippenham. The following year was Albert's 40th as a professional musician and saw him tour with the Rhythm Kings.

During August 2001, the band began a tour of North America for the first time. A year later Hogan's Heroes began a 56-date tour and released a second album 'Tear It Up'. On November 29, 2002, Albert was part of the band gathered together for a tribute concert celebrating the life of George Harrison. In the same year, he won a Grammy award for Best Country Instrumental Performance for 'Foggy Mountain Breakdown' from the CD 'Earl Scruggs and Friends'.

Albert Lee rehearsing with James Burton.
Vince Eager collection.

Four years later, he was present in 'Primal Twang: The Legacy Of The Guitar'. He performed at the Crossroads Guitar Festival during 2007, and later in the same year appeared with the Rhythm Kings at the Ahmet Ertegun tribute London concert.

Throughout his long musical career, Albert has played, and still continues to play guitar, mandolin and piano with a wide range of artists as well as in his own band.

ALVIN LEE

Alvin Lee had a vision of how he wanted to play electric guitar from an early age and arguably stuck to it throughout his career. He aimed to take his blues and jazz influences and play them 'a bit more crazy, rocking them up a bit' and with the similar excitement he heard in Chuck Berry's rock 'n' roll music, particularly 'Sweet Little Rock 'n' Roller'. That, to him, was the basis of British blues. The music form was recycled and taken back to America in the late 1960s, although he didn't feel at the time he was part of a 'British Blues Boom'.

Alvin Lee (real name Graham Anthony Barnes) was born at Wollaton Park, Nottingham, in 1944 to Sam and Doris. He was the youngest of three children having two elder sisters. His father worked at the Department of Works and his mother ran a small hairdressing business from a back room in their prefabricated 1950s bungalow. Both parents were ardent fans of swing jazz, blues and country and it is understood that Doris played guitar a little.

On YouTube, a 'Rockspective Documentary' features Alvin, and he reveals his father was an avid collector of blues records, especially chain gang prison songs and they were often heard around the family home. Sam also listened to Big Bill Broonzy and Lonnie Johnson.

When Alvin was about 12 years old, he fondly remembers being woken one night by his father who had been to see Big Bill Broonzy at a Nottingham club. To Alvin's surprise, Sam brought the blues man back home. Alvin sat on the floor listening to the giant, Big Bill, play, and suggests this was a great influence on him, admitting his first interest was in country blues. Alvin said he was impressed with how Big Bill would keep a rhythm going on guitar as well as playing with his fingers.

Initially, Alvin did not play guitar, taking up the clarinet for about a year. He may have been influenced by his brother-in-law playing clarinet in a local dance band. Uncomfortable with the instrument, he switched, around the age of 12/13, to guitar, preferring the sound of the American swing and jazz guitarist Charlie Christian to Benny Goodman on clarinet.

Alvin told *Beat Instrumental No. 60* of April 1968 that his first guitar was a Spanish model but he 'swapped it for an electric Guyatone when he was 13.' This was bought by his parents and, mother Dot says, on the very informative German website www.alvinlee.de: '[Alvin] was over the moon [with the Guyatone] and so happy, we could see that this was his instrument without a doubt.' She added: 'He practiced every single minute he could and got on like crazy with [the guitar] so quickly. It was then that I knew the talent was there, and nothing could stop him … He just loved playing his music which he was dedicated to.'

Alvin became familiar with major guitar chords after being taught by a family friend, and for him the 1950s were a time for absorbing guitar influences, most notably from Django Reinhardt, Barney Kessel, George Benson, Segovia, and Merle Travis, but especially Chuck Berry, Scotty Moore and Franny Beecher.

Alvin was around 13 years old when joining Ivan Jaye and the Jailbreakers. He hated school and left when he was 15. He only ever had one job and that was working at the Raleigh cycle factory in Nottingham, but this lasted only a week before he quit.

By 1960, he was a member of the Atomites, replacing the original guitar player and teaming up with bass player Leo Lyons. This would be a working relationship lasting for many years. The Atomites changed their name to Ivan Jaye and the Jaycats when Ivan Jaye joined the band. The new line-up was Alvin on lead guitar, Roy Cooper on rhythm guitar, Ivan Jaye on vocals, Pete Evans on drums and Leo Lyons on bass. At this time, Alvin was playing a Burns Vibra-Artist guitar with a rosewood neck. Leo Lyons recalls Alvin and himself often tuned their guitars using a tuning fork.

Paying on HP, the band acquired three Vox amplifiers: Two Vox AC15s for lead and bass; and an AC10 for the rhythm guitar. After a disagreement, Alvin briefly left the band and went to London, auditioning for the Outlaws, an instrumental outfit being put together by record producer, Joe Meek. Alvin was unsuccessful in his venture, returning to Nottingham. However, in 1961, with Alvin back in the fold, Ivan Jaye and the Jaycats moved to London. They auditioned for Joe Meek and recorded several songs for him. This was besides performing up and down the country wherever possible, and playing, as a backing band, for a number of solo artists such as Eden Kane. Eventually, after some very scary encounters with gangs, the band returned from the capital to Nottingham with Leo Lyons becoming their manager.

In late 1961 or early 1962, Alvin moved from the earlier Burns guitar to a Grimshaw. On www.grimshawguitars.co.uk,

---

The Burns Vibra-Artist guitar was manufactured 1960–1962 and featured Tri-sonic pick-ups with three volume controls, three tone controls, one 3-way selector and one rhythm/solo. The standard finish was cherry with, initially, a maple fingerboard later changed to rosewood. The guitar was Jim Burns' first creation for his own company and retailed at £78.

The Grimshaw website states: 'SS [short scale] de-luxe 1958. List price, 1958 £52 10s, case extra. Tremolo unit, £10 fitted.' In the website's history section it mentions: 'The most popular model of the 1950s was the SS (short scale) Deluxe, the styling on this was a cross between a Gibson ES 335 and a Gretsch White Falcon, with an individual Grimshaw-style of un-equal cutaways and finished in adventurous colours such as white, cherry red and blonde, unusual when most guitars were dark sunburst.'

there is a photograph with the caption 'Alvin Lee with [an Emile Grimshaw] SS de-luxe, fitted with Bigsby trem.' Several photographs taken by Leo Lyons show Alvin with the guitar.

By 1962 the band was a three-piece, the Jaybirds, Ivan Jaye having left and a replacement for him did not stay for very long. Roy, the rhythm guitarist, departed not long afterwards, Alvin becoming vocalist and guitarist.

In June 1962, the Jaybirds played for a six-week stint in Hamburg, Germany, at the Star Club initially as a four-piece, as they took a rhythm guitarist with them. A van full of equipment was taken to Hamburg but only guitars were used, as Fender amps and a drum kit were provided by the venue. They played a mixture of numbers by Chuck Berry, Eddie Cochran, Elvis Presley, Carl Perkins and Little Richard. These were performed during several-hour-long sets lasting until early morning. Often, they stretched out songs jamming and including individual solos and this was how the Ten Years After sound was nurtured.

On their return from Hamburg, first Leo and then Alvin, began building their own speaker cabinets. Also, Alvin and Leo invested in Mullard and Leak 50-watt hi-fi stereo amps to power their home-built cabinets. With the help of a local electronics wizard, the pair built their own 100-watt PA system with a small mixer, two microphone inputs and two 12-inch speaker cabs for either side of the stage.

Around 1963, drummer Pete Evans left and was replaced by Dave Quickmire. The band was playing regularly but barely surviving. Their repertoire included Ray Charles 'What'd I Say' and 'I Gotta Woman'; Barrett Strong's 'If You Gotta Make A Fool Of Somebody'; 'The Star Club Twist'; a spin on Joey Dee's 'Peppermint Twist'; and 'Twist And Shout', the Isley Brothers song. At the same time, they added Woody Herman's 'Woodchoppers Ball', an attempt at big band swing.

After many disappointments in the music industry, the Jaybirds found work with Larry Parnes backing some of his stars including Dickie Pride, Johnny Gentle, Vince Eager, Lance Fortune, The Vernons Girls, Gary Mills, Ricky Valance, Wee Willie Harris. Throughout this time, the Jaybirds built a reputation as good players and many local musicians went to see them.

In 1965 drummer Dave Quickmire departed and Ric Lee was persuaded to leave his outfit, the Mansfields, and join the Jaybirds. Manager Leo Lyons struggled to find venues for the band to play as he was often told their fees were too high and the music focus at that time was on Soul music. To give another dimension to the Jaybirds, a decision was taken to add a keyboard player resulting in Alvin's friend Chic Churchill, from a Mod/Soul band the Sons of Adam joining the line-up in 1966. Leo remembers that about this time Alvin managed to obtain of a 50-watt Marshall head and used that with the homemade speaker cabinet.

Moving to London again, the band backed such artists as the Ivy League, while Leo and Alvin undertook some session work in several Denmark Street studios, including Regent Sound. Leo played with a jazz band, run by guitarist Denny Wright during the evenings in a Chelsea club. Denny played in Lonnie Donegan's backing band and when he was away on tour, Alvin joined Leo in the jazz club. Eventually, Leo retired from his management role and handed it over to Chris Wright.

Around the mid-1960s both Leo and Alvin met Charlie Watkins and began using Watkins 100-watt Solid State amplifiers. Said Leo: 'We got very involved with the Watkins brand, went down to the factory and tried out different amps. They worked fine and we had huge cabinets. Charlie was a wonderful man. He provided a PA and let us have whatever we wanted.'

Alvin Lee with Grimshaw guitar.
Photograph courtesy of Leo Lyons.

The blues scene, developing in the UK in the late 1960s, arguably opened up by the 'John Mayall With Eric Clapton Bluesbreakers' album, was welcomed, in particular by Alvin and Leo, who commented: 'It showed we could play the music we really wanted to perform, high energy blues, jazz, rock 'n' roll whatever you want to call it, and have the opportunity to jam. We also realised we needed to come up with some of our own blues-flavoured songs and we did that quite quickly. Of course, we were familiar with the Cream, having toured a little with them, and with Peter Green's Fleetwood Mac, as well as Jimi Hendrix.'

The new music form encouraged several name changes for the Jaybirds. First was, Blues Trip, then they played at the Marquee as Blues Yard, before finally settling, in 1967, on Ten Years After, a name chosen by Leo Lyons who recalls: 'I was looking through the Radio Times and saw an advertisement for a book about the 1956 Suez Crisis. Alongside was the phrase, "Suez, Ten Years After". I thought part of that could be a really good name, and would intrigue people, so we adopted Ten Years After.'

Establishing a reputation as a good live band, Ten Years After supported John Mayall's Bluesbreakers around 1967 and secured a residency at the legendary Marquee Club, as well as playing many of the noted blues clubs around the capital such as the Cricketer's Arms. Leo mentions that for some of the Marquee gigs Alvin played through a Marshall head and Watkins WEM cabs.

An invitation to the famous Windsor Jazz & Blues Festival, on August 12, 1967, playing in front of 20,000, led to their first recording contract. Decca Records auditioned the band for a possible deal but that came to nothing. Meanwhile, Decca had established Deram Records and Ten Years After were signed by the label on the recommendation of Decca staff producer Mike Vernon.

Alvin commented, this was a fine example of 'one hand not knowing what the other was doing.' The band was given a deal for an album which was quite unusual at the time. It was more common for a band to have hit single first before being asked to make an album.

Ten Years After's first album was recorded in September 1968 at Decca Studios, Broadhurst Gardens, West Hampstead, London and produced by Mike Vernon and Gus Dudgeon. Released in October of the same year, Alvin has stated the album was basically a live set. They were familiar with the numbers and 'just went into the studio and played them.'

The album had some original material – out of nine tracks five are attributed to Alvin – one of them is co-written with Gus Dudgeon and another with Chick Churchill. The album was reissued in 2002 with six bonus tracks, five being penned by Alvin Lee.

In the late 1960s, Ten Years After became part of the so-called 'British Underground' with bands playing in different styles and Alvin describes the period as 'great and very exciting.' He enjoyed the freedom where band members did not have to don suits and constantly smile. They just did what they wanted to do.

Beat Instrumental's 1967 Gold Star Awards, published in Beat Instrumental No. 58 of February 1968 saw Alvin positioned at no. 8 under the 'Lead Guitarist' list, with Eric Clapton at no. 1. Two months later, he told the magazine he rated every guitarist in the jazz class, particularly George Benson, and Wes Montgomery. He admired the 'big league of Clapton, Hendrix and Green' but has a special word of praise for Thunderbird Albert Lee. Alvin's musical tastes were wide, confessing: 'I can listen to most types of music, if it's good, but I do prefer blues and jazz.'

He admitted that he wasn't into fast-playing guitarists, preferring Peter Green's subtle touch. On seeing Green perform with John Mayall's Bluesbreakers at the Marquee Club, Alvin was very impressed. Peter was the only guitarist Alvin had ever seen turning the volume control down during a solo.

Ten Years After busily promoted their first album at home and in Europe. Unexpectedly, the debut album received airplay on San Francisco's underground radio stations and was greatly admired by listeners. One of them was the celebrated impresario and rock concert promoter Bill Graham, who ran the Fillmore East and Fillmore West auditoriums. He was a champion of music and invited Ten Years After to play at his venues. This was a dream come true for both Alvin and Leo as they always wanted to play in America. 'It was fantastic,' recalled Leo. 'We loved American music. We loved American cars and American guitars.' Before leaving, they agreed a new album was needed.

Without any new material, they decided to record a live album that was, initially, only intended for release in the States. Funds for this venture were hastily scraped together and 'Undead' was recorded live on May 14, 1968, at Dick Jordan's Klooks Kleek Club in West Hampstead, London. Released on August 10, 1968 in the USA, and May 14, 1968 in the UK, it comprised five tracks, with three being written by Alvin. Andrew L. Cope in Black Sabbath and the Rise of Heavy Metal Music (2010) argued that 'Undead' amply illustrated Alvin Lee's 'eclectic' use of the pentatonic scale mixed with other modalities. A 2002 reissue of the album includes nine tracks.

Notes about the recording were revealed by engineer Roy Baker in an article 'Ten Years After Live' published in Beat Instrumental No. 63 of July 1968. He said: 'We've carted a classical machine out of the studio, fitted it with limiters echo [sic], and so on, doctored the wiring, and set the whole thing up in the Decca studio's canteen, which is linked up to the club just down the road. The acoustics in Klook's set a lot of recording problems, and to make matters even more difficult we could only put up one screen to separate the mikes. Otherwise, the audience wouldn't be able to see a thing. We've got mikes in the chandeliers to catch the audience reaction, wires going everywhere and back, equipment filling every square inch …'

For the encore at the gig, Alvin Lee starts with a guitar intro and then, out of the blue, sings 'I'm Going Home', the rest of the band playing an appropriate backing behind him. Thereafter, this was to become the title of a band anthem.

For the recording Alvin used the Gibson ES 335, an

Alvin is pictured with a Gibson cherry ES 345 in a posed photograph that includes Leo Lyons and drummer Pete Evans in the early 1960s. Alvin told Beat Instrumental No. 60 *of April 1968 that he'd been using a Gibson cherry ES 335 for three years and it was over ten years old. He does not mention the Gibson ES 345. It is unclear whether Alvin bought the cherry ES 335 from a friend or a store in Nottingham. Tony Bacon in* The Gibson 335 Guitar Book *(2016) states: 'The guitar that [Alvin] Lee chose for his speedy jazzy bluesy workouts was a [Gibson] dot-neck cherry ES 335, which he bought in his hometown of Nottingham, England in 1963 for £45.'*

There are several problems with these statements regarding the ES 335 guitar and may need some clarification. First, as Tony Bacon rightly points out in his book, the Gibson ES 330, ES 335 and ES 345 guitars were offered only in two finishes until 1960: sunburst or natural. He adds: 'In that year [1960] cherry was offered – although a lone '58 (only just: it was shipped on December 15) and a few '59 ES 335s in cherry have turned up.'

Whether Alvin's ES 335 guitar was the rare 1958 or one of those from 1959 is open to speculation but probably most unlikely.

Additions were made to the guitar during the early part of Alvin's ownership and these included the fitting of a Bigsby and a Stratocaster pick-up between the two humbuckers. The two humbucking pick-up covers were also removed and a little later, stickers – including one for 'Ban the Bomb' – were applied to the front of the guitar which he nicknamed 'Big Red'.

The guitar's original neck was replaced in the early 1970s following damage sustained on stage and a new neck fitted. No information about the serial number has been located from the time of the repair.

Alvin Lee, in Amsterdam, Netherlands, 1974.
Gijsbert Hanekroot / Alamy Stock Photo.

8x10 Watkins cab and the Marshall 50-watt head.

Ten Years After toured America for the first time in 1968 using rented amps. They played the Fillmore East and West and other noted venues where audiences were mesmerised by Alvin's rapid-fire guitar playing as well as the rest of the band's energetic contributions to the overall sound.

For their second tour of America, Ten Years After bought several sets of Marshall gear, continuing to use it at home and abroad over the ensuing years. Leo adds: 'Alvin wasn't that much of an effects guy. He got a sound from his guitar and played it. In the early days though, Alvin occasionally used a Binson echo unit.'

'Stonedhenge', the band's second studio album, was recorded in September 1968 and released February 22, 1969. There are ten tracks, seven being written by Alvin, including one co-written with Mike Vernon who was also the producer.

The band reached a pinnacle when appearing at the Woodstock Music and Arts Festival, held in Upstate New York, in August 1969. Playing on the third day of the event, Ten Years After followed Country Joe & the Fish. Alvin used the dot neck Gibson 335 played through the band's own Marshall heads and cabs.

One freelance writer commented about the band's performance in a Los Angeles magazine: 'At Woodstock, [Ten Years After] arrived unheralded. Simply an English group playing what Alvin Lee, vocalist-lead guitarist, terms "blues-based rock with jazz tendencies". But, their impact was instantaneous. The drums of fame began beating at once throughout the rock generation to celebrate the advent of a new combo with a genuinely unique sound.'

Michael Wadleigh's film about the Woodstock event, which came out a year later, catapulted Ten Years After to international stardom and made sure they would be playing arenas and stadiums in America over the next few years. Alvin Lee once told *Guitar World* the following about his guitar solo in the ten-minute performance of 'I'm Going Home', featured in the movie: 'The solo sounds pretty rough to me these days. But it had the energy, and that was what Ten Years After were all about at the time.'

About being called 'Captain Speedfingers', Alvin admitted he never really tried to play fast, stating the technique developed from the adrenalin rush of the many gigs he performed long before Woodstock, adding there were many guitarists faster than him, amongst them Django Reinhardt, Barny Kessel, John McLaughlin and Joe Pass.

At the Isle of Wight Festival in 1970, Alvin played a Gibson sunburst ES 345 with a Bigsby which he used during the second half of the year. Leo Lyons suggested there was no particular reason for him using the ES 345, adding: 'I think he just wanted to try out another guitar.' Leo recollects the ES 335 dot-marker neck was broken through Alvin throwing the guitar across the stage around 1970.

Alvin told David Sinclair in *Sounds Guitar Heroes* (1983) that he broke the headstock of the ES 335 and it was sent away to Gibson for repair, minor modifications and a body re-spray that went over the stickers. He employed another ES 335 which had small block markers, a trapeze tailpiece, but no extra pick-up. This second ES 335 was used until about 1974 when picking up the original one, now having a replaced neck, a stopbar tailpiece and a knob to access the Stratocaster pick-up.

On www.alvinlee.com/equipment, there are notes from Alvin about his guitar modifications: 'I always liked the Strat sound but when I play a Strat I find my little finger on the right hand keeps turning the volume down unintentionally. I figured that by adding a Strat back PU to my ES 335 I would have the best of both worlds. I've always liked messing about with electronics. I built my own amp and speaker cabs when I was 16 and as soon as I got my first ES 335, I took off the humbucker covers to get a bit more edge and turned the bridge PU round the other way for extra bite.'

Commenting about the guitar's stickers Alvin said: 'When I was on stage at Woodstock a sticker somehow got passed to me while I was playing and I just slapped it on. The peace stickers came to me in a very similar manner in 1967 at the Fillmore West, in San Francisco, and the rest just somehow appeared.'

The single 'Love Like A Man' released in 1970 reached no. 10, and was the band's only success in the UK Singles Chart. In 1971, another single, 'I'd Love To Change The World' peaked at no. 40 on the Billboard Hot 100.

Further albums were released during the early 1970s: 'Sssh' (1969); 'Cricklewood Green' (1970); 'Watt' (1970); 'A Space In Time' (1971); 'Rock & Roll Music To The World' (1972); 'Positive Vibrations' (1974).

Whilst on the many tours of America, Leo notes that Woody Herman was one of a number of musicians who watched them: 'He wanted to see us play our version of his "Woodchoppers Ball", I guess. We met Stan Getz, Miles Davis, Larry Carlton, Les Paul and John McLaughlin, amongst many others.' Leo recalls that whilst on the road, Alvin really only carried one guitar, his ES 335, but in America he often bought a number of instruments from dealers when they brought them backstage after a gig.

The remainder of the 1970s saw Alvin leave and rejoin Ten Years After on several occasions. He teamed up with American Gospel singer Mylon LeFevre for an album 'On The Road To Freedom' released in November 1973. Amongst the musicians contributing were George Harrison, Steve Winwood, Jim Capaldi, Mick Fleetwood and Ron Wood. Later in the decade he formed Ten Years Later and toured in Europe and the USA.

During the 1980s, the Tokai guitar company built Alvin an ES 335-type guitar, and in the following decade one was provided by the Heritage company. Associations during the 1980s were forged with vocalist Steve Gould and ex-Rolling Stone Mick Taylor, with tours being undertaken. Amongst Alvin's albums released in the 1990s were 'Zoom' and '1994'. A studio album 'Alvin Lee In Tennessee', released in 2004, saw him involve such musicians as Scotty Moore and D.J. Fontana.

Gibson produced a Nashville Custom Shop replica of Alvin's ES 335 in 2005 and he worked with the company's artist relations officer, Pat Foley, as well as the Custom Shop's Edwin Wilson to produce the guitar. The Custom Shop had both the guitar and case long enough to make a convincing model which featured aging, the extra single coil pick-up and stickers. In total, the production run was limited to 50 guitars, numbered 'nn' on the label in body. The guitar included small

Ten Years After c. 1972 with Alvin Lee and Leo Lyons (left).
Pictorial Press Ltd / Alamy Stock Photo.

block markers, crown inlay on headstock, black pick-guard, six saddle bridge and separate stopbar tailpiece. Alvin's signature was on the rear of the headstock.

Production of 'Big Red' models did not stop there. In 2006, Gibson's Memphis factory turned out a non-aged ES 335 but displaying stickers. A year later another model appeared minus stickers.

In later years, Alvin, as may have been predicted, no longer used the original ES 335, having become too much of a risk and valuable to take on the road. One collector had offered him $500,000 for the instrument but this was declined.

After releasing the album 'Still On The Road To Freedom' in 2012, he gave an insight into what had been employed in the studio for an interview with Damian Fanelli posted on *Guitar World* of December 19, 2014: [I used] mainly a Gibbo ES 335 and a Martin acoustic. I used a Wal bass and a Gretsch baritone guitar for bass, as well as Pete Pritchard's Music Man and a dog house double bass called Charlie Boy. Amp wise, I used a WEM 15 Dominator and a very old Yamaha I bought from Mick Abrahams. I also used the original Pod, which is better than the new ones, as a preamp into a Fender champ and Mustang. Plus Guitar Rig and Amplitude and too many others to mention.'

Alvin Lee died on March 6, 2013, from unforeseen complications following a routine surgical procedure for atrial arrhythmia.

To honour the 50th Anniversary of Woodstock and to recognise, once more, the band's explosive performance of 'I'm Going Home' at the festival, Gibson announced the release of the Alvin Lee ES 335 '69 Festival' model. Built with all the stickers, aging characteristics, and modifications of the original instrument, as it was played at Woodstock, only 50 of these models were released worldwide. Features of particular note are the Pearloid Dot inlays; the Bigsby B-7 tailpiece; authentic Medium C-Shape neck profile; Indian rosewood fingerboard; two Custombucker (Alnico III) uncovered pick-ups; A Seymour Duncan SSL-1 Single Coil Middle pick-up; and Black Top Hat knobs w/Silver Inserts.

A Gibson promotional video for the 'Festival Guitar' featured Ten Years After's bass player Leo Lyons and Loraine Burgon, Alvin's partner (1963–1973). Loraine commented that the aging on the guitar was 'remarkable' and that 'Alvin would have been very pleased.' Leo Lyons added that he remembered when Alvin bought the original guitar. 'It was no big deal. [Guitars] then were just the tools of the trade. Alvin liked that particular guitar because Chuck Berry played one.'

John Lennon, with Rickenbacker 325.
Pictorial Press Ltd / Alamy Stock Photo.

JOHN LENNON

As one quarter of the cultural and musical phenomenon that was the Beatles, John Lennon was always known as the straight-forward 'tell it like it is' member of the group. His guitar playing can be similarly described, often being simple yet effective in getting the point of the song across or providing support for other guitarists to play lead. As a result, John is perhaps overlooked as a great rhythm guitarist.

John first became interested in playing music around the age of ten when he heard a house guest at his Aunt Mimi's playing a mouth organ. The guest said that if John could learn a song that night, he would buy one for John. Learning two, John received the gift.

John's interest in music was further developed by his mother, Julia, who could play the banjo. She taught John a few chords when he was about 15. This coincided with the rise of skiffle music, which fascinated John and induced him to form a band with a friend. John played a Gallotone Champion, that he had ordered from a newspaper for £10. Yet, his training on the banjo forced him to play the guitar in this way, with just five strings and a different tuning.

John's band the Quarry Men began to perform in the summer of 1957. At one appearance at a village fete, John met Paul McCartney and later invited him to join the band, which continued with other line-up changes into 1958. A major recruit in early 1958 was George Harrison on guitar.

During the year, the band made their first recording at a primitive studio in Liverpool with a cover of Buddy Holly's 'That'll Be The Day' and an original penned by Paul and George – 'In Spite Of All The Danger'. John sang and played his guitar on the tracks. Despite this achievement, the Quarry Men went their separate ways for a time before being drawn back together.

George Harrison had joined the Les Stewart Quartet and were about to begin a series of gigs at a coffee bar when they disbanded. George and another guitarist decided to call on John and Paul to fill the dates. This spurred John into buying a Hofner Club 40 from Hessy's Music, Liverpool, for £30.

The three principal members of the Quarry Men were ready to persevere with the band and started in 1960 by recruiting Stuart 'Stu' Sutcliffe. A friend of John's from Art School, he was persuaded to buy a bass guitar.

Along with a number of other Liverpool groups, the Quarry Men, now renamed the Silver Beetles, auditioned for Larry Parnes, to support one of his artists. This main job was later filled by another band, but the Silver Beetles were asked to support Johnny Gentle on a tour of Scotland. John had his Hofner Club 40 during this period.

Afterwards, the band was recommended to a German promoter, who owned clubs in Hamburg. After recruiting a drummer, Pete Best, the Silver Beetles left Liverpool and John took his Hofner for gigs at the Indra club, later moving to the Kaiserkeller. Yet, he did not have his own amp and shared George's new Selmer Truvoice model, purchased following the Scottish tour.

From a Hamburg shop, John chose a 1958 Rickenbacker 325 and this would be his main instrument into the mid-1960s. He bought a 16-watt Fender Deluxe amp, with a 12-inch speaker.

John did not use his new Rickenbacker in Germany for too long as problems with the promoter forced the group to return to Liverpool. Now renamed the Beatles, the band's stint in Hamburg had allowed them to create a style that was different from other Liverpool bands. Playing a gig in Liverpool before the end of the year, they impressed the crowd, which included a local promoter who immediately booked them for a number of shows in the new year.

Before the band left Germany, an agreement was reached with another promoter to appear in Hamburg. As April 1961 approached, the Beatles were informed that the deal was to be honoured and the members travelled for appearances to begin April 1. John was proudly playing his Rickenbacker through his Fender amp for the duration of their stay.

While in Germany, the band was approached to record some songs with their fellow performer at the Top Ten club, Tony Sheridan. The Beatles managed two songs on their own, with John singing 'Ain't She Sweet' and there was an instrumental – 'Cry For A Shadow', composed by John and George. Tony Sheridan recalls in Andy Babiuk's *Beatles Gear: All the Fab Four's Instruments, from Stage to Studio* (2002) that John used the former's Gibson ES 175 for the latter song.

The Beatles returned to England in early summer, playing a number of gigs around Liverpool and at the Cavern Club, which had first welcomed them early in the year. John was still using his Rickenbacker, but made some modifications to improve its playability. This entailed switching the original vibrato tailpiece with a Bigsby B5.

The Beatles' growing reputation caught the attention of local music store proprietor Brian Epstein. He saw them several times and managed to agree a deal for him to become their manager.

Epstein promised to prioritise obtaining a record deal for the Beatles and through his store contacts managed to get Decca to listen to them in very early 1962. Although recording a large number of songs (with a few originals), the label was not happy with the group's equipment and insisted they used the studio's amplifiers.

In Liverpool, the band's popularity was soaring and was

The Rickenbacker 325 was part of a new range of designs introduced by the company in the 1950s and specifically was a three-quarter scale guitar with a semi-hollow body. John's guitar was quite rare, being one of only a handful produced in 1958 with the company's mapleglo finish, and had appeared at a trade show in America before reaching Germany.

partially satiated by the release of their first single. This was a joint effort with Tony Sheridan recorded in Germany – 'My Bonnie'.

Decca contacted Epstein and said they were ending their interest in the band. The manager decided to try other labels and roused the attention of George Martin at Parlophone. Before a test could be organised, the Beatles were signed to appear in Hamburg again and departed in early April 1962. John and the band only carried their luggage and instruments as the venue was providing amplification. Both guitarists were furnished with Fender Bandmaster heads and cabs for the duration.

Whilst performing in Germany, Brian Epstein contacted them to confirm a session with George Martin at Abbey Road. Taking place in early June 1962, John used his Rickenbacker through the Fender Deluxe amp. Four songs were recorded: 'Love Me Do', 'PS I Love You', 'Ask Me Why' and 'Besame Mucho'. As at Decca, the band came under fire from the Parlophone engineers for the state of their amps. George Martin suggested a new drummer was necessary and Ringo Starr replaced Pete Best.

The situation with the amps was soon resolved when Epstein worked out an endorsement deal with Jennings Musical Industries for a set of Vox amplifiers. John had to give up his Fender Deluxe as part of the deal and received an AC30 model with tan tolex covering.

Returning to Abbey Road in late summer, the Beatles had another attempt at recording 'Love Me Do'. They also ran through 'How Do You Do It?' which was later a hit for Gerry and the Pacemakers. John used his Rickenbacker and AC30 for 'Love Me Do', and also played a harmonica.

Soon after the session, John acquired a Gibson J-160E acoustic guitar with pick-up. It had been ordered from Rushworth's Music, Liverpool, earlier in the summer. There is a possibility that the guitar was taken to a third session at Abbey Road soon after arriving in England as the group returned for yet another attempt to record a satisfactory single. On this occasion 'Love Me Do' and 'PS I Love You' were taped and eventually became the Beatles' first single, released early October 1962. The latter track features John on acoustic guitar, whilst on the former he plays harmonica.

For the remainder of the year, the Beatles promoted their new single and played gigs, not only in Liverpool, but across the country. The band was heard on radio stations and even appeared on TV programmes. In November and December, they played a small number of gigs at the Star Club in Germany. Around this time, John had let a friend refinish his Rickenbacker in black.

George Martin called the band into the studio in late November to record a new single for release early in the new year. John put forward, 'Please Please Me', which was originally quite slow in tempo. Martin told the band to speed it up and everyone was happy at the result. John provided a harmonica part to begin the track, then played rhythm on his Gibson acoustic. He used the guitar on the B-side, 'Ask Me Why'. The single proved to be the band's breakthrough, reaching the top of the charts.

In support of both singles, a British tour was arranged for early 1963. To prepare for this, both John and George's AC30s were sent away for refurbishment and returned re-covered in black tolex. John took his Rickenbacker and Gibson J-160E on the tour, which began on February 2, 1963.

As 'Please Please Me' grew in popularity, George Martin arranged for the Beatles to attend a session on February 11, 1963, to record their first album. Owing to the touring schedule, the record had to be completed over one day. Several original songs were mixed with covers that were used in the band's live set. John used his Rickenbacker, Gibson acoustic and harmonica in the studio, as well as his Vox amplifier. He played rhythm guitar on most tracks and added several harmonica parts.

With the single reaching the top of the chart, the Beatles performed 'Please Please Me' on the 'Thank Your Lucky Stars', a week after completing the album session. John appeared playing his Gibson acoustic alongside George.

John stuck to the Gibson for recording the new single, following the end of the British tour. 'From Me To You' was written on the road and featured John on harmonica, as well as rhythm guitar. The record was the band's first undisputed no. 1 hit in the UK.

Following a tour with Roy Orbison, the Beatles were back in the studio to record 'She Loves You'; 'I'll Get You' was the B-side. John and Paul wrote both songs, with John providing lead vocals, rhythm guitar using his Gibson, and harmonica parts. John played guitar through his Vox AC30, although later in the summer, Vox gave the Beatles new amps which were the same as the ones in use but with slight external differences.

After a break towards the end of September, the Beatles were back on the road for more gigs, even spending a week in Sweden, and appeared on several TV and radio shows. John continued to use his Rickenbacker, which received some maintenance during the downtime, and his Gibson acoustic; amplification continued to the Vox AC30. Even though the Gibson was an ever-present companion for John, the guitar was stolen after a London show.

Before the end of the year, John and George took delivery of two new Vox AC50 amplifiers. They had been specially produced for them in an attempt to combat the screaming fans at their shows. The AC50 had a separate 'head' which connected to a speaker cabinet containing two 12-inch speakers.

By mid-January, the Beatles had completed their Christmas Tour dates, but were soon whisked off to Paris for a two-week engagement at the Paris Olympia theatre. John used his Rickenbacker 325 and had George's Gibson acoustic as well, playing both through his new Vox AC50. The amp was soon shipped out to America as the band played the 'Ed Sullivan Show' in recognition of the single 'I Want To Hold Your Hand' reaching no. 1 in the chart. John again played rhythm on his Rickenbacker.

John's prominent use of Rickenbacker was not lost on the company and whilst the band was in America a meeting was arranged. Initially wanting the Beatles to use Rickenbacker amps, the company soon had to move on to guitars when it became clear that Vox could not be ousted. A new 12-string guitar model was brought along, the 360-12, and, although John initially tested the instrument, he suggested that George would be better suited to the guitar and he ultimately took possession, using the 360-12 extensively over the coming years. John was not left out, and Rickenbacker made him a brand new 325 in black to replace his road-worn original. This was later shipped to him and he also ordered a 12-string 325.

The new Rickenbacker 325 arrived whilst the band was on a break in Miami, following performances in New York and Washington. John used his old guitar for these gigs, but following the arrival of the new instrument he retired the 1958 Rickenbacker. John first played his new 325, which was slightly different from the original, on a second appearance on the 'Ed Sullivan Show', recorded in Miami.

By late February, the Beatles were back in England and returned to Abbey Road Studios to record more tracks. 'You Can't Do That' ended up as the B-side to 'Can't Buy Me Love', the group's next single which was recorded in France the previous year. John played the rhythm part for 'You Can't Do That' on his new Rickenbacker 325 and also added the lead break. Another track recorded at this time was 'I Should Have Known Better' where John features the harmonica and Gibson J160-E acoustic. Both of the tracks were primarily composed by John and sung by him. Another track completed was 'And I Love Her', written by Paul, and on the song, John played the Gibson.

These recordings formed the basis of the album 'A Hard Day's Night', which was also the soundtrack to the film of the same name starring the Beatles. John used his Rickenbacker 325 and the Gibson acoustic for both projects.

By this time 'Beatlemania' was in full swing. At gigs, girls would scream hysterically and drown out the band's sound. The Vox AC50s were evidently not powerful enough and the Beatles turned to the company to provide more power. Three prototype 100-watt Vox AC100s were hastily produced to be taken on an American autumn tour. John took the Rickenbacker 325 and 325-12, which had arrived in England earlier in the year. Whilst in America, John was able to replace his Gibson J160-E with another model, which was virtually identical to the predecessor, but with slight detail differences.

Up to the end of the year, the Beatles were in the studio recording tracks for 'Beatles For Sale' and touring Britain. John continued to use his preferred equipment over this period and for the Christmas shows which occurred in London during late 1964/early 1965.

Following a short break, the Beatles were back at Abbey Road to record new tracks for their upcoming album and film – 'Help!'. Early in the sessions, which began in mid-February, both John and George sent road manager Mal Evans to buy a pair of Fender Stratocasters. He managed to find two in the same custom colour – Sonic Blue. John had his guitar for the start of the 'Help!' sessions and used it for playing rhythm on the first recorded track, 'Ticket To Ride'.

After these sessions, the Beatles began filming the new movie, also finding time to complete the album. John continued to use his 1964 Rickenbacker 325 and the J160-E.

When the film and album were completed, the band took to the road for gigs in Europe and Britain in the summer. John's guitars were as above and amplification was still provided by the Vox AC100. In Spain, a local guitar company gave him a traditional acoustic which he would use several times throughout the years.

Another summer American tour was arranged and the group flew out in early August. Their first engagement was on the 'Ed Sullivan Show' and John used his Rickenbacker through the Vox AC100. A new addition for him was a Vox Continental Organ which was used on 'I'm Down'. The organ would continue on the tour, but had to be replaced after the second date in Toronto due to some over-enthusiastic playing from John. The first gig had taken place at Shea Stadium, New York, where John had an unchanged line-up of instruments, with the Gibson J160-E waiting in reserve. The Beatles played eight more dates in America before returning to England.

The Beatles had an extended break before entering Abbey Road to record a new single and album. In mid-October they started with 'Run For Your Life' and 'Norwegian Wood (This Bird Has Flown)', two of John's compositions. The latter saw John using his Gibson acoustic with a capo for the rhythm track. This was the first instance of many for the group as they tried to coax new sounds from their guitars with the capo. George added an interesting touch to the song with his sitar.

The band worked on 'Day Tripper' and 'We Can Work It Out' and these were chosen for the singles released in time for Christmas. John devised the distinctive riff opening 'Day Tripper' but George performed it on the recording using his Fender Stratocaster. John completed the backing on his 1964 Rickenbacker 325, and used a harmonium on 'We Can Work It Out'.

Not only did the singles pioneer the double A-side, but also the promotional music video. As the Beatles were constantly requested to make appearances across the world, the decision was made to film them performing their latest songs and send this out across the globe. For 'Day Tripper', John played his 1964 Rickenbacker 325 and 'We Can Work It Out' sees him on the harmonium.

A song illustrating a shift away from the band's traditional song-writing subjects was John's 'Nowhere Man', which deals with an existential crisis he was having at the time. He plays a Gibson acoustic on the track and the solo in partnership with George; both using their Fender Stratocasters. Continuing with the theme of self-reflection was 'In My Life', an autobiographical reminiscence of John's early years. The song features an impressive piano solo by producer George Martin which was speeded up to sound like a harpsichord.

The new album – 'Rubber Soul' – was another giant hit and was critically acclaimed. It would also prove to be a turning point for the group as they started to chase new and interesting sounds for their songs.

1966 started with over three months' rest for the band, following several years' hard work. John was back in the studio with the band in early April and brought along a new guitar. This was an Epiphone Casino in sunburst finish which would go on to become his guitar of choice for the next few years. He had new amps, as Vox had delivered a new 120-watt Solid State model (7120), consisting of amp head and 4x12 in. cabinet, and the band had bought two Fender Showman amps. These were formed from an 85-watt head and 1x15 cabinet.

John continued to use his 1964 Gibson J160-E acoustic

and this was utilised for the rhythm guitar part of 'I'm Only Sleeping'. It was the first track of his to appear on the album 'Revolver' when completed and released in August 1966. The sessions picked up where 'Rubber Soul' had left off by the band's increasing use of recording techniques to broaden their range of sounds. The 'Revolver' track that highlights this the most is John's 'Tomorrow Never Knows', featuring a number of tape loops, slowed and quickened, to create interesting effects.

Even though John contributed the majority of the ideas for five tracks on the album, he was particularly struggling to create new material. Nevertheless, he was able to provide suitable backing to these songs and those of both Paul and George. John's rhythm guitar on 'I'm Only Sleeping' provides a solid foundation for George's reversed lead guitar part and his vocal. The recording had the speed altered to sound different and was double-tracked using the recently invented technique (actually for these sessions) of Automatic Double Tracking (ADT). Similarly, on 'And Your Bird Can Sing', John's backing on his Epiphone Casino provides the basis for George and Paul to play lead sections in unison but in different octaves.

The sessions yielded two new songs for release as singles, 'Paperback Writer' and 'Rain'. The former did not feature a guitar part by John, but he was seen in the promotional video playing his new Epiphone Casino and also for 'Rain' when he did record a backing.

At the completion of the sessions, the band started a tour of Europe, the Far East and USA. This would prove to be the last time they performed live for paying audiences. The first dates were in Germany before the Beatles travelled to Tokyo for three days at the Budokan arena, then made their way to Manila. After a month in England, the Beatles went back to the USA for a string of performances which concluded in San Francisco.

John mainly used his Epiphone Casino for the set, which comprised songs from 'Beatles For Sale' and 'Rubber Soul'. He travelled with his Gibson J160-E as spare and amplification was provided by the Vox 7120 for the European dates, whilst in North America, the US distributor gave the band a new model, the 'Super Beatle', which was generally similar to the aforementioned amp.

The 1966 world tour was difficult for the Beatles and particularly for John as he was overshadowed by his infamous 'we're more popular than Jesus' quote taken during an interview with a British journalist earlier in the year. Thanks to a media bombardment during the band's time in the US, especially in the southern states, feelings turned against the group and there were fears for their safety. At the end of the dates, the Beatles formally decided amongst themselves to no longer perform in public and concentrate on producing studio material. Sessions for a new album would start in late November 1966 and during the interim the band again had time off. John travelled to Spain and had a part in the film 'How I Won the War' and between scenes was able to write new songs.

'Strawberry Fields Forever' was the first song the Beatles attempted upon their return to the studio in late November 1966. It was one side of the double A-side single released in early 1967, the other track being 'Penny Lane'. The first song evolved over several weeks as John was not happy with the finished takes. He eventually decided that he liked part of take seven, with Mellotron introduction by Paul and rhythm guitar by George, and the second half of take 26. This featured trumpets and cellos orchestrated by George Martin. Even though the two sections were in different keys and tempos, John boldly asked if they could be joined. The result achieved by George Martin was a delicate shift in the initial tone of the recording to become disconcertingly eerie and dreamlike.

When released, the song was well-received, yet it was the first Beatles single to not top the British charts. 'Strawberry Fields Forever', much like 'Tomorrow Never Knows' from 'Revolver', highlighted the band's search for new and interesting sounds using studio techniques. This experimentation also inspired other musicians to take bold steps with their own recordings to sound new and different.

During this period, John particularly moved away from using the guitar as a prominent sound on recordings. When he did play a rhythm part, the Epiphone Casino would be chosen or the Gibson J160-E, with one of the band's various Vox amplifiers. Two of John's tracks on the new album – 'Sgt Pepper's Lonely Hearts Club Band' – 'Lucy In The Sky With Diamonds' and 'Being For The Benefit Of Mr Kite!' feature no discernible guitar part. John made sure that they contained unique sounds that fit in with the themes of the lyrics: a dreamlike melody played by Paul on a Lowrey organ to the former and fairground noises picked at random from stock noises of the latter. The solo on his third, 'Good Morning Good Morning', was played by Paul on his Fender Esquire but the song has a brass section (Sounds Incorporated) playing prominently throughout. The final track on the album, 'A Day In The Life', was John's, with a middle section provided by Paul. John's part is the only prominent example of his guitar on the album and sees him play the Gibson J160-E.

The Beatles continued to record following the completion of 'Sgt Pepper's Lonely Hearts Club Band'. They had committed themselves to a soundtrack for an animated film ('Yellow Submarine'). Paul had also devised a film scenario which would ultimately become 'Magical Mystery Tour'. For the project, the band had to leave Abbey Road due to capacity issues and booked time at Olympic Studios, being assisted by Jimi Hendrix's future sound engineer Eddie Kramer. Whilst there, the band recorded 'Baby, You're A Rich Man' which had

Epiphone was a successful and well-regarded company in its own right before taken over by Gibson in 1957. The brand was then repurposed to offer budget versions of Gibson's models, although the instruments remained of high quality. The E230TD 'Casino' was introduced in 1961 and shared the same specifications of Gibson's ES 330 model. The Casino was a thinline hollow-body guitar with 24.75 in. scale and 16 in.-wide body made from laminated maple and birch. The neck was mahogany with rosewood fingerboard and trapezoid inlays. Gibson P90 pick-ups were fitted and there was a Tune-o-matic bridge with trapeze tailpiece. Originally, the headstock was small as with pre-takeover Epiphones but was later elongated.

been partially written by John, with Paul adding the chorus. On the track, John played a clavioline. This was a keyboard that featured several settings to alter the tone of the sound produced and had its own amplifier and speaker unit.

Before the band took a break for the remainder of the summer, Brian Epstein had arranged for them to appear on the 'Our World' TV special which was broadcast across several countries using a satellite connection. One of John's songs, 'All You Need Is Love', was chosen for the appearance. John was set to play his Gibson J160-E but chose to concentrate on his vocal instead. He had commissioned the Fool art collective to paint the guitar, which was becoming a particular trend at the time; George played his self-painted Stratocaster on the programme.

Returning to work in early September, John brought 'I Am The Walrus' for the 'Magical Mystery Tour' soundtrack. Like the other songs recorded for the project, it featured little guitar and favoured orchestral backing or the use of the Hammond organ, piano and Mellotron.

After filming 'Magical Mystery Tour' at the end of September, the Beatles produced their single for the Christmas market, 'Hello Goodbye' and later made an accompanying video at the Saville Theatre in London. For this, the band wore their Sgt Pepper costumes, and mimed a performance to the song. John used a new Martin D-28 acoustic guitar which would become prominent in future songs.

The Beatles arranged to spend time in India during early 1968 with the Maharishi Mahesh Yogi, who they had met in mid-1967, to learn more about his Transcendental Meditation technique. Prior to departure, the group recorded two new tracks: 'Lady Madonna' and John's 'Hey Bulldog', which would later appear on the 'Yellow Submarine' soundtrack. The Beatles were filmed recording 'Hey Bulldog', but the footage was to be used for a promo video to accompany 'Lady Madonna'. The track was scheduled for release whilst the band were away. Footage shows John playing the piano on 'Hey Bulldog' and he perhaps used the Epiphone Casino for a rhythm track. At one point, he has George's Gibson SG Standard, yet George performed the lead guitar parts using the guitar through a Fender Showman, whilst the Epiphone was plugged into a Vox amp.

John's time in India was particularly fruitful as he created a large number of songs, many of which would be taken up when the Beatles returned to the studio in the summer. Additionally, John's guitar playing attained a new dimension. Folk musician Donovan, who was also present, taught John how to play 'fingerstyle' guitar and this technique would be used on the subsequent recordings. John had his Martin D-28 with him during his almost two months in India and was also pictured playing Donovan's Gibson J45.

Entering the studio in late May 1968, recording sessions for the new album, which was simply titled 'The Beatles' and later became known as the 'White Album', lasted four-and-a-half months and produced enough songs for a two-disc set. John contributed 13 of the songs. The sound of these was quite diverse and ranged from the acoustic 'Julia' to the rock of 'Revolution 1' and 'Everybody's Got Something To Hide Except Me And My Monkey', the blues of 'Yer Blues' and the experimental 'Revolution 9'. The 'fingerstyle' method of playing was employed on 'Dear Prudence' and 'Julia'.

John used his Epiphone Casino prominently on the album, along with his Gibson J-160E, with amplification coming from either Vox units or new Fender amplifiers. The Casino was stripped and a light coat of finish applied leaving the guitar with a natural look, as was the Gibson J-160E. The Casino would be seen in this state on the videos for the new single 'Hey Jude' and B-side 'Revolution', with John playing through Fender Deluxe amps. In the midst of recording the 'White Album', the band had broken their agreement with Vox, mainly due to the death of Brian Epstein the previous summer, and had welcomed overtures from Fender. The company soon sent amps for the group and a Bass VI, which was used by both John (on the songs 'Back In The USSR' and 'Helter Skelter') and George on the record.

C.F. Martin developed the 'Dreadnought'-style guitar in the early 20th century to provide guitarists with a richer and louder sound through a larger body. The D-28 model was introduced with the body style in the early 1930s and featured rosewood back and sides with spruce top and bracing, with mahogany neck and ebony fingerboard.

Despite the immediate success of 'The Beatles', or 'White Album', the group was particularly dissatisfied with the direction they were going. Tensions, which built during the sessions for the 'White Album', increasingly became a problem. John was ready to leave as 1969 began. This was in part due to the stresses caused by the foundation of Apple Corps, the search for a new manager following Brian Epstein's death, and his divorce from wife Cynthia and subsequent relationship with Japanese artist Yoko Ono.

With Yoko, John had released his first album away from the Beatles – 'Unfinished Music No. 1 – Two Virgins' – that comprised a series of avant-garde recordings completed at his home studio. A second album of similar recordings was made soon after, 'Unfinished Music No. 2 – Life With The Lions'. The first side comprised the track 'Cambridge 1969', recorded at the university during a performance by Yoko, with John using his Epiphone Casino through a Fender Bassman amp to create a 'feedback' accompaniment to Yoko's vocals.

John and Yoko formed a band for an appearance on the Rolling Stones' film 'Rock and Roll Circus' which was recorded at the end of 1968. The Dirty Mac band – John, Yoko, Eric Clapton (lead guitar), Keith Richards (bass) and Mitch Mitchell (drums) – performed John's 'Yer Blues'. John played his Epiphone Casino through a Triumph 100-watt head and 4x12 in. cabinet.

At the start of 1969, the Beatles assembled to start new recording sessions which were to be filmed as part of a documentary on the creation of the new album and culminating with a live performance (or performances). In general, the group did not work harmoniously, and for a number of reasons John was quickly losing interest in the Beatles. Yet, George was the first to leave the sessions following an argument and took some persuasion to return. Recording was moved from the original venue at Twickenham to the purpose-built studio in the Apple offices on Savile Row.

A large number of tracks were started during the sessions, although few of John's were released on the finished album, originally titled 'Get Back', then 'Let It Be', released in mid-1970. These were: 'Dig A Pony', 'Across The Universe' and 'One After 909'. The latter had been penned in the early 1960s and was resurrected at this time. John predominantly used his Epiphone Casino through a Fender amp, with his Martin D-28 acoustic also employed, along with George's J200. John made an interesting addition to the sound of George's track 'For You Blue' with a lap steel guitar made by Hofner. John played the Fender Bass VI on 'Let It Be' and 'The Long And Winding Road'. The sessions were capped by a performance on the roof of the Apple offices and John used his Epiphone Casino with a Fender Twin Reverb amplifier.

After the 'Get Back/Let It Be' recordings were completed, John married Yoko Ono and went on honeymoon to Amsterdam, where the newlyweds staged a 'bed-in' for peace. John took along his Gibson J160-E and used the guitar during his week-long stay. A similar 'bed-in' took place in Montreal during late May and early June and the guitar was again present, being used for the future single 'Give Peace A Chance'. Recordings made in Amsterdam also appeared as part of the 'Wedding Album', released in late 1969.

Shortly after returning to London, John decided to commemorate his recent experiences in song form and enlisted Paul to help him record 'The Ballad Of John And Yoko'. John played both rhythm (Gibson J160-E) and the distinct lead parts (Epiphone Casino) as George was on holiday at the time.

John was in the studio with the Beatles over the summer months working on 'Abbey Road' and contributed three songs: 'Come Together', 'I Want You (She's So Heavy)' and 'Because'. The album's second side contained a medley of ideas that were not fully completed and John had three pieces featured: 'Sun King', 'Mean Mr Mustard' and 'Polythene Pam'. John used his Epiphone Casino and Fender amp throughout, apart from a Framus 12-string acoustic on 'Polythene Pam'. 'I Want You (She's So Heavy)' particularly stands out for John's guitar performance in the blues style, playing the riff and some solo sections. 'Because' featured several distinct sounds: a harpsichord by George Martin, Moog from George and John played his Casino through a Leslie speaker. This was a favoured sound on the album for both John and George. The final track on the record saw Paul, George and John (in that order) trade solos over two bars three times each.

Shortly before the record was released at the end of September 1969, John told the other Beatles that he was leaving the band but the decision was not publicised for business reasons. The group officially disbanded during the spring of 1970 after Paul announced his own intention to leave the group.

In mid-September 1969, John formed the Plastic Ono Band. This was the result of an invitation to appear at a rock 'n' roll concert in Toronto. John quickly rounded up Eric Clapton, Klaus Voormann (bass) and Alan White (drums) for the appearance and their first rehearsal was on the plane from London. The Plastic Ono Band performed eight songs which were a mixture of classic rock 'n' roll songs and John and Yoko's compositions: 'Blue Suede Shoes', 'Money', 'Dizzy Miss Lizzy', 'Yer Blues', 'Cold Turkey', 'Give Peace A Chance', 'Don't Worry Kyoko (Mummy's Only Looking For Her Hand In The Snow)', and 'John John (Let's Hope For Peace)'. These tracks were released on the album 'Live Peace In Toronto 1969'. John took his Epiphone Casino and played through an unidentified amp which was likely supplied by the concert promoter.

John took the Plastic Ono Band (now with Ringo on drums) into the studio to record 'Cold Turkey' and 'Don't Worry Kyoko (Mummy's Only Looking For Her Hand In The Snow)' which were later released as a single. The band gathered again in London during mid-December to play a special concert in aid of the charity UNICEF. Joining them on stage was the American group Delaney & Bonnie and Friends which had recently recruited Eric Clapton to join them on their European tour, as well as George who had been introduced to the band by Eric. John played his Epiphone Casino on the night through a Fender head and cabinet.

After a break in Europe over Christmas, John and Yoko returned to London in late January and immediately headed for the studio to record 'Instant Karma!'. He played the piano and George guitar, although the instrument does not seem to have made the finished Phil Spector-produced recording. The latter was in London after being asked to pull together the recordings for 'Let It Be'. 'Instant Karma!' was a hit for John in both the UK and America and has gone on to be one of his most recognisable solo recordings.

In the early summer of 1970, John and Yoko became involved with primal therapy under Arthur Janov. This was a form of psychoanalysis whereby the patient relived traumatic events from their lives and expressed their feelings about these during sessions in order to come to terms with them. John and Yoko spent a number of months in LA with Janov before returning to England.

John's experience with the treatment inspired many of the tracks on his debut solo album 'John Lennon/Plastic Ono Band'. It was recorded over a short period in late September/October 1970. The album's sound was in contrast to much of the late-Beatles material as the arrangements were quite sparse and simple to highlight the lyrics. John was the only featured guitarist and likely used his Gibson J-160E for the acoustic parts and the Epiphone Casino the electric, with amplification from the Fender amps the Beatles were latterly using. He played piano and organ on several of the album's tracks.

John's guitar playing is highlighted on tracks such as 'Hold On', which has a delicate rhythm part, 'I Found Out' for the distorted intro and rhythm sections, 'Working Class Hero' with the dynamic acoustic backing, while 'Well Well Well' and 'Look At Me' have an intricate fingerstyle part. John played on Yoko's companion album 'Yoko Ono/Plastic Ono Band' and the track 'Why Not' features a blues riff accompaniment with a slide, similarly on the song 'Touch Me'.

Less than six months later, John was working in the studio on his next album. This would have a 'fuller' sound compared to his previous effort and included several guitar players in addition to John: George Harrison, Joey Molland and Tom Evans from the Apple-signed band Badfinger, Ted Turner from Wishbone Ash, Rod Lynton and Andy Davis; apart from George, everyone else played acoustic guitar. With this line-up, John was not featured as much on guitar, but did perform on 'It's So Hard', delivering a rare guitar solo, and 'How Do You Sleep?' on which he played the rhythm part on his Epiphone Casino.

Some of the recording process was filmed and subsequently released, providing an interesting document of John at the time. Several of John's guitars are displayed in his home studio. He has a number of resonator guitars – one was used by George on 'Crippled Inside' – a Fender Telecaster with Bigsby vibrato unit, a Gibson J45 acoustic and a Hagstrom BJ12 H33 12-string acoustic, as well as his 1964 Gibson J160-E. A Fender Bassman head and cab are visible but do not appear to be in use and no other amps can be seen in the room.

The most well-known song of John's career was recorded during the album's sessions – 'Imagine'. The arrangement was quite sparse with just piano, bass drums and very light strings. John wrote the song on a Steinway & Sons upright Model Z piano, which he had recently bought. He likely recorded the song on that, as a performance with Yoko's white Steinway & Sons baby grand piano (which John had bought for her birthday) was not deemed to be suitable by producer Phil Spector.

The album – 'Imagine' – enjoyed great success worldwide and was no. 1 in both Britain and America. Shortly before the album's release in September, John and Yoko moved to New York City. Soon after, John went into the Record Plant and recorded 'Happy Xmas (War Is Over)' which was released only in America in December 1971 (the UK release would follow a year later).

Whilst a number of John's recent songs had political overtones, he was particularly inspired by the various causes he encountered in America and these would inform many of the tracks on 1972's 'Some Time In New York City'. On December 10, John was at the Crisler Arena to join a protest against the excessive sentence given to John Sinclair for drug possession. The song bearing the man's name was performed on a National-style resonator with slide, whilst another new song, 'Luck Of The Irish', was played using a Martin D-28. The latter guitar, which John had recently acquired as a replacement for his Beatles-era instrument, was also present seven days later when he performed at the benefit for the victims of the Attica State Prison riots at the Apollo Theatre. Additionally, he had the guitar for an appearance on the 'David Frost Show' during which he performed 'Attica State' and Yoko's 'Sisters, O Sisters' whilst 'John Sinclair' was played on the resonator.

Around this time, John acquired a Gibson Les Paul Junior in sunburst finish with single P90 pick-up and wraparound tailpiece. He visited luthier, Ron DeMarino to have a humbucker pick-up installed, but the latter suggested a Charlie Christian pick-up instead. This type had first been installed on Gibson ES 150 guitars during the mid-1930s and was known for having a full, warm sound. John used the Les Paul Junior during a week hosting the 'Mike Douglas Show' in February 1972 and ran the guitar through a Marshall head and cabinet. A highlight of these appearances was the performance of John and Chuck Berry on 'Memphis Tennessee' and 'Johnny B. Goode'. John played his Martin D-28 on several acoustic tracks during his stint on the show.

John further modified the Gibson by having the wraparound tailpiece replaced by a stopbar tailpiece and Tune-o-matic ABR-1 bridge. During the 'Mike Douglas Show', the tuners were the Kluson Deluxe type with pearloid keystone buttons (in place of the original in-line tuners with white buttons). These were subsequently swapped with Schaller tuners. The sunburst finish was removed and the guitar was refinished in cherry.

The Les Paul was in this new state when John played a charity concert for Willowbrook State School at Madison Square Garden on August 30, 1972. Backed by the band Elephant's Memory, which had performed this role from John's arrival in America, John played a selection of songs from the late-Beatle period to his and Yoko's recent solo work. Providing backup for the Les Paul was John's Epiphone Casino. The concert was both filmed and recorded and was later released.

John performed on the Jerry Lewis Muscular Dystrophy Association's Labor Day Telethon and used the same guitar line-up; John plugged into a Fender Dual Showman head and cabinet. At the end of 1972, John co-produced Yoko's double album, 'Approximately Infinite Universe', with Elephant's Memory accompanying.

The critical reception to John's 'Some Time In New York City' and the concerts at Madison Square Garden was negative and contributed to his withdrawal from music for several months. Although Elephant's Memory was to be used for a world tour following the Willowbrook concert, John's step back from music, along with immigration problems with the US government, saw these plans disintegrate and the band moved on. John's relationship with Yoko also became strained by mid-1973 and this inspired him to write a number of songs which he quickly recorded and later released as 'Mind Games' in late 1973.

For the 'Mind Games' sessions, John assembled a new group of musicians including guitarist David Spinozza and pedal steel player Pete Kleinow. As a result, John mainly provided a solid foundation for these players to accompany the song. There were some instances where John was more elaborate on the guitar, such as on 'Intuition' where he plays a slide solo, 'Out The Blue', with a melodic acoustic guitar introduction to the song and 'Meat City' has a driving distorted rhythm guitar part. John likely used his Martin D-28 for the sessions and may have used the Gibson Les Paul Junior or Epiphone Casino for the electric parts.

Despite John's attempts at reconciliation with Yoko, she decided they needed to spend time apart and he left for Los Angeles during the summer of 1973. Around this time John had been subjected to legal action from the publishers of Chuck Berry's 'You Can't Catch Me' over similarities between that and the Beatles' 'Come Together'. By the end of the year the court had ruled in favour of the publishers and the settlement required John to record three songs to which they held the copyright. John spent some time in A&M Studios working on this project with Phil Spector but little useable work was done due to overconsumption of alcohol by all concerned. John had perhaps acquired a black Fender Telecaster around this time as

he would be seen with one going forward.

By mid-1974, John was ready to ditch the hedonistic lifestyle of LA and return to New York. He was inspired to write a number of songs and went into the Record Plant during the late summer to record them. John assembled another band, including guitarists Jesse Ed Davis and Eddie Mottau. Yet, the sound of the album – 'Walls And Bridges' – tends towards the piano sound of John, Nicky Hopkins and Ken Ascher, as well as the horn sound of Bobby Keys and the 'Little Big Horns'. John could be the featured guitarist on 'Going Down On Love', as he doubles the melody of the vocal in a manner he has done before, in addition to the slide part on '#9 Dream' and the riff on 'Surprise Surprise (Sweet Bird Of Paradox)'. 'Steel And Glass' is a revamped version of 'How Do You Sleep' from the 'Imagine' album and John could be playing the acoustic intro, and the same could be said for 'Nobody Loves You When You're Down And Out', whilst 'Beef Jerky' sees John and Jesse Ed Davis trade lead guitar parts.

The main single from the album 'Whatever Gets You Thru The Night' was recorded in collaboration with Elton John. The

John Lennon playing with the Dirty Mac at the Rolling Stones' Rock and Roll Circus 1968. The temporary supergroup also included Eric Clapton, Mitch Mitchell, and Keith Richards.
Everett Collection Inc / Alamy Stock Photo.

track eventually reached no. 1 in the American chart and to celebrate, John appeared with Elton on stage during the latter's concert at Madison Square Garden during late November 1974. For this, John took along a black Fender Telecaster, modified with a Gibson embossed bridge humbucker placed in the neck position and he played through a Fender combo amplifier.

At the end of 1974, John returned to the project he had begun with Phil Spector in late 1973. Several tracks had been recorded and these were covers of old rock 'n' roll songs from the 1950s and 1960s. Due to a number of reasons, some of the recordings were unusable and John was obliged to record some again or overdub others. For this he used many of the musicians from the 'Walls And Bridges' sessions. The album – 'Rock 'n' Roll' – was released in early 1975 and was successful on both sides of the Atlantic. John promoted the album in Britain with a pre-recorded appearance on the 'Old Grey Whistle Test', performing 'Stand By Me' and Little Richard's 'Slippin' And Slidin'. For both tracks he used a black Fender Telecaster with standard neck pick-up. This appears to be a later model (late 1960s/early 1970s) owing to the decal on the headstock.

In mid-April 1975, John made his last public performance at the tribute to Lew Grade show in New York. The latter was a British businessman who had bought Northern Songs, John and Paul's music publishers. Both had been involved in legal actions against Grade and John's appearance was quite pointed as the band wore face masks on the backs of their heads. Three songs were performed on the night, 'Slippin' And Slidin', 'Stand By Me' and 'Imagine', and for all, John used his Martin D-28.

By this time, John had reconciled with Yoko and she had become pregnant with their son Sean, who was born later in the year. John made the decision to step away from the music business to concentrate on raising Sean as Yoko tended to business matters. John did not abandon the guitar entirely as he was pictured playing a Yamaha GJ52 acoustic guitar for Sean and Yoko, as well as posing with his National Resonator and eldest son Julian.

In mid-1980, John felt ready to return to music and made a number of demos in preparation for going into the studio during the summer. He continued to play his Martin D-28 but had added a new accustic, an Ovation Legend 1651 which he used during the sessions. John had also purchased the Sardonyx 800 DII which was made in the New York area by luthier Jeff Levin. It featured a small wood body, with metal pieces attached in parallel, an ebony fretboard, humbucker pick-ups and complex wiring system to deliver a number of tonal options. Another new guitar for the sessions was a Hamer Special in white with humbucker pick-ups and also acquired around this time was a Fender 'The Strat' in candy apple red with matching headstock and gold hardware.

The sessions produced the album 'Double Fantasy'. It was a joint project with Yoko and alternately featured each other's songs. John assembled a new group of musicians but the constituents were generally players featured on 'Walls And Bridges'. There were two guitarists – Earl Slick and Hugh McCracken – and they provided much, if not all, of the lead parts on the album. John continued to be the rhythm guitarist, either on acoustic or electric guitar, also playing some piano and keyboard.

'Double Fantasy' was released in November 1980 but the sessions were fertile enough for another album of songs to be accumulated, later released as 'Milk And Honey'. John was working on Yoko's track 'Walking On Thin Ice' on December 8 and had previously recorded a particularly experimental guitar part for the track. Upon arrival at his apartment following the sessions he was shot in the back and died on his way to the hospital.

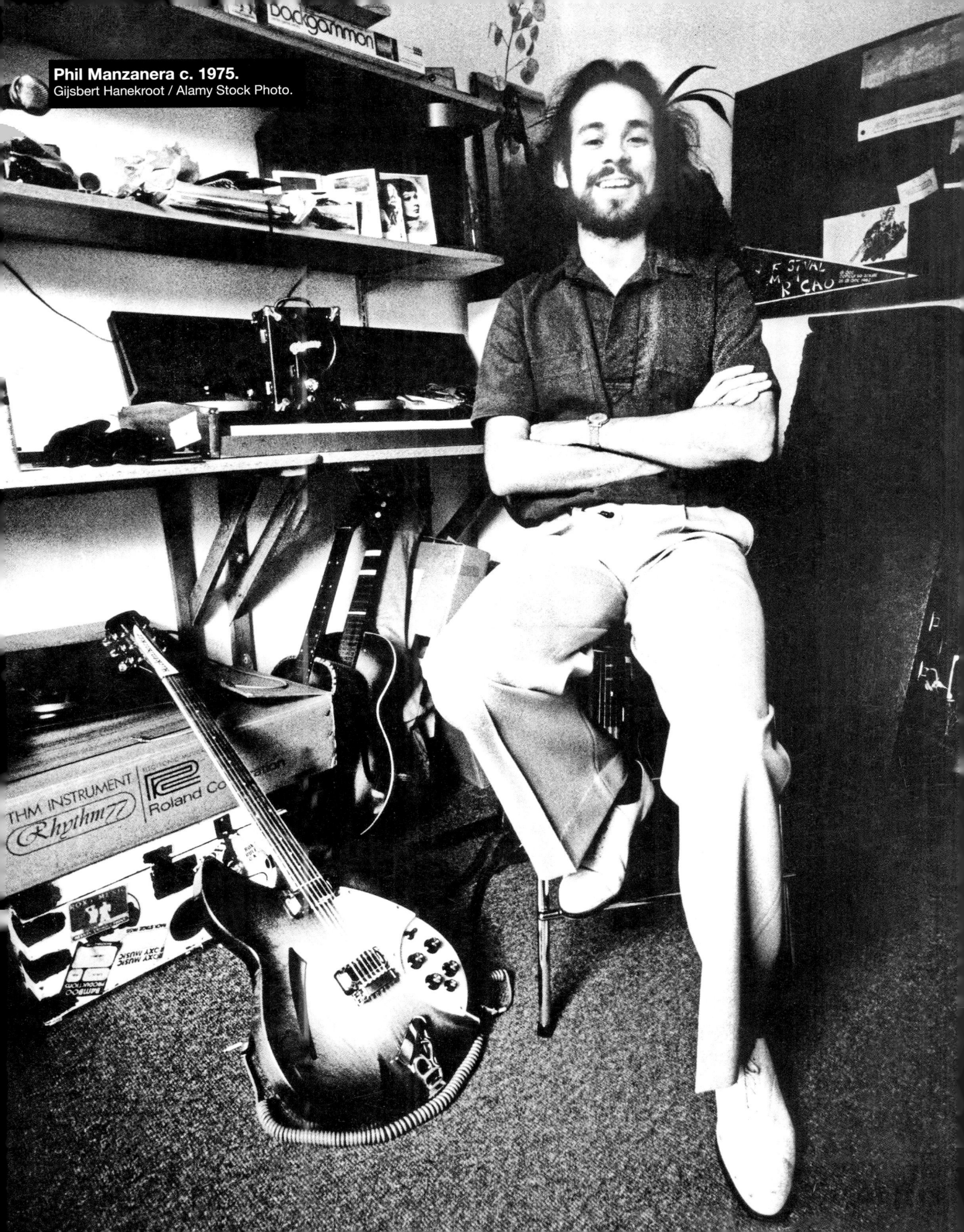
Phil Manzanera c. 1975.
Gijsbert Hanekroot / Alamy Stock Photo.

PHIL MANZANERA

With his distinct red Gibson Firebird VII and 'bug eye' glasses, Phil Manzanera created a distinct sound and image as part of 'art rock' group Roxy Music. Songs like 'Amazona' and 'In Every Dream Home A Heartache' showcase his ability to shape interesting sounds using his instrument and effects. Phil also worked successfully with noted musicians, such as Brian Eno and David Gilmour, and recorded several acclaimed solo albums, including 'Diamond Head', 'K-Scope', 'Primitive Guitars', 'Firebird V11' and 'The Sound Of Blue'.

Phil was born in London, though travelled with his parents around North and South America during his early years owing to his father's employment. Whilst Phil's father was English, his mother was Colombian and she owned a Spanish-style guitar which interested Phil in music at an early age. Living in South America, Phil was also inspired by local Latin music. He recalled on ultimateclassicrock.com (March 2009) that his mother taught him some Cuban folk songs on the guitar in 1957.

In his early teens, Phil became a boarder at Dulwich College but kept up his interest in music. During the late 1960s, Phil was able to immerse himself in the 'blues boom' and 'psychedelic' period, whilst also taking an interest in other musical forms recommended to him. Phil acquired his first instrument in the early to mid-1960s and he told *Sounds International* (November 1978): '... I bought a cello guitar with a Hofner pick-up and later nearly bankrupted my father by getting a Hofner Galaxie for £50 ...'

To learn guitar, Phil purchased an instructional book and also listened to records to try and reproduce the solos. In the same publication, he admits: '... I could never do it properly and there was always someone who could play better. So, I gave that up and decided I would just have to try and play my own way and that if people didn't like it, that was just too bad.'

Towards the end of his school years, Phil joined with several like-minded friends to form a group which ultimately evolved into Quiet Sun. The band had a 'progressive' sound and played several gigs in 1970–1971. Phil upgraded to a Gibson ES 335 around this period. With Quiet Sun not progressing to his liking, Phil looked for other musical employment. He auditioned for a newly formed group, Roxy Music, though ultimately lost out to former the Nice guitarist David O'List. Although playing with the band for a few months, David left, allowing Phil to become a member.

After about a month, recording sessions began and yielded the first album. Phil had his ES 335, though he revealed in *Making Music* magazine (June 1986): 'None of the other guys from Roxy liked it ... The sound was a bit too mature ... well, unrock, if you like ... the others said what you need is a Strat as well ...' In the article 'Finding 9 New Year's Resolutions in Bacon's Archive' by Tony Bacon and available on reverb.com, Phil describes an unusual source for the Stratocaster – Brian Eno's milkman. The guitar was white, featured a rosewood fingerboard and had 'JH Experience' on the back. Also, in conversation with Roland UK on youtube.com (October 2010), Phil noted from the start of his Roxy Music career a Roland Chorus Echo unit was in use. He said: 'We used it non-stop. Because you could actually slow the thing down and you could play a few tricks doing what it was not meant to do. You always take equipment and do what you're not meant to do with it. When I get a new piece of equipment, I go through it and find what's unique about it and try to build something around the uniqueness of it. I don't want it to do the normal things.' In some instances, Phil's guitar sound was further manipulated by Brian Eno using a VCS3 synthesizer.

'Roxy Music' was released in June 1972 and was well-received, achieving a top ten position in the UK charts. The band appeared on the 'Old Grey Whistle Test', performing 'Ladytron', and Phil used the white Stratocaster ('Exp' can be glimpsed on the reverse) and stars appeared in place of the standard inlays (later photographs indicate these were stickers). The guitar was with Phil when Roxy Music performed the single 'Virginia Plain' on 'Top of the Pops' during August – the record peaked at no. 4. Phil has stated that the ES 335 was present on the original recording.

Though Phil had been persuaded to acquire a Fender Stratocaster, he was still on the look-out for a new guitar which would fit Roxy Music's striking visual image.

Around early 1973, he came across an advertisement in *Melody Maker* for a red Firebird guitar. Intrigued, he went to an American family's house in Regent's Park and bought the instrument virtually on sight. The guitar was a custom-colour Gibson Firebird VII from 1964 and he played it on the second Roxy Music album, 'For Your Pleasure'. In celebration of 50 years of the Firebird, *Guitarist* magazine (issue 368, June 2013) talked to Phil of the initial experience of using the Firebird VII during the sessions. He said: '... it was a fantastic recording guitar. Those pick-ups are different ... they have a very contained sound, which doesn't spread a lot around the edges into other frequencies ... it sits very nicely within the whole spectrum.' A highlight of Phil's playing on 'For Your Pleasure' is the track 'In Every Dream Home A Heartache' which is in two sections. The first focuses on Bryan Ferry's spoken lyrics, mainly with synthesizer background, whilst the second has an extended guitar solo by Phil which begins quite clean in tone but then distorts thanks to the use of a flange effect and phasing near the end.

Preceding the album was the single-only 'Pyjamarama' and Phil utilised open E tuning, though with the B string also an E. Remembering the song in *Making Music* (op. cit.) Phil commented: 'It was one of the first times I'd used notes ringing through, leaving the same notes here and there and changing a few other notes in the chord. It's a nice way of getting a big sound ...' In the same article he revealed that he was using Revox tape machines to create Automatic Double Tracking (ADT) and this was linked to a foot pedal, controlling the speed of the tapes. The tape machines are seen in use on the

Phil Manzanera playing white Fender Stratocaster with Roxy Music.
Philippe Gras / Alamy Stock Photo.

group's 1973 performance on the German TV programme 'Musikladen' – with Brian Eno manipulating the sound during the solo section of 'In Every Dream Home A Heartache' – and Phil's new Hiwatt Custom 100 heads and cabs stand behind. He had a new guitar which he used on the song, a 1958–1960 Gibson Les Paul Standard. This belonged to bassist John Porter who had swapped a Gibson Les Paul Custom for the guitar with Free's Paul Kossoff. However, the guitars went back to their original owners around 1974. Phil used the Les Paul on the 'Old Grey Whistle Test' performance of the song.

Roxy Music had cemented their place in music by mid-1973. Yet, this came at the cost of Brian Eno departing following creative differences. A new dimension was added with the inclusion of Eddie Jobson on violin. Roxy Music recorded 'Stranded' at the end of summer 1973 and Phil had his first writing credit on the song 'Amazona'. Similar to 'In Every Dream Home A Heartache' in structure, Phil's guitar backed Bryan Ferry's lyrics with a funk-style rhythm before descending into a psychedelic solo. Commenting on the track for the release of a 'Greatest Hits' record, in the *Mail on Sunday* (published June 25, 2009, reproduced on bryanferry.com) Phil said: '… I was very proud of it. I had this riff and a bit in 7/8 time signature … I used a specially built guitar version of the VCS3 synthesizer that Eno had been using and I really only got it to work once and the result is on this track. It created an underwater sound and I think it is rather unique.' A second composition from Phil was featured as the B-side to the lead single for the album, 'Hula Kula'. On the song, Phil developed a Hawaiian-themed acoustic instrumental with slide lead playing. Further writing credits were received on Brian Eno's solo record, 'Here Come The Warm Jets', as Phil contributed to 'Needles In The Camel's Eye' and 'Cindy Tells Me', whilst also playing on 'The Paw Paw Negro Blowtorch'. Pictures from the sessions show Phil with the white Fender Stratocaster.

In November 1973, Roxy Music released both the album 'Stranded' and single 'Street Life'. At the end of the month, a 'Top of the Pops' appearance performing the single saw Phil using the Firebird VII. The band returned to 'Musikladen' and several of the album's tracks were played and have since been made available on the programme's youtube.com channel. Phil appears to have the same equipment as with the previous appearance, though he remained seated throughout, perhaps to improve his control of the pedals.

Phil experienced a busy 1974. Over the summer, Roxy Music recorded 'Country Life' and he had two co-writing credits on the album – 'Out Of The Blue' and 'Prairie Rose'. The former has become a particular favourite of Phil's and features phased guitar parts. A recording of the song was made on the American TV show 'Midnight Special' during the supporting tour. He was playing a natural Fender Telecaster from 1951. For *International Musician and Recording World* in May 1975, Phil commented on his current guitars: 'There's … an old Telecaster from 1951 … the Telecaster is the best rhythm guitar in the world …' Another new guitar mentioned was a Rickenbacker 12-string. He mentioned the effects he was using: 'Over the last three years I've been developing what loosely could be described as a guitar synthesizer, but it all blew up on me on the last European tour, I couldn't bring it to America – it's being fixed. Basically, it's a very sophisticated envelope shaper and filter, which was built for me by the person who originally built the VCS3, Jerry Rogers. I had these special pedals built which control the knobs on the synthesizer, so instead of having to do it with your hands, you can do it with a pedal that goes up and down and sideways.' Other pedals included an MXR phase shifter and fuzz, whilst the Revox continued in use for ADT and echo.

Also in 1974, Phil collaborated with Brian Eno on 'Taking Tiger Mountain (By Strategy)', playing guitar and helping with production. He received a writing credit on 'The True Wheel' which has a solo apparently using ADT. Brian Eno returned the favour to Phil by helping with tracks for his debut solo album 'Diamond Head' released in spring 1975. This featured several music styles and was split between vocal and instrumental songs. The musicians were particularly productive in the studios and completed the material with time left for Phil to bring together his former Quiet Sun bandmates. They recorded some of the old material and this was presented as 'Mainstream', also in 1975. The *New Musical Express* afforded the 'album of the month' title to the record and there are some strong moments from Phil, particularly on the lead track 'Sol Caliente'. Phil was likely using much of the previously mentioned equipment across the sessions.

The fifth Roxy Music album, 'Siren', was recorded in 1975. This featured 'Love Is The Drug'. On the 'Top of the Pops' appearance, Phil was using his Telecaster. 'Whirlwind' and 'Nightingale' on the album had a co-writer's credit with Bryan Ferry. A film was made of a performance in Stockholm (January 1976) on the supporting tour; the band also played 'Diamond Head' from his solo album. Phil was mainly using a Non-Reverse Gibson Firebird with three humbucker pick-ups, as well as the Telecaster. He most likely had a Pete Cornish pedal board by this time. In an interview with Tony Bacon on reverb.com, Pete relates that in 1975 he produced a board for Phil with an 'old Sound City fuzz, an MXR Phase 90, an echo send and return, and an output selector, which I remember was for the bright and normal channels of his Hiwatt.' Pete devised a system which automatically detected the input power supply voltage and distributed this accurately (either 18 or 9 volts) to the equipment. A number of recordings were made from the tour dates and assembled for the live album 'Viva!'.

Around mid-1976, the members of Roxy Music took a break and this gave rise to various solo endeavours. Phil continued his collaboration with Brian Eno and the pair formed the group 801, with Bill MacCormick (bass), Francis Monkman (keyboards), Simon Phillips (drums) and Lloyd Watson (slide guitar). The new band rehearsed for several weeks and went on to play three gigs, the last was recorded at the Queen Elizabeth Hall. The standard practice of close-miking was discarded and the outputs were taken directly to the recording equipment which significantly improved the quality. The show featured a mix of material from Phil and Brian, as well as Quiet Sun and covers of the Beatles' 'Tomorrow Never Knows' and the Kinks' 'You Really Got Me'. '801 Live' appeared at the end of the year and achieved moderate sales across the world. Phil was pictured using the Gibson Non-Reverse Firebird in addition to a Yamaha SG 3000 guitar. Amplification continued to be

Hiwatt.

801 (billed as Phil Manzanera/801) went on to complete a studio record 'Listen Now' which was released in September 1977. Lloyd Watson left the project and several guests contributed, including Godley & Creme, Tim Finn, Eddie Jobson, etc. Lol Creme was kind enough to lend Phil two Gibson Les Pauls over this period. Phil told *Sound International* magazine of November 1978: 'Actually, I use a lot of Lol's guitars [on 'Listen Now'], in fact I've got more of his instruments than he has. I've been looking after his two 1953 and '57 Gold Top Les Pauls for about a year now and using them on recording …' Another long-term loan to Phil was the previously mentioned Les Paul Custom (1957 model) belonging to John Porter. In the *Guitar Magazine* (January 1992, vol. 1, no. 9) he elaborated that the guitar had a 'four-way rotary switch for tone selection and the most fantastic sound … I ended up using the '57 from the second Roxy album right up to "Avalon", as well as using it on most of the solo albums …' Another striking feature of the guitar was a mother-of-pearl inlay on the front of the instrument below the tailpiece. Phil later admitted he had to return the Les Paul Custom around the early 1990s owing to the increased value of such guitars. A short tour was mounted in support of 'Listen Now' and an album was made from the concert in Manchester during 1977, though not released until the late 1990s.

Bryan Ferry produced his first solo album of original songs in 1977 – 'In Your Mind'. Phil was credited on guitar for the album, along with Chris Spedding and Neil Hubbard. Phil and Chris were on the subsequent tour of America and Asia in 1977. A date in Tokyo was filmed and shows Phil mainly as the rhythm guitarist playing a red Yamaha SG 3000. In 1978, Phil returned to solo work and completed 'K-Scope'. Again, it was a mixture of instrumental and vocal songs.

The decision was made to reunite Roxy Music in the late 1970s and between 1978 and 1979 the group recorded 'Manifesto'. Phil had four writing credits: the title track; 'Trash'; 'Still Falls the Rain'; 'My Little Girl'. 'Trash' was the lead single and the video saw Phil returning to the Firebird VII, as did the film for the following release 'Dance Away' and the remixed version of 'Angel Eyes'. In a live recording of the band in Manchester during 1979, Phil again had the guitar, along with a Gibson Les Paul Gold Top with humbuckers and appears to be using a Mesa Boogie combo amp through a wireless system.

With two of the singles and the album performing particularly well in the UK and US, the band continued, and 'Flesh And Blood' was completed for release in mid-1980. Phil had three credits, including the lead single 'Over You'. On vivaroxymusic.com, he is quoted as saying the song was the first to be recorded in his own Gallery Studios: 'I rang up Bryan and asked if he'd like to check it out. We decided to have a jam together, Bryan on bass and me on guitar with rhythm box [early drum machine]. Within five minutes, we had written this track and it reached number three in the charts [sic, the single actually reached number five].' Televised performances of the song were made on 'Musikladen', where Phil had the Firebird VII, and 'Le Collaro Show' in France which had him with the Les Paul Custom. The other credits on the album were 'No Strange Delight' and 'Running Wild'.

The next single was 'Oh Yeah' and Phil was seen on 'Top of the Pops' with the Custom again, whilst on 'Musikladen' he returned to the Firebird VII. At the end of 1980, an appearance was made on the 'Rockpop' TV programme and the band performed songs from the new album and from those preceding. Phil used the Les Paul Custom throughout and had the Mesa Boogie paired with a Fender combo amp (single speaker). This appearance also marked an early performance of 'Jealous Guy' following John Lennon's murder. The song was later released as a single and became Roxy Music's first UK no. 1.

Roxy Music travelled to the Bahamas to record the (at present) final studio album, 'Avalon' in 1981/1982. Phil shared guitar credit with Neil Hubbard as the pair split lead and rhythm duties respectively. Phil collaborated on the track 'Take A Chance With Me'. From promotional material and performances of the period, Phil was playing a red Stratocaster with maple neck and the Les Paul Custom. A concert film of a performance in France from the 'Avalon' tour saw Phil with the same equipment as the 1980 German concert, with the addition of the Stratocaster mentioned earlier.

Phil had been a professional musician for around ten years in 1982 and to mark this milestone, he produced a solo album featuring tracks that represented the various stages of his musical development. 'Primitive Guitars' mainly featured Phil on all instruments (bass and a drum machine), though John Wetton played bass on 'Europe 80-1', and he created thematically different soundscapes with his guitar adding different textures.

In the mid-1980s, Phil teamed with Andy Mackay and singer James Wraith to record as the Explorers. With a pop/rock sound, the trio recorded a self-titled album, which yielded four singles: 'Lorelei'; 'Venus Di Milo'; 'Two Worlds Apart'; 'Falling For The Nightlife'. In promotional clips and appearances for these Phil was seen with the Firebird VII, a white Guild S-300 and a white Stratocaster with rosewood fingerboard. The group toured and live footage from a Spanish concert shows Phil with the Les Paul Custom, red Fender Stratocaster and Mesa Boogie with Fender combo amp pairing. The Explorers recorded a follow-up album, yet this was not released until 1988, then only in America as 'Crack The Whip' credited as Manzanera Mackay.

Phil released a compilation of his own material in 1986 – 'Guitarissimo' – followed by a collaboration with John Wetton, 'Wetton Manzanera' in 1987. This embraced a similar sound to the Explorers, though his next release was a return to instrumental music. Under the title 'Nowamowa' (Polish for 'Newspeak') with the musicians Paul Williams and Andy Grossart, Phil recorded 'The Wasted Lands', which on later CD reissues had Phil credited as using an unidentified midi guitar system. This could have been the Casio PG380, which was a Stratocaster-like guitar (built by Ibanez) with Floyd Rose tremolo, two single coils and a bridge humbucker with coil-split. A hexaphonic pick-up was installed next to the bridge for the synthesizer, which had 64 voices, and a built-in turner was also provided. Phil was seen with a black Casio guitar in a French TV appearance promoting the single – 'A

Million Reasons Why' – from his 'Southern Cross' album of 1990, in addition to his performance at the 'Guitar Legends' concert in Seville during October 1991. Over two dozen of the world's top guitarists played in concerts taking place over a week. Phil performed 'Lagrima' and 'Frontera' from 'Diamond Head', an instrumental track called 'Sphinx' (using the Casio) and went on to play with Jack Bruce on Cream's 'Sunshine Of Your Love', as well as with Bob Dylan on 'All Along The Watchtower'. Several of the night's guitarists, including Keith Richards, Steve Cropper and Robert Cray, joined Phil for a jam on Otis Redding's 'Can't Turn You Loose'. On the night, Phil also used a natural Stratocaster and his Les Paul Custom.

A collaboration with Brazilian musician Sérgio Dias created the album 'Mato Grosso'. In the album credits, the use of the Casio guitar on the record is confirmed. Phil continued his foray into Latin music with a concert in Havana with the local band Moncada. Recordings from the date were made and released as 'Live at the Karl Marx' in 1992. In 1993/1994, Phil produced Brazilian rock group Os Paralamas do Sucesso on the album 'Severino'. To the end of the decade, Phil was involved in several other projects involving Latin artists. For the first episode of the 'Red Dwarf' sixth series in 1993, Phil's hands were used in a sequence where main character Dave Lister has an alien double. To distinguish between the two, the crew ask for a demonstration of his guitar abilities which proves the difference, in that the alien could actually play the instrument, whereas Dave Lister could not. The guitar in question was a 'genuine Les Paul copy' – an Antoria Pro Star. In 1999, Phil released the solo album 'Vozero', which featured several instances of him on lead vocals.

Roxy Music celebrated their 30th anniversary in 2001 and a reunion was held for a world tour through to 2002. Phil detailed his equipment for the tour on his website manzanera.com. In addition to the Firebird VII and Les Paul Custom, he also had a new Les Paul Custom made specifically for him, again with mother-of-pearl inlay, though of an iguana. Two new white Fender Stratocasters joined the rig and these were 'Roland-ready' models with midi pick-up and dedicated output. Phil had acquired these specifically to use with a Roland VGA-7 amplifier, of which he had two that were set individually for the Gibsons and Stratocasters. The amps modelled several well-known brands, as well as cabinets, in addition to guitar types – for example acoustic, 12-string, or modified tunings – and Roland/Boss pedals. These settings were accessed by a large pedalboard, of which Phil had two for the respective amps and had pre-sets for his requirements. A film of the Apollo concert was released in 2002 and this was followed by the 'Live' album in 2003. The success of Roxy Music's return led to further engagements in 2005 as the group performed at the 'Live 8' event, in addition to the Isle of Wight Festival.

In the midst of the Roxy Music schedule, Phil recorded his sixth studio album '6PM' in 2004. This was a mixture of songs and instrumentals, with vocals again provided by him. There are several standout moments on the record, including the title track, 'Green Spiky Cactus', 'Broken Dreams', etc. Pink Floyd guitarist David Gilmour contributed to 'Sacred Days' and Phil returned the favour on 'Take A Breath', 'This Heaven' and 'Then I Close My Eyes' from David's 'On An Island' record, whilst also assisting with the production. A number of David's tour dates featured Phil ('Live in Gdansk' and 'Remember That Night' at the Royal Albert Hall being captured on film). He was seen performing with the 'iguana' Les Paul Custom, black Stratocaster with maple neck and David's Gibson Country and Western acoustic, which marked a rare public appearance by Phil on acoustic. He looked to be using Hiwatt heads through WEM cabinets and these could have been borrowed from David as well. Two years earlier, the pair had appeared together at the 'Strat Pack' concert in celebration of 50 years of the Fender Stratocaster. Phil performed on David's set following his solo spot where he played '6PM' using a white Fender Stratocaster with maple neck and his Roland amp set-up.

Phil's next album was '50 Minutes Later' (2005) which continued in a similar vein to '6PM', whilst 2008's 'Firebird V11' was inspired by Phil's iconic instrument. The Gibson Studio in London hosted the launch of the record and in early 2009, Phil performed the material, in addition to his other work, at Ronnie Scott's club using the guitar and the Roland VGA-7. In the late 2000s, a new Roxy Music album was expected, yet this failed to appear and several of the intended tracks surfaced on Bryan Ferry's 'Olympia' album in 2010. Phil had a writing credit on 'BF Bass (Ode To Olympia)', whilst providing guitar parts for three other tracks: 'Song To The Siren'; 'Reason Or Rhyme'; 'Whatever Gets You Thru The Night'. Roxy Music did reunite for the band's 40th anniversary in 2011.

For 2015's 'The Sound of Blue', Phil returned to the concept explored on 'Primitive Guitars' of creating pieces that reflected periods or events in his life. In the press release for the album, he said: 'When I write instrumental music, I think about a possible narrative for each track. During the writing of "The Sound of Blue", it started evoking memories and emotions that I hadn't revisited in years …' Whilst 'Primitive Guitars' featured Phil mainly on all instruments, the new record had contributions from Sonia Bernardo on vocals, Andy Mackay playing saxophone and VCS3, Yaron Stavi on bass and the drummer was Javier Weyler. The album also had a cover of 'No Church In The Wild' by American rap artists Jay-Z and Kanye West which featured a sample of Phil's guitar riff on the track 'K-Scope'. Minus Andy Mackay and with other musicians, Phil played with The Sound of Blue band for a number of appearances in 2016 and 2017. 'Live At The Curious Arts Festival' and 'Live In Japan' from these dates were released subsequently and Phil was mainly using a wine-red Les Paul Studio with a pair of Fender Hot Rod DeVille amps, as well as a pedal board/multi-effects unit. In November 2018, Phil and Andy Mackay produced 'Roxymphony' with an orchestra and choir performing reinterpreted Roxy Music songs. Phil was using a black Epiphone Flying V on the night.

Roxy Music briefly reunited during 2019 for the band's induction into the Rock and Roll Hall of Fame. Phil's most recent project is a collaboration with Tim Finn of Split Enz, 'Caught By The Heart'.

Phil Manzanera playing his red Gibson Firebird VII while performing with Roxy Music at the Fuji Rock Festival, 2010.
WENN Fights Ltd / Alamy Stock Photo.

HANK MARVIN

From his column in *Beat Instrumental Monthly No. 21* of January 1965, Hank Marvin enthused about his first, new, signature guitar manufactured by Burns London Ltd. Many people had asked him numerous questions about the instrument. He said that the attention didn't trouble him, 'because there is nothing like playing your own "tailor-made" guitar.' He told readers he had first thought about the idea some two years earlier and mentioned it to his old music teacher, Ike Isaacs, a guitarist who happened to be involved with model development at Burns.

Isaacs arranged a meeting with company owner, Jim Burns and his technicians; work on Hank's new instrument beginning soon afterwards. Hank knew exactly what he was after: 'I wanted it to remain in tune even with a wide-range tremolo arm, with, if possible, more variation in the tone controls. [Jim Burns] knew the shape I wanted but that was no great problem.'

Burns' Romford factory technicians built around 30 prototype models before Hank finally accepted one as his own signature model. He conceded: 'The months of waiting was a nuisance I know, but it all seemed worthwhile …' One of the 30 prototypes is held in the Burns Guitar Museum.

By the early 1960s, Hank had become a well-known Fender player using Vox amplifiers and it has often been speculated why one of the two companies did not develop a signature guitar for him. That did not happen, and the opportunity was embraced by Burns, the association with Hank doing the company no harm. At the start of the 1960s, Hank was a role model for thousands of budding guitarists intently listening to all the Shadows' records and watching his every finger move on the fretboard.

Burns produced three models for Hank, the Burns Marvin, the Burns Double Six 12-string; and the Burns Marvin S prototypes. Although Hank mentions a signature guitar at the beginning of 1965, a Marvin prototype can be identified in pictures taken in the studio during early November 1963. Jim Burns has confirmed the first Burns guitars were delivered to Hank and Bruce in November 1963. They were finished in white polyester, had Brazilian Mahogany bodies, steamed beach necks and fingerboards from Indian rosewood. Production of the Marvins began in 1964 and their serial numbers began with the number '5'.

Beat Monthly No. 14 June 1964 mentions: '[Hank] has now at last achieved one of his ambitions, that of having a guitar named after him. The guitar itself is called the Burns Marvin.'

Beat Monthly No. 15 July 1964, in 'Talking Guitars No. 3 Burns' by Tony Webster, mentions the cost of the Burns Marvin was £162 15s 0d. In the same article, Webster says: 'Finally, there is the Double Six. A 12-string model with a special Burns tuning. For a new sound just try the Burns Double Six. It is priced at £131 5s 0d.'

Whilst the Marvin model's shape was influenced by the Fender Stratocaster, Burns added new features such as a scrolled headstock shape, which was Hank's idea, and a Rezo-tube vibrato, with a knife-edge bearing and six individual tubes to anchor the strings instead of Fender's metal block. Hank states on the current Burns website: 'The Marvin was a fine guitar, which I played on record, stage and screen from 1964 thru to 1970 when, unfortunately, my guitars were stolen, never to be seen again, well not by me!'

A prototype Double Six was produced in 1963 with the design resembling guitars in the Burns Split Sound Range and including a floating cradle bridge but this was abandoned. The production Burns Double Six 12-string was often described as virtually a 12-string 'Marvin'. As well as the 'normal' tuning, a special set of 'octave below' strings could be acquired. This altered the guitar to a 12-string bass, producing a unique sound. With a 25½-in. scale length, 21 frets, three Tri-Sonic pick-ups, volume and tone controls, and a 3-way selector switch, the Double Six appeared in green sunburst, red sunburst as well as solid white and black finishes. The fingerboard (some were bound) was rosewood and there was a black scratch plate incorporating the engraved Burns name which varied in size during the production period. A few Double Six guitars were fitted with a tremolo system. Costing £131, the Double Six became a popular guitar at the time with a number of celebrity owners including Elvis Presley. Hank had two variations of the Double Six with vibrato system: a green one with a modified Rezo-tube and a red one with a floating bridge.

Hank is known to have played versions of a Double Six from around late 1963. When promoting Cliff Richard's single 'Don't Talk To Him', Hank used a red sunburst prototype Double Six. He has one at the Olympia on May 24, 1964, in a live performance with the Shadows backing Cliff Richard singing 'I'm The Lonely One'. He is with a green prototype Double Six in the film 'Wonderful Life' (released July 1964), performing part of the accompaniment for 'On The Beach' (written by Welch/Richard/Marvin and released June 1964).

Three Marvin S prototypes – two green and one white –

The Hofner Congress was a small-bodied arch top of 19.5 in. length by 14 in. and 3.1 in. body depth. The guitar, without any cutaways, almost had the appearance of a parlour guitar but with a full size 25.5 in. scale length. The top featured a plain maple veneer with plain or slightly flamed maple veneers being used for the back and sides. Hofner did not produce an electric version of the guitar though Hank Marvin later fitted a pick-up to his instrument which he played through a tiny amplifier borrowed from a friend. Binding was only featured on the body top and there were double dot markers on the 5th, 7th and 9th frets with a single one on the 12th fret. Selmer distributed versions of the guitar between c.1953 and 1973.

were built by Baldwin-Burns (the Baldwin Piano and Organ Company took over Burns in 1965) between 1965 and 1966. Amongst the features were non-contoured bodies, acoustic pockets, bound body edges, a 'Marvin' neck, a 'scroll' headstock, and black 3-piece laminate scratch plates, displaying the 'Baldwin-Burns' legend. A 5-way selector switch was fitted on the two green guitars; the white one a rotary type selector. The white prototype did not have a vibrato unit. Whilst these prototypes were used by the Shadows on their 1967 Australian tour, the guitars were never put into production and not retained by the band, allegedly falling short of their expectations.

A TV performance of the instrumental single 'The Rise And Fall Of Flingel Bunt', released in May 1964 and written by all four members of the band, was the first time all three Shadows guitarists – John Rostill, Hank Marvin and Bruce Welch – appeared with Burns guitars. The Shadows used green Marvin guitars in the films 'Rhythm and Greens' (1964) and 'Finders Keepers' (1966). Hank's Marvin differed from Bruce's in the following ways: the pick-up and selector positions were changed; and the scratch plate was re-shaped around the tremolo unit.

Around 1965, Hank commented to Jim Burns that his Marvin guitar was a little heavy for live performance. Thus, a new model with an obeche body was made, with a rosewood fingerboard, white binding on the maple neck and the strap button was repositioned, and it was accepted by the guitarist.

Much of Hank's early life and career as well as his, and the Shadows', major successes enjoyed during the 1960s are adequately detailed in Bruce Welch's *Rock 'n' Roll: I Gave You the Best Years of My Life* (1989).

Hank was born Brian Robson Rankin during 1942 in Newcastle upon Tyne. He studied piano from the age of eight and gained a good solid grounding in music. He attended Rutherford Grammar School for Boys and was nicknamed 'Hank' because, according to Bruce, 'he was bandy-legged and walked like a cowboy.' At 14, Hank bought a banjo from a French teacher, James Moody, after some bartering, for £2 10s which he promised to pay in instalments. Hank liaised well with his art teacher and he excelled at the subject. The banjo was a five-string Windsor G instrument and Hank purchased an instructional manual and taught himself to play, mastering the finer points of tuning.

Hank was fascinated by New Orleans and Chicago jazz and listened to it intently. He appreciated Benny Goodman, Sidney Bechet and Monty Moonshine, all accomplished clarinet players. In fact, Hank had wanted to play clarinet but, put off by the price of the instrument and lessons, he dismissed the idea. Pete Deuchar, who ran a local jazz club, Vieux Carre, gave Hank advice on how to play the banjo and, in time, John Tate helped him play guitar.

Amongst Hank's other influences were Lead Belly and folk roots music, often frequenting specialist record shops in Newcastle that sold that type of music. He also read numerous jazz journals. He collected newspaper clippings, featuring Fats Waller, Jimmie Rogers and Lonnie Donegan, pasting these into a scrapbook. Attending concerts at Newcastle City Hall, he listened to a string of contemporary jazz performers and amongst them were George Melly, Humphrey Lyttelton and Chris Barber.

Around the mid-1950s, Hank joined together with a few friends and played banjo in a band called the Riverside Skiffle. The name was eventually changed to the Crescent City Skiffle Group and the band played in local jazz clubs.

Hank and Bruce Welch played their instruments together at school whenever there was an opportunity. Hank developed an ability to pick out notes played on a guitar from a record. His band, the Crescent City Skiffle Group eventually split up and he joined Bruce's band the Railroaders, and they built up a reputation around Newcastle. They were rated highly by the *Newcastle Evening Chronicle* and worked two or three nights a week earning £6 or £7 on each occasion. To begin with, Hank played banjo in the Railroaders, though in 1957, on his 16th birthday, he was presented with a Hofner Congress cello-bodied guitar which had cost 16gns.

With the Railroaders, Hank was persuaded to play in a more rock 'n' roll style. The band tried to replicate guitar sounds produced by James Burton and Scotty Moore but this was obviously difficult given the far superior equipment used by the Americans. Two other guitars played by Hank during the late 1950s included a solid-body Antoria LG50, bought in London for £35, and a Vega.

Until around 1958, Hank was known to play guitars through a Selmer Truvoice Stadium amplifier, introduced by the company in the mid-1950s. Once Bruce and Hank moved from Newcastle to London, they became part of the short-lived Chesternuts with Pete Chester, son of comedian Charlie Chester. Afterwards, Bruce and Hank performed for four hours, three nights a week, as a singing duo the Geordie Boys at the 2i's coffee bar and they were often joined on stage by well-known artists of the day. Hank steadily built up a strong reputation as a very competent guitarist who was acknowledged as such by quite a number of people.

After a short stint with the newly reformed Vipers (one of the leading British skiffle bands), Hank teamed up with Bruce in the Drifters and backed Cliff Richard on a tour headlined by the Kalin Twins. This developed until the Drifters changed their name to the Shadows and they supported Cliff Richard on record, toured with him, as well as making some recordings of their own.

Fed up with his troublesome Antoria guitar, which also had

Built by Guyatone in Japan, the almost Les Paul-shaped Antoria LG50 was branded, imported and marketed in the UK by James T. Coppock Ltd. Featuring bird's-eye maple, the guitar had dot inlays in the fretboard. Between 1960 and 1962, Jennings Musical Instruments introduced a Vox-branded LG50 'Shadow' guitar built by Guyatone. The Japanese company was founded by Mitsuo Matsuki (born around 1915) and the original company name was Matsuki Manufacturing. The 'Guya' and 'Guyatone' names were first put on lap steel guitars and amplifiers. By 1951, the company name was Tokyo Sound Laboratory and towards the end of the decade a number of solid-body electrics were introduced.

a 'bent' neck, in 1959, Hank coaxed Cliff Richard to buy him a 'good' guitar. This had to be a Fender Stratocaster as Hank had seen his hero Buddy Holly with one on an album sleeve. A Fender catalogue was obtained from the States and a top-of-the-range model was ordered in fiesta red, with gold hardware and a bird's-eye maple neck. The price paid was £120. According to Tom Wheeler in *The Stratocaster Chronicles: Celebrating 50 Years of the Fender Strat* (2004) this was organised by Cliff Richard's manager, whilst he was in New York's Manny's guitar store.

Hank's guitar arrived in a tweed case with red crushed-velvet lining and it really impressed him. The only disappointment was that the guitar strings were quite heavy but this problem was soon solved. Hank found the Fender to be quite light and the contours made it comfortable. He really enjoyed using the tremolo arm, becoming a part of the unmistakeable Shadows' sound. Hank recalls playing the guitar on 'Saturday Dance', and a number of Cliff Richard's releases.

In *Beat Instrumental No. 41* of September 1966, Hank looked back to the late 1950s British guitar scene: '… the British guitarists then showed a lamentable lack of feeling. If they could play the melody, it was simply a series of single notes, rather like just taking off a saxophone solo. No feeling, no soul at all. Up in Newcastle, we'd been following the way American stars like Scotty Moore got the twanging sounds and the way he bent his notes. We got some of these phrases off and simply copied them, but we got the knowledge that real feeling was all important. No, the standards back in 1958 were very poor. Even among the better, more gutsy, players.' A little later in the same article he added: 'The origin of much of this "feeling" in music comes from the old Country and Western banjos and violins. They had some really fantastic music … slurred and sliding notes and marvellous phrasing.'

Once the US trade embargo was lifted in 1959 and UK firms were able to buy instruments from America, JMI supplied the Shadows with Fender guitars around 1961. Hank obtained another fiesta red guitar but this time it had a rosewood fingerboard and chrome hardware. This belonged to Fender's second phase of Stratocaster construction, stretching from 1959 to late 1965. The guitar had off-white or clay dots, instead of black, on the fingerboard. Hank is known to have used the 'rosewood' guitar in April 1961 when performing 'The Frightened City' and 'FBI'. Meanwhile, the maple-neck Strat was handed back to Cliff Richard and sprayed white. Hank confesses that he preferred the maple-neck Strat over the rosewood one.

As a backup guitar, Hank used a Gretsch Country Gentleman from around 1961. It may be identified on a stand when the Shadows performed with Cliff at the 1961 Wembley Poll Winners concert. On www.alturnertivemusic.com, Doug Turner recalls that whilst he was working for Arbiters in London, who imported Gretsch guitars from America, he delivered a Country Gentleman to 'a little guitar shop in Charing Cross Road.' Several months later he discovered that it was purchased by Hank Marvin. Later in 1972, Doug saw a Gretsch Country Gentleman for sale in Baldwin's Guitar Shop near Tottenham Court Road Tube Station. The guitar was being sold for Hank Marvin and Doug bought it. Much later Doug had the opportunity to talk to Hank about the guitar and it was confirmed the guitar bought in the early 1960s was the same one sold at Baldwin's. Hank was also able to reveal the Gretsch was used on the Shadows' first solo album 'Nivram' (released September 1961) and on Cliff Richard's 'A Girl Like You' (released June 1961).

With regard to amplification, Hank, in mid-1958, acquired a Vox AC15 admiring its small size and reliability seemingly in preference to the more prestigious Fender amps and this started a long association with the company. Vox had only put the AC15 into production in early 1958 and gradually, as the Shadows played larger venues, there was a need for more amplification. On asking Vox if a 'twin' AC15 could be built, Vox launched the AC30/4 using two 12-inch speakers with four inputs.

Although the band had been impressed by the Fender Twin, introduced in 1956, they found it lacked the same richness of tone as the Vox AC15. According to Peterson & Denney (*op. cit.*), the Shadows took delivery of three AC30s during late 1959 'after extended speaker testing to confirm reliability.'

Paul Rossiter on www.tvsspecialtyproducts.com uses meticulous observation, watching films, live and television performances, to detect that the Shadows used, in the period October 1960 up until 1968, seven different variants of the Vox AC30 amplifiers. These, he notes, were also used for many of the Shadows' greatest hits. The list of variants includes overall design, the number of inputs, speaker types, coverings and cosmetic additions and finishes.

A *Beat Monthly No. 3* July 1963 advertisement feature illustrates the Shadows with AC30 Twins (6 inputs in three channels). One amplifier retailed for £110 gns. The advertisement announced: 'It is an undisputed fact that VOX

Fender custom colours: At the launch of Fender Stratocasters in April 1954, they first appeared in a shaded two-colour sunburst, though Tom Wheeler (op. cit.) states by 1956 non-stock finishes were specified in Fender literature to be 'the player's choice'. Then, around 1957, Fender offered custom colours at a 5% extra charge. In 1961 the colour chart contained 14 colours plus blonde and most of those available mirrored choices offered by USA automobile manufacturers. Colours which did not appear on the chart could be provided on special request.

In Tom Wheeler (op. cit.) Hank states: 'Few of us [in the 1950s] had heard of blues players like Albert King or B.B. King, and we'd never heard of finger vibrato apart from classical guitar … I was overjoyed when I realized that not only could you give the tremolo bar a real mad woggle, but I could actually use it to produce a vibrato effect to help the notes sing more. I learned to play holding the vibrato bar in the palm of my hand while I picked so I could shake it while I was playing.'

Hank Marvin pictured with the Hank Marvin Signature Limited Edition guitar.
Courtesy Barry Gibson.

amplifiers are featured by more than 90% of Britain's foremost Radio … Television … and Record Artistes and Groups.'

After Burns was acquired by Baldwin in late 1965, the Burns Marvin guitar underwent changes and amongst these were alterations to the neck and a 'flattened' scroll headstock was introduced and, later, Bar-Magnet type pick-ups were fitted. The guitar retailed for £148. Marvins built during the first few months after the Baldwin takeover displayed either the Burns or Baldwin or both brand names. The Double Six also underwent various minor alterations to the bridge styling, neck and head stock finishes, retailing at £139.

The former Burns guitars, albeit with modifications, were only built under Baldwin until 1970. This was due to a number of reasons: the guitars didn't sell well in the US because of Baldwin's inexperience with selling guitars; problems with the polyester finish; and high import tariffs on completed guitars. Following the acquisition of Gretsch in 1967, Baldwin focussed their attention on marketing that range of guitars.

In *Beat Instrumental Monthly No. 22* of February 1965, Hank mentions the experimentation with radio mikes fitted to the backs of the Shadows' guitars had been unsuccessful, explaining: 'We tried them out at rehearsals for "Aladdin" at the Palladium and heard great jamming noises. The units apparently clashed with the radio mikes which were essential to the show – so the units just had to go. It was a pity. You can imagine the freedom we would have had.'

Mention of 'Aladdin' reveals the versatility of the Shadows: playing instrumentals; writing songs; and appearing in pantomime. The 'Aladdin' pantomime, staged over the Christmas period 1964/1965, featured the Shadows, Cliff Richard, Arthur Askey, Una Stubbs, Charlie Cairoli and Alan Curtis. Hank said: 'We do two shows a day, one matinee and one evening performance, every house is jammed full, and the reaction from the kids and the adults is tremendous.'

By the time Hank's column for *Beat Instrumental No. 23* of March 1965 had appeared, the Shadows' single 'Mary Anne' had been released. It was written by Jerry Lordan and featured vocals. Hank pointed out: 'It seems that many people are under the impression that vocal records are completely new to us. True, this is the first time we've had a vocal issued as an "A" side single release. When we were known as The Drifters, we had two vocals released … Since then we've concentrated on instrumentals, but a while back we featured ourselves singing again [on "I Want You to Want Me" which was] on the back of "Atlantis".'

Beat Instrumental Monthly No. 24 of April 1965 ran the article 'Song-writing Now' and included the following: 'Hank Marvin and Bruce Welch of the Shadows are well known in the song-writing field and are concentrating more and more, it seems, on this side of their work. After having completed the score for the "Aladdin" pantomime at the London Palladium, they are getting their heads together for songs for both Cliff's and their own forthcoming films. Yet, their song-writing is often done with the help of John Rostill and Brian Bennett and all four Shads have formed their own publishing company, Shadows Music Ltd.'

Under the heading '50 years of Echoes', Paul Rossiter (*op. cit.*) looks at Hank's echo units. During the 1960s Hank used a Meazzi Echomatic 1; Meazzi/Vox Echomatic 2; Vox Long Tom; and Baby Binson. Rossiter submits the Shadows used models of the Meazzi Echomatic 1; a five head and a six head and both had emitted a unique pattern of echoes.

About the Meazzi, Tom Hughes in *Premier Guitar* August 27, 2014, writes: 'Italian amplifier company Meazzi became much better known for its Echomatic delay units than for its amps. British guitarist Hank Marvin made great use of the first Echomatic for his famous "rippling echo" effect with his band the Shadows. The first version of the Echomatic used a rotating-drum system … But after having problems with the rotating drum Meazzi switched to a tape loop system.' Based on the Meazzi system the Vox Echo was developed by Dick Denney. Two versions were built, the Shadow Echo, with three playback heads, and another, with six.

After selling out to Baldwin, Jim Burns involved himself in several other 'come-back' projects over the ensuing years: Ormston Steel Guitars London Ltd 1966–1970; the Hayman Range 1970–1975; Burns UK Ltd 1974–1977; and Jim Burns Actualizers Ltd 1979–1983. In 1992 Barry Gibson re-launched the Burns name, initially with Jim Burns as a consultant, and the company still thrives today.

Beat Instrumental No. 37 of May 1966 listed the stringed instruments Hank had in his possession at that time: a five-string banjo; a four-string banjo; a battered old Zenith guitar; a Gretsch Country Gentleman; a Gibson 12-string acoustic; a Gibson Jumbo; a six-string Fender bass; a Burns 12-string electric; a Burns Double Six with six bass strings; plus the Burns Marvin guitars used on stage, one in green and one in white.

When asked about fuzz-boxes he replied: 'We've got some lying around. It's a great sound but you must use the box sensibly … the important thing is not to over-do it, otherwise the effect is lost.' He added: 'I'd just like to mention the foot-pedal, too, for guitarists. I first heard it used from Big Jim Sullivan and I realised how fabulous it is. It's a straight pedal. Push forward and you get maximum volume, push back and it's lessened. Turn to the left and it puts on full bass; turn to the right and it turns up treble. It gives a crying effect, sounds great on melodic numbers. It's great for getting full control without using your fingers. We find it's not so good on stage – easier to set up properly in a club or recording studio where the visual effect doesn't matter so much.'

When asked about the future role of the guitar he replied: 'People keep talking about the guitar losing popularity and so on, but I just can't see it. I would say the general standards among British players just get higher all the time.'

Talking to Pete Goodman for *Beat Instrumental No. 41* of September 1966, Hank admitted: 'I've been trying to get new ideas and sounds. It's really a gradual evolution of my general thinking … I'm really interested in the foot pedal because you can get a really marvellous sound going with that.'

Following the first break-up of the Shadows in 1968, Hank released a self-titled solo album a year later. At the same time, the Shadows reformed for a Far East tour and released a live album. Marvin, Welch and Farrar was formed in 1970. Shortly before opening at the Palladium with Cliff Richard and Olivia Newton-John, Hank had a number of guitars stolen: the white obeche-bodied Burns guitar, two green sunburst Burns Marvins, a 12-string Gibson and an acoustic six-string. This prompted a return to playing Stratocasters and he is noted as having a Sunburst one, that was later painted black. He undertook trials with different pick-ups, including the Gibson humbucker, DiMarzio FS-1 and Fender wide-range humbucker as well as wiring modifications. During the Marvin, Welch, Farrar period, Hank is known to have used: a Baldwin Marvin; a 1957 Fender Sunburst Stratocaster bought from Tony Hicks of the Hollies; a Gibson Les Paul Custom; a Gibson Les Paul Deluxe; and a Roger Giffin Custom guitar.

Amongst Hank's echo units listed by Paul Rossiter in the 1970s and later, were the Binson Echorec; Maestro Echoplex; Watkins WEM The Shadow Echo; Binson EC3; MXR Digital Delay; and Roland RE-201 (301 and 501); Roland RE-3 digital rack unit; the Alesis Q2; and TVS3.

Jim Burns' company Actualizers Ltd produced the Marvin between 1980 and 1983 in an attempt, perhaps, to relive the glory of former days. A simpler version of the original Marvin, it included 22 frets, a tone and volume controls, 3-way selector switch and single-coil pick-ups, though, for an extra cost, a version could be obtained with two Burns Humbuckers and a Burns single-coil pick-up. Some early guitars have Hank Marvin's signature on the headstock and he is known to have played this version of the guitar on at least one occasion. Available in white and black as well as red, green or brown sunburst, it retailed between £300 and £390.

In 1985, CBS sold the company acquired from Leo Fender in early 1965, to Fender Musical Instruments Corporation. A year later, the new Fender company introduced the USA '57 and '62 Vintage Reissue Stratocasters. Fender boss Bill Schulz was given the first '57 fiesta red reissue manufactured and Hank Marvin received the second one, with the serial number V000002. Before Hank left England to live in Perth, Western Australia, it was presented to him at a special party in London on February 12, 1986. The event was attended by other noted players including Eric Clapton, Steve Howe, Jeff Beck, David Gilmour, Richard Thompson and Stuart Adamson. Fender boss, Bill Schultz was present. Hank played the guitar on 'Cliff And The Shadows Reunited', released in 2009.

Commenting on some of the features on the reissue signature guitar, built by George Blanda, Hank told *Guitar Player* in September 1987: 'I wanted a slightly wider neck because with a lot of Strats you can pull the first string easily off the fingerboard. There's a Teflon nut to make things a bit more slippery, no string trees and it uses the American Standard bridge. When you use the tremolo on them as much as I do – and sometimes I use it quite radically – they just go out of tune quite easily. But, this one stays very much in tune and it sounds wonderful.'

Since its inauguration from 1992, Burns London Ltd has produced a number of true replicas of the celebrated 1960s guitars such as the Marvin model, becoming known as the Legend; the Legend 'S' Type and the Apache Limited Edition, 2001. During late 1999, Burns introduced a range of Korean-built guitars including the Marquee, a budget version of the Marvin, the Double Six, and the Marquee Special.

In addition, Burns, in association with Hank Marvin, have launched the 40th Anniversary Marvin, the Burns Marvin Shadows Custom, the Apache; and the Gold Dream Model. This strongly acknowledges Hank Marvin's influence on guitar playing and Jim Burns' important place in British guitar manufacture.

The last quarter of the 20th century and first years of the 21st century were marked for Hank by: song-writing for the Shadows and Cliff Richard; the Shadows' entry in the 1975 Eurovision song contest; Shadows reunions; solo single and album releases; solo tours; and collaborations with other artists. He has played lead guitar on a Roger Daltrey album; co-wrote an Olivia Newton-John hit; joined forces with French keyboard player and composer Jean-Michel Jarre; and performed a duet with French guitarist Jean-Pierre Daniel.

Amongst the guitars used by Hank during this latter period were: a Roland Synthesizer guitar, a Giffin Custom, and several Burns guitars. The amplifiers employed have included Mesa Boogie, Matchless, Cornell, and Pinnacle.

During 2009, Cliff Richard and the Shadows joined together once more to record many of their greatest hits from the late 1950s to the mid-1960s. A sell-out arena tour, captured for DVD, was also undertaken and saw them perform in the UK, Europe, Australia, New Zealand and South Africa. On the tour the Shadows used JMI amps.

Forming Hank Marvin's Gypsy Jazz band, Hank in some ways has returned to his much earlier fascination with jazz, particularly appreciating the work of Django Reinhardt. He released 'Django's Castle' with Nunzio Mondia and Gary Taylor in 2014 and has undertaken several tours playing at festivals and jazz clubs. When speaking about gypsy jazz, Hank naturally admits the music owes a lot to Django Reinhardt's playing and adds the guitars he invariably uses have a longer scale length than a 'normal' acoustic. And his way of playing or picking strings is different. He explains on www.hankmarvingypsyjazz.com: 'I was a loyal up-picker, though not all the time. Now I get sensitivity with down strokes. Gypsy jazz is played with a lot of down strokes. It is very difficult for a number of us who haven't been brought up in that style. I now play more down strokes than I used to. One thing about playing an acoustic instrument with down strokes is that it gives strength to the note and a lot of authority to the sound. At the end of the day, all these ways of playing probably don't matter too much as long as you produce some good music.'

The Shadows: l to r, John Rostill, Hank Marvin, Brian Bennett, and Bruce Welch.
Allstar Picture Library Ltd / Alamy Stock Photo.

JOHN MCLAUGHLIN

An innovative and widely respected guitarist in the genres of jazz and 'fusion', John McLaughlin has used a diverse group of instruments and equipment over his career spanning several decades.

As the youngest of five children (three brothers, one sister), John benefitted from his siblings' interest in music. A brother's fondness for classical music initially sparked John's enthusiasm and this was followed by his sister learning the piano, which he quickly joined in with at age nine. John was introduced to the guitar two years later through his brothers and this was a cheap Spanish-style instrument. Talking to *Guitar* magazine in 1975 he commented: 'It was quite a thrill … I fell in love with the guitar at that moment … The instrument fascinated me and when I realised I could do it, it was something super special.'

John was also fortunate that his brothers were at the forefront of British interest in American blues music and they had records by Muddy Waters, Lead Belly and Sonny Terry. By 14, John was listening to classical Spanish guitar, then Django Reinhardt. Whilst learning by ear for much of this period, John's foray into the more complex music led him to find a guitar teacher for detailed instruction on the instrument. In his mid-teens John was exploring jazz and was particularly enthralled by Tal Farlow.

Though John already had a solid grounding with the guitar, he was not impervious to the skiffle boom that swept Britain in the late 1950s and formed his own band with school friends. John was still playing an acoustic guitar but had managed to acquire and fit a pick-up which was amplified by his record player. When John was 16, his mother agreed to help with the purchase of an unidentified flat-top guitar. John was in a couple of bands that played jazz music. His tastes had developed further, particularly to include Miles Davis and John Coltrane.

From his early teens, John had favoured a career as a musician and when he left school at 16, turning professional was his ambition. In *Bathed in Lightning: John McLaughlin, the 60s and the Emerald Beyond*, George Harbertson (a school friend of John's) is quoted as recalling John purchased a second-hand guitar around this time: 'it cost £65 … John explained to me that it was the same kind of guitar Django Reinhardt played.' Frequenting many jazz nights in Newcastle, John often sat in with jazz bands and joined Big Pete Deuchar's Professors of Ragtime. In a low-quality image of the band available online, John has a guitar which is possibly the one mentioned above and appears to be a Levin archtop – a brand associated with Django Reinhardt – looking similar to a 315 M2.

Around this time, John often visited his brother, who was studying at the University of Manchester. The vibrant jazz scene in the city was part of the attraction and Pete Deuchar's Professors of Ragtime later found work there. The band had a spell playing the London jazz clubs before John decided to leave. He found a job at Selmer's on Charing Cross Road. Perhaps this decision was taken as John was recently married and with two young daughters.

Between 1959 and 1962, John primarily worked at Selmer's and developed a reputation amongst working and budding guitarists in the London area as one of the best. John did play with some groups during this period but this was mostly as a guest or to help friends. He was recruited for Georgie Fame and the Blue Flames in May 1962. The band started with a regular gig at the Flamingo Club, resulting in consistent bookings across London, as well as further afield. Yet, John found the group's repertoire limiting and, around March 1963, he left to join the Graham Bond Organisation featuring renowned bassist Jack Bruce and drummer Ginger Baker. A photograph from the period shows John with a Gretsch 6125 single pick-up 'Anniversary' model.

One of the first engagements for the quartet was a session backing former Larry Parnes act Duffy Power on a cover of the Beatles' 'I Saw Her Standing There' in late February 1963. This was John's first documented recording session and sadly his guitar part is completely buried in the mix, with vocals and Graham Bond's organ prominent. A second version, which was the one released, was recorded later though John did not attend the session and Big Jim Sullivan stepped in, but again the guitar is missing. John has much more prominence on a jam recorded at Abbey Road and later released as 'Untitled Abbey Road Blues Instrumental' on the compilation 'Wade In The Water: Classics, Origins & Oddities'. An early live recording was made of the joint Bond/McLaughlin song 'The Grass Is Greener' and this also appeared on 'Solid Bond', along with a cover of Sonny Rollins' 'Doxy'.

John's tenure with the Graham Bond Organisation lasted only six months as the demands of the road and poor financial recompense took their toll. Initially attempting to regain his employment at Selmer's, John was obliged to continue with his music career elsewhere and played a solo engagement before taking up a rhythm guitar position with former Shadow Tony Meehan. This was on a package tour alongside Joe Moretti on lead guitar, John Paul Jones on bass, Glenn Hughes on baritone saxophone and Chris Hughes on tenor saxophone. Before this group disbanded at the end of 1963, a single was recorded – 'Song Of Mexico' b/w 'Kings Go Fifth' – which just broke into the top forty early in 1964.

Brian Auger called on John and Glenn Hughes to join a quintet for a residency in a London club during early 1964. Though the band dispersed when the contract expired, a brief reformation was staged for a month gigging in Germany during late spring/early summer. In the meantime, John had begun working as a session musician, being employed by Rolling Stones manager Andrew Loog Oldham for his extra-curricular activities producing demos for other artists. Later in the year, John appears to have been re-hired at Selmer's, though continued to perform with bands in the evening and at sessions, such as for Dionne Warwick and Burt Bacharach, who were working on the film soundtrack 'What's New Pussycat?'.

By 1964, John was with Ronnie Jones and the Night-Timers,

then the Ray Ellington Quartet. The latter was only a brief association and John was in the Night-Timers in early 1965 when Ronnie Jones was replaced by Herbie Goins. John played on the first single 'The Music Played On' and wrote 'Cruisin' which was the B-side for the second single 'No. 1 In Your Heart', though he had left at the time of the release in mid-1966. In a brief break by the band at the end of 1965, John was hired to back Wilson Pickett on a tour of England. John left the Night-Timers in spring 1966 after a residency in Switzerland.

Following a meeting with old friend Duffy Power, John joined forces with him to help with new material. 'Little Boy Blue' and 'It's Funny' were two songs later released and credited to the pair. This was a short-term project and John returned to session work as his main employment in 1966. During an interview with *Jazz Journal* (November 1996), John recalled playing a Gibson L4C with an added Charlie Christian pick-up (the guitar had no pick-up when new) at this time as well as the Gretsch.

Early in 1967, John performed for a short time with the Danny Thompson Trio and a gig was recorded and later released. John went on the road with the Four Tops as a backing musician, whilst also continuing with sessions for a variety of artists. A particularly interesting track from this time was 'The Koan' which was on fellow session guitarist Big Jim Sullivan's 'Sitar Beat' album. In mid-1967, John was a member of Pete Brown's First Real Poetry Band and played a number of gigs with them through to early 1968.

John became extremely frustrated with the session work, despite the lucrative opportunities. He decided to quit – even though an occasional foray into the studio occurred subsequently – and he later told *Guitar Player* magazine (April 1996): 'It was great money, but I was dying, couldn't stand it. One day I cut everything and was poor again. I had to sell my guitar, a great carved-top Gibson L4C …' Photographs reproduced in *Bathed in Lightning* and a brief clip of John with Time Is Now (see below) suggest the guitar was sold in late 1968/early 1969, rather than late 1967/early 1968. The book also records several contemporaries noticing John using a small practice amplifier, at least for gigs, which could have been a DeArmond R5 or R15 model.

A more creative outlet for John's talent came when pianist Gordon Beck added John to his trio, forming a quartet to record versions of several contemporary hit songs. 'Experiments With Pops' covered 'These Boots Are Made For Walkin', 'Norwegian Wood', 'Sunny', 'Up Up And Away', 'I Can See For Miles', 'Michelle', 'Good Vibrations' and 'Monday, Monday'.

In mid-1968, John joined Gunter Hampel's Time Is Now band, playing on the continent to the end of the year. John helped old bandmate, Jack Bruce with five of seven tracks for his album 'Things We Like', which was released in 1970.

Ex-Rolling Stones manager and Crawdaddy club owner, Giorgio Gomelsky had independent record label Marmalade for a few years in the late 1960s. John was recommended to him for a record. In early 1969, this was completed at Advision Studios with Tony Oxley (drums), Brian Odgers (double bass) and John Surman (saxophone). 'Extrapolation' featured ten pieces that allowed John to finally commit his ideas freely on tape. Most tracks featured electric guitar, though two had an acoustic instrument, 'This Is For The Two Of Us To Share' and 'Peace Piece'. The front and rear cover photographs have John playing an acoustic guitar, which in later versions is more clearly identified as a Gibson Hummingbird with added pick-up.

The recording of 'Extrapolation' marked a turning point in John's career and his musical direction. Around a month after the album was completed, American jazz drummer Tony Williams finalised plans for John to join a new band he was forming with organist Larry Young – The Tony Williams Lifetime. He had befriended John on a previous visit to England. John arrived in New York during mid-February 1969 and immediately began rehearsals. Only two days later, John was invited by Miles Davis to contribute to tracks being recorded and later released as 'In A Silent Way'. Despite self-admitted nervousness at playing with Miles, who was one of his musical influences, John shines on the album and is integral to Miles' 'electric period' which started with this record.

Though Miles was impressed with John's contribution and asked him to permanently join his band, John preferred to continue with the Tony Williams Lifetime as this allowed more creative freedom than would have been the case with Miles. The trio began playing live around New York and in May recorded their first album, 'Emergency!'. An early photograph of the band in the studio shows John with the Gibson Hummingbird, which he is quoted in *Bathed in Lightning* as playing on 'In A Silent Way', as well as a jam with Jimi Hendrix near the same time (this has later seen release as a 'bootleg'). The use of the acoustic in the electric setting, however, was not desirable because of uncontrollable feedback and John was obliged to buy a solid-body guitar. This was a Fender Duo Sonic II, which was a student model and appears to be the 24 in. scale version with 22 frets. John acquired the guitar around late summer 1969 and likely used it on Miles' 'Bitches Brew' sessions and later was photographed with the Fender in hand for the Monterey Jazz Festival in September 1969.

The year ended with further live dates for the Tony Williams Lifetime, including a support slot for the Who, and John was also involved in sessions with Miles Davis. These continued into the new year and were eventually used on 'Jack Johnson' (also known as 'A Tribute to Jack Johnson') and 'Live-Evil'. Early in 1970, John reached an agreement with American producer Alan Douglas to record an album and teamed with Buddy Miles, Billy Rich and Larry Young to record 'Devotion'. This moved away from the music of the Tony Williams Lifetime and perhaps could be described as being 'rock' oriented. John has a 'rock' guitar sound for much of the album and also employs a Wah-Wah pedal for a number of passages. A picture on the inside cover of the record has John apparently with his Duo Sonic II, though a humbucker now appears in the neck position.

Jack Bruce joined the Tony Williams Lifetime in spring 1970 and the band played in America before travelling to Europe in the summer for a number of dates in Britain and Germany. The group was partway through recording the second album – 'Turn It Over' – when Jack joined and he appears on

John McLaughlin with Gibson Doubleneck.
Pictorial Press Ltd / Alamy Stock Photo.

California-based luthier Rex Bogue approached John McLaughlin in the early 1970s to build a custom guitar. Playing a Doubleneck at the time, John requested a particularly ornate instrument, mainly made from maple with ebony fingerboard and 'tree of life' inlays on each fretboard. Completed in mid-1973, John used the Doubleneck for around a year before the guitar fell and split in two. A similar guitar was released by Ibanez as the 'Artwood Twin' in 1975.
Pictorial Press Ltd / Alamy Stock Photo.

John McLaughlin performing with the custom-made 'New York Skyline' Paul Reed Smith guitar at the Sarajevo International Guitar Festival, November 2014.
Jasmin Brutus / Alamy Stock Photo.

a few tracks. Sometime early in the year, John swapped his Duo Sonic II for a Gibson Les Paul Junior and this was also modified with a neck pick-up. From the few pictures of this band line-up, John appears to be using a Marshall stack at one concert, whilst a fragment of an appearance on the German TV show 'Beat Club' which was never shown has John with Orange amplifiers.

Despite being lauded for live performances, the Tony Williams Lifetime failed to translate this to the records. Not well-received upon release, they have since seen renewed appreciation. By the end of 1970, John had left the band and in early 1971 he recorded his second solo album for Alan Douglas. 'My Goal's Beyond' featured John on an Ovation classical acoustic guitar for all songs and this was also visible on the album cover. Shortly after this project's completion, John decided to form his own outfit. Being particular about the importance of the drummer in a band, John first recruited Billy Cobham and went on to enlist Rick Laird on bass, Jan Hammer on keyboards and Jerry Goodman on violin (the latter had also contributed to 'My Goal's Beyond').

The Mahavishnu Orchestra came together in summer 1971 and following a small number of gigs, the band was in the studio recording 'The Inner Mounting Flame'. John was pictured on the back cover of the record, perhaps for sessions connected with the album, using a late 1960s/early 1970s Gibson Les Paul Custom with two pick-ups. The tone on many of the songs suggests a Marshall amplifier was now used by John (and certainly was live later in the year). Certain passages utilise a Wah-Wah pedal (particularly on 'The Dance Of Maya'), whilst a fuzz pedal might also be present. John played an acoustic – perhaps the Ovation – on 'A Lotus On Irish Streams'.

Both with the Tony Williams Lifetime and the Mahavishnu Orchestra, John was using arpeggios as a feature of his music and this perhaps influenced his next guitar. In an article appearing on www.guitar.com, John comments on how he acquired a Gibson EDS 1275 Doubleneck guitar. 'I called Gibson and I said "I understand you do a Doubleneck and I'd really like a Doubleneck." Of course, there were no chorus pedals in those days, just amps and wah pedals, and that was it. And the 12-string was great for chords and arpeggios, and so they built me an SG Doubleneck …'

Touring mainly around north-east USA to the end of 1971 supporting other bands, the Mahavishnu Orchestra soon developed a reputation for high quality performance and often eclipsed the main act. This helped album sales when the record was released before Christmas and into 1972. During the year, the band continued to perform across America, with John mainly using his Gibson EDS 1275 and Marshall, with an Ovation acoustic and Wah-Wah pedal present. In the summer, the group travelled to Europe and several live appearances were recorded at the BBC, in Germany and France.

Whilst in London, the Mahavishnu Orchestra completed sessions for the second album, 'Birds Of Fire'. This continued in a similar manner to 'The Inner Mounting Flame' though John likely switched to his EDS 1275, whilst acoustic was present on 'Thousand Island Park'. The album cemented the group's popularity, reaching no. 15 in the US chart following release in early 1973. Yet, there was disharmony between John and the musicians and a proposed third album was shelved in favour of a live recording made in Central Park, New York, during early August 1973 – 'Between Nothingness And Eternity'.

Sometime in early 1973, John received a second Gibson EDS 1275 which he again custom ordered, though was unhappy when it was received. On www.theguitarcolumn.com, an article published in 2009 quotes John as saying Gibson failed to build the instrument he requested and only 'Sweetest is my Lord' was inlaid on the fretboards from his specification. He is pictured with this guitar during a collaboration with Carlos Santana in 1973, as the pair recorded 'Love, Devotion, Surrender' and also toured. This disappointment led John to take up an offer from luthier, Rex Bogue to build a custom Doubleneck guitar. Appearing in the middle of 1973, it had a maple body, multi-piece maple and rosewood neck topped by an ebony fingerboard inlaid with 'tree of life' motif, two humbuckers for each neck controlled by individual volumes, a master volume and master tone, with coil splits and a preamp also included. John used the Rex Bogue Doubleneck for around a year before the guitar was damaged and had to be replaced.

The original line-up of the Mahavishnu Orchestra dissolved at the end of 1973, though John decided to continue with the name. He recruited Jean-Luc Ponty on violin, Ralphe Armstrong on bass, Narada Michael Walden on drums and Gayle Moran on keyboard. The band travelled to London in early 1974 to record 'Apocalypse' with the London Symphony Orchestra conducted by Michael Tilson Thomas and produced by George Martin. The group subsequently toured the material with a small string section and John was primarily seen using his Rex Bogue custom with a pair of Mesa Boogie Mark I combo amplifiers.

At the end of 1974, 'Visions Of The Emerald Beyond' was recorded and released in early 1975. This saw a mix of the styles from the first band to 'Apocalypse' and John had Wah-Wah for certain sections, whilst the guitar sound was 'direct' with the Mesa Boogie perhaps used. When playing later in the year, John was pictured with a Gibson Les Paul Deluxe in natural finish and had a Hiwatt head running a Fender cabinet.

Before recording 'Inner Worlds' (minus Jean-Luc Ponty and Gayle Moran) and disbanding the Mahavishnu Orchestra, John started a new project – Shakti – featuring Indian musicians. Three albums were completed in the mid-1970s and tours were undertaken over the same period. John used an acoustic guitar and this was specially commissioned from Gibson. Inspired by the Veena and Sarod, John's guitar had six normal strings and seven additional strings running diagonally across the sound hole for drone sounds. The fretboard was also scalloped. The initial guitar featured a crown headstock inlay, whilst John was also seen with a similar second guitar that had a cutaway, 'The Gibson' inlaid at the top of the headstock as well as a fleur-de-lis.

After Shakti was concluded, John reunited with old friends, such as Billy Cobham, Jerry Goodman, Carlos Santana, Jack Bruce, etc, to complete tracks for his next solo album, 'Electric Guitarist'. In both the album art and publicity material, John is with a Gibson Byrdland, though the fretboard is plain and without the usual block inlays as the fretboard was scalloped. John supported the release with live dates to the end of 1978 and into 1979. He was seen using a contemporary Gibson ES 345 in walnut with dot inlays – again the fretboard had been scalloped – and Varitone, as well as a sunburst guitar of the same model mostly through Marshall amplifiers.

Playing with Jaco Pastorius and Tony Williams in Cuba for a festival, this performance was later released (along with some studio recordings) as the 'Trio Of Doom'. 'Electric Dreams' with the One Truth Band (formed by John, consisting of L. Shankar on violin, Stu Goldberg on keyboards, Fernando Saunders on bass, Tony Smith on drums, Davis Sanborn on saxophone and Alyrio Lima providing percussion), followed in 1979.

Despite having his last two albums incorporating 'electric' in their titles, John had perhaps tired of amplifying his guitar as he began favouring the acoustic, particularly playing in the Spanish style. As the 1970s drew to a close, he teamed up with Larry Coryell and Paco de Lucia for a number of concerts in Europe playing acoustic, with John using an Ovation with normal headstock. In 1980, John and Paco enlisted Al Di Meola for the trio and a recording of a concert in San Francisco (in this instance John played an Ovation with slotted headstock). Around this time, John relocated to France and continued to use the acoustic when recording his next album, 'Belo Horizonte'. During 1982, John was seen performing live mainly with a classical guitar and in the same year he released 'Music Spoken Here'. A reunion with Paco de Lucia and Al Di Meola occurred at the end of 1982, though this was only in the studio and the sessions produced 'Passion, Grace & Fire' which was available to the public in early 1983.

John decided to return to the electric guitar in 1984 and at the time he was armed with the latest digital guitar synthesizer. This was a Roland G303 instrument which he used with a Synclavier II. The guitar was modified to carry the Synclavier control panel by a bracket on the bottom horn and was also fitted with hexaphonic pick-ups, which gave separate outputs for each string. Talking to *Guitar Player* in September 1985, John commented: 'The Synclavier allows me access to the new realms of creative synthesis. This is very exciting to a guitarist who is trying to create new sounds. And now, once I have a particular timbre on the strings, its own characteristics begin to affect the way I play, almost as if I am playing another instrument. You do have to modify your technique to a certain extent, but once you get used to it, the tracking is superb. You just have to give the guitar the right instructions.'

John recorded with the Synclavier on 'Mahavishnu' and was seen playing the guitar at Montreux in 1984, along with a white Gibson Les Paul Special (double cutaway). John was using a Roland Jazz Chorus amp at the time. 'Adventures In Radioland' followed in 1986, though John reduced his use of the guitar synthesizer. Before making the record, John reunited with Miles Davis to work on the 'Aura' project, which had been instigated by Danish musician Palle Mikkelborg, and followed this with sessions for 'You're Under Arrest'. For these, John used a Gibson Les Paul Deluxe. He had a 1958 Gibson Les Paul Standard and a video of him playing the guitar at the North Sea Jazz Festival is available on YouTube.

At the end of the 1980s, John again returned to the acoustic guitar and had a classical instrument made by Abraham Wechter (who built the Shakti guitar) with a Florentine cutaway and slotted headstock; a Fishman blender pick-up was installed. John played the guitar with the Los Angeles Philharmonic for 'The Mediterranean Concerto' orchestrated by Michael Gibbs and later recorded the piece with the London Symphony Orchestra conducted by Michael Tilson Thomas. Afterwards, John formed a trio (with Trilok Gurtu, percussion, and Kai Eckhardt, bass, later replaced by Dominique Di Piazza) playing amplified acoustic and used his Wechter guitar with Fishman pick-up which had an output for each string. This was sent into a preamp in the guitar then to a Photon MIDI processor. The trio made an album in 1989 of a live performance at the Royal Festival Hall and a studio album – 'Qué Alegria' – was created in late 1991. This acoustic period was capped by 'Time Remembered – John McLaughlin Plays Bill Evans' for which he joined forces with the Aïghetta Guitar Quartett [sic].

Joey DeFrancesco (Hammond organ) and Dennis Chambers (drums) joined John at the end of 1993 to record a live album in Tokyo. Acquiring a sunburst Gibson Johnny Smith model archtop by this time, John used this with a Sony DPS-M7 multi-effect processor. He chose to stop using amplifiers and went directly from this to the venue's PA system. In 1995, John began favouring a cherry version of the Johnny Smith guitar, though both had Bigsby tremolo units. Before the end of the 1990s, John was using two Sony DPS-M7s and his old sunburst Gibson ES 345 with scalloped fretboard when he revisited his Shakti project for 'Remember Shakti'.

A custom guitar was built for John by Mike Sabre around 2003/2004 to allow ease of travel. The instrument, which was unusually shaped with two top 'horns', had a mahogany body and neck, maple centre top and rosewood wings, ebony fretboard compound radiused from 12 in. to 16 in. with 22 frets. The scale length was 24.5 in. and a Johnny Smith mini-humbucker pick-up was fitted, as well as RMC Midi pick-ups for each string at the bridge. Volume and tone controls served the Johnny Smith pick-up and a volume control affected the RMC units.

An instructional music theory DVD set was created by John in 2004 and for this he wanted an interface that scored the notes as he played them. He turned to a Godin LGXT guitar with Midi output to achieve this and began a long-lasting relationship with the company. Later, using Freeway SA and Passion RG2 models, which had a 13-pin and USB output for recoding purposes – John was an early user of Logic software.

By the end of the 2000s, John was touring with a pedalboard and used an MXR chorus and MXR delay, in addition to a Mesa Boogie V-Twin preamp pedal, yet this was later changed to a Seymour Duncan Twin Tube Classic and John has recently added a Zen overdrive.

In 2008 John formed the 4th Dimension and later recorded with the band under the name which included Gary Husband on keyboards and Etienne Mbappé on bass, first with Mark Mondesir on drums, later with Ranjit Barot. The first album was 'To The One' on which John paid tribute to early influence John Coltrane. 'Now Hear This' and 'Black Light' followed in 2012 and 2015 respectively. Around 2010, John began using PRS guitars and first had a dark amber example with flametop and custom inlays. Later, another PRS guitar was built for John featuring the New York skyline inlaid on the fretboard, whilst a Doubleneck was manufactured for John's farewell American tour in 2017. This was auctioned after the tour concluded to raise money for musical therapy helping traumatised children.

Tony McPhee, April 18, 2010.
Courtesy Alexander Kretz (alaksey).

TONY MCPHEE

Tony McPhee was a rare commodity – an incredibly adventurous lead guitarist who could pen amazing songs as well as engineer and produce them. Not many guitarists boasted these talents. In a forward to Martin Hanson's *Hoggin' the Page: The Groundhogs' Classic Years* (1988), the Damned's Captain Sensible loudly proclaims Tony was 'the British Hendrix.' Some accolade indeed and not without some foundation many would argue. Tony inspired such diverse bands as the Fall, the Datsuns and Queens of the Stone Age to play his material on stage or on record.

Born March 23, 1944, in Humberston, Lincolnshire – though moving a little later with his family to Tooting, South London – Tony started to unleash his guitar virtuosity on the world at 14, when he obtained an acoustic instrument. This was a Telesforo Julve Spanish guitar bought by his mother as a Christmas present from Taborns music store in Tooting.

Following a visit to the WEM music shop in Clapham South, Tony discovered the electric strings on the Telesforo needed to be replaced by nylon ones otherwise the bridge might be damaged. But, a little later, keen to amplify the guitar, he swapped back to electric strings, attaching throat microphones to the guitar bridge. An old valve radio was used as an amplifier and Tony was surprised and elated when he heard the results. Said Tony: 'My guitar teacher, Sam Weller in Clapham, thought the Telesforo played better than his guitar which was about 100 years old. My brother Sam ended up with it, but I don't know what happened to it afterwards.'

Whilst Tony had been impressed with the electric guitar sound heard on Bill Haley's 'Rock Around The Clock' in 1955, he was completely mesmerised a year later when his ears were assaulted by Scotty Moore's two electric guitar breaks on 'Hound Dog'.

Tony was captivated by the earthy and energetic Lonnie Donegan and the hugely talented Buddy Holly. He welcomed hearing blues recordings by Alan Lomax in 1959 and this, he admits, was life-changing.

The guitar lessons with Sam Weller only lasted for a short period then Tony began to attentively listen and play along to a number of instrumental artists including the Shadows, the Fireballs and the Hunters. 'I learned to tune the guitar by getting the bass note E in tune, using a tuning fork hit on my head, and using the frets to tune up from there. It was standard practice before guitar tuners.'

Tony practised meticulously and his first public performance was in 1959 at an annual school Christmas concert. 'At these early gigs, it was completely acoustic guitars and vocals, no amplification.' The nine-piece band, the 'Worried Nine' eventually slimmed down to a four piece. Tony sought further guitar tuition at a night class at Ensham Girl's School, learning clever chord changes and how music was constructed.

Telesforo Julve was from a family of classical and flamenco guitar builders that produced guitars in Valencia, Spain, from the turn of the 19th century until their factory closed in 1972. This was after decreasing sales in a shrinking market.

Leaving school in 1960, Tony's first job was in a soldering team made up entirely of females, before he moved to Post Office Telephones to become an engineer. At this point he was in a band that eventually became known as the Seneschals and included close friend Dave Wetton.

Tony paid fifty-five guineas (on hire purchase around 1960) for his first coveted electric guitar, The Futurama II. Bought from Selmer's Music Shop, it was brown sunburst with a white scratch plate. 'There were three pick-ups, with a white rocking switch on each one, so if I was unlucky I could turn them all off at the same time. It had a tremolo arm, but I broke it on the way back from buying the guitar so I had to improvise a new one.'

Tony gave the Futurama II to Dave Kelly around 1968.

Tony bought a Selmer Truvoice 30-watt amp around 1961 and from www.vintagehofner.co.uk, we learn: 'Selmer had taken over a small company called RSA in December 1947, and this company had been producing a range of PA amplifiers since 1946 under the RSA and Selmer names. It was therefore easy to expand the RSA production into guitar

Tony McPhee, April 18, 2010.
Courtesy Alexander Kretz (alaksey).

amplification in the mid-1950s with the introduction of such models as the early RSA (non-Selmer) Truvoice Model TV19. The TV19 (Auditorium/Stadium) and TV6 (Popular) model designations on early Selmer Truvoice amps was a throwback from that era.'

Tony purchased a cherry red Gibson SG from Selmer's in 1962 for 173 guineas. 'The guitar had a side action tremolo which I liked and that was different. I admired the Gretsch sound, but was not keen on the Bigsby. I liked the Fender sound but preferred the Gibson overall. It was about the ergonomics rather than the look.'

The early repertoire of Tony's band, the Worried Nine, included material by Buddy Holly, Roy Orbison and Everly Brothers and they grew in stature, playing to larger audiences.

During the early 1960s, Tony frequented London's Marquee club watching amongst others Cyril Davis and his All Stars. Tony turned professional in 1963 and joined another band, Dollar Bills, playing their first gig at the well-known 2i's coffee bar. Performing cover versions of hits by Elvis, Coasters and the Shadows, they travelled around the country. But, as Tony had immersed himself in the blues, particularly the country players of the 1920s and 1930s, the repertoire began to change with the inclusion of numbers by Little Walter, Jimmy Reed, John Lee Hooker.

By 1963, the band changed the name to John Lee's Groundhogs. All the band were listening to blues records acquired from the Swing Shop in Streatham, also frequented by Keith Relf, Eric Clapton and John Mayall. Tony would eventually meet Jo Ann Kelly in the store and, a little later, using his Ampex recorder, taped an EP with her.

At the end of 1963, the band included John Lee (John Cruickshank), Bob Hall, Tony McPhee, Dave Boorman and Pete Cruickshank. In the following year, the band, now playing blues, began to appear at Studio 51, Oxford Street's 100 Club and further afield at Newcastle's Club A Go Go.

During March 1964, the band supported the Animals and Pretty Things at the 100 Club. On May 7, they backed Champion Jack Dupree, Little Walter, and Memphis Slim. In June, Tony received an offer to join Chris Barber's jazz band though turned it down. A good break came in July 1964 when the band assisted John Lee Hooker during the last week of a tour. Hooker said: 'John Lee's Groundhogs are definitely my favourites. They're tremendously nice fellows and very good to work with.' Numbers played included 'Shake It Baby', 'Hi Heel Sneaker', 'Boom Boom', and 'Dimples'.

In 1964, Tony was using the Gibson SG guitar with a banjo string on the top E, loaning a Vox AC30 for the Hooker tour. Said Tony: 'John Lee Hooker influenced me to have my guitar strung over my right shoulder and to forget using a plectrum. This has never stopped and is something I continued for the rest of my career.'

At the end of the short tour, John Lee's Groundhogs signed with Anglo-America, and for another tour with Hooker. By this time, Tony was being described as a 'really great guitarist whose work with a bottleneck has to be heard to be believed.'

The band's pianist, Bob Hall, was replaced by Tom Parker. Appearing on a BBC programme 'Beat Room' on November 9, 1964, with the Kinks, Tony was impressed with Dave Davies's guitar sound – the guitar being plugged into an Elpico amplifier then fed into a Vox AC30.

After the tour, the band made several recordings at Philips Studios in London, and then went on tour with Jimmy Reed. At a blues festival, Tony and fellow band member Pete Cruickshank were both invited by Howlin' Wolf to have a drink back at his hotel where they met Sleepy John Estes and Hubert Sumlin, amongst a big crowd of US blues players.

During 1965, the band made an album with Hooker and this was recorded mostly in first takes by Mickie Most. Whilst released in the States, it did not appear in the UK until 1971. There was a shift in the British music landscape during the mid-1960s with blues being temporarily left behind in favour of Soul music. The band followed, with two people leaving, while Tony, perhaps surprisingly, temporarily accepted the situation and played more rhythm guitar using the Gibson SG pushed through the Selmer Truvoice amp. Starting to write original material, Tony's first song to appear on vinyl, a Soul music influenced number, 'Over You Baby' was the flip side of 'I'll Never Fall In Love Again'.

In the short period that Eric Clapton left John Mayall's Bluesbreakers, Mayall offered Tony the job at £40 a week but it was turned down. In February 1966, Tony played lead – with the Gibson and Selmer – on some tracks for a Champion Jack Dupree album. Eric Clapton also played on the disc, recorded in Denmark Street.

Recording some tracks around June 1966 for Mike Vernon's Purdah label, these showcased Tony as a lead vocalist for the first time. Struggling a little during July 1966, Tony briefly joined the band Truth, then later, Boz and the Boz People. But,

---

Winfield Scott 'Scotty' Moore III (1931–2016) was an American guitarist and recording engineer. He was part of Elvis Presley's band during the first part of the singer's career stretching from 1954 to the beginning of his Hollywood years. In Elvis: The Man and His Music *(1981), Erick Kjeseth states, 'The majority of major guitar players associated with Elvis were Gibson oriented.'*

The Czechs had been producing the guitar (later known as the Futurama), initially at Blatn, from 1955, under the trade name of Resonet and calling the model 'Grazioso' which was designed by a Mr Ruzicka. During 1958/1959, the Selmer company began importing this solid guitar, and they titled it Futurama. With import restrictions in operation in Europe at that time, the Futurama was the nearest one comparable and obtainable, to a USA Fender Stratocaster, this side of the Atlantic. Having three pick-ups it was given the title 'The world's most advanced Electric guitar' and sold for 55 guineas. In 1959 the Futurama Solid Guitar was replaced by the Futurama III manufactured by a different Czechoslovakian company. Later a Futurama II was produced.

he had to temporarily return to permanent employment while launching a part-time band, Herbal Mixture.

Performing Soul numbers, the band signed to Columbia, recording a few tracks over a period in IBC Studios. They adopted a different inventive style, particularly the track 'Machines', released in December 1966 that featured an imaginative guitar solo by Tony. The only guitar effects were provided by a distortion box that Tony (who was keen on electronics) had designed and built into a Vox AC30.

New Musical Express made Herbal Mixture's offering their record of the week. A track that inspired Tony at this time was 'Hey Joe' by Jimi Hendrix. He also played on an Eddie Boyd album and tracks by Champion Jack Dupree. Herbal Mixture folded in Summer 1968 while Tony stepped into the John Dummer Band, appearing on John Peel's 'Top Gear' in July 1968. Guitar solos were shared between Tony and Dave Kelly though Tony left before the release of an album 'Cabal' in January 1969. He signed to Liberty, packed in his day job and launched a new Groundhogs. At this period, the music landscape was switching to blues rock. The band included Tony, Pete Cruickshank (bass), Steve Rye (harmonica) and eventually Ken Pustelnik (drums).

When recording the 'Scratching The Surface' album at Marquee Studios in 1968, Tony wrote two songs for the album and used his Gibson SG and the Vox AC30. In 1969, John Peel loaned Tony £100 via Jo Ann Kelly to buy a Hiwatt PA for a tour. The first time they used it, at a large venue in Bath, the band couldn't be heard as the speakers were wrongly wired. Tony quickly rectified the problem and everything worked fine afterwards.

Tony played on an album by Hapshash and the Coloured Coat, a band that featured psychedelic poster artists Nigel Weymouth and Michael English. Producer Mike Batt said Tony 'played some great stuff.'

Other highlights for the band in 1968 included Tony writing sleeve notes for a Big Joe Williams album, and another link up with John Lee Hooker for a tour, Hooker stating he wouldn't work with anyone else. Early in 1969, the band toured with Champion Jack Dupree, Aynsley Dunbar and Jo Ann Kelly.

The year 1969 marked the period of blues rock in the UK and Tony said at this juncture sticking to blues was restrictive. Steve Rye left the Groundhogs and now, as a three-piece, the band became tighter as a unit and entered a very successful period.

Tony produced a multi-artist blues album, 'I Asked For Water She Gave Me Gasoline' where he appeared on four tracks. The next album, 'Blues Obituary', saw Tony as producer while his guitar style became excitingly varied, perhaps leaning towards a more rock-based sound. Played on the album was a nine-string German Framus guitar that Tony had acquired from a junk shop for £15. 'I played slide on the guitar for one track on "Blues Obituary", "Light Was The Day". Again, it was another guitar I gave away to a friend.'

At the National Jazz and Blues Festival at Plumpton racecourse during August 1969, Tony used his Gibson SG but when playing with a bottleneck switched to a Fender Stratocaster. 'I had acquired two second-hand Strats, one in black and the other in slate-grey. Both got nicked from the back of a van in Bridgend. Eventually, I bought a Tokai from a Shrewsbury music shop as it was less "nickable". Around this period, I was using a 100-watt Laney, which in time was also nicked.'

The Groundhogs' album, 'Thank Christ For The Bomb', was destined to become a classic. Dealing with war and a variety of other subjects, Tony wrote all the songs, and intended them to suggest a mood or feeling. 'My first manager, Roy Fisher, came up with the album title. He was looking for a gimmick. Earlier, John Lennon had proclaimed the Beatles were "more popular than Jesus" which had caused a furore. There was also a lot of concern over the development of the atom bomb. So, putting religious sensibilities and the bomb together "Thank Christ for the Bomb" was certain to attract attention. From this idea, I was inspired to write songs with themes of war. I found the stories of the First World War more resonant and felt compelled to proclaim injustice.'

The second theme of the album is more personal. At the time, Tony was living in a one-room flat in south Kensington with his partner Christine. 'Looking out of a window at the overgrown garden inspired one song. My outsider, eccentric persona, whether real or imagined, produced the others. I would sit by a window with a Harmony acoustic guitar, noodling and looking for riffs. If I found one, I would have to play it over and over again to remember it because I had no recording equipment at home. I always found writing lyrics harder than composing music. I used a variety of inspirations, including incidents from real life. When I admonished two old women for being racist to a bus driver, I was told to "get the lice out of my long hair." I developed that incident into a song lyric. Mostly, the lyrics and riffs were all in my head, refining them as I played the songs over and over again. Some may have been written down on a scrap of paper or in an old exercise book.'

On the track, 'Soldier', Tony employed a finger-picking style of playing, explaining: 'I feel I have an advantage with my pick style because if you play with a plectrum, it will always sound staccato. Playing with your fingers, you can use the thumb, the nail or even the fingertip and this gives you more tones. Also, finger-picking is cheap, you don't have to buy picks. And, your

---

www.gibson.com states: 'With its streamlined mahogany body and sharply pointed offset double cutaways, the SG Standard is still a radical-looking instrument today. So just imagine how it must have appeared back in 1961 when it rolled out of the factory, originally as the entirely revised Les Paul model. The new instrument was a bold design for Gibson back in the day, and it's a bold performer [57] years later.'

The Fender Stratocaster, a double-cutaway guitar, was designed in America by Leo Fender and others. It first appeared in 1954 and was the first guitar to feature: three pick-ups; a spring tension vibrato system; and a contoured body.

Tony McPhee playing at The Ferry in Glasgow on Sunday June 10, 2012.
Photograph by Norman Smart.

fingers are nearer to the strings so you don't have to move your hand around as much.'

'Thank Christ For The Bomb', recorded at De Lane Lea Studios, was completely divorced from the blues as Tony confirms: 'Yes, "Blues Obituary" had been the album to mark this departure. I was trying to develop my own style, away from the formulaic ideas and restrictions of three-chord blues.'

Tony had all the album material written before the band went into the studio and there was a different approach to the music. 'I worked out the bass lines for the songs and then showed them to Pete Cruickshank. I wanted something more complex to harmonise with my riffs. If the riff started in F#, the bass would start in E, to produce a different sound to what everybody else was playing at that period. I wanted instruments playing different notes at the same time, harmonising rather than just being rhythmic.'

The Groundhogs appeared on 'Disco 2' and John Peel's 'In Concert' series. For John Peel's show, Tony used his Gibson SG, played probably, he says, through Marshall amps. The bass player had an EB3 pushed through bass cabs built by Tony. John Peel liked 'Thank Christ For The Bomb' and following release in June 1970, he regularly played tracks. This helped it to sell, peaking at no. 9. In reviewing the album, *Melody Maker* praised Tony's ability, stating: 'He [is] one of the most original and calculating guitarists in Britain.'

Amongst a number of festivals, played by the Groundhogs at home and abroad during 1970 was the Folk, Blues and Jazz Festival held at Krumlin near Halifax. Tony and Pete (the bass player) played through 100-watt Hiwatt stacks provided by the festival organisers. A photograph from the festival was used inside the double cover of the album 'Split'. Tony has a white Fender Stratocaster which he had borrowed from future brother-in-law Daryl Payne. Tony said the c.1960 Fender Strat, with a rosewood board, worked better on some tracks than the Gibson.

At Krumlin, it was said, 'Tony McPhee's heavy bluesy material went down well.' The Groundhogs also played favourably at the Isle of Wight Festival on the Thursday before the mayhem of subsequent days. Tony married his partner Christine in September 1970; unique guitar-maker Tony Zemaitis, a friend of Jo Ann Kelly, was a witness. In the middle of 1970, Tony had experienced a 'mental aberration' during a very hot day and after trying cannabis for the second time (the first time having produced no effect). The 'aberration' was probably due a

Tony McPhee, September 3, 2011.
Courtesy Jeremy Stewardson.

Tony McPhee playing at the Pacific Arts Centre, Birkenhead, February 26, 2006.
Photograph by Tony Sherratt.

mixture of heat stroke and a bad reaction to cannabis. He never experimented with the drug again.

Nonetheless, a door was opened in his mind, creating 'Split – Parts One To Four' for the new album 'Split'. Some fans may argue that these tracks are not only some of the best ever produced by the band, but also amongst the best in the ever-fickle rock landscape.

'Split' was completed in a couple of weeks and on some tracks featured double-tracked guitars. Tony acquired a Wah-Wah pedal just after 'Thank Christ For The Bomb', and this is used to remarkable effect on 'Split – Part Two'. Tony was a great Hendrix fan, particularly admiring the 'Machine Gun' track. 'It was a Schaller Wah-Wah and it was nicked during the 1970s from the Newcastle City Hall stage. Even though everybody was searched on the way out, it was never found.'

Opening 'Split' side 2 is 'Cherry Red' – also destined to become a classic – and was recorded in one take. For this track Tony used his Gibson SG, a Laney 100-watt amplifier, and a Dallas Arbiter Add-a-Sound with Tony's own distortion pedal wired inside. In the past, Tony had used both Marshall and Hiwatt amps. The Marshall was a 50-watt amplifier with two built-in cabinet speakers. By the end of March 1971, he had switched to Laney. 'There's not much to choose between makes, though this Laney stuff gave out what it claimed to do and was OK. I especially liked the LA 100BL. I've made some alterations to improve the tone because I'm interested in a good sound as well as volume.'

Tony commissioned Tony Zemaitis to make a guitar for him. It was the first one the guitar maker had produced with a metal front and it cost Tony £175. Tony played the guitar on a 'Top of the Pops' performance of 'Cherry Red'. Tony Zemaitis also made a bass guitar for Groundhogs' bassist Pete Cruickshank.

During 1971, the Groundhogs supported the Rolling Stones for nine shows, playing to large audiences. That year saw 'Split' reach no. 5, but the album was plagued with pressing and distribution problems. 'They quickly ran out of copies,' informed Tony.

The Groundhogs started recording 'Who Will Save The World?' in December 1971 at De Lane Lea where Tony, as well as playing guitar, used a Mellotron and harmonium. 'The Mellotron was in the studio and had two keyboards. I was told it had been used by the Beatles. I had first come across the Mellotron at De Lane Lea and hadn't really played much keyboard but as it was there, I experimented. I would often take advantage of whatever was lying around in studios, hence the cow bell at the beginning of "Cherry Red". I thought a Mellotron would be useful in addition to the guitar as an extra instrument so bought one. I discovered it was crap, the springs that pulled the tape down kept getting stuck and I had to free them up by hand all the time, so it got sold.'

On the 'Who Will Save The World?' album, Tony used his Gibson SG and a 15-watt Quad amplifier. For effects, he employed an Astronic Equaliser. The band never really played many of the tracks live though the album reached no. 9. Tony was not satisfied with 'Who Will Save The World?', as he was touring so much and didn't have time to work fully on the songs.

Surprisingly, given the band's high regard amongst fans, the Groundhogs undertook their one and only American tour in 1972. They played at the Poconos Music Festival with Humble Pie and Black Sabbath in front of 200,000. Tony took with him two large Laney cabinets, a Gibson SG and Strat. Unfortunately, the Groundhogs' tour was cut short after Tony broke his wrist.

During the summer of 1972, Wilf Pine became the Groundhogs' manager and drummer Ken Pustelnik was sacked and replaced by Clive Brooks. Tony had his arm in plaster for three months and wrote the new Groundhogs album, 'Hogwash', with the help of a Mellotron; Martin Rushent was the producer. One track on the album '3744 James Road' became another band anthem. With his right hand, Tony plucked the root notes (A and D) with his thumb and used the index and middle finger to play the riff.

To be heard on 'Hogwash' was a Mellotron, ARP synthesizer as well as a Yamaha acoustic, Gibson SG and the Zemaitis. Tony removed the Gibson SG's side Vibrola and scratch plate to fit instruments that controlled external effects. A tour in November and December 1972 following the release of the album – praised by *New Musical Express* – included Tony playing Mellotron, synthesizer and guitar, and with him undertaking some of the technical work. A year later Tony bought equipment from De Lane Lea studios transferring it to his home at Haverhill.

He appeared as a solo artist on the 'Old Grey Whistle Test' in April 1973 and around the same time released a solo album 'Two Sides Of Tony (T.S.) McPhee'. He attempted to play all the required instruments himself but as he could not play drums used a Bentley Rhythm Ace drum machine. He produced and engineered the album. This was followed up with a solo tour which saw him playing guitars for an hour, then an hour of keyboards, ARPs and an RMI electric piano.

Said Tony: 'We had played with Edgar Winter on the US tour and listening to him got me into keyboards. Our manager, Wilf Pine had previously suggested that I do an album with blues on one side and electronic on the other. That's how I started working on the "Two Sides Of Tony (T.S.) McPhee".'

The follow-up to 'Hogwash' was 'Solid', recorded at Tony's studio and showcased further use of a Synthi Hi Fli and Mellotron; he also played bass on the album. A Groundhogs tour was started in November 1973 and an equipment list (with values) for the band included the following for Tony: 1, Mellotron and volume pedal (£600); 3, ARP 2600 synthesizers (£3,000); 3, ARP keyboards (£600); 1, Schaller Wah-Wah pedal (£15); 1, Dallas Arbiter octave splitter (£35); 1, phaser (£400); 1, Synth(i) Hi Fli and pedals (£300); 1, Swiss echo and pedal (£150); 1, Gibson SG 6-string guitar (£200); 2, Fender Stratocaster (£400); 1, Zemaitis 6-string guitar (£250); 1, Fender Mustang 6-string guitar (£100); 1, Harmony Regal Acoustic guitar (£70); 1, Yamaha acoustic guitar (£50). Amps the band used on stage included 10 Quad 303s with a total output of 900 watts, controlled by an Alice mixer desk.

During 1974, the band and their management had a feud with *Melody Maker* over poor reporting whilst there were encouraging reviews from *New Musical Express* and *Disc*. In the following year the band left World Wide Artists and disbanded in 1975.

From April 1975, Tony envisaged having a solo career like Rory Gallagher, recording a new solo album and then going out on tour with a new band. Instead, he turned to reforming Groundhogs with drums, bass, and a second guitar. He was told by a Chrysalis executive, that he wouldn't get any gigs under his own name.

The band went into Tony's home studio and recorded 'Crosscut Saw'. New guitarist Dave Wellbelove took a solo break on several tracks. He used a Fender guitar and amplifier. Tony thought the amplifier so piercing that he couldn't walk in front of it. He called Dave's guitar the 'Immaculate Conception'; Dave was always polishing it.

Tony had a very workman-like attitude to his guitars, considering them mere tools. He rarely found a guitar that could accomplish everything he wanted it to do so, using his electronic skills, he would move, add, remove switches

> The Wah-Wah effect can be traced back to the 1920s, with trumpet or trombone players discovering they could produce an expressive crying tone by moving a mute in and out of the instrument's bell. Bradley J. Plunkett at Warwick Electronics Inc. created the first electronic Wah-Wah pedal, though similar effects had been used in the 1950s by Chet Atkins, Peter Van Wood and Big Jim Sullivan.

> Lyndon Laney founded Laney Amplification in 1967 and built the first amp in his father's garage. One of his first sales was to Black Sabbath's Tony Iommi and manufacturing was carried out in Birmingham's Digbeth area but later settled in Cradley Heath, before moving to Halesowen.

and effects as he felt necessary. He thought having a second guitarist was 'handy', as it left him to concentrate on his solos. Generally, he liked Dave's guitar work, although sometimes he felt it could be a bit 'sweet'.

Whilst there is a snatch of synth heard on 'Crosscut Saw', it is basically a guitar album. Promotion was via a 30-date tour between February and March 1976. This came after Tony had been off the road for almost a year.

The band appeared on 'Old Grey Whistle Test' with Tony using a cordless guitar, fixed with a transmitter – originally bought for his solo tour. This had enabled him to play guitar and move from one keyboard to another. 'I had a BBC transmitter which I worked mostly with the Gibson SG, but could be used with others. A jack from the guitar fed to a transmitter in my back pocket. There was a receiver, on the floor by my feet, connected to a 50-watt Marshall amp.'

The 1976 tour featured Dave Wellbelove on a few solos and the band's performances were recorded but not released until years later as 'Groundhogs Live In 1976'. Disappointingly, press reaction to the Groundhogs was proving a problem as music journalists were rejecting bands from the 1960s and championing Punk instead.

The year 1976 was eventful both musically and personally for Tony. His long track 'The Hunt', from the solo album 'Two Sides Of Tony (T.S.) McPhee', was featured on BBC's 'Open Door' in a documentary on the fledgling Hunt Saboteurs. He dropped the Mellotron but still used an ARP synthesizer; he split with wife Christine, took up with Sue; and switched to using Orange Amps. Dave, the guitarist, left and in came Rick Adams.

The Groundhogs' follow-up to 'Crosscut Saw' was 'Black Diamond' recorded at Tony's home studio. The 'Black Diamond' cover featured photography by Gered Mankowitz. With the advent of Punk, the album received poor reviews and the Groundhogs folded in 1977. Tony formed new bands Terraplane, Turbo and eventually the Tony McPhee Blues Band. 'The same old equipment was used, Gibson SG, sometimes the Strat, a Marshall 50-watt amp and various Wah-Wah pedals.'

When 'Hoggin The Stage', a live album, was released 1984, this encouraged Tony to bring back the Groundhogs. During a tour in Scotland, the much-loved Gibson SG, which had guided Tony through many of his successful years, was stolen.

'I lost the SG in Irvine. It had been packed away after the gig and one of the roadies decided to take it out to have a play, leaving it unattended in the dressing room. If it had been in the van, it would have been safer because the vehicle was put in a lock up. I have never given up hope that one day it will be "found". I've even written a song, using the serial number 54146 as the title.'

Albums which followed included 'Razor's Edge' then 'Back Against The Wall' – the last album of original Groundhogs material recorded.

'Razor's Edge' was recorded in 1984 at Alaska Studios, in London. Having been eight years since the previous original album, Tony had been persuaded by various people that it was time to get back into the studio. He was still using the Gibson SG, as well as a Fender Mustang, and a Marshall 50-watt combo. The albums came together following Tony's usual style of producing numbers as the demand arose. He liked the phrases 'I Confess' & 'Razor's Edge' and wrote songs to fit.

'Back Against The Wall' in 1986 featured Dave Anderson, an original Hawkwind bassist, and Mick Jones on drums, the trio forming the longest-lived touring line-up of the Groundhogs. Recorded at Dave's studio for his Demi-Monde label, the album contained classic dark lyrics and a homage to Tony's stolen Gibson SG. Tony played a Gibson SG loaned from the roadie who was responsible for the original one being stolen; the loaned SG was later stolen in Tamworth. Other gear included a Marshall 50-watt combo, a Guild 20-watt circa 1958, Selmer TV12, Tokai Stratocaster, Yamaha acoustic FG180, Boss Super Overdrive, and Chorus, Ibanez analogue delay, Cry Baby Wah-Wah, and Rotosound Strings, all nicely listed on the back of the album.

As a solo artist in the early 1990s, Tony recorded 'Foolish Pride' then 'Slide TS Slide'. He also toured Europe opening for Jefferson Starship playing a Yamaha acoustic through the PA.

Tony suffered his first stroke in 1993 and mostly recovered. Solo albums and a temporary reforming of the classic line-up of Groundhogs followed. The band appeared at a Punk Aid concert, 'Beautiful Days Festival' and toured for 18 months. After that, Tony played acoustic blues on tour with Alvin Lee and Edgar Winter.

Tony had further strokes in 2001, 2009 and again in December 2018. The third stroke in 2009 reduced his dexterity and took his speech, giving him severe, persisting dysarthria, which affects the mouth muscles and tongue. Joanna Deacon took over vocals, leaving Tony to concentrate on guitar playing. He retired from playing live in 2014 after a gig at Skegness Rock & Blues Festival. Tony passed away in June 2023.

Tony Zemaitis (1935–2002) was born in London and began his working life as a cabinet maker before turning to guitar building after his National Service in 1957. From the early 1960s, a number of leading guitarists began buying his guitars. In 1970, he introduced metal shields on guitar tops as an attempt to eliminate microphonic noise gathered by a guitar's pick-ups. Tony Zemaitis's first metal top prototype was acquired by Tony McPhee; Ronnie Wood had the second. Gun engraver Danny O'Brien produced and undertook designs on the tops and other metal parts.

Described as an electro-mechanical, polyphonic tape replay keyboard, the Mellotron was originally developed and built in Birmingham, in 1963. It was manufactured by Bradmatic/Mellotronics (1963–1970) and Streetly Electronics (1970–1986, 2007–present). The Mellotron worked by pulling a section of magnetic tape across a head. Different portions of the tape could be played to access different sounds. The instrument became more popular after usage by the Beatles.

MICKY MOODY

When young lads show an interest in a subject that could lead to a successful career, dads usually give their wholehearted support. This was the case when Micky Moody decided he wanted to be a guitarist.

'When I was 12 years old in 1962, I cajoled my dad, a Middlesbrough Dorman and Long steel erector, to buy me a guitar. I wanted an electric one, something like a Rossetti Lucky 7 that could be bought mail order from a Bell's Musical Instruments Ltd catalogue. Dad said: "No, when you learn to play, I'll buy you a proper guitar".'

Micky's interest in guitars started after his parents took him to a pantomime at the Globe Theatre in Stockton in 1959 where Cliff Richard and the Shadows were starring in 'Babes in the Wood'. At the end of the show, the Shadows did a set which left a deep impression on Micky.

'I've talked about the gig to Bruce Welch who had an uncle in Stockton. I said that sparked me off to become a guitarist. My sister had a couple of the Shadows singles, "Wonderful Land" and "Man of Mystery".' There were no musicians in Micky's family. His sister tinkered with playing piano but did not persevere and it was eventually sold. 'I was told my paternal grandfather had the only German accordion in Middlesbrough. Whether he could play it or not, I don't know.'

To buy a guitar, Micky and his father went to Greenwood's, a local pawn shop. Micky was attracted to a Watkins Rapier instrument but his dad asked the shop assistant: 'What have you got for a couple of quid?' He held up an acoustic with an incredibly high action and that was purchased for £2 10s (£2.50p).

To try and make sense of playing the guitar, Micky acquired *The Complete Guitar Method* by Dick Sadler and struggled to tune the instrument via pitch pipes. Making little progress, a tutor was sought. On Sunday nights, Micky's parents spent some time at a local club. They saw Johnny Goffin, the guitar-playing half of that night's act, and asked him if he gave guitar lessons. Confirming that he did, Micky began lessons with him at his house in South Bank. Each lesson, lasting about an hour, cost 6s (30p) and a guitar book, Mel Bay's *Modern Guitar Method*, was acquired for 8s (40p).

Johnny Goffin played a jazz, big-bodied guitar and he used that to tune Micky's instrument. 'I found it difficult to press the strings down but managed to play the Shadows' "Apache" on one string, the top E.' After two weeks, Micky was ready to quit but his dad persuaded him otherwise. Goffin was not a full-time professional teacher, working during the daytime at an ICI plant. He had other pupils, and was established as a teacher. Micky does not remember many other guitar teachers around in the area at that time.

Initially, Goffin didn't show Micky how to play chords, that came later. He had to learn the notes on every string, then he was set little tunes like 'Little Brown Jug', and taught exercises such as the Diminished scale. Micky changed his guitar strings when Goffin told him they were 'dead'. Strings were purchased from Hamilton's Music Store at 45 Corporation Road, Middlesbrough. The store sold pianos and musical instruments upstairs and accessories, and records downstairs. There were cards in the downstairs window advertising local bands and Micky dreamed of being in there one day.

Mel Bay (1913–1997) was a musician and publisher. Whilst playing guitar, Bay began writing instructional books due to the difficulty encountered by budding guitarists in playing chord forms in rhythm sections, and the poor note-reading ability prevalent among guitarists at that time. These books became the basis of the Mel Bay instructional method and the Mel Bay publication house. Guitar Player *magazine called him 'the George Washington of the guitar'. Sales of his* Modern Guitar Method *are estimated to be more than 20 million copies. Bay established the structure for modern guitar and helped increase the guitar's popularity.*

Goffin taught Micky how to count and play in time, but he hated the exercises. To Micky it was like maths and he hated the subject at school. He persevered with his 'starter' guitar, playing with all fingers and using a plectrum. Goffin told him off for playing with his thumb over the bottom string. Then, the elder man said it was time to progress to another guitar.

Micky's dad was called upon to help purchase a Harmony Roy Smeck electric guitar. 'It was advertised in a local paper for £42, and my dad gave me £40. When I tuned up with it at Johnny Goffin's, he was impressed.

Micky was ignorant about how electric guitars functioned. 'I thought they were plugged into a wall socket and the sound came out of the pick-ups.' Shortly afterwards his dad bought him a Harmony amplifier from an advert in a local newspaper. 'My dad's mate, Micky Lynch, an electrician, went with me to test it out. It was all valve and about 20-watt.'

At school, Micky was friendly with Paul Rodgers (later of Free and Bad Company) and Colin Bradley. Along with two others, they formed a band, initially titled the 'Titans', then 'Intrepid' until 'Roadrunners' was settled upon after Bo Diddley's song 'I'm A Roadrunner Baby'. Paul Rodgers had an acoustic guitar, but eventually played bass while Colin had a Hofner Congress cello-bodied guitar and boasted knowing a number of chords. Several drummers also passed through the lifespan of the Roadrunners. Colin's elder brother, Joe, drove them to gigs around the local club circuit in Middlesbrough, Stockton and Hartlepool, and generally helped them out. They scraped through contemporary hits such as the Beatles' 'Can't Buy Me Love' and the Stones' 'Not Fade Away'.

Between 1963 and 1965, Micky would attend lessons with Goffin and learn to read music. 'I wanted to play beat group music and found the lessons tedious to say the least, playing

Micky Moody on the stage at the Bock auf Rock - Norstedt Festival with a Tokai Stratocaster August 28, 1993.
dpa picture alliance / Alamy Stock Photo.

"Little Brown Jug" over and over again.' Nonetheless, he persevered and grasped an elementary understanding of the guitar, and his talents developed from there. There was no criticism from Micky's schoolmates about him playing guitar in a band, in fact everyone thought it was 'hip'.

Needing more volume, Micky replaced the Harmony amp with a Pick-a-Bass in turquoise, bought by his dad from Hamilton's music shop. 'Yes, it was a bass amp but that's all Dad could afford. I liked its appearance. It was turquoise – an American Cadillac colour.'

For Micky's next guitar, his dad said he would lend him £100, so off they went to Burdon's in Stockton. Moody snr also added that if Micky didn't progress, he would take the guitar back to the shop and ask for a refund. 'I wanted a Gibson Les Paul SG but settled on a Harmony H78 with three pick-ups and a Bigsby.'

Micky was consciously making a study of lead guitarists and thanks to a tip from a guitarist in a band from Oldham stopped using heavy gauge strings. 'The band members were a bit older than us and their guitarist said I reminded him of Eric Clapton on the album "Five Live Yardbirds". Then he said, "Let me give you a piece of advice, try using a plain third instead of a wound third." I did and after that my fingers thought they were on holiday. I'm forever grateful to that guy.'

During the mid-1960s, Micky saw a number of shows in the North East featuring Chuck Berry, the Stones and Long John Baldry. On Thursday April 7, 1966, Micky saw Eric Clapton with John Mayall's Bluesbreakers at Billingham KD club. 'It was just before the Bluesbreakers album came out on July 22, 1966. Eric was in the same clothes that he was later seen wearing on the album cover – fur coat, Levi jeans, but with spats over his boots. Watching the equipment being unloaded we thought they were bringing a wardrobe into the venue as we'd never seen Marshall stacks before. All the local guitarists turned out to see "God" as he was known at that time.'

Micky left school at 14 at the end of July 1965; he wasn't 15 until August 30. He hated school and on leaving took an apprenticeship as a mechanic then as a heating engineer but these jobs only lasted a few weeks. 'I walked out of both of them and my dad went ballistic. Eventually, I think Mum and Dad realised I wanted to try and make it as a musician.'

One of the Roadrunners' drummers introduced the rest of the band to Muddy Waters and Howlin' Wolf. 'You can imagine what we sounded and looked like. We wore nice white shirts and sang old blues numbers in high adolescent squeaky voices.'

Micky was lead guitarist with the Roadrunners, his influences arising from around 1961 when he went to the local Woolworths' record department and listened to instrumentals by Johnny and the Hurricanes, especially 'Walk Don't Run'. Guitarist, Dave Yorko was a major influence as well as the lead guitar work of Chuck Berry, the Rolling Stones and George Harrison.

For a brief period, Micky had a Gibson ES 345 paid for by some cash left to him by his grandmother. Unfortunately, the HP payments had not been made by a previous owner. 'My dad was furious when he found out. I'd made the deal without him knowing. This did not stop him retrieving the cash from the unscrupulous seller, a local cafe proprietor.'

Goffin was not impressed learning that Micky was in a band. 'He scoffed when I showed him some Chuck Berry licks, saying: "What's that, Chinese?" He didn't want to know and I said to myself, right I'm out of here. By the time I quit, I could read music, but never felt very comfortable. My timing was OK.'

In July 1966, the Roadrunners attended the Windsor Jazz and Blues Festival, seeing Cream (before the three musicians performed under that name). The Roadrunners travelled down in a converted van with bunks, driven by Joe Bradley; his wife also went along.

Micky Moody when in Wildflowers with Telecaster in Finsbury Park, London, 1967.
Micky Moody collection.

'We went to Ivor Mairants Music Centre in Rathbone Place and I bought a Telecaster. I loved those guitars after seeing Steve Cropper and Jeff Beck playing them. The guitar cost £124 but I couldn't have it until the following week after my dad had signed the HP forms. Why we made another trip to London a week later instead of buying the same guitar in Middlesbrough I don't know.'

Micky played the guitar through a Gibson Varitone amp. A little later with his dad's help once again, he acquired a 50-watt Marshall head and a 4x12 in. cabinet. 'God bless my dad. He often said: "I'm not made of money you know." It was great that he had faith in me. With my mum, he came to watch us occasionally in local clubs, but we were a bit loud for them playing, amongst other things, rocked up Soul numbers. They were more used to the Bachelors. Sometimes we wore gangster suits wanting to copy the Move and pulled a few stunts in front of an audience.'

The Roadrunners moved to London in 1967 amidst Flower Power and Kaftans, changing their name, perhaps appropriately, to the Wildflowers. 'We passed an agency audition but didn't get many gigs. Paul Kossoff was working in Selmer's and we became friends. Sometimes he let me play his 1959 Les Paul.'

Frustrated with the situation in London, Micky moved back to the North East, taking a job in a Millets store. That didn't last long, and he signed on, his parents exclaiming: 'Whatever.'

Micky sold his Marshall amp and Fender Telecaster, buying a second-hand Telecaster with a humbucker. His dad didn't understand that logic. He also bought a cheap classical guitar, a Giannini from Hamilton's music store, after listening to Andres Segovia on the radio. He took classical lessons from a local teacher in Stockton called Gladys Kirkham. 'I got into acoustic blues like Robert Johnson's material and became fascinated with slide and open tunings.'

A friend in the North East, vocalist John McCoy, wanted to put a band together, Tramline, and Micky was recruited. He used the old Telecaster and played through an Impact 100 stack.

The Pick-A-Back and Pick-A-Bass were WEM's first "piggy-back" units, introduced circa 1963 during the transitional Watkins to WEM period. The 14-watt valve head seems to have been an early version of the ER15, although it is not marked as such. Two inputs, two channels, each with volume, bass and treble controls. The head was common to both models: the cabs bore the model name, and the Pick-A-Back had 2x10 speakers as opposed to the single 12" unit in the Pick-A-Bass.

Tramline was described as a hard-rocking, blues-based quartet and in 1968 Chris Blackwell signed them to his Island label. Their first album 'Somewhere Down The Line' was produced by Blackwell and they received some exposure on John Peel's 'Top Gear'. A second album, 'Moves Of Vegetable Centuries' was recorded and the band was featured on the Island sampler 'You Can All Join In'.

Micky recalled, 'Tramline did the Reading Festival on August 12, 1968 and we were on the same bill as Traffic, Spencer Davis, John Mayall, Fairport Convention and Jethro Tull. We also drove down from Middlesbrough to play for £15 at the Marquee. Once we appeared with Ten Years After. One of the tracks, "Mazurka", on the Tramline first album I helped to write. It was in 6/8 time and inspired by a Segovia track on an album of the classical guitarist's Paul Kossoff had swapped me for a BB King LP.'

On Tramline's demise, around 1969, Micky saw an advert placed by Lucas and the Mike Cotton Sound, a top Soul band. They wanted a lead guitarist and Micky was invited for an audition. Other guitarists considered were Dave O'List formerly of the Nice and Jimmy Roache who played for a short time with Jon Hiseman's Colosseum.

'I got the job. I knew many Soul numbers and within two weeks I was on a package tour, backing Gene Pitney. Amongst the places we played were the Batley Variety Club and the Showboat Club in Middlesbrough. I must admit I found it a little unnerving hearing all these women screaming at us.'

In this band, Micky played a Telecaster, through the Impact head but with only one cab. One of the roadies said he didn't need two cabs when playing in a Soul band. Micky bought his first Cry Baby Wah-Wah pedal in 1969.

After the Mike Cotton Sound, Micky teamed up with Zoot Money for a few months, then joined Juicy Lucy along with vocalist Paul Williams in a revamped line-up.

'Just before joining this band, I turned down the chance of buying Robin Trower's Les Paul for £300, but once in Juicy Lucy I played my Telecaster for a while then part-exchanged it for a Les Paul Deluxe Gold Top.'

The Juicy Lucy line-up included steel guitarist Glen Ross Campbell, formerly of the cult band, the Misunderstood, who were championed by John Peel. 'I was a fan of his then suddenly I'm in a band with him. He helped me develop a slide style. At this period, I was influenced a lot by Freddie King, Ry Cooder and Bill Harkleroad (Zoot Horn Rollo in Captain Beefheart's Magic Band). I loved the slide guitar on the track "Big Eyed Beans From Venus" on Captain Beefheart's album "Clear Spot". In Juicy Lucy, I mainly played rhythm but sometimes was given a lead part. Eventually, I swapped the Gibson Les Paul Deluxe for a Gibson SG Standard and played through a 50-watt Marshall. Then I swapped the SG for a Gibson ES 335. This was after seeing Henry McCullough playing one.'

Following on from the JTM-45 (1963–1964), JTM-45 Mark II (1965–1966), Bluesbreaker Combos Models 1961 and 1962 (1964/1965 to 1972), 18-watt combos (1965), Marshall Amplification began introducing their first 50- and 100-watt amplifiers from 1966. The new JTM 50 amplifier featured EL 34 power tubes (instead of KT66s), producing a higher output but requiring a larger output transformer. This rendered a brighter, louder sound. Amplifiers from this period are easily identifiable by their Plexiglass front panel, earning them the nickname 'Plexi'.

Before the demise of Juicy Lucy, where Micky made contributions to three albums, he played as a session musician on Bobby Harrison's solo album. Bobby was one-time vocalist and drummer with Procol Harum and also a member of Freedom. The collaboration between the two led to the formation of Snafu, playing American-inspired funk and R&B-flavoured rock. The name Snafu came from a line in the TV series 'The Phil Silvers Show'; Captain Beefheart also mentions Snafu in the song 'Big Eyed Beans From Venus'.

Micky made three albums with Snafu, played on Graham Bonnet and Gerry Rafferty albums and performed in Status Quo drummer John Coghlan's band, Diesel. 'John Coghlan wanted to do something a bit different to Quo. Included in the band were John Fiddler from Medicine Head, Gordon Edwards a keyboard player from the Pretty Things and, sometimes, Rick Parfitt joined the line-up.'

In Snafu's performance on the pop programme 'Supersonic', Micky has a Gibson ES 335. He made writing contributions to the band as well as playing guitar and mandolin. In 1976, David Coverdale, then with Deep Purple, saw Micky at a Snafu gig, told him he didn't think Purple would last much longer and was planning a solo album. Did he want to play guitar? 'I told him I was no Ritchie Blackmore or Tommy Bolin. At the time I was into Ry Cooder and Little Feat.'

Micky appeared on David Coverdale's two solo albums. On the first one 'White Snake', recorded in London and Munich, and released on February 9, 1977, he co-wrote four of the nine tracks and contributed guitars (slide and Wah-Wah), percussion and backing vocals. On the second, 'Northwinds', recorded in London and released on March 1, 1978, he co-wrote three of the eight tracks, playing guitars and adding backing vocals.

'My contribution to the writing included devising chord sequences. I didn't write out the music, I just used a tape recorder to put down the ideas. Sometimes David would bring words and chords and then there would be a discussion about where we were heading with the song. Riffs have always been a part of my playing. Sometimes I don't honestly know where they come from. I draw on something else, then develop it in my own way. There are many different ways they come to life.'

On the two solo albums, which reveal a cross section of moods and themes, Micky used two ES 335s – a sunburst and a cherry – and played them through a Fender Tremolux. Following on from the albums, Whitesnake, the band, was formed, where Bernie Marsden and Micky Moody played guitar. For Micky this was his first involvement in the blues rock phenomenon of two lead guitars.

'I suggested having two lead guitars to David. For me, this style started with the Yardbirds in 1966 when Jeff Beck and Jimmy Page played dual lead guitars on the single "Happenings Ten Years Time Ago". It was considered groundbreaking for the time, though I recall it only made a modest showing in the record charts. I, along with many others, was also influenced by the dual guitars of the Allman Brothers especially "At Fillmore East" album.'

The birth of Whitesnake and their first release, an EP 'Snakebite' in June 1978, coincided with domination of Punk. 'What was happening elsewhere in the music scene was never given a second thought. You have to remember that blues rock music continued throughout the Punk period especially with bands like ZZ Top.'

At the end of the 1970s, Micky added guitar on Roger Chapman's first solo album 'Chappo', playing slide on a Dobro. He was present in Whitesnake during the late 1970s and early 1980s for classic albums such as 'Snakebite' (1978); 'Trouble' (1978); 'Live At Hammersmith' (1978); 'Lovehunter' (1979); 'Ready And Willing' (1980); 'Live … In The Heart Of The City' (1980); 'Come And Get It' (1981); 'Saints And Sinners' (1982); 'Slide It In' (1984).

Micky made significant contributions to a number of Whitesnake classics such as 'Love Hunter' and 'Fool For Your Loving'. 'My take on "Fool For Your Loving" is that I was influenced in supplying the main riff by a section in Jimi Hendrix's "Purple Haze".'

For Micky, the Whitesnake sound was not established until the third album. Amongst his guitars used with the band were a 1953 Gibson Gold Top and a 1958 Gibson Les Paul that he bought from Mick Ralphs for £2,000. Micky sold his cherry ES 335 and used Marshall 100-watt amps.

'Whitesnake was great when John Lord and Ian Paice joined, but for me the band had wound its course by 1984 and I left. John Sykes joined in my place; Bernie had left before me. David Coverdale wanted to take the band to a new level in America. To be honest, I'd had enough of being a rock star. I was kind of burnt out.'

In 1985, Micky turned to writing a book with Bob Young, *The Language of Rock 'n' Roll*, revealing life behind the scenes of bands on the road. Later, he would write two more on his own, *Playing with Trumpets: A Rock and Roll Apprenticeship* (2006) and *Snakes and Ladders: My Autobiography: A Rock 'N' Roll Odyssey to Whitesnake* (2016).

In his own words, after the Whitesnake experience, he was somewhat disillusioned with the music business and retreated into a world of normality and low-profile appearances peppered with occasional session work.

By the end of the 1980s, he had put together a three-piece band to play small venues, turned out for some shows with Frankie Miller, then teamed with his old Whitesnake chum, Bernie Marsden to form the Moody Marsden Band. They gigged and recorded a live album, 'Never Turn Your Back On The Blues'.

Micky toured with Chris Farlowe, Roger Chapman and the Shortlist while the Moody Marsden Band would become a fairly regular port of call for him throughout the 1990s. In his choice of guitars, he switched from Gibsons to favour Fender

The Gibson Les Paul Deluxe followed the 'new' 1968 Les Pauls a year later and featured 'mini-humbuckers'. The mini-humbucker pick-up fitted into the pre-carved P-90 pick-up cavity using an adaptor ring developed by Gibson in order to use a surplus supply of Epiphone mini-humbuckers. The first incarnation of the Deluxe featured a one-piece body and a slim three-piece neck. Interest in the Deluxe was indifferent and in 1985, Gibson cancelled it. In 2005, the Deluxe was re-introduced. Micky is seen playing the guitar live in the 1971 film 'Bread'.

Micky Moody (far right) playing his Harmony H78 guitar with the Roadrunners in 1965.
Micky Moody collection.

Micky Moody at the 1977 Reading Festival.
Lebrecht Music.

Stratocasters, but by the time the Moody Marsden outfit came to record its first studio album, he'd acquired a PRS 22-fret, 10-top, though played his 1968 Gibson SG Special for slide work. 'Our Gibson Les Pauls would often trade licks and the Allman Brothers influence would be proudly displayed.'

The 1990s concluded with Micky and Bernie touring and recording together in a band, the Company of Snakes, which would eventually develop into M3, a celebration of Whitesnake songs which also included the latter band's bass player, Neil Murray.

The 21st century began with Micky releasing his first solo album 'I Eat Them For Breakfast' where he handled a selection of guitars, including a 1958 Gibson Les Paul, a 1965 Gibson ES 335, and a 1976 Martin D-28. Not long afterwards, Micky teamed up with his old Juicy Lucy bandmate singer, Paul Williams, to pay tribute to three of his favourite blues artists: Howlin' Wolf, Muddy Waters and Elmore James. They recorded a selection of their songs performed in a laid-back manner, titling the album, 'Smokestacks, Broom Dusters And Hoochie Coochie Men'. On this album, he used a Gibson ES 335 sunburst, a Tokai Strat, a National Resonator guitar and a Martin acoustic.

During the first decade of the 21st century, Micky wrote and produced some library music for television. 'I discovered I had quite a few tunes, both acoustic and electric, that were gathering dust so I decided to put them to good use, recording a couple of instrumental music albums. These appeared as "Acoustic Journeyman" and "Electric Journeyman" and I had a lot of fun making them.'

Micky's final farewell to rock music came in the shape of Snakecharmer, a band which comprised 'established names' on the rock scene. He quit after one album and a round of gigs and festivals, quoting the old adage 'too many cooks spoil the broth.'

'These days I take it easy, and stay at home a lot, still enjoying my music and guitars. I sold my 1958 Les Paul and had a replica made. I have an ES 355 from 1963 with a stopbar tailpiece and sometimes play slide with several of my Flying Finn guitars, hand-made by Matti Nevalainen of Finnish Guitar Works in Tampere, Finland. They are pretty unbeatable.'

'Though reluctant to travel, I currently tread the boards in a band with my wife, singer and artist Ali Maas. I adore playing our style of music, a blend of cool rock, blues, featuring "swampy" rhythms and melodic acoustic tunes. We also stamp our style on some selected Whitesnake classics. I believe I've contributed a lot since my first gig back in 1964. The music never leaves one's soul, it just matures like a fine wine.'

Jimmy Page on stage in Germany in March 1973.
Gijsbert Hanekroot / Alamy Stock Photo.

JIMMY PAGE

In a career spanning well over 50 years, Jimmy Page has influenced countless guitar players, with his memorable riffs, standout solos and low-slung Gibson Les Paul defining rock music for many.

Jimmy became interested in guitar around age 12 and, luckily, a Spanish-style instrument had been left in his home by a former occupant. Initially interested by skiffle music, he soon turned his taste to the rock 'n' roll of Chuck Berry, Elvis and Buddy Holly. Jimmy had lessons for a time, before moving on to learn his favourite songs by ear, particularly solos. Quickly finding an acoustic did not match his ambitions, Jimmy worked a part-time job to afford a Hofner President, which he fitted with a pick-up. Yet, he soon decided he preferred a solid-body guitar and obtained a Grazioso Resonet Futurama. This was made in Czechoslovakia and was heavily influenced by the Fender Stratocaster.

Jimmy soon developed a reputation as a budding guitarist and performed in several local groups. During one gig, when he was in Red E. Lewis and the Redcaps (performing early rock 'n' roll songs), Chris Tidmarsh approached him to join a band. Jimmy accepted and the outfit later became Neil Christian & the Crusaders. For around two years, Jimmy was with the group and in 1962 a single was produced for Columbia – 'Road To Love' b/w 'The Big Beat Drum'.

After playing the club circuit with Neil Christian & the Crusaders, Jimmy decided to further his studies at Art College and left the band, though the lure of playing music proved too strong. At one gig, Jimmy was approached by record producer Mike Leander to work sessions for various new bands. The first was for the Carter Lewis Group on 'Your Momma's Out Of Town' and another early example was 'The Worryin' Kind' by Brian Howard with the Silhouettes. Soon after, Jimmy was involved with former Shadows Jet Harris and Tony Meehan on their single 'Diamonds' playing an acoustic guitar. The single climbed to the top of the UK charts in early 1963.

Jimmy became one of the most in-demand session guitarists and over the next few years played on hundreds of records. These included: Dave Berry, P.J. Proby, Everly Brothers, Paul Anka, Jackie DeShannon, Petula Clark, Them, Lulu, Burt Bacharach, the Kinks and the Who. In *Beat Instrumental No. 28* of August 1965 Jimmy was featured for the first article of a new series on session musicians. He noted that he was working around eight sessions a week and was given the chords for the song but had free reign for solos. His favourites at the time were on 'Money Honey' by Mickie Most and 'Once In A While' by the Brook Brothers. Jimmy had made his first solo record at this point – 'She Just Satisfies' with B-side 'Keep Moving' on Fontana. For these, Jimmy played guitar and bass, also the vocal for both tracks and harmonica on the B-side. A feature of the latter was a fuzz effect. This had been custom-made for Jimmy by Roger Mayer, who was an electronics engineer, employed by the Admiralty and just starting out with instrument effects. The fuzz can also be heard on the Who B-side 'Bald Headed Woman' to the first single 'I Can't Explain', which also had Jimmy playing rhythm guitar.

One of Jimmy's primary guitars for his heavy workload in the session scene was a Gibson Les Paul Custom 'Black Beauty', with Bigsby tremolo, that he purchased during the early 1960s. Talking to *Beat Instrumental No. 41* of September 1966 he explained the origins of the guitar: 'I bought a guitar which went wrong, so I took it back to the shop. They had this Les Paul in the window. I hadn't seen it before, although the bloke in the shop told me that it had been there for quite some time. I thought "this is for me. It looks different and if it's been there for a few weeks not many people can be interested in it".' Jimmy favoured the guitar for several years and mainly used a Burns amplifier (likely a 2x12 in. combo). He also acquired a Danelectro 3021 guitar, used a Harmony Sovereign acoustic and a Vox Phantom XII electric 12-string.

In 1965, Andrew Loog Oldham formed Immediate Records and enlisted Jimmy as a producer. In this role, he worked with John Mayall and the Bluesbreakers (with Eric Clapton) on the single 'I'm Your Witchdoctor', as well as Nico (later of the Velvet Underground) on her first single 'I'm Not Sayin'. Jimmy went on to work with American singer/song-writer Jackie DeShannon, Johnny Hallyday and Donovan for the label.

With several years in the background of the music scene, Jimmy was ready to have a more prominent profile by the mid-1960s. Jeff Beck asked him to join the Yardbirds, and Jimmy jumped at the chance. In an interview with *Beat Instrumental No. 41* of September 1966, Jimmy explained: 'I just helped them [the band] out one night … they had a show on … Jeff asked me if I could stand in and I said I would.' Yet, there was a catch to this – Jimmy had to take over on bass. He said: 'I had an hour's practice, that's all. If the Marquee [gig] had gone badly I would have been worried about the future but, as it happened, I got by OK, and it set me up for future dates.'

Jimmy inherited a sunburst Epiphone Rivoli bass from outgoing Yardbirds bassist Paul Samwell-Smith. He can be seen with the instrument (which is going through a Marshall stack) at a Paris gig during June 1966.

This spell on bass was only to be temporary. Original rhythm guitarist, Chris Dreja was to learn the bass on the upcoming American tour and switch instruments with Jimmy when the band returned to England. When asked if his arrival was to change the Yardbirds' sound, Jimmy was adamant this was not the case, commenting: 'I think that [the sound] will move more to free-form. Mind you, it will be highly organised. The whole thing must be done tastefully otherwise the Yardbirds' sound will be ruined. Jeff and I have had quite a few work-outs round at my place and they have been pretty successful. We have learned a couple of Freddie King solos note by note, and when we play them in unison it sounds good. We'll be doing quite a lot of this sort of thing, playing in unison or in harmony.' Jimmy thought the spell on bass had been a positive influence on his guitar playing: 'I don't think it did me any

Jimmy Page, with Gibson Doubleneck, plays at the ARMS Benefit at Madison Square Garden in New York City, August 12, 1983.
Michael Brito / Alamy Stock Photo.

harm at all. I was becoming very stale [on the guitar]. Once I was back on stage again, even though I was playing bass, I was thinking in terms of a guitar and I found that I was covering new ground. As soon as I got back on the six-stringer … I found that I was doing new things.' Jimmy added some information on his attitude to practice: 'I try things out for practice. But I don't consciously practice, I don't think I could play a scale to save my life.'

Even though Jimmy favoured his Les Paul Custom, he was aware that life on the road could be detrimental to the instrument and decided to play a white 1959 Fender Telecaster with rosewood neck, gifted to him by Jeff Beck. Early footage of him with the guitar was captured when the Yardbirds appeared in the film 'Blow-Up' performing 'Stroll On' (a version of 'Train Kept A-Rollin') using a Vox amplifier. The Telecaster was also likely used on the band's next single 'Happenings Ten Years Time Ago'.

This proved to be the only record released by the Beck-Page line-up of the Yardbirds as the former left the group in the midst of an American tour at the end of 1966. A change in management occurred in early 1967 as Peter Grant replaced Simon Napier-Bell and Mickie Most was brought in as producer. The first track recorded was 'Little Games' which was not a group composition. Aimed at a mainstream audience, the song failed to attract attention when released in April; the B-side 'Puzzles' features an impressive outro solo from Jimmy. The Yardbirds continued to record in early 1967, assembling a number of eclectic tracks for the album 'Little Games' released only in America during July. Jimmy's standout contribution was 'White Summer', recorded on acoustic guitar in 'DADGAD' tuning and influenced by Indian music. He achieves a similar sound with the electric guitar on the track 'Glimpses'. The interest in Indian music had been developed during the very early 1960s and Jimmy had even purchased a sitar.

At the start of 1967, the band toured in Australia and New Zealand, then returned to Europe during March when they performed for a German TV show. Jimmy's Telecaster was now fitted with circular mirrors on the body and pick-guard, whilst he displayed a new method of playing the guitar – using a violin bow to sound the strings. The band played through provided Echolette amps. Later in the year, answering a question from a fan in *Music Maker* magazine, Jimmy commented that he was using Vox amplifiers, a 100-watt head and two AC30s. He also noted the use of a banjo string for the high E. A feature of Jimmy's set-up not mentioned was an MkII Tonebender pedal.

The Yardbirds experienced much of their success in America and this continued to be their focus through late 1967 and early 1968. Three more singles were produced for that market: 'Ha Ha Said The Clown', 'Ten Little Indians' and 'Goodnight Sweet Josephine'. All were written by others and failed to chart. The B-side to the last-mentioned song was 'Think About It' and this was a better offering written by the band, featuring a distinct guitar riff from Jimmy. Another impressive track, worked into their set, was 'Dazed And Confused', though based on a Jake Holmes song.

The general lack of success, as well as the pressure from touring, contributed to disillusionment within the group. Singer Keith Relf and drummer Jim McCarty left and formed a new band following a final US tour in early summer 1968. Jimmy initially wanted to continue as the Yardbirds with replacement personnel whilst retaining Chris Dreja on bass. However, he decided on a new line-up. He recruited Robert Plant on vocals, followed by session player John Paul Jones on bass and John Bonham on drums. After several rehearsals, the new band toured Scandinavia in September 1968, still as the Yardbirds due to contractual obligations. Jimmy continued to use his Telecaster, though this was now without the mirrors and a 'psychedelic' design incorporating a dragon was painted on the guitar. This change dated from early 1968 and a performance of the Yardbirds from French TV at the time shows Jimmy's Telecaster with this new appearance.

The band returned to London and recorded a number of songs for a debut album. Financed by Jimmy, he wanted to have creative control in light of his experience latterly with the Yardbirds. Eventually, a deal was reached with Atlantic Records. The album featured the heavy rock Jimmy was developing in the late Yardbirds period as well as blues and acoustic tracks (most of 'Babe I'm Gonna Leave You' and 'Black Mountain Side', which was similar to 'White Summer'). Jimmy used his Telecaster for the album's electric parts in partnership with a Supro Coronado 35-watt combo amp. This was originally a 2x10, yet Jimmy's had been modified to carry a single 12 in. speaker. A Gibson J200 (a 1965 model with Tune-o-matic bridge) was used for the acoustic parts and Jimmy played a pedal steel guitar on 'Your Time Is Gonna Come'.

Before booking British dates in the run-up to Christmas 1968, the group was obliged to discard the Yardbirds moniker. Several stories exist as to how the new name was chosen, but nevertheless, this was Led Zeppelin. Yet, owing to the lukewarm reception in Britain of the Yardbirds, the new band did not have enough credit to receive many bookings and played less than two dozen gigs, with several being in the London area. Jimmy and manager Peter Grant decided a better idea was to concentrate on building from the Yardbirds' popularity in America, where the market was much more rewarding. Therefore, a tour was organised for the Christmas period and into the early New Year. Arriving on the West Coast on January 23, the band played in cities in that area for around a month before heading over to the East Coast for another month of dates. For the gigs, Jimmy continued to use his Telecaster, though an unusual choice was made for amps. The band apparently reached an arrangement with Rickenbacker to take the company's new Solid State 'Transonic' amps, though in addition to using a 200-watt head and cabinet, Jimmy had an Arbiter 100-watt head coupled to another Transonic cab.

As Led Zeppelin crossed the country, their reputation grew and this was further stimulated by advance promotion of the first album 'Led Zeppelin' which was released in the USA during mid-January. When the tour concluded towards the end of February, the band could look on the expedition as a success.

Work was still needed to promote the band at home, and in March Led Zeppelin embarked on a tour of Britain, along with a few Scandinavian dates. A recording of a Danish performance was made for TV and captured the group playing 'Communication Breakdown', 'Dazed And Confused', 'Babe

I'm Gonna Leave You' and 'How Many More Times'. Jimmy plays his Telecaster through the Arbiter 100-watt head and Transonic cab, as well as an unidentified cab, with a MkII Tonebender and Wah-Wah pedal also employed. Soon after, Led Zeppelin was filmed for 'Supershow' (a documentary film, featuring many contemporary artists) and Jimmy used WEM equipment whilst performing 'Dazed And Confused'. Rounding off a trio of recorded performances was an appearance on 'Beat Club'. Though 'Babe I'm Gonna Leave You' was synched to a backing track, Jimmy had his Telecaster with a Selmer amp posed behind.

The group returned to America in April to enjoy the success earned from the release of the first album, starting with four nights at the Fillmore West and Winterland. Earlier in the year, during the first US tour, James Gang guitarist Joe Walsh approached Jimmy with a Gibson Les Paul Standard and 'insisted' that he buy the instrument. Though initially reluctant to take another Les Paul – still owning the Les Paul Custom – Jimmy relented and the guitar became his main instrument from the second US tour onwards. Walsh had refinished the guitar and the neck profile had been made slimmer. The original tuners were still in place, though by the autumn these changed to gold Grovers, and both pick-up covers remained. The bridge cover was later removed to reveal 'double white' humbucker bobbins. Jimmy initially adopted the practice of 'top wrapping' the strings, whereby the strings were inserted into the tailpiece away from the headstock then pulled over the tailpiece, reducing the break angle over the bridge, though he later reverted to the normal method. Another change made to Jimmy's set-up was the adoption of Marshall amplifiers, done for reasons of servicing, i.e. they could be repaired or replaced in most locations.

Though the band had a busy touring schedule, time was found to record tracks for a new album. Photographs of Jimmy in Olympic Studios, London, before leaving for America caught him using his Les Paul with a Vox head through the Rickenbacker Transonic cab. There was also a Vox CO2 'Long Tom' echo unit atop another Rickenbacker cab. Sessions continued throughout the American tour and between dates in Britain over the summer. Jimmy favoured his new Les Paul using Marshall amplifiers and the Vox echo unit. He had his Danelectro for use mainly on his showcase 'White Summer/Black Mountain Side' medley, though also as a backup to the Gibson.

Led Zeppelin was in America for the summer festivals between early July and the end of August. The second album – 'Led Zeppelin II' – was completed at this time and the group had a month off before promotional duties saw them return to the road. A handful of dates were made in Europe before the group was in America for the fourth time in a year. 'Led Zeppelin II' was released in the midst of this and was immediately successful, reaching the top of the US charts, as well as in the UK during early 1970.

The start of the new decade saw the band performing several British dates. One, at the Royal Albert Hall, was filmed for a proposed release at the time, though this was abandoned until recently. Jimmy used his Les Paul, as well as the Danelectro, with a recently acquired custom-built Hiwatt DR103 100-watt head in partnership with four Marshall cabinets. He also had the Vox echo and a Wah-Wah pedal. A special appearance was made by his Les Paul Custom during the encore and this had bridge and neck pick-up covers removed – revealing 'double black' and 'zebra' (black and white) bobbins respectively. Jimmy's initial reluctance to take the guitar on the road was starting to subside and the Les Paul Custom would make the American trip for the spring 1970 tour. At this point, the instrument had been modified with two extra switches near the original to allow greater control over the pick-ups, as the factory wiring only allowed the middle pick-up to be active with the bridge in the middle setting. Yet, Jimmy's fears proved prophetic as the guitar was stolen in Minneapolis and remained missing, despite his pleas for its safe return. Incredibly, around 2015, the guitar resurfaced and was reunited with him.

In the preceding European tour and that of the US in April and May, Jimmy continued to use the set-up mentioned above. Upon the band's return, Jimmy and Robert Plant retreated to Wales to prepare songs for the third album, 'Led Zeppelin III'. Jimmy was pictured with a Harmony Sovereign acoustic, as well as a Cromwell archtop, both dating from his session days. The band rehearsed and recorded the material at Headley Grange using the Rolling Stones Mobile Studio, then returned to London for further studio work. This was broken up by touring commitments, playing in Iceland, the Bath Festival and Germany before ending the summer in the USA; the album was ultimately mixed there. 'Friends' has Jimmy playing his acoustic in 'C6' tuning, with the accompanying strings serving to give the song an 'Eastern' flavour. Another showcase for Jimmy's playing was the slow blues 'Since I've Been Loving You'. Jimmy has a 12-string acoustic on 'Tangerine' and 'That's The Way', whilst adding pedal steel guitar with a Wah-Wah effect to the first-mentioned and a dulcimer on the latter. To help record his acoustic guitar parts – Jimmy told *Guitar World* in 1991 – he used an Altair tube limiter, which had been recommended by noted American 12-string guitarist Dick Rosmini.

Jimmy Page at a London recording studio, c. 1965.
From Original Negative / Alamy Stock Photo.

Jimmy Page with Danelectro guitar c. 1977.
Pictorial Press Ltd / Alamy Stock Photo.

The album was released following the summer US tour, which finished in late September, and continued the band's success. Following two years of hard work for the band up to this point, as well as the death of John Paul Jones' father, requests for further gigs through to early 1971 were declined and, after some time off, a start was made on tracks for a new album. These were largely completed by March, though delays in mixing postponed release until the year end. Though untitled, the album was almost universally known as 'Led Zeppelin IV' and carried on from the predecessor in mixing styles and instruments. The first track on the album was the heavy rock 'Black Dog', highlighting a distortion effect on Jimmy's Les Paul. Engineer Andy Johns later explained to Universal Audio webzine in May 2002 that he ran the direct signal through two Universal Audio 1176 compressors to achieve saturation without the use of amplifiers. Jimmy branched out and played mandolin for the first time on 'The Battle Of Evermore', borrowing one belonging to John Paul Jones. Further experimentation was made with alternate tunings and 'Going To California' had an acoustic played in 'Double Drop D', whilst 'When The Levee Breaks' had an open F tuning, with Jimmy playing slide. A complete mixture of styles was found on perhaps the band's most celebrated song 'Stairway To Heaven', which ended the first side. This utilised an acoustic before going to electric 12-string and then the solo in a heavy rock section. Jimmy stated that the solo was played using his Fender Telecaster from the Yardbirds days. Even though the Les Paul had captured his affection, another reason for the change was that the Telecaster had been refinished while he was away on tour in early 1970. He said the work completely changed the guitar's character.

By March 1971, Led Zeppelin was ready to return to gigging and an intimate tour of smaller British venues was arranged. Much of the new material was included, with the complex 'Stairway To Heaven' also chosen. To allow a seamless transition between all the parts, Jimmy acquired a Gibson EDS 1275 Doubleneck and used this for future performances. Following the British tour, Led Zeppelin had just a handful of European dates before travelling to America in August for over 20 shows. Jimmy's live set-up appears to have been in transition at this point, with Marshall heads visible alongside the Hiwatt, whilst the Vox echo was replaced by an Echoplex EP3. The guitar line-up was stable and his Les Paul, Danelectro and Harmony acoustic were on the road with him. Shortly after the US dates were completed, the band made their first Japanese trip and completed a series of gigs to the end of September. Then, following the release of the fourth album in November, the band played across Britain to the end of the year.

An Australian tour and a gig in New Zealand were Led Zeppelin's first engagements of 1972. These saw Jimmy with a new amplifier line-up. He retained three Marshall 4x12 in. cabinets from the previous version but dispensed with the Hiwatt and adopted two Marshall 100-watt heads – a Super Bass and Super Lead. Also in use were two orange 1x15 in. cabinets and a 200-watt Orange Matamp head, employed for a Sonic Wave theremin. Echo continued to be provided by the Echoplex EP3 and Jimmy also had a Wah-Wah pedal. Jimmy's guitar collection expanded, with photographs from 'Houses Of The Holy' sessions revealing a Martin D-28 acoustic. For the summer US tour he had acquired a Giannini GWSCRA 12-P Craviola 12-string acoustic.

Whilst the album was completed shortly after the end of the US tour, the record did not appear until March 1973. The band began working the material into the live set from mid-1972 and was the main constituent of the songs played on the Japanese and British tours in late 1972 and early 1973. At the release of 'Houses Of The Holy', Led Zeppelin performed multiple dates in Europe before embarking on an extensive American tour. This ended with three nights at Madison Square Garden which were filmed and recorded for release as 'The Song Remains The Same' (1976). Jimmy played his Les Paul for much of the set through the rig mentioned earlier. It had not outwardly altered – apart from the addition of a theremin and the Orange cabs were painted black. Appearing towards the end of the show was a recent addition – another Les Paul. This had a red top and was a late 1960s or very early 1970s Deluxe Gold Top, refinished and routed to fit humbucker pick-ups (exposed 'double blacks').

The 1973 US Tour was one of the band's most successful to date, in both financial terms and reception of the show, which added more theatrical elements than hitherto. Yet, the heavy workload caused band members to take an extended break from touring, through to 1975.

Sessions for the sixth album, 'Physical Graffiti', were completed by the spring of 1974. Music from these was mixed with some older compositions to create a double album – Led Zeppelin's first. One of the new tracks created was 'Custard Pie' and the song featured a part created by Jimmy on his ARP 2500 synthesizer. This was visible in contemporary photographs taken in his home studio, as were two rarely seen guitars: a Fender Stratocaster in two-tone sunburst finish (a mid-1950s model); a Gibson ES 5 in natural finish with three P90 pick-ups and master tone, signifying a pre-1955 model. Another new song, 'Kashmir', saw Jimmy employing 'DADGAD' again, whilst 'In My Time Of Dying' utilised open A for slide guitar parts. Jimmy multi-tracked several guitars for 'Ten Years Gone'. He played with a Leslie speaker of sections of 'Night Flight' and 'The Wanton Song'.

Even though the album was completed by autumn 1974, release was delayed by production problems and not available until February 1975. This left the band time to organise a supporting American tour for early 1975, with warm-up concerts in Europe, followed by a series of gigs at Earls Court, London. Jimmy kept a similar backline to the 1973 US tour, though the Orange head was replaced by another Marshall, these three being two 1959 100-watt Super Leads and one 100-watt Super Bass. A new guitar was also on the road – a 1959 Les Paul Standard, which became known as No. 2 and served as a backup to the original Les Paul Standard (No. 1). The Danelectro appeared during the set as did the EDS 1275 and Martin D-28 acoustic.

Led Zeppelin was set to continue promoting 'Physical Graffiti' with a tour of the US in August 1975. Yet, Robert Plant was involved in a serious car accident shortly before departure and this was cancelled. Despite being in a wheelchair for a time, Robert participated in sessions organised during the downtime at the end of the year in Germany. The band had just two weeks in the studio and completed several tracks that made up the 'Presence' album, in shops the following March. One of Jimmy's favourite tracks was 'Achilles' Last Stand' which featured several guitar parts, including slide, and a solo Jimmy ranked alongside 'Stairway To Heaven' as his best.

Seeing out 1976 with the long-delayed release of 'The Song Remains The Same' film of the 1973 Madison Square Garden concert, Led Zeppelin planned to return to America in 1977 for a 50-date tour over three legs. Jimmy continued with the 1975 backline and many of the same instruments, though two Martin acoustics joined the line-up, in addition to an early 1950s Telecaster with maple neck, refinished in a chocolate colour and with a 'B-Bender' device installed.

The tour was cut short following the death of Robert Plant's son, Karac. For over a year, the band spent time away from music. Afterwards, they travelled to ABBA's Polar Studio in Stockholm. Over three weeks in late 1978, Led Zeppelin recorded tracks for 'In Through The Out Door', which saw John Paul Jones and Robert Plant take a greater role in the arrangement of the songs whilst Jimmy concentrated on guitar parts. For two of the tracks – 'In The Evening' and 'Carouselambra' – Jimmy used a Gizmotron. This was a device invented by Kevin Godley and Lol Creme (of 10cc) and fitted to the guitar top to sound the guitar strings using wheels connected to a motor. Keys above the wheels were depressed to make the string sound in a manner similar to a violin bow.

Despite returning to the studio, the band was reluctant to begin touring again. In the summer of 1979, two shows were arranged at the Knebworth Festival. Just two songs were played from 'In Through The Out Door', though this provided Jimmy an opportunity to change guitars. On 'Hot Dog' he had the chocolate Telecaster, which now had the rosewood neck from the Jeff Beck-gifted guitar. 'In The Evening' saw a switch to a Fender Stratocaster in lake placid blue. 'Misty Mountain Hop' from 'Led Zeppelin IV' also had Jimmy with an early Gibson RD Artist Custom. The remainder of the set was performed using his favoured guitars and equipment.

The new decade began with Led Zeppelin set to reclaim their status as the biggest act in rock and dominate the American market. As a warm-up to this, a European tour was arranged to run in late June and early July 1980. With American dates set for the end of the year, rehearsals were being undertaken when John Bonham died in September. By the end of the year, the rest of the band had decided to go their separate ways rather than continue with another drummer.

With this decision made, Jimmy made plans to form a new group with Chris Squire and Alan White of Yes and Dave Lawson of Greenslade. Known as XYZ, this project had faltered by the middle of the year. Soon after, Jimmy was approached by film director Michael Winner, who wanted him to produce the soundtrack for the upcoming film 'Death Wish II'. This was not Jimmy's first involvement with such work, as for much of the early 1970s he was involved with Kenneth Anger's 'Lucifer Rising' film. For some parts of the 'Death Wish II' soundtrack Jimmy utilised a Roland G808 guitar with GR300 synthesizer unit. Later, he promoted a successor product, the G707 guitar with GR700 synthesizer.

Some of the music produced during the 'Death Wish II' sessions was later performed as part of the ARMS (Action into Research for Multiple Sclerosis) concert which was organised by Ronnie Lane, who was suffering from the disease. Taking place at London's Royal Albert Hall in September 1983, Jimmy played a set of music from 'Death Wish II' as well as an instrumental version of 'Stairway To Heaven'. Mainly using his Telecaster, he turned to the EDS 1275 for the closing song. The gig was very well received, leading to a decision for a short American tour to be mounted at the end of the year. For this, Jimmy took a white Fender Telecaster, his Les Paul and Danelectro. His amp choice is difficult to discern, though appears to be one of several Fender combos on stage.

For the American leg, Paul Rodgers was the vocalist. In 1984, Jimmy and Paul decided to collaborate in a new band, the Firm, with bassist Tony Franklin and drummer Chris Slade. An eponymous debut album was recorded during the year and released in early 1985, reaching the top twenty in both the British and American charts. Before the end of 1984, the Firm toured Europe and then, in support of the album, played a number of USA gigs. Jimmy primarily used the chocolate Telecaster. His amps were concealed as part of the stage design, though a Marshall head could be glimpsed.

Another collaboration undertaken during 1984 was with long-time friend Roy Harper. Jimmy played with him at the Cambridge Folk Festival using his Telecaster. They were also featured on a segment for the 'Old Grey Whistle Test' where Jimmy played an Ovation acoustic. Roy Harper's album 'What Ever Happened to Jugula?' also had guitar contributions from Jimmy.

In mid-1985 Jimmy reunited with the surviving members of Led Zeppelin to perform at the Live Aid benefit concert; drummers Phil Collins and Tony Thompson were invited to play with them. Jimmy used his Les Paul (likely through a provided Marshall JCM800 head and stack) for 'Rock And Roll' and 'Whole Lotta Love', then turning to his Doubleneck for 'Stairway To Heaven'. The trio would reunite for a second time in 1988 for the 40th anniversary of Atlantic Records.

The Firm followed up the debut album with a second, 'Mean Business', in 1986. The band toured the US in the months following the record's release in February. Despite the relative success of the Firm, Jimmy and Paul decided to concentrate on solo projects. In early 1987, Jimmy recorded his first solo album – 'Outrider' – which was released in the summer of 1988. Several songs featured guest vocalists John Miles, Chris Farlowe and Robert Plant, as well as a number of instrumentals. Reaching the top thirty in both the UK and US, the record has several standout solos and riffs from Jimmy. In support of the release, Jimmy took a band consisting of John Miles, drummer Jason Bonham and bassist Durban Laverde on the road in America, in addition to a handful of British dates at the end of 1988. The band played much of the 'Outrider' album along with a handful of Led Zeppelin songs. Jimmy mainly used his red-top Les Paul, now fitted with a 'B-Bender', but also had his No. 1, Danelectro and Doubleneck. New additions to the line-up included a 1989 Paul Reed Smith 'Special' (solid mahogany body and neck with rosewood fingerboard) and a Washburn Woodstock 12-string acoustic. A backline of four Marshall half stacks was present and Jimmy had a recently (around mid-1980s) acquired pedal board, housing his Wah-Wah pedal, a chorus and distortion effect, along with the controller for his Echoplex.

Jimmy started the 1990s by performing as a guest with Aerosmith at the Monsters of Rock concert, also making an appearance at the band's Marquee Club gig; in both instances he used his red-top Les Paul. In 1991, he embarked on an album project with former Deep Purple and Whitesnake singer David Coverdale. The collection of songs completed by the pair was well received on both sides of the Atlantic, breaking into the top five when released in 1993. The delay from the completion of the 'Coverdale/Page' album to the record being available in shops saw a proposed American tour scrapped. The duo, along with backing band, only made an outing in Japan, performing several concerts at the end of 1993. Jimmy continued to use the red-top Les Paul and other guitars from his collection, though there were some new additions. An all-gold Les Paul (early 1990s classic model) had been fitted with a TransPerformance system. This allowed Jimmy to select from several pre-set tunings via a keypad on the face of the guitar. Jimmy upgraded his pedal board to a custom-made unit by Pete Cornish. The specifications of this are given on www.petecornish.co.uk and, briefly, the unit was designed to combat signal losses through long lengths of cable and the pedals themselves. Thus, the guitar input was fed into a high impedance unit then into a similar one for each of the various pedals to preserve the integrity of the guitar tone. The pedals are listed as fuzz (later removed) MXR phase, Yamaha chorus, Boss chorus, Wah-Wah and Digitech whammy, as well as an output to the Echoplex. On tour, Jimmy had several Marshall heads on top of a row of single height 4x12 in. cabinets, whilst an appearance was made by the Orange Matamp.

Two videos were recorded for the singles 'Pride And Joy' and 'Take Me For A Little While'. In the first, Jimmy uses a dulcimer before moving on to a sunburst Gibson J200, then his new gold Les Paul; he also demonstrates his proficiency with the harmonica. The gold Les Paul dominates the screen time in 'Take Me For A Little While', though a Gibson 'Style U' harp guitar from Jimmy's collection has a part in the video.

During 1994, Jimmy reunited with Robert Plant for an MTV 'Unplugged' session. This was recorded in Morocco, Wales and in a London studio and featured several Led Zeppelin songs. A handful of new tracks with an eastern flavour were performed acoustically utilising Moroccan and Egyptian musicians on location and in the studio. Jimmy brought out several of his acoustic guitars, including the Martin D-28, Ovation Doubleneck, Washburn Woodstock 12-string and a new custom-built Andy Manson triple-neck acoustic with mandolin, 12-string and six-string necks. A handful of electric songs were performed and for these Jimmy used his No. 1 Les Paul, which now had an exposed bridge pick-up, though this was now a 'double black' (the original had failed in Australia during 1972 and the cover was returned soon after), as well as the gold Les Paul. No. 1 had the wiring modified to allow Jimmy to achieve an 'out of phase' sound similar to that made famous by Peter Green. No. 2 had been altered in a similar way, though more extensively, much earlier. Amplification was provided by a Vox AC30 (with top boost) and, in the studio, a Fender Vibro-King 3x10 in. combo. The set was later released as 'No Quarter: Jimmy Page and Robert Plant Unledded'.

In 1995, Jimmy and Robert Plant embarked on an extensive American tour during the first half of the year, followed by European dates during the summer. Jimmy mainly used his No. 1 Les Paul, the gold and red-top Les Pauls, along with the Ovation Doubleneck and Gibson Doubleneck. New additions included an Ovation 6-string acoustic, two Washburn EA-20 12-string acoustics – one in natural finish, one in sunburst, both with cutaway – and a Fender Stratocaster in sunburst with lace sensor pick-ups. A change was made to the amplifiers. Several Petersburg P-100 100-watt amp heads replaced the Marshalls and two Vox AC30s were also utilised. Later in the year, the band returned to America and in the new year played gigs in South America and Japan.

Jimmy and Robert continued to collaborate in 1997, recording the 'Walking Into Clarksdale' album. Released in spring 1998, the record was another chart success for the pair and much of the year was spent promoting it, in Europe and America over two legs. Jimmy continued to use similar instruments to the previous tour, though the all-gold Les Paul was joined by a similar instrument in dark red and a sunburst Paul Reed Smith McCarty featured on one song. An unidentified black jumbo six-string acoustic played a part on 'Going To California'. Another change was the Petersburg amps were replaced by Fender Tone Master 100-watt heads with matching 4x12 in. cabinets, whilst the Vox AC30s remained and a modern Marshall, perhaps a JCM 800, was added. Jimmy also returned to using a theremin.

In 1999 and 2000, Jimmy collaborated with US band the Black Crowes on a few live dates, resulting in the album 'Live At The Greek', though due to contractual obligations only Led Zeppelin material was included. No. 1 was the main guitar, with the Danelectro, red top and gold Les Pauls also featuring. The amps were changed from the Page/Plant tour to be just one Fender Tone Master head and cab with two Orange AD30 30-watt amp heads and a Petersburg P100 head into 4x12 in. cabinets.

Though a long US tour was scheduled, Jimmy was forced to cut short his involvement due to back problems. For the first half of the 2000s, Jimmy's public musical appearances were limited, then in 2006, Led Zeppelin was inducted into the UK Music Hall of Fame. By 2007, plans had been formulated to reunite the surviving members for a tribute concert to Atlantic Records founder Ahmet Ertegun, who had died the previous year. To play the drums, the band enlisted John Bonham's son Jason.

For the concert, Jimmy changed his amp line-up, now omitting the Fender and adding two Orange AD50 50-watt amps, whilst also using two of his old 100-watt Marshall heads, as well as two Petersburg P100s. He continued to favour the No. 1 Les Paul. An ES 350 was used on 'In My Time Of Dying' and this was custom-built for Jimmy by Gibson. Another new instrument was a Gibson Les Paul Custom with three pick-ups and a Bigsby which was played on 'For Your Love'. This was a prototype for his signature 'Black Beauty' model which saw a release in the following year.

Alan Parker with Gibson Les Paul Custom guitar. Photograph by Peter Tuffrey.

ALAN PARKER

Many guitarists pick up the instrument, hoping one day to earn a lasting reputation and untold wealth through hit records and live performances. Guitarist Alan Parker has followed a different route. Initially working in bands, he then became a session guitarist and also turned his attention to library music and film scores. However, he admits, sometimes these have all overlapped each other.

Alan was born on August 26, 1944, at Willersley Castle, a late 18th-century country mansion in Matlock which, between 1940 and 1946, served as a Salvation Army maternity hospital. His parents were moved there from bomb-torn London for a few months. He was an only child; his mother was a cleaner, his father a cabinet maker. There were no family connections with music. He started playing guitar when he was 11 after wanting to play a trumpet but his parents were not able to afford one.

'A family friend said he had a guitar, a Gibson Kalamazoo, in the loft and he gave it to me. I cycled to his house and brought the guitar back on a piece of string round my back. I still have the guitar.'

Alan found a local guitar teacher called Charles Johnson in Walthamstow and attended lessons once a week. He had played recorder at school and, not long after beginning guitar lessons, discovered he had perfect pitch. 'Where it came from, I don't know. The tutor recognised it straight away and I learned to read music very quickly by the time I was 12.'

With Charles Johnson, Alan read and played specific guitar pieces, including work by Eddie Lang (1902–1933), the father of jazz guitar, and Andres Segovia (1893–1987) the virtuoso Spanish classical guitarist. School bored Alan, and from age 11 he was completely absorbed with the guitar. He rarely handed in homework because after tea he'd spend the rest of the night up in his bedroom playing guitar.

After taking lessons for about 18 months, Johnson suggested Alan should enter guitar competitions staged annually by the BMG – the Banjo, Mandolin and Guitar Federation – at Wigmore Hall and St Pancras Town Hall. As a result, Alan won two cups and two medals.

One of the competition adjudicators was distinguished classical guitarist Julian Bream (1933–2020) who played a significant role in improving the public's perception of the classical guitar as a respectable instrument.

'He chatted to me and was impressed at what I was doing on the acoustic classical side. Afterwards, I went to his house in Guildford for coaching and further lessons for about a year.

Gibson produced a US-built budget line of guitars which were branded Kalamazoo (the company's base for much of the 20th century) during the 1930s, and again in the 1960s. Prior to, and during, the Second World War, the Kalamazoo budget line comprised guitars, banjos and mandolins.

Perfect pitch is a rare auditory phenomenon characterised by the ability of a person to identify or recreate a given musical note without the benefit of a reference tone. Researchers estimate the occurrence of perfect pitch to be 1 in 10,000 people.

He did this for nothing. This brought me into the classical side of guitar. I still had the Gibson Kalamazoo and also borrowed a guitar from my teacher – a Martin Coletti, a lovely old cello guitar.'

Alan left secondary school at 15. He'd done very well at maths, okay at English, geography he couldn't be bothered with, history he liked, and he did very well at art, enjoying making and drawing things.

He knew he wanted to be in the music business but aware he couldn't make a living from playing classical guitar. The main classical guitarists, Julian Bream and John Williams were struggling to secure a decent living, so Alan thought his own chances were slim. He took a job as a computerised bookkeeper with a tea merchant, though this didn't last long. Around the same time he swapped over to playing electric guitar.

'I started to play gigs with a number of bands at parties and weddings and other functions. We performed a variety of Bessie Smith songs and early rock 'n' roll. There were no rehearsals, I just turned up and off we went.'

When playing at an infamous pub, the Two Puddings, he was asked to form a resident band. He accepted, though at 15 this was illegal. His parents bought him a Vox solid electric guitar with a tremolo arm and this was played through a Selmer Truvoice amplifier. His band played early rock 'n' roll with Alan organising all the song arrangements. He found this easy and everyone in the pub loved the music. 'The Two Puddings was one of the Kray twins' favourite haunts and they thought we were great.'

After almost a year, the famous theatre director, Joan Littlewood (1914–2002) from the nearby Theatre Royal, Stratford, realising Alan's talents, asked him if he'd like to work on musical arrangements for the theatre orchestra. When he handed in his notice at the pub, the Krays said they didn't want him to leave. He argued that he was only young and wanted to move on and establish himself. It was an opportunity he couldn't miss. 'They spent about ten minutes thinking it over. It was the longest ten minutes in my life and then they agreed I could go.'

Alan took the theatre job for about six months and then left. He had made the acquaintance of a number of guitarists working in the Mecca Palais bands, including those of Joe Loss, Johnny Howe and Cyril Stapleton. Guitarists in these bands in the 1950s had become prominent and busy playing the hits of the day. If they were called upon for session work in studios, the band leader would ask another guitarist to deputise for them. For a period, Alan was a 'dep'.

'There were no rehearsals and I'd be thrown a deep wad of music. I had to sight read and adapt very quickly. Obviously, there were a few mistakes but I just got on with it. At this time, I was about sixteen-and-a-half. It was an incredible grounding, marvellous experience and an eye-opener into the music business.'

From 'dep' work, Alan moved to join the Johnny Howard band full-time, playing pop songs and a few ballads at the Royal Ballroom Tottenham, six nights-a-week, Monday to Saturday. There were a few hundred people dancing happily each night. On Sunday afternoons, the band appeared at an American officers' club in Bayswater, but there was no dancing, entertainment only being provided.

'The Johnny Howard band did a live recording on Sunday mornings at a BBC theatre in Charing Cross for Brian Matthew's 'Easy Beat' programme. Johnny called in other session guitar players for this slot, and I got to know, amongst others, Vic Flick and Ernie Ford who were full-time session guitar players.'

Work for session players was organised by 'fixers' and they included Charlie Katz and Harry Benson who were contacted by a studio or a producer to round up the necessary musicians for a recording. The session musicians did not know who they were working for until they arrived at a studio.

'I became involved with session work when I was about 17 – not full-time, it gradually built up until I was going to nearly every studio. Amongst these were Decca, EMI, Lansdowne and Regent Sound – one of the first I worked in with Clem Cattini. I got in with this type of work because in the early 1960s there weren't many session guitarists around.'

Alan worked sessions with a Gibson ES 345 TD and a Fender Stratocaster played through a Fender Deluxe Reverb single 12 with no effects. He's a firm believer in sticking a lead in the amp and finding the required effect within an amp. For acoustic work, he had a Martin D-45 and later a Knight custom guitar. He's mainly used Ernie Ball strings on electrics and Martin's own strings on their acoustics.

When Alan first started session work, the pay was £7.50 for a three-hour session. He worked seven days a week, even fitting in an odd early morning jingle 8 to 9 am. He was very busy, even turning work down. 'Chronologically I've lost track of all the pop records I've played on. Two that immediately spring to mind are the Fortunes "You've Got Your Troubles" (1964), written by my pals Roger Cooke and Roger Greenaway; and Dusty Springfield's early records including "You Don't Have to Say You Love Me" (1966). I did a lot of work with record producer and A&R man at the Philips label, John 'Johnny' Charles Franz (1922–1977). The problem with band members playing on their records was that they took too long to get it right in the studio. Producers said "let's bring in session guys." This caused quite a controversy as it became generally known that some pop stars did not play on their records.

'After finding out who the session guys were, [the press] followed us around. On emerging from a studio, they asked "Who have you been playing for today?" Can't say, we'd answer, as they attempted to concoct a story to ridicule a band.'

The 1960s were a crazy time, but Alan concentrated hard on his flourishing career where his session work, library and film music opportunities all began to absorb him. 'I didn't want to know about the rock 'n' roll lifestyle. My head was totally into a long career.'

At the time that Alan turned to library music, it was forbidden by the Musicians' Union to make recordings in the UK. This didn't bother Robin Philips of Keith Prowse Music who recorded sessions in Cologne, Germany, about twice a year. KPM along with De Wolfe were the large library music organisations of the time. Initially, Alan went to Cologne as a session guitarist. 'Robin would also take a rhythm section, guitar, bass and drums along with a lead fiddle and lead trumpet player. We'd spend four or five days there.'

Alan's introduction to writing Library music came on one of these KPM sessions. 'We'd finished early with the studio time free the following day. Graham Walker, Robin's assistant, encouraged me to compose some music for the spare session.' Alan busied himself all night and well into the morning and the music he'd written was recorded. In the early 1960s, he admired guitar instrumentals and his first efforts were similar to Chuck Berry's music, but with no words. They were put on an album and sent out to agents worldwide who presented them to film, television and other relevant sources.

Those first tracks were well received and they still generate cash for him even today but he admits to cringing when listening to them.

He believes he was the first guitarist to move into composing library music. He added that some guitarists could not be bothered to step into this area. He also argues being able to read and score music was a massive asset.

On his first library tracks, a Gibson Les Paul was used with a

---

First built in 1958 the ES 345 TD (Thinline double pick-ups) was an upscale version of the ES 335. The ES 345 features a multi-position 'Varitone' switch adjacent to the lead tone and volume controls, adding various combinations to the guitar's circuit, adding colour to the sound. The guitar also featured an optional stereophonic output jack, gold-plated hardware, large split parallelogram fingerboard inlays and a thicker three-ply edge binding than that of the ES 335.

The Fender Deluxe Reverb was introduced in 1963 and incorporated an onboard spring reverb tank to the newly designed Fender Deluxe. The latter amp was built from early 1948 to 1966. The Deluxe Reverb was a 22-watt tube amplifier and most often featured a Jensen C-12Q series 12-inch loudspeaker.

Stanley(Dick) Charles Knight, born 1907 started as an amateur player and became proficient on the banjo and clarinet while working as a machinist. One day there was a freak accident and he severed part of every finger on his left hand. So he thought, I can't play guitars so I'll make them.

Alan Parker, extreme right with Blue Mink.
Pictorial Press Ltd / Alamy Stock Photo.

hired Fender Deluxe Reverb, though without the Wharfedale speaker fitted in his own amp. Alan's contribution to KPM library music developed from there. 'Robin said do you fancy doing an album. I didn't have a clue what it might be used for but he said produce something folky, but commercial, a bit random, light-hearted and spirited. I harnessed all my skills and pulled it together. One of the tracks was eventually used for a Yorkshire Television series whilst the rest was sent on its travels around the world.'

By 1964, Alan was orchestrating for artists and started to work for famous American film composers Jerry Goldsmith (1929–2004) and Dominic Frontiere (1931–2017). He had met them through being booked on their session work.

'I got to know Jerry Goldsmith very well and wanted to learn how to orchestrate in the special way he did. He orchestrated from a conventional size orchestra but got different sounds from them. I went to the Royal College of Music to study under Sir David Willcocks (1919–2005) but only lasted about three months. He said I can't teach you to orchestrate in the way that you want to and probably nobody in this country can. He suggested I go to America to the University of California, Los Angeles, because some of the lecturers were film composers. They lectured one or two days a week. In 1964 I went to UCLA for six months and learned a hell of a lot, taking everything in.'

In between other activities, Alan continued as a session guitarist throughout the remainder of the swinging 1960s. He played guitar on Dave Clark hits and on virtually everything by the Walker brothers, 'Make It Easy On Yourself' (1965), and the 'Sun Ain't Gonna Shine Anymore' (1966).

During 1968, Alan played lead guitar on Donovan's 'Hurdy Gurdy Man'. John Paul Jones, later of Led Zeppelin, did the arrangements and suggested the lead part. In the studio, Alan retuned the top two strings, so they were slightly out of tune. 'I played the part with a Gibson Les Paul through the Fender Twin Reverb. Generally, ideas were suggested for guitar parts but it was mostly left up to me to make my own interpretations. In some cases, the contributions have given the tracks a massive uplift. Looking back, it's nice to have been involved with such iconic pieces, and iconic riffs. Songs give great pleasure, all around the world, every day. That is what is so powerful about music. It can

> An electric sitar is designed to mimic the sound of the sitar, a traditional musical instrument of India. Depending on the manufacturer and model, these instruments bear varying degrees of resemblance to the traditional sitar. Most resemble the electric guitar in the style of the body and headstock, though some have a body shaped to resemble that of the sitar (such as a model made by Danelectro). The instrument was developed in the late 1960s by Danelectro, when many western musical groups began to use the sitar. The sitar is generally considered a difficult instrument to learn. By contrast, the electric sitar, with its standard guitar fretboard and tuning, is a more familiar fret arrangement for a guitarist to play. The twangy sitar-like tone comes from a flat bridge adding the necessary buzz to the guitar strings.

reach every corner of the earth.'

The closing years of the 1960s were marked by Alan meeting Jimi Hendrix and becoming a member of Blue Mink. Alan states he and Jimi played together at Olympic Studios in London. 'I got on well with him. He was very open, no edge of any sort. He had a total command of the guitar. Whatever he heard in his head he could transfer to the instrument.'

The chance meeting arguably left an impression on Hendrix as a little later, he gifted Alan with his 1951 Epiphone FT-79 acoustic guitar. This had been bought for $25 in 1967 with money earned from the Monterey Festival appearance. It had been Jimi's main home guitar while in London, used for practice and composition. Alan states he later used the Hendrix instrument as a high-strung guitar on a number of top recordings. Eventually he sold it along with the hard case (stencilled with 'A. Parker') that he'd found for it.

'How everyone came together to be involved with Blue Mink was an accident. We were all session musicians and session singers. We found out, over a good period of a year between 1967–1968, that we were all meeting up in the studio to work on the same session. Fixers were booking us almost like we were a group. Barry Morgan of Morgan Sound Studios in High Road Willesden said this is crazy, we should make a record of our own. Barry and Monty Babson said we could have the studio free for a day as long as they could have the rights to try and place a record.'

Those involved with Blue Mink were Alan on guitar; Roger Coulam (keyboards); Madeline Bell (vocals); Roger Cooke (vocals); Herbie Flowers (bass); and Barry Morgan (drums).

'Cooky had one or two good songs. We went in one morning between 10 and 1, and laid down four backing tracks. In the afternoon we put vocals on and some extras. Amongst the four tracks finished in one day were "Melting Pot" and "Banner Man". I played all guitars on these tracks mostly using a Fender Telecaster with palm levers. I got quite fond of those because, with the help of a palm lever, instead of bending up to a third you could bend to a fifth. I also used them on my Gibson Les Paul.'

'Melting Pot', written by Cook and Greenaway, with 'Blue Mink' on the B side, written by Alan Parker, was released at the end of 1969, peaking at no. 3 in January 1970. 'The troubles started when the records started selling in large numbers. We were not a working group. We all had our own careers. Some appearances became hilarious because, initially, not all of us could appear on TV spots. On one TV show where we mimed, we even had a tape operator deputising for lead singer Roger Cook. In the end, because we had top five hits and albums, we decided to take roughly a year out from sessions. We did one tour, performing at all the main venues in England including Wakefield and Batley Variety Clubs. None of us really liked this pop star thing but venues were sold out wherever we appeared. At one place we played in Wales, we had Tommy Cooper as support. Booker T and the MGs toured with us and I got on incredibly friendly with Steve Cropper. We compared notes. He was a lovely man, so were the others. Madeline said Steve told her, he wanted to "cut my fingers off." On tour, I used both a Telecaster and a Les Paul through my Fender Twin.'

Work in its various forms for Alan during the 1970s was in some ways a continuation of the previous decade. During 1970, Alan became a member of CCS. Formed in 1970 by musical director John Cameron and record producer Mickie Most, CCS consisted largely of session musicians, and was created primarily as a recording outfit. The personnel also included Peter Thorup (vocals); Harold McNair (flute); Herbie Flowers (bass); Roger Coulam (keyboards); Barry Morgan (drums); plus Don Lusher and Bill Geldard, (trombone). Some of the musicians were also members of Blue Mink.

CCS are best known for their instrumental version of Led Zeppelin's 1969 track 'Whole Lotta Love', which got into the UK Singles Chart in 1970, and was used as the theme music for 'Top of the Pops' for most of the 1970s, and, in a remixed version, between 1998 and 2003.

'During a break, whilst playing with the "Top of the Pops" orchestra, I had my Gibson ES 345 stolen. At the time, the Who were on the programme, so I borrowed Pete Townshend's SG before and after they appeared. There is a clip somewhere showing me, after playing the intro, running to give the guitar back to Pete on stage. Then, after the Who played, I ran to collect the guitar so I could play out the theme tune.'

Blue Mink made several appearances in the US and before one concert the band was introduced on stage by Elton John and Dusty Springfield. 'In America we were represented by Universal and we appeared with Bill Withers and the Pointer Sisters. Our reception was mixed because of the racial prejudice in existence at the time. At the Troubadour Club, when we came on with a black singer, the audience turned their backs on us. It shocked us and Madeline was really upset. We did a week there and some nights were better than others.'

Although busy with Blue Mink from 1969 to around 1975, Alan managed to appear as a 'dep' with the Jack Parnell band for Frank Sinatra at the Royal Festival Hall during February 1971.

A year later, Alan recorded a KPM library music piece that was used as the theme music for the children's animated TV programme 'Sir Prancelot'. 'I bought a Danelectro sitar guitar and wrote the piece in KPM's basement studio in Denmark Street.' In time, Alan would produce in excess of 50 albums of library music.

During 1974, David Bowie contacted Alan to help him with a few tracks for his album 'Diamond Dogs'. 'That's me on lead guitar on "Rebel Rebel". David said I want to do a number with a Rolling Stones' riff. I think he wanted to pull Mick Jagger's leg a bit. He had part of the "Rebel Rebel" riff and I finished it off. I suppose by this time I had become known for my good melodic lead sound. I have to admit the riff makes the song. It's iconic. I also played on a number of other tracks.'

'Rebel Rebel', recorded 14–16 January 1974 was released in February 1974, several months before 'Diamond Dogs'.

'Sadly, in the past, about 20 guitarists claim to have played on "Rebel Rebel" as well as performing the solo on the Walker Brothers' "No Regrets" (1975). One guy who tried to register was only three years old at the time of "Rebel Rebel". Thankfully, all my performances are now registered with PPL.'

Over the ensuing years, composing and orchestrating became the main focus of Alan's creative output. 'My introduction to serious composing was through library music. I can hear what I

Alan Parker with a Dobro guitar. Photograph by Peter Tuffrey.

Alan Parker with sitar. Photograph by Peter Tuffrey.

Alan Parker with Gibson Byrdland guitar. Photograph by Peter Tuffrey.

want to hear and voice it. I can orchestrate for any instrument, horns, clarinet, violins anything. Jerry Goldsmith, who I'd met in the 1960s, eventually became a friend and let me orchestrate one or two things for him. Initially, I gulped but dived in and swam out. I conducted his orchestra on "First Blood" in 1982. At first when conducting an orchestra, I got some strange looks. "What is an electric guitarist doing conducting us?", I thought some musicians were asking. Once I had proved myself my reputation changed in an instant.'

During 1982, Alan had an unfortunate accident where an index finger was badly gashed. 'I can still play guitar but it's not quite the same.' A year later he wrote his first feature score. This was for 'Jaws 3'.

One reviewer noted that Alan had previously provided music for British television including 'Vander Valk' and 'Minder' and then added: 'John Williams' original shark motif is, however, integrated into the score. The soundtrack album was released by MCA Records … The soundtrack was later released on CD by Intrada and was limited to only 3,000 copies. Alan Parker hits on [the] famous John Williams shark motif, then takes off on his own. Exciting score anchors with rousing, fanfare-theme for Florida Seaworld locale. Tender moments for Kay & Mike appear but bulk of score spells danger. Parker scores for full orchestra, often gives spotlight to vibrant French horn passages. In balance are ample moments for expected see-saw cellos & basses.'

Later Alan would work on, 'American Gothic' (1988), 'What's Eating Gilbert Grape' (1994) and 'Stormbreaker' (2006).

Despite diversifying from guitar playing over the last few decades, Alan is still extremely active in all other aspects of his creativity today. He believes, without question, the guitar still has a future and when asked to give advice for budding guitarists, he simply answers: 'Be adaptable and know your instrument inside out.'

MIKE PENDER

Sometimes, the sound of a particular guitar can influence a guitarist enough for them to continue using the instrument for much of their career. This happened with Mike Pender and his use of Rickenbacker 12-string guitars. He first heard a six-string Rickenbacker when he saw John Lennon with one in Hamburg; and a 12-string in 1964 when George Harrison played one during a performance of the Beatles' 'Hard Day's Night' single.

'The first 12-string I acquired was in 1964. Sadly, five years later it was stolen but I bet there's not a professional musician from the 1960s, or even later, who has not had a guitar nicked. Even though I have acquired other Rickenbacker 12-strings, I do miss that first guitar and even more so as time goes on. I live in hope that one day I might see it return.'

Mike was born in Bootle during 1941, the son of a dock worker. 'The Pools, Littlewoods and Vernons, and the Docks provided work for both men and women around where I lived.' Mike has an elder sister, and whilst the family name is really Prendergast, it has been shortened to Pender. His parents had Irish ancestry though they were not musical. A maternal aunt and uncle had some ability. His uncle Dennis played accordion and aunt Nance played piano. 'I used to listen to them as a kid. I can say that I was aware of music at a young age. I liked country music. In fact, it was played a lot around where I lived.'

Mike recalls first seeing a guitar around the age of ten. This was on Sunday visits to his paternal grandparents' Victorian terraced house near Liverpool city centre. A guitarist, playing at a local pub on Saturday nights, left his instrument – an electro acoustic – overnight at their house. 'I have no details about why this occurred. I didn't even ask. My grandparents had no connection with music. I haven't a clue about the make of the guitar only that I picked it up and was curious about how it was played.'

As a youngster, Mike was interested in good wholesome activities like watching cowboy films, on Saturdays at a local cinema, the Commodore; playing football; and trainspotting, often travelling as far afield as Perth or Dundee. 'Trainspotting belongs to one of the really enjoyable periods of my life. Dad always gave me ample money to go off on jaunts. Travelling was unbelievably cheap in those days. Mam and dad were quite laid back and never put pressure on me to do well at school or had any pretensions on what I should be on leaving. I enjoyed an ideal, relaxed family atmosphere. Even I didn't know what I wanted to do on leaving school.'

Mike was fond of songs by Hank Williams, Faron Young, Jimmie Rodgers and Frankie Laine. 'At family parties or gatherings people would sing and I liked that kind of atmosphere. I would be embarrassed when my mam asked me to sing for everyone. I would perform a 1952 Guy Mitchell song, "Wise Man or a Fool".'

The second time Mike picked up a guitar was around 1954 and this was at his friend John Bargens' house. 'Me and a few mates would try in vain to make some sounds from John's guitar. A little later, I traded in my impressive collection of American comics for a battered acoustic. Tuning was achieved with a tuning fork. This guitar really helped me to play. After obtaining a book showing simple chord shapes, I became familiar with G and C. But, it was the A, E and D that really got me into playing. These are the simple chords that you can play and sing along to quite easily.'

Leaving the battered acoustic behind, Mike progressed to a 6-string Framus/Zenith Tango 5/57. Pictures exist of Elvis Presley playing this model. Mike's guitar was bought at Christmas 1955 on HP by his dad, from Liverpool city centre music store Rushworths Music House. In the 1950s and 1960s, the store was known as the 'largest music house in Europe'.

Mike played football for Bootle Schoolboys and the team met Liverpool Schoolboys at Anfield in the W.R. Williams Cup final. Although the game was lost, Mike still has a much-coveted runners-up medal from the match. He left St Winefride's Secondary Modern School at 15 in 1956 with no qualifications and by his own admission was 'given an average report.' To begin with, he was an office boy with a major shipping company, Rea's Tugs, where he delivered mail, carried in a large satchel, to shipping companies like Cunard and the East India Company. This was in and around Liverpool city centre. 'I mostly travelled on the overhead railway called the "Dockers' Umbrella" locally. I enjoyed the work, everybody was friendly, and happy-go-lucky.'

Once Mike had left school, the interest in music took over; his football boots being discarded. He had met John McNally through mutual friends and they both had blonde Hofner Club 60 guitars. 'My Hofner was bought on HP from Frank Hessy Ltd's music store in Liverpool and it didn't have the greatest actions but I persevered with it.'

The pair practised regularly in the parlour at Mike's or John's house, mostly playing instrumentals. Mike was particularly impressed by Arthur Smith's 'Guitar Boogie' which he learned to play note-for-note. 'I suppose that instrumental really decided me on becoming a lead guitarist. I liked all those fiddly, melodic bits at the top end. John comfortably slipped into rhythm and I played lead. It just happened that way. Playing lead came to me naturally and John was impressed. While we lived in a rough and tumble, mucho-macho area, lads didn't put

Zenith guitars were built by Framus in Germany and re-badged Zenith by the importers (major instrument distributors Boosey & Hawkes). On www.framus-vintage.de website, the following specifications for the 5/57 Tango, built from the beginning of the 1950s, are included: 'dark auburn, later brown, or natural finish and several golden finishes; laminated arched body; single plywood binding; rosewood fingerboard with inlays; white Celluloid headstock.'

us down for being in a band, in fact they were pretty impressed we could play guitar and sing.'

Mike was mesmerised when Elvis Presley and rock 'n' roll burst upon the music scene, particularly when he heard 'Heartbreak Hotel', released in January 1956. 'I loved that record. I admired Elvis' vocal as well as Scotty Moore's guitar playing. Sometimes I would pose with my guitar in front of a wardrobe mirror in my parents' bedroom and believe I was a star. Never in my wildest dreams did I think I would ever be one. Music was for pretending not making a career.'

The mid-1950s were a time when skiffle was popular in the UK and groups abounded with makeshift instruments, but this was not for Mike. 'I was never interested in skiffle or Lonnie Donegan but knew lads who became part of that scene, using their mothers' washboards to create music.'

In 1957, Mike saw the John Wayne western film 'The Searchers' (released September 1956) at the Regent cinema in Crosby, Liverpool and the title was used for the original and first real performing line-up of the Searchers. This included Mike Pender and John McNally on guitars; Joe West on bass; and Joe Kennedy on drums. 'Joe West was the instigator of the group but could hardly play anything. We were really amateurish performing instrumentals and with me singing on a few songs. We only played a handful of small-time gigs. Wherever we went, there always seemed to be a piano, which we used to tune the guitars to concert pitch. John's and my guitar were played through a Watkins Dominator bought by Joe West's parents who were quite well off. This was the first time I ever played an electric guitar through an amplifier. Joe played bass through a homemade amp. After a while, the Watkins amp was stolen, causing the band to break up. There was no way we could buy another amplifier.'

On March 20, 1958, Mike saw Buddy Holly's second show at the Liverpool Philharmonic Hall and admits it was a life-changing experience for him. 'Des O'Connor was the compere and there were plenty of other Artists on the same bill. I was in the stalls, quite close to the stage. On the way home, I had an overwhelming urge to establish another version of the Searchers. I dreamed of having an American Fender Stratocaster just like Buddy which he played I believe through a 50-watt Fender Bassman amp with 4x10 in. speakers. I firmly believe that Buddy's Liverpool appearance was the catalyst for the birth of the Mersey sound, encouraging many local lads to form bands. It is significant that Buddy's "That'll Be the Day" was the first song the Quarrymen recorded in the Summer of 1958.'

Mike's jobs towards the end of the 1950s and early 1960s included working with John Fiddie's Ltd, a floor-laying company (from around 1958 to 1959), and then Birchall's, a book-printing firm, where he was employed in the bookbinding department.

'At the end of the 1950s, I was listening to and admiring the Shadows' guitar instrumentals. I liked tuneful melodic guitar music. I was also fascinated to watch and hear Vic Flick playing with the John Barry Seven when they appeared on "Six Five Special" and "Oh Boy!".'

On teaming up with Tony Jackson, Mike located John McNally once more and together they performed briefly as a three-piece. Tony Jackson was a competent vocalist who had been performing Elvis' songs and John and Mike taught him how to play bass as well as singing. For at least one gig they called themselves Tony and the Searchers. 'I recall that Tony got me and John an amp, though I don't remember the make and later he built his own bass amp because he was a great electrician and good at making things.'

Norman McGarry joined forces with the trio briefly on drums. This was roughly about 1959 and then Chris Crummey (later Curtis) joined. One of the first gigs played before Johnny Sandon joined was early in 1960 at the Reo, an old cinema in Fazakerley. From September 1960 until February 1962, Bill Beck (stage name Johnny Sandon), was lead vocalist, the group becoming known as Johnny Sandon and the Searchers. Mike and Tony still sang on some numbers then shared main vocal duties when Johnny joined the Remo Four. 'In a way it was a blessing for us he left, as we had to step up and say, come on we can handle vocals on our own.'

Around 1960, Mike bought a cherry red Burns Vibra-Artist guitar, sometimes known as a Burns Tri-sonic, with a tremolo arm, from Hessy's in Liverpool. 'That was the place to go. All the groups went down there. You could buy anything, straps, strings and any other accessories. With this guitar, I was able to play instrumentals like "3.30 Blues", "Walk Don't Run" and a handful of Shadows' hits.

'We played gigs in Liverpool, including the Casbah, Wavertree Town Hall, Orrell Park Ballroom, Litherland Town Hall, the Cavern and the Iron Door, which became our second home.'

The Iron Door opened on April 9, 1960, in a butter-packing warehouse at number 13 Temple Street and existed until 1964. 'Iron Door-owner, Les Ackerley became our manager. He also managed Freddie Starr and the Midnighters (before Freddie became a comedian). Playing a major role in the Searchers' development, Les said he believed in us and we could be as good as the Beatles who were the idols of Liverpool.

'Our first appearance at the Cavern was on April 5, 1961.

The Watkins Dominator amplifier with its unusual V-front made its debut in 1956. The turquoise and cream amplifiers pushed out a mere 17-watts and included a black control panel centred in the top of the amp; an Elac 10-inch speaker, two channels, four inputs and tremolo. Two EL 84s provided the output power.

Per Gjorde in Pearls and Crazy Diamonds: Fifty Years of Burns Guitars 1952–2002 *(2002) mentions the Vibra-Artist was the 'first' originally-produced design by Burns London … The guitar had [three] Tri-Sonic pick-ups with three volume controls, three tone controls, one 3-way selector and one rhythm/solo switch … The standard finish was cherry with fingerboard in maple (later rosewood) and black scratch plate. They were made in fairly large quantities. Retail price, £78.*

Mike Pender with Jetglo Rickenbacker 620 twelve-string.
Photograph by Peter Tuffrey.

Mike Pender with Fender Stratocaster from 1963.
Photograph by Peter Tuffrey.

Mike Pender with two of his guitars: Aria Pro II Aquanote 12-string and Yamaha Pacifica PAC 303-12 II 12-string.
Photograph by Peter Tuffrey.

The Aria Guitars company website, history section, states Shiro Arai, born in 1930, began to import classical guitars, Augustine guitar strings and musical scores for himself and students in 1954. Recognising an increasing demand for guitars he founded Arai & Co. in August 1956. 'The name, "ARIA", which means expressive melody, was first used in 1958 when Arai exported Japanese-built classical guitars fitted with steel strings to South East Asia in 1963. Also, the letters of his name "ARAI" were just switched around to "ARIA" as he recalled,' says the website.

We first supported the Beatles at the Cavern on July 26, 1961, when they had guest nights. By this time, John and I were playing through a single Fender amp. We did lunch-time sessions for the office workers and changed our set from what we did at night. We were one of only a few bands who could change direction and do this. Most of the others just stuck to the rock 'n' roll music, "Johnny B. Goode" and all those types of songs. With Johnny Sandon as lead vocalist, we were able to do this. The other Liverpool groups were friends of ours like Rory Storm and the Hurricanes, Swinging Blue Jeans, Gerry and the Pacemakers and we got to know the Beatles really well.'

For a period, when the band first started performing, Mike was still working at Birchall's but when they left for Hamburg, his boss told him if things didn't work out, he could return to his old job.

In October 1962, the Searchers appeared at the Star Club, Hamburg, for four weeks. 'Horst Fascher, booking agent for the club had seen us at the Cavern and invited us over there. We had to borrow cash before making the journey. It took two days to reach Hamburg from Liverpool, and we only carried our guitars. The PA and backline, of Fender amps, were supplied by the club. My wages at Birchall's were £10 a week, with overtime; at the Star Club they were £50. We really learned our trade in Germany during several stints there and became a really good band. Big stars from the States, including Ray Charles, Bill Haley and Jerry Lee Lewis, played at the Club, which opened at 4 pm and closed at 4 am, the last spot being 3 am. We often played the last set. There were usually four English groups there at any given time, and performed for three separate hours a night, three shows each.

'One afternoon while we were rehearsing, Jerry Lee Lewis came bounding in, jumped on stage and asked me if I knew the intro to "How's My Ex Treating You?". This was the B side of "Sweet Little Sixteen" released in July 1962. I confessed I didn't know it. "No matter I'll play it myself," he said. It was disappointing not to play something with him.'

Early 1963, saw the Searchers recording an 11-track demo tape at the Iron Door which eventually became known as 'the Home of the Searchers'. On receiving a copy of the demo, Pye Records' producer, Tony Hatch, was impressed and travelled up from London to meet the band. Decca showed no interest.

The Searchers' line-up of Pender, McNally, Jackson and Curtis were signed by Pye Records in March 1963. In June of the same year, the Searchers released 'Sweets For My Sweet', written by Doc Pomus and Mort Shuman. Chris Curtis had unearthed a Drifters' album featuring the song which had been a minor hit for them. Tony Hatch produced the Searchers' record at Pye's Marble Arch Studios and it went to no. 1.

'Chris was so good at finding songs and boasted an incredible record collection. He spent all his money on records and had them stacked all over the house where he lived with his mother. Before recording tracks, John and I would sit on our own devising and learning our rhythm and lead parts then come together with an original arrangement that included fills, breaks and everything else. John was a good rhythm player and stamped his style on the song and once I knew that, I put the lead parts on top. Whilst Chris discovered the songs and was a dominant influence within the band, he did not have any input into the guitar arrangements. For the first two or three singles, Pye didn't spend a lot of money on us. We did the songs in about three takes over sessions not lasting longer than 45 minutes and I believe we played the guitars through our Fender amps which we'd brought along with us.'

A second single 'Sugar And Spice' written by Tony Hatch under the pseudonym Fred Nightingale was released shortly afterwards and reached no. 2. In the ensuing years the band made appearances on 'Thank Your Lucky Stars' and other TV shows such as 'Ready Steady Go!' as well as being regularly heard on radio.

Performing at the Star Club and on the Searchers' first two singles, Mike used the Burns guitar. After Tito Burns became the band's manager, he helped Mike exchange it for a Gibson ES 345. 'I remember Tito telephoning Ivor Mairants at his music shop in Piccadilly Circus to ask him to make sure he did me a good deal.'

Before the end of 1963, another single 'Sweet Nothin's' appeared as well as three albums, 'Meet The Searchers' and 'The Searchers At The Star Club, Hamburg', and 'Sugar And Spice'. In December 1963, Mike found time to marry the love of his life, May.

The Searchers' first big year was 1964, with lots of hit singles, EPs and LPs, TV shows, concerts and world tours. In January of that year, the Searchers released 'Needles And Pins' and Mike says the track features his Gibson ES 345 with John McNally's Club 60 behind. 'Although we did receive a demo of "Needles & Pins", we first heard the song on our second trip to the Star Club after which I sang it in our set, before we actually recorded it. For our version, we doubled my Gibson just to enhance the A-chord riff.'

Rickenbacker's first 12-string, one of three prototypes made in July 1963, went to Suzi Arden, a showband singer, fiddle player and guitarist. Francis Cary Hall, Rickenbacker's owner, had been contacted by London-based, Rose-Morris & Co. Ltd (Rose-Morris) about importing Rickenbackers from July 1962. A deal was clinched by Rose-Morris in December 1963. Rose-Morris' manager, Roy Morris and Maurice Woolf made Hall aware of the Beatles' popularity and suggested presenting the band with guitars. F.C. Hall handed George Harrison the second of the three prototype Rickenbacker 12-string guitars, built in December 1963, during the first week of February 1964 whilst the Beatles were on their first US tour. Rose-Morris received a sample Rickenbacker 12-string in June 1964 and soon afterwards a further batch of 25 guitars followed. The company catalogued it as model 1993 and priced it at £222 10s.

'Needles', with Mike, not Tony Jackson, as the lead vocalist, reached no. 1 within a few weeks. 'At first I was not comfortable being lead guitarist and lead vocalist but grew into it gradually.'

Mike played his Gibson on several more singles 'Don't Throw Your Love Away' and 'Some Day We're Gonna Love Again'. Tito Burns took the Searchers to the USA for a short promotional tour in January 1964 where they made a successful appearance on the 'Ed Sullivan Show'.

'Until the explosion of British music in the 1960s, it was difficult for artists to make a big impression in America. The Beatles made it easier for other groups coming through like us, Gerry and the Pacemakers and a few others. I took my Gibson ES 345 to the States and we played through Fender amps. Before we went on stage during the big tours, we just tuned by ear because your ear became accustomed to the correct sounds. John and I would tune up to each other so that both guitars were exactly the same.'

For much of 1964 and into 1965, Tito had the Searchers headlining major tours with many other top stars, amongst them Roy Orbison, Bobby Vee, Dusty Springfield, Brian Poole and the Tremeloes and Dionne Warwick.

Mike was extremely impressed when he saw George Harrison playing a red Rickenbacker 12-string on the single 'A Hard Day's Night' on TV. The disc was released in July 1964.

A short time before the Searchers recorded 'When You Walk In The Room', written by Jackie DeShannon, Mike played the opening riff on a 6-string and it didn't sound right. The riff for this song needed to be a different sound and Mike was convinced it had to be played on a Rickenbacker 12-string.

'Crane's music shop in Liverpool was pretty upmarket in those days, and I knew they had a Rickenbacker 12-string in stock. To my amazement, they did me a straight swap for my Gibson ES 345, which at the time I thought was a great deal. Crane's obviously knew their guitars and probably got the better of it, but I wanted that Rick!'

Ideally, Mike wanted the 360/12 model he'd seen George Harrison play. But, when Crane's showed Mike the Rose-Morris 360/12 1993 model he changed his mind.

'I much preferred the 'f' sound hole to the 'slash' type on George's guitar.'

Mike was just one of a number of 1960s lead guitarists who fell in love with electric 12-string Rickenbackers and their 'jangling' sound. Besides George Harrison, they included Pete Townshend, Brian Jones and Roger McGuinn. Later came Tom Petty, Peter Buck, and Bruce Springsteen.

'The Rickenbacker Rose-Morris 360/12 (Model 1993) was, without doubt, my second love … I was very lucky to get one, as demand exceeded supply at the time … "When You Walk In The Room" played on a 12-string has become one of the most instantly recognisable guitar riffs from the 1960s, even providing the inspiration for Tony Hatch's famous "Crossroads" theme.'

'When You Walk In The Room', released in September 1964, reached no. 3 in the UK and no. 35 in the USA.

Mike used his Rickenbacker 12 for the Searchers' next single 'What Have They Done To The Rain' which he states was a protest/anti-war song and a major departure for the band. The song was written by Malvina Reynolds, and the Searchers based their version, released in November 1964, on a recording by Joan Baez.

'It is, arguably, one of the first British folk-rock records, pre-dating artistes like Donovan, and electrified Bob Dylan and the Byrds in the US, who some say adopted our Rickenbacker-led sound and vocal harmony.' The single reached no. 13 in the UK and no. 29 in the US.

During 1964, the Burns guitar company presented Mike with a white Double Six and a white Burns Marvin. 'I used the Double Six on some recordings, in particular our live recordings in Sweden, as well as for TV shows and concerts.'

Tony Jackson, the band's lead vocalist and bass player, left in July 1964 and was replaced by Frank Allen, formerly of Cliff Bennett and the Rebel Rousers. Mike was now firmly established as the lead vocalist.

From 1963 to 1966, the Searchers were a household name and enjoyed 15 UK chart singles (including three number ones), seven hit EPs (including two number ones), and four top twenty LPs (including one number one). During 1966, drummer Chris Curtis was replaced by John Blunt, staying until 1969 when Billy Adamson took over.

'From around 1963, we used Vox amplification similar to most British bands. Vox actually gave us some amps during this period.' In *The Vox Story: A Complete History of the Legend* (1993), David Peterson and Dick Denney mention: 'As a guitar unit, [the AC50 MK2] answered the need for more clean volume and plenty of treble, which was needed to overcome the unbelievably noisy crowd reaction to the new generation of vocal/instrument groups. The great majority of these (the Searchers, the Hollies, the Dave Clark Five and Billy J. Kramer, who all had hits in 1963) used Vox amplifiers exclusively …' A picture in the above-mentioned book shows the Searchers on stage at the New Musical Express Poll-winners concert, Wembley 1964 with an all-Vox backline. Mike is playing the Gibson ES 345.

Mike's Rickenbacker 12 was stolen in late 1969 from the Lafayette nightclub in Wolverhampton and he temporarily used a sunburst Danelectro Bellzouki 12-string.

During a Searcher's USA tour in 1974, Mike bought a Rickenbacker 456 6/12 'comb converter' in maple glow from Manny's Music shop in New York.

Despite the loss of original members, Tony Jackson and Chris Curtis and a lack of chart success, the Searchers continued to thrill audiences around the world for the remainder of the 1960s, and during the ensuing decades.

Mike bravely accepts some harsh comments made by Paul Du Noyer in his book *Liverpool – Wondrous Place: Music from the Cavern to Cream* (2002), about what happened to the Searchers, and to other Merseyside bands, in and around 1966: 'The Mersey beat acts were mostly working-class lads, whose values were those of traditional entertainers. They never had the scholarly obsession with the obscure blues that Jagger, Richards and others had. They liked the bright, accessible pop of Tamla-Motown and the Brill Building. They had no interest in the emerging counter-culture; their roots were in semi-pro show business. When pop became rock, and rock went weird around 1966, the Liverpool groups were left behind; and with the rise of the deejay-dominated discos, the beat groups weren't even needed for dancing to …'

The Searchers released their final singles for Pye in 1967 and then moved to Liberty before joining Sire Records in 1978. Whilst touring in America in 1974, Mike bought a 1963 Fender Stratocaster in Kansas City. 'From what I've been told, it's quite a rare and collectable model. It even has the original bridge cover.'

A well-crafted album 'The Searchers' released by Sire Records in 1979 received critical acclaim. 'The album was very well received by self-confessed admirers of our '60s sound such as Tom Petty and the Heartbreakers.' 'Hearts in Her Eyes' was

---

Burns introduced the Double Six prototype in 1963 and it was originally designed to fit in with the Split Sound range (Jazz Split sound and Split Sonic). However, the design was changed to match visually with the Marvin range. Models produced 1964–1965 had Tri-sonic pick-ups with volume, tone and 3-way selector. The guitar had a rosewood fingerboard; colours included green or red sunburst as well as some white and black. Elvis Presley is pictured performing with a green sunburst Burns Double Six in a musical scene from MGM's 1966 release 'Spinout'.

The Danelectro Company of Neptune, New Jersey, made the unusual-looking 12-string guitar called the Bellzouki based on an idea put forward by Italian studio player Vinnie Bell. Introduced around 1961, the Danelectro Bellzouki 710 had a teardrop-shaped body, one volume and one tone control along with a 3-way toggle for tone selection. The models had one or two Lipstick pick-ups. In time Danelectro introduced two revised models, the 7020 and 7021.

The Rickenbacker string converter models, 336/12, 366/12 and the 456/12 were devised by musician and inventor James E. Gross. A 'converter comb' mounted to the body of a 12-string could be manipulated to turn the guitar into a 6-string (or any number in between). When engaged the 'converter comb' pulled strings down away from a guitarist's right hand, leaving only the required number of strings to be picked. After Gross had approached Rickenbacker owner F.C. Hall with the idea, the inventor gave a demonstration at the July 1966 NAMM show. Production had started on the 'converter comb' guitars by the winter of the same year. Rickenbacker 'converter comb' publicity read: 'Now, one instrument—the most versatile guitar ever made—ends the need for carrying extra guitars. By means of an exclusive, patented converter on the brilliant Rickenbacker 12-string guitar, any combination of strings can be played.'

Mike Pender with Rickenbacker 456/12 Convertible.
Photograph by Peter Tuffrey.

released as a single, and got some great reviews and built up some airplay.

Peter Trollope gave the album a good review in the *Liverpool Echo* on October 31, 1979. He described the Searchers 'as a group that refused to die' and 'as fresh today as they were in the glorious Mersey beat heyday.' Trollope continued: 'Mike and John are the guitarists from the original line-up – it is their playing that gives the group its unique sound.'

The Searchers were invited to perform in front of the Queen as part of the '25 Years of British Pop' segment of the Royal Variety Show on Monday, November 23, 1981. During the late 1970s, Japanese guitar company Aria, with a factory on the outskirts of London, presented the band with new guitars. 'Frankie had met Aria's chairman, who just happened to be a Searchers fan. John and I chose a 12-string and a 6-string. I was a bit cheeky and also asked for a 12-string acoustic. The 12-string electric Aria was quite impressive, with a great action – very important on a 12-string – and not too big a body. The electric 12-string Aria Pro-11 got stolen but the company gave me a replacement in 1993, a 12-string Aria Pro-11 Rev Sound in a stunning blue colour.'

Mike left the band in 1985, after protracted legal battles, to form Mike Pender's Searchers. His new band continues to enjoy enormous success at home and abroad with Mike (82 at the time of writing) fronting the band on vocals and guitar.

The 12-string Aria Pro-11 Rev Sound guitar was damaged during a flight to Australia for a Mike Pender's Searchers tour in 2006. 'I didn't have another guitar so the Australian promoter bought me a 12-string Yamaha; the Aria was repaired once I returned home.'

Before Mike performed in the first of a number of shows called 'ReelinandaRocking' in 2002, he treated himself to a new Rickenbacker. 'I bought a 660 12-string in jetglo which has the separate tailpiece and separate "bed" for each string. I now use this for all my major gigs and tours.'

Andy Powell with a Music Man Silhouette guitar.
Photograph courtesy of David Moffitt.

ANDY POWELL

Andy Powell is still enthusiastic playing guitar with internationally acclaimed Wishbone Ash. This is over 50 years since he first attended an audition that would result in the band's formation. He is the only constant member of a line-up that has often changed. For a number of years, Wishbone Ash has been managed solely by Andy as a private company. The band regularly plays its inimitable, melodic, hard rock to discerning audiences around the world. He is a survivor from the heady days of early 1970s rock, where drugs were present everywhere. He states: 'I'm just high on life. I keep fit and like to be engaged in life. Drugs and alcohol can lead you away from celebrating the essence of life.'

Although born during 1950 in the East End of London, Andy grew up in Hemel Hempstead, designated a new town in 1946 with modern housing estates and facilities. During the Second World War, his father had worked in an armaments factory later becoming an engineer for Vauxhall Motors in Dunstable, Bedfordshire. Besides being a housewife, his mother kept accountancy books for a local garage and worked in a school canteen. Andy has a brother Len, who is four years his junior.

'My parents never played an instrument,' began Andy, 'but my dad was a virtuoso whistler. In fact, almost everyone around me, including the milkman, rag and bone man and postman seemed to constantly whistle.' Curiously, this had an impact much later, on how he would use vibrato when developing a melodic guitar style. In some instances, he has whistled licks to various guitar partners to get a melody across.

'I have always been interested in a melodic guitar sound. Whenever I'm improvising on stage, I'm always thinking melody. That's what people pick up on with my guitar style.'

From 1955, Andy attended Hobbs Hill Primary School where he said the art classes always captured his imagination. During his early years, he listened to the BBC's 'Children's Favourites' with 'Uncle Mac' (Derek McCulloch) and was familiar with material from America by Burl Ives, old bluesmen and other performers. In the 1950s, his family never possessed a record player but his aunt Rene had a radiogram where he heard Peggy Lee.

As the 1950s progressed, Andy realised the impact of Lonnie Donegan, 'loosening up' music from the stranglehold of light music heard on the BBC. For Andy, Lonnie was the father of 'letting it all go.'

Andy first became guitar conscious at a cousin's wedding party. A band performing at the event included a guitarist with a blood-red semi-acoustic instrument playing through a Vox amplifier. Before the end of the decade, Andy was enamoured by Chuck Berry's guitar sound, riffs and the poetry of the lyrics.

As the 1960s dawned, anything from America's popular culture made a huge impact on Andy. He felt the influence of the Shadows' instrumental music, considering Hank Marvin to have a special touch. He was hugely impressed with Hank's red Fender Stratocaster with its gold hardware and tremolo arm. Until this time, he was only familiar with the poor British versions of American instruments, seen with his mates on their regular trips to local music shops.

At ten years old, Andy fell under the spell of Django Reinhardt, watching him play lead guitar with just two fingers. 'He had an ebullient gypsy-style passion and emotion.' A year later, Andy passed the Eleven-Plus to attend Apsley Grammar School but found there was little opportunity to study music. Undeterred, and with an ever-growing interest in the guitar, he marvelled at a salmon pink Stratocaster seen in a local music shop window. Regular jaunts to view guitars were now being made to London music shops such as Macari's and Selmer's.

Around 1962, Andy was inspired by a neighbour to make his own guitar and was ably assisted by his dad and uncle. He believed this was the best way to have an in-depth understanding of how the instrument functioned. 'Making a guitar was hugely important for me, being involved with the woodwork and the electrics. It not only assisted me in creating my sound but also how it might be improved and progressed.'

Andy's uncle Jim was the manager of a timber suppliers and wood yard in Brentwood. From there, he obtained a piece of maple wood for the guitar neck and a lump of mahogany for the body. Andy created the guitar from memory, on the family's dining room table, and it was shaped like a Fender Strat. 'The mess created in the house was unbelievable. Dad helped with some of the brass metal work which he'd chromium-plated at the Vauxhall car plant. Later, I built a Les Paul-shaped guitar which I amusingly titled my "Les Powell".'

The guitars were played through a homemade amp put together utilising television components. Later, he progressed to use some of the English-built amps like those by Selmer and Burns.

Whilst Andy bought Bert Weedon's *Play in a Day*, he never learned more than three chord patterns in different keys. He had no formal guitar or music tuition and trusted his ear to tune the guitar and pick out guitar parts he wanted to play.

Andy's first band was a four-piece line-up and he was lead guitarist. 'We played mostly instrumentals and our first performance was in 1963 at the Ovaltine factory in King's Langley.' A year later, Andy was in a band, the Dekois and they opened for the High Numbers, later to change their name back to the Who, at Watford Trade Hall in August 1964.

'I was definitely impressed with the High Numbers' professionalism and they had a great impact on me. I came away from the gig thinking that to be a rock musician you must have attitude, a strong work ethic and unswerving determination to be successful.' Working hard didn't bother Andy as he always strived to earn cash from various jobs: a newspaper round; working in a fish and chip shop; in an electrical shop; and selling ice cream.

By 1966, Andy made regular visits to Soho's Flamingo Club and was a fan of the Action, Creation, Spencer Davis Group, Georgie Fame, and Albert King who he noticed played a strangely-shaped Gibson guitar called a Flying V. King was mostly known for playing a 1959 Korina V, though he did play other models.

Leaving school in 1968 with eight O-Levels and two A-Levels, Andy felt no pressure from his parents to enter university or pursue what may be termed a conventional career. At this period, he was playing in seven- or eight-piece bands with horn sections and a Hammond organ, feeding his interest in Tamla Motown, Soul and R&B. The bands included the Sugarband and the Ashley Ward Delegation and they played around St Albans, Watford and Hemel Hempstead.

For a while, he played a Hofner Coronado and a Burns short scale Jazz guitar with a floating vibrato system which he found to be well made, very comfortable to play and helped him form a lead guitar style. It was bought for £40, which was hard-earned cash from his many jobs.

The following year, 1969, was eventful for Andy and saw him have a flirtation with working in a John Lewis Partnership retail store; sell his Burns guitar to finance a journey to Marrakesh, which lasted only six weeks; and answer an advertisement in

> *Chuck Berry was born in 1926 in St Louis, Missouri, United States. During the early 1950s, he absorbed the guitar riffs and showmanship of T-Bone Walker. With the help of Muddy Waters, he started recording for Chess Records, 'Maybellene' being released in 1955. Other hits during the remainder of the decade included 'Roll Over Beethoven' (1956); 'School Days'(1957); 'Rock And Roll Music' (1957); 'Sweet Little Sixteen' (1958); 'Johnny B. Goode' (1958); and 'Little Queenie' (1959). Amongst the guitars used by Berry were: a Kay Thin Twin K-161; a 1956 Gibson hollow body ES 350TN; a 1957 Gibson ES 350T; a Gibson ES 335; and a Gibson ES 345.*

Melody Maker magazine for a lead guitarist in a band. To the audition, Andy had taken along the second homemade guitar.

Already members of this band were Martin Turner, a bass guitarist, and Steve Upton, a drummer. The manager was Miles Copeland III, son of Miles Axe Copeland Jr, a CIA officer from Birmingham, Alabama. Another candidate for the lead guitar role was Ted Turner (no relation to Martin) who had been unsuccessful in an attempt to slot into a guitarist role with Jon Hiseman's Colosseum.

Ultimately, at rehearsals in the home of Miles Copeland's parents in St John's Wood, it was decided to run with two lead guitarists and so Wishbone Ash was born. Andy has often been asked how did two lead guitarists mesh together in a band. His answer has always been straightforward, given his previous musical experiences:

'I'm always an ensemble player first. I can step out and solo and do the guitar god thing but the music as a whole is much more important. I always want to support the song, and the melody. Before Ted and I came together, I had been used to both playing a solo and a supporting role with horn or brass sections or a Hammond organ. I used to sit down with the trumpet or sax player and we would sing or whistle parts to each other, get our heads round the fact that trumpets are tuned to Bb and then transpose an arrangement accordingly. We were trying to replicate what was happening in Motown and Stax productions in our own English way. At the same time, I particularly liked Pentangle, admiring their guitarists, John Renbourn and Bert Jansch. Fairport Convention impressed me too as I liked the whole British folk scene.'

After a jam session, Ted and Andy immediately got on well together. They both liked the same music. They were very young and gladly accepted they would be sharing roles.

'We played to our strengths, because we wanted to move this new professional band forward. As with many things, it required hard work to bring it all together, involving both the bass player and drummer moulding a true band spirit. The British Blues Boom had happened in the mid-1960s and Jeff Beck, Eric Clapton and Jimi Hendrix had just about done everything with guitar by 1969. We wondered where else can you go. We wanted to try and push it a little bit further, using the guitars in a slightly more intelligent way.

Andy Powell playing a Hofner guitar at the Ovaltine works social in Kings Langley, Hertfordshire. Photograph courtesy of David Moffitt.

'The first song we wrote as a band was "Blind Eye". The idea was to produce a staccato riff that would grab everyone's attention. We were playing in clubs with three or four bands on the bill so we needed something special. As soon as we heard that track played back, we were impressed and thought, let's continue in that way. There's always a bit of twin lead guitar in everything we do. It's become our hallmark, our stamp. The Allman Brothers formed around the same time as us but we were completely unaware of what they were doing. Our main influences were Peter Green's Fleetwood Mac and before that Blossom Toes. For me, they were the first bands I heard playing two guitars together. Two guitars played in synergy is ear candy and you want to hear more. Ted tended to play solo in our more bluesy numbers while I played the more frenetic pieces. I could never have predicted then that the two-guitar sound would still be relevant today, 50 years later.'

The Burns Short Scale Jazz guitar was produced between 1962 and 1965 and featured TriSonic pick-ups, volume and tone controls, a 3-way selector switch, a standard red sunburst finish (though a selection of colours was available); rosewood fingerboard and black scratch plate. According to Pearls and Crazy Diamonds: Fifty Years of Burns Guitars 1952–2002, *later models were fitted with the series two vibrato unit.*

Initially, Andy played his second homemade guitar in the band but soon bought an all-mahogany Gibson SG Special finished in cherry, with a stopbar tailpiece and two P90 single coil pick-ups. 'I'd play the SG strapped high up on my chest and it had a rather unstable neck you could bend to create vibrato effects when chording.'

The guitar was pushed through a 60-watt Laney amplifier which Andy bought on credit.

In Wishbone Ash's early days, Andy lived in a rat-infested London flat above a convenience store. Some of the early gigs in 1970 found the band in France but Andy was stricken with pleurisy and returned to his parents' home. Whilst there, he had serious doubts about his career as a guitarist, but drummer, Steve Upton, talked him round.

On May 18, 1970, Wishbone Ash supported Deep Purple at the Civic Hall, Dunstable. During the afternoon, Andy had a small impromptu jam session with Ritchie Blackmore. Later, Richie heard Wishbone's set and was impressed enough to recommend them to Purple's producer Derek Lawrence. This was a major break for the band with Miles Copeland following up and cutting a deal with Don Shane, head of Decca/MCA Records. Ultimately, Wishbone Ash gained a fantastic American record deal, so elusive for many British bands.

Through Miles Copeland, some prestigious session work came Andy's way. He is heard on several tracks George Harrison produced for Cilla Black. 'I played one of George's 6-string Harptone guitars in the studio.'

In preparation for recording the first album, Andy became absorbed in creating arrangements, guitar parts and openings. Some of these are showcased on the album, particularly on the track 'Errors Of My Way'.

During 1970, Wishbone Ash played a number of festivals: at Bath and at the Plumpton Racecourse, as well as appearing on BBC 2's 'Disco 2'. They also appeared on the same bills as Atomic Rooster, ELP, the Who and Van der Graaf Generator.

The band's first album was recorded at De Lane Lea studios, during September 1970 and released in December of the same year. For recording, Andy used Fender Concert combo amplifiers for their clear, warm tone. In time, he would acquire a vintage 1959 tweed-covered Fender Bassman combo and use this regularly in the studio.

'Sometimes playing through two Fender amps – one with full bass the other full treble – I found they gave a great fat sound. On the first album, Ted played a Gibson SG Junior but generally as a rule we liked to have a Gibson and a Fender playing together. That gave us the high end cut of a Fender and the warmth of a Gibson, to add more texture to the twin lead guitars.'

Wishbone Ash began touring America in March to April 1970, sharing the same bill on those dates as Eric Burdon, Badfinger, the James Gang, the Allman Brothers and Elton John, and playing venues such as the Fillmore West, San Francisco. In September 1971, Wishbone Ash released a second album, 'Pilgrimage'. Andy played the SG on the first and second albums. A short tour of the US followed the record's release with the band appearing on the same bill as Steve Miller, Love, and Humble Pie. At the Satsop River Festival, Seattle on September 3, they performed

Andy Powell playing a Telecaster.
Photograph courtesy of David Moffitt.

Andy Powell with a Royal Flying V.
Photograph courtesy of David Moffitt.

in front of an audience numbering over 100,000.

In 1972, Andy made two very important decisions in his life: he got married to Pauline and chose to adopt the Gibson Flying V as his instrument of choice. Both continue to play a major part in his life today.

'In the spring of 1972, I had a call from Cliff Cooper at his London Orange shop saying he had for sale two brand new and boxed (but five years old) Gibson Flying Vs that he'd imported from the USA. Apparently, nobody over there wanted them. I'd never seen one in the flesh up until that time, though had seen Dave Davies and Jimi Hendrix playing them on TV. I plugged one of them into an OR-100. The guitar was a cherry red colour, with a Vibrola system, and I knew instantly this was for me. I gladly handed over £300 and took the guitar home to my bedsit and marvelled at it for a while. At that time, the V was unpopular with American players because of a feeling the company was trying to compete with Fender by producing futuristic-looking rock instruments and they didn't like that. The classic Gibson guitars had developed with jazz and the V was a step too far. Another small consideration was that for some people the Vs were difficult to play sitting down but that has never bothered me. I quickly discovered the V had all the components of a Gibson, with a thick mid-range and also because of the fins there was a nice vibrant high-end. The other advantage was the guitar had a Vibrola. I had first admired Hank Marvin using a tremolo and was able to use that feature with the V. The majority of players today, Jeff Beck being a prime example, use that as an important part of their performance.'

Shortly after Andy's Flying V purchase, the band started using Orange amps on stage. 'We bought a selection of 100-watt heads and even 200-watt heads, together with separate reverb units. The cabinets were later upgraded with JBL K120 speakers. We shipped the amplifiers almost every day during an American tour and our tour managers had to use their best negotiating powers with airport staff.'

Andy fondly recalls that 1972 was the year the band's album 'Argus' was recorded at De Lane Lea studios and concedes nothing else they did would be quite as significant. Martin Turner wrote most of the words and everyone in the band, to varying degrees, crafted the music. 'I played my Flying V through Fender amps. Ted played a 1959 Les Paul and a 1950s Fender Stratocaster. The guitar lines are very lyrical and melodic. Ted and I worked out most of the songs on acoustic guitars in a place we had just off Ladbroke Grove. For me the "Blowin Free" track had a wonderful exuberance and perhaps may have influenced Steely Dan's "Reelin' In The Years" and Thin Lizzy's "The Boys Are Back In Town". "Argus" was not just a collection of songs. They are inter-related with themes carried over from song to song. It's really a concept album by default. Just before "Argus", we were starting to break into America so the music was constructed for performing in stadiums. We needed to slow down and open out like Pink Floyd's music does.'

Declining sales of Gibson Les Paul models by 1960 led to a new guitar design appearing, the SG. In the following year the Custom, Standard, Special and Junior models received the new, exciting shape. The Gibson SG Special was available in 1961/1962 in a cherry or cream finish. The guitar had a nickel-plated, wrap-around tailpiece and two single-coil P-90s were present; they were covered with rectangular black plastic. A bound rosewood fingerboard was used with dot inlays and an unbound headstock with the Gibson logo in pearl inlay.

'Argus' was voted by *Sounds* as the Best Rock Album of 1972, also Top British Album by *Melody Maker*.

In the early 1970s, Wishbone Ash members moved to America with Andy settling in Connecticut, where he still lives, eventually becoming an American citizen. During American tours, Ted and Andy regularly went round pawn and guitar shops picking up 1950s and 1960s instruments at very low prices. Known dealers would turn up at sound checks with guitars.

Fender first introduced the Concert amp in 1959. Comprising two channels, the amp came in a 4x10 in. configuration with vibrato being the only effect. In subsequent years, 1960–1965, the Concert amps changed cosmetically and electrically.

'Often, I bought a Flying V and Ted picked up a Les Paul. Thrown into deals were a Gibson mandolin or lap steel guitar. I once bought a 1952 Telecaster from Larry DiMarzio for $300 and also picked up 1958 and 1959 Korina wood Flying Vs. I paid around $2,000 for the 1959 V with an original case. Eventually I acquired Stratocasters from every one of the classic years, 1954 to 1963. Ted and I liked to coax out of these early guitars the essence of what they had been built for. The Telecaster was once owned by Roy Buchanan and I've played that a lot on record. Most guitar dealers were fans and like us were guitar enthusiasts. They knew what they were picking up. Ted and I also acquired guitars from various sources ourselves. Both the Fender and Gibson vintage guitar sounds are clearly heard on our early 1970s recordings.'

A change to the band occurred in 1974 when Ted Turner left and Laurie Wisefield (ex-Home) joined. The first album recorded with Laurie was 'There's The Rub'.

'This was a daunting period because Ted and Laurie's guitar styles were different. Laurie came with a country influence. He was more of a guitar picker so the learning curve of us playing together was massive for both him and me. He had to learn single string soloing blues style while I had to learn country pick, with two and then three fingers. I got that style of playing from Richard Thompson. Laurie had been into that before me. The pair of us coming together produced some interesting results.'

Laurie quickly accompanied Andy on the pawnshop excursions. On one occasion, Laurie picked up a 1954 Fender Stratocaster for a mere $300. Many of the instruments 'found' were used on recordings making the collecting obsession exciting and relevant.

Wishbone Ash albums released throughout the rest of the 1970s were: 'Star Truckin'; 'Locked In'; 'New England'; 'Front Page News'; 'No Smoke Without Fire'.

Guitars used by Andy during this period included a white Gibson Firebird VII with three pick-ups and gold hardware which he subsequently sold to Stephen Stills. 'The reason behind this came through Miles Copeland saying my signature guitar was a Flying V and people came to concerts to see me playing it. "Sell it", he said. "That's not your trademark guitar". My friend, Fred Renz, once told me, "Without the V, it cannot be".'

At regular intervals, throughout their time together, Wishbone Ash had to weather the changes taking place within the fickle music industry. 'Not long after we started there was Glam Rock, followed by Punk Rock, then came the New Romantics and about the same time the New Age of British Heavy Metal. We had to decide how to take our music and help it slide through these changes. Primarily, it did help relying heavily on a guitar sound and we kept that as a constant belief. A producer once said to me "It's all about the guitars, Andy. As long as you remember that you'll be OK" and I did and I have. I must confess I have an undying passion for guitars, I can't stop touching them, picking them up and playing them. I'm also one of those people who are extremely loyal to an idea. Once I commit myself to an idea, I commit. I'm like that in life too.'

At the outset of the 1980s, Martin Turner was replaced by bassist John Wetton who had experience with Family, King Crimson and Uriah Heep. After appearing on the 'Number The Brave' album, John Wetton was replaced by Trevor Bolder formerly of the Rats, Spiders from Mars and Uriah Heep. Other personnel changes included the departure of Laurie Wisefield, and bass and lead guitarists were brought in on a contractual basis. At one point in the decade, the band faced bankruptcy but with some clever negotiating this was avoided.

An interesting place in the world where Wishbone Ash performed for several dates during December 1981 was India. 'On one occasion we used some of the equipment left by the Police who had toured over there. Guitars and amps were piled on a three-wheel truck, covered up and then precariously moved around to the venue. We played there again on several other occasions.'

Towards the end of the 1980s, Miles Copeland III, contacted three of the original 1969 members of the band with a master plan (Ted Turner was to be contacted much later). He wanted them to produce an instrumental album and 'Nouveau Calls' (a pun on 'no vocals') was released in December 1987. Afterwards, the band felt comfortable enough together again to continue and they produced one more album 'Here To Hear' released in 1989 before they embarked on an American tour as well as fitting in a couple of shows in Brazil.

Earlier in November 1988 and then May 1989 Andy, and Ted Turner, performed together in an ambitious 'Night of the Guitars Tour' organised by Miles that featured a number of prominent guitarists. Amongst the other guitarists featured were Leslie West from Mountain, Alvin Lee from Ten Years After and Robby Krieger from the Doors. Later, Phil Manzanera from Roxy Music and Jan Akkerman from Focus joined for the European dates. Each guitarist performed three songs with a rhythm section of Clive Mayuyu and Livingstone Brown.

Long-time drummer, Steve Upton left before the recording of 'Strange Affair', released in 1991 and this was the last album to feature founding members Martin Turner and Ted Turner who left in 1991 and 1994 respectively.

All this ultimately led to Andy taking full control of the band, hiring musicians when needed for tours and recordings, along with juggling this role with a number of other diverse activities. This continues today and Wishbone Ash are still appearing all over the world at festivals, and in theatres, art centres and clubs.

During his long and eventful career Andy has owned over a dozen Gibson Flying Vs including three or four from 1967 as well as Korinas and various custom models. A number of other guitars he plays have been built by independent luthiers such as Ray Cooper of Berkhamsted. He has built Andy a Strat-style instrument with a compressor built into the body as well as a Telecaster-style guitar. For the body of this guitar, part of an old top from a demolished pub was used.

Sam Li, a reputable luthier, who was formerly based in Gerrard Place, Soho, London made a Flying V-style guitar for Andy, so too did another guitar maker, Kevin Chilcott. Kevin built the V-style guitar to include a piezo pick-up system, in addition to the regular magnetic pick-ups, so that Andy could obtain acoustic guitar sounds from it as well. Two Vs were built from aged Honduras mahogany with ebony fingerboards. Jon Case, another Wishbone Ash fan and guitar builder, has provided Andy with a V-style guitar featuring a Fishman piezo system.

Andy is frustrated that Gibson have never produced a signature Flying V for him. He has spoken to Gibson at length about this and many fans have lobbied the company on his behalf but no interest has been shown. It would be a fitting tribute to one of the instrument's greatest champions.

Gibson introduced the Flying V guitars – made of Korina wood – from 1958. The guitar was part of a modernist line designed by the company president Ted McCarty; the others being the Explorer and Moderne. McCarty considered these would add a more futuristic aspect to Gibson's image but the line was discontinued in 1959 due to poor sales. Guitarists Lonnie Mack and Albert King were early supporters of the Flying V. By the mid-1960s there was a renewed interest in the V and Gibson reissued the guitar with a mahogany body in 1967.

Orange was founded by Cliff Cooper in 1968 when he opened the Orange Shop in London's New Compton Street. The outlet sold second-hand guitars and amplifiers. Tasting success, Cliff then started building his own amps which were initially constructed under a sub-contract to Mat Mathias, running Matamp in Huddersfield. From the late 1960s, the Orange brand had a meteoric rise and became used by many large acts including Fleetwood Mac. Cliff Cooper eventually moved the manufacturing operation closer to home in London.

Keith Richards with Gibson ES 355 guitar in rare factory black finish. He is pictured on stage at the Barclaycard British Summer Time, Hyde Park, London on Saturday July 6, 2013.
Suzan Moore / Alamy Stock Photo.

KEITH RICHARDS

Often described as the epitome of the 'rock 'n' roll' ethos, Keith Richards certainly does little to take away from this sentiment, particularly in regard to his guitar playing. Being influenced by the music in his youth, Keith has kept true to rock 'n' roll throughout his career with the Rolling Stones and in his solo work. His choice of guitars and amps is similarly consistent with this and in the most part he has eschewed guitar effects and studio trickery. He has defined his own style of playing through the use of open G tuning from the late 1960s to the present.

Keith became interested in music from an early age. His grandfather Gus had been in a band and a number of musical instruments were in his house, which Keith often visited.

Despite this early interest, Keith was relatively late in acquiring his own guitar. At 15, he persuaded his mother to buy a £15 Rosetti acoustic model and he devoted all his time to mastering it, mainly by listening to the hits of the day and learning all the parts by ear. The first song he could play all the way through was Elvis Presley's 'That's All Right Mama' and soon formed a lifelong affection for Chuck Berry. Yet, Keith was reluctant to join a band despite his growing proficiency on the guitar.

Gaining a place at art college after leaving secondary school, Keith was encouraged by like-minded classmates to join a group. More importantly, they introduced him to the blues. The music served as a connection with old primary school chum Mick Jagger, who Keith bumped into one day at Dartford station. Mick was carrying a bunch of obscure blues records and this helped to reacquaint the pair.

Mick was enthusiastic about forming a band and with Keith they recruited mutual friend Dick Taylor. Buying a Gallotone Valencia archtop guitar, Keith added a pick-up, amplified through a homemade unit. The trio frequented the growing blues scene and met Brian Jones at a concert organised by Alexis Korner. A proficient slide guitar player, Brian impressed the budding bandmates. Alexis encouraged Mick, Keith and Dick to record a demo and this was achieved in a primitive studio. They performed, under the name Little Boy Blue and the Blue Boys, 'La Bamba' and several Chuck Berry songs. Around this time, Keith bought his first amplifier – a 4-watt Selmer 'Little Giant' with an 8-inch speaker.

Brian invited Mick to a rehearsal with a band he had formed. Keith joined Mick and the pair ended up playing with them. Brian was impressed by both and immediately offered to join them and start a new group; Ian Stewart also left the old outfit for the new one. The band then started to rehearse in London.

Keith dropped out of art college, whilst Brian held a number of jobs briefly before giving up on employment. Mick continued with his studies at the London School of Economics. Keith, Mick and Brian moved into a flat in Edith Grove, Chelsea, allowing Keith and Brian to spend the majority of their free time listening to music and learning songs. As a result, the pair developed an intuitive understanding of each other's playing.

Keith preferred listening to Chicago blues at this time.

Initially, the band struggled to book any gigs, but as the popularity of 'trad jazz' fell off, clubs looked to present new acts, especially those performing blues. Alexis Korner helped out and booked them at the Marquee Club as part of his own residency there. Performing on July 12, 1962, the Rolling Stones went through a number of songs by Elmore James, Chuck Berry and Jimmy Reed. Keith used his Gallotone through the 'Little Giant' amp. The band won a residency at the Ealing Jazz Club and this encouraged Keith to upgrade his amp to a Harmony H306.

Keith and the others arranged their first recording session for October 1962 at Curley Clayton Sound Studios, Highbury. They captured performances of tracks by Muddy Waters, Jimmy Reed and Bo Diddley. The tape was sent to record companies but without encountering any interest.

Around December 1962, the Rolling Stones found a replacement for Dick Taylor, who had left to concentrate on his art college studies. Bill Wyman was hired to play bass on the recommendation of part-time drummer Tony Chapman. Bill brought a spare Vox AC30 with him and this impressed Keith. Shortly after Christmas, Charlie Watts became their full-time drummer.

Following a busy schedule over the festive period, Keith's guitar failed at a gig and, despite initially repairing the problem, he decided to upgrade to a Harmony Meteor, which cost £74. About a month later, Keith acquired a Harmony 1270 12-string acoustic.

In February 1963, the Rolling Stones gladly accepted a residency at the Station Hotel, Richmond, and gradually built up a fanbase. They arranged another recording session and chose IBC Studios in Central London. Playing similar songs to the previous date, the band again failed to attract any record company interest. Throughout this period, Keith played his Harmony Meteor with Harmony amp.

During the spring of 1963, ex-publicist Andrew Loog Oldham met the Rolling Stones with his business partner Eric Easton. Both were impressed with the group at the gig they attended and soon signed them up to a management deal. Dick Rowe from Decca Records saw the band and arranged for recordings to be released by the company.

Two new Vox AC30 amplifiers were bought and Keith began playing his Harmony through one of these. They were used on the recording sessions for the band's first single, 'Come On' (a Chuck Berry cover), with the B-side 'I Want To Be Loved', released in June 1963. The single was moderately successful, reaching no. 21 in the charts. In promoting the record, the Rolling Stones appeared on television for the first time and Keith used his Meteor.

Throughout the summer, the Stones struggled to find a new single, yet a chance encounter by Oldham with John Lennon and Paul McCartney led the song-writing duo to offer 'I Wanna Be Your Man'. The track was released later in the year and reached no. 12.

During the autumn, the band embarked on their first nationwide tour, albeit sharing the bill with the Everly Brothers and Bo Diddley. Keith took his Harmony Meteor and Vox AC30 to use over the six weeks.

By the end of 1963, Keith and Mick had left Edith Grove and taken up residence with Oldham in Hampstead. They were encouraged to start writing their own songs instead of relying on covers. Although an early effort – 'That Girl Belongs To Yesterday' – was a hit for Gene Pitney in late 1963, Keith and Mick did not write a song they thought worthy as a Rolling Stones single until 'The Last Time', released in February 1965.

Earlier, in 1964, the Stones recorded several covers, some of which would be used on a forthcoming album. Then, the band went on another package tour. Keith was still using his Harmony with the Vox AC30. During a brief respite in the schedule, he turned to his Harmony 12-string to record Buddy Holly's 'Not Fade Away' and this reached no. 3 in the charts.

By spring 1964, enough tracks were recorded for the self-titled debut album. Only one track was credited to Keith and Mick (with two collectively to the Rolling Stones), 'Tell Me (You're Coming Back)' and this saw Keith provide a memorable introduction on his Harmony 12-string. It was also used on several other tracks. The Meteor was present and played through the AC30. The album was an immediate hit, reaching no. 1 after just a week.

Although Keith had relied on his Harmony Meteor over the previous year, the success of the tours and the album allowed him to upgrade to a 1962 Epiphone Casino with small headstock and Epiphone-branded vibrato unit.

Keith acquired the guitar in time for the Stones' first American tour during June 1964. He had his Harmony 12-string on hand, but relied on rented amplifiers for appearances and these were mainly Gibson models. With the group only having a couple of songs charting in America, their reception differed between venues. Yet, a highlight for the Stones was a session held in Chicago at Chess Records, the home of their favourite artists, such as Chuck Berry, Howlin' Wolf and Muddy Waters.

Keith used his Casino during the session and played with a Fender amp provided by the studio. One of the recordings was a cover of the Valentino's 'It's All Over Now'. This became the group's first British no. 1 when released in the summer of 1964. The song features a distinct solo from Keith.

The band returned to England and throughout July and August continued to promote the album and latest single with performances on TV and across the country. In mid-August the EP 'Five By Five' was released featuring songs recorded during the Chess sessions.

Despite only recently acquiring his Epiphone Casino, Keith bought a number of new guitars at the end of the summer. His main purchase was a second-hand Gibson Les Paul Standard from a London music shop. It had been modified with a Bigsby vibrato unit added in place of the original stopbar tailpiece. Additionally, Keith purchased a new Fender Telecaster in white with rosewood fingerboard, and a Framus 5/97 Jumbo six-string acoustic.

Towards the end of October, the Stones returned to America and embarked on a series of concerts and radio appearances which promoted the release of the '12 x 5' album in the USA. Keith appeared mostly with his Gibson Les Paul, but also had his Fender Telecaster on hand. Amplification was provided by rented Fender heads and cabinets.

The band made an appearance on the 'Ed Sullivan Show' and performed 'Around And Around' and 'Time Is On My Side'. During their stay in Los Angeles, the band booked sessions at the RCA studio and recorded several covers and an original, 'Heart Of Stone'.

By the end of 1964, several of Keith and Mick's songs had been recorded by other artists. Three of the twelve tracks on the group's second album 'The Rolling Stones No. 2' were credited to Jagger/Richards – 'What A Shame', 'Grown Up Wrong' and 'Off The Hook'. Around the time of the album's release, in mid-January 1965, the Stones were in the studio recording 'The Last Time'. Keith played the rhythm guitar part on the track, whilst Brian provided the riff. The chords were played on the Framus acoustic, then Keith added the guitar solo using his Gibson Les Paul.

The group recorded the track at RCA Studios in LA before heading to Australia and the Far East to tour. Keith used the Gibson as his main guitar with a Fender head and cab provided by the promoter. As a result of their exposure to Fender amps on the tour and on previous American engagements, Keith and Brian decided to order a pair of Fender Showman 85-watt amplifiers with two 15 in. speakers.

At the beginning of March 1965, both 'The Rolling Stones No. 2' and 'The Last Time' enjoyed great success and the band headlined a British tour. This was quickly followed by dates in Scandinavia, the New Musical Express Poll Winners Concert and a trip to Paris. Keith still favoured his Les Paul and transported his Fender Showman around to the different venues.

The same combination of equipment was used for the early stages of the North American tour undertaken between late April and late May, including another session at Chess studios. Perhaps influenced by Keith's prominent use of the Les Paul at the time, Gibson sent Keith and Brian some equipment. The main items were two Firebird VII guitars. Two Titan amps were provided and along with several Maestro Fuzz-Tone effects units. Both Keith and Brian also received a Gibson Heritage six-string acoustic guitar.

Both guitarists favoured the Gibson Firebird VII guitars and took them to a recording session at RCA studio when working on a new song, '(I Can't Get No) Satisfaction'. Keith played the song's distinctive riff and used the Fuzz-Tone effect, initially as a reference for a horn part he envisaged. Yet, Andrew Loog Oldham liked the sound and, as a new single was required urgently, he encouraged the band to add the finishing touches necessary for the release. The American market received the single before the UK, but the top of both charts was reached nevertheless.

The Firebird VII was prominent on several Stones TV appearances during their time in the USA, particularly on 'Shindig!', when performing 'The Last Time'. The spot on the show was noteworthy for the inclusion of Howlin' Wolf which was done at the Stones' request.

Whilst Brian continued to use his Firebird VII on the Stones'

Keith Richards with Epiphone Casino guitar.
Heritage Image Partnership Ltd / Alamy Stock Photo.

return to Britain, Keith reverted back to his Epiphone Casino and the Les Paul for British and European concerts. He is seen with the former as the band performed '(I Can't Get No) Satisfaction' in late July on 'Ready Steady Go!'.

Over two days in early September, the Stones flew out to LA to record a number of original songs at RCA Studios. Keith used most of his current line-up of guitars, excluding the Les Paul, to record his guitar parts, but mainly favoured his Casino. Included in the recordings was the band's next single 'Get Off Of My Cloud', which continued the band's run of no. 1 singles in both the USA and Britain. Three of the other songs were used soon after on the Stones' album 'Out Of Our Heads' which reached no. 2 in the charts, being kept off the top spot by the Beatles' 'Help!'. Through the rest of September, the band toured Germany and then returned to Britain for shows through October.

Rounding off 1965 was an extensive American tour, comprising 41 concerts. Keith favoured his Epiphone through the Fender Showman during this period, although he was sometimes seen with the Gibson Firebird VII. Before leaving America, the Stones spent two days recording at RCA Studios. Nearly all of the material was original and would be heard on the 'Aftermath' album, released in April 1966.

The sessions also saw the appearance of a Gibson Hummingbird acoustic which had been relatively recently introduced by the company. It had a spruce top with mahogany back and sides, as well as neck, and rosewood fingerboard. The guitar was the main acoustic heard on the tracks recorded during the sessions, such as 'Mother's Little Helper'.

'19th Nervous Breakdown', recorded at RCA, became the band's first single of 1966. Released in February, it climbed to no. 2 in both Britain and America. Keith used his Epiphone Casino, playing the introduction and rhythm part, as well as the recurring lead line, for which he turned to the Fuzz-Tone.

Throughout the month, the Stones promoted the new single. On 'Top of the Pops', Keith first played his new Guild M-65 'Freshman' guitar. This was a relatively small hollow-body (13½ in. across) made with a maple top and rosewood back and sides; the neck was mahogany with rosewood fingerboard using a 24¾ in. scale. Whereas the standard M-65 had only one pick-up, Keith's was fitted with two and these were DeArmond 2000-B types.

Keith received a new Gibson Firebird VII Non-Reverse guitar later in the month, yet he appears to have preferred the new Guild and primarily played this guitar on the Australian tour that began in late February. He took his Fender amp for the concerts, which concluded in early March.

The creative relationship between Keith and Mick continued to sow seeds in early 1966 as the band went back to RCA Studios to record more original songs. The sessions marked Brian's break away from the guitar as his primary instrument. He tried to find more exotic sounds, which left Keith as the sole guitarist for the most part. He used his Guild through the Fender amp and Gibson acoustics for many of the songs recorded, including: 'Lady Jane', 'Under My Thumb', 'Paint It, Black'.

The above-mentioned tracks (apart from the last for the British release) were amongst those included on the Stones' next album 'Aftermath'. Released in mid-April 1966, this followed the group's brief European tour and climbed to no. 1 in the UK and no. 2 in the USA. A month later the single 'Paint It, Black' was released and was similarly successful.

Keith Richards with Gibson Korina Flying V at Hyde Park, London 1969.
Trinity Mirror / Mirrorpix / Alamy Stock Photo.

The Stones toured America over the summer with 32 shows in just over a month. Keith travelled with his Guild M-65 and a recently acquired Sonic Blue Fender Telecaster with maple fretboard. The Gibson Hummingbird was used when necessary. Amplification continued to be from the Fender Showman and the Fuzz-Tone effect was used for 'Satisfaction' and '19th Nervous Breakdown'.

As the tour wound down, Keith and the band travelled to LA for sessions at RCA before they returned to England. The principal recording from this was the next single 'Have You Seen Your Mother, Baby, Standing In The Shadow?'.

The end of the Stones' summer in the USA was marked by an appearance on the 'Ed Sullivan Show', where they performed 'Paint It, Black', 'Lady Jane' and 'Have You Seen Your Mother, Baby, Standing In The Shadow?'. For the first-mentioned, Keith played the song using yet another new guitar – a Gibson Les Paul Custom with three humbucker pick-ups. On 'Lady Jane', Keith used his Gibson Hummingbird and, turned to an upright piano on 'Have You Seen Your Mother, Baby, Standing In The Shadow?'.

The band went back on the road for a British tour in late September/early October. Keith took his new Les Paul Custom and this was his main guitar throughout, with the Hummingbird serving the acoustic songs. A soundhole pick-up was installed for amplification. Both Keith and Brian received new amps from Vox for the tour and these were new UL760 60-watt heads utilising both Solid State and tubes coupled to cabinets fitted with 2x12 in. speakers.

The Stones finished 1966 with a stint in Olympic Studios in London, recording a number of songs, including the future double A-side singles 'Let's Spend The Night Together' and 'Ruby Tuesday'. Keith favoured his recently used guitars for the sessions, but also had on hand a new Guild 12-string acoustic and a Fender Precision bass which he added to the song 'Yesterday's Papers'.

Early 1967 was spent promoting the new singles in Britain and America, with Keith using his Gibson Les Paul Custom and returning to the piano on 'Ruby Tuesday'. At the end of the month, the Stones' 'Between The Buttons' album was released and this subsequently climbed to the upper reaches of the charts on both sides of the Atlantic.

Even with an album in the charts, the band returned to the studio for most of February, recording songs that would later appear on 'Their Satanic Majesties Request'. Keith mainly used his Les Paul Custom through the Vox, but following a break for a holiday in Morocco, he added a Gibson ES 330 to his collection. Despite the new addition, Keith relied on his Les Paul Custom for the European tour undertaken during the spring of 1967. Vox supplied both Keith and Brian with new amps at this time. These were completely Solid State 200-watt 'Supreme' models, with 4x12 in. speakers.

Mid-1967 saw the culmination of the court case involving Keith and Mick. The support the pair received from the public during this time led to the recording of the song 'We Love You' and the B-side 'Dandelion'.

The sessions at Olympic were understandably disjointed, but in July a new effort was made to push forward and recordings were made through to October. Keith was using his Gibson electric and acoustic guitars along with his Fender Telecaster through the Vox Supreme amp. He acquired a Vox Wah-Wah pedal which was used on an unreleased track. The year 1967 ended with the completion of 'Their Satanic Majesties Request' which performed well in spite of mixed reviews.

The Stones took a break over the festive period and in the new year Keith and Mick began writing songs and preparing to return to the studio. American producer Jimmy Miller was recruited to help with the new album. Keith reinvented his guitar playing by adopting open tunings, particularly D at this time. He thought he had become stale and wanted a new challenge.

An early test was also provided for Jimmy Miller. Keith liked the sound of the demo he had made for 'Street Fighting Man' – originally to be the group's next single – on his new Philips cassette recorder and tasked the producer with transferring the rhythm track to 4-track tape. It was eventually performed again and Keith played his Hummingbird in open D tuning whilst Charlie used a toy drum kit and Brian added sitar. Keith also used his Fender bass on the song.

The band used the same method to record 'Jumpin' Jack Flash', chosen for release ahead of 'Street Fighting Man'. Keith used his Gibson Hummingbird in open D tuning, but added a capo to the first fret. The band made a music video to promote the song across the world and Keith is seen with his Gibson Les Paul Custom, which he had decorated with a 'psychedelic' design, plugged into a Triumph Silicon 100 amplifier.

Throughout the spring of 1968, the Stones continued to record at Olympic Studios, cutting several tracks which would appear on the 'Beggars Banquet' album. Keith favoured his Les Paul Custom through a Vox amp, but his Fender Telecaster and Gibson ES 330 were also used, along with the Triumph amp. He can be seen with some of this equipment in the film 'Sympathy for the Devil', made by French filmmaker Jean-Luc Goddard. He captured the band recording the song of the same name over two days and would later cut the footage together with other unrelated material.

Towards the end of the sessions, Keith spent time with American blues guitarist Ry Cooder. He used open tunings to emulate some of the early bluesmen and particularly employed open G, which Keith would later adopt. Keith became close friends with Gram Parsons of the Byrds and assimilated the latter's country style of playing.

The 'Beggars Banquet' album was completed by mid-1968 but a dispute with the record label over the cover delayed the release until December. In the meantime, the Stones had begun sessions which would yield songs for the next album, 'Let It Bleed'. Keith continued to use his Gibson Les Paul Custom and Hummingbird guitars, as well as open tunings.

The year ended with the group recording a TV special – 'Rock And Roll Circus' – which was subsequently shelved by the band and not released until the 1990s. Keith had his Les Paul Custom through Triumph and Vox amplifiers but turned to a Gibson J200 acoustic for some tracks. Keith played a Fender bass for the Dirty Mac which was a group formed by John Lennon with Eric Clapton on guitar and Mitch Mitchell on drums.

The Stones returned to the studio in February 1969 and

recorded tracks such as 'Midnight Rambler', 'You Got The Silver' (sung by Keith) and 'Let It Bleed'. Keith continued to use previously mentioned guitars and equipment, but did use a Maton SE777 hollow-body electric guitar on several tracks, including 'Gimme Shelter' which was one of the last songs finished for the album.

With nearly a year elapsing from the release of their last single in Britain, the Stones quickly produced 'Honky Tonk Women' following the completion of the 'Let It Bleed' sessions. The song marked a major change for Keith as he primarily favoured open G tuning with the sixth, or low E, string removed from the guitar; the open notes were then G-D-G-D-B. Keith thought this allowed him to create more interesting rhythm parts and moved the sound away from that of a traditional guitar as the harmonic relationships changed.

'Honky Tonk Women' saw new recruit Mick Taylor contributing lead guitar to the track. He had joined the band following the departure of Brian in the spring of 1969.

As the summer approached, the Stones planned a concert in Hyde Park but this sadly turned into a memorial for Brian who died just two days before the show. Approximately 250,000–500,000 people turned up to see the band play a selection of mostly recent tracks, with Keith using a newly acquired Gibson Flying V – made from Korina wood – and his Gibson ES 330 through a Hiwatt DR201 200-watt amp. Mick Taylor used Keith's 1959 Gibson Les Paul Standard which he had acquired some time before joining the band.

The end of 1969 saw the Stones tour America. Keith took a number of his guitars, some of which were new additions. Foremost, was a 'Plexiglas' guitar from Dan Armstrong which was the prototype for a production run and had been sent to Keith specially. He had bought another Les Paul Custom earlier in the year but more recently acquired were a 1959 Gibson Les Paul Standard (with plain top) and a Gibson ES 355 in walnut finish. For acoustic tracks, Keith used his Gibson Hummingbird and also a National resonator.

Originally, Hiwatt amplifiers were to be used on the tour but problems arose following shipping to the USA. Ampeg was contacted and gave the band their new SVT models. These were prototypes and after initial problems, Ampeg sent technicians on the road with the band to keep them going.

After the end of the tour in late November, the Stones cut three tracks in Muscle Shoals Studio, including 'Brown Sugar'. This was mainly composed by Mick Jagger in open G tuning, although Keith played the guitar part on the final recording.

The year ended with two sets of two shows in London at the Saville and Lyceum theatres. Keith continued to use his Dan Armstrong guitar and the second Les Paul Custom, pairing these with Hiwatt amps for the Saville gig and the Ampeg at the Lyceum.

The Stones had some time off during early 1970 before going into Olympic Studios to record new tracks in the spring. Several of these would later appear on the next album 'Sticky Fingers'. No new items of gear had been acquired at this point and Keith continued to use previously mentioned equipment.

Following further spells in the studio during the summer, the band returned to the road and played a number of European gigs to the end of the year. Keith mainly played his 'Plexi' guitar or his Gibson Les Paul Custom through Ampeg SVT amps. A Martin D12-20 acoustic guitar was also used.

Keith continued with this line-up for the British tour undertaken during the first half of March 1971. Shortly afterwards, the band became tax exiles and relocated to the south of France. Keith rented the villa Nellcôte and established a recording studio in the cellar, using a mobile facility the band had commissioned early in 1970. The sessions proved extremely fruitful, forming the 'Exile On Main Street' album.

A new guitar for the sessions was a 1954 Fender Telecaster with maple neck that Keith had been gifted for his birthday at the end of 1970. He used the guitar, which became one of his favourites, with open G tuning and removed the low E string to create his now favoured set-up and subsequent signature style. Further modifications have been made over the years such as the addition of a humbucker in the neck position and a single coil pick-up from a lap steel guitar at the bridge, which has been changed to brass with individual saddles.

Towards the end of recording for the album, a burglary deprived Keith of several guitars including his Les Paul Custom (not painted), Les Paul Standard, Flying V, Dan Armstrong 'Plexi' prototype and a Telecaster with rosewood neck. Keith quickly set about replacing the instruments and soon he had a new Les Paul Custom with Bigsby tremolo and another Les Paul Custom with Alnico V pick-up in the neck and P90 at the bridge. He bought another 1959 Les Paul Standard with flametop and two Telecasters, both with maple necks.

The end of 1971 and early 1972 was spent adding the finishing touches to the tracks recorded in France at Sunset Sound in Los Angeles. At the start of the summer Keith returned to LA after a spell in Switzerland for the birth of his daughter as rehearsals began in preparation for the Stones' tour of America to support the 'Exile In Main Street' album. Keith took many of his new guitars on tour, mainly as the result of the wide variety of tunings he employed for songs from this period; he also used a capo frequently. Amplification continued to be Ampeg SVT with 4x12 in. cabinets and the company provided a technician to keep them in service.

From late November until mid-December, the Stones were recording in Jamaica. Many of the songs were later assembled for the 'Goats Head Soup' album. A new addition to Keith's arsenal at this time was a Gibson Les Paul Junior with double cutaway, whilst he also used some effects to change his guitar tone, such as phaser and Leslie speaker.

In the New Year, a tour of the Far East was organised and to warm up the group played a charity concert in LA for earthquake victims in Nicaragua. Keith introduced a new guitar during the concert – a mid-1960s Gibson SG Custom with Maestro Vibrola. He also had a custom five-string guitar built by his guitar tech Ted Newman Jones. This saw action during the concert and was made from mahogany and rosewood, with a bolt-on neck, and had a P-90 pick-up in the neck position and a humbucker at the bridge.

After adding finishing touches to 'Goats Head Soup' in London during the summer, the Stones recorded promotional videos for songs on the album. 'Dancing With Mr D' and 'Silver Train' sees Keith playing the Gibson SG Custom with Ampeg SVTs, whilst on 'Angie' he switches to a Gibson

Hummingbird. 'Angie', with 'Silver Train' as the B-side, was the first single from the album and was successful in America, reaching no. 5 in Britain. The album went to the top of the charts at home and in America.

The band's second tour of the year began in Europe during early September and ran through to mid-October. Keith's equipment was similar to the last two tours, with the addition of another Jones custom, which had comparable specifications to the predecessor. A departure from the roster was the Gibson SG Custom which Keith abandoned. Most of the guitars were present for recording sessions, taking place at the end of the tour in Munich. The tracks created were co-produced by Keith and Mick and would later form part of 'It's Only Rock 'n' Roll'.

The sessions continued in mid-February 1974 and Mick Taylor arrived with a 'Synthi Hi-Fli' guitar effects unit. Both he and Keith used this on tracks for the album, with Keith particularly using the Wah-Wah for 'Fingerprint File'.

As with 'Goats Head Soup', a trio of promotional videos were filmed for tracks from 'It's Only Rock 'n' Roll'. The title track sees Keith with a Gibson Firebird Non-Reverse and for 'Ain't Too Proud To Beg' and 'Till The Next Goodbye' he plays his Gibson Les Paul Junior.

The album, 'It's Only Rock 'n' Roll', was a worldwide hit, but the band suffered a blow with the departure of Mick Taylor, who felt frustrated at his role in the Stones and wanted to break out on his own. He had left the group by the end of the year and Keith shouldered the guitar duties for sessions at Musicland Studios in Berlin.

Following a Christmas break, the Stones assembled in Rotterdam to record while also holding auditions for a new guitarist. Many big names were considered, but there was a focus on finding an American guitarist. Wayne Perkins was very close to getting the job, as was Harvey Mandel, but the Stones ultimately chose Ronnie Wood, who they had worked with earlier in 1974.

Ronnie, initially, only partially joined as his band Faces was still active until the end of the year. He participated in sessions during mid-1975 using his Zemaitis guitars and hardtail Fender Stratocaster. Ronnie was one of the early supporters of Zemaitis, and custom-ordered a guitar for Keith. This was a five-string with mahogany body and neck with ebony fingerboard and one pick-up. The top was decorated with pearl inlays of a skull, dagger and revolver. Other new additions at this time were two Travis Bean guitars and a bass, which used aluminium for the necks.

On June 1, 1975, the Stones were scheduled to begin a tour of North and South America but the second half was ultimately cancelled. Keith took a number of guitars on the road – Fender Telecasters, Zemaitis custom, Gibson Les Paul Junior and Travis Bean – and continued to use Ampeg SVT models, although these were customised examples with white covering and floral grill cloth.

On tour, Keith bought a new black 1975 Fender Telecaster Custom, featuring a Fender wide-range humbucker (designed by Seth Lover, inventor of Gibson's model) in the neck position. Used prominently, this was played as a five-string. Between gigs, Keith and Ronnie decided they were close enough to Kalamazoo to visit the Gibson factory. The pair left with an L6S, an S1 and a J200 acoustic.

The rest of 1975 and early 1976 was spent mixing the 'Black And Blue' album at various locations. Several promo films were recorded and Keith is seen with his Gibson L6S in 'Fool To Cry', 'Hot Stuff' and 'Crazy Mama' and the Zemaitis custom guitar in 'Hey Negrita'.

The album was toured in Europe during the summer of 1976. Keith had settled down with his favoured guitars – Fender Telecasters, Gibson Les Paul Junior and Zemaitis custom. Amplification continued to be Ampeg SVT. Yet, this was soon to change. The band was putting together a live album – 'Love You Live' – and wanted to play a smaller gig for one side of the record. A date at the El Mocambo club in Toronto was arranged and due to the size of the venue smaller amps were required.

Keith had played Carlos Santana's Mesa Boogie Mark One, and enjoyed the sound, believing the amp was versatile. Contacting Mesa Engineering, he acquired a pair of Mark Ones for himself and Ronnie. These had 100-watt and 60-watt settings, with a single 12 in. speaker. There were normal tone and volume controls in addition to a five-band EQ.

As 1977 ended, the band booked time in a Parisian studio to record tracks for the next album, 'Some Girls'. These sessions spilled into early 1978 as a number of tracks were completed. The only new addition for Keith was a custom-made Telecaster-type guitar with mahogany body and complete rosewood neck. It is visible in the videos for 'Far Away Eyes' and the single 'Miss You'. A third video was shot for the single 'Respectable', released later in the year. Keith is with a Gibson Melody Maker in sunburst finish. It was from c. 1960 and a model aimed at student players, being of simpler construction, and with single coil pick-ups.

'Some Girls' was released in June 1978. Promoting the album, the Stones toured America during June and July and Keith played many of the previously mentioned guitars through his Mesa Boogie Mark

Keith Richards with Fender Telecaster at the TD Garden in Boston, Massachusetts, 2013.
Michael Dwyer Ltd / Alamy Stock Photo.

One and the Ampeg SVTs.

Over the course of 1978, Ronnie had recorded a number of his own tracks and during early 1979 these were assembled for release as the album 'Gimme Some Neck'. Keith had contributed to some of these songs and Ronnie also asked him to join a touring band for the album in America – the New Barbarians. Keith agreed and took several new guitars with him, including a prospective signature guitar made by his guitar tech Ted Newman Jones. The others were two Gibson Les Paul Juniors (one a double cutaway), a Telecaster Deluxe and a Travis Bean.

For the remainder of 1979, Keith was with the Stones building on tracks that would be heard on 'Emotional Rescue'. The project was completed in early 1980 and released in June.

There were still some songs left from the sessions, as well as several others stretching back several years, and the decision was taken to release these before an American tour in 1981. 'Tattoo You' was preceded by the lead single 'Start Me Up', which had originally appeared during the 'Some Girls' sessions, and the video has Keith with a new guitar. This was another Telecaster and it dated from the mid-1960s, with a maple neck and sunburst finish. The guitar was modified through the addition of a humbucker above the bridge position, with stock neck and bridge pick-ups, but soon after this was changed to have the humbucker in the neck position.

Several other Telecasters accompanied Keith on tour and he had his Gibson Les Paul Juniors. A switch was made away from Ampeg to Mesa Boogie for amplifiers and Coliseum

160-watt heads were used with Cerwin-Vega 4x12 in. cabinets, before being switched for Mesa 4x12 in. cabinets. This set-up continued to the European tour which took up two months from late May to late July 1982.

Over the next year, the Stones recorded tracks for the 'Undercover' album and Keith favoured custom guitars made by Doby and Jesselli. One of them was prominent in all the videos for the singles 'Undercover Of The Night', 'She Was Hot' and 'Too Much Blood'.

Much of 1984 was spent on a break from the Stones, but Keith and the band reassembled early in 1985 for the 'Dirty Work' album. Although in possession of an extensive collection, Keith bought another Telecaster before the sessions. Dating from 1959, it featured a rosewood neck, as well as maintaining the stock pick-up configuration despite Keith's preference for a humbucker in the neck position. He bought a Fender Twin amplifier and this found extensive use on the sessions.

A break in activity occurred for the Live Aid performance, but the Stones did not appear and Keith, with Ronnie, backed Bob Dylan during his performance, playing a Martin acoustic.

The 'Dirty Work' album was finished in late 1985 and appeared during March 1986. There were two videos for the singles 'Harlem Shuffle' and 'One Hit (To The Body)'. In the former, Keith had a blonde Fender Telecaster with a maple neck and for the latter he turned to a red Fender Custom Telecaster with a rosewood neck.

Mick decided to concentrate on solo projects and Keith and the band also took time off. Keith was involved with the celebrations for Chuck Berry's 60th birthday in late 1986. He played guitar during the two concerts, using his black Fender Telecaster Custom through a Mesa Boogie combo connected to a Mesa Boogie cabinet.

Deciding to produce a solo album, Keith assembled a group of musicians – called the X-pensive Winos – to work with in late summer 1987, including guitarist Waddy Wachtel. The 'Talk Is Cheap' album was released in late 1988 and was successful, receiving many positive reviews. The first single was 'Take It So Hard' which was promoted with Keith's first solo video. In this, he is playing his 1954 Fender Telecaster.

Keith and Mick reunited at the end of 1988 and decided to bring the band back together in 1989. For the 'Steel Wheels' sessions, Keith favoured his Telecasters through his Fender Twin amp. For acoustic songs he used a recently acquired Velázquez classic guitar. At the end of summer 1988, the band spent three months on a North America tour, which turned out to be their most successful to date. Keith's guitar line-up was quite stable and he favoured the Fender Twin amp connected to a Mesa cab.

In 1992, Keith recorded tracks for his 'Main Offender' album and then toured with the X-Pensive Winos. The first single was 'Wicked As It Seems' and in the video he is playing a recently acquired Fender Esquire, which still has six strings, although the number was later reduced to five. Equipped with an Anderson humbucker in the neck, the guitar is plugged into an unidentified small vintage amp. The Esquire was seen in the promo for the follow-up single 'Eileen' (now as a five-string) and Keith is playing in a studio setting as well as on the road during the 'Main Offender' tour. His rig for this continued to be Fender Twin amps through Mesa cabinets.

During the Stones' 'Voodoo Lounge' period, Keith had cemented his preference for Telecasters or Stratocasters, although there were occasions when guitars from the collection were taken out.

Before the end of the century the 'Bridges To Babylon' album was completed and the band went on another extensive tour. Alongside the regulars in Keith's guitar collection came two new instruments. First was a Gibson ES 355 in cherry, then a backup in the form of another ES 355 in rare factory black finish.

Early in the 21st century, the Stones celebrated their 40th anniversary with a greatest hits compilation – 'Forty Licks' – and worldwide tour. Keith had most of his usual guitars with him but also played several custom-made examples.

In 2005, the album 'A Bigger Bang' was released and the Stones again went on a worldwide tour in support. Keith carried well over 40 guitars on the road and continued to use his Fender Twin amps, although no longer with the Mesa cabs, being mic'd instead. Despite the rise in popularity of pedals and pedalboards, Keith has remained free of them and only has MXR phase and delay pedals for certain songs from the 1970s.

In between Stones projects, Keith found time to appear with the Crickets (of Buddy Holly fame) after their induction into the Musicians Hall of Fame in 2008. He played with the group on a number of songs during their performance and used his black Gibson ES 355. Keith was present at the 2012 celebration of Chuck Berry's song-writing at the JFK Presidential Library. He made an impromptu appearance with Elvis Costello on the song 'Promised Land' and used a Gibson Super 400 through a 65 Amps combo.

The '50 and Counting' tour, celebrating the band's 50 years together, occurred in 2012/2013. Starting off with dates in France and England, the tour moved over to North America. Towards the end there was a performance at Glastonbury, where the band was joined by former member Mick Taylor.

In 2014, the Stones continued the celebrations, although the tour was named '14 on Fire'. The dates took in cities in the Far East and Europe before heading to Australia and New Zealand at the end of the year.

Despite this busy schedule, Keith found time to record his third solo record, 'Crosseyed Heart', released at the end of 2015. This reached the top ten in the UK and no. 11 in America.

Keith was back on the road with the Stones in mid-2015 touring North America and at the end of the year the band was in the studio recording their first album in ten years. Yet, 'Blue And Lonesome' featured no original material and the band returned to their origins by recording many blues tracks. This approach was just as popular as it had been in the 1960s and the album was a global success when released at the end of 2016.

The Stones continued to play to audiences across the world through to the end of 2019 with the last tour – 'No Filter' – spanning 45 dates in Europe and North America, having started in 2017; the band entertained over 2,000,000 fans. In recent years Keith has settled on his favourite guitars and plays through the Fender Twin.

MICK RONSON

Mick Ronson's life was very short. He died aged 46 in 1993. He did, however, make a significant contribution to rock music. It's an influence that still finds much applause and celebration today.

Mick was born in Hull on May 26, 1946, the first son of George and Minnie Ronson. When Mick was five, his mother bought a piano. This immediately captivated his attention and he was lucky to find a teacher (in fact it was Trevor Bolder's grandmother) that would encourage him to develop. Mick attended Maybury Junior School. Whilst there, he began to play violin and recorder but this was short-lived. An ambition to become a cello player also came to nothing.

At 14, Mick left school and found work on a mobile grocery van. His interest in the guitar started when he was 17. He admired the playing of Duane Eddy. At this early stage, Mick played a Rosetti acoustic which had cost him £14. He was capable of teaching himself the basics. Mick told Dutch music magazine *Music Maker* in 1988 that he did not practise when turning to the guitar: 'It's because I used to play classical piano and violin and I learned to hate practising the scales. When I took up the guitar I decided not to practise anymore, just play.'

Mick's first band was the Mariners. They played the music of Chuck Berry, Eddie Cochran and that of the early British beat groups such as the Rolling Stones. Mick's first appearance with the Mariners was at a Beverley pub – on November 22, 1963. Even at this stage, Mick was being described as 'an excellent guitarist'.

In May 1964, the Mariners appeared first on the bill when the Rolling Stones played at Bridlington Spa. During the early 1960s, Mick had stints with other bands including the Buccaneers and the King Bees. Around mid-1964, he joined the Crestas. They played around Yorkshire, featuring cover versions of songs popular at the time. At a Ferriby gig, Mick received a nasty electric shock. Although hospitalised, he was able to make a successful recovery and continue his career.

Recalling his early lead guitar playing influences, Mick singled out George Harrison. He told the American music magazine *Hit Parader*, in March 1975: 'George Harrison, he influenced me a lot. Harrison was a great guitarist, really excellent. I told you about my classical background; so the beautiful melodies he was playing really grew on me. Every time George Harrison is playing, he does exactly the right thing for the song. He never had a "big guitar sound", he didn't play everywhere, just in the right sections.'

By 1966, Mick had decided that he must push his ambitions further forward. He moved to London and, at the outset, lived with a family friend in a Chinese restaurant. Much of what happened to him during this short period in London is revealed in letters he sent to a girlfriend. We learn that work was hard to find. Yet, he did play for a time with a band called the Voice. They were managed by Micky Most and he replaced Miller Anderson. Mick mentions that he played through Marshall amplifiers. Whilst in London, he was able to watch Jeff Beck performing. Mick was hugely impressed. He played with a band, the Wanted. This was besides working in a garage.

By September 1966, Mick had returned frustrated to Hull. He found a job with Hull Council's Parks Department. His mother, Minnie, mentions in Weird and Gilly's *Mick Ronson: The Spider with the Platinum Hair* (2003): 'He never had the guitar out of his hand.' Besides appreciating the music of Jeff Beck, Mick admired Jimi Hendrix.

Shortly after his return to Hull, Mick joined a newly reformed local band, the Rats. Bass player Geoff Appleby told Weird and Gilly: '[Mick] was just playing normal sort of rock guitar, that Chuck Berry-type lead guitar. He was only just experimenting with the new Eric Clapton-style of guitar playing, as it were then … When I first heard [Mick], I knew his guitar playing was magic and outshone any other guitarist in the area. What impressed me most was the way he handled the Wah-Wah pedal.'

On www.maggironson.com (Mick Ronson's sister's website) bass player Keith Cheesman mentions: 'It was the mid-60s and a new style of guitar playing was evolving. String bending was the name of the game and only a handful of guitarists had mastered it … In Hull and the surrounding area, and probably for miles around, Mick was the first to master this style. He was also the first to learn the trick of using a banjo string for the top E and moving all the strings up one to create a light-gauge string set.'

Included in the Rats' repertoire was the Yardbirds' 'The Nazz Are Blue', and the Cream's 'I'm So Glad' and 'I Feel Free'. In April 1967, the Rats played in France. Whilst there, band members recall that Mick constantly played the Django Reinhardt/Stephane Grappelli's live album. Unfortunately, the Rats' time abroad was not a success. A short stint in London also brought no luck. But, they continued to be appreciated locally. In late 1967, the band recorded a single at Fairfield Studios in Hull. It was titled 'The Rise And Fall Of Bernie Gripplestone'. The single was a band composition, though was not released at the time.

On March 17, 1968, the Rats played at the Cat Ballou Club in Grantham. They were on the same bill as Jeff Beck, Mick's hero. During this period, Mick bought a black 1968 Gibson Les Paul Custom. His sister Maggi told Weird and Gilly: 'I remember him saying to me about the action being nice and slack, it wasn't too tight and he could really get a good old bend of the strings.' In time, he had the black finish stripped off the top and he removed pick-up covers.

For a short period, the Rats became Treacle, but reverted back to their original name. Early in 1969, they made several recordings at Fairview studios. Their choice probably reflected the music the band was performing. They included Jeff Beck's 'Jeff's Boogie' and 'Morning Dew'. The tracks were not released at the time. Live performances of the band included numbers by Led Zeppelin and Jimi Hendrix. They played gigs up and down the country. Mick still worked during the day as

Mick Ronson with 'stripped' Gibson Les Paul Custom c. 1973.
Pictorial Press Ltd / Alamy Stock Photo.

a Hull Council gardener. He bought his guitar strings from Hammonds' department store in Hull.

Mick befriended, Michael Chapman, a local singer/songwriter and guitar player. Chapman had released one album, and needed a lead guitarist for a second. Mick was chosen even though there was some reticence from the record company. One of Chapman's roadies, Pete Hunsley was responsible for stripping the black paint off the front of Mick's Gibson Les Paul. Chapman's album, 'Fully Qualified Survivor', was released in March 1970. Mick's guitar playing is particularly noteworthy on several tracks including 'Kodak Ghosts'. The Rats recorded once more at Fairview, though the tracks remained unleased for a number of years.

David Bowie released the 'David Bowie' album in November 1969. To promote it, he formed a backing band, the Hype. Mick Ronson left his Hull Council job and became the band's lead guitarist. This was in early February 1970. Bowie was instantly thrilled with Mick's guitar playing. On Maggi Ronson's website, Tony Visconti says: 'Mick Ronson just floored us. When David and I met him, we knew he'd fit in looks-wise, but we had no idea what was coming until he picked up his Les Paul and played for us.'

Bowie and Mick played together on John Peel's Sunday Show, recorded on February 5, 1970. Amongst the songs were 'The Prettiest Star' and 'Width Of A Circle'. Mick lived with Bowie and wife Angela, along with other musicians (including Tony Visconti). This was in a large house, Haddon Hall, in Beckenham. The Hype first performed as Bowie's backing band on February 22, 1970, at the Roundhouse, in London. They opened for Fat Mattress. On March 6, 1970, Mick was thrilled to appear on home soil at the University of Hull with Bowie and the Hype. There was a second appearance at the BBC on March 23, 1970, when Bowie played on 'Sounds of the Seventies'.

Mick first recorded with Bowie early in April 1970. This was on a reworking of the track 'Memory Of A Free Festival'. It was released as a single during June 1970. On the B-side, Mick sang some backing vocals. Work began on Bowie's album, 'The Man Who Sold The World' during April and May 1970. It was Bowie's first album to showcase Mick as his lead guitarist. Mick played a significant part at the recording sessions. Tony Visconti told Weird and Gilly: 'I have to go down on record in saying that if it wasn't for Mick and his desire to show the world that he was a great guitarist, who knows what would have happened.' Tony and Mick played recorders on 'All The Madmen'. For the same track, Mick wrote the violin-sounding parts that were played on a Moog synthesizer. These sections showcased the work of Ralph Mace. During the recording of the album, Mick learned a lot about production techniques from Tony Visconti. Whilst recording 'The Man Who Sold The World', Mick played guitar on a session for Elton John. The David Bowie album was released in April 1971.

For a period, Mick left Bowie. He became part of a new incantation of the Hype. Amongst the members to begin with were Woody Woodmansey, Tony Visconti and Benny Marshall. The new band became Ronno for a time and they played gigs around the country. They released a solitary single, '4th Hour Of My Sleep'. In the early 1970s, Mick took lessons on music theory from the Hull lady who once taught him piano.

When Bowie embarked on his next album, 'Hunky Dory', Mick returned to London to help him out. He was accompanied by Trevor Bolder and Mick 'Woody' Woodmansey. Recording took place between June and August 1971. Mick is noted as producing some outstanding solos where each guitar note counted and enhanced the song. Besides guitar, he was responsible for backing vocals, work with a Mellotron and some string arrangements. Noteworthy examples of arrangements are 'Changes' and 'Life On Mars'. Rick Wakeman contributed to the album on piano. During the summer of 1971, Mick produced some songs and did string arrangements (his first) for Dana Gillespie. A band called Milkwood also asked him to create string arrangements.

Work on David Bowie's 'The Rise And Fall Of Ziggy Stardust And The Spiders From Mars' began at Trident Studios in September 1971. Bowie signed a new recording contract with RCA Records in New York. He was accompanied to the US with wife Angela and Mick. They met Iggy Pop, Lou Reed and Andy Warhol. This was besides seeing Annette Peacock who was noted for her work with the synthesizer.

Around the Ziggy Stardust period, Bowie, Mick and the rest of the band changed their hairstyles and appearance. Contributing to this was Angie Bowie and hairdresser, Suzi Fussey. Suzi was offered the job of hairstylist/personal assistant and eventually became Mick's wife.

Television performances of the band in 1972 included the 'Old Grey Whistle Test' (February 8), 'Lift off With Ayshea' (June 15) and 'Top of the Pops' (July 5). Bob Harris commented to Weird and Gilly: '[With Bowie] I thought that Mick was important to the way everything sounded. His guitar work and his presence were an integral part of it and, without that, it just wouldn't have worked in the same way.'

Two days later, Bowie and the band embarked on a UK tour. Many up-and-coming guitarists found inspiration in the concerts they attended. Mick Rock in his book *Ziggy Stardust* (1984) heaped more praise on Mick: 'From the outset, Ronno's star shone brightly. He was never simply a sideman; he was Ziggy's pal and anchor. He understood Ziggy and could structure the interpretation of his music.'

In mid-1972, Mott the Hoople accepted David Bowie's song 'All The Young Dudes'. When the band recorded the album of the same title, Mick helped out on a track, 'Sea Diver'. He was responsible for writing the brass and string arrangements and conducting the players.

'The Rise And Fall Of Ziggy Stardust And The Spiders From Mars' album was released on June 6, 1972. Mick contributed guitar, piano and vocals. During a concert on June 17, 1972, at Oxford Town Hall, Mick Rock photographed a classic rock moment. Bowie performed a fellatio act with Mick's Les Paul. Mick Rock commented in the *Ziggy* book: 'It becomes a classic rock 'n' roll gesture, like Hendrix setting his guitar on fire or Pete Townshend smashing his guitar.'

Bowie and Mick worked on Lou Reed's album 'Transformer' in August 1972. Although Mick and Reed initially found understanding each other's accents a slight problem, they eventually worked well together. Mick contributed string and bass arrangements, lead guitar, piano, recorder, and backing vocals. Mick and Bowie produced the album.

Ziggy and the Spiders went to America for a tour which began in September 1972. Mick was given the task of auditioning a piano player. Jazz musician Mike Garson only played for a few seconds, but immediately became part of the Bowie entourage. Mick and Garson would continue to have a mutual respect for each other in the years ahead. Whilst in the US, the single 'The Jean Genie' was recorded. In a 1992 interview, Mick would state the song was done in two takes and he used a very small amplifier. The Bowie US tour which lasted until early December was a complete success. Mick's outstanding guitar playing was greatly admired by full-house crowds. Mike Garson told Weird and Gilly: '[Mick's] melodic concept and the way he saw tones and motion with the guitar, plus the love that he had for it … he's still the guy that moved me the most.'

In Toronto, Mick worked with the Pure Prairie League. He did string arrangements for certain songs on their album 'Burstin' Out', played bass guitar and added backing vocals. Bowie's single 'The Jean Genie' was released in November 1972.

The first month of 1973, was spent performing in the UK and working on 'Aladdin Sane'. Mick played acoustic and electric guitar, piano and added backing vocals. This was besides being heavily involved with the arrangements and mixing of the album. His muscular, heavy guitar work is featured on a number of tracks. On February 14, 1973, Bowie's US tour began. It was sold out everywhere with many matinees arranged. Praised frequently, was the stage presence of Bowie and Mick. Both worked together well, complementing each other's dynamic performance.

The US Ziggy tour ended on March 12, 1973. The next stop on the schedule was Japan. 'Aladdin Sane' was released on April 13, 1973. The Far Eastern tour ended on April 20. An eight-week tour of the UK began on May 12. Phil Collen (Def Leppard) attended one of the shows. He told Weird and Gilly: 'Every guitar player would play standard chords, but Mick would play a root note and just sustain it.'

In an interview with *Melody Maker* on June 9, 1973, Mick said that on stage he used 'Two Gibson Les Paul Custom guitars, with another as spare, placed on a convenient stand.' His amplifier was 'a Marshall 200-watt with one 120-watt Marshall cabinet containing four 12-inch Celestion speakers. I use a Cry Baby Wah-Wah pedal and an American Tonebender.' Amongst his other guitars were a Yamaha acoustic, a Brazilian Carlos Robelli acoustic, a black Gibson SG Special and a Fender Mustang.

Mick's Tonebender was a Mk1 fuzz. The Wah-Wah, a Vox, in the early days, then a Jen Cry Baby, a little later.

On www.kemper-amps.com, JJ notes: 'Mick used a 200-watt Marshall Major [a 1967 version which became nicknamed 'The Pig']. This version of a Major was different to Ritchie Blackmore's Marshall Major … Live-the vol was cranked to full. This is why the two outer KT88 valves were removed. The Marshall Major Pig was a mindblowingly loud amp!' Additionally, JJ mentions: 'Mick also used a Marshall cab … After the first American tour, Mick switched his Celestions to JBLs [James Bullough Lansing Sound Incorporated], likely as they handled the Pig more efficiently. Mick's sound became brighter with the JBLs.'

Further information may be found on www.fuzzfaced.net: 'In 1967, following the continuous demand for more powerful amplifiers, the first 200-watt amplifiers, the Marshall 200, came to light. [They were created] under the supervision of Ken Flegg … Since these heads had a large cabinet and small front panel, which at first glance resemble the snout of a pig, the Lead of the first series of Marshall 200 (1967 model) was nicknamed "The Pig".'

Bowie called time on the Ziggy act at the Hammersmith Odeon on July 3, 1973. A highlight of the concert was Jeff Beck joining Mick and the others on stage for a short jam session. Bowie and Mick got together later in July to record 'Pin Ups' in France. The album featured a number of songs from the 1960s that had influenced not only Bowie but Mick as well. On 'Pin Ups', Mick is noted as playing guitar, piano, adding vocals and arrangements. Later, Mick would say 'Pin Ups' was the Bowie album he enjoyed working on the most.

Commenting on his work with Bowie, Mick told *Sounds* magazine in February 1990: 'I'm not denying that I was chiefly responsible for the sound of the David Bowie records from the seventies. I'm not trying to brag about it, it just so happens that I was an integral part of the band, as well as on stage and in the studio.'

On Maggi Ronson's website, producer Ken Scott comments: 'Would everyone know [Bowie's] name if not for his pairing with Mick Ronson? Quite possibly not. Ronno was a major part of the team that brought David to the forefront of modern music.'

In July 1973, Mick started recording his debut album. Mick said Bowie's manager, Tony Defries told him: '[O]kay, we can make you a big star, get you a deal with RCA, all that. So I said "Wonderful", and went off to make my own record.' 'Slaughter On 10th Avenue' was released in February 1974. Mick is credited with playing guitar, piano, vocals, and undertaking arrangements. He is also noted as conductor. Mick's sister, Maggi, then only 16, added some backing vocals. Mick co-wrote two of the seven tracks. Mick's debut concerts were at the Rainbow Theatre, London, on February 22–23, 1974. The band comprised Mark Carr-Pritchard on second guitar, Trevor Bolder on bass, Mike Garson on keyboards and Ritchie Dharma on drums. The London Symphony Orchestra was present and the event was filmed. MainMan management gave lavish promotion, even producing a short film and establishing a fan club. The album, released on March 1, 1974, climbed to no. 9 in the UK album charts.

To promote 'Pin Ups', Bowie made a film 'The 1980 Floor Show' for the US weekly rock show 'The Midnight Special'. Performances to be included in the film were staged at the Marquee Club, London. These were recorded on October 18, 19, and 20, 1973. Bowie used the same musicians that had participated in the 'Pin Up' recording with the addition of a second guitarist, Mark Carr-Pritchard. Mick was credited with electric guitar and backing vocals. His last session with Bowie for a number of years occurred in November 1973. This was on the recording of '1984/Dodo'.

Mick's solo tour to promote 'Slaughter On 10th Avenue'

began during April 1974. Around the same time, he helped out on Bob Sargeant's album, 'First Starring Role'. This was besides producing two tracks on Dana Gillespie's album 'Aint Gonna Play No Second Fiddle'.

In July 1974, Mick started work on his second solo album 'Play Don't Worry'. For this, Weird and Gilly note that he played eight instruments. In addition, he was responsible for arranging, conducting and producing all the songs. Sister Maggi, wife Suzi and Ian Hunter contributed backing vocals on 'Girl Can't Help It'.

But, not feeling comfortable as a front man/solo artist, Mick turned his attention elsewhere. He joined Mott the Hoople in 1974. Ian Hunter and the other band members were very pleased to have him with them. Amongst the tracks he recorded were 'Saturday Gigs' and 'Lounge Lizard'. Mick was part of Mott the Hoople's European tour which began in Sweden on October 10, 1971. Afterwards, there was a British tour that started in November. The band played a mixture of Mott the Hoople songs as well as some of Mick's solo tracks. Mick enjoyed playing live with Mott the Hoople but this was short-lived. The band broke up at the end of December 1974.

Ian Hunter began recording his solo album 'Ian Hunter' in January 1975 and Mick was there to help and played a number of instruments. These included lead guitar, organ, Mellotron, mouth organ and bass guitar. This was besides co-writing 'Boy' with Hunter. Mick took credit for the arrangements and co-producing the album with Hunter. There was a Hunter/Ronson tour to promote the album. The set list included some of Mick's solo songs.

During February 1975, Mick's second solo album, 'Play Don't Worry' was released. One track from the album, 'Angel No. 9', particularly showcases Mick's rocky lead guitar playing. He performed the song with the stripped top Gibson Les Paul Custom on the 'Old Grey Whistle Test', April 11, 1975. 'Play Don't Worry' was another track Mick played.

Contractual difficulties put paid to a Hunter/Ronson album in 1975. Then, Mick met Bob Dylan and was invited to go on tour with him. This, becoming known as the 'Rolling Thunder Revue', stretched between October 1975 and May 1976. Mick received an enthusiastic reception for his guitar playing. Bob Dylan's friend, Bob Neuwirth said on Maggi Ronson's website: '… Mick's brilliance was the way in which he adapted to what everyone else was doing around him. He played every style of music, too – Beck, Hendrix, you name it. Mick Ronson was quite simply a tour de force!'

Amongst the other musicians involved were Scarlett Rivera, Joan Baez, T-Bone Burnett, and Roger McGuinn. During a break in the tour in December 1975, Mick recorded songs for an intended solo album.

On the Dylan tour, Mick befriended ex-Byrds front man, Roger McGuinn. He helped with the latter's album 'Cardiff Rose'. Mick was credited with playing no less than eight instruments. He added backing vocals and produced the album. Around the same time, Mick played some great lead guitar on a David Cassidy track, 'Getting It In The Street'.

Dylan released an album in September 1976 that included songs from the 'Rolling Thunder Revue' and Mick is featured. He appears in a film, 'Renaldo and Clara', which captured elements of the tour. This was released in 1978.

During the latter half of 1976, Mick spent time playing with other musicians in the US and in the UK. He appears on Michael Chapman's 'The Man Who Hated Mornings'. Chapman noted that Mick turned up one day at the recording studio with his Les Paul and a Mesa Boogie amplifier. Mick played a solo on the album track 'I'm Sober Now'. Other work involved adding guitar to John Mellencamp's album 'Chestnut Street Incident'. He rehearsed with Sparks, though the association came to nothing.

Living in Woodstock, Mick gathered together musicians for the Mick Ronson Band. Some recordings were made, though not available until some years later. He involved himself in work with Topaz, Roger Daltrey and Benny Mardones, and Van Morrison. In an 'Old Grey Whistle Test' feature 'The Bearsville Picnic', from 1977, Mick was interviewed by Bob Harris. Revealed, were Mick's plans to involve himself with more production work, particularly with British bands, and win a record deal for himself.

Whilst in London during 1978, Mick helped out the Rich Kids, which included Glen Matlock and Midge Ure. He made a number of contributions and suggestions. He produced their debut album 'Ghosts Of Princes In Towers' (released in October 1978) and played keyboards on four tracks. He joined the Rich Kids on stage at two gigs. Embracing the Punk/New Wave movement, Mick assisted another band, Slaughter and the Dogs. He gave much encouragement and advice to guitarist Mick Rossi. Mick Ronson played on two of the band's tracks on the album 'Do It Dog Style', (released in June 1978). For the sessions, Rossi recalls Mick used his Les Paul and a Mesa Boogie amp. In the same year, Mick lent a hand to Hull band Dead Fingers Talk by producing their album 'Storm The Reality Studios'.

During the Autumn of 1978, Mick was invited to help Annette Peacock with her second solo album, 'X-Dreams', released in September of the same year. He is featured on four tracks. Annette told Weird and Gilly: 'There was an understanding between Mick and I, a mutual respect and admiration.'

Before the end of 1978, Mick would work with Corky Lang (of Mountain) and on Ian Hunter's fourth solo album, 'You're Never Alone With A Schizophrenic', appearing in March 1979. Mick co-wrote the opening track 'Just Another Night' and added guitars, vocals and percussion. The album was produced by Mick and Ian. Mick also suggested the album's title. Afterwards, between June and November 1979, Mick went on the road with Ian to promote the album. They toured under the heading 'The Ian Hunter Band featuring Mick Ronson'. This culminated in the live album 'Welcome To The Club', produced by both performers (appearing in April 1980). Mick is noted as playing lead guitar, Moog synthesizer, mandolin and adding vocals.

Ian made these comments about Mick's playing: 'His approach to recording was slow and beautiful. He wasn't really a rock player – he was classically trained. Sometimes he would listen to a track for about an hour without touching the guitar. He'd form the whole solo completely in his head, and then it would slowly emerge through his fingers. About the time when

I'd be ready to get up and leave, he'd play this absolutely amazing line.'

Mick made contributions to Ellen Foley's debut album, 'Night Out' (June 1979). He played guitar, keyboards and percussion and can be heard on background vocals. Mick was responsible for the string arrangements and both he and Ian Hunter produced the album. After Ellen's album, Mick went to Connecticut to assist David Johansen with his second solo album, 'In Style'. He took credit for his guitar work and co-producing the album with David.

The 1980s began with a busy itinerary for Mick. He worked with the Iron City Houserockers on their album 'Have A Good Time But Get Out Alive'. He was part of the production team for the album as well as on certain tracks playing piano and mandolin. In April 1980, Mick appeared with Ian Hunter on 'Rockpalast'. He is seen playing a red Gibson Les Paul Custom with stripped top and headstock and both pick-up covers removed. He also plays mandolin. This was a period when he would later admit to an interviewer that he didn't want to play the guitar. Nonetheless, whilst living in Woodstock, he plays lead guitar on 'Gotta Go Home' on the Johnny Average Band's album 'Some People'.

Ian Hunter enlisted Mick to co-produce (with Mick Jones of the Clash) his fifth studio album 'Short Back 'n' Sides', issued in August 1981. Mick Ronson contributed lead guitar, keyboards and vocals to the album. In the same year, Mick joined the band the New York Yanquis, recoding some demos and undertaking a short tour in the US. After this project, Mick was associated with Meat Loaf's second album 'Deadringer' (guitar on 'More Than You Deserve') and a soundtrack for the film 'Indian Summer'. The film was never made but a soundtrack album was released in 2001.

Ian Hunter toured in 1981 to promote the 'Short Back 'n' Sides' album. At one point Mick was called upon to play keyboards. This fell into that period when he was trying to step back a little from playing guitar. He did not appreciate the way guitar playing was going at the time. Weird and Gilly quote Ian Hunter's comments: '[Mick] used to say, "They may as well be draftsmen or something, because they're not saying anything. They're just going up and down the fretboard." He just felt, if that's the way it was going to be, then he would rather not play. So he didn't.'

In the early 1980s, Mick worked with A&M Records. Sven Gusevik in *Ronson Goes Solo: Part Two of the Mick Ronson Story* (December 1989) states under the heading 'Mick Ronson in 1982': 'Ronson spent two years in Canada, working primarily with young bands – making demos

Mick Ronson with David Bowie c. 1972.
Pictorial Press Ltd / Alamy Stock Photo.

and producing the odd record along the way.' One of the most successful bands he worked with was the Payolas, on their 'No Stranger To Danger'. Mick produced the album as well as contributing guitar, keyboards and vocals.

Mick worked on John Mellencamp's album 'American Fool' (released in 1982). He made significant contributions to the track 'Jack and Diane' which was no. 1 in the US. In September 1983, Mick joined David Bowie on stage at Toronto's National Exhibition Stadium, during the 'Serious Moonlight Tour'. He used a prototype guitar belonging to Bowie's guitarist Earl Slick and performed 'The Jean Genie'. On YouTube Mick comments: 'I was playing Slick's guitar ... I had heard Slick play solos all night so I decided not to play solos and I just went out and thrashed the guitar. I really thrashed the guitar, I was waving the guitar above my head and all sorts of things. It was funny afterwards because David said, "You should have seen [Earl Slick's] face ..." meaning he looked petrified. I had his prize guitar and I was swinging it around my head and Slick's going "Waaaa ... watch my guitar," you know. I was banging into it and it was going round my head. Poor Slick. I mean, I didn't know it was his special guitar, I just thought it was a guitar, a lump of wood with six strings.' It is noted that for the Bowie tour, Earl Slick used DiMarzio guitars.

Gusevik (*op. cit.*) mentions that in 1984, Mick teamed up with singer/song-writer Lisa Dalbello: 'Ronson approached Lisa after watching some old videos of her on national TV. Her band at the time "stinked" – according to Mick, so they recorded the album ['Womanforsays'] alone.' Mick and Lisa produced the album which was released in 1984. Mick played guitar, keyboards and bass.

For the film 'Teachers' (1984), Mick co-wrote with Ian Hunter the track '(I'm) The Teacher'. Mick worked with Hunter on the song 'Good Man In A Bad Time' which was included in the soundtrack for the film 'Fright Night' (1985). Between 1985 and 1987, Mick made demos, performed and was involved in working with a number of bands. Amongst many of these were: One the Juggler, Sandy Dillon, Steve Harley, Midge Ure, Andi Sexgang, Lisa Dominique, XDavis and David Lynn Jones.

Mick spent time in Nashville helping to produce country singer David Lynn Jones' first album 'Hard Times On Easy Street' (1987). Maggi Ronson told Weird and Gilly: 'He enjoyed the Nashville experience, for sure. I know he liked the country scene very much ...' During 1987, Mick joined Ian Hunter for a short tour in Canada. The pair worked together for some songs on Urgent's album 'Thinking Out Loud' (issued 1987).

Mick produced an album, 'Johnny D. Is Back' for Dutch band Fatal Flowers in early 1988. He also played guitar on a track on the Toll's 'The Price Of Progression' LP. In the same year, Mick once again teamed up with Hunter and eventually embarked on a 60-date tour that would end in London during mid-February 1989. Weird and Gilly mention two interesting points about Mick's guitars in 1988. Whilst working with the Fatal Flowers, 'The band convinced Mick to play on the recordings and he pulled out his old Ziggy-era Les Paul one last time for the occasion ...' During the Ian Hunter tour, the authors mention a squealing lead coming from 'Mick's blue [Fender] Telecaster.'

In 1989, Mick worked with Andi Sexgang. In Stockholm, Mick produced the Swedish band EC2's album. The first ever album credited to the Ian Hunter–Mick Ronson moniker, 'Yui Orta', was recorded in 1989 and released in the same year. Mick and Ian co-wrote three of the songs. On www.allmusic.com, Donald A. Guarisco writes: 'As usual, Mick Ronson plays an important role, making a substantial contribution to the song-writing and supplying an array of tasty guitar licks.' Mick and Ian promoted the album throughout a long tour.

Commenting about his guitar set-up, Mick told *Guitarist* magazine in 1990: 'Right now, I like the combination of Mesa Boogie's head and Marshall cabinet. If possible, I don't want to use any effects. Sometimes they change the guitar tone. To get the best sound you have to link the guitar directly to the amp.'

Mick produced the Fatal Flowers' album 'Pleasure Ground', issued in 1990. He undertook further work with EC2, and played guitar and keyboards on Secret Mission's 'Strange Afternoon' which appeared in 1991.

Mick involved himself in a few projects, playing and producing, in Sweden in 1991. In the same year, Mick was diagnosed with liver cancer. It was inoperable. Yet, he undertook a short Scandinavian tour with Graham Parker in the autumn of 1991. In the following year, Mick teamed up with Morrissey to produce his solo album, 'Your Arsenal'. It was issued in July 1992 and was an instant success. In a review of the album on www.allmusic.com, Stephen Thomas Erlewine states: 'Guitarist Alain Whyte's riffs swagger with a self-absorbed arrogance, and producer Mick Ronson gives the music a tough, stylish sheen ...' Morrissey said in a 'Modern Rock' live radio interview: 'I was obviously a fan [of Mick's] twenty years ago when he worked with David Bowie, and I actually saw Mick in 1972 ... so for me, it was just an enormous compliment that he actually agreed to produce the record ...'

Whilst producing the Morrissey album, Mick appeared on April 20, 1992, at Wembley Stadium for the tribute to Queen's Freddie Mercury. He performed songs with Ian Hunter and David Bowie. During 'Heroes', Mick played a blue Fender Telecaster and employed an EBow.

Mick briefly worked with David Bowie on his album 'Black Tie White Noise', recorded over a period in 1992. Mick played lead guitar on Bowie's version of the Cream's 'I Feel Free'. Mick then turned to working on his album 'Heaven And Hull'. The album brought several people together to provide vocals: David Bowie, John Mellencamp, and Chrissie Hynde. Guest musicians included Martin Chambers, Brian May, John Deacon, and Roger Taylor. Sham Morris helped Mick write four of the album's songs and was involved with production.

On October 20, 1992, Mick was interviewed for the BBC documentary called 'Hang On to Yourself' at the Hammersmith Odeon. He explained that to create his hallmark sound he often put the Wah-Wah into a 'cocked' or 'parked position' to create what he described as a 'Honking' sound. He revealed that he had always been a nervous person but on stage his guitar playing made him grow considerably in confidence. In fact, he became another person.

Mick helped the Wildhearts on one of their tracks, 'My Baby Is A Headfuck', which appeared on the album 'Earth Vs

The Wildhearts' (released August 1993). On Maggi Ronson's website, Ginger from the band recalls: 'Mick turned up at the studio with his guitar case. We expected him to open it and reveal the beautiful Les Paul he was famous for playing, but instead he pulled out this grubby blue Telecaster. We were a little shocked when he told us he didn't have a Les Paul – not even a Gibson endorsement like we had.'

Mick died at his home in Hasker Street, London, on April 29, 1993. He was 46. His album 'Heaven And Hull' was unfinished at the time of his death. A number of people grouped together to complete the production. They included Frankie LaRocka, Joe Elliott, Sham Morris, Sam Lederman, Steve Popovich, and Suzi Ronson. The album was released in May 1994. In reviewing the album in *Rolling Stone*, Alec Foege wrote: '"Heaven and Hull" brims with the kind of muscular but melodic guitar leads that earned Ronson a cult following among musicians.'

A tribute concert to Mick was held at the Hammersmith Odeon on April 29, 1994. Amongst those who appeared were the Rats, Dana Gillespie, Glen Matlock, Gary Brooker, Bill Wyman's Willie and the Poor Boys, Mick Jones, Bill Nelson (lead guitar on 'Ziggy Stardust'), Joe Elliott, Ian Hunter, Roger Taylor, Phil Collen (lead guitar 'Moonage Daydream'), Tony Visconti and Roger Daltrey. Bob Harris compered the evening.

On May 15, 1994, a 'Mick Ronson Memorial Concert' was organised in Japan by the band Yellow Monkey. This was the first of three concerts staged between 1994 and 1996. On August 9 and 10, 1997, 'The Mick Ronson Memorial Concert II' was held in Hull and was well attended. Weird and Gilly mention 600 Japanese fans were present. In some areas of the city banners were stretched across the streets displaying the words 'Welcome to Kingston upon Hull – Mick Ronson's home town.' They were printed in English and Japanese. Amongst those appearing at the concert were many who had been at the first concert: Ian Hunter, Joe Elliot, Mick Jones, Steve Harley and Phil Collen.

Since Mick's death, and the birth of the internet, many reflections have appeared about Mick's playing and the equipment he used. On www.theproaudiofiles.com there is an article, dated February 1, 2019, by Mark Marshall, 'The Anatomy of Mick Ronson's Guitar Tone'. One piece of equipment Mark mentions is the Maestro Echoplex: 'In some live performances from the Ziggy Stardust tour you can hear Mick use a Maestro Echoplex. Later in his career, Mick used a Roland Space Echo, not only for the echo but also as a preamp to push his amp harder.'

The Mick Ronson Memorial Stage was officially dedicated on Sunday, August 10, 1997. On www.hunter-mott.com, it is mentioned: 'The proceedings opened at midday, with a short formal presentation from the Hull Council director of leisure services and the Lord Mayor. Kevin Cann, Maggi and Minnie Ronson also made some nice speeches, and there was a special award presented to the Yellow Monkey for all their efforts. A mixture of local bands and "name" bands played throughout the afternoon.'

On www.guitarhangar.com, there is an article titled 'Rick Tedesco and the Hunt for Mick Ronson's Ziggy Stardust Les Paul'. This tells how guitar collector and dealer, Rick Tedesco undertook painstaking research in 2000, before locating Mick's Les Paul in the Hard Rock Café in Australia. It had been donated by Mick Ronson in the late 1980s. Rick Tedesco states: '[I] proceeded to work on procuring the guitar for purchase. We eventually landed a deal where I would supply them with several guitars to replace that one.'

Rick loaned the Les Paul to the Cleveland Rock and Roll Hall of Fame Museum in mid-August 2001. After two years, Rick got the guitar back and it was played on a few of his projects. In 2004, he set in motion the production of a Mick Ronson tribute Les Paul guitar. He also acquired more Mick Ronson gear. This included guitars, the Marshall Major head and a few pedals. A video was made featuring Rick talking about the collection.

In an article 'Gibson Remembers Mick Ronson' from May 24, 2007 (on www.gibson.com), Russell Hall wrote: 'There's seldom a guitar talent so unassuming as Mick Ronson. Even during his years as the flamboyant foil for David Bowie's Ziggy Stardust character, Ronson's searing solos and crunchy riffs were less about showmanship than about serving the song at hand. The quintessential sideman, Ronson used little more than his trusty Les Paul and a Cry Baby Wah-Wah to garnish the song-writing efforts of such brilliant writers as Bowie, Ian Hunter, and Lou Reed.'

During November of the same year, Mick received the Tommy Vance Inspiration Award at the *Classic Rock* Awards. It was accepted on Mick's behalf from Joe Elliott and Ian Hunter by Lisa and Suzi Ronson.

In 2014, Rick Tedesco sold the original Mick Ronson Les Paul guitar to another collector. In Hull's East Park on June 2, 2017, a new memorial to Mick was unveiled. This was an 8ft guitar sculpture designed by student Janis Skodins. Mick had worked as a gardener in the same park. It has since become known as the Michael Ronson Garden of Reflection.

On Maggi Ronson's website, Ian Hunter comments: 'Professionally it was a privilege to play with Mick, personally it was a privilege to have known him. He was a nutcase but his legacy is pure class. Guitarists will emulate him as long as rock 'n' roll is around.'

Mick Taylor on stage at the Sportshalle in Cologne, Germany during 1973 as part of the Rolling Stones Tour of Europe.
Gijsbert Hanekroot / Alamy Stock Photo.

MICK TAYLOR

One of the standout blues guitarists of the 1960s, Mick Taylor built his reputation with John Mayall and the Bluesbreakers before becoming Brian Jones's replacement in the Rolling Stones. Like his predecessor, Mick added another dimension to the group's style with his dynamic guitar playing over several classic albums in the early 1970s. After his departure from the Stones, Mick released two solo albums and returned to his blues roots, performing to appreciative audiences around the world.

Mick's mother and father were interested in music and there was a piano in the family home which he played when around nine years old. Mick then took to the guitar and was shown some chords by an uncle, who owned an instrument.

Whilst in his mid-teens, Mick formed his first band, the Juniors. In 1964, a single was released – 'There's A Pretty Girl' – and Mick is pictured with the band holding a Hofner Super Solid two-pick-up guitar. The Juniors subsequently evolved into the Gods with Ken Hensley, Joe Konas and John and Brian Glascock.

The group opened for John Mayall's Bluesbreakers in 1965. Guitarist Eric Clapton had failed to appear and Mick offered his services, taking up Eric's Gibson Les Paul Standard and playing through a Marshall 1962 combo amplifier. Mayall was impressed by Mick's performance. Peter Green subsequently became the Bluesbreakers' lead guitarist following the departure of Clapton. When the former left to found Fleetwood Mac in 1967, Mayall remembered Mick when he answered the bandleader's ad in *Melody Maker* and he joined the band.

Mick was with the Bluesbreakers for two years, playing on several albums: 'Crusade'; 'The Diary Of A Band Volumes 1 And 2'; 'Bare Wires'; 'Blues From Laurel Canyon'. With the Gods and John Mayall, Mick had upgraded from the Hofner to a 1959 Gibson Les Paul Standard with Bigsby tremolo. He had two of these, purchasing the first from Central London in 1965, followed by a second in 1967 which he bought from Keith Richards.

Mick is credited with a handful of songs on the Bluesbreakers' albums. 'Snowy Wood' is his first, appearing on 'Crusade' (on which he delivers an Albert King-style solo), followed by 'No Reply' on 'Bare Wires' where Mick displays his skills with a Wah-Wah pedal. 'Hartley Quits' on the same album is an extended guitar workout, whilst on '2401' from 'Blues From Laurel Canyon', Mick turns his hand to a pedal steel guitar.

Well-regarded by the end of the 1960s, Mick was a top candidate to replace Brian Jones when he left the Rolling Stones in mid-1969. At the time, Mick had finished a tour of America with the Bluesbreakers and was about to become redundant as Mayall decided to take the band in a new direction. Therefore, when Mick Jagger was in contact, Mick was free to attend sessions for the 'Let It Bleed' album. After a couple of days, Mick was officially enlisted with the group.

Mick's earliest contribution to a Stones song was adding slide to 'Country Honk' using a Selmer lap steel guitar. He added some riffs to 'Honky Tonk Women' using a Gibson SG Standard. Mick had acquired the guitar around 1968 and favoured this for several years. In an interview for Gibson's website in 2010 he commented: '… I just remember loving that guitar … I preferred that SG [to his Gibson Les Paul] because it had a very wide neck, and a very flat neck, and the action was absolutely superb. And the sound was good too. And it had a Bigsby arm on it, which I didn't use a lot in those days, but I like that kind of effect, as well.'

Mick's SG Standard was an early 1960s model which had been originally fitted with a 'sideways' Vibrola, though this had been removed and the Bigsby unit installed. Despite favouring the SG, Mick also had a Fender Stratocaster and Telecaster, along with a Martin acoustic that he used in the studio.

Mick's first public performance with the Stones was at the free Hyde Park concert staged on July 5, 1969, which turned into a memorial for Brian Jones who had recently passed away. Mick played his Gibson SG Standard with Bigsby along with the 1959 Gibson Les Paul Standard ex-Keith Richards using a Hiwatt DR201 200-watt amplifier connected to 4x12 in. cabinets.

For the end of the year, the Stones organised an American tour. Mick took his Gibson SG and Les Paul Standard, whilst also using a Fender Telecaster in white and a Gibson ES 355 which belonged to Keith. Amps were initially to be Hiwatt but problems were experienced and a switch was made to Ampeg. These were prototype SVT models. A number of the concerts were recorded and tracks from them released as 'Get Your Ya-Ya's Out!' in late 1970. Mick's SG makes an appearance on the album cover.

The Stones went into Olympic Studios to record new tracks in spring, 1970. Several of these would appear on 'Sticky Fingers'. Mick continued to use equipment mentioned above for the sessions, but did add some guitar parts using a Watkins Copycat tape echo. The recording sessions later moved from Olympic Studios to Mick Jagger's house 'Stargroves' using the band's mobile recording studio, commissioned earlier in the year.

Mick has several standout moments on 'Sticky Fingers', such as 'Sway', featuring a slide part and an outro solo. 'Wild Horses' has Mick's acoustic guitar tuned in the Nashville style, and another solo at the end of 'Can't You Hear Me Knocking' uses Keith's ES 355.

Towards the end of 1970, the Stones toured Europe and Mick was seen playing his Gibson SG or Les Paul. The latter was used for slide parts, such as 'You Gotta Move', from 'Sticky Fingers' and part of the touring set list. Amplification was provided by either the Ampeg SVT units or Fender models.

After completing a British tour during the first half of March 1971, Mick and the Stones moved to the south of France to help ease the increasing burden of taxes imposed on them. Keith rented a villa – Nellcôte – and soon after recording sessions began in the cellar using the mobile studio. A large number of tracks were assembled for 'Exile On Main Street'. Equipment used continued to be as mentioned previously.

Mick received a writing credit for devising the 'Ventilator Blues' riff. He provided excellent guitar parts, such as on 'Casino Boogie', and played bass on a couple of tracks – 'Torn And Frayed' and 'I Just Want To See His Face'. Mick continued to use the slide, heard on 'All Down The Line' and 'Stop Breaking Down'.

As the Nellcôte sessions wound down, several guitars were stolen from the property. Keith was the main victim, though Mick lost his 1959 Gibson Les Paul with Bigsby. He gifted his brother-in-law the SG Standard at the end of the year.

The album was mixed in LA during the winter of 1971/1972, then the Stones assembled in LA during the early summer to prepare for an American tour.

Mick moved on to another Gibson Les Paul Standard, which had been fitted with a Bigsby at some point but was now removed, whilst amps continued to be Ampeg SVT models. The Les Paul had been purchased by Keith in the late 1960s and featured on the cover of 'Get Your Ya-Ya's Out!'.

In late November, the band went to Jamaica to record songs for 'Goats Head Soup'. Mick utilised a Wah-Wah and Leslie speaker on the track 'Doo Doo Doo Doo Doo (Heartbreaker)', whilst making a writing contribution to 'Winter'.

In early 1973, the Stones toured New Zealand and Australia and began with a show in LA to benefit earthquake victims in Nicaragua. Mick continued to favour his Gibson Les Paul Standard, yet he had a similar guitar that he used with a figured maple top. Both guitars had their pick-up covers removed.

The Stones recorded promotional videos for songs on 'Goats Head Soup'. For 'Dancing With Mr D', Mick has a Gibson ES 345 and also used it for 'Silver Train' where he plays the slide riff and solo. For 'Angie' he has a Gibson Hummingbird acoustic for one version of the video, although another was produced with Mick playing the piano part.

The second tour of the year began in Europe during early September and continued through to mid-October. Mick mostly used Gibson Les Pauls over the dates, but did add a late 1950s Fender Stratocaster with rosewood neck. He used the Strat when making a guest appearance with Mike Oldfield during a London performance of 'Tubular Bells'.

Although not present for the initial recording sessions for the 'It's Only Rock 'n' Roll' album that took place at the end of 1973, Mick was with the band in the studio for the follow-up dates in early 1974. He contributed a standout guitar solo on 'Time Waits For No One' using his Fender Stratocaster and a 'Synthi Hi-Fli' effects processor.

Mick contributed to the solo album of the Stones' new associate Ronnie Wood from the Faces. He played guitar on 'Take A Look At The Guy', whilst also contributing bass and electric piano parts on 'Shirley' and synthesizer on 'If You Gotta Make A Fool Of Somebody'. All of these appeared on 'I've Got My Own Album To Do' released in September 1974.

Three promotional videos were filmed for songs taken from 'It's Only Rock 'n' Roll'. Mick is seen with a Gibson Les Paul Standard on 'Ain't Too Proud To Beg', switching to a Martin 12-string for the acoustic 'Till The Next Goodbye'. The title track has Mick with a Fender Bronco, which Keith had briefly used.

The 'It's Only Rock 'n' Roll' album was a hit across the globe, but Mick was not happy with his position within the Stones and decided to quit the band at the end of 1974.

Mick joined forces with bassist Jack Bruce, Carla Bley, Bruce Gary and Ronnie Leahy. The group performed on a small tour of Europe during 1975 before breaking up in 1976. A performance by the band was captured on the 'Old Grey Whistle Test' and Mick uses a Gibson ES 355 with Marshall amplifier.

Mick signed a solo record deal in the late 1970s and produced his debut album. Simply titled 'Mick Taylor', the record was released in mid-1979 and was well-received. The final track – 'Spanish/A Minor' – is an extended showcase of Mick's guitar playing. The cover features Mick standing next to a Fender Stratocaster with a maple neck.

At the start of the 1980s, Mick joined the Alvin Lee Band for a tour of Europe – playing a Gibson Les Paul Standard – then in 1982, he reunited with John Mayall for a series of gigs in America, with a live album ('The 1982 Reunion Concert' from the Washington show) and film of the New Jersey gig later released. In the latter, Mick has a sonic blue Fender Stratocaster with rosewood fretboard, a Gibson Les Paul Standard (from the Rolling Stones years) and another Fender Stratocaster in white with maple neck and rail pick-ups. Mick also has two Marshall amplifiers and an Ampeg combo.

Soon after the Bluesbreakers tour, Mick was asked by Bob Dylan to play guitar on the Mark Knopfler-produced album 'Infidels'. Mick went on the ensuing tour of Europe and he continued to use his Les Paul and Marshall amplifiers. A new addition was a sunburst Fender Stratocaster with maple neck.

At the start of the 1990s, Mick recorded a new album, 'Stranger In This Town', mainly consisting of blues covers. He toured to support the record and for the gig in Toronto he had a sunburst Gibson Les Paul Custom (without pick-up covers) and Fender Stratocaster-style instrument in white with a rosewood neck. Amplification was provided by a Marshall head and cab alongside a Fender combo. Mick also used a glass slide.

Mick collaborated with American musician Carla Olson in the early 1990s and played guitar on her 'Within An Ace' and 'Reap The Whirlwind' albums, as well as 'Too Hot For Snakes' (also released earlier on a different label as 'Live'). This was a recording of their concert at the Roxy Theatre, Hollywood, in 1990.

A second solo album – 'A Stone's Throw' – was released in 2000 and featured mostly original material. Mick's skills with a slide were demonstrated on several songs, such as 'Secret Affair', 'Twisted Sister' (on both resonator and electric guitars), 'Never Fall In Love Again', 'Losing My Faith', 'Blind Willie McTell'. He uses a Wah-Wah pedal to good effect on 'Blues In The Morning' and 'Late At Night'.

Mick reunited with John Mayall in 2003 for the bandleader's 70th birthday celebrations. He performed on several songs using a Gibson Les Paul Standard with flametop (likely a historic reissue model) through a Fender 'The Twin' amp, with a Wah-Wah pedal also in evidence (one is on the floor, whilst two 'Cry Baby' 95Qs are in reserve behind the amp).

Mick Taylor with Fender Stratocaster on stage, Amsterdam, Netherlands, 1975.
Gijsbert Hanekroot / Alamy Stock Photo.

In 2007, Mick paid tribute to Jimi Hendrix, performing with Experience Hendrix on the song 'Red House'. Mick had played the song at various gigs over the years – even featuring the track on his 'Stranger In This Town' record – and in this instance used a Gibson Les Paul Standard, with a Wah-Wah on certain passages, as well as a metal slide for others.

Returning to his roots in the early 2010s, Mick obtained a Gibson Les Paul Standard with Bigsby tremolo that was aged and customised to appear like a vintage instrument. This guitar was prominent for several projects, such as a gig with Ronnie Wood in 2010 benefitting the 100 Club in London, as well as a tribute to Jimmy Reed in 2013. The Stones celebrated their 50th anniversary in 2012 and Mick was invited on the '50 & Counting' tour of 2012/2013. He mainly played the Les Paul mentioned earlier, as well as a white Fender Stratocaster with rosewood fingerboard.

Mick Taylor and his Gibson SG.
Album / Alamy Stock Photo.

PETE TOWNSHEND

In a career spanning 60 years, Pete Townshend has been at the forefront of rock music and performance. As the driving force behind the Who, he has created a considerable body of work, including 'My Generation', 'Tommy', 'Who Are You', etc. Pete's theatrical guitar style has been inspirational to many musicians and fans, yet remains distinctly unique.

Pete has a strong musical background. His paternal grandparents were working musicians – a flautist and singer – whilst his father and mother also performed, playing clarinet/saxophone and singing respectively, in the RAF band the Squadronaires. Pete's mother later gave up singing but remained involved in managing the affairs of the group. During summer holidays, the family often resided at holiday camps when his father played with the group. In 1955, Pete's father, Cliff, recorded 'Unchained Melody' which performed modestly but served as inspiration to his son.

Following a dalliance with the piano, Pete was finally interested in the guitar thanks to Bill Haley's 'Rock Around The Clock'. His first instrument was gifted to him by his grandmother. Soon after, Pete joined his first group – the Confederates, with John Entwistle – and played local shows. Pete upgraded to a Czech-made electric guitar and a small Watkins amplifier. Developing a reputation as a noteworthy guitarist locally, Pete was approached by schoolmate Roger Daltrey to join the Detours and the band first performed in 1962. Pete used a Harmony 'Stratocruiser' and painted it red. The Detours' reputation and popularity in the local area steadily grew into 1963. This success allowed Pete to purchase a Fender Pro amp.

The Detours played covers of contemporary songs, mainly pop, then R&B and blues in 1964. Pete experimented with other playing styles and notes in his autobiography: 'Working from my Chet Atkins study pieces, I began to master The Pirates' [Johnny Kidd's band, who the Detours were supporting at the time] rockabilly finger picking played by Mickey Green. I started playing a mix of rhythm and lead – what came to be called power chords – often with a jangling open string to give the sound more colour.'

Pete made a tentative foray into song-writing, providing the Naturals with 'It Was You', which was released in 1964. Early in the year, the Detours discovered another band had the same name and changed theirs to the Who. Roger switched to vocals, having provided guitar parts previously, whilst John Entwistle was on bass and the regular drummer Doug Sandon was replaced by Keith Moon around the time of the name change. The Who hired a new manager (Peter Meaden) who decided to push the group to the new R&B/Soul youth movement ('Mod'). A recording audition was secured and the group – briefly rechristened the High Numbers – released 'Zoot Suit/I'm The Face' for Fontana in mid-1964. This failed to find an audience and the Who changed managers, employing filmmakers Chris Stamp and Kit Lambert. American producer Shel Talmy, recently experiencing success with the Kinks, was invited to produce the Who. Pete wrote 'I Can't Explain' for the band's next single on the Brunswick label. Appearing in early 1965, the record peaked at no. 8 a little later.

Early in 1964, Pete acquired a Rickenbacker 1998 (US designation 345) with three pick-ups and Rose-Morris f-holes (denoting an export model). In *Who I Am*, Pete recalls that he set the central pick-up very close to the strings in order to achieve a signal boost when selected; he also stuffed the body with paper to reduce unwanted interference. Pete bought a Fender Bassman head with a Marshall 4x12 in. cabinet. He used this with the Fender Pro to keep pace with growing venue sizes and the need for high stage volumes.

Whilst Pete took measures to reduce unwanted feedback, he attempted to create music by using it, at the appropriate moment. This was aided by the louder volumes and the powerful amplifiers supplied to the band by Marshall, which were custom-built to Pete's requirements. This kept the sound bright and capable of distortion at high volume.

After leaving school, Pete enrolled at art college and this education aided his performance. He brought a new concept to shows – the destruction of the instrument as part of the music itself. This had roots in the work of Gustav Metzger which was familiar to Pete. In *Who I Am*, Pete said: 'I was experimenting all the time, trying to find new ways to play my guitar on stage … I fell upon my Rickenbacker with all manner of scraping, banging, bending and wrenching, which resulted in howling acoustic feedback. Encouraged … by the work of Gustav Metzger … I secretly planned to completely destroy my guitar if the moment seemed right.' Whilst commenting on there being a plan, the first instance appears to have been accidental. An exuberant performance at the Railway Tavern, Harrow and Wealdstone, in September 1964, led to Pete accidentally burying and breaking the headstock in a low ceiling. In anger, Pete went on to completely destroy his Rickenbacker.

Introducing the Who and Pete to a national audience, *Beat Instrumental No. 25* of May 1965 said: '[Pete] has developed quite … a style. The guitar has become his slave. He makes it moan, scream, mumble and, sometimes in fact, it seems that it can do quite well on its own. This illusion occurs when Pete is characteristically bringing his arm round in a wide arc above his head ready for the next stroke, usually up. The fingers on his left hand stop the required notes and the power in his set-up does the rest.' The article also records the use at the time of another Rickenbacker – a 360/12 and the Fender amp head with Marshall cabinet combination.

The Who wanted to capture their live sound on the next record, 'Anyway, Anyhow, Anywhere', especially Pete's guitar and feedback effects. Offered as a single in late 1965, the song was another top ten record for the group. For promotion, an appearance was made on 'Ready Steady Go!' and Pete played his Rickenbacker 360/12. In *Beat Instrumental No. 32* of December 1965, Pete commented about the guitar: '"I was getting frustrated because of the limitations of the line-up.

The only melody in our music was the guitar and voices. All sorts of discussions went on as to whether or not to expand. There was even talk of having two drummers at one time!" Now Pete feels better about the overall sound because he uses his Rickenbacker 12-string ALL [sic] the time, not just here and there. This gives the group a much fuller sound.'

A busy summer followed for the Who and included gigs across the country, in addition to an appearance at the Jazz and Blues Festival, Richmond. A debut appearance was made in America on 'Shindig!', including the new song 'My Generation'. Pete had worked on this during the summer and early recordings date from late August following a brief Scandinavian tour. Soon after the band's return their van was stolen, containing £5,000 worth of equipment, though much was later recovered by the police. The Who recorded the final version of 'My Generation' in mid-October, along with 'The Kids Are Alright'. The record reached no. 2 in the UK charts following release at the end of the month. 'My Generation' became a defining song by the band, in addition to the times, due to the lyrical content. Pete still favoured the Rickenbacker during this period. Towards the end of the year, he acquired a Danelectro (along with John, who obtained a bass) besides a Harmony 12-string acoustic. The completion of the first Marshall 100-watt amplifier heads also occurred. Pete initially had a single solid stack containing eight 12 in. Celestion speakers, but quicky had to reconsider for transport purposes and used a pair of 4x12 in. cabinets secured together. The bottom cabinet had a straight front, whilst the top was angled, as well as partially open at the back.

The release of the band's debut album ended 1965, with 'My Generation' matching the performance of the single in the album charts. A number of gigs either side of Christmas were arranged in support. The record marked the end of the Who's work with Shel Talmy as a dispute led to a separation. Despite this setback, and the turmoil caused by legal wrangling through 1966, the Who was in the studio early in the year to record 'Substitute', becoming a UK no. 5 hit during the spring. Later, a promotional video of the song saw Pete using a blonde Fender Telecaster with a rosewood neck. In late 1965 and into 1966, Pete used the guitar – in addition to a red Telecaster during the second tour of Sweden later in the year – and a sunburst model with maple neck in the early spring. On the first Swedish tour, Pete had a Gibson ES 175 and the blonde Telecaster appeared with a Danelectro neck. In *Beat Instrumental No. 41* of September 1966, Pete confessed that he had considered having another amp rig custom-made but acknowledged that the ones he used were adequate. An unidentified head model had been trialled for a time without success. Pete wanted to use 'tweeters' to deliver unique high frequencies but he realised 'certain acoustic "high spots" just behind the bridge of any guitar would give a very high screech. This isn't feedback but an interaction,' he said.

In between tour dates and recording sessions – some producing the singles 'I'm A Boy' and 'Happy Jack', the latter has Pete playing a cello – he was often at work in his home studio, in which he learned keyboards, using a Hohner Cembalet, and drums. Pete had several apartments during this period, though always set up a room for recording. *Beat Instrumental No. 36* of April 1966 carried a number of details for the equipment in use. He started with two tape recorders and a microphone, recording tracks from one to the other, building a demo. He stressed the importance of a good pair of headphones and was using an unspecified pair that cost £4. He recorded rhythm parts first followed by lead and played guitar directly to the recorder's input. Pete's new recorders at the time cost £170 each and were stereo. He utilised his Marshall heads with a dummy load and the output was plugged into the recorders. These delivered sound to a pair of old Marshall speaker cabinets with tweeters. *Beat Instrumental No. 50* of June 1967, named the recorders as Revox models, whilst noting further additions: two Vortexion recorders, costing £200 each; Nagra portable tape recorder for £300.

With legal issues regarding recording mainly resolved towards the end of 1966, the Who produced 'A Quick One' for the Christmas market. A feature of the recording contract was Roger, John and Keith were required to write a share of the material, whereas Pete had been the main song-writer up to this point. In the event, he continued to be the main contributor and the final track on the album, 'A Quick One, While He's Away' was the beginning of Pete's later project, 'Tommy'. A photograph from the sessions shows two of Pete's Rickenbackers, a six-string and a twelve, and Marshall cabinets set-up with partitions. On John's track 'Cobwebs And Strange' Pete played a penny whistle and banjo.

In early 1967, the Who busily promoted the album, with two appearances on 'Top of the Pops', playing 'Happy Jack' twice, and on the German programme 'Beat Club'. The latter also yielded two performances, one in Germany during January, with Pete using his Telecaster with Selmer amps (likely provided), the other being in March at the Marquee Club, London. Pete had his Marshalls on this occasion and a red Fender Stratocaster with rosewood neck. January 1967 ended with a double bill at the Saville Theatre, headlining over the Koobers and the Jimi Hendrix Experience, the latter having earlier received Pete's recommendation of Marshall amplifiers. Pete used a Gibson ES 345 with stopbar tailpiece. *Beat Instrumental No. 48* of April 1967 recorded Pete using this guitar with two Fender Showman amps in order to take advantage of the stereo system. Pete mentioned he had a Rickenbacker 12-string that had once belonged to a member of the Byrds. This had a custom fuzz effect installed, which he had tired of using.

After a spell in Italy during February, the Who's maiden trip to the US occurred for a residency with several other acts at the RKO Theatre in New York, organised by DJ 'Murray the K'. The Who managed to improve their standing in the country, whilst Pete had a minor revelation when there. Andy Neil and Matt Kent in *Anyway, Anyhow, Anywhere: The Complete Chronicle of The Who, 1958 to 1978* (2007), quote Pete saying: 'I discovered Fender Stratocasters are very strong and cheap out in the States. Once I chopped a Vox Super Beatle amplifier in half with one. They're made out of chipboard … and I chopped right through the whole thing. It was a 4x12 in. cabinet, and it fell in two bits. I picked up the Stratocaster and continued playing … it was still perfectly in tune!'

In the spring, 'Pictures Of Lily' was released and the Who

Pete Townshend plays a Rickenbacker 1997 (Rose-Morris) on 'Ready Steady Go!' 1966.
Pictorial Press Ltd / Alamy Stock Photo.

appeared in Sweden and West Germany. Pete was seen with a Stratocaster partnered with a Telecaster neck (featuring a large decal on the headstock) and two 100-watt Marshall heads with two cabinets, as well as two Sound City cabs. From earlier in the year, Pete had taken to stacking his amp heads on a stool to the left (from audience) of the stacked cabinets, perhaps to reduce the risk of damaging the expensive and fragile heads. A Grampian spring reverb unit was now employed and placed on top of the amps.

The Who returned to America in mid-June 1967, mainly to appear at the first Monterey International Pop Festival. Not travelling with their amps, the band had to use the provided Vox Super Beatle 120-watt heads and cabinets, whilst Pete had a sunburst Stratocaster with a maple neck. The guitar went on to prove his earlier assessment as to the robustness of the instrument when several heavy blows to the stage were required before the body disintegrated. Returning to England between July and September, the Who then embarked on their first US tour. Again, using rented amplifiers, these were mainly Fender, though a Sunn model was seen on occasion. Pete picked up a Gibson EDS 1275 Doubleneck guitar towards the end of the tour and was using this through to early November. It was not immune to mishap (either deliberate or accidental) as a contributor to www.thewho.net notes Pete playing a gig in Scotland with just the six-string portion of the guitar. Also, Pete's autobiography features him on the cover with the guitar, which at first glance appears normal. Actually, the instrument has been repaired as the 12-string neck is pitched at an angle and a crack along the centre of the body is just visible. The US tour ended with an appearance on the 'Smothers Brothers Show' and the destruction of a Vox Cheetah guitar. Keith decided to upstage Pete by stuffing his bass drum with as many cherry bombs as possible. Unfortunately for Pete, this detonated very close to him at the climax and permanently damaged his hearing.

'The Who Sell Out' album was recorded during the autumn and inspired by Pete's demo 'Jaguar'. The latter paid homage to the car manufacturer, in addition to the recently shut-down pirate radio stations, with their advertising jingles slotted between rock songs. The sound of the tracks on the record was generally clean and featured several acoustic parts (particularly 'Sunrise') with Pete using Harmony models in the studio. His electric parts were created on the Stratocaster, though the solo on 'Our Love Was' sounds like a humbucker-equipped Gibson. Amplification was from Marshall and Fender models. Whilst praised by critics at the time, the album was disappointing commercially, but has continued to garner praise to the present; a 'Super Deluxe Edition' of the album has been released recently. 'I Can See For Miles' was the album's lead single and particularly successful in the US, reaching no. 9; in the UK it peaked at no. 10. The US placing was perhaps helped by a short tour in November 1967.

A disappointing start was made to 1968 due to problems encountered in Australia and New Zealand. The amps and PA equipment had to be rented and did not reach the standard expected. Pete appears to have travelled with at least a Stratocaster. Following a short break, the band was back on the road with a handful of gigs in England before again departing for America in February, performing through to April. The Who had agreed to endorse Vox equipment whilst there, though later used Sunn 100-watt heads and 2x15 in. speakers.

The Marquee Club welcomed the Who in late April with a gig featuring Jethro Tull in support. Pete briefly used a Coral Hornet guitar (similar in appearance to a Fender Jaguar) before switching to his Gibson ES 345. He told *Melody Maker*: 'I use [the Gibson] for recording. At the end [of the concert], I thought "what the hell" and smashed them both [the Coral had developed a fault earlier]. The Gibson Stereo [ES 345, apparently referred to as 'Stereo' by many musicians at the time] cost £200 …' The concert marked the start of Pete's exclusive use of two Sound City 100-watt heads and were modified by Dave Reeves, then working for the company and later to start Hiwatt Amplification. These were with Pete when the Who returned to the US for the summer concert season, stretching over three months.

Commitments to touring in the first half of 1968 stifled Pete's creative output. Yet, before jetting to America in June, 'Dogs' was recorded and released shortly after, though proved commercially disappointing. The following single 'Magic Bus' – a leftover from the 'My Generation' sessions – performed similarly in the UK but did modestly in the States, reaching no. 25.

Around mid-1967, Pete had taken Gustav Metzger to a Who gig. The artist commented to Pete, who explained in *Who I Am*: '… according to his thesis I faced a dilemma; I was supposed to boycott the new commercial pop form itself, attack the very process that allowed me such creative expression, not contribute to it. I agreed. The gimmicks had overtaken me.' Though not immediately dismissing his act, Pete began to consider his next musical avenue and this was partially explored in 'A Quick One, While He's Away', namely being a suite of music with a central theme. Throughout 1968, Pete had developed one concerning a 'deaf, dumb and blind boy' from his birth and journey to a young adult and through trauma in his early life to spiritual awakening. Yet, when he achieves a following after being cured of his afflictions, he finds even more disillusionment and isolation, but with his future still ahead of him. The story was illustrated by Pete using various pieces of music reflecting the tone of the scenes presented. Recording began in September 1968 and continued into early 1969. To help with demos and finished recordings, Pete upgraded his acoustic to a Gibson J200 in sunburst from 1968, whilst for electric parts he favoured another contemporary Gibson, an SG Special with two P90 pick-ups. This model was to become his principal instrument, particularly in live performances. Pete was also pictured recording with a Fender Electric XII through a Sound City head, though he perhaps used other amp models. Some piano and organ parts were added by him. The double album – 'Tommy' – was preceded in release during mid-1969 by 'Pinball Wizard' (top five in the UK and top twenty in the US).

The Who concentrated on the American market following the completion of 'Tommy' and travelled there in the summer. Pete was mainly seen with Gibson SG Specials and Sound City amps, though later changed to Hiwatt 100-watt heads. These had four inputs with individual volume and master volume controls. He also started using a fuzz pedal and WEM Copicat delay. This rig was used for performances at the Woodstock and the Isle of Wight festivals during August.

Touring 'Tommy' in America, Britain and Europe continued to the end of the year and into early 1970. A number of live shows had been recorded through 1969, yet the task of choosing a definitive collection proved too much. A decision was taken to set aside two dates in order to record them for a live album. These were February 14 at Leeds University and February 15 at Hull. Though the band played a mixed set, mainly favoured towards 'Tommy', the finished record 'Live At Leeds' featured several of the group's recent releases as well as covers. Pete continued to use gear mentioned above.

Despite the band feeling constrained by 'Tommy', much of the set list continued to be taken up by the music through 1970, with the Who appearing in Britain (particularly the third Isle of Wight Festival in August) Europe and America. Pete was developing ideas for the next project, including continuing to question the method by which music as art was created. During the year he purchased an EMS VCS3 synthesizer and planned to incorporate sounds created by the unit into the Who's live show. By early 1971, Pete's idea was another story set to music. This was a dystopian version of Britain where citizens were immersed in a virtual reality and had their needs provided by the government. A rebel to the system took over the programme to wake up the masses through rock 'n' roll. Though not an unfamiliar concept in the modern world, Pete's idea was lost on many at the time and the project ultimately faltered. Yet, Pete had a box full of demos and the band teamed with producer Glyn Johns to record 'Who's Next' at Olympic Studios. Pete departed from his usual guitars and played a 1959 Gretsch 6120 Chet Atkins model with a Fender Bandmaster (from the same year), both of which had been gifted to him from Joe Walsh, for much of the record. Pete's interest in synthesizers also came into the studio and the VCS3 found use on 'Won't Get Fooled Again', and an ARP2500 synthesizer appeared on 'Going Mobile'. Acoustic parts were played on the Gibson J200 and a Guild 12-string acoustic. When on the road in the summer of 1971, he kept with the SG Special and Hiwatt amps, though Gibson did make an SG Special for him with a Tune-o-matic bridge and stopbar tailpiece, likely to improve intonation and tuning stability.

In 1972, the Who pursued separate interests for several months. Pete produced 'Who Came First' in honour of spiritual leader Meher Baba. The band did tour Europe during the summer, with Pete's rig little altered, apart from the addition of a contemporary Gibson Les Paul Deluxe. During early 1973, Pete organised a concert for friend Eric Clapton, who was undergoing rehabilitation, at the Rainbow Theatre, London. Pete performed alongside Eric and had the Gretsch 6120, possibly with a Fender amp. The guitar was used on a 'Top of the Pops' performance of the UK single '5.15', taken from the next album 'Quadrophenia'. Pete spent much of 1972 and 1973 working on the material. This followed a similar path to 'Tommy' in telling a story, in this instance being the band's early days and their 'Mod' followers, particularly 'Jimmy' a disillusioned youth who tries to find purpose in his life, initially through the 'Mod' movement.

Recorded in mid-1973, 'Quadrophenia' also made use of the ARP synthesizer and this would go on to cause problems when the band came to perform the material live at the end of the year. Using tapes, the band had to synchronise to them, yet they were beset by technical issues, which came to a head at a concert in Newcastle. The frustration Pete felt resulted in the destruction of an early 1970s Gibson Les Paul Custom in cherry sunburst with embossed pick-up covers. The album mainly had Pete using the Gretsch with the addition of a mid-1950s Fender Stratocaster with maple neck which had been a gift from Eric Clapton. Pete had a white SG Special for performances at the time, though for the 'Quadrophenia' tour he started using a Les Paul Deluxe almost exclusively.

A film of 'Tommy' had been mooted from the inception of the idea, though this did not occur until the mid-1970s, with Ken Russell directing. Pete worked on the soundtrack, which included some new material. He took a break from this to perform his first solo concert (for a charitable cause) at the Roundhouse in April 1974, playing a number of tracks using a backing tape, made in his home studio. Several guitars were present, including the Gibson J200, Gretsch 6120 and Fender Stratocaster.

Much of 1974 was taken up by 'Tommy'. In 1975 the Who returned to the studio and recorded 'The Who By Numbers' which appeared in October. A new guitar present for the sessions was a 1958 Gibson Flying V which was another gift from Joe Walsh. Live dates at the end of the year saw several Gibson Les Paul Deluxes in use. In 1976, Pete had most of them modified to feature a DiMarzio Dual Sound humbucker between the two original pick-ups, with a coil split switch and a selector for the DiMarzio. Pete later told *Sounds International* (April 1980) that he rarely used the humbucker, except for some instances in the studio, adding he liked the look of the three pick-ups. Furthermore, some work was carried out shaping the necks at the heel and behind the nut, whilst Pete's guitar tech Alan Rogan fitted a strap lock system, consisting of a threaded strap pin with large washers secured either side of the strap. Pete had Deluxes in cherry sunburst, gold and wine red. All were later numbered from 1–9, mainly to allow Alan Rogan to distinguish between those set up for certain songs. The Who toured the UK at the end of 1975 and played a number of dates in the USA in 1976.

In 1977, Pete recorded 'Rough Mix' with Faces bassist Ronnie Lane. During the middle of the year, the Who began work on assembling a documentary film about their career named 'The Kids Are Alright', which would take two years to complete. For the film, the band performed a live set, first at Kilburn, then at Shepperton Studios to an invited audience; the first gig was declared to be below the Who's standards. The second concert took place in May 1978 and Pete used two wine-red Les Paul Deluxes (no. 1 and no. 5) with his Hiwatt amps and cabs. This proved to be the last performance with Keith Moon who died in early September.

Before Keith's death, the Who recorded 'Who Are You'. This saw a return to the synthesizer, using an ARP 2600 model which featured on several tracks. Guitars were as live, in addition to the Gretsch, whilst Pete chose to use Mesa Boogie amps. Pete had a Mark II combo, sometimes with an extension

Here (and next page), Pete Townshend smashes guitar into Marshall amplifier speaker cabinets at Windsor Jazz & Blues Festival, Windsor Racecourse, Saturday July 30, 1966. Pictorial Press Ltd / Alamy Stock Photo.

cabinet, whilst also using a Mesa Boogie preamp rack unit. 'Who Are You' peaked at no. 6 in the UK and no. 2 in the US.

The Who decided to carry on after Keith's death and recruited ex-Small Faces drummer Kenney Jones as well as John 'Rabbit' Bundrick on keyboards. Starting off in London with a residency at the Rainbow Theatre, the band travelled to Europe, then America for several nights at Madison Square Garden. Before the end of 1979, a second leg focussed on the East Coast of America. The weight of the Gibson Les Pauls had started to become a problem for Pete, so when Alan Rogan found a Schecter Telecaster-style guitar with humbuckers, Pete immediately began using it. He acquired a few other similar guitars, then commissioned London-based luthier Roger Giffin to construct more with similar specifications.

Though busy with the Who at the end of the 1970s, Pete was able to create material for a solo album 'Empty Glass', completed in spring 1980. Pete used many previously mentioned pieces of equipment, in addition to a Roland GR-300 synthesizer, particularly on the opening track 'Rough Boys'. The Who produced 'Face Dances' at the end of the year, in addition to Pete releasing another solo album 'All The Best Cowboys Have Chinese Eyes' in 1982. For the latter he was pictured on the cover with the 1958 Gibson Flying V. Also from 1982 was 'It's Hard' which proved to be the Who's last album for 24 years and the final one for John Entwistle who died in 2002. The band struggled to make the record and Pete became particularly disillusioned. This led to a farewell tour in 1982. The main change for this was that Pete started using the Hiwatt heads with Mesa Boogie 4x12 in. cabinets.

The band briefly reunited for the Live Aid event in 1985, whilst in the same year Pete released 'White City', which was inspired by his early life. Pink Floyd guitarist David Gilmour made a guest appearance on 'Give Blood' and 'White City Fighting'. For live dates, up to the end of the decade, Pete favoured Washburn and Takamine electro-acoustics, played into the PA system, to reduce the volume on stage, in an attempt to preserve his hearing. In the late 1980s, Pete adapted Ted Hughes' 'The Iron Man' story to music and this later became a stage presentation, in addition to a Hollywood film, 'The Iron Giant'. Around this time, Pete began using a Synclavier synthesizer when song-writing. He was pleased with the range of the technology which allowed virtually unhindered creative possibilities.

The 25th anniversary of the Who was marked in 1989, and a live album from several US dates followed in 1990. Pete made a major change to his stage gear by adopting Eric Clapton's

signature Stratocaster, using several examples, some of which had Kahler tremolos and others Floyd Rose systems, whilst others remained stock. The guitars had Fender lace sensor pick-ups and were joined by a Fishman piezo pick-up from the mid-1990s. The guitar sound was fed through a preamp into the mixing desk and then the PA. He also had Rickenbacker 12-strings and Takamine acoustic guitars.

Pete suffered a serious wrist injury in the early 1990s which delayed progress on his next solo project 'Psycoderelict'. This tells the story of an aging rock star whose career is resuscitated by controversy. Pete toured for the record in 1993 using arrangements mentioned earlier. He was seen during a performance on 'Late Night with David Letterman' using a Gibson J200 in natural which he proceeded to destroy during 'Pinball Wizard'.

The Who returned to the stage in 1996 to perform 'Quadrophenia', initially at Hyde Park, then extended across to America and elsewhere. Continuing to play shows with the Who in the late 1990s, Pete made a return to Hiwatt heads and cabs, whilst also employing a Boss overdrive pedal. In the early 2000s the Hiwatt served as a backup to a Fender Vibro-King with extension cabinet. Pete and Roger recorded 'Endless Wire' during 2006 and toured in support. A new addition at this time was a custom pedalboard made by Pete Cornish and featuring echo, overdrive and a compressor. Pete has continued to be active with the Who in the 2010s, with few changes made to his equipment. The group's 12th album, 'Who', appeared in 2019.

Pete Townshend has Gibson Les Paul Deluxe '1' performing 'Pinball Wizard' in 'Tommy' film, 1975.
Album / Alamy Stock Photo.

Bert Weedon in dramatic pose with Hofner guitar.
Pictorial Press Ltd / Alamy Stock Photo.

BERT WEEDON

Herbert Maurice Weedon, the man who influenced thousands of guitarists worldwide, was born on May 10, 1920, in Burgess Road, East Ham, London.

Several significant developments influencing Bert's musical career occurred around this time. The first jazz record was released by the New York Victor label during May 1917. This was a recording of the Original Dixieland 'Jass' Band's 'Dixie Jass Band One Step' and 'Livery Stable Blues'. British jazz is said to have begun with the Original Dixieland Jazz Band tour in the country during 1919. In 1922 regular British wireless broadcasts for entertainment began from the Marconi Research Centre at Writtle, near Chelmsford.

The 1920s witnessed some of the greatest jazz music ever made and amongst the virtuoso performers were Louis Armstrong, Jabbo Smith and Johnny Dodds. Jazz dance bands included a bandleader up front; musicians divided into sections of rhythm, brass, wind instruments, sometimes strings; and singers.

The establishment of radio and record companies released musicians from an existence confined to theatres and music halls. In turn, pop fans could play their favourite tunes at home. The British weekly music magazine, *Melody Maker*, founded in 1926 by Leicester-born composer Lawrence Wright, created an appreciation of American jazz soloists for British players. In the 1920s, jazz became more focussed and more separate as a musical force with British jazz musicians scraping a living in dance bands.

Bert was the youngest of two brothers and his father, also called Bert, was a tube train driver on London's District Line. Bert senior had a collection of 78 rpm records that included artists such as Jimmy Rogers and Carson Robinson. With the guard of his train (named Walmisley), he performed in an amateur song and dance act under the name of 'Wal and Bert' at railway social events and masonic halls.

Initially, Bert junior took about three or four piano lessons but was disinterested. In a note sent to Bert senior, the piano teacher wrote: 'Don't spend any more money on Bert's education as he will never be a musician.' Bert turned his attention to stringed instruments and, at the age of nine, tinkered on his father's ukulele. A couple of years later, when a full-size guitar caught his attention one Sunday afternoon in Petticoat Lane market, the course of his future was set. He returned to view the guitar a number of times, the stall-holder often telling him to 'clear off', until it was bought for 15 shillings (75p).

During the early 1930s, the guitar was a rare instrument and Bert admitted the only time anybody saw a guitar was in the hands of a cowboy during a western film where he would be warbling 'Home on the Range'.

Bert located a guitar teacher, James Newell, in Manor Park, who charged a shilling (5p) a lesson. Although jazz was loved by Bert, Newell instantly expressed a distaste, saying he would only teach classical guitar. After playing Chopin's Prelude No. 7 on a gut-strung Martin guitar, Bert was astounded by what he heard. He eventually learned a lot from Newell: how to read and write music as well as basic harmonies and major and minor chords. After each lesson, Newell gave Bert free philosophy lessons and so he became familiar with a number of religions including Yoga and Buddhism. Bert continued with lessons from Newell for about four years.

www.tunelectric.com states in Big Bands during the 1920s and 1930s, the guitarist was part of the rhythm section, playing nothing more than a supportive role. Their guitars were acoustic and their sound blended with other instruments. The guitarist felt increasingly trapped but amplifying the instrument changed all that. The guitar could replace a horn section, enabling a small trio or quartet to achieve a Big Band sound. 'Eddie Lang was one of the 1920s most recorded guitarists and was a huge influence on the first generation of players … His style was unique and showed a sophisticated approach to chord voicing and solo playing.'

Bert was aware of jazz and guitar developments in the 1930s and spent much of his time practising classical guitar and playing jazz with local dance bands. On leaving school at 14, he worked in a variety of office jobs as a clerk, though intended to become a professional musician as soon as possible. Around 1937, he formed a band named 'Butch Townsend and His Cold Shoulders' with the local butcher's son, Dennis Townsend. Later, outfits were styled Bert Weedon & the Blue Cumberland Rhythm Boys and Bert Weedon & His Harlem Hot Shots.

On www.bertweedon.com, Bert states whilst he was going to and from gigs people would say: 'What have you got there, son?' He would answer: 'It's a guitar,' and they responded: 'What's that then?' Frustration aroused in him a desire to show the outside world the guitar was a great instrument.

From the age of 15, Bert's hero was Django Reinhardt (1910–1953). Together with violinist Stephane Grappelli, Reinhardt formed the Paris-based Quintette du Hot Club de France in 1934. The band was among the first to play jazz with the guitar featured as a lead instrument.

Bert's eagerness to learn more and more about the guitar continued through the 1930s. Mo Foster in *Play Like Elvis* (2000) quotes the following entry from jazz and classical guitarist teacher and composer Ivor Mairants' diary: 'Sunday May 3rd 1938 HM Weedon (Bert) of 1 Ashland Road, East Ham E6 £4 for term of six lessons.' Foster also notes: '1938 saw 17-year-old Bert Weedon thrilled at the sight of Jack Abbott constructing his first ever hand-built guitar: the Abbot Victor guitar.'

During the Second World War, Bert Weedon volunteered for the rescue services and served with them through the worst of the London blitz. In this period, he was a semi-professional musician and proudly played as rhythm guitarist with Django

Reinhardt and Stephane Grappelli (although not on any recordings). Later, when Reinhardt left the band, Bert took over the guitar role, with George Shearing on piano. Bert worked for a period with Grappelli at Hatchetts restaurant. Stephane told Bert to 'play like Bert Weedon, and you will be a star. Do not be a copyist.'

By the end of hostilities, Bert had turned fully professional and was playing in bigger and better dance bands, including the Ted Heath Orchestra, the Squadronaires and Harry Gold and his Pieces of Eight. Bert said that most of the big bands didn't carry a guitarist but every time one was needed for broadcasts or recordings, they called on him. Bert also found time in the immediate post-war years to play together with Julian Bream some Spanish music on classical guitar for a London production of a play, 'Blood Wedding' written by Lorca. In existence is a film from 1949 showing Bert as a Flamenco guitarist.

On www.gypsyjazzuk.com, it is mentioned that Bert used an Abbott-Victor Ritz on many radio recordings between 1946 and 1948. The site also adds: 'Bert Weedon – Victor Ritz arch top acoustic guitar, 19 fret rosewood fingerboard with pearl block position markers, burst finish, hollow body, hard case … Bert Weedon traded this guitar back to Jack Abbott for the top of the range Music Master Model.'

A prestigious job came Bert's way when he joined Cyril Stapleton (1914–1974) and the BBC Show Band making him widely known to the general public and, in particular, within recording circles. With Cyril Stapleton, Bert was heard on a number of radio shows, in particular 'Workers' Playtime' and other BBC 'Light Programme' features.

A temporary, but serious setback occurred when Bert contracted consumption (tuberculosis) a potential killer at the time. He was hospitalised in Plaistow for three months though with the help of a new drug, Streptomycin, pulled through, and recovered. Whilst in hospital, Bert was visited by Julian Bream, who he had performed with some time earlier.

A doctor advised Bert not to continue playing in smoky nightclubs and dance halls and this encouraged him to find work in a few of the major studios. Having a good reputation as an accomplished guitarist with sight-reading skills, he was soon recording with Ambrose, Mantovani, Ray Martin and Harry Leader. He backed major British stars of the 1950s: Alma Cogan, Dickie Valentine and Eddie Calvert. Also a number of Americans: Frank Sinatra, Tony Bennett, Judy Garland and Nat King Cole. Frank Sinatra suggested Bert ought to relocate to America. He predicted Bert would make a big hit there. Bert answered: 'I said I'd rather stay in England because I'm a big fish in a small pond. In America, there were, great, great guitar players. I'd be a smaller fish in a huge pond. So, I stayed here.'

For Bert, the 1950s were challenging, productive and enjoyable. Cyril Stapleton made him aware of rock 'n' roll which was dominating the musical scene, playing a copy of Bill Haley's 'Rock Around The Clock' some months before it was released in Britain.

Bert was excited, recognising rock 'n' roll's influences of standard 12-bar blues, country music and several other styles. Afterwards, he quickly became a rock 'n' roll session guitarist, playing on Tommy Steele's 'Rock With The Cavemen' as well as backing tracks to the hits of Marty Wilde, Johnny Kid and Adam Faith.

In 1956, Bert began recording in his own right, eventually leaving session work behind; his first single – with the Sydney Torch Orchestra – 'Stranger Than fiction', (a 78 rpm release only), written by Arthur 'Guitar Boogie' Smith, appeared on Parlophone.

An advertisement placed in *Record Mirror* on June 2, 1956, showed Bert with a Hofner Club guitar and stated the instrument could be heard on Parlophone, playing 'The Boy With The Magic Guitar', his second single release. According to the advert, Bert could be seen and heard in a demonstration at Selmer House on June 2, 1956.

The *Record Mirror* of August 24, 1957, carried the header 'Bert Weedon Steps Out as a Solo Guitar Artiste' and, pictured with a Hofner guitar, Bert said: 'I am not going out with the Stapleton band, I am concentrating absolutely on solo work, and I am glad to say I kicked off to an excellent start.' He had a lot of television work lined up (he had first appeared on TV in 1946). Earlier in August 1957, he had been on the 'A to Z' BBC programme, and on August 25 he was doing a spot in the Commercial TV advertising feature, 'Slater's Bazaar'. He was following this with an appearance in 'Emney Enterprises' (BBC TV, August 29), and again in 'Slater's Bazaar' (September 8) and in the Autumn Prelude feature (BBC TV, September 15).

Radio engagements included 'Guitar Club' in September 1957. Bert added he had completed a guitar tutor, *Play in a Day*, which was to be published by Chappell Music Ltd in September 1957. The guitar's popularity had grown considerably in the 1950s and there were too many pupils for too few teachers, so the book was launched to an eager market. Teenagers were scraping their cash together to buy cheap acoustic guitars and play in skiffle bands. Bert Weedon was the man to teach them the way forward.

Play in a Day, with its red cover, featuring a photograph of

> *Information is provided about Jack Abbott Jr on www.gypsyjazzuk.com: '[He] was the very first British luthier who built archtops. It seems he became a real expert and made very good instruments. He mainly built banjos but a few guitars as well. His production was not very big so Abbott guitars are really hard to find. At some point after the war, he was associated with someone called Victor and designed and supervised a series of guitars branded Abbott-Victor. Jack continued making instruments until the mid-1950s when he retired … [He] was persuaded out of retirement in 1970 to make around 200 banjo ukuleles for the George Formby Society … Jack died in February 1994.'*

> *As leader of the BBC Show Band, Stapleton became a fixture on the English musical scene, broadcasting across the nation throughout the mid-1950s. A number of players in his ensemble went on to fame in their own right, including Bert Weedon.*

Bert with his Hofner guitar, became a resounding success, and went on to be the best-selling guitar tutor in the world. Cover text informed the purchaser, he or she would be taught to play skiffle, jazz, Latin American rhythms and 'special effects' as well as rock 'n' roll. Printed in several languages and published all over the globe, the book eventually sold more than 2 million and earned Bert the coveted title 'The man who taught the world to play the guitar'.

The official Bert Weedon website notes Bert originally wrote the book because he remembered the difficulty he had had as a guitar beginner not knowing a thing about the instrument or how to play it. 'He was determined there would be a tutor that anyone could understand and learn from without a teacher, and by anticipating all the questions that a beginner would ask and by answering them in his book, he was able to help most of today's top pop idols on their way to stardom,' stated the website. Amongst the topics covered in the book are: how to hold the guitar; how to tune the guitar; rudiments of music; position playing; chord shapes; amplifiers; group playing; and care of the instrument.

Some of the artists who have benefitted from the book are: Eric Clapton, Mark Knopfler, Brian May, Pete Townshend, Mike Oldfield and many more.

According to Neville Marten, editor of *Guitar Techniques* magazine: '[Bert, in *Play in a Day*] presumed intelligence on the part of his reader and assumed that he or she was prepared to take a journey that might take some time to complete. It was based on reading notation and on learning "band"-style guitar, which might involve playing rhythm or taking single-line solos. It was about learning the art of being a musician. Today's learner is drawn to the internet. On YouTube, they can see players showing them how to break down this song, that riff or solo. They very rarely think about notation and there seems little intent on making people better "musicians".'

Parlophone released five more of Bert's guitar singles up to 1958; Saga released a solitary single also in 1958. Bert's biggest single success occurred in 1959 when Top Rank released a cover version of 'Guitar Boogie Shuffle', written by Arthur Smith. This became the first major hit for a British solo guitarist, peaking at no. 6 during the early summer of 1959.

Record Mirror of November 18, 1961, noted that Bert, after releasing 15 singles on the Top Rank label, had switched to HMV Pop inside the EMI group. His first release was 'China Doll' which he showcased on ABC TV's 'Thank Your Lucky Stars' on November 25, 1961. Between 1961 and 1967, Bert released 14 singles on HMV Pop.

He was friendly with two brothers, Ben and Lew Davis, who owned Selmer's in London's Charing Cross Road. The pair introduced Bert to the Hofner Committee guitar. Bert states in Gordon Giltrap and Neville Marten's *The Hofner Guitar: A History* (2009): '[Ben said] I'd like you to have this guitar and play it for us. I was doing a lot of radio work and occasional TV shows, so I started to play the Hofner Committee. And when I looked at it, I thought it was such a beautiful guitar ... Then [Hofner] brought out a thinner model, the Golden Hofner (shipped to Selmer's c. 1960), and then the Verithin. And as they brought out each model, Ben Davis said to me, "Would you play this one and bring the old one back", and like a fool I gave them all back.'

Bert argued that playing Hofners influenced a number of guitarists, including Paul McCartney and John Lennon, to favour the guitar range: 'I was doing quite a lot at the time [late 1950s/early 1960s], and papers like *Melody Maker* and *New Musical Express* used to advertise "Bert Weedon plays a Hofner" and all the up-and-coming guitarists bought them because of that.'

Bert presented the British children's television show 'Tuesday Rendezvous (1961–1963) with Muriel Young and Wally Whyton. Bert's single 'China Doll' was the show's theme tune. He demonstrated guitar innovations during a regular spot on 'Five O'Clock Club' (1963–1966), a children's television pop programme on Rediffusion. He said: 'I would often try and introduce a pick-up or a vibrato arm or an echo chamber. I suppose I was an innovator in those days ... I think my use of the Bigsby influenced the Hofner factory to fit them as standard on some models. The tremolo arm at that time was a very important development in guitar playing, a very innovative and exciting sound.'

Mike Oldfield was one of many guitarists inspired by Bert's televised guitar lessons: 'I saw him on television when I was seven [1960] and immediately persuaded my father to buy me my first guitar. If it wasn't for Bert, I might never have taken it up in the first place.'

Paul McCartney commented: 'George [Harrison] and I went through the Bert Weedon books and learned D and A together.'

Gradually Bert switched to using Guild guitars and explained: 'I had a Starfire and they asked me to help them

---

Arthur 'Guitar Boogie' Smith (1921–2014) was a former American textile worker who elevated himself to become a celebrated and respected country music instrumental composer, guitarist, fiddler and banjo player. He wrote the instrumental 'Guitar Boogie' in 1945, selling over three million copies. It was subsequently renamed 'Guitar Boogie Shuffle' and became a rock 'n' roll hit for Frank Virtue and the Virtues in 1958.

Guild Guitars
During 1945 Alfred Dronge and Barney Sagman opened their music store, aptly titled Sagman & Dronge, in New York's Park Rowe. The store existed for two years before Alfred took control and re-titled the business Alfred Dronge Music. After Alfred Dronge entered a partnership with George Man, ex-Vice President of Epiphone Company, the two men registered their new company in 1952 as Guild Guitar Company. A year later the first Guild Guitars were built at 536 Pearl Street in New York. During the first year of operation the company produced full-depth hollow electric guitars but over the next few years the company manufactured its first flat tops and the acoustic archtops.

design a Bert Weedon model. I was thrilled about that, because I think that was the first American guitar ever named after a British guitar player.'

Bert featured regularly in *Record Mirror* during the early 1960s making comments about music, performers, guitars and equipment. In *Record Mirror*, March 31, 1962, he took part in a questions-and-answer piece. Here are two of the questions and his answers: Question: *Has the guitar influence on pop music changed?* Answer: 'Not at all. So many guitars have been sold – but the market is still big. It is much bigger than the piano. And the interest is there. I reckon I get thirty letters a day from guitarists asking for help and 100 letters a day from the fans. When I gave a guitar tuition course on television, they said would I come and collect the mail. They said I'd better hire a truck. There were six sack-loads and about 10,000 letters. That's why they're bringing back this course.'

Question: *Do you mind passing on advice to possible competitors?* Answer: 'Not at all. I reckon guitarists must help each other more than any other instrumentalists. I had help when I was young. And I figure that if they know as much as I do then I have got to do better myself. Guitarists are a matey crowd.'

A sequel to Bert's *Play in a Day* was available in January 1963 when *Play Every Day* was published and retailing at 5s (25p). The book dealt with the complicated task of playing guitar really well. Bert said the method outlined was amazingly easy to follow and the new book was bound to turn some of the beginners from the first book into guitar experts. 'I hope it'll help the fairly advanced players,' said Bert, adding: 'I'll just have to rely on my longer time in the business to give me a head start.' Video and DVD versions of the books appeared later.

In *Record Mirror* November 23, 1963, Bert and Duane Eddy were interviewed together. For the magazine Norman Jopling reported: '… they both use Guild. The firm have just made a special model for Bert called appropriately enough "The Bert Weedon". This guitar is now being manufactured commercially in the States, and Bert reckons it's the best guitar in the world. New features include double cutaway body, and a block of wood inside the frame to prevent string vibration with the magnets. And a more delicate neck. "I think I'll stick to my guitar" said Duane – who had just tried Bert's. "Mine's easier to play – and Bert is a better player than I am".'

Hans Moust in *The Guild Guitar Book: The Company and the Instruments 1952–1977* (1995) acknowledges Bert was in great demand as a session musician during the early days of rock 'n' roll and that was the reason Boosey & Hawkes, who were the sole importers for Guild guitars, got together with Bert around 1963. At that time, Bert was already playing a Guild Starfire III. The Bert Weedon Model, introduced in 1963, was made for the UK market only. 'The instrument had all the features of the Duane Eddy Standard, including a Bigsby tailpiece, but in a fully hollow double-cutaway format … The oldest known Bert Weedon model – Bert's personal guitar with a serial # 24039 – dates from the early part of 1963 …' wrote Moust.

Bert played some of his guitars through Burns or Selmer amps. He was pictured in a music paper advertisement with a Hofner Golden/Deluxe guitar and Truvoice Professional amplifier. He made a $33\frac{1}{3}$ record demonstrating a Selmer Truvoice Echo Chamber, with commentary by David Gell. Bert is seen on the record label with a Hofner V3 Solid, a Selmer Selectortone, and a Truvoice Echo Chamber.

In *Record Mirror* January 25, 1964, Bert was featured in an advertisement for the New Bert Weedon Zero-One Electric Guitar. Publicity material about the guitar stated it was obtainable from both Boosey & Hawkes and Besson & Company Ltd. The advertisement stated the guitar had been 'specially designed for the young player by Britain's top solo guitar star'. The Zero-One included: a 21-fret fingerboard; two f-shaped sound holes; a raised scratch plate which held two pick-ups; two volume controls; one tone control; and two on/off pick-up switches. The headstock displayed the 'Bert Weedon Zero-One' logo and three-on-a-side tuners.

Bert's successes in the singles market declined in the 1960s with the explosion of the Beatles, Rolling Stones and many other bands but he was still very popular, when making cabaret, concert and TV appearances.

Bert made his first LP 'King Size Guitar', released on Top Rank, in 1960. Three more albums appeared before the 1970s, during which time he enjoyed considerable success. In 1973, 'Bert Weedon Remembers Jim Reeves' sold over 250,000 copies. Three years later, '22 Golden Greats', released on Warwick, reached no. 1 and earned him both gold and platinum discs. At one point, the album knocked Led Zeppelin off the top of the album chart. Albums would subsequently appear on a variety of labels including: HMV; Fontana; Contour, Polydor EMI; Cheron; Celebrity; Dansan; Everest; and Pickwick.

During later years, Bert became known for playing Fender Stratocasters, Yamahas and Parker Fly guitars, pushed mostly through Marshall amplification. He enjoyed playing the Parker Fly because it 'was so light.'

On the Bert Weedon website, Bert said that on his electric guitars he used thin gauge strings 'on my Parker guitar (9-42 gauge), and a slightly thicker gauge (10-46) on my Fender Stratocaster, Yamaha and Bert Weedon Guild guitar.'

He was first initiated as a member of the Grand Order of Water Rats in October 1983, becoming King Rat in 1992, helping to earn thousands for various charities. In the same year, he was featured on 'This is Your Life' where Eric Clapton, Brian May and Hank Marvin paid tributes to him.

Bert was a Barker of the Variety Club of Great Britain from the late 1950s and the organisation staged a tribute luncheon in Bournemouth for him in 1999. Other charity organisations he was involved with include Active Hearts, Barnardo's, Save the Children, NSPCC, and the Children with Leukaemia Fund.

He was awarded an OBE in the 2001 Queen's Birthday Honours List. During his lifetime Bert was voted Britain's top guitarist on nine occasions in popularity polls. He often said: 'I'm the luckiest man in the world, 'cause I get paid for doing something that I love doing and I'd do it for nothing anyway. But I don't tell any agents.'

Bert Weedon died on April 20, 2012, but the continuing popularity of his instruction books and DVDs mean his influence will be enjoyed by budding guitar players for a very long time to come.

Bert Weedon holding a Guild semi-acoustic with Bigsby. Bert's name is featured on the Pick-guard.
Pictorial Press Ltd / Alamy Stock Photo.

Ronnie Wood and his Zemaitis Metal Front guitar, 1971.
MARKA / Alamy Stock Photo.

RONNIE WOOD

Over a career spanning nearly 60 years, Ronnie Wood has developed a role as a versatile guitarist and musician. Most recognisable as a member of the Rolling Stones, Ronnie easily switches between rhythm and lead roles and is equally adept as a slide and pedal steel player. He began his career with the Birds, yet found fame as bassist with the Jeff Beck Group and as guitarist for Faces in the early 1970s.

Ronnie was interested in music from an early age thanks to his family's ability with various instruments. His father played harmonica and piano, while an aunt played piano as well. Ronnie's parents often held parties that revolved around musical entertainment, as did his two older brothers, Art and Ted. Ronnie looked up to his brothers and, in an effort to impress them, he would learn any musical instrument that was left lying around following one of their gatherings.

Around age eight, Ronnie took to the guitar and persevered with a borrowed one for a time. He was helped by his brother's friends, who drew chord shapes on a piece of paper for Ronnie to learn. Disappointed when giving the guitar back, Ronnie's dedication was rewarded by his brothers after they presented him with an acoustic guitar around age ten. Although difficult for him to play, he was not deterred and would listen to records of the day, learning the songs by ear. Favourite artists at this time included Big Bill Broonzy, Chuck Berry and Wes Montgomery.

Despite learning the guitar, Ronnie's first position in a band – the Thunderbirds – was as the drummer. Yet, he soon moved back to the guitar and bought his first electric one for £25 around age 14. This was a Roger Model 54 solid body with two pick-ups; amplification was from a Bird type. The band played an eclectic range of songs, including releases by the Beach Boys and Chuck Berry, as well as Motown.

The Thunderbirds group found some success on the London scene and was signed to Decca Records as the Birds. The band's first single 'You're On My Mind' was written by Ronnie and released in November 1964. In his autobiography, *Ronnie* (2008), he comments about the song: 'I just picked up my guitar, turned on the tape recorder and played what I felt. Of course, I was heavily influenced by the music I was listening to at the time, but I believed then, and still do today, that it's not what you steal, it's how you steal it.'

The Birds appeared on battle of the bands-style TV programme 'Ready, Steady, Win' in late 1964 and this helped the group's second song, 'Leaving Here', a Motown cover, to enter the charts. Ronnie upgraded to a Fender Telecaster and Vox AC30. The Telecaster can be seen with a black and yellow paint design of the film 'The Deadly Bees' as the Birds perform 'That's All I Need You For'. Ronnie later upgraded to Marshall amps and had a custom-made 8x12 in. cabinet with 200-watt head. The group only released a handful of singles before disbanding in late 1966.

Ronnie united with Jeff Beck and was joint lead guitarist for a short time in the Jeff Beck Group, before eventually persuaded to play bass. He picked up a Fender Jazz bass in London and used this for recording 'Truth'. The record mainly featured covers, though did contain some original material, and was released in August 1968. Earlier in the year, the group toured America and Ronnie used his Fender with a Marshall stack.

During 1968, Ronnie joined the Creation as guitarist for a brief period, with one single being promoted before the band folded. Towards the end of the year, Ronnie returned to America for another tour with the Jeff Beck Group. A second run of dates was scheduled for early 1969 before being cancelled, allowing a new album to be recorded. 'Beck-Ola' was released in June 1969. Ronnie was co-writer on three of the seven tracks and continued to play bass.

Despite the success of the album and another tour of America, friction within the band forced a split. Ronnie joined forces with vocalist Rod Stewart to form Faces alongside members of the Small Faces. This was following the departure of guitarist Steve Marriott from the latter's line-up. Just before this, Ronnie had participated in sessions for Rod Stewart's solo album, 'An Old Raincoat Won't Ever Let You Down', and played guitar and bass.

In Faces, Ronnie initially used a red Fender Stratocaster with a rosewood neck, before moving on to a Tony Zemaitis custom guitar. This had a Les Paul-style body with an engraved metal top, and a mahogany neck with ebony fingerboard. Ronnie received a similar guitar, with three humbucker pick-ups, soon after and later ordered another possessing a pearl mosaic top, as well as three single coil pick-ups. Also in the line-up, with Faces, was a Fender Stratocaster from 1955, which was a 'hardtail' model with no tremolo system, and a Dan Armstrong 'Plexi' guitar. Ronnie was initially seen using Hiwatt and Fender amplifiers live before favouring Ampeg SVTs.

Faces produced four albums – 'First Step' (1970), 'Long Player' (1971), 'A Nod Is As Good As A Wink … To A Blind Horse' (1971) and 'Ooh La La' (1973) – before going their separate ways in the mid-1970s.

Ronnie helped Rod Stewart complete his solo albums over this period and was co-writer of several tracks, in addition to providing guitar parts and some bass. He played guitar on Rod's hit single 'Maggie May'. Another venture was the soundtrack for 'Mahoney's Last Stand', which was recorded with Faces bandmate Ronnie Lane in 1972, although not released until 1976.

The success of Faces' last two albums, in addition to several popular US tours, allowed Ronnie to buy the Wick in Richmond. With 20 rooms, he was able to build his own state-of-the-art studio in the house's basement. The fruit of this was his first solo record, 'I've Got My Own Album to Do', released in 1974. Several guest musicians, as well as members of Faces, featured: George Harrison, Mick Jagger, Keith Richards and Mick Taylor. Ronnie completed enough tracks for a second set – 'Now Look' – released in mid-1975.

Ronnie Wood plays slide on his 1972 Zemaitis Disc Front guitar.
Pictorial Press Ltd / Alamy Stock Photo.

Late in 1974, Mick Taylor left the Rolling Stones. Ronnie decided to help out and performed on some sessions during mid-1975. The song 'Hey Negrita' was developed from a riff contributed by Ronnie whilst auditioning with the Stones and later appeared on the 'Black And Blue' album.

Ronnie's participation with the band on stage came with the North and South American tour, beginning June 1, 1975. Only the North American portion actually went ahead and Ronnie played, on these dates, his Zemaitis guitars, along with the 1955 Fender Stratocaster. He used the Stones' new Ampeg SVT amplifiers, which had been custom covered in white with a flower pattern on the grill cloth.

The Stones promoted the tour to the press by arriving at the meeting on a flat-bed truck playing 'Brown Sugar'. This was Ronnie's first Stones' appearance and he used his 'hardtail' Stratocaster with Ampeg amp. Ronnie also played bass on the tour, particularly when the band performed 'Fingerprint File', as Mick Jagger had the guitar part with Keith on the track. Furthermore, Ronnie used a Gibson acoustic for relevant songs.

Between gigs, Ronnie and Keith decided they were close enough to Kalamazoo to visit the Gibson factory and spent the day trying out guitars. The pair eventually left with an L6S, an S1 and a J200 acoustic. Ronnie subsequently appeared in Gibson advertising material of the period as a result.

In early 1976, Ronnie was with the band recording promotional videos for songs from the upcoming 'Black And Blue' album. In 'Fool To Cry', Ronnie is with the metal front Zemaitis custom, for 'Hey Negrita' he switches to the Zemaitis with the pearl top, then the three-humbucker Zemaitis was brought out for 'Hot Stuff' and 'Crazy Mama'.

Ronnie had quickly bonded with Keith, both personally and musically, and the pair soon developed an intuitive understanding with their guitar parts. In *Ronnie*, he says: '… if an idea suddenly popped into my head, or into Keith's head … one of us could go right ahead and play something and the other would pick up on it immediately and react to it. Mick and Charlie would pick up on that, too, right away, because we were all speaking the same musical language.'

Keith was also complementary of the new guitarist and, in *Ronnie*, it is noted: 'Keith sensed what was happening on that tour [North America, 1975] … because he was telling people that the band had finally found the right chemistry. He was saying, "Woody is made for two guitars but he hasn't had the chance to do it until now. His strength, like mine, is to play with another guitar player".'

During the summer, the Stones toured Europe and Ronnie travelled with the guitars mentioned earlier, along with two new additions. One was a Gibson Firebird VII (a model which both Keith and Brian Jones had played in the band during the mid-1960s) and the other was a Gibson Les Paul Special.

Recordings were made of the live performances over the tour and these were eventually produced into an album – 'Love You Live'. The band thought that the intimacy afforded by a small gig was lacking and decided to stage one in Toronto, at the El Mocambo, during early 1977. For this, the SVTs were thought to be too loud and Keith suggested Mesa Boogie amps, as he had been impressed when trying one. He ordered a pair, for both himself and Ronnie, and these were used on the night. They had 100 watts output, which could be reduced to 60 watts, and a single 12 in. speaker.

The band ended 1977 in the studio recording tracks for 'Some Girls'. A number were completed during the sessions, which continued through early 1978. Before the album was released in June, the single 'Miss You', with 'Far Away Eyes' as the B-side, became a worldwide hit. For the video accompanying the latter, Ronnie was playing his new Sho-Bud lap steel guitar. The 'Miss You' performance sees him with a new Zemaitis Les Paul-style guitar, which did not have an engraved metal top, and a Marshall stack. Another promo video was filmed for the third single from 'Some Girls', 'Respectable', and in this Ronnie has a mid-1970s Fender Stratocaster with a natural finish.

'Some Girls' was promoted in America through a nationwide tour. Ronnie had two new guitars on the road: a Zemaitis with a specially engraved top commemorating the tour; a Gibson Les Paul Custom in black with two pick-ups. These were used, along with several other of the previously mentioned guitars, through the Mesa Boogie Mark I amp and the Ampeg SVTs.

In tandem with the Stones' sessions in Paris during early 1978, and later in LA following the US tour, Ronnie recorded a number of solo tracks. These featured members of the Stones on occasion and were later collected for his album 'Gimme Some Neck', released spring, 1979. The album was a relative success and Ronnie toured America with a band – the New Barbarians – including Keith Richards, Ian McLagan, Bobby Keys, Stanley Clarke and Zigaboo Modeliste.

Following the tour, Ronnie returned to work with the Stones on tracks that would appear on 'Emotional Rescue', released in June 1980. Yet, the band still had material left over, in addition to tracks stretching back a number of years, and the decision was made to release these quite soon after 'Emotional Rescue'. 'Tattoo You' appeared in August 1981 and was supported by an American tour. This lasted nearly three months, beginning in late September. Ronnie had his Zemaitis guitars with him and also used Fender Stratocasters, along with a Tokai Stratocaster copy. This was bought with the express intention of fitting a Floyd Rose tremolo system. Ronnie acquired two guitars whilst on tour: a Fender Stratocaster 'Mary Kaye' model; a Gretsch Falcon. Ampeg lost out to Mesa Boogie for the tour and 160-watt Coliseum heads were used with Cerwin-Vega 4x12 in. cabinets, before a switch was made to Mesa Boogie cabs. These continued in use, along with the majority of the guitars, to the European tour of 1982.

Ronnie began endorsing ESP guitars around 1983. He had a Stratocaster-style model from the company during the recording of the band's 'Undercover' album, released at the end of the year. A blue ESP guitar with maple neck was used during the videos for the singles, 'Undercover Of The Night', 'She Was Hot' and 'Too Much Blood'.

'I Think I'm Going Mad' was recorded at this time, although not included on the 'Undercover' album. In his autobiography, Ronnie states that he played saxophone on the track, as he had recently become interested in learning the instrument and had done so over a two-week period. Ronnie adds that he performed saxophone parts on his 1981 solo album '1234', which featured guest musicians such as Bobby Womack, Waddy Wachtel and Nicky Hopkins.

The Stones dispersed for most of 1984 and reconvened in early 1985 to record 'Dirty Work'. Ronnie continued to use guitars from his collection and added two new acoustics. These were Zemaitis six- and 12-string models with a heart-shaped soundhole. In the same year, Ronnie used a Martin acoustic during Bob Dylan's appearance at Live Aid, as he backed him along with Keith for a couple of songs. Bob broke a string during 'Blowin' In The Wind' and Ronnie selflessly gave up his instrument so Bob could continue; for a short time until a replacement acoustic arrived, Ronnie played 'air guitar'.

The band brought the 'Dirty Work' album to a close with the recording of two promo videos for the singles 'Harlem Shuffle' and 'One Hit (To The Body)'. Ronnie had a custom-made Gibson L5S, with just a bridge pick-up, in the former and a sunburst Gibson J200 acoustic in the latter.

The Stones took time off following 'Dirty Work' to pursue personal projects. Ronnie went on tour with Bo Diddley and songs captured on the dates were later presented on the 'Live At The Ritz' album. Increasingly, Ronnie used ESP guitars, both Stratocaster and Telecaster types, as well as his Gibson L5S.

Mick and Keith brought the Stones back together in 1989 for the 'Steel Wheels' sessions. Ronnie continued to play ESP guitars, along with other guitars in his collection, through either Mesa Boogie or Fender amps. Bill Wyman was absent for a period, due to his recent marriage, and Ronnie filled in on bass for a time as well. Ronnie returned to the guitar for the North American tour of 1989, which turned out to be extremely rewarding for the band. He continued to use instruments from his arsenal through Mesa Boogie amplifiers. The tour was extended through Europe in 1990.

As the Stones went their separate ways again after the 'Steel Wheels' project, Ronnie recorded his fifth solo album, 'Slide On This' and supported the release with a tour. He appeared with Faces bandmate Rod Stewart for the appearance on MTV's popular 'Unplugged' series. Ronnie used a Gibson J200, his Zemaitis acoustic and a Takamine six-string electro-acoustic.

The next Stones album was 'Voodoo Lounge' (1994) and Ronnie stuck to the guitars he had at this time, although there was the addition of a Gibson Firebird V, which would appear with him on a number of occasions.

Early in 1997, Ronnie was with the Stones recording 'Bridges To Babylon', then up to the end of the century an extensive tour was undertaken. The year saw Gibson release Ronnie's signature J200 acoustic model, of which 100 were built in two finish options. The guitar was similar to the standard model, only either side of the soundhole were two pickguards, both with a flame motif, and flame inlays; his signature was present on the headstock front.

Before the Stones embarked on their worldwide tour celebrating the 40th anniversary of the formation of the band, Ronnie released another signature model, this time with Duesenberg. The instrument was a semi-hollow body version of the Zemaitis pearl top guitar, but with a Bigsby vibrato unit.

In his autobiography, Ronnie reproduced a set list for the tour with the guitars used on each song included. He mainly favoured his 1955 Stratocaster, though he also had a 1954 Stratocaster, a 7-pedal steel guitar, a Fender lap steel, a sitar guitar, Gibson Firebird V, his Duesenberg signature and an ESP Telecaster copy with B-Bender, as well as his Gibson J200 and Zemaitis six-string acoustic.

Ronnie started the new millennium with his sixth solo album, 'Not For Beginners', featuring guest musicians Bob Dylan, Scotty Moore and Kelly Jones. Following the album was a live performance in London, which was filmed and released on DVD as 'Far East Man'. Joining Ronnie on stage was Slash (for several songs) and Andrea Corr, as well as daughter Leah and son Jesse. Ronnie performed most of the set using his 1955 Stratocaster and turned to his three-humbucker Zemaitis for the Faces' hit 'Stay With Me', which saw Ronnie using a metal slide.

'A Bigger Bang' was the first Rolling Stones record in eight years when released in 2005. Yet, Ronnie missed some sessions and was only credited on 10 of 16 songs. He was ever-present for the 'Bigger Bang' tour, which comprised 147 performances across the globe. Ronnie's guitars were mainly those mentioned for the previous Stones tours, with favour bestowed on the 1955 Stratocaster. The main change was that Mesa Boogie amps were dispensed with and a pair of Fender Vibro-Kings were brought in. These were 60 watts with three 10-inch speakers.

Following this marathon tour, Ronnie made several guest appearances with other musicians, such as Pearl Jam, Red Hot Chilli Peppers and Beverley Knight. A solo album, 'I Feel Like Playing' was released in 2010 and featured collaborations with Slash, Billy Gibbons and Waddy Wachtel.

The Rolling Stones celebrated the band's 50th anniversary in 2012/2013 with a large tour of 30 dates. Through to the end of 2019, the band continued to perform to audiences across the globe with gigs arranged in each year. During 2016, the Stones released 'Blue And Lonesome', which was a return to the group's roots and consisted of covers of blues songs.

Gibson released Ronnie's signature L5S in 2015 and these guitars were limited to 300 worldwide. He had been associated with the model since the 1970s, although he thought the design could be simplified to produce a more versatile guitar. Ronnie's L5S had a multi-ply maple body, five-ply walnut/maple neck, with ebony fingerboard and block inlays, stopbar tailpiece, and two humbuckers (Burstbucker 1 in the neck and Burstbucker 2 in the bridge positions) controlled by single master tone and master volume controls.

In 2019, Ronnie recorded 'MadLad: A Live Tribute To Chuck Berry', featuring vocals from Imelda May. He performed the album on a small tour of Britain late in the year and he had a Rozeo 'Ladybug' guitar, as well as his L5S and a vintage L5 with one pick-up (neck), accompanied by a lap steel, with amplification from a pair of Fender Hot Rod Deluxe amplifiers.

In February 2020, Ronnie played guitar with Eric Clapton at the tribute concert for Ginger Baker. Performing several songs, Ronnie had both his signature L5S and 1955 Stratocaster.

Ronnie Wood playing a Fender Stratocaster with the Rolling Stones in Philadelphia on September 25, 1981.
MediaPunch Inc / Alamy Stock Photo.

Bert Weedon holding a Guild semi-acoustic with Bigsby. Bert's name is featured on the Pick-guard.
Pictorial Press Ltd / Alamy Stock Photo.

Ronnie Wood pictured playing a Gibson Les Paul Special alongside Keith Richards at Carter-Finley Stadium July 1, 2015 during the Zip Code Tour.
AFF / Alamy Stock Photo.

Jimmy Page, Eric Clapton, and Jeff Beck during the ARMS tour in Los Angeles, California on December 5, 1983.
Kevin Estrada / MediaPunch / Alamy Stock Photo.

BIBLIOGRAPHY

Babiuk, Andy *Beatles Gear: All the Fab Four's Instruments, from Stage to Studio* (2002)

Babiuk, Andy and Greg Prevost *Rolling Stones Gear: All the Stones' Instruments from Stage to Studio* (2014)

Bacon, Tony *Million Dollar Les Paul: In Search of the Most Valuable Guitar in the World* (2008)

Bacon, Tony *50 Years of the Les Paul: A Half-Century of a Guitar Icon* (2002)

Bacon, Tony and Howe, Steve *The Steve Howe Guitar Collection* (1999)

Bacon, Tony *The Gibson 335 Guitar Book* (2016)

Bacon, Tony and Day, Paul *The Gibson Les Paul Book: A Complete History of Les Paul Guitars* (1993)

Bacon, Tony *The SG Guitar Book: 50 Years of Gibson's Stylish Solid Guitar* (2015)

Bacon, Tony, and Day, Paul *50 Years of Fender: Half a Century of the Greatest Electric Guitars* (2000)

Bay, Mel *Modern Guitar Method* (1990)

Blake, Mark *Pink Floyd: Pigs Might Fly* (2013)

Bloom, Jerry *Black Knight: Ritchie Blackmore* (2008)

Bragg, Billy *Roots, Radicals and Rockers* (2017)

Brown, Joe *Brown Sauce: The Life and Times of Joe Brown* (1986)

Carter, Walter *The Martin Book: A Complete History of Martin Guitars* (2006)

Celmins, Martin *Peter Green: The Authorised Biography* (2003)

Chapman, Rob *Syd Barrett: A Very Irregular Head* (2010)

Christie's *The David Gilmour Guitar Collection Sale Catalogue* (2019)

Clapton, Eric *Eric Clapton: The Autobiography* (2008)

Cope, Andrew L. *Black Sabbath and the Rise of Heavy Metal Music* (2010)

Davies, Dave *Kink: An Autobiography* (1996)

Du Noyer, Paul *Liverpool: Wondrous Place – Music from the Cavern to Cream* (2002)

Farren, Mick *Gene Vincent: There's One in Every Town* (2004)

Finch, Peter *The Roots of Rock: From Cardiff to Mississippi and Back* (2016)

Foster, Mo *Play Like Elvis: How British Musicians Bought the American Dream* (2000)

Foster, Mo *British Rock Guitar* (2011)

Frampton, Peter *Do You Feel Like I Do? A Memoir* (2021)

Giltrap, Gordon and Marten, Neville *The Hofner Guitar: A History* (1993)

Gusevik, Sven *Ronson Goes Solo: Part Two of the Mick Ronson Story* (1989)

Hanson, Martin *Hoggin' the Page: The Groundhogs' Classic Years* (1988)

Harper, Colin *Bathed in Lightning: John McLaughlin, the 60s and the Emerald Beyond* (2014)

Hinman, Doug *The Kinks – All Day and All of the Night: Day-by-day Concerts, Recordings and Broadcasts, 1961–1996* (2004)

Howe, Steve *All My Yesterdays* (2020)

Hjort, Christopher *Strange Brew: Eric Clapton and the British Blues Boom* (2007)

Hunter, Dave *Acoustic Guitars: The Illustrated Encyclopedia* (2003)

Iommi, Tony *Iron Man: My Journey Through Heaven and Hell with Black Sabbath* (2012)

Kjeseth, Erick *Elvis: The Man and His Music* (1981)

Kershaw, Eric *Dance Band Chords for the Guitar* (1946)

Leigh, Spencer *Puttin' On the Style: The Lonnie Donegan Story* (2003)

Leigh, Spencer *Things Do Go Wrong Eddie: Gene and the UK Tour* (2008)

James, J.D. *Paul Kossoff: All Right Now – The Guitars, the Gear, the Music* (2017)

Johnston, Richard and Boak, Dick (revised and updated from the original by Mike Longworth) *Martin Guitars: A History* (2008)

McLenehan, Cliff *Marc Bolan 1947–1977: A Chronology* (2002)

Meiners, Larry *Flying V: The Illustrated History of this Modernistic Guitar* (2001)

Moody, Micky *Playing with Trumpets: A Rock and Roll Apprenticeship* (2006)

Moody, Micky *Snakes and Ladders: My Autobiography – A Rock 'n' Roll Odyssey to Whitesnake* (2016).

Moust, Hans *The Guild Guitar Book: The Company and the Instruments, 1952–1977* (1995)

Neil, Andy and Kent, Matt *Anyway, Anyhow, Anywhere: The Complete Chronicle of the Who, 1958 to 1978* (2007)

Page, Jimmy *Jimmy Page* (2014)

Page, Jimmy *Jimmy Page: The Anthology* (2020)

Petersen David and Denney, Dick *The Vox Story: A Complete History of the Legend* (1993)

Power, Martin *Hot Wired Guitar: The Life of Jeff Beck* (2014)

Rock, Mick *Ziggy Stardust* (1984)

Rosen, Steven *Free at Last: The Story of Free and Bad Company* (2001)

Sadler, Dick *The Complete Guitar Method* (n.d.)

Shadwick, Keith *Led Zeppelin: The Story of the Band and their Music, 1968-1980* (2005)

Smith, Sid *In the Court of King Crimson* (2003)

Summers, Andy *One Train Later: A Memoir* (2007)

Taylor, Phil *The Black Strat: A History of David Gilmour's Black Fender Stratocaster* (2008)

Townshend, Pete *Who I Am* (2012)

Wall, Mick *Black Sabbath: Symptom of the Universe* (2014)

Weedon, Bert *Play in a Day* (1957)

Weedon, Bert *Play Every Day* (1963)

Weird & Gilly *Mick Ronson: The Spider with the Platinum Hair* (2003)

Welch, Bruce *Rock 'n' Roll: I Gave You the Best Years of My Life* (1989)

Wheeler, Tom *The Stratocaster Chronicles: Celebrating 50 Years of the Fender Strat* (2004)

Wood, Ronnie *Ronnie* (2008)

Wyman, Bill *Rolling with the Stones* (2002)

Young, Bob and Moody, Micky *The Language of Rock 'n' Roll* (1985)